REASON, MORALITY, AND LAW

Reason, Morality, and Law

The Philosophy of John Finnis

Edited by

JOHN KEOWN AND ROBERT P. GEORGE

OXFORD

UNIVERSITY PRESS

OXFORD

UNIVERSITY PRESS

Great Clarendon Street, Oxford, OX2 6DP,
United Kingdom

Oxford University Press is a department of the University of Oxford.
It furthers the University's objective of excellence in research, scholarship,
and education by publishing worldwide. Oxford is a registered trade mark of
Oxford University Press in the UK and in certain other countries

Published in the United States of America by Oxford University Press
198 Madison Avenue, New York, NY 10016, United States of America

British Library Cataloguing in Publication Data
Data available

Library of Congress Cataloging in Publication Data
Data available

ISBN 978–0–19–967550–0 (Hbk.)
ISBN 978–0–19–873810–7 (Pbk.)

Editors' Preface

It is a sign of the high esteem in which John Finnis is held that we had no difficulty securing contributions from the distinguished scholars whose essays grace this volume in his honour. (Indeed, we were in the enviable, albeit awkward, position of having to decline offers from other distinguished scholars who had got wind of the project.) The essays, which reflect the remarkable breadth of his scholarly achievements, range across philosophy of law, moral philosophy, political philosophy, philosophy of religion, constitutional law, medical/health law, bioethics, and Shakespeare.

This, then, is a *Festschrift*. But it is not a typical *Festschrift*. It includes scholars who are, more or less, sympathetic to the ideas about natural law that he has articulated, and scholars who are critical of those ideas (and in some cases, of the natural law tradition broadly). Moreover, it was always our intention to invite John Finnis to offer some sort of response, and he kindly agreed. But, to his surprise as much as ours, his 'Reflections and Responses' developed into a serious engagement with the main arguments, or other important issues raised, in almost all the essays, and thus into something of the substantial length we now see. This venture was timely: his *Collected Essays*, and a second edition of *Natural Law and Natural Rights*, both of which include important new material, appeared in 2011. Contributors to this volume have written their essays in light of those publications.

The influence of John Finnis's work, especially among younger scholars, is growing globally, particularly in the UK and the US. We trust that this volume will promote even greater interest in, and understanding of, his thought, not least by clarifying points of agreement and disagreement with leading thinkers representing a wide range of perspectives.

We end on a very sad note. One of the contributors was to have been a brilliant, younger scholar of natural law: Dr Amanda Perreau-Saussine of the Faculty of Law in the University of Cambridge and of Queens' College, Cambridge. Amanda died before she could complete her essay. *Requiescat in pace.*

Acknowledgments

We thank all those who contributed essays to this volume, and especially John Finnis for his thoughtful and highly detailed response to the arguments they present. We are also grateful to Alex Flach and Natasha Flemming of Oxford University Press for their help with this volume from conception to birth.

One of us (JK) carried out much of his work on this volume while a Herbert Smith Visitor in the Faculty of Law at Cambridge University. He is grateful to Herbert Smith and to the Cambridge Law Faculty, not least to David Wills, the Squire Law Librarian. The other (RPG) worked on the volume in Princeton, his institutional home, and at Harvard, where he is a Visiting Professor in the Law School. He is grateful to Sherif Girgis and Ryan Anderson for their help.

Contents

PHILOSOPHY OF LAW

PHILOSOPHY, RELIGION, AND PUBLIC REASONS

REFLECTIONS AND RESPONSES

List of Abbreviations

Acta Vat. II	*Acta Synodalia Sacrosancti Concilii Oecumenici Vaticani II* (Rome: Vatican Polyglot Press)
Aquinas	1998d: John Finnis, *Aquinas: Moral, Political, and Legal Theory* (1998) (Oxford: OUP)
CEJF I	2011c: *Reason in Action: Collected Essays of John Finnis volume I* (Oxford: OUP)
CEJF II	2011d: *Intention and Identity: Collected Essays of John Finnis* volume II (Oxford: OUP)
CEJF III	2011e: *Human Rights and Common Good: Collected Essays of John Finnis* volume III (Oxford: OUP)
CEJF IV	2011f: *Philosophy of Law: Collected Essays of John Finnis* volume IV (Oxford: OUP)
CEJF V	2011g: *Religion and Public Reasons: Collected Essays of John Finnis* volume V (Oxford: OUP)
Conc. Trid.	*Concilium Tridentinum Diariorum, Actorum, Epistularum, Tractatuum,* ed. Societas Goerresiana, volume V, ed. S. Ehses (Freiburg im Breisgau: Herder, 1911); volume XII ed. V. Schweitzer (Freiburg im Breisgau: Herder, [1930] 1966)
CUP	Cambridge University Press
DH	Second Vatican Council, *Dignitatis Humanae* (Declaration on Religious Liberty, 1965)
FoE	1983a: John Finnis, *Fundamentals of Ethics* (Oxford: OUP; Georgetown: Georgetown University Press)
In Pol.	Aquinas, *In libros Politicorum Expositio [Commentary on Pol.]*
MA	1991c: John Finnis, *Moral Absolutes: Tradition, Revision, and Truth* (Washington, DC: Catholic University of America Press)
NE	Aristotle, *Nicomachean Ethics*
NDMR	1987g: John Finnis, Joseph Boyle and Germain Grisez, *Nuclear Deterrence, Morality and Realism* (1987) (Oxford: OUP)
NLNR	1980a: John Finnis, *Natural Law and Natural Rights* ([1980] 2nd edn, 2011) (Oxford: OUP)
OUP	Oxford University Press (including the Clarendon Press)
Pol.	Aristotle, *Politics*
Sent.	Aquinas, *Scriptum super Libros Sententiarum Petri Lombardiensis [Commentary on the Positions of the Church Fathers] of Peter Lombard* (c. 1255)
ST	Aquinas, *Summa Theologiae [A Summary of Theology]*(c.1265–73)

List of Contributors

Joseph Boyle is Professor of Philosophy at the University of Toronto.

Gerard V. Bradley is Professor of Law at the University of Notre Dame.

Roger Crisp is Uehiro Fellow and Tutor in Philosophy at St Anne's College, Oxford, and Professor of Moral Philosophy at the University of Oxford.

Julie Dickson is CUF Lecturer in the Faculty of Law, and Fellow and Senior Law Tutor at Somerville College, Oxford.

Richard Ekins is Tutorial Fellow in Law at St John's College, Oxford.

Timothy Endicott is a Fellow in Law at Balliol College and Professor of Legal Philosophy and Dean of the Faculty of Law in the University of Oxford.

John Finnis is emeritus Professor of Law and Legal Philosophy in the University of Oxford, and Biolchini Family Professor of Law at the University of Notre Dame.

Anthony Fisher OP is Archbishop of Sydney, Australia, and Adjunct Professor of Bioethics in the University of Notre Dame Australia.

Kevin L. Flannery SJ is Professor of the History of Ancient Philosophy at the Pontifical Gregorian University.

John Gardner is Professor of Jurisprudence, and Fellow of University College, Oxford.

Robert P. George is McCormick Professor of Jurisprudence at Princeton University and Visiting Professor of Law at Harvard University.

Luke Gormally is a former Director of The Linacre Centre for Healthcare Ethics, London.

Neil M. Gorsuch is a Judge of the United States Court of Appeals for the Tenth Circuit.

Leslie Green is Professor of the Philosophy of Law, and Fellow of Balliol College, Oxford, and Distinguished University Fellow at Queen's University, Canada.

Germain Grisez is emeritus Professor of Christian Ethics at Mount St. Mary's University.

John Haldane is Professor of Philosophy at the University of St Andrews.

Sir Anthony Kenny is emeritus Fellow of St John's College, Oxford.

John Keown is the Rose Kennedy Professor in the Kennedy Institute of Ethics at Georgetown University.

Maris Köpcke Tinturé is Fellow and Tutor in Law at Worcester College, Oxford.

Matthew H. Kramer is Professor of Legal and Political Philosophy at Cambridge University, and Fellow of Churchill College, Cambridge.

Patrick Lee is John N. and Jamie D. McAleer Chair in Bioethics at the Franciscan University of Steubenville.

Timothy Macklem is Professor of Jurisprudence at the Dickson Poon School of Law, King's College London.

Cristóbal Orrego is Professor of Jurisprudence at the Pontifical Catholic University of Chile.

Thomas Pink is Professor of Philosophy at King's College London.

Joseph Raz is Professor of Law at Columbia Law School and Research Professor at the Dickson Poon School of Law, King's College London.

N.E. Simmonds is Reader in Jurisprudence in the Faculty of Law, and a Fellow of Corpus Christi College, Cambridge.

Jacqueline Tasioulas is Fellow in English, Clare College, Cambridge.

John Tasioulas is Quain Professor of Jurisprudence at University College London.

Christopher Tollefsen is Professor of Philosophy at the University of South Carolina.

Jeremy Waldron is Chichele Professor of Social and Political Theory, and Fellow of All Souls College, Oxford, and University Professor at New York University School of Law.

Introduction

The Achievement of John Finnis

Robert P. George

> There are human goods that can be secured only through the institutions of human law, and requirements of practical reasonableness that only those institutions can satisfy.

With these words, John Finnis, while still in his late 30s, began his masterwork, *Natural Law and Natural Rights*—the book that would not only revive scholarly interest in the venerable, but deeply misunderstood, idea of natural law and natural rights, but also powerfully challenge dominant ways of thinking among philosophers of law and moral and political philosophers in the analytic tradition.[1]

Future intellectual historians will no doubt present the book, together with Professor Finnis's other philosophical writings, as part of the broad revival in more or less Aristotelian approaches to moral and political thinking that gained prominence beginning in the late 1970s. And they will be right to do so. Like Elizabeth Anscombe, David Wiggins, Philippa Foot, Alasdair MacIntyre, and many others, Finnis adopted or adapted Aristotelian methods to overcome the defects of utilitarian and other consequentialist approaches to ethics, on the one side, and Kantian or purely "deontological" approaches, on the other.

Like utilitarians, and unlike Kantians, these thinkers (who can even be called neo-Aristotelians) hold that ethical thinking must be deeply linked to considerations of human well-being or flourishing—Aristotle's *eudaimonia*. But such thinking, they maintain, cannot treat the human good as subject to aggregation and calculation in a way that could somehow render coherent and workable a norm directing people to choose the option (or act on the rule) that will, for example, produce the greatest happiness of the greatest number or the net best proportion of benefit to harm overall and in the long run. So, like Kantians, they reject the belief that ethics is a matter of technical reasoning (or "cost–benefit analysis") aimed purely and simply at producing the best possible consequences. Unlike Kantians, however, they also reject the idea of a purely deontological ethics, with its reduction of moral thinking to the domain of logic. To be sure, they accept the idea of morality as a matter of rectitude in willing, but they argue that morally wrongful choosing is not merely a matter of inconsistency in thought. Rather, immorality consists in choosing (and thus willing) in ways that are contrary to the good of human persons.

---

[1] *NLNR.*

A critical moment—one might say *the* critical moment—in Finnis's intellectual biography occurred when, nearly 15 years before the publication of *Natural Law and Natural Rights*, he encountered the work of Germain Grisez. It was Grisez's "re-presentation and very substantial development" of Aquinas' understanding of the first principles of practical thinking, the understanding articulated in the "treatise on law" of the *Summa Theologiae*, that made it possible for Finnis to deploy with the rigor rightly demanded in the analytical tradition of philosophy an Aristotelian approach to problems in philosophy of law and moral and political philosophy.[2] According to Grisez and Finnis, Aquinas correctly understood that the underived (*per se nota* and *indemonstrabilia*) first and most basic principles of practical reason direct human choosing and acting towards intelligible human goods—the various irreducible aspects of human well-being and fulfillment which provide more-than-merely-instrumental reasons for action—and away from their privations. These first principles (and the basic human goods to which they refer in directing our choosing and acting—friendship, knowledge, critical aesthetic appreciation, skillful performances of various types, etc.) are not themselves moral norms. (Knowledge of them is moral knowledge incipiently, but only incipiently.) Rather, they guide and govern *all* coherent practical thinking, whether it results in morally upright action (e.g., visiting an ailing colleague in the hospital simply as an act of friendship) or immoral action (e.g., telling a lie to protect the reputation of a friend who has done something disgraceful).

Moral norms, whether general ones, such as the Golden Rule ("do unto others as you would have them do unto you"), or more specific ones, such as the prohibition of lying even to protect the reputation of a friend, are specifications of the obligation to honor the dignity of all human persons (including oneself) by respecting human well-being in its fullness—i.e., the basic goods of human persons considered integrally. And so what Grisez and Finnis, who (together with Joseph M. Boyle, Jr.) would later collaborate extensively in developing the moral theory pioneered by Grisez, call "the first principle of morality" enjoins us to choose and otherwise will in ways that are compatible with a will towards integral human fulfillment.[3] And just as the various "basic human goods" are specifications of the first and most general principle of practical reason, which Aquinas formulates as "good (*bonum*) is to be done and pursued and bad (*malum*) is to be avoided," the various moral norms which we strive to live by and transmit to our children are specifications of the first and most general principle of morality. These norms of morality governing human choosing are not mere projections of feeling or

---

[2] Grisez, "The First Principle of Practical Reason," 168–96. In the Preface to *NLNR*, on p. vii, Finnis acknowledges his intellectual debt to Grisez, noting that "[t]he ethical theory advanced in Chapters III–IV and the theoretical arguments in sections VI.2 and XIII.2 are squarely based on my understanding of his vigorous re-presentation and very substantial development of the classical arguments on these matters."

[3] This development is discussed intensively in Joseph Boyle's essay herein (Essay 4), in Finnis's response to it (Essay 28), and Grisez's essay too (Essay 27). In *NLNR*, Finnis did not formally articulate the first principle of morality—something he accounts as a "failure" in the post-script to the book's 2nd edition (see p. 419). This was, however, soon rectified in his writing, as a result of collaboration with Grisez and Boyle in the refinement and development of their "new" natural law theory. As Finnis points out, in 1983 "openness to integral fulfillment" is accorded the status of the "master principle of morality" in his *Fundamentals of Ethics (FoE)*, 70–4, 120–4, and 151–2. A more formal articulation of the principle first appears in Grisez et al., "Practical Principles, Moral Truth, and Ultimate Ends," 126–9.

emotion, nor are they imposed upon reason extrinsically; rather, they are the fruit of reasoning about the human good and its integral directiveness, and are, in that sense, as Finnis says, requirements of (practical) *reasonableness*.

When Finnis arrived in Oxford in the early 1960s as an Australian Rhodes scholar holding an LL.B. from the University of Adelaide, he was fortunate to be able to write his doctoral dissertation (on the idea of judicial power) under the supervision of Herbert Hart, holder of the University of Oxford's Professorship of Jurisprudence and the preeminent anglophone legal philosopher of his time. Hart had recently published his own masterwork, *The Concept of Law*.[4] Much of what Finnis would go on to achieve in legal and political philosophy would be rooted in critical engagement with Hart's thought. This was an engagement that Hart welcomed. Indeed, in his role as editor of the prestigious Clarendon Law Series of Oxford University Press, Hart would commission Finnis (who in the mid-1960s became his colleague on the Oxford law faculty) to write *Natural Law and Natural Rights*, even specifying the title. While resisting most of Finnis's criticisms of his work, Hart had a keen appreciation of the power of his young colleague's intellect and the force of his arguments.

Although Hart's sympathies tended to run in a moderate empiricist, and to some extent utilitarian, direction, there is a sense in which his work (especially *The Concept of Law*) prefigured the Aristotelian revival. Despite his firm commitment to what he regarded as "legal positivism"—which he understood as a strict commitment to the "conceptual separation of law and morality"—Hart was a severe critic of Jeremy Bentham's externalist and reductionist view of law (or the concept of law). Bentham supposed that the social phenomenon (or set of phenomena) we know as "law" is best understood on the model of "orders backed by threats"—orders issued by a sovereign who is habitually obeyed, but who obeys no one. On this understanding, laws function as *causes* of human behavior. They do not create obligation, at least in the normal, normatively flavored sense of that word. Rather, they merely oblige—by way of threats of punishment for non-compliance. They oblige in the way that an armed bandit obliges a victim to turn over his wallet when the villain points a loaded pistol at the victim's head and says "your money or your life."

Now, Hart's objection to Bentham's account was not moralistic; rather, he argued that it failed *descriptively*—it did not "fit the facts."[5] In particular, it did not account for the ways in which laws characteristically function in the lives of citizens and officials as frequently providing certain types of intelligible *reasons* for action, what he would later describe as "content-independent peremptory reasons."[6] To "fit the facts" an account of law must pay attention to the practical point of laws and legal institutions, and draw the distinctions between various types of laws and their various functions. But this, in turn, required the legal theorist, or descriptive sociologist[7] of law and legal systems, to adopt what Hart called "the internal point of view," that is, the practical viewpoint of citizens and officials for whom the laws provide *reasons* for acting by, among other

---

[4] Hart, *The Concept of Law*.
[5] Hart, *The Concept of Law*, 78.   [6] Hart, *Essays on Bentham*, Ch. 10.
[7] On the very first page of *The Concept of Law* Hart invites the reader to regard the book as an exercise in "descriptive sociology."

things, enabling them individually and/or collectively to pursue certain objectives and accomplish certain goals (e.g., transporting themselves on the highways, getting married, creating a binding commercial contract, establishing a charitable trust).[8]

Thus, Hart's "concept" (and philosophy) of law, having identified and adopted the internal point of view, begins to move away from the voluntarism (law as will) that lies at the heart of Benthamite legal positivism, and towards a recognition of law as *rationally* grounded—that is, as providing reasons that guide choosing. Law (and laws), according to Hart, cannot be reduced to *causes* of human behavior, nor can it accurately be described as the sheer imposition of (the) *will* (of a sovereign). It is characteristically (though not always) reasoned and reasonable. At least, it is capable of being so, and will be so in the central or "focal" cases in which law functions in the ways that make it intelligible as a product of human deliberation and judgment in the first place. And yet, Hart himself drew short of committing himself to any such conclusion. He wished to retain the core of legal positivism even while jettisoning Bentham's externalism (and strict voluntarism) and reductionism. It was precisely for this drawing short, this refusal to identify fully reasonable (i.e., just) law as the focal case of law, and the point of view of the morally motivated legal official and citizen as the focal case of the internal point of view, that Finnis criticized the otherwise powerfully compelling philosophy of his teacher.

For Finnis, the focal case of a legal system is one in which legal rules and principles function as practical reasons for citizens as well as judges and other officials because of people's appreciation of their virtue and value, i.e., their *point*. Aquinas' famous *practical* definition of law as an ordinance of reason directed to the common good by the persons and institutions having responsibility for the care of the community here has its significance in *descriptive* legal theory. As Finnis observes,

> if we consider the reasons people have for establishing systems of positive law (with power to override immemorial custom), and for maintaining them (against the pull of strong passions and individual self-interest), and for reforming and restoring them when they decay or collapse, we find that only the moral reasons on which many of those people often act suffice to explain why such people's undertaking takes the shape it does, giving legal systems the many features they have—features which a careful descriptive account such as H.L.A. Hart's identifies as characteristic of the central case of positive law and the focal meaning of "law," and which therefore have a place in an adequate concept (understanding and account) of positive law.[9]

Yet, as I have noted, Hart himself, in *The Concept of Law* and elsewhere, refused to distinguish central from peripheral cases of the internal point of view. Thus, he treated cases of obedience to law by virtue of "unreflecting inherited attitudes" and even the "mere wish to do as others do" as indistinguishable from morally motivated fidelity to law.[10] These "considerations and attitudes," like those which boil down to mere

---

[8] As Finnis points out, Hart in *The Concept of Law*, "gives descriptive explanatory priority to those who do not 'merely record and predict behavior conforming to rules', or attend to rules 'only from the external point of view as a sign of possible punishment', but rather '*use* the rules as standards for appraisal of their own and others' behavior,'" *NLNR*, 12, quoting Hart, *The Concept of Law*, 95–6.

[9] *CEJF* IV.7, 204.   [10] Hart, *The Concept of Law*, 198.

self-interest or the avoidance of punishment, are, Finnis argues, "diluted or watered-down instances of the practical viewpoint that brings law into being as a significantly differentiated type of social order and maintains it as such. Indeed, they are parasitic upon that viewpoint."[11]

Now, this is not to suggest that Finnis denies any valid sense to Hart's insistence on the "conceptual separation" of law and morality.[12] It is merely to highlight the ambiguity of the assertion of such a separation and the need to distinguish, even more carefully and clearly than Hart did, between the respects in which such a separation obtains and those in which it does not. Still less is it to suggest that belief in natural law or other forms of moral realism entail the proposition that law and morality are connected in such a way as to confer upon judges as such plenary authority to enforce the requirements of natural law or to legally invalidate provisions of positive law they judge to be in conflict with these requirements. The scope and limits of judicial power is a separate issue—one that has been the focus of criticism of Hart's jurisprudence by another of his eminent former students, Ronald Dworkin, who has faulted Hart's positivism for excessively narrowing the authority of judges and other officials to bring moral judgments to bear in the enterprise of legal interpret-ation.[13] Finnis has not signed on to Dworkin's critique of Hart's jurisprudence—a critique that is sometimes regarded as proceeding from a natural-law vantage point of its own—and parts of Finnis's work suggest reasons for believing that Dworkin's critique is in important ways misguided. For Finnis, the truth of the proposition *lex iniusta non est lex* is a moral truth, namely, that the moral obligation created by authoritative legal enactment—that is to say, by positive law—is conditional, rather than absolute. The *prima facie* moral obligation to obey the law is *defeasible*. Finnis does not claim that unjust laws are in no legitimate sense laws,[14] nor does he argue that judges enjoy as a matter of natural law some sort of plenary authority to invalidate or even to subvert or ignore laws that they regard (even reasonably regard) as unjust.

We see, then, that Finnis takes on board Hart's key insights deriving from his critical engagement with Benthamite legal positivism and pushes them to their logical conclusions—conclusions that move legal philosophy beyond legal positivism, even in its comparatively modest Hartian iteration, into a recognition of law as, in a meaningful sense, connected with reason's quest for justice and the common good (law as reason and not merely will). In the process, he strikes a blow against a familiar caricature of natural law whose wide acceptance (including, incidentally, by Hart

---

[11] *NLNR*, 14.

[12] See generally *CEJF* IV.7.

[13] Finnis comments on Dworkin's critique, in *Taking Rights Seriously*, of the "positivism" of Hart and Joseph Raz in an illuminating endnote to Chapter 1 of *NLNR*, arguing that the debate "miscarries" because Dworkin "fails to acknowledge that their theoretical interest is not, like his, to identify a fundamental 'test for law', in order to identify (even in the most disputed 'hard cases') where a judge's legal (moral and political) duty really lies, in a given community at a given time. Rather, their interest is in describing what is treated (i.e., accepted and effective) as law in a given community at a given time, and in generating concepts that will allow such descriptions to be clear and explanatory, but without intent to offer solutions (whether 'right answers' or standards which if properly applied would yield right answers) to questions disputed among competent lawyers."

[14] *NLNR*, Ch. 2.

himself as well as by Hans Kelsen and others) had provided apparent grounds for its quick dismissal by serious scholars and students of jurisprudence.

The achievement of John Finnis goes well beyond his signal contributions to philosophy of law. It certainly includes his work with Grisez and Boyle in developing the understanding of practical reasoning and moral judgment that has come to be known, problematically, as the "new"[15] natural law theory and (not unrelatedly) his critical writings against moral skepticism, utilitarianism and other forms of consequentialism in ethics, and ethical theories that purport to lay aside considerations of human well-being in identifying norms of conduct for the moral life.[16] It also includes significant work in political philosophy, some of it directed to pulling the rug out from under the most influential forms of "liberal" political theory of our time, namely, those "anti-perfectionist" theories (often underwriting an ideology of expressive and/or possessive individualism), such as the theory of justice and "political liberalism" advanced by the late John Rawls, proposing that political decisions may not legitimately be based on controversial ideas of what makes for or detracts from a valuable and morally worthy way of life, or that in decisions pertaining to constitutional essentials and matters of basic justice, liberty may not legitimately be limited except on the basis of "public reasons" (where the concept of a public reason strictly excludes reasons drawn from "comprehensive" philosophical and religious views—however reasonable those "comprehensive views" may be).[17]

Finnis's contributions in political philosophy go beyond the criticism of major works by influential contemporary liberal thinkers, such as Rawls, Dworkin, and the late Robert Nozick. *Natural Law and Natural Rights*, especially Chapters VI–XI, constitutes a major affirmative contribution to thought about (1) justice and its requirements, (2) the content (and scope) of the political common good; (3) rights, including human rights, and their identification; (4) the rational grounds for honoring legal and political authority and recognizing legal and political obligation; and (5) the nature and social functions of law. In all of these areas, his analysis and prescriptions are notable not only for their analytical rigor and precision, but for their attention to the complexities of the subject matter. (For example, Finnis carefully explores, in *Natural Law and Natural Rights* VII.4, the relevance of (a) need, (b) function, (c) capacity, (d) desert, and (e) consideration of who may have created or at least foreseen and accepted a risk of loss or harm, in analyzing problems of distributive justice.) In all of these areas, what was originally presented in *Natural Law and Natural Rights* has been expanded, deepened,

---

[15] The substance of the account of natural law offered by Finnis et al. is hardly new. Its core can be found in Aquinas, and much of that, in turn, Aquinas draws from Aristotle. It is true that Finnis, Grisez, and others have developed the Thomistic theory of natural law in various ways, and articulated the theory in a modern philosophical idiom. But to develop a theory is not to reject it. It is, rather, to accept its substance and draw out its further implications. That is what they have done by, for example, showing how reflection on the integral directiveness or prescriptivity of the principles of practical reason that are presented by Aquinas enables us to identify moral principles and norms that distinguish options for choice that are fully in line with all that reasonableness demands from options that, in one way or another, fall short or afoul of the full demands of practical reasonableness.

[16] See especially *FoE*.

[17] See Rawls, *A Theory of Justice*; Rawls, *Political Liberalism*; Nozick, *Anarchy, State, and Utopia*; Dworkin, *A Matter of Principle*.

and in various ways enriched by papers Finnis subsequently published, most of which are included in the five volumes of *Collected Essays of John Finnis* published in 2011 by Oxford University Press. Taken together, the chapters of the book and the various essays represent an important and distinctive contribution to the contemporary debate about the selection of political principles and the proper design and healthy functioning of political institutions.

In normative ethics and political theory, Finnis has been a force second to none in defending the moral inviolability of human life in all stages and conditions and the norm against making the death or injury of a human being the precise object of one's choosing. And so he has written powerfully against abortion, infanticide, euthanasia, and the intentional (including the conditional) willingness to kill or maim noncombatants (including captured or subdued enemy soldiers) even in justified wars (whether the weapons used are nuclear or conventional). Similarly, he has been a leading voice in defense of the historic understanding of marriage as a conjugal partnership—the union of husband and wife. In many cases, his views have put him at odds with the socially liberal orthodoxy prevailing in the universities and other intellectual sectors of the culture; in a few, they have placed him in dissent from what are regarded today as conservative positions. Like his hero Socrates, in an analogy his commendable humility would cause him vehemently to reject, he has followed arguments wherever they lead, and has never hesitated to state and defend a view because it flies in the face of the intellectual, moral, or political dogmas of the day. The accolades and honors that have come his way were not purchased by conformity to allegedly enlightened opinion or by silence in regard to what he judges to be its grave defects. His powerful and very public dissent could hardly have been contrived to gain him a personal chair in Oxford or election as a Fellow of the British Academy. In this, as in so many other ways, he has always been an inspiration to those (like the two editors of this *Festschrift*) fortunate enough to have been his students and to young scholars in the various fields of his interest and influence who know his work and the witness to the unconditional pursuit of truth it represents.

And this takes us to one last area of his interest and influence, an area in which the truths pursued are truths about ultimate things. While still a young philosopher, in a milieu dominated by the secularism he had hitherto shared—and one that was already showing signs of hostility to dissent—he made the move from secularism to (Catholic) Christianity, under the influence of classic philosophers as well as Christian saints. It was not that he came to faith and therefore saw the world differently. If anything, the reverse was true. The closed horizon of secularism artificially constrained the questions which, pursued with Socratic relentlessness, undermine secularism itself and inaugurate a journey of faith that might well lead to the rational affirmation of spiritual realities and an openness to entering into some form of communication and friendship with a transcendent source of meaning, value, and indeed all that there is. It was, in other words, reflection on the world—and the manifold orders of intelligibility (the natural, the logical, the moral, the technical) in which it presents itself to us and yields to our questioning and investigating—that led John Finnis to conclude that there are more things to be understood (and engaged) than can be immediately perceived with the senses or accounted for by empirical inquiry or technical analysis. Like so many other notable modern philosophers who have made the journey from secularism to Catholicism—Elizabeth Anscombe, Alasdair MacIntyre, Michael Dummett, Peter Geach, Nicholas Rescher—it was reason and reasoning that brought him to faith.

Faith was not to be, for Finnis, purely a matter of personal piety detached from his exertions as a philosopher. It could not be, since the lines of questioning that must be pursued in practical philosophical disciplines—ethics, political philosophy, philosophy of law—will, unless for no adequate reason we choose to cut them off, take us to the deepest questions of meaning and value. Reason itself—if it is anything more than a computational power—is a spiritual capacity, one that is not reducible solely to material and efficient causes. And reason cannot be a merely computational power if it is indeed capable of grasping more-than-merely-instrumental reasons for action (and their integral directiveness)—reasons (including moral norms) that are capable of guiding choices that are truly free. And if we are indeed rational and free creatures—i.e., *persons*, beings whose fundamental makeup (nature) is oriented to deliberation, judgment, and choice—then we are not merely material, but also spiritual creatures—creatures whose integral good includes not only our bodily (biological) health, but our intellectual, moral, and spiritual well-being as well. Obviously, these anthropological facts, if facts indeed they are, cannot but be highly relevant to questions of ethics, political philosophy, and philosophy of law, as well as to theology (including, centrally though not exclusively, of course, moral theology).

Finnis's work in moral theology prompted the highest authorities of the Catholic Church to summon him to service on its most important theological council, the International Theological Commission. There he worked especially on the philosophical and theological currents that were washing away the concept of intrinsically morally wrongful acts. In his own voice, and not purporting to speak for the commission, he published a small but lastingly valuable book on the subject entitled *Moral Absolutes*.[18] Here, in my view, we have a supreme example of the value of rigorous philosophical work marshaled in the cause of understanding the data of revelation and illuminating and enriching the teachings of faith. The work vindicates the claim famously advanced by Pope John Paul II in the opening sentence of his encyclical letter *Fides et Ratio*: "Faith and reason are like two wings on which the human spirit ascends to contemplation of truth." The truth-seeking achievements of John Finnis have been made possible by his willingness to use both wings.

Bibliography

Dworkin, Ronald, *Taking Rights Seriously* (Cambridge, MA: Harvard University Press, 1977).

Dworkin, Ronald, *A Matter of Principle* (Cambridge, MA: Harvard University Press, 1985).

Finnis, John, *Fundamentals of Ethics* (Oxford and Washington, DC: Oxford University Press and Georgetown University Press, 1983).

Finnis, John, *Moral Absolutes: Tradition, Revision, and Truth* (Washington, DC: Catholic University of America Press, 1991).

---

[18] Finnis, *Moral Absolutes: Tradition, Revision, and Truth* (1991c).

Finnis, John, "The Truth in Legal Positivism," in Robert P. George (ed.) *The Autonomy of Law: Essays on Legal Positivism* (Oxford: Clarendon Press, 1996), pp. 195–214.

Finnis, John, *Natural Law and Natural Rights* (Oxford: Clarendon Press, 1980); 2nd edition published in 2011.

Grisez, Germain, "The First Principle of Practical Reason: A Commentary on the *Summa Theologiae*, 1–2, Question 94, Article 2," *Natural Law Forum*, Vol. 10 (1965), pp. 168–96.

Grisez, Germain, Joseph M. Boyle, Jr., and John Finnis, "Practical Principles, Moral Truth, and Ultimate Ends," *American Journal of Jurisprudence*, Vol. 32 (1987), pp. 99–151.

Hart, H.L.A., *The Concept of Law* (Oxford: Clarendon Press, 1961); 2nd edition published in 1994.

Hart, H.L.A., *Essays on Bentham* (Oxford: Clarendon Press, 1982).

Nozick, Robert, *Anarchy, State, and Utopia* (Oxford: Oxford University Press, 1974).

Rawls, John, *A Theory of Justice* (Cambridge, MA: Harvard University Press, 1971).

Rawls, John, *Political Liberalism* (New York: Columbia University Press, 1993).

REASONS, GOODS, AND PRINCIPLES

1

Value: a Menu of Questions

Joseph Raz

For a long time John Finnis and I taught a joint seminar every year. Many students were lured to attend expecting to witness fierce intellectual conflicts between two academics known to adhere to diametrically opposed philosophical traditions. I would like to think that their disappointment at the general absence of the expected clashes was compensated for by an example of productive debate among people with diverse opinions. But that is too self-congratulatory a view. Perhaps closer to the truth is that while we tend to have radically different views on many specific moral and political issues we share a general approach to the understanding of theoretical ethics and practical reason. One way of characterizing the approach is as a value-based account of practical reasons. Finnis was happy to write about values in *Natural Law and Natural Rights*, but in much later writing used 'goods' or 'intelligible goods' or 'human goods' instead. As he does not suggest that the difference in terminology resulted from a difference in content I will use both 'value' and 'goods'. I take this opportunity to reflect on some of the issues that the value-based approach raises. This is a preliminary inquiry, ending with unanswered questions. My hope is that there is some point in articulating the questions, and some of their presuppositions.

I. Value and Action for a Reason

Fundamental to the value approach to practical reason[1] is the view that some actions, activities, or omissions (for brevity's sake I will use 'actions' to refer to all these categories) have some value properties, some good- or bad-making properties, and that those properties constitute reasons for or against the actions. The reasons referred to here are normative reasons, considerations that give a point to the actions for which they are reasons, make them desirable, and so on. There is no non-circular explanation of what normative reasons are. The notion is explained contextually, and most helpfully by contrast with the other concept the word 'reasons' is used to express, namely reasons as the factors that explain what the reasons are reasons for, as when we explain that the reason I lost the 100m race is that I had a stomach bug. Whenever I refer to (normative) reasons I will be referring to *pro tanto* reasons. As Finnis explains, values provide *pro tanto* reasons.[2] I will not be concerned here with the converse claim that nothing else provides reasons for action. Actions are not the only

---

[1] Among many other simplifications I adopt here is the concentration on reasons for action alone. Practical reasons can also be reasons for intentions or for emotions.

[2] *NLNR*, 62.

bearers of value properties. Moreover, often they have value properties in virtue of their relations with something else which has such properties: they may be constituent elements of more complex phenomena that are good, and therefore good in being component elements of more complex goods, or they may facilitate the production of some other goods, by creating opportunities for their production, creating favourable conditions for their production, or simply causing them. More indirectly they may be good because they have one of these relations to things or events that are good because they themselves bear these relations to other goods. Hence Finnis explains: 'What "gives a reason" is the good that is referred to in spelling out the reason'.[3]

This last formulation (clarified in the wider context to have the meaning I spell out below) and some others require cautious treatment. For example, Finnis writes that 'to say that such knowledge is a value is simply to say that reference to the pursuit of knowledge makes intelligible (though not necessarily reasonable-all-things-considered) any particular instance of the human activity and commitment involved in such pursuit'.[4] Two caveats are needed for a proper understanding of these two quotations. I believe that both caveats merely bring out Finnis's meaning.

To see the need for these caveats a crucial point about the relations of reasons to values has to be borne in mind. In their actions people and other living beings can be attracted to good options without recognizing their value. They may, for example, seek warmth, shelter, protection from predators, food and water, both for themselves and for others, because they are, as we might say, 'hard wired' to do so. This is evident in the behaviour of living beings that are incapable of rational action, incapable of realizing the grounds for their choices. But it is also true, though in a more limited way, of humans. Sometimes they too flinch from fire instinctively, and not only through apprehension of the harm it may cause. They turn their head automatically when hearing a loud or sudden noise, and while there are good reasons of prudence to do so, that is not why people do it. These actions are a genetically determined behaviour pattern.

Their ability to act because they perceive the value of the action is distinctive of rational beings with a fully developed ability to act for reasons (I formulate it this way to allow that some humans and some animals of other species have a more limited capacity to act for reasons). Actions that manifest that capacity do not necessarily have any value at all. But they are actions taken because the agents believed that they have some value. That is, I believe, the intended meaning of Finnis's observation that actions are made intelligible by being 'involved in such pursuit'.

Needless to say, given that people's **beliefs** in the value of their actions are involved in the exercise of their capacity for rational action the possibility that their action possesses no value is inescapable. It follows from the possibility that those beliefs are false. People act for a reason whenever they act in the belief that their actions have some value, whether these beliefs are true or false, at least so long as their beliefs that their actions have value are intelligible.

---

[3] *NLNR*, 443.   [4] *NLNR*, 62.

Possibly this last qualification is not needed. All that needs saying is that people act for a reason when they act because they believe that the action has some value. Of course there will be cases in which people will **claim** that the reason for their action was this or that, using words we normally use to designate some evaluative property, but where in fact they do not refer to any value property. Their command of the relevant words may be defective, leading them to choose the wrong word. Or their mastery of the concepts (either the concept of value, or that of the specific evaluative property concerned) may be defective and incoherent so that it makes no sense to attribute to them the assertion that would normally be expressed with the words they used. The crucial point is that people may have false beliefs about what is of value.

I assume that the possibility that people may (and sometimes do) have false beliefs about the value of various options needs no argument. But are such beliefs intelligible? Perhaps they are intelligible only when true, for they are made intelligible by it being the case that things are as they represent them to be? That is a mistake. We do understand what people say even when we do not know whether what they say is true. Moreover, we would not be able to know whether what they say is true unless we know what they say, and if we can know what they say independently of knowing whether it is true, we can also understand what they say independently of knowing whether it is true. That is why expressions of false beliefs (to be distinguished from the unintelligible use of words which cannot be understood as assertions of beliefs) are intelligible. And that is why actions for false beliefs about what is of value are also intelligible.

We should therefore be careful in understanding what Finnis is saying when he writes that 'to say that such knowledge is a value is simply to say that reference to the pursuit of knowledge makes intelligible (though not necessarily reasonable-all-things-considered) any particular instance of the human activity and commitment involved in such pursuit'.[5] Acting in pursuit of value makes the action intelligible. But so does (and Finnis does not deny this) action in the false belief that what it pursues is valuable. So, assuming for the sake of argument that knowledge is not of value, people's actions in pursuit of knowledge may nonetheless be intelligible; for example, if they pursue knowledge in the mistaken belief that it is valuable. In other words, we cannot infer the value of knowledge from the intelligibility of its pursuit. And the same goes for other beliefs in the value of this or that.

II. The Difficulty of Harmony

With these clarifications behind us I want to examine some questions about value, focussing on knowledge. I choose knowledge not only because it is Finnis's chosen central example, and not only because I have an independent interest in the question whether there is value to knowledge. It is also easier to examine than Finnis's other examples of basic values. So before looking at knowledge let me explain why it is a relatively easy case to consider.

---

[5] *NLNR*, 62.

Finnis's original list of basic values[6] consisted, apart from knowledge, of life, play, aesthetic experience, friendship, practical reasonableness, and religion. We were assured that other supposed basic goods are but 'ways or combinations of ways of pursuing (not always sensibly) and realizing (not always successfully) one of the seven basic forms of good, or some combination of them'.[7] On its face at least some aspects of the list are surprising. For example, some friendships and some religions or aesthetic experiences are without merit at all. Good friendships are good, and good religious experiences or lives are good, but not all friendships nor all religious experiences or religious lives, one is inclined to say, derive any value from being friendships or from being religious.

It is clear, however, that when invoking friendship and religion Finnis intended to invoke only those of their manifestations that are good. He explains them in terms of harmony between people (friendship) and between people and the divine (religion). That explains what, in Finnis's view, is the good of those forms of good, and the explanation is open to question. Harmony came to assume greater prominence in Finnis's later listings of basic goods. At times one almost gets the impression that he thinks that there is only one value, harmony, and the different values are merely harmony between different elements of the world. My comments about the difficulty with harmony below will explain both the appearance of reduction to one value (harmony) and why it is misleading.

The question that troubles me is whether the proposition 'harmony is intrinsically, i.e. non-instrumentally, good' is a conceptual truth or not. If not, then in the current jargon it is, if true at all, a metaphysical truth. I doubt that it is a conceptual truth. Nor does Finnis take it to be one. Finnis defends the claim that knowledge, friendship, and the things that constitute the other basic values are good by arguing that it is self-evident that they are. Conceptual truths may be self-evident truths, but I doubt that Finnis's defence of self-evidence is meant to vindicate reliance on it in coming to realize conceptual truths.

But, if not a conceptual truth, I doubt that 'Harmony is a non-instrumental good' is true at all. Of course, sometimes it is good. But if it is only sometimes good then it is not harmony by itself that is good, but only harmony combined with (or in the context of) something else. There is something else that is making it good, or it is good only when combined with that something else.[8] Think of harmony as a property of a tune, or a painting. It need not make the tune good. It may make it boring.

Perhaps there are at least two concepts of harmony, one relatively formal and the others relatively substantive (I am using these terms in a non-technical way). The formal concept of harmony has it that anything is harmonious if it comprises parts or components that are arranged, or that function, as they should be (or combined so as to produce a good effect), and any number of items are harmonious if they are arranged

---

[6] Currently he prefers the list he provided in *Reason in Action*, 244n.

[7] *NLNR*, 90.

[8] If it is merely a component of a good, and not one that is intrinsically good in itself, then it is an instrumental or, more accurately, a facilitative good, because it makes the realization of the intrinsic good more likely.

or function as they should be or in ways that will produce a good effect. The substantive notions specify certain relations among the elements of an object such that it is (formally) harmonious if they obtain.[9]

The problem is that saying, e.g. that friendship is good because it is a (formally) harmonious relationship is empty for it amounts to saying that friendship is good because it is a relationship that is as it should be. But saying that friendship is good because it is a (substantively) harmonious relationship is not, in the context in which the statements are made by Finnis, much more help. It is doubtful that there is only one substantive relationship between people that makes their relationship into a (good) friendship. It is likely that there are many different kinds of friendships marked (if harmonies are what makes for good friendships) by different kinds of harmonies. Further kinds of harmonies may make plays good, may make societies good, may make the relationships among states good, etc. Perhaps what is common to all of them is that they are all instances of the formal notion of harmony, but that is uninformative about what exactly makes them good. And unfortunately Finnis does not investigate the different substantive relationships that he implicitly invokes.

This omission means that we do not know what are the basic goods in Finnis's view. They are friendships when they are good friendships, religions that are good religions, and so on—but when are they good we are not told. That has the additional consequence of making it impossible to examine whether they are basic goods, and also impossible to examine whether harmony plays the role in making them good that Finnis claims. That last point may be important. I think, for example, that I live in harmony with many people, including many of whose existence I am unaware, who are not my friends. I also feel that there is much more to friendship than harmony, much more that makes friendships good as friendships than the harmony between the friends. But to find out in what ways I am wrong we need substantive accounts of the different harmonious relationships various goods embody.

The advantage of the case of knowledge is that its examination can avoid these issues.[10] I turn to Finnis's use of it in my attempt to clarify my own mind about the nature of values.

III. The Place of Self-evidence

A question that seems to me fundamental is what makes knowledge valuable? I suspect that Finnis took himself to have dealt with this question in his discussion of the self-evidence of basic values. But I believe that that issue does not touch my question. There

---

[9] There is something appealing in this suggestion, but it is unlikely to be a correct explanation of 'harmony' as it stands, and I am not endorsing it.

[10] So can the examination of some other of the items on Finnis's list of basic goods. However, they all raise complex issues that cannot be examined here. Just by way of example: A much debated question concerns the status of life. Is human life a value (so that there is always a *pro tanto* reason to bring another life into being), or is it that longevity is a value (so that there is always a *pro tanto* reason to prolong the life of any human being) or is life not a value at all, being 'merely' a precondition for the existence of anything of value in human life? The normative implications of these three possibilities (and there are others) closely overlap, yet they diverge in some cases. So far as I am aware Finnis has not discussed in detail the case for and against each of them. For my view see Raz, *Value, Respect and Attachment*, Ch. 3.

are two matters that may be self-evident (and I express no view whether either is): it may be self-evident whether something, say knowledge, is valuable. It may also be self-evident what makes knowledge valuable. My question ('what makes knowledge valuable?') has nothing to do with the doubts about the value of knowledge. It seeks an explanation of its value (if it has one), an explanation of the claim that it has value. The claim that that too is self-evident is (if true) reassuring. But it does not actually give us the answer to the question. It is good to know that the answer is self-evident, but we also want to know what it is.

It is no use saying that because the answer is self-evident we already know it. Finnis rightly alerts us to the fact that not everyone knows all the self-evident truths. And he provides a personal example of this fact: as we know, he himself has changed his mind on the list of the basic goods, even though that these are the basic goods is (according to him) self-evident. But be that as it may, we need not assume that the question (what makes knowledge valuable) is posed by someone who does not know the answer. It is simply a request for the answer to be articulated. (Think of it by analogy to an exam question.) But is there an answer to the question 'what makes knowledge valuable?'? And if there is, must it be possible to express the answer in words?

Some may suspect that the question has no answer. An answer to the question what makes A good could only refer to some other good, B, and state that A is good because it is B. Such explanations are frequently available and helpful, but their availability depends on A being a derivative good, something whose goodness derives from the fact that it is B. Basic goods cannot be explained in that way. They are basic, not derivative. But while it is true that basic goods cannot be reduced to other goods, it is possible that they can be explained, meaning that what makes each one of them the good it is can be explained. These explanations, if available, will be circular in that they will explain evaluative concepts using evaluative concepts. We know that the fundamental concepts all thought relies on cannot be explained in a non-circular way, but some wide circles have explanatory power.

Finnis underlines the intelligibility of values and reasons. Does that commit him to the possibility of explaining what it is about any value that makes it a value? I do not think that he explains what makes knowledge a value. So perhaps he thinks there is no answer to the question. He may be thinking that the fact that the value of knowledge is self-evident makes it intelligible without there being an explanation in language of what makes it a value. This is not a view shared by everyone who believes that some of our knowledge is self-evident. An alternative view is that one can acquire knowledge that P by coming to realize that P is self-evident only if one can understand P. We can have knowledge without understanding what we know. Some objects of knowledge may not be possible objects of understanding. For example, it is possible that green being the colour of grass is not something we can understand. Those who have the concept 'green' know some such truths, for the normal way of having the concept is to be able to identify green objects by looking at them. Blind or colour blind people can have the concept without having that ability, but their knowledge of the colour of things is parasitic on others having it in the normal way: they know that among green things are those that sighted people can recognize as green by looking at them. However, 'knowledge' and the concepts of other basic values do not seem to be concepts whose application can be recognized perceptually. At least they are not concepts whose application is primarily by perceptual recognition. There may be other truths whose understanding is not a possibility. But I agree with Finnis in his insistence on the intelligibility of value, and that seems to imply that it is possible not only to know that something is a value but also to understand what it is that makes it a value. It is of course possible to know without understanding that something is of value. But that knowledge presupposes the possibility of understanding.

Why must value be intelligible? A more subtle argument is called for, but, briefly, it seems plausible that the primary way of identifying what has value is by pointing to features that make it valuable, features relevant to an explanation of what makes the valuable object valuable. The primary way of identifying that something is of value is that it has features or relations that make it valuable, features and relations that we can understand. It cannot be identified by possession of features that are irrelevant to an understanding of what makes it valuable. Compare explaining why rudeness is bad by the fact (let us assume that it is a fact) that it increases the addressees' body temperature with an explanation in terms of its hurting the addressees' feelings and impeding friendly interactions with them. The first cannot possibly be a way of identifying what conduct is rude, or that rudeness is bad, unless one was reliably informed of the connection between rudeness and body temperature by someone (possibly oneself) who could establish its existence because he is able to identify rudeness and its character in the primary way, the way that contributes to an explanation of what makes it bad.

I should underline that I assume neither that there is one privileged explanation (there are many and different ones that would be appropriate in different contexts), nor that anyone who knows of the value of something understands what makes it valuable (there are secondary, derivative ways of identifying what is of value). A more difficult question is whether (as I have been assuming in this description of the case for the intelligibility of value) the understanding of what makes anything of value valuable assumes the ability to explain that in language. After all, we learn the nature of the different values not so much by explicit definition and instruction (though they can help) as by developing through experience and reflection, observation and imitation, a sense of what they are. Arguably, no complete understanding of basic values can be acquired by definition alone, however complex.

These observations, however, while suggesting that the answer to the question what makes knowledge good cannot take the typical form of a definition, do not in the least suggest that the answer is ineffable, and that no explanation(s) in language would do. It may be true, for example, that the best way to teach someone what our values are (what we take to be of value) is to have them live with us and observe, yet surely we can also tell them in words what those values are. And we can do so in a way that enables the learner to apply the newly acquired concepts to new instances, in a variety of contexts, and that requires some understanding of the concept. So, experience suggests that it is possible to explain what makes something of value valuable, even if it is not possible to give a comprehensive explanation on any single occasion.

Why am I belabouring these points? Because Finnis's emphasis on the self-evident character of the value of knowledge raised in my mind not (or not only) the question whether self-evidence plays a role, but a desire to understand the role it plays: its significance and function. Self-evidence is often invoked to rebut scepticism. I think that at best it has only a small role in that drama. Scepticism, when serious, is not a brute doubting, or disinclination to believe. It is rooted in sophisticated arguments about various impossibilities: the so-called metaphysical impossibility of things like values, or properties like having value, existing, or rather being part of the fundamental furniture of the world, arguments about the impossibility of knowing what they are, given the ways knowledge can be acquired, and so on. Explanation and refutation, not self-evidence, assure us against scepticism. My preceding comments aimed to suggest that self-evidence as a source of knowledge or as a fundamental justifying condition does not provide an understanding of value. Rather it presupposes such an understanding. Following Descartes we should say that certainty can be reached when contemplating a clear and distinct idea, or proposition. So we need an answer to the question what makes knowledge a good before we can trust any sense of certainty, or feelings of self-evidence that knowledge is a good. Self-evidence plays a role, if at all, only after all the hard work is done.

IV. Various Reasons for a Single Value?

When presenting knowledge as his central case of a basic value, Finnis explains that he considers only the non-instrumental value of knowledge,[11] and that he considers all knowledge as valuable in itself, in the sense that there is (non-instrumental) value in seeking, and in achieving, knowledge of any proposition.[12] Instrumental value and instrumental reasons used to be taken as relatively simple and unproblematic kinds of value and reasons. But recent writings have shown it to be otherwise. I have written at length on the subject and will here understand the 'instrumental' to be the 'facilitative', namely preparatory, facilitative, or causally efficient steps towards something one has an undefeated reason to pursue, whether or not it is among one's goals. So understood, knowledge can have instrumental or facilitating value, though (a) not all knowledge has it, and (b) that value is derived. The case Finnis presents is for the basic value of knowledge.

Finnis tells us that 'to think of knowledge as a value is not to think that every true proposition is equally worth knowing'.[13] This last claim deserves scrutiny. I take it to mean that different instances of knowledge may have different value and that there may be reasons of different strength to acquire knowledge of different items of knowledge. Obviously, there may be value in knowing some truths that does not depend on or derive from the value of knowledge, and that may make knowing them more valuable than knowing others. For example, knowledge of some moral truths may be part of what it is to be a moral person. That may make knowledge of those truths more valuable, more important, than knowledge of some other truths. That may be due to the fact that having that knowledge is valuable as an instantiation of two distinct values (with apologies for the awkward way I put the point). But it may appear that all

---

[11] *NLNR*, 59.   [12] *NLNR*, 60.   [13] *NLNR*, 62.

instances of one value would be of equal importance, and that one value would generate one reason, a reason of the same strength wherever it applies. After all, if the value provides the reason and the value is the same, how can the reason vary in any respect, including in its strength? How can knowledge of different propositions differ in how valuable it is *qua* knowledge?

One way it can be so is where the value in question can be realized to different degrees: Some paintings may be of greater artistic merit than others. They are all valuable because of their artistic merit, but they have that value in different degrees. Various experiences may be valuable because they are enjoyable, but they may be enjoyable to various degrees. Possibly at least some paintings and some experiences are of different degrees of value because even though they all realize but one value they realize it to various degrees. The possibility that a single value property can be realized to various degrees is problematic and requires analysis. But we can sidestep this matter here, since knowledge does not admit of degrees. So if knowing that P is more valuable than knowing that Q, this is not because there is a higher degree of knowledge in knowing that P than in knowing that Q.[14] The difference, it would seem, is not in the knowing but in the known. But that difference cannot affect how valuable knowing that item is *qua* **knowledge**.

But perhaps this is too quick. Perhaps the value of knowledge is a kind of generic value, and there are various specific values subsumed under it. Take as an example a possible difference in value between knowledge of eclipses and knowledge of the French Revolution. If there is a difference in the value of these species of knowledge it cannot be in their object. It cannot be that knowing about eclipses is more (or less) valuable than knowing what happened, and why, during the French Revolution because somehow the laws of nature are more valuable than the events of the revolution. This does not even make sense. Nor can it be due to the fact that the different types of knowledge have different functions in the life of different people: arguably it is more important (more valuable?) for historians to know history than to know science. That is due to the role knowledge of this or that has in their lives. It marks a difference not in the value of scientific versus historical knowledge as such, but in their value to this person or that. Finnis mentions separately the possibility of varying degrees in value that different areas of knowledge have for one person or another. The variations in value I am trying to understand are variations in the value of knowledge, not in its value for X or Y.

Arguably there is another difference between scientific and historical knowledge. The first but not the second presupposes a reasonably high level of competence in mathematics. The second but not the first engages the empathy of those who possess the knowledge. Do we not have here at least the possibility that different kinds of knowledge, while being the same in being knowledge, vary in value because they

---

[14] I assume that we can dismiss the suggestion that knowing that P can provide one with more knowledge (with a greater quantity of knowledge) than knowing that Q, on the ground that given that any proposition entails or contributes to the entailment of an indefinite number of other propositions there is no purely quantitative measure of how much one knows. If what matters is knowing what it is important to know then it is no longer knowledge alone which determines the value.

require different mental capacities? It is common to think that the possession of, and some of the uses of, many of our capacities are intrinsically valuable. Possibly when people assign different value to different types of knowledge they are influenced by awareness of the different abilities they require. Note that such views cannot underpin the claim that knowledge is valuable in itself. These abilities exist independently of their role in securing knowledge, or some types of knowledge, and they can be manifested in other contexts too. Admittedly, some kinds of knowledge are occasions for the display or use of those abilities. However, not all uses of valuable abilities have any value at all (some murders involve impressive use of important abilities). The use of empathy or other abilities in some knowledge is valuable only if that knowledge is otherwise valuable. True, if knowledge is valuable in itself then, other things being equal, knowledge that involves empathy may be (by that fact) made better than knowledge that does not.

But generally speaking that would be only marginally relevant. We do not normally think that knowledge is admirable as a display of mental powers and abilities. We see that most clearly when considering cases where we do admire people for having the ability to get to know something: 'Jim is so clever', we may say, 'starting from scratch he got on top of quantum mechanics in less than a week'. True, but normally when we find knowledge valuable considerations of this kind are far from our thoughts. To conclude, the engagement of different abilities in different cases of knowledge can make some of them marginally of greater value than others, but (a) only if the knowledge in which the abilities are engaged is independently valuable and (b) it cannot explain the familiar view that knowledge of history is more important than knowledge of local gossip and like opinions.

Another possibility to consider is that knowledge of different areas, or different kinds of knowledge, may be constituent elements of different more complex values. This seems highly likely. A variety of valuable occupations, pastimes, styles of life, and the like require a degree of mastery of knowledge of various areas (think of a clinical psychologist, a stock broker, a youth guide, a hang glider or just about anything). This does not affect the reasons one has to pursue knowledge in any particular area unless one pursues the form of activity of which it is a component. Arguably, however, knowledge of some subjects or areas is part of the ideal of a good human life. That would provide everyone with reason to pursue such knowledge, and arguably, other things being equal, knowledge of these matters is of greater importance than knowledge of other areas. Possibly it is more valuable because other knowledge in itself has no value. After all, knowledge that is part of the ideal of a good life would be valuable even if knowledge is not valuable in itself. If it is not then the argument for the superior value of that knowledge does not show that some cases of knowledge can have different value as knowledge.

V. Is Knowledge Valuable?

Knowledge that is part of an ideal of a good human life would be valuable as part of that ideal even if knowledge is not valuable in itself. It could be that knowledge that is a constituent part of the good life is valuable not merely as a component of the good life, but also in itself. Think of an example: assume that knowledge of what makes life good is part of the ideal of a good life.[15] It seems reasonable that it is part of the good life because it is good in itself, and that it is good in itself not because it is knowledge, but because it is knowledge-of-this-matter. Having this knowledge constitutes an orientation towards the world and life in it. It is not mere theoretical knowledge. But some kinds of purely theoretical knowledge may be intrinsically valuable, on analogous grounds. For example, knowing how things work where one is in the world, and I mean both having the knowledge that enables one to understand people and other animals, their conduct and social processes, and having the technical knowledge that enables one to understand how the machines and tools one uses and those that service one's needs work, having that knowledge also affects, meaning constitutes part of, one's mode of being in the world, one's orientation to oneself, other people, and the environment one lives in.

Could it be that when knowledge is valuable in itself what makes it valuable are factors of these kinds? There may also be other features that make some knowledge valuable. Perhaps some knowledge is formative of ways of relating to the world, of living in the world. Some knowledge may be valuable because it opens valuable opportunities for those who have it. And there is of course knowledge that is good for this person or that because of its role in their life, and there is always the important facilitative value that so much knowledge has.

So, being part of a valuable orientation towards oneself and the world makes some knowledge valuable. Being part of options for various activities and pursuits may make some (possibly different areas of) knowledge valuable, and some knowledge may be valuable for one person or another, because of its relations to their chosen relationships and pursuits. As these diverse grounds do not all apply to the same kinds or domains of knowledge their existence does not contribute to a case for thinking that knowledge is good in itself. Moreover, all of this leaves much knowledge without value at all. Some cats were born on 20 November 720 A.D. But is there any value at all in knowing how many? There appears to be an indefinite number of truths, knowledge of which is without value, and which, moreover, are not objects of human curiosity. If Finnis is right then there is some value in having such knowledge. But not knowing what, in his view, makes knowledge valuable makes it difficult to assess his view.

Bibliography

Finnis, John, *Natural Law and Natural Rights* (Oxford: Clarendon Press, 2011).
Finnis, John, *Reason in Action: Collected Essays of John Finnis* volume I (Oxford: OUP, 2011).
Raz, Joseph, *Value, Respect and Attachment* (Cambridge: CUP, 2000).

---

[15] I am not assuming that no other knowledge is part of the good life.

2

Finnis on Well-being

Roger Crisp

In the 1970s, a lively philosophical debate developed concerning what it is that makes life good for the person living it—that is, concerning well-being or self-interest. According to Derek Parfit, theories of well-being can be placed in one of three categories:

> On *Hedonistic Theories*, what would be best for someone is what would make his life happiest. On *Desire-Fulfilment Theories*, what would be best for someone is what, throughout his life, would best fulfil his desires. On *Objective List Theories*, certain things are good or bad for us, whether or not we want to have the good things, or to avoid the bad things.[1]

The theories Parfit has in mind appear to be what one might call *substantive* theories of well-being—theories answering the question, 'What does well-being consist in?'. Thus understood, the theories are not mutually exclusive. So it might be claimed that (a) happiness is what would be best for someone, (b) happiness is what would best fulfil a person's desires, and (c) happiness is good for us, whether we want to have it or not (since it does not follow from my wanting certain things that will in fact make me happy that I want happiness). The substantive question is of course important. But any answer to it raises further *explanatory* questions: 'What is it about this thing, or these things, that *makes*, or make, them good for a person? What is (or are) their good-making property (or properties)?'

Like other graduate students in Oxford in the mid-1980s, I took it that the canonical statement of a contemporary objective list theory was that of John Finnis.[2] Finnis answered both the substantive and explanatory questions with characteristic clarity and force.[3] Well-being, he argues, consists in seven basic goods, and these items are good because of their intrinsic nature, not because they make us happier, fulfil our desires, or whatever. My impression is that, during that period, hedonism was considered by most philosophers to be dead in the water. The debate, then, was between desire and objective list theorists. Over the last two decades, I have come to believe that hedonism has greater resources to defend itself than many have thought. Like Finnis, I have never seen any plausibility in desire theories. The fact that something fulfils a desire of mine is a mere psychological fact about it. In itself (that is, purely in so far as it

---

[1] Parfit, *Reasons and Persons*, 493.

[2] Let me take this opportunity to thank John for the warm welcome he gave me as a British Academy Postdoctoral Research Fellow at University College in 1989. Our conversations about Aristotle and other matters were one of the intellectual highlights of those now regrettably distant days.

[3] See especially *NLNR*. All page references in the text are to this work.

fulfils a desire), it gives me no reason to pursue the item in question, and cannot add to its goodness for me. Of course, by fulfilling some desire, I may acquire something good in itself (knowledge, perhaps, if knowledge is a good), or avoid something bad in itself (such as the unpleasantness of frustration). But these goods and bads are best accounted for by other theories. The real debate, then, is the one that dominated philosophical discussion until the emergence of desire- and preference-accounts of well-being in the late 19th century: that between hedonism and objective list theories. In this chapter I propose to examine Finnis's version of the objective list theory from a hedonist point of view. My conclusion will be somewhat sceptical, but it will at least leave hedonism in as strong a position as objective list accounts.

Before moving on to discuss Finnis's list of basic goods, let me note some further, welcome points of agreement between us. One rather obvious one is that we both accept the notion of well-being, which has been questioned by, among others, G.E. Moore and T.M. Scanlon.[4] It is possible for a person's life to go well or badly for her, and it is an important task for philosophy to work out what that going well or badly consists in. One might even claim that it is hard to think of any more important question, whether for philosophy or humanity as a whole.

Like Finnis, I believe that the truths about well-being are self-evident (32, 59, 65, 67–8, *passim*). Finnis, however, reads more into the notion of self-evidence than I would. According to him, self-evident truths are 'indemonstrable' (32). Though I accept that one cannot *derive* a proposition, in so far as it is self-evident, from other propositions (70, 73, 75), as J.S. Mill put it: 'Considerations may be presented capable of determining the intellect either to give or withhold its assent to the doctrine; and this is equivalent to proof'.[5] I take it that much of Finnis's argumentation is indeed to be understood as an attempt to provide such considerations. He does not merely present us with the seven basic goods and ask us to consult ourselves as to their goodness. Consider, for example, his reference to Nozick's case of the experience-machine as bringing out what is wrong with hedonism.[6]

Nor, *pace* Finnis (59; though cf. 65), need self-evident truths be *obvious*. Consider an example of Robert Audi's: 'If there never have been any siblings then there never have been any first cousins'.[7] A truth is self-evident to the extent that warrant for believing it consists in understanding that truth itself, and that understanding may require a good deal of time and reflection. And, I shall suggest below, such a truth may be inaccessible to many, however much time and reflection they give to its assessment.

What is it that enables us to grasp such self-evident truths? Finnis prefers not to speak of 'intuition', because the insight in question 'is not made in the absence of data, nor by any "noticeable" intellectual act'.[8] By 'data' here, Finnis may well have in mind the kinds of 'considerations . . . capable of determining the intellect' I mentioned above, and I see no reason why ethical intuitionists should not allow that such considerations can facilitate the grasp of self-evident truths. As for 'noticeability', Finnis surely does

---

[4] Moore, *Principia Ethica*, 99–102; Scanlon, *What We Owe to Each Other*, 109–43.
[5] Mill, *Utilitarianism*, 1.5.20–3.   [6] *NLNR*, 95–6; *FoE*, 37–42.
[7] Audi, 'Intuitionism, Pluralism, and the Foundations of Ethics', 114.
[8] *FoE*, 51.

not intend to claim that our grasp of self-evident truths is somehow beyond the grasp of consciousness. Consider again the claim about siblings above. It seems quite possible to attend to the process leading up to the grasp of such a truth, and indeed that grasp itself. *How* we can grasp such truths, of course, is a very difficult question, but it is also a different one. In other words, I take Finnis, despite his unwillingness to use the term 'intuition', to be an intuitionist, who believes that human beings have a rational capacity to grasp the truth of certain theoretical and practical self-evident propositions.

I am in sympathy also with Finnis's linking evaluation with normativity, that is, goodness with reasons for action. But I would prefer to put at least a whisker between the two notions. Finnis claims that 'Knowledge is something good to have' is a 'practical principle' (63). If his claim is conceptual, it seems mistaken. Consider an extreme aesthete, who believes that our only reason for action is to promote beauty in the world. She might accept that knowledge is good for someone to have, but deny that this goodness grounds any reason for action on her part or on that of others. This is, I admit, a peculiar view; but it is not an incoherent one. We should not, then, accept a so-called 'buck-passing' account of goodness, according to which goodness is a 'purely formal, higher-order [property] of having some lower-order [property or] properties that provide reasons'.[9] Nevertheless, in the case of well-being, I agree with Finnis that the fact that something promotes my well-being is in fact a reason for me to incorporate it into my life. So we may insert the premise missing in the argument from the claim about the goodness of knowledge to a normative conclusion:

1. Knowledge is something that promotes my well-being.
2. I have a reason to seek anything that promotes my well-being.
3. Therefore, I have a reason to seek knowledge.

Having registered these points of agreement, let me move to discuss Finnis's seven basic goods (86–90).

I. Knowledge

Though this comes second in Finnis's list, after *Life*, he discusses it first, dedicating a whole chapter to defending its place on his list. The value ascribed to knowledge by Finnis is, of course, non-instrumental: knowledge is valuable in itself, not merely as something that will, say, promote my survival (62). Nor is all knowledge equally valuable: it is more valuable to know whether the claims in some important philosophical book are true or false than to know how much printer's ink was used to produce the book in question.

Finnis's primary argument for the value of knowledge, as for the value of other items on his list, is by appeal to (what I would call) the reader's intuition:

> It is obvious that those who are well-informed, etc., simply *are* better-off (other things being equal) than someone who is muddled, deluded, and ignorant, that the state of the former is better than the state of the latter, not just in this particular case or that,

---

[9] Scanlon, *What We Owe to Each Other*, 97.

but in all cases, as such, universally, and *whether I like it or not*. Knowledge is better than ignorance. Am I not compelled to admit it...? (72)

I feel no such compulsion. Knowledge is some kind of attitude to propositions. It used to be widely accepted that it was justified and true belief, but of course so-called Gettier examples have thrown that view into serious doubt.[10] But whatever it is, most accept that knowledge is not to be understood merely as an occurrent, conscious mental state. Reading this sentence, you are aware of your knowledge that full moons do not always happen on Tuesdays. But this is knowledge you had before reading the sentence. Indeed, it was knowledge you had while deeply asleep last night. Now imagine that God creates some being with great knowledge, far beyond that any human has or will attain. But this being has no awareness or conscious life of any kind. In my view, it makes no difference to this being whether it has knowledge or not. Indeed, its life is of no value to it at all. Or consider a case in which someone who does know a great deal about many important things begins to suffer from some medical condition which causes her to fall into a very deep sleep for increasing numbers of hours a day. She is likely to be very distressed at the effect of this on the value of her life, and I cannot imagine her comforting herself with the thought: 'Well, at least I will still have my knowledge while I'm asleep.'

It might be claimed that knowledge when it is combined with conscious awareness is a constituent of well-being. This claim, however, will leave it mysterious why knowledge which remains purely dispositional can add value to a person's life if it is not affecting her consciousness at that time, while it cannot add such value when she is asleep. The link between knowledge and conscious awareness would need to be made considerably tighter. Could the value of knowledge, then, be as an element in occurrent states of reflection or contemplation of what is known? Imagine that God makes the previously non-conscious knower aware of what she knows, and that she spends her time contemplating various important truths. She has no purpose in doing so, and gains no enjoyment from it. Again, I myself can see no value in such a life. We now have a clash of intuitions, that is, a disagreement about *apparently* self-evident truths. How we should approach such disagreement I shall return to below.

In the case of knowledge, Finnis has an argument independent of appeal to intuition, to the conclusion that any sceptical argument about the value of knowledge will be 'self-defeating' (73–5). The self-defeatingness in question Finnis calls 'operational self-refutation',[11] and this arises when some proposition is *inevitably* falsified by assertion of it. One example is 'I do not exist'.[12] And, Finnis claims, the assertion that knowledge is not a good in this category is self-refuting, since, if one makes that assertion with the intention of contributing to a serious rational discussion, 'one is implicitly committed to the proposition that one believes that one's assertion is worth making, and worth

---

[10] Gettier, 'Is Justified True Belief Knowledge?', 121–3; see Russell, *Human Knowledge: Its Scope and Limits*, 170–1.

[11] See *CEJF* I.3, with reference to Mackie, 'Self-Refutation—A Formal Analysis', 197. Finnis's essay is a development of his 'Scepticism, Self-refutation, and the Good of Truth'.

[12] A better one might be 'Nothing exists'.

making *qua* true ... [and] thus ... to the proposition that one believes that truth is a good worth pursuing or knowing' (74–5).

Even by Finnis's own lights, the scope of this argument is limited. It does not apply to the sceptic who, though she sincerely believes her position, is uninterested in serious rational discussion, and is making her assertion just to be playful or annoying. But it is not clear why even those who wish to participate in such discussion have to believe that knowledge is good in itself for their assertion to be not only intelligible but reasonable.[13] They may indeed wish to acquire knowledge, but purely for instrumental reasons. Or, though they see serious rational discussion as itself aimed at the truth, they may believe the value of it for them lies solely in the enjoyment they take from the dialectical struggle with their opponent. The claim that knowledge is not a good, then, is not operationally self-refuting.

II. Life

Finnis, as appropriate for an Aristotelian, tends to see basic human goods in the light of the activities in which they are allegedly implicit. So in the case of life, the first human motivation he mentions is the drive for self-preservation. But he goes on to include in this category not mere biological survival, but 'every aspect of the vitality (*vita*, life) which puts a human being in good shape for self-determination' (86).

The phrasing Finnis here uses itself suggests that what he has in mind by life is not something valuable in itself, but a set of necessary conditions for pursuing genuinely non-instrumental goods, such as that of self-determination. Consider another case of divine creation, in which God creates some being with the various relevant aspects of 'vitality': bodily and mental health, freedom from pain, and indeed various desires. But for some reason—perhaps because the opportunities are not available—this being never engages in any non-trivial activity or experiences enjoyment of any kind. Can we allow that nevertheless her life contained something of value for her merely through the presence of the aspects of vitality?

III. Play

By 'play', Finnis means 'performances which have no point beyond the performance itself, enjoyed for its own sake' (87), and which can be seen as distinct from any

---

[13] Finnis offers an extended version of his argument in *CEJF* I.3, 72–3. The dubious step in this argument, I suggest, is: (4) 'I assert that *p*' entails 'I believe that *p* is worth asserting.'

This premise is said to lead to: (6) 'I assert that *p*' entails 'I believe that truth is [a good] worth [pursuing or] knowing.'

In his elucidation of (4) (*CEJF* I.3, 74), Finnis seeks to draw an analogy between the case he is discussing and a Moorean paradox implicit in the assertion: '*p*, but I do not believe that *p*'. There is no paradox, however, in asserting *p* but denying that *p* is worth asserting. Consider: 'I assert that a piece of string two inches long is twice as long as a piece of string one inch long. But I do not believe that it is worth asserting this.' It might be objected that it *is* worth my making this assertion, since it is playing a role in my argument. But Finnis explicitly notes that he is speaking not only of assertion, but of judgement. I accept and judge to be true a very large, perhaps infinite, number of propositions about pieces of string. The vast majority (perhaps apart from the one I just made) I judge not worth asserting—indeed, worth not asserting.

'serious' (that is, non-playful) context. (So play can take place in contexts such as the drafting of legislation, but it is to be conceived of independently of the activity of drafting itself.)

The reference to enjoyment here might be taken to imply at least a partially hedonistic conception of the value of play. But a later passage makes clear that no such implication was intended:

> The experiences of...creative play...are pleasurable..., but it is because we want to...create...that we want the experiences. What matters to us, in the final analysis, is...significantly patterned or testing performances (and performing them)...If these give pleasure, this experience is one aspect of their reality as human goods, which are not participated in fully unless their goodness is experienced as such. But a participation in basic goods which is emotionally dry, subjectively unsatisfying, nevertheless is good and meaningful as far as it goes. (96–7)[14]

Finnis appears to be working with two different conceptions of play. According to the first, play consists in enjoyable activity. Consider someone who is taking great pleasure in seeing whether while sitting at her desk she can flip coins into her waste-paper basket. Here it is hard to see why such activity, stripped of enjoyment, should be valuable. According to the second, play consists in successfully engaging in certain especially complex or difficult activities (see also 408–9). But here the idea of play drops out. As the passage above makes clear, these activities need not be enjoyed. And there seems little reason to restrict them to the domain of the non-serious, especially since there is no independent place on Finnis's list for serious complex or difficult activities. In other words, brilliantly drafting some piece of legislation, even if the drafter gains no enjoyment from it, is the kind of activity Finnis has in mind.

Here we are speaking of what James Griffin calls the value of 'accomplishment': 'We all want to do something with our lives, to act in a way that gives them some point or substance.'[15] That accomplishment adds to the value of a person's life is a highly plausible view. But let me mention some hedonist arguments against it.[16]

(1) Accomplishment, like many other allegedly non-hedonistic goods, is, as Finnis himself points out, something human beings tend to enjoy. Much more worrying for a hedonist would be an alleged non-hedonistic good which is widely accepted as a constituent of well-being and never enjoyed.

(2) Consequentialists standardly make room for common-sense moral principles within their theory by giving them a 'secondary' status.[17] Rather than directly trying to maximize utility, for example, I might produce more utility overall by following certain non-consequentialist principles requiring me to refrain from harming others, to keep promises, and so on. Likewise, a hedonist may claim that aiming at accomplishment, on the basis of a belief in its intrinsic value, will be more productive of enjoyment overall than aiming directly at enjoyment.

---

[14] See also *FoE*, 47.   [15] Griffin, *Well-Being*, 64.
[16] See Crisp, *Reasons and the Good*, 117–25.
[17] See e.g. Mill, *Utilitarianism*, 2.24.

(3) Our beliefs about values are the product of evolution. Many years ago, during the Stone Age, those who achieved more in the field would have been rewarded by their companions with a larger share of goods, including social esteem. This practice is likely to be the origin of our admiration for accomplishment. Of course, this does not debunk the claim that accomplishment is valuable in its own right. But it may throw it into some doubt.

(4) I have already suggested that a life consisting only in unenjoyed contemplation of truth is not clearly valuable. The same claim might be made about accomplishment. Consider someone who writes a great novel, but takes no pleasure in writing it and does so purely to make money.

(5) The value we place on accomplishment seems to depend on the perspective we take on it. In our own case, we take a view internal to our own life, and from that point of view what we accomplish seems to matter significantly. But there is also an external point of view, and, as Thomas Nagel puts it, 'In seeing ourselves from outside we find it difficult to take our lives seriously.'[18] We might imagine our novel writer comparing herself to God: what is writing even *War and Peace* compared to creating a universe? What if we could all write as well as Tolstoy?[19] Again, we do not here have a knock-down argument against the claims of accomplishment. But the defender of accomplishment has to defend the perspective she is taking in a way that a hedonist does not (since the hedonist need not be committed to claims about 'importance' or 'meaningfulness').

(6) Accomplishment depends on valuing agency—what people do—over what is allowed or what happens. So if Michelangelo had allowed some pupil of his to paint the ceiling of the Sistine Chapel, and it had turned out to be even more wonderful than it is now, the credit would have gone to the pupil not to Michelangelo for allowing it to happen. The attaching of such significance to the doing/allowing distinction has been widely questioned in recent philosophy, so here is another place where there is work to do for the defender of accomplishment.

(7) And yet another defence must be mounted in the territory of the freedom of the will. If accomplishment is 'determined', its value becomes dubious, though it may be that some version of compatibilism is sufficient to justify our continuing to see it as a good. Otherwise, of course, a version of libertarianism is required. To supply either of these views is a tall order, and again not one that the hedonist has to fulfil.

IV. Aesthetic Experience

This value is not to be subsumed under the heading of 'Play', although beauty can be found in some forms of play. Beauty is also found in nature, and appreciation of it may not involve action as usually understood.

Note that a sceptic about the value of such experience as a component of well-being is not required to claim that beauty itself is valueless. The question is whether merely

---

[18] Nagel, *The View from Nowhere*, 214.
[19] Nozick, *Anarchy, State, and Utopia*, 241, 245.

experiencing (or, rather, as Finnis notes, *appreciating*) that beauty is good for the subject. Several of the arguments above apply also to aesthetic experience. The main difficulty here is that it is not clear why such experience, when it is devoid of any kind of enjoyment for its subject, should be considered of value *for that subject*. Consider once again the divinely created and conscious contemplator of truths. Will value be added to her life merely because she can recognize the aesthetic value of certain objects, without taking any pleasure in such recognition?

V. Sociability (Friendship)

Here Finnis has in mind a value with the breadth of Aristotelian *philia*, ranging from peaceful cohabitation with fellow citizens to full personal friendship:[20]

> Indeed, the good that is common between friends is not simply the good of successful collaboration or co-ordination, nor is it simply the good of two successfully achieved coinciding projects or objectives; it is the common good of mutual self-constitution, self-fulfilment, self-realization. (141)

It is not clear whether Finnis wishes to go so far as to interpret Aristotle literally, and to agree with him, when he says that a friend is 'another self'.[21] I suspect that he means by 'mutual self-constitution' not the blending of one's person's identity into that of another, but the shaping of an individual self through the engagement with another in some common project.

Friendship, as Finnis brings out well, involves non-egoistic motivation. One friend will act for the sake of the other's well-being, and value the well-being of the other for the other's own sake (143).[22] Because we admire such caring relationships from the moral point of view, we must take care not to allow such admiration to seep into our judgements of well-being. As Finnis notes, considerations of morality are posterior to issues of well-being (59).

Because friends care for one another, it is hard to see how a hedonist could construct a thought-experiment in which some friendship occurs in the absence of pleasure and pain. If I claim to be your friend, and am not devastated when something very bad happens to you, then I am not your friend. But what we can do is, in thought, focus just on those aspects of friendship that are not themselves constituted by experiences of pleasure and pain. And here it may become hard to see how engaging in joint activities with another whose fate one cares about can matter to well-being in its own right. Imagine I am digging a ditch with a stranger. Suddenly, we are overcome by deep concern for one another's well-being (perhaps engendered by God). Why should this

---

[20] The account in IV.2 is developed further in VI.2–4. Because of its breadth, I take it to include the good of marriage (*pace* Finnis, 'Introduction', *Collected Essays I*, 9–10).

[21] Aristotle, *Ethica Nicomachea*, 1166a31–2.

[22] Finnis suggests also that a friend will treat the other's well-being as an 'aspect' of her own well-being. Again, he need not be read as suggesting that another's well-being can become my own. Rather, his point is that one friend will judge how well her life is going for her partly by how well the friend's life is going for her. One individual's well-being can affect another's without becoming in some mysterious sense part of that other's well-being.

deep concern have as a result that our joint activity adds to our well-being in a way that previously it did not?

VI. Practical Reasonableness

Here Finnis has in mind the exercise of reason in decision-making about actions, including actions directed at shaping one's life or character as a whole. It involves an inner aspect, consisting in an attempt to bring harmony to one's emotions and dispositions to action. At this point, Finnis appears to be deviating from the ancient paradigms of Plato and Aristotle and heading in the direction of a greater psychological realism. Those earlier writers recommend harmony of the soul as an ethical ideal, so that someone who was still in the process of shaping their own character would to that extent be deficient. But no real human being can achieve that ideal, and therefore it is reasonable to recommend the striving to reach the ideal as itself a good. (Presumably, the more successful the striving—as striving—the greater the value.) The external aspect of practical reasonableness is authenticity in action, in which one's free decisions are realized in the world.

I take it that Finnis is assuming that practical reasonableness must be at least in good part shaped by recognition of the other basic values themselves. A pure egoist, motivated only by concern for power, say, might well instantiate order in her freely chosen actions; but that concern is not itself reasonable, and so neither is her practical reasoning. But this enriched conception of practical reasonableness could plausibly be seen as a species of accomplishment, and so open to the doubts raised above in the discussion of the non-hedonistic conception of play.

VII. 'Religion'

The 'scare quotes' are Finnis's, since he sees the term as inadequate to cover the relation of the orders found in one's own life and community to the larger order of the cosmos, and to the possibility of superhuman agency at a level far beyond human freedom and intelligence. Finnis raises the obvious atheist doubt at this point, but suggests that it would be unreasonable to deny that it is especially important to have thought 'reasonably and (where possible) correctly' (89) about our relation to the cosmos, primarily because, if the order of the cosmos is indeed divine, our own lives and actions will be in serious disorder if they are not in harmony with that cosmos as far as possible. Even the atheist Sartre must accept that '"man" is and is-to-be free', thus recognizing an order of things '"beyond" any individual'.[23]

As we have seen, order is central to Finnis's conception of practical reasonableness, and it is tempting to see the value of 'religion' as an extension of that value to cover not only the internal ordering of the agent's inner life and action, but the ordering of that life to reflect whatever metaphysical view of the universe the agent reflectively arrives

---

[23] Finnis's own theistic account is set out, in a reconsideration of practical reasonableness, religion, and play, at *NLNR*, 407–10.

at. Further, since this broadened conception of practical reasonableness can also be seen as an accomplishment, my earlier objections remain relevant.

Objections can be raised, then, to each of the items on Finnis's list of seven basic values. But one major objection to the list as a whole is that it makes no independent room for the value of pleasure or enjoyment (and so also fails to recognize the disvalue of pain or suffering[24]). This objection is not in itself hedonist, since many pluralist objective list theorists will allow hedonic goods onto their list.[25] As we have seen, like Aristotle, Finnis believes that full participation in the genuine basic goods of life will be pleasurable, but 'in the final analysis' (96) pleasure itself is of no value (and, we may presume, Finnis sees no disvalue in pain or suffering in itself).[26] But, as we have seen also, we can imagine cases of full participation in values such as that of accomplishment (non-hedonic 'play') in the absence of pleasure. Consider religion. It may take a great deal of effort to work out one's conception of one's place in the universe, and it may be psychologically troubling or even traumatic. It is not clear why engaging in such reasoning is in any sense lacking as reasoning (though of course it is of course lacking in the value of enjoyment).

Finnis's main objection to hedonism as a theory of well-being is based on Robert Nozick's famous thought-experiment, the so-called *experience machine* (95–7)[27]:

> Suppose there were an experience machine that would give you any experience you desired. Superduper neuropsychologists could stimulate your brain so that you would think and feel you were writing a great novel, or making a friend, or reading an interesting book. All the time you would be floating in a tank, with electrodes attached to your brain ... Would you plug in? *What else can matter to us, other than how our lives feel from the inside?*[28]

Like Nozick, and unsurprisingly given his list of basic goods, Finnis believes that no sensible person will wish to plug into the experience machine, because one wants to *do* certain things, to *be* a certain kind of person, and actively to *live* in a real world with real values.

A hedonist may respond that, in an admittedly fictional sense, one will be acting in the machine, and that there is no reason why we must assume the machine will determine one's choices for one, so in a non-fictional sense one will continue to exist in the machine as the kind of person one was. Further, of course, a hedonist will reject the idea that one's well-being can be affected in ways that do not affect one's own conscious states: what you don't know can't hurt you. And many of the arguments above regarding accomplishment can be used against the evaluative assumptions of the experience-machine objection.

---

[24] At 410, Finnis claims that in the '"final analysis" ... even atrocious miseries ... are really serious *only* to the extent that they contribute to or are caught up into a good play of the game of the God who creates and favours human good' (my italics).

[25] See Griffin, *Well-Being*, 67. For an interpretation of Griffin's view as close to an objective list theory, see Crisp, 'The Road to Objectivity', 131.

[26] Aristotle, *Ethica Nicomachea*, 1175b24–7.

[27] See *FoE*, 38–42.

[28] Nozick, *Anarchy, State, and Utopia*, 142–3.

Rather than develop these responses further, I wish to conclude by asking what is the rational response to what will almost certainly remain a stand-off between Finnis and the hedonist on the correct view of well-being. Essentially, what we have is a fundamental disagreement between two non-inferential beliefs (that is, apparently self-evident intuitions). In his *Methods of Ethics*, Henry Sidgwick—fully aware of the possibility of error and disagreement—asked what conditions an apparently self-evident proposition should meet if it is to reach 'the highest degree of certainty attainable'.[29] The first three conditions are fairly straightforward: the terms of the proposition must be clear and precise; the proposition must be seriously reflected upon; and propositions taken to be self-evident must be consistent with one another. The fourth, however, is more troubling:

> Since it is implied in the very notion of Truth that it is essentially the same for all minds, the denial by another of a proposition that I have affirmed has a tendency to impair my confidence in its validity . . . [I]t will be easily seen that the absence of such disagreement must remain an indispensable negative condition of the certainty of our beliefs. For if I find any of my judgments, intuitive or inferential, in direct conflict with a judgment of some other mind, there must be error somewhere: and if I have no more reason to suspect error in the other mind than in my own, reflective comparison between the two judgments necessarily reduces me temporarily to a state of neutrality. And though the total result in my mind is not exactly suspense of judgment, but an alternation and conflict between positive affirmation by one act of thought and the neutrality that is the result of another, it is obviously something very different from scientific certitude.

Sidgwick is especially talented at close and honest introspection. Here we see him describing how hard it is to suspend one's own judgement on some matter when one is confronted with disagreement by an 'epistemic peer'—that is, someone whose judgement on that matter one has no reason to think more liable to error than one's own. Consider the following case:

> *Birds.* You and a friend are wandering together in the countryside. The light is good. Both of you have recently been attending a course for novice ornithologists, and each of you knows that the other is roughly equally good at bird-identification. At the same moment, each of you sees a bird on a tree-branch about ten meters away. You believe it to be a redwing, while your friend says it is a song thrush.[30]

Now you might *feel certain* that the bird is a redwing. But you are quite aware not only that your friend might feel the same way about her identification of it as a song thrush, but that the epistemic entitlement each of you has to your claim is equal. If you now reflect upon Sidgwick's fourth condition, you may—indeed, if Sidgwick is right, you *should*—accept that you just do not know whether the bird is a redwing or a song thrush—it is roughly equally likely to be either. But that will not stop you thinking: 'It's a redwing!' This is the 'alternation and conflict' of which Sidgwick is speaking.

[29] Sidgwick, *The Methods of Ethics*, 338–42.
[30] Crisp, 'Reasonable Disagreement: Sidgwick's Principle and Audi's Intuitionism', 151.

The epistemic upshot of the application of Sidgwick's condition to the debate between Finnis and the hedonist is that each of them is required to suspend judgement on their position on well-being *unless* they have some plausible theory of error to justify the conclusion that their opponent is not an epistemic peer. I submit that at present neither of them can have such a theory. We know far too little about the sources of evaluative and normative opinion, and hence of sources of error in such opinion.

Does this mean that we can be certain about nothing in ethics? Almost. I am inclined to think that if there is some evaluative or normative proposition on which nearly everyone agrees, we are entitled to claim at least near-certainty for that proposition (though we must always remember that we can be mistaken, even if in fact *everyone* agrees, and has always agreed, with the proposition in question). Consider the following propositions:

> *P1*: An hour of agonizing and undeserved suffering makes a person's life go, in respect of that suffering, worse.
> *P2*: A person has a reason to avoid such a period of suffering.

As I have suggested, it may be an implication of Finnis's view of pleasure as valueless that pain and suffering are also neutral. So he might disagree with these two propositions. But he would almost certainly be in a *tiny* minority, to the extent that it would not be implausible to argue that he has somehow been misled by argument to a mistaken conclusion. But anyway, these propositions do not take one very far in practical ethics. Only *P2* concerns reasons for action, and it speaks only of one reason each of us has among others. Further, it concerns the reason an individual has to avoid herself suffering. A version of egoism according to which each of us has no reason, in itself, to relieve the suffering of another person is quite consistent with *P2*.

I see no good epistemic reason to deny Sidgwick's fourth condition (though I fully accept that I cannot be certain of it, given that many of my epistemic peers disagree with it!). Does that mean the end of practical philosophy? Far from it. Return to my simple case of disagreement over the identification of birds. You might give a reason for your view: 'I'm sure it had a creamy strip over its eye.' Now your friend might respond: 'I'm sure it didn't. And it didn't have any redness on its flanks either.' Or she might say: 'Ah, I didn't look for that. Perhaps you're right.' In other words, there is no reason why disagreements between epistemic peers cannot be taken further, with each party to the debate continuing to assert their own position, giving reasons, offering arguments, pointing to salient features of the situation or the case at hand, or whatever. Further, in the case of judgements about well-being and the practical implications of well-being, it is hard to deny that one approach likely to bring us closer to agreement, and to the truth, is that of philosophy.

Bibliography

Aristotle (1894), *Ethica Nicomachea* (ed. I. Bywater, Oxford: Clarendon Press).

Audi, Robert (1996), 'Intuitionism, Pluralism, and the Foundations of Ethics', in Mark Timmons & Walter Sinnott-Armstrong (eds), *Moral Knowledge? New Readings in Moral Epistemology* (New York: OUP), 101–36.

Crisp, Roger (1989), 'The Road to Objectivity', *Philosophical Books* 30: 129–36.

Crisp, Roger (2006), *Reasons and the Good* (Oxford: Clarendon Press).

Crisp, Roger (2012), 'Reasonable Disagreement: Sidgwick's Principle and Audi's Intuitionism', in Jill G. Hernandez (ed.), *The New Intuitionism* (London: Continuum), 151–68.

Finnis, John (1977), 'Scepticism, Self-Refutation, and the Good of Truth', in P.M. Hacker & J. Raz (eds), *Law, Morality, and Society: Essays in Honour of H.L.A. Hart* (Oxford: Clarendon Press), 247–67.

Finnis, John (1983), *The Fundamentals of Ethics* (Oxford: Clarendon Press).

Finnis, John (2011), *Natural Law and Natural Rights* (2nd ed., Oxford: OUP).

Finnis, John (2011), 'Introduction', in *Reason and Action: Collected Essays Vol. I* (Oxford: OUP), 1–15.

Finnis, John (2011), 'Scepticism's Self-Refutation', in *Reason and Action: Collected Essays Vol. I* (Oxford: OUP), 62–91.

Gettier, Edmund (1963), 'Is Justified True Belief Knowledge?', *Analysis* 23: 121–3.

Griffin, James (1986), *Well-Being: Its Meaning, Measurement, and Moral Importance* (Oxford: Clarendon Press, 1986).

Mackie, J.L. (1964), 'Self-Refutation: A Formal Analysis', *Philosophical Quarterly* 14: 193–203.

Mill, J.S. ([1871] 1998), *Utilitarianism* (4th ed., repr., ed. R. Crisp, Oxford: OUP).

Moore, G.E. (1903), *Principia Ethica* (Cambridge: CUP).

Nagel, T. (1986), *The View from Nowhere* (New York: OUP).

Nozick, R. (1974), *Anarchy, State, and Utopia* (Oxford: Blackwell).

Parfit, Derek (1984), *Reasons and Persons* (Oxford: Clarendon Press).

Russell, Bertrand (1948), *Human Knowledge: Its Scope and Limits* (London: George Allen & Unwin).

Scanlon, T.M. (1998), *What We Owe to Each Other* (Cambridge, MA: Belknap Press).

Sidgwick, Henry (1907), *The Methods of Ethics* (7th ed., London: Macmillan).

3

Reasoning about the Human Good, and the Role of the Public Philosopher

John Haldane

I

The published writings of John Finnis constitute one of the most substantial and significant contemporary presentations, both theoretical and practical, of natural law reasoning about values and principles pertaining to the conduct of life, both individual and communal. They are marked by a degree of rigour of examination and argument characteristic of anglophone 'analytical' philosophy, but also by adherence to a pre-modern tradition of 'right-reason' particularly in the form associated with Thomas Aquinas. Further to this, and contrary to the temper of modern times, they acknow-ledge the legitimate role of authority in morals beyond that of experience or expertise. This possibility arises out of two circumstances: that in which it is necessary for some practical project that someone or some office should be in command; and that in which someone has been put in command by a higher authority for the sake of the common good. Evidently these two circumstances may coincide but equally they may not.

To maintain further that natural reason and a magisterium based on revelation presenting moral teaching as doctrine may not only be harmonized but shown to be mutually supportive, is exceedingly unusual in the secular academy. To do so at the level of particular ethical and social questions is rarer still; and to draw the conclusions that Finnis has done in such areas as sexual conduct, the beginning and ending of life, warfare, state authority, and the limits of liberty, is quite exceptional and challenges the assumption widespread in the secular academic sphere that natural law and traditional morality lack intellectual credibility.

Here I am not concerned to expound Finnis's account of natural law for the purpose of criticizing or defending it, though I shall suggest that where some have seen opposition(s) between the kind of view he has presented as deriving from Aquinas, and that described as 'traditional' Thomistic natural law theory, there are opportunities for synthesis. Further, I wish to suggest that advocates of 'old' and 'new' natural law might do well to incorporate something of the phenomenological approach to value. Put in terms of theories and methods I suggest that there is no difficulty in combining the metaphysics of animate substance, the rationality of practical agency, and the personalistic phenomen-ology of value and that there is much to be gained from doing so, particularly in the context of contemporary debates about morality and public policy.

The phenomenological approach is associated historically with the Austrian school of value theory (axiology) deriving from Husserl and including such figures as Max

Scheler and Nicolai Hartman; but, as Husserl's teacher Franz Brentano recognized, it is at least pre-figured in the writings of the Scottish moral sense philosophers, in particular Francis Hutcheson and Adam Smith. Aspects of both traditions, as well as of early 20th-century English moral intuitionism, were drawn upon in what is perhaps the most interesting attempt at a theoretical and practical value-ethics, that presented in the writings of the Hungarian philosopher Aurel Kolnai. Like Finnis, Kolnai was a convert to the Catholic faith, and while an admirer of Aquinas he was not a member of a Thomist school. Again like Finnis he emphasized that knowledge of various goods is available on the basis of experience and reflective insight without recourse to moral theory or metaphysics. Where Finnis writes of 'insight' Kolnai speaks of 'intellectual perception', each meaning to suggest a form of knowledge that arises within the individual but is not deduced or otherwise derived from premises, even though it is grounded in lived experience.[1]

The matters introduced thus far are theoretical, but as the title and mention of morality and public policy indicates I am also concerned with how arguments should be made in the public sphere and with the role of the philosopher, or other theorist of value and conduct, in contributing to public debates. John Finnis has been such a contributor, particularly in relation to the ethics of nuclear deterrence, and the making and taking of human life. He has also reflected on the question of what, if any, are reasonable constraints on the premises and modes of argument that may be deployed in debating public policy. To understand his broad approach, to see how distinctive it is among contemporary philosophical positions, and to assess what it offers by way of example it will be useful to contrast his writings with those of John Rawls, Jurgen Habermas, and Richard Rorty. To narrow the range I shall refer, fairly briefly, to four essays: Rawls's 'Idea of Public Reason Revisited',[2] Habermas's 'Religion in the Public Sphere',[3] Rorty's 'An Ethics for Today',[4] and Finnis's 'Religion and Public Life in a Pluralist Society'.[5]

These were all written within a five-year period against a common background of debate about the place of philosophical and religious beliefs in public discussion of moral and political issues and they can be related to one another geometrically, either as representing corners of a square or as points or regions on a line. Speaking schematically, Finnis represents a broad and deep rationalism, Rawls a narrower and shallower one, Habermas a pragmatic, cultural hermeneutic, and Rorty the rejection of all rationalism, even the weak form of Habermas's reason-constrained pragmatism, in

---

[1] See for example *CEJF* I.Introduction, 2–3: 'insight is not, properly speaking, an inference, a deduction from premises, or even a conclusion from data or experience [though it is grounded in lived experience] . . . Understanding that knowledge is not only possible but desirable, a benefit, a good to be pursued, and that being ignorant or mistaken is undesirable, a lack, deficiency, a bad to be avoided, is another simple, original, and foundational act of insight; in that sense it is not reasoned to'; and Kolnai, 'Morality and Practice I', 85: '[there is] a pre-moral order bearing a general sign of good, and further defined and characterized by the reaction of moral pressure from the part of that order and the loyalties it commands', also Kolnai, *The Utopia Project*, '[one] apprehends [right kinds of action, good and bad in objects and conditions, etc] by "intuition", i.e. a kind of intellectual perception with inseparable emotive accent'.

[2] Rawls, 'Idea of Public Reason Revisited'.

[3] Habermas, 'Religion in the Public Sphere'.

[4] Rorty, 'An Ethics for Today'.   [5] *CEJF* V.2.

favour of rhetoric. In describing Rorty's position in that way I do not mean to prejudge its merit, for if he is right about reason then rhetoric is all we have—and all we could have by way of resources for argument. From that perspective Rawls's political liberalism remains unduly rationalistic and impartial, while from Finnis's point of view it illegitimately restricts the sources and scope of rationality.

II

Before considering the scope of public reason and the need for public philosophy, however, I need to address the question of how there can be anything to say about norms, values, and requirements other than describing and/or endorsing the attitudes and commitments of individuals or groups. In another essay from the same period as those mentioned and on the same broad themes, Simon Blackburn positions himself in relation to Rorty, describing features of the latter's relativist and pragmatist general philosophy and the 'liberal irony' it is taken to enjoin. I shall return to the 'liberal' part of that later but so far as 'irony' is concerned the idea is that the underlying philosophical positions require the ironist to recognize that everything he might choose to say by way of analysis and argument is historically conditioned, provisional, and open to rejection as other sets of views and values come to seem more useful.

This of course is far more than modesty or fallibilism, for the point is not that we have to recognize that our thoughts arise out of historical and social contexts and may be open to improvement or correction; rather it is that they could *never* be right or rationally warranted since there simply is no objective standard of truth or warrant. Blackburn cites Rorty as a prominent example of a non-cognitivist because Blackburn is concerned that any non-objectivist is open to the challenge that his or her first order moral and political claims are undermined for want of the possibility of corresponding to objective reality. As one who holds that moral statements do not purport to represent how the world is but serve to express speakers' attitudes to things, thereby disposing them to act positively or negatively towards them, Blackburn is troubled that his own 'expressivism' may be similarly dismissed as unable to support moral claims particularly as these might be advanced in public debate. He writes:

> The rhetoric is telling: the expressivist is billed as little better than a relativist or nihilist. He doesn't really believe in truth in ethics. He has no proper conception of authority. He thinks that duties, obligations and the rest are fictions... The expressivist is actually no better than the ironists and the debunkers. Only something more robust, a realism about moral fact, will restore us to the self-confidence that we want.[6]

Blackburn goes on to argue that the expressivist is perfectly capable of speaking about truth in ethics, of achieving confidence in his judgements, and in arguing for them:

> The right way to hear the issue of objectivity is in the, first-order, ethical way. Then indeed someone might think the opinion [that cruelty to animals is wrong] is 'subjective' in a number of ways. He might think it whimsical, deriving from something very

---

[6] Blackburn, *Liberalism, Religion and the Sources of Value*, 6–7.

specific to me ... He might be vaunting a society where cruelty is a prelude to bravery in battle.

But I reject all of this ... I have taken in all the facts, seen the situation in the round, and I am reasonably sure that no hidden subjective agenda, such as a desire for my own advantage, is driving the attitude. This is all that objectivity is, or can be.[7]

There are two points to note in this. First the suggestion that the concern with moral objectivity can be met by reference to conditions on the *forming* of judgements; and second the claim that there is nothing else that objectivity could consist in. Let us call the first the 'requirements of conscientiousness', including attention to facts and their contexts, consideration of prejudice, adoption of due disinterest, and so on. Suppose with Blackburn that he has satisfied these requirements and thereby avoided subjectivity in the first-order sense, 'subjectivity' in this case carrying a pejorative connotation: is it possible that even though conscientiously arrived at his judgement is mistaken?

Here it is important not to focus on the particular example of thinking cruelty to animals to be wrong, an opinion with which we are likely to concur (though perhaps for diverse reasons)[8]; for agreement in judgement is no guarantee of correctness, even in Blackburn's theory. It is more proper, therefore, to consider the general question of whether judgements meeting the requirements of conscientiousness might be mistaken. Again the question must be distinguished from another, namely whether one should always follow one's conscientiously determined judgement. Let us suppose with Aquinas that even an erring conscience binds (*Summa Theologiae*, Ia IIae, q.19, a. 5). The issue is whether, once first-order objectivity is exhausted, sense can still be made of mistaken judgement, or, as we might also put it, of erroneous conscience. Ordinarily considered, without reference to philosophical theory, the answer would seem to be that we can. Indeed it is a mark of reflective humility to consider that one may be wrong, morally speaking—this being something different from generalized moral scepticism. But that answer assumes that there is a difference between the standards appropriate to the *formation* of a judgement and those required for its *truth*. The conscientious person seeking to know what is right conducts his or her enquiry with due regard to proper methods in the belief that this raises the likelihood of a correct answer but knowing that it does not guarantee it, for correctness requires objectivity in the second-order sense of truth about the way things really are.

This, however, brings us to the second point, namely Blackburn's claim that there is no possibility of this second kind of objectivity. His reasons for thinking this are full-bloodedly philosophical, having to do with problems surrounding the idea of mind-independent moral facts, and the problem of seeing how, even if such existed, they could play any explanatory role in accounting for moral thought and motivation.[9] It has been characteristic of anglophone metaethics in the 20th century to put the issue of objectivity in terms of a distinct ontology of moral facts with resultant criticism and

---

[7] Blackburn, *Liberalism, Religion and the Sources of Value*, 8–9.

[8] See for example Aquinas, *Summa Contra Gentiles* III, c. 112, who argues that we may use animals for our benefit and that cruelty to brute animals is prohibited because it may lead to its being practised against human beings.

[9] See Blackburn, *Ruling Passions*, especially Ch. 9.

defence of the idea and efficacy of irreducibly moral properties. So pervasive has this been that many have grown accustomed to seeing the issue in this way and therefore assume that any attempt to present objectivism by reference to earlier historical figures must construe them as sharing this identification of moral objectivity with the idea of existent moral properties.

The example of Kant presents an obvious challenge to this identification, but that has served to place him in a distinctive and isolated part of the theoretical terrain. Otherwise it is widely assumed that the question of objectivism from Plato to Moore is best represented as a dispute about what exists. Of course in some sense that is true, but the distinctive feature is the claim that to say that some moral statement is true in virtue of the way things are is to say, or imply (knowingly or unknowingly) that the truth of moral statements requires the existence of specifically moral entities: objects, properties, or facts. So conceived moral objectivism does seem exotic and unnatural, as if it tries to explain what we are familiar with in terms of something quite extraordinary. However, this way of viewing the issue is historically atypical and quite unnecessary as consideration of natural law approaches shows.

III

Following recent usage I spoke earlier of 'old' and 'new' natural law theories and it is with the latter that John Finnis is firmly associated as one of its primary proponents. In his way of presenting natural law reasoning it is a theory of practical rationality which contends that as well as directing actions towards previously given ends reason can determine, or reveal, what our ends should be. So put it may sound as if practical reason is conceived of as a kind of value-detecting faculty which when oriented towards arrays of objects and states of affairs detects those possessing goodness (or badness), but that is to lapse back into the identification of objectivity with realism. Additionally and more misleadingly it conceives the operation of reason in relation to values as if it were an exercise of speculative or contemplative thought, forgetting its essentially practical and hence active ('for-action') nature.

Instead we are invited by Finnis to see that the identification of proper ends for action is internal to the operation of practical reason. In thinking about what to do one may consider what one desires or what others may require of one, but in so far as thinking amounts to an exercise of practical *reason* it must address the question what is good and ought to be pursued and what is bad and is to be avoided, and that question is directed as much to what we desire as to what may be proposed by others or by the situation. As the business of thinking what to do proceeds, certain possibilities may commend themselves but without it yet being clear why this should be so and whether the commendation is sound. For any possible end, the question arises: is it rationally desirable? And either directly or by stages this brings us to the issue of intrinsically intelligible goods. These may be encountered in particular or general form and then more or less specifically, but experience testifies to a set of basic human goods whose status as such is self-evident to reflection. Thus deliberation concerns not only *means* but *ends*, these being goods that constitute intrinsically intelligible reasons for action. Correlatively, sound practical thinking involves distinguishing between actions that are reasonable not just with regard to some particular aim but reasonable all things considered and those that are all-in-all unreasonable.

Here are sample statements drawn from writings separated by 30 years:

principles of natural law include ... (i) a set of basic practical principles which indicate the basic forms of human flourishing as goods to be pursued and realized and which are in one way or another used by everyone who considers what to do, however unsound his conclusions; and (ii) a set of basic methodological requirements of practical reasonableness (itself one of the basic forms of human flourishing) ... enabling one to formulate (iii) a set of general moral standards ...

... Aquinas [whom Finnis endorses] asserts as plainly as possible that the first principles of natural law which specify the basic forms of good and evil and which can be adequately grasped by anyone of the age of reason (and not just by metaphysicians) are *per se nota* (self-evident) and indemonstrable. They are not inferred from speculative principles. They are not inferred from facts. They are not inferred from metaphysical propositions about human nature, or about the nature of good and evil, or about 'the function of a human being'; nor are they inferred from a teleological conception of nature or any other conception of nature. They are not inferred or derived from anything.[10]

The 'ultimate first principle of natural law' [good is to be done and pursued, and evil is to be avoided], occupying the same sort of place in practical thinking as the principle of non-contradiction in all thinking, directs only that we act to some intelligible point, and the substantive first principles have their directness precisely in and by picking out the kinds of point (end, good, value) that have the requisite intelligibility—intelligibility as desirable because beneficial for anyone: life, marriage, knowledge, friendship, practical reasonableness, and likeness to and harmony (indeed *assimilatio* with [making oneself alike]) the transcendent source of all reality and value.[11]

There is no canonical source for 'old' natural law, though traditional Thomist moral philosophers and theologians would contend that Aquinas's writings on law and reason and nature, principally *Summa Theologiae* Ia IIae, qq. 90–7, are precisely that. Prescinding from the interpretation of Thomas, however, it is reasonable to propose two ideas which individually or conjointly constitute 'older' accounts of Thomistic moral theory. The first concerns the derivation of particular norms or prescriptions. It invokes as a self-evident truth the principle previously alluded to that 'good is to be done and pursued and evil is to be avoided' which serves as the major premise of a series of deductive syllogisms the second premises of which consist of identifications of particular goods and evils, thereby yielding various prescriptive conclusions. On this account, while the major premise is indubitable and the inferences are deductive the overall arguments are non-demonstrative since the minor premises are contingent and known empirically, hence without certainty. Finnis, by contrast, claims that particular principles, such as that knowledge is good and ought to be pursued, are, like the first principle itself, self-evident truths and are not derived from it but are recognized directly.

---

[10] *NLNR*, 23 and 33–4.   [11] *CEJF* I.1, 30.

The second idea to be found among traditional Thomists is that claims about what pertains to the human good are to be derived from an account of human nature. Studying the human subject one identifies common patterns of action and reaction directed towards certain conditions and thereby identifies inclinations the realization of which generally benefits the human agent. There is much scope for refinement in this characterization since it calls for a distinction between what happens as a matter of statistical regularity and what happens in line with the nature of the agent. Again it has to address the issue of whether what is found to be generally beneficial, e.g. acting fearlessly in the face of danger, should be affirmed as good for all, even when particular cases appear to lead to loss, or simply affirmed as good for the most part '*ut in pluribus*'. The source for this style of reasoning is, of course, Aristotle's *ergon* argument (*Nicomachean Ethics* 1097b22–1098a20); but to cite that is not to progress with the issue of interpretation since similar questions may be directed to it.

As was seen, Finnis sets himself against the idea that for Aquinas principles of natural law reasoning are derived from accounts, metaphysical or empirical, of human nature but that is not to say that he thinks the facts of human nature are irrelevant. He writes, in the same place as the first two of the quoted paragraphs, that 'Of course, Aquinas would agree that "were man's nature different, so would be his duties". The basic forms of good grasped by practical understanding are what is good for human beings with the nature they have'.[12] This, however, raises the question of how it should be that what is identified by insight as self-evident and in that sense is a priori should correspond to the nature of the agent qua animate substance, knowledge of which would seem to be a posteriori. Finnis has proposed a suggestion which might be adapted to provide an answer, but before considering that let me offer a brief account of the Thomistic metaphysics of animate substance as I read and subscribe to it, suggesting how this leads to the derivation of statements of value from those of fact, or better how it subverts the fact/value distinction.

It is a principle of Aristotelian/Thomistic philosophy of nature that acts are specified by their objects, powers by their acts, and substances by their powers[13]: thus *seeing* is identified as the kind of act it is by reference to its proper objects, light or colour, to which it is responsive; *sight* is identified as a detective capacity whose character is specified by its acts; and a *seer* is identified as something possessed of the power of sight. Typically sentience will involve more than one modality but the further nature of the subject is again arrived at by proceeding from *acts* via *powers* to the *agent*. One question that immediately arises is what is meant by 'specification' and 'identification': are these epistemological, conceptual or metaphysical notions?

To answer this, consider a further element of Aristotelian/Thomistic philosophy, the idea of a *nature*, as that which answers to the question *what is it?*, posed of some observed or inferred entity E. In principle this might (perhaps) be anything but the

---

[12] *NLNR*, 34.

[13] See, for example, Aquinas, *Commentary on Aristotle's De Anima*, Book II, lecture 6, 304 and 308: 'Potentiality is nothing but a capacity to act or be acted upon; it essentially involves a relation to actuality and can only be defined in such terms. And if this is the case with acts and potencies, acts in their turn connote something prior to themselves, i.e. their objects ... so we proceed from objects to acts, from acts to faculties, and from faculties to essence'.

paradigm is an enduring object that interacts with other objects in apparently regular ways. An answer to the question *quid est*? will give the *quiddity*, the 'what-it-isness' of E. Assuming that E has material aspects but also that these are configured in ways that constitute a characteristic structure, which in the case of an active entity will be part of its functional organization, then we can see that the specification of the nature or quiddity of E is an identification of its essence: thus to deal for simplicity with unicellular organisms biology aims to give definitions of the likes of the yeast cell or the ecoli bacterium. This is the bare identification of their natures but there will in addition be characteristics of such entities which while not part of their specific definitions are common to individuals having the same essence and which are con-nected to their nature non-contingently. This is to say that if some individuals lack such characteristics this will be due to a developmental defect or to injury, or to some other disabling or inhibiting cause. Finally, there will be additional features possessed or lacked simply as a matter of contingency, typically due to the effects of environment; though even here the fact and character of these will typically bear some intelligible relation to the essence and natural characteristics of the thing. Thus we have the threefold classification: nature (*essence*); proper attributes (*propria*); and contingent features (*accidents*). In the case of a particular yeast cell its *essence* may be that of sugar mold fungus (*Saccharomyces cerevisiae*); its *propria* include growing aerobically, forming buds, and mating; its *accidents*, size, location, and other contingencies.

Note again, the use of 'specification' and 'identification' to which is now added 'definition'. In the latter case it should be clear that what is at issue is not nominal but real definition, or if one wishes to say that conceptual work is going on then it is work intended to represent the actual structure of things as they are, independently of our experience of them. Of course experience is necessary to provide the data upon which such conceptual activity goes to work, but essential definition is neither just a concaten-ation of observed features nor a linguistic stipulation; rather it seeks to abstract the underlying nature of the objects given in experience and to distinguish among observed features those that arise from that nature (*propria*) and those that attach contingently to instances of it (*accidents*). It is in the same way that we should understand the business of identifying and specifying acts, powers, and agents. The business has an epistemological dimension but it is at the same time concerned with things as they are and not merely as we discover them, or choose to arrange our discoveries. The sequence *act-power-agent*, like that of *propria-essence* (or again *agent-power-act* or *essence-propria*) is not simply a contingent epistemological ordering but a necessary metaphysical one. In fact there is at least the possibility of cases in which epistemologic-ally the order of things proceeds from knowledge of the nature of an agent to inferred conclusions as to its powers and acts.

Finally there is the matter of immanent teleology. As described, the natures of living things include functional organization directed towards characteristic activities. These are given a foundational taxonomy in Aristotle's *De Anima* and discussed by Aquinas in his *Commentary* on that work and elsewhere in his own elaborated philosophy of nature. Here it is unnecessary to go into the details of this as a few examples of characteristic activities suffice. Living things exchange matter with their environment and replicate; some have powers of relocation and of perception, and among these some have capacities of thought and deliberation. In each case we might examine the objects over which these powers are defined and the means by which they are exercised, but here the main point to note is that such powers are associated with natural tendencies. That is to say it is not just that an entity E has an ability to do A but that it has a tendency towards doing so as part of developing and sustaining its form of life. Here there is a complex of active and passive potentialities: propensities to act and liabilities to respond, but for convenience let me just abbreviate this by speaking of a single capacity C aligned to an inclination towards achieving a state S. We may say then that C is a 'natural function' of A if it is part of the essence of A or is a proper attribute of A, if it serves to achieve S, and if it exists in order to achieve S. Equally we can say that S is a 'natural end' for A (and of C). On this account the exercise of C is, other things being equal, conducive to, or constitutive of the natural good of A. It will not always be good for A to exercise C, and there may be some other natural capacity, involuntary or voluntary, by which C is withheld or impeded for the benefit of A; but it will be an abuse of C for A to exercise the capacity so as to frustrate the realization of its natural end, or to achieve an end which is liable to impede the realization of S. So, for example, there is something prima facie wrong with an agent that uses the capacity to ingest material in order to prevent the end of nutrition, say by eating stuffs which will either be regurgitated or pass through the body entirely unabsorbed, or to pursue an end that will non-accidentally impede it. Such is the nature of certain forms of *bulimia*, *rumination*, and *pica*, the pathological consumption of indigestible materials such as stones, all of which are aptly categorized as eating disorders.

In this last phase I have moved explicitly into the area of value or normativity, thus far not emphasizing rational agency. What the latter adds is the ability to exercise a faculty, or to refrain from doing so on the basis of consideration of ends and deliberation between them. Here, of course, 'ends' is ambiguous between chosen outcomes and proper objects and it is part of the traditional Thomistic account that the capacity for choice does not itself create the desirability of ends but should respond to them. Certainly rationality has ends peculiar to it but in so far as these connect with organic functions they should be harmonized with them either cooperatively or by subsuming them into the rational order, as when eating is ordered according to a reasonable diet or into a practice of shared meals.

Like 'definition', 'specification' and 'identification' as they have featured above should be seen not in epistemological or evidential terms as opposed to conceptual or metaphysical terms. If one had to choose then it would be more accurate to say that they are metaphysical notions but they are non-contingently related to observation insofar as the idea of what is involved in a nature is abstracted from experience and testimony regarding the operations of things. Here there is a difference with the understanding of natural kinds and essences associated with the semantic views of Putnam and Kripke. In the case of the latter, at least as advanced in some presentations, there is an implied divide between what a thing is and how it is encountered, sometimes put in terms of real and manifest natures. On this account everything that is predicable of an entity is either essential or accidental (in the sense of metaphysically contingent), and since it can be imagined that some cats, say, lack tails, or fur, or claws, the 'nature' is pared down to something such as a genotype. From this perspective, to say that things are specified via their acts and powers will look to be an epistemological claim about how we fix the reference of a kind term and these features will not enter essentially into the real definition of the nature or its proper attributes. In the view I am describing and recommending, by contrast, it is an inessential but necessary feature of cats that they eat and mate and are sentient; that is to say that it is a priori true that cats as a kind eat, mate, and sense, and non-contingently true of the cat population *ut in pluribus*, for the most part. Where these attributes are lacking, some explanation is called for which will be of the sort that identifies a disability, or an impediment, or a pathology. If on the other hand serious examination and considered analysis led one to conclude that such attributes were simply and non-defectively absent from an animal that would be reason to conclude that, whatever it is, it is not after all a cat.

All of this bears on the issue of natural law reasoning because of the seeming opposition of Finnis who holds that claims about intelligible goods are self-evident and not inferred from 'metaphysical propositions about human nature, or about the nature of good and evil, or about "the function of a human being"; nor are they inferred from a teleological conception of nature', and who thus differs from those who propose that rational prescriptions can and should be got from such resources. Finnis himself essays one kind of reconciliation. He writes in discussion of Aquinas and of competing interpretations of his view:

> Natural inclinations are not, for Aquinas, the fundamental reality in relation to which propositions about what ought to be done have their truth . . . But, to prepare for [the] specification of the primary or basic human goods, St Thomas refers directly to the inclinations natural to man . . . What then is this constitutive role of the natural inclinations in the explanation of reasoning to justify oughts (specifically moral or otherwise)? . . . [T]he inclinations are ontologically more proximate to the nature whose specific character makes what-is-good-for-a-specific-type-of-being indeed good for that being. Indeed, we come to know the essence or nature of such a being by knowing its potentialities and capacities: '*per obiecta cognosc[i]mus actus, et per actus potentias, et per potentias essentaim animae* [so we proceed from objects to acts, from acts to powers, and from powers to essence] . . . But [this] principle must be taken as a whole, and when it is so taken, it discloses both (A) the reason why 'ought' is not derived from 'is' (according to Aquinas), and (B) the reason why 'ought' is derived from 'is' (according to Aquinas).[14]

In brief, the idea is that propositions regarding human goods are known not derivatively but by insight as self-evident, and that this is compatible with the objects-acts-power-essence principle since we come to know our nature through first knowing our acts, and the objects of human inclination and will are the primary goods. On the other hand, since acts flow from natures the value of human goods is derived from the nature whose realization and perfection they promote or constitute. In short, practical principles prescribing the pursuit of certain goods are *epistemologically prior* and underived, but *ontologically dependent* upon the nature of the agent.

---

[14] *CEJF* I.9, 144–7.

This reconciliation is consistent with the act-essence axiom but I think that because of the strength of his attachment to the idea that principles of practical reason are knowable in themselves and without proof (*per se nota et indemonstrabilia*) Finnis gives insufficient consideration to the possibility that one might also invoke knowledge of natures to argue for certain directions of action, and that there may be circumstances in which this course is likely to be more helpful and a corrective to an overly aprioristic interpretation of understanding practical principles directly in virtue of their very content. Finnis allows that in order to understand such principles one will have had to form the relevant concepts and that this will be done from experience, including acquaintance with aspects of one's nature, but this addresses the issue of concept formation. What it does not consider is the possibility that such concepts may be too thin or ambiguous to allow one to draw much from their deployment in the specification of human goods, or, relatedly, too uncertain to resolve debates about their interpretation and application.

The looming charge is of an empty formalism but I am not pressing that so much as identifying the role of anthropology in a broad sense in guiding us to conclusions about how to act. It might be thought that this is liable to fall short because of the is/ought gap and certainly Finnis thinks it is a merit of his account of practical principles that it avoids this since they are intrinsically prescriptive. I do not deny that they are such, but I hold that so too may be claims deriving from metaphysical propositions about human nature, as these are understood along the lines sketched above. First, to say that an action exercises a natural capacity directed towards an end constitutive of human flourishing is to say that, other things being equal, it is good and choice-worthy. While to say or recognize this in the context of practical reasoning, rather than anthropological theorizing, is to say that, *ceteris paribus*, it ought to be done. I entirely agree with Finnis on the great importance of distinguishing speculative and practical thought and reason, and of seeing the latter as dynamic and heading towards the taken-to-be-good. In that framework, discovering that something pertains to the perfection of one's nature is learning where the target one was looking for actually lies and is like a traveller seeking a destination: the recognition of it is reason (rational cause) to direct one's course towards it.[15]

IV

Before turning to the issue of the role of the public philosopher let me return briefly to the subject of value-phenomenology. Finnis presses the claims of underived and self-evident practical principles specifying basic human goods, these providing intrinsically intelligible reasons for action. I have pressed, if somewhat briefly, the claims of practical judgements derived from propositions about human nature, natural functions, and immanent teleology. But there is, I think, a third route towards value-governed action, and that is reflection upon the lived experience of good and bad, understood not in

---

[15] For further discussion of these matters and other aspects of Aquinas's account of action and value see Haldane, 'Is Every Action Morally Significant?'

terms of exercises of rational insight into the truth of propositions, or as metaphysical-cum-empirical reasoning, but directly as responsive consciousness.

By way of analogy, consider a situation in which someone proposes as guidance in the making of a work of art or a performance certain principles of aesthetic action, such as that compositional unity is to be promoted; and let us allow that it is intrinsically intelligible that in itself this provides a reason for aesthetic action. One might wonder, however, what the promotion of compositional unity amounts to, which is a question about general interpretation and particular application. Suppose also that someone else proposes to complement or enrich this guidance by talking about aspects of human nature and the way in which the exercise of certain capacities directed towards their proper ends conduces to human flourishing. Certainly, if it issues from serious and detailed study this will be able to be made more specific, but again while it is intelligible that this is indeed action-guiding it remains at some distance from a major, if not the only, mode of operation in art-making, which is direct conscious engagement with the materials to hand, literal and metaphorical. A more apt and immediately telling kind of guidance is that provided by another artist viewing things in the studio or seeing or hearing things in the rehearsal room or auditorium. Here the aim is to get the practitioner to experience things in a certain way so as to bring into imaginative view possibilities that would carry forward her project. Now what can be said and done by another can in principle be achieved by the artist herself. So she would do well to ask such questions as what does this mean? What is going on here? What am I trying to say? How does this appear? What does it evoke? Should this be chosen and that eliminated, this increased and that diminished? And so on. Confining the case for convenience to the visual, this mode of aesthetic reasoning is ineliminably experiential and takes the form of considering ways in which things appear to consciousness. To move to the perspectives of the artist, critic, or teacher as they may try to help someone visually understand the work, the general mode of guidance is the invitation to 'see it like this'—where further direction is then supplied—in the hope that recognition of what, why, and how worthwhile the thing is will then dawn.

Returning to practical reasoning as it was previously discussed, and considering moral reasoning as a species of this, the question arises whether there is scope for something analogous to posing the sorts of questions and giving the sort of advice proposed in the aesthetic case. The answer seems obviously that there is and indeed it is something we are familiar with. A conscientious deliberator will ask herself whether she is feeling as she ought to about another or herself; someone wondering how and whether to act may ask whether what he feels is disgust and anger or fear and frustration, and again which if any of these is appropriate to the object or situation. Someone resolute in their affections or repugnance may have their minds changed by being brought to see things in a new light. Another, generally unsure and easily confused, may be helped by being taken through a series of scenarios real or imagined and invited to focus first on one and then another feature in order to develop and refine his sensitivity and sensibility.

It may be said that this hardly constitutes another means of coming to recognize goods or arriving at practical judgements and is only a metaphorical way of describing the deployment of concepts in practical reasoning; but that omits the essentially experiential character of the process and the engagement of the affections. Consider again Kolnai:

> To assert the objective existence [of good and evil] presupposes engagement with metaphysics; pure ethics must content itself with assuming it, just as logic refrains from asserting the existence of truth and falsity, let alone proving it, but simply sets forth what can be established on this assumption. It is hard to see how we can properly engage in ethics unless our experience of good and evil and the conflict between them is deeply felt and beyond doubt.[16]

And later he explains that moral consciousness relates to the ways in which human actions bear upon values of which we are pre-morally aware, being occasioned by a certain emphasis

> [which] has to be understood in terms of devotion to value, of feeling the presence of values in one's own action, or some moment of it. The feeling can issue, or express itself, in a variety of evaluative stances, recognitions, decisions or projects—in feeling the value of the objects or ends one has in mind, in feeling obliged to do something, in feeling the *urgency* of some matter, and so on. All ethical phenomena of this kind have a common source in the fundamental fact of emphasis.[17]

Nothing said in the previous section outlining different approaches to natural law ethics precludes acceptance of these points but, notwithstanding the recognition that value concepts are formed out of experience, little attention is given to the character of value consciousness and of moral experience in particular. As with the metaphysical approach to values and directives, my suggestion is not this should be seen as a rival basis for ethics rather that it should be viewed as complementary to what has been presented, and a necessary complement both because moral consciousness is a reality which needs to be taken account of, and because it is a resource in making arguments in support of particular claims and policies. In summary: (1) *traditional natural law* addresses the metaphysics of value and refutes the claim that there are unbridgeable gaps between facts and values, and between values and requirements; (2) *new natural law* addresses the issue of practical rationality in respect of the conceptual and epistemological status of certain principles specifying intrinsically intelligible goods; and (3) *phenomenological value theory* addresses the question of the distinctive nature of the experience of value and the special emphasis that marks moral consciousness.

As well as providing a required supplement, the last contribution serves to counter the impression of reductionism that might be given by the first, for especially in contemporary anglophone analytical philosophy in which 'naturalism' frequently connotes scientific materialism, talk of 'natures' may be thought to indicate a reduction, conceptual or ontological, of human values to something such as biological utility. That interpretation would be erroneous but the temptation to assume it is less likely if it is insisted that what is demonstrated metaphysically is something that is also recognized in greater richness in value-consciousness; but by the same token it is one and the

---

[16] Kolnai, 'Ethical Value', 17.
[17] Kolnai, 'The Gradation of Ethical Value-Emphases', 63–4.

same reality that is converged upon by these approaches, and the distinctively moral dimension of human values is embedded within a larger pre-moral but still ineliminably normative domain of natural goods. Interestingly, though he eschewed talk of 'natural law' for fear of the spectre of naturalism in the reductionist sense, Kolnai nevertheless was himself drawn to recognize a convergence of the sort I have proposed. He wrote:

> the functioning of nature must be 'good' for it is only in that frame of reference, against that background, that we come to contrast good and bad at all, and it is things conducive to the undisturbed processes of life, to security, unfolding, etc., that we call good, and destruction, obstruction, deformation etc. bad. We are not thereby committed to interpret all dimensions of good and bad in such terms, or committed to an interpretation in such terms of all standard meanings of good and bad, and notably to any rash explanation of the morally good and bad in terms of biological concerns or their rational governance, but we must vaguely assume some sort of congruity between the natural and the moral good rather than a relation of strict irrelevance.[18]

V

Finally I turn to the role of the public philosopher and to issues that have dominated recent discussion of reasoning in the *public square* about matters of common *public interest* with a view to influencing *public policy*. I take the public philosopher simply to be a philosopher who seeks, or at any rate is willing, to practice to a significant degree, if not exclusively, publically in the three respects indicated: *locus*, *subject-matter*, and *goal*. As is widely known, however, there is a fourth respect which has become the subject of considerable discussion since it was first introduced by John Rawls in the elaboration of his account of political liberalism. This is the idea that reasoned contributions to public debates about public policy should be subject to the constraint that they are formulated either immediately or in due course in terms of *public reason*.

Rawls's thinking on the subject went through a number of developments and revisions from its first appearance in lectures in the late 1980s through its presentation in *Political Liberalism* in 1993 to the publication of 'The Idea of Public Reason Revisited' in the *University of Chicago Law Review* in 1997, and its incorporation in his *Collected Papers* and again in *The Law of Peoples* both in 1999. Evidently Rawls saw the need to further clarify his thoughts and in particular to address the matter of religious public discourse which on the one hand might rest on claims of revelation and so be deeply contested and viewed as beyond rational argument, but on the other had in some cases, as in the example of the abolition of slavery, been important and perhaps decisive in advancing the cause of liberty and equality.

In his last multiply published version of 'The Idea of Public Reason' Rawls describes it as having a definite structure (which he elaborates largely in terms of other aspects of his theory of political liberalism) and as being public in three ways (which are more specifically political than those I introduced):

---

[18] Kolnai, 'Morality and Practice I', 83.

as the reason of free and equal citizens, it is the reason of the public; its subject matter is the public good concerning questions of fundamental political justice [constitutional essentials and matters of basic justice]; and its nature and content are public, being expressed in public reasoning by a family of reasonable conceptions of political justice reasonably thought to satisfy the criterion of reciprocity.[19]

Again there is reference to specific doctrines of Rawls's larger political creed but the general point is evident that Rawls ties public reason to political offices, law-making and legal interpretation, and the requirements of political justice. From one point of view this seems overly restrictive since one might think that public reason is at issue in public contexts that are not necessarily political in the narrow state-related sense. On the other hand one may welcome the fact that these elaborate conditions are confined to this sphere. In the event, however, many who have responded to his discussions have elided the 'public' in the broad sense with the 'political' in its institutional-cum-constitutional meaning. This, I think, is evidence of a growing tendency to suppose, and thereby to contribute to its generally being supposed, that every social question is an issue for the politics of the state. Be that as it may there is good reason to extend the consideration of public reason to the public in the broader understanding since it is already a matter of contest what sort of considerations may be brought forward in discussing policies within elements of civil society and in public fora more generally conceived of, such as public broadcasting discussions contributed to by non-political agents.

Earlier I mentioned three other publications relating to these themes: Habermas's 'Religion in the Public Sphere', Rorty's 'An Ethics for Today', and Finnis's 'Religion and Public Life in a Pluralist Society'. Habermas takes the broader view, conceiving the public sphere in terms of civil society understood as a secular realm in which matters of public good are the subject of rational-critical debate. While Rawls was only prepared to allow religious discourse subject to the proviso that any argument expressed in such terms subsequently be translated, by its advocates, into secular idiom, Habermas is sensitive to the fact that the origins of the public sphere(s) are in large part religious—as in the effort to reconceive a common space subsequent to the fragmentation of Western Christendom by the Reformation. Additionally he believes that the language in which debate is conducted has been and is liable to continue to be enriched by originally religious concepts, albeit de-theologized. In that respect, and with regard to the political sphere proper, he shares with Rawls the requirement of translation into secular idiom, though not in the sense of a pre-existing secular language only a non-eliminably-religious one. Significantly, however, according to Habermas the burden of such translation is not to be placed exclusively upon the religious speaker. Rather, in recognition of the fact and continuing potential of enrichment from outwith secular discourse it is for society as a whole to find ways of taking-in what religious discourse has to offer it.

Habermas's greater accommodation of religious discourse is due in part to his hermeneutic sense of the religious origins of modern sociopolitical concepts and practices; but he is also moved by the consideration that we now inhabit a post-secular

---

[19] Rawls, *The Law of Peoples*, 133.

culture, that is to say one that has given up the belief and hope in enlightenment rationality just as the enlightenment gave up belief and hope in Judaeo-Christian revelation. In this respect he is more sceptical of reason than is Rawls but far less so than Rorty, who differs also in his response to the decline of rationalism; for whereas Habermas responds by adopting a position of discursive humility Rorty treats it as license for unbridled advocacy of his own version of pragmatic liberalism. The following gives something of the substance and character of his last thoughts:

> Most of Western philosophy is, like Christian theology, an attempt to get in touch with something other than ourselves. [I repudiate that tradition which means] ceasing to ask both metaphysical questions about the ground or the source of our ideals and epistemological questions about how one can be certain that one has chosen the correct ideal... There is nothing already in existence to which our moral convictions should try to correspond... There is no such thing as intrinsically evil desire. There are only desires that must be subordinated to other desires in the interests of fairness.[20]

To set this in context, Rorty's starting point was the observation that:

> Pope Benedict XVI has complained that it is becoming very difficult for the Church to say what it believes. Very soon, the pope has written one will not be able to affirm that homosexuality constitutes, as the Catholic Church teaches, an objective disorder in the structure of human existence... I hope this will happen. I hope that the pope's fears will be confirmed because I think that condemning homosexuality has produced a great deal of unnecessary, pointless human misery.[21]

Although his attack here and at later points is upon traditional religion, in particular Catholicism (presumably because it is the most conspicuous and pervasive form of traditional Western theism), it is clear that his target more generally is realism, in the sense of there being a reality independent of our conceptions and desires which may serve as a standard of correction or endorsement of them. Talk of epistemological questions being concerned with 'certainty' is self-serving here since the realist or objectivist may only seek reasonable warrant; all the same he or she is appealing to the idea that standards of warrant are objective and that knowledge requires truth. From this point of view the efforts of Rawls and to a lesser extent of Habermas to fashion principled sets of requirements on public discourse are residues of rationalism. Rorty speaks of 'the interests of fairness' but by his own account these can be no more than interests or sentiments; that is to say there is no metaphysical or rational foundation for the idea of fairness. At best there is pragmatic or utilitarian calculation, though even with this one may wonder why each should count for one when it comes to the satisfaction of desires. Furthermore, like Habermas and to a degree like Rawls,[22]

---

[20] Rorty, 'An Ethics for Today', 9, 10, and 15.
[21] Rorty, 'An Ethics for Today', 7–8.
[22] See Rawls (1999), 104–5, where he writes that 'the Catholic doctrine of double-effect agrees with the Law of Peoples for the conduct of war that civilians are not to be attacked... Resting on the divine command that the innocent must never be killed this doctrine says that one must never act with the intention of attacking the enemy state by the means of taking the innocent lives of its civilians. Political

Rorty misunderstands the way in which moral rationality is related to religious teaching in the Catholic tradition, though one would have thought that the terms of his own gloss, namely 'an objective disorder in the structure of human existence', would have alerted him to the fact that what is proposed is presented in the mode of philosophical reason rather than in that of scriptural declaration. For a better account we should return to Finnis who writes as follows:

> The inquiry into human flourishing can proceed without adverting to the question of divine existence... Accordingly, when one pursues (a) the inquiry into the principles of practical understanding that direct us towards the basic aspects of human flourishing, and (b) the inquiry into the rational requirement... that one remain open to each of those first principles, and likewise (c) the inquiry into the implications of that requirement, implications we call morality, one can proceed, rather as one does in the natural sciences, without adverting to the *further question* [of whether these principles being true and our having the capacity to recognize them point to a creative cause].[23]

At the same time, however, he proposes the reasonability of making the argument from moral order to God and then of investigating how the fact of a providential Creator might bear upon the significance of that order as being, as well as intrinsically good, related to a supernatural purpose: namely uniting one's practical reason with Divine wisdom. Moreover he argues that put in these terms and in this mode such thinking is an exercise of public reason. So too, he claims, is the natural law style argumentation in which he has engaged both at the level of first principles and at that of specific moral and social prescriptions—and I would assume he would say the same with regard to the metaphysical reasoning which I presented above.

What then of the charge that this represents an invocation of comprehensive doctrine and thus violates the application of the principle of toleration to philosophy itself? Finnis offers some general psychological and cultural observations on the ways in which we can fail to recognize or refuse to accept moral principles or more commonly apply them, and considers that if the theistic conclusion is warranted then it is reasonable to suppose that a providential deity 'might communicate those same moral principles in a way that renders them more clearly accessible and more palpably warranted. And that anticipation is satisfactorily met, fulfilled, as one aspect of the public revelation in Jesus the Christ'.[24]

Finnis continues further in this vein exploring the potential for grounding ideas of universal human dignity and religious liberty, but all that need be observed in this context is that this is but one instance of an ongoing interplay of philosophical and religious ideas and arguments, presented at least on occasion in the public square about

---

liberalism allows the supreme emergency exemption; the Catholic doctrine rejects it, saying that we must have faith and adhere to God's commands.' Rawls nowhere quotes Aquinas on the matter but had he consulted relevant parts of the *Summa Theologiae* he would have seen that the doctrines of (a) the wrongness of taking innocent human life (Ia IIae q. 94, a. 2), (b) double-effect (II II, q. 64, a. 7), and (c) just war (II II q. 40, a. 1), are given natural law style rationales, as well as being keyed to theological ideas. It is clear that what Rawls terms 'the Catholic doctrine of double-effect' is intended by Aquinas to have a fully sufficient natural reason foundation.

[23] *CEJF* V.2, 42.   [24] *CEJF* V.2, 47.

matters of common public interest with a view to influencing public policy. In these respects they are contributions of an occasionally public philosopher; but by Rawls's account they would violate the requirements of public reason. Finnis rightly challenges the idea that one should only advance reasons that all reasonable people could reasonably be expected to endorse on the grounds that it licenses anyone who thinks their belief is true to expect that under idealized conditions of inquiry others will share that belief. While on the other hand if conditions are as at present there is no guarantee that what reasonable people could reasonably be expected to endorse is in fact reasonable. There is a more extensive case to be made against Rawls's account of public reason from the point of view of 'natural law' ethics and politics but this is not the occasion to present it.[25]

The general lesson to be taken from Rawls, Habermas, and Rorty, however, is that secular liberalism and the varieties of public philosophy it favours are in retreat (or distancing themselves) from moral reasoning as traditionally understood, regarding it either sceptically or else with disfavour on grounds of its threatening to propose principles and values that would require it to distinguish between substantial conceptions of the human good. For reasons external to philosophy, having to do with demography, economics, and international relations, there is also a real prospect that the culture produced and sustained by secular liberalism may not survive much longer, at which point the best we can hope for is respectful open contest over ideas. Independently of that possibility, however, what it is reasonable now and always to expect of a public philosopher is that he conscientiously advance in public fora whatever good reasons he believes he has identified and can argue for regarding the flourishing of individuals and of communities. Finnis has done precisely that in articulating and applying his version of natural law reasoning. All I would add in light of earlier discussion is that in making arguments about human values generally, moral values in particular, and public policies consequent upon them, one will do best if one draws upon the full resources of *metaphysical*, *practical-reasonable*, and *phenomenological* considerations,[26] both moving between them as appropriate, i.e. as the argument itself requires, or as is suited to the condition of the audience, and also seeking as a philosophical good the task of integrating them.[27]

Bibliography

Aquinas, Thomas (1951) *Commentary on Aristotle's De Anima*, translated by Kenelm Foster, O.P. and Sylvester Humphries, O.P. (New Haven, CT: Yale University Press).

Aquinas, Thomas, *Summa Contra Gentiles*, translated by Anton C. Pegis, James F. Anderson, Vernon J. Bourke, and Charles J. O'Neil. 5 volumes (Notre Dame, IN: University of Notre Dame Press, 1991)

---

[25] See Haldane, 'Political Theory and the Nature of Persons'; Haldane, 'The Individual, the State and the Common Good'; and Haldane, 'Public Reason, Truth and Human Fellowship'. Versions of these and related essays are assimilated in Haldane, *Practical Philosophy*.

[26] For some discussion of Kolnai's moral philosophy in relation to social and political issues see Haldane, 'Ethics, Politics and Imperfection'.

[27] In this connection an interesting model, though somewhat different in its ingredients, is the axiological and methodological synthesis proposed by Wiggins, *Ethics*, especially Chapters 1, 9, and 11.

Aquinas, Thomas, *Summa Theologiae*, translated by Thomas Gilby, et al. 59 volumes (London: Eyre and Spottiswoode; New York: McGraw-Hill, 1964–1981).

Blackburn, Simon (1998) *Ruling Passions: A Theory of Practical Reasoning* (Oxford: Oxford University Press).

Blackburn, Simon (2005) *Liberalism, Religion and the Sources of Value* (Lawrence: University of Kansas).

Finnis, John (1980) *Natural Law and Natural Rights* ([1980] 2nd ed. 2011) (Oxford: Oxford University Press).

Finnis, John (2011) *Reason in Action: Collected Essays of John Finnis* volume 1 (Oxford: Oxford University Press).

Finnis, John (2011) *Intention and Identity: Collected Essays of John Finnis* volume II (Oxford: Oxford University Press).

Habermas, Jurgen (2008) 'Religion in the Public Sphere: Cognitive Presuppositions for the "Public Use of Reason" by Religious and Secular Citizens', in *Between Naturalism and Religion* (Cambridge: Polity), 114–47.

Haldane, John (1991) 'Political Theory and the Nature of Persons: An Ineliminable Metaphysical Presupposition', *Philosophical Papers*, 20, 77–95.

Haldane, John (1996) 'The Individual, the State and the Common Good', *Social Philosophy and Policy*, 13, 59–79.

Haldane, John (2007) 'Public Reason, Truth and Human Fellowship', *Journal of Law, Philosophy and Culture*, 1, 101–16.

Haldane, John (2008) 'Ethics, Politics and Imperfection', *New Blackfriars*, 89, 389–98.

Haldane, John (2009) *Practical Philosophy: Ethics, Society and Culture* (Exeter: ImprintAcademic).

Haldane, John (2011) 'Is Every Action Morally Significant?', *Philosophy*, 86, 375–404.

Kolnai, Aurel (1950s) *The Utopia Project* (unpublished).

Kolnai, Aurel (2002a) 'Ethical Value', in *Early Ethical Writings of Aurel Kolnai*, edited by Francis Dunlop (Farnham: Ashgate), 17–32.

Kolnai, Aurel (2002b) 'The Gradation of Ethical Value-Emphases', in *Early Ethical Writings of Aurel Kolnai*, edited by Francis Dunlop (Farnham: Ashgate), 59–96.

Kolnai, Aurel (2008) 'Morality and Practice I: The Ambiguity of Good', in *Ethics, Value and Reality* (New Brunswick, NJ: Transaction), 63–94.

Rawls, John (1996) *Political Liberalism* (New York: Columbia University Press).

Rawls, John (1999) *The Law of Peoples* with 'The Idea of Public Reason Revisited' (London: Harvard University Press).

Rorty, Richard (2011) 'An Ethics for Today', in *An Ethics for Today: Finding Common Ground Between Philosophy and Religion* (New York: Columbia University Press), 7–26.

Wiggins, David (2006) *Ethics: Twelve Lectures on the Philosophy of Morality* (Cambridge, MA: Harvard University Press).

4

On the Most Fundamental Principle of Morality

Joseph Boyle

The ethical theory John Finnis has adopted and developed includes an account of moral principle. In this approach to morality, fundamental moral principles justify more specific moral considerations, such as the norms guiding actions of specific kinds and the procedures for determining the all-things-considered judgments often needed to complete moral assessment. Thus, according to this conception of a moral principle, an act of killing an innocent person is wrong because features of actions of that kind, considered in the light of the basic moral principle, vindicate that moral judgment. In this contribution, I will consider this conception of moral principle. My specific concern is with a set of closely related issues raised by the several mature formulations by Finnis and his collaborators[1] of what Finnis has called the "master principle of morality."[2] One of these formulations is an interpretation of the traditional directive that one should always act in accord with "right reason." The gloss is that right reason is practical reason *unfettered* in its direction of choice and action by non-rational motivational factors that are not integrated with reason. So, the basic principle thus formulated would be: never choose except in accord with unfettered reason.[3] More commonly, the master principle is stated as a moral ideal: In voluntarily acting for human goods and avoiding what is opposed to them, one ought to choose and otherwise will those and only those possibilities whose willing is compatible with a will towards integral human fulfillment.[4]

Finnis's discussion of these formulations suggests how they are related—as distinct but logically equivalent propositions that articulate moral principle from different perspectives. Both formulations appear to rely on the notion of "the integral directiveness

---

[1] Finnis developed his approach to moral theory in broadly collaborative work, some of which appears in co-authored publications; for simplicity I will generally refer to all work having Finnis as author or co-author as his, without thereby denying the contributions of others, especially of Germain Grisez. I am happy to have been one of Finnis's collaborators on some of the works in which the views I address here were developed.

[2] See *FoE*, 72, 76, 124, 127 and 151 for the original use of this name.

[3] See Grisez et al., "Practical Principles, Moral Truth and Ultimate Ends," 121; *CEJF* I.14, 215–16. In his contribution to this volume Grisez (Essay 27, 444) has proposed the following formulation: "When one's feelings incline one to choose what reasons indicate is not to be chosen or not to choose what reasons indicate is to be chosen, one ought to choose in accord with reasons."

[4] Grisez et al., "Practical Principles, Moral Truth and Ultimate Ends," 128; *NDMR*, 283; *CEJF* I.7, 129; *CEJF* I.13, 210. Grisez, "The True Ultimate End of Human Beings," 57, argues that the integral fulfillment referred to in the formula cannot be limited to humans but must allow for a community including God and other intelligent beings. This improvement of the principle by restating it in terms of integral communal fulfillment does not directly affect the matters I will address here.

of practical reason," which was proposed as a definition of moral truth,[5] but has not been clearly distinguished from the notion of unfettered reason. However, the integral directiveness of practical reason is not precisely the same idea as that of unfettered reason; the latter makes reference to factors that prevent reason's working from being integral. So, the former idea is simpler. I will proceed, therefore, on the assumption that the traditional rule of following right reason (understood as following the integral directiveness of practical reason) can be usefully distinguished from Finnis's interpretation of it as "unfettered reason."[6]

Similarly, the integral directiveness of practical reason is not the same idea as that of integral human fulfillment: the latter refers to the ideal outcome that would come to be and unfold as the result of the whole set of possible good choices by everybody. The former notion, therefore, underlies the ideal of integral human fulfillment. This suggests that the integral directiveness of practical reason is a candidate to be the subject in the most basic formulation of the principle of morality.

I. The Integral Directiveness of Practical Reason and Free Choice

A. Morality and free choice

The relationship between moral principle and free choice is the essential element of the context in which Finnis's conception of moral principle emerges. Specific moral norms, and so also moral principles, guide choices.

To make a choice an agent must consider alternatives. That consideration is deliberation. Deliberating is a form of practical reasoning. Deliberating begins in articulating the causal and other connections between what one can do and an objective one considers realizing. The deliberation leading to free choice is called for by the fact that more than a single objective emerged as desirable in such a way that one has hesitated to do one action because of one's interest in doing the other. One way to resolve the hesitation is by *thinking* about the options, and then selecting in response to the results of the thinking.

In choosing, the acting person selects one of the options presented in deliberation; that is, one responds to one of the judgments directing the choice of an option. One responds in choosing by beginning to realize the goal promised in the option selected rather than an alternative by executing the performance one believes will contribute to that. Choices made with the intention of a goal one will realize only if conditions outside one's power obtain activate performances designed to make oneself ready to carry out that intention should those conditions obtain.

---

[5] Grisez et al., "Practical Principles, Moral Truth and Ultimate Ends," 126.

[6] It will become clear that these two ideas are very closely related: I suspect that the normative principle stated in terms of integral directiveness of practical reason and some plausible claims about human motivation imply the unfettered reason formulation, and that the latter formulation implies the former. Even if these formulations are, in the end, less distinct than I suppose, I focus on them separately to allow distinguishing the relationship of the distinctive application of practical reason to free choice, in which its integral directiveness is operative, from the relationship between the first moral principle and the factors preventing its integral working.

When the choice is free, the rational and other considerations motivating the option chosen are not sufficient to determine it towards that option. One settles that for oneself by choosing. For this reason, one is responsible for the action chosen; the action done would not have been done without one's choice, and that choice—the selecting and initiating—lacked sufficient causes prior to one's own choosing.

Since free choices are creative in the way just specified, and are therefore irreducible to other volitional responses to practical judgments, they constitute a domain of reality that is *sui generis*. The creativity involved in human free choice is analogous to divine creativity: God's creation is the irreducible source of the reality of all creaturely reality; one's choosing freely is the naturally irreducible source of the actions for which one is responsible.

The exercise of human freedom, though creative, is not necessarily arbitrary since choice is responsive to practical judgment, and practical judgments can be thoroughly informed by practical reason. Practical reason, in turn, is human intelligence directing action to goals that are worth realizing. This use of human intelligence to guide the creation of the *sui generis* domain of reality constituted by free choices is necessarily irreducible to its use in other domains. It is neither discovering and explaining facts about established creation, nor imposing rationality on the activities of thinking, nor shaping artifacts by intelligent manipulation of things. These uses of human intelligence are in turn used in practical thinking, but do not exhaust its distinctive task of directing human freedom.[7]

This conception of morality as the direction of human free choices is at least as widely denied as is the reality of free choice. Finnis's suppositions that human beings can make free choices and that moral norms direct free choices have been defended at length, by Finnis and his collaborators and by others in the broader natural law tradition they seek to develop. Consequently, I proceed in the following on Finnis's supposition that moral standards are what provide the rational guidance of the distinctive creativity which we humans exercise in making free choices, and consequently, that moral goodness is the reality created by choosing in accord with those standards.

B. Practical reason and its principles

Moral judgment is plainly a form of practical judgment, that is, it is a judgment that directs one person to shape a part of one's unfolding life; it does this in a special way— to shape one's life in accord with moral truth. Moreover, moral judgment presupposes options, and options cannot be articulated without thinking practically. Minimally, articulating an option involves judging that the goal it includes promises benefit.

A judgment that a goal promises a benefit does not contain the specific, imperative prescriptivity of a moral judgment, but like a moral judgment it is directive: one judges that a certain way of acting (including refraining from acting) *is to be* undertaken. That supposes that one has a **reason** to shape one's future in the way proposed by the reason.

---

[7] The two points made in this and the preceding paragraphs are taken from St. Thomas Aquinas, interpreted and made his own by Finnis in *Aquinas*, 20–3.

Understanding practical reason as the capacity to make such judgments presupposes a cluster of simple ideas about human action: that in acting one seeks to bring about a goal by doing something that one believes to be both in one's power to do and capable of contributing to the realization of the goal. In thinking practically one takes note of the causal relationships between what is in one's power and what can foster or instantiate a desirable goal. Making use of these beliefs, one projects and anticipates that realizing the goal by action will be beneficial or useful. Although the realization of the goal is an individual event, one is interested in realizing it because one anticipates that it will instantiate some property or feature whose instantiation in or promotion by the goal that will constitute a benefit or an empowerment. Thus, one goes on a diet anticipating a healthier future.

Finnis follows Aquinas in holding that the features in virtue of which a goal is capable of motivating action are such because they are *judged to be good*, that is, because instantiating them by realizing the goals in which they are anticipated is judged to be a future worth bringing about, a future that includes the self the acting person determines himself or herself to be by so choosing. On this account, having reason to pursue these goals does not stop at the brute fact that an agent simply desires goals having these properties. The obtaining of these properties in the goals people realize by action is judged good, desirable—fit to be desired—or perfective, not simply noticed as what one wants.

If the beneficial features of goals—that is, those features that are simply desirable and not desirable only because they enable further benefit—can be gathered into a set of genera of "goods," and if these goods are common to human beings, then there could be a list of basic human goods—a list of the properties of possible goals in which human beings reasonably find the fulfillment that is available to human beings and their communities. Finnis again follows Aquinas in proposing such a list, and largely accepts the appropriateness of the items on Aquinas's list: survival, marriage, knowledge, social relationships, religion as well as practical reasonableness itself are on both lists.

Finnis also follows Aquinas in holding that there is a more fundamental practical principle that is presupposed by the directive force common to any of the human goods considered practically. Aquinas proposed as the first principle of practical reason the proposition that good is to be done and pursued and evil is to be avoided. He held that this proposition is known through itself on the basis of the concept of the good as what all things desire, that is, as the desirable.[8]

If one accepts that this proposition is the most basic practical truth (although a minimally informative one), then it appears to function in practical thought much as does the principle of non-contradiction in thinking more generally. And like this principle, it plausibly is known through itself—that is, judged to be necessarily and un-derivatively true: the good relevant for human action is to be done and pursued. We are directed to pursue what we practically judge to be good and to avoid its contrary.

---

[8] *ST*, 1–2, q. 94, a. 2.

As already suggested, the concept of the good as the desirable, and the prescription that good is to be done do not by themselves contain the content of good; this definition and principle do not indicate what is practically good. That practical content—the actual elements that make up human good—is what the basic human goods provide; thus these goods are also practical principles, basic practical propositions, directing that these properties are to be realized in goals human beings can aim to bring about.

These practical principles are neither unattached, indubitable intuitions nor conclusions of inferences from facts about human nature. Since they are directions towards the fulfillment of the various dimensions of human beings, the workings of human nature provide data which, when understood practically, provide the concepts needed for the formulation of each of the basic human goods.[9]

The basic human goods are irreducible in their practical diversity; each good marks a domain of human fulfillment that is not a means to other, higher ranked goods, whether among the basic human goods or distinct from them and unifying them as a more ultimate good. Any such super-good would necessarily be a construct from the basic human goods, since the first principle directs human beings to the basic human goods and to them alone. So, instances of the various categories of good are incommensurable in their goodness with instances of other goods. Similarly, the various possible instantiations within any category of basic good are often themselves incommensurable. The basic categories of good are generic and allow instantiations of properties that are not simply more or less of the very same intelligibility. For example, health, an aspect of the good of life, can be pursued by promoting irreducibly distinct and sometimes opposed goals. Medical procedures undertaken to lower mortality are for the sake of promoting the good of health, as are those undertaken to lower morbidity. Many procedures undertaken for the former predictably cause morbidity, and vice versa. There is no common property of healthiness that ranks such actions.[10]

C. Integral directiveness defined

The considerations in section B indicate the essential contours of the practical reason presupposed by free choice. Considerations about human good are presupposed by having options. However, these considerations do not settle which option is to be preferred. Each option is supported by something judged to be beneficial or valuable for realizing benefits. In this situation of competition between goods, the rational appeal of each cannot by itself settle which to prefer.

Therefore, the specific rational direction which moral norms provide for the exercise of freedom in choosing is not simply the direction provided by the goods motivating any of the options among which one must choose. However, since the common elements of practical reason are presupposed by choice, moral guidance makes

---

[9] For Finnis's discussion of this "induction" of basic practical propositions from the data provided in humanity's natural inclinations, see *CEJF* I."Introduction," 2–3, 5; I.1, 32–3, 38–9; I.9,148; I.11, 177–9; I.15, 244.

[10] See *NDMR*, 251–61; *CEJF* I.15.

reference to the human goods, the foundations of practical reason. Similarly, the goodness of choosing in accord with moral standards incorporates in some way the realization of basic human good. This essential reference to human good, however, does not settle how one is to be good precisely in choosing to realize some instance of human good rather than a different instance of a good that is perhaps in a different category of basic good.

If, as many people suppose, instances of the basic human goods were strictly comparable in goodness, then the principles of practical reason themselves would be sufficient to resolve the competition between options based on human goods. On that supposition one option would be seen to be better or worse than the others, or they would be found to be equal in goodness. Among such comparable goods the prescription that one is to do good will have application: the rational pursuit of good, in the light of the logic of comparatives, mandates doing the greater good and avoiding the greater evil; it also directs us not to hesitate among options revealed not to differ in goodness. Through the logic of comparison, the principles of practical reason would acquire some minimal directive content in choice situations, but only if goods were commensurable.

Finnis accepts that the content available to practical reason is entirely that provided by the basic human goods, and that the first principle of practical reason provides no special content of its own that might be relevant to evaluating choices. He proposes, however, that in the context of choice it is possible to distinguish two ways these principles can work: practical reason can be directive in a partial, limited or selective way or in an "integral" way.

In formulating a single goal and the means to realize it, or in acting in the absence of the competition among goods needed for free choice, the difference Finnis has in mind does not (and I believe is not meant to) apply; practical reason directs the person towards realizing, through something the person can do, a goal instantiating or contributing to the instantiation of a basic human good. In that simplest case of deliberation and action (where the result of the "practical syllogism" is held to be an action[11]), practical reason operates without reference to a framework that could discriminate partial from integral direction. The emergence of options, which calls for deliberation and choice among them, provides that context.

When one deliberates among options, one's reflection necessarily takes practical note of some impacts on some of the human goods implicated in the options—for example, one cannot avoid attending with interest to the goods grounding the desirability of the alternate goals that will be realized or not depending upon one's choices. Similarly, the person deliberating will find it difficult to avoid considering with interest those side effects negatively affecting emotionally salient and favored goods, such as staying alive and uninjured.

---

[11] See Anscombe, *Intention*, 57–67 for her account of this Aristotelian dictum. Aristotle and Anscombe appear to be dealing with only the single strand of practical reasoning that moves from desirability feature, through something a person can do to realize it, to action. The kind of deliberation and choice that is needed when there are options among which selection is required is not considered. The single strand of practical thinking Anscombe so plausibly explains is an element in the more complex practical reasoning Finnis holds to exist when deliberating about which of competing options to select.

The deliberation undertaken in the face of options is completed in practical judgments; when the deliberation does not succeed in removing all but one option as a live possibility, deliberation will lead to several judgments about what to do. The reflection leading to these judgments is wide ranging and broadly comparative, involving at least some attention to the goods and evils involved in the options. The context of this sort of reflection requires that it consider more than how to realize a good by acting for a goal we can achieve.

I propose that when reflection on options is carried out as fully and thoroughly as possible, the judgment expressing that reflection is based on the integral directiveness of practical reason. That is, when all the relevant principles of practical reason are fully and consistently applied in deliberating to all aspects of options, the direction practical reason provides is integral. All the impacts on all aspects of human good of the action we deliberate about doing will be attended to practically if the result of deliberation incorporates the integral directiveness of practical reason.

That integral directiveness unfolds in critical reflection on the entire set of motivations towards and away from aspects of the options among which one deliberates. Those motives may include factors not related to willing basic human goods. When reflection reveals that, it becomes clear that these factors are not a basis for rational action. Similarly, that deliberative reflection scrutinizes the goals that emerge in the conflicting options. Aside from the possibility that the goals might be desirable because of factors that are not thoroughly good, pursuing a goal because it promises to instantiate a basic human good often affects the rest of one's life. Choosing to pursue a goal involves forswearing other actions and possibilities, and so can limit one's further pursuit of that good in other goals and of other human goods. Such reflection may lead the person to articulate other possibilities, options having similar goals but perhaps different ways to achieve them and different, less objectionable side effects.

By contrast to the integral working of practical reason, a person deliberates in a partial or selective way when the result of deliberation—the judgment that this option is to be chosen—is based on practical reflection that fails to give force to the rational appeal of some aspect of an option or of the set of options that affects human good. A choice responsive to a judgment based on a selective application of the principles of practical reason is not informed by all the intelligible good available. Such a judgment, therefore, proposes to shape the future only partially in accord with what is good, on the basis of motivating factors responsive to what is not intelligibly good or not responsive to what is intelligibly good. In the next part of this contribution, I will discuss how such non-rational factors can "fetter" the working of practical reason, and how those factors can be exposed.

In the book *Nuclear Deterrence*, Finnis, Grisez, and I articulated the attitude towards goods expressed in the notion of the integral directiveness of practical reason as a matter of *respect* or *appreciation* of the goods,[12] especially of those not directly in one's sights in acting. But that should not be understood as the claim that the goods themselves and the first principle of practical reasoning have within them a

---

[12] *NDMR*, 283.

deontological character that constrains the pursuit of good and the avoidance of evil. Good is to be pursued and evil is to be avoided; that together with the content provided by the basic human goods, comprises (is the entirety of) what practical reason directs. The direction of choice by the integral application of practical reason might appear to be a deontology of goods, because it directs us to attend practically to goods affected by our actions without limitation to the goods to be realized in the goals we pursue by adopting certain behaviors as means. However, that direction is the direction of the good as what is to be done and pursued and of evil as what is to be avoided, but now considered in its full directiveness, both towards the goods and away from the evils in the entire set of effects on basic human goods by all aspects of what we might choose to do.

The appeal of the goods fostered or instantiated in goals is salient in deliberation; we begin to deliberate because we judge several goals are worth pursuing. That interest in each of the competing goals is only a step away from action, which one would spontaneously do except for the interest in the alternative. But the rational appeal of other goods affected by aspects of prospective actions, that is, by the side effects and by the means, is not so central to the interests that provoke deliberation. For example, giving practical reality (as within one's power to do so) to the recognition that harming someone as a means or side effect is an evil to be avoided can remain in the background of one's practical reflection. The practical prescription that these harms are evils to be avoided might falsely appear to be a constraint on pursuing one's interests rather than thorough-going rationality in the pursuit of good.

Such thorough-going rationality will direct the person to take note of side effects and means and to allow their relationship to good and its contrary to be given practical effect as far as possible. There are practically significant limitations here, since in choosing we inevitably set aside the pursuit of some goods or the avoidance of some evils as a result of choosing to pursue other goods or avoid other evils. So, giving practical effect to, that is, making real by one's actions, all that is judged good and evil in alternatives for choice is beyond human power. However, we will complete deliberation integrally only in judgments that, while taking into account the inevitable limitations of human power, incorporate the directiveness of all the goods involved.

D. The integral directiveness of practical reason provides the criterion for morally good choice

The integral directiveness of practical reason carries through to completion a process of practical thinking that is unavoidable in deliberating among options for choice. Carrying that process through to its end allows a fully rational assessment of the options for choosing. All the impacts on goods of all aspects of the options will be considered, not just noted theoretically. Their rational appeal is given voice and attention as human power allows. A free choice responsive to such an outcome of deliberation will be as reasonable as a choice can be, since it will be responsive to all that is reasonable and to nothing besides that (since integral reflection will expose such things as failing to provide reasons to act).

One might wonder why this idea of choosing reasonably should provide the criterion for morally good choices, and so constitute the basic principle of morality. Since the analysis has now arrived at the point where the truth of a fundamental principle is proposed, I cannot claim to provide anything like a demonstration. Several considerations must suffice.

Free choices can be responsive to a practical judgment that results from practical reason functioning integrally or to a judgment that results from something short of that. The former choices are as fully in accord with all that rational reflection can deliver as is possible for beings whose creativity involves doing some good, but not all, at the price of *not* doing some other good or causing some harm.

That form of rationality is distinctive since it directs free choices—the creative choices constitutive of this domain. The rationality directing the creative choices constitutive of this domain necessarily is not reducible to that of logical consistency, or to that of the rationality of decision making among commensurables, or to other decision-theoretic prescriptions for social cooperation. Volitional responses to those judgments are settled by them, if there is not a breakdown in a person's motivational operations: recognizing incoherence leads naturally to willing the coherent; recognizing a greater good or univocally more rational course of action naturally evokes pursuit of that greater good or of the more rational course. Practical reason directing choice by way of an integral judgment does not settle one's choice as these forms of rationality would do wherever they were applicable. It indicates that an option is fully reasonable, but the judgment is not sufficient, because of the complexity, multiplicity, and incommensurability of the factors considered, to settle what the person will choose and do.

The fact that choices can respond to practical reason working integrally, joined with the fact that the direction this working of practical reason provides is appropriate to the irreducible reality constituted by free choices underlies the basic prescription that only choices responsive to practical reason working integrally should be chosen.

Perhaps one could dispense with claiming that this prescription provides a "moral" standard, and say simply that it articulates a basic norm for choosing in accord with appropriate rationality. Even so, something can be said about the propriety of this rationality constituting the ultimate *moral* standard.

There is a clear sense in which choosing in accord with the integral directiveness of practical reason provides the standard for what one should choose, that is, what one **ought** to choose, understanding "ought" as it is ordinarily associated with moral obligation. The goods that will not be served, or will be harmed, by refusing to choose in response to a selective, non-integral application of practical reason nevertheless remain goods to be done; the judgment to which a selective use of practical reason leads remains directive, and indeed it is possible that a person will choose the option thus recommended. These goods *ought not*, however, to be pursued in choices responding to this result of selective deliberation. The rational force of that obligation is rooted in the integral directiveness of practical reason; that force gives one reason to override not only the de facto urgency of desire but also the prescriptivity of the good that remains in the option one sets aside because of the selectivity of the deliberation supporting it.

II. Unfettered Practical Reason

In part I, I proposed that the integral directiveness of practical reason provides a basic moral standard. This account of moral principle obviously does not indicate how more specific moral principles and moral norms are to be justified by reference to the basic principle. Moreover, this formulation invites but does not answer the question about what could prevent practical reason from operating fully and integrally as a person deliberates in the face of options for choice.

The idea that a person's practical thinking can be fettered or not addresses both these issues, and in so doing provides a somewhat less abstract version of the basic moral principle than the version formed on the idea of the integral directiveness of practical reason.

What sort of reality is this fettering of practical reason? A fetter is literally a chain or shackle on a person's foot. Fetters restrain or confine. So, practical reason is fettered if it is confined or restrained. This does not mean that the acting person does anything or makes any choice to fetter his or her practical reason, but simply that this thinking is somehow chained down. There are deliberate choices to fetter one's practical reason, but, like all choices, they will presuppose the workings of practical reason, with its directiveness either functioning integrally or selectively (and rather clearly functioning selectively in this case). So, not all fettering of practical reason can be a human action.[13]

The general proposition that unfettered reason is practical reason operating without limitations or restrictions adds a thought to the idea of the integral directiveness and suggests another. The added idea is that the dynamic of practical reason is towards its full and integral use, and that this dynamic will carry through to its end unless prevented. The suggested idea is that there are identifiable kinds of factors that prevent the integral directiveness of practical reason from functioning, and thereby cause it to operate only selectively.

The idea that practical reason includes a dynamic towards the result its integral directiveness would reach is justified in the context of deliberating about options among which one must make a free choice. The application of practical reason in choice situations involves applying it widely. There is no point short of its integral application that provides a natural limit on its use.

Perhaps there are factors which can sometimes overcome practical reason so that deliberation and choice become impossible. Insanity, states of diminished consciousness, and, perhaps sometimes, overpowering fear or desire might make practical thought, deliberation, and choice impossible. Such situations are not cases of reason fettered, but rather of reason altogether overcome and absent. What fetters reason must

---

[13] This conclusion may appear contrary to several statements in Grisez, et al., "Practical Principles, Moral Truth and Ultimate Ends," 124; "Thus, the vengeful person chooses, fettering reason by one of its own practical principles . . ."; and at 125: "Immoral choice fetters reason by adopting a proposal act without adequate regard for some of the principles of practical reason, and so without a fully rational determination of action." This appearance arises on the assumption both that these statements are more than elliptical statements that bad choices manifest the fettering of practical reason (rather than creating it); and that these statements affirm that all fettering of practical reason is by or in choosing. Here I am rejecting the latter assumption, since some fettering must be prior to choice, because choice responds to a practical judgment, which in the case of an immoral choice must be a fettered judgment.

constrain, not overwhelm, it. Consequently, a fettering factor must be capable of influencing practical judgments such as that an option should be chosen. Unless fettering factors work within this structure of practical thinking, the factors that might render a free choice immoral would not be capable of functioning within the context in which free choices are possible.

Factors capable of constraining the full working of practical reason will be found among the cognitions and motivations that can somehow figure into deliberation, choice, and action. The direction practical reason proposes is ultimately based on the basic human goods; that direction cannot fetter its own working. Distorted conceptions of a genuine human good are certainly possible and relevant to reason's being fettered, but it is not practical reason itself that generates the distortion. Rather it directs that good is to be done, and indicates the goods that are to be done. Something beyond these directions is needed if they are to be constrained. Similarly, the volitions responsive to practical judgments about human goods will not fetter practical reason's working except to the extent they are responsive to something besides the goods, for example, such as fragments or appearances of goods. Consequently, other cognitions and motivations are the likely fettering factors.

Those other cognitions include non-practical judgments about such things as human power and causal connections. However, these judgments as such do not constrain practical reason but delineate possibilities for action and the limits of human power; practical reason uses these judgments for its purposes. And as we saw, practical reason working soundly from its principles does not fetter itself.

Like other animals, humans also acquire information from sensory experience, both external and internal to the organism's body. That information can be stored in memory and manipulated in imagination. Such information is often practically relevant, and that relevance can be articulated by practical reflection on the information. Insight into that information allows propositional formulation and reference to human goods and to human possibilities.

We humans not only understand sensory information; like other animals, we react to it: information that registers as repulsive or dangerous or desirable triggers appropriate motivation; like other animals, we behave in response to those motivations. What medieval philosophers called "sensory appetite" indicates this class of motivations. These are motivations responsive to sensory information, understood broadly as including imagination and memory. Given that we are animals, such sensory motivation is closely connected to some of the basic human goods such as survival, health, and the affectionate elements of human sociality.

However, the internal and external factors whose awareness by non-human animals triggers motivations such as fear in the face of what registers as impeding danger, anger in response to threats, or desire for the satisfying do not always, in the case of humans, point in the direction towards which practical reason, integrally applied, directs. One can be motivated by fear to avoid doing what is completely reasonable but dangerous; one can be motivated by desire for satisfactions that are in the situations in which they are sought either unhealthy, or selfish, or irreligious, or otherwise unwise.

This kind of motivation is the likeliest source for the factors that can fetter practical reason. This is so because other elements of motivation, deliberation, choice, and action seem incapable of constraining practical reason, and because it is clearly possible, as the examples in the previous paragraph suggest, for these motivations to operate within a person's exercise of practical reasoning without simply overwhelming it.

One's wanting something or fearing something obviously affects one's deliberation about actions dealing with the desired or feared realities. Ordinarily, they play a role within deliberation, perhaps by suggesting options, by highlighting and favoring some outcomes at the expense of others, by bringing deliberation to a (perhaps premature) close, and by other such influences. These influences point to objects that can be understood practically as goals instantiating goods. Sometimes these motivations accurately indicate a goal in which a genuine human good is instantiated—as when one reasonably judges some rest as a way to realize the good suggested by sensory reluctance to continue to carry on exhausting labor, and chooses that option after careful reflection on the situation. In this case the sensory motivation is integrated with practical reason. Sometimes, however, the goods articulated on the basis of the suggestions of sensory motivation are incomplete or distorted, and the very urgency of the motivations prevents full critical reflection upon the underlying fragments of human good. In such cases the goal articulated and the good which provides reason for its pursuit are inadequate; they are not integrated with practical reason directing integrally. The exhausted person who is reluctant to carry on, but who knows that the labor is morally imperative, and whose wish for rest prevents careful consideration of the alternative—carrying on—provides an example.

I suspect that precise mechanisms through which sensory motivations can limit or distort the integral direction of deliberation but not simply overwhelm practical reason are manifold and more complex than my examples suggest. The examples used by Finnis to exhibit this notion suggest this complexity.[14] However, it is not necessary to sort out these complexities for Finnis's central claims about the fettering of practical reason to be credible. These claims include the following: (1) that the directiveness of practical reason can be fettered; (2) that reflection can identify the fettering factors, namely, sensory motivation that is responsive to imagination and sensory awareness, but not integrated with practical reason; and (3) that identification allows the judgment that these motivations unreasonably shape the results of deliberation affected by them.

Examples can clarify these claims. The desire to stay alive is obviously connected to the good of life; however, the urgency of this desire is not measured by the good of life or by the integral working of practical reason operating when a choice about what to do to survive is called for. Absent that urgency, the choice to kill an innocent, or to deny one's faith, or treacherously to betray a friend in order to save one's own life or that of a beloved person (or even something much less dramatic such as spending the family fortune to stay alive a bit longer) will be understood clearly as choices not simply responsive to the basic human good of human life, but as choices shaped by emotionally dominated self-interest or failure to subordinate feelings of terror to the goods affected by choices raised by the fearful prospect. In the presence of that urgency, the selective application of practical reason results in a judgment that for the sake of the

---

[14] See Grisez et al., "Practical Principles, Moral Truth and Ultimate Ends," 123–4; *NDMR*, 284–7; *CEJF* I.14, 215.

good of life one should, for example, choose to kill an innocent person. Choosing on the basis of such a judgment is acting on the basis of fettered reason. Unfettered, integral reason is needed to correct that judgment and rule out and condemn that choice.

In this example, the urgency of desire to stay alive fetters reason without suppressing it altogether (as could happen if the terror of being killed simply overcame one's rational powers). Perhaps this urgency distracts the person from fuller, more integral deliberation; perhaps it leads the person to overlook the precise directives of practical reason as they bear upon the evils to be avoided, evils that are pursued as instrumental goods in the choice to, say, kill or betray for the sake of saving one's life.

The urgency of this motivation naturally favors some options that arise in the face of death. When that urgency is not integrated into the direction provided by the human goods, it can prevent the full and integral application of practical reason to those options. Of course, that more reasonable result can be reached by conscientious deliberation that can expose any such limiting of practical reason. Exposing such fettering of practical reason allows a practical judgment fully expressing the directiveness of practical reason functioning integrally and well in proposing what is to be chosen.

The importance for moral reasoning of the idea that practical reason can be fettered and can become unfettered emerges by noting how these conceptions can be used to generate more concrete moral principles and specific moral norms. An example shows how this can be done: sensory motivation favors goals in which goods are anticipated for oneself and for those near and dear, and slights the harms to others that are the means or side effects of pursuing these goals. Sometimes favoring the benefits of one's goals to oneself and others is completely reasonable: doing this accepts responsibility for one's own life, serves goods that otherwise cannot be served, and accepts harmful side effects to others only as reasonable or unavoidable. But plainly that favoring and slighting often are not integrated into practical rationality. Invoking the considerations of fairness expressed in exercises of imagination such as the Golden Rule serves to clarify the difference between the integrated and non-integrated functioning of our natural tendencies to favor some persons and to slight the interests of others.

So fairness as exhibited in the use of the Golden Rule emerges as a moral principle by considering facts about human motivation, and then directing that they be assessed in the light of an imaginative exercise in which the connection between the motivations and the relevant human goods is exposed. The demands by the goods of sociality to act for peace and potential friendship with those we affect by action, together with the fact that the basic human goods are understood to provide fulfillment not only for oneself and one's own but for human beings as such, should be shaping practical judgments affecting others. The imaginative experiment which the Golden Rule enjoins shows when the sensory motivations involved in such actions are or are not integrated with practical reason's integral working.

This is but one instance of a moral principle that depends upon and implements the idea of unfettered practical reason. Another well known instance is provided by the example of choosing to kill an innocent to save one's own life. Here unfairness exists, but another fettering limitation on practical rationality as well. For the life I save is an instance of the good of human life, and the life I destroy for the sake of that instance of good is also an instance of that same good. These are incommensurable, but one is subordinated to the other, as if they were commensurable, without good reason, but not without a natural preference we can all understand, yet not accept as fully good.

These cases exemplify what Grisez, and his collaborators including Finnis, call "modes of responsibility."[15] By specifying some aspect of sentient motivation which, when not incorporated into a fully reasonable direction for action, skews and constrains practical reason, one can, by exposing it and testing to determine its possible integration or non-integration into practical thought, distinguish the integrated from the non-integrated workings of the motivations in question. In making this separation based on facts about human motivations and tests to reveal their failure to fit into a plan of integral practical rationality, one has moral guidance with enough content to generate—articulate more or less philosophically—more specific moral norms; in the fairness example, norms of justice and fair play emerge concerning such matters as distributing benefits and burdens of social cooperation and helping the needy; in the example of killing innocents to survive, a norm emerges immediately that excludes without exception the intentional killing of the innocent even for the sake of one's own survival.[16]

In a word, the formulation of the first moral principle in terms of unfettered reason is an essential expansion of the formulation in terms of the integral directiveness of practical reason. Only this expansion makes clear which intermediate moral principles and specific moral norms follow from the most basic moral considerations.

III. Integral Human Fulfillment

The version of the first principle most commonly invoked by Finnis is that stated in terms of integral human fulfillment. Choices and any other volitions for which humans are responsible are said to be morally good if and only if they are consistent with willing this ideal.

The ideal is constructed by considering a community comprising all human beings, and indeed, in Grisez's more recent formulations, all rational creatures and God. All choices in this morally ideal community would be shaped by moral truth, so the fruit of all these choices would be "the fulfillment of all persons in all the basic goods."[17]

Finnis provides several clarifications to prevent misunderstanding. First, the fulfillment of all people in all the goods is not the individualistic fulfillment of each of them alone. The goods can be shared by all humans and in some way by all rational creatures; some goods, like friendship, involve fulfillment of people as members of communities. Second, integral human fulfillment is not a vast, final state of affairs to which common action could be a means, since the basic human goods are open ended. Third, integral

---

[15] Grisez, "Appendix I: Human Acts and Moral Judgments," 861–9, provides the most systematic attempt to locate the sources of fettering factors and to test for their inappropriate influence on deliberation.
[16] See *NLNR*, 100–30, for the development of the modes of responsibility and some of their more specific implications. See also *NDMR*, 284–95.
[17] Grisez et al., "Practical Principles, Moral Truth and Ultimate Ends," 128. This is the original statement of the integral human fulfillment formulation.

human fulfillment is not a further good, a super good beyond the basic human goods, but their fully rational unfolding in a morally ideal community.[18]

With some hesitation, I propose that the idea of this formulation is the following: considerations made simply in terms of the integral directiveness of practical reason (even as expanded to include the unfettering of reason) provide only the procedure for determining that a choice is morally good. The procedure delivers a criterion for goodness in choice and so moral goodness. It remains entirely cognitive, practically cognitive but still propositional. Only the choice to conform to the criterion constitutes a reality that is morally good. That realization of moral goodness is essentially related to the fulfillment of persons in human goods, since choices select among options in which goods are instantiated or fostered. The actualization of moral goodness will therefore include the fulfillment of persons in human goods, and the ideal projected in this formulation invites the largest possible view of what that fulfillment would be. It delineates what reality, specifically the domain of reality constituted by free choices, would be like insofar as all the morally good choices shaped it as fully as possible.[19]

Indicating something of the shape of a reality created by good choices is a valuable addition to the dialectic concerning moral principles. In particular, it is useful for showing that the version of natural law Finnis espouses is not indifferent to realizing human good. Its focus however is on the realization of human good in and through choice and in accord with practical reason functioning integrally. The ideal of integral human fulfillment is, therefore, important for responding to results-oriented moralities such as utilitarianism and its structurally similar egoist rivals, and for clarifying that "goodwill" cannot be understood independently of human good, as Kant appears to have held.

However, while the principle that one ought to choose only those possibilities whose willing is compatible with a will towards integral human fulfillment is a correct construction from the first moral principle, its construction suggests that it is limited in the ways it can function as a basic moral principle.

First, the construction of the ideal moral community involves a number of concepts people might lack who nevertheless have the capacity to deliberate and make free choices. Ideas about the fulfillment of all persons in all intelligible goods likely have not occurred to many who have choices to assess morally. If this principle is known through itself (and not a deduction from the requirement that one ought to choose in accord with the integral directiveness of practical reason), the concepts in virtue of which it is so are not those available to all people (and so it would be, in Aquinas's vocabulary, "known through itself but not to all," and perhaps only to the wise or at least the learned). If this is correct, one can be morally good without knowing this truth. But one cannot be morally good without some understanding of what it is to choose in accord with the dictates of conscience. The ideas connected with unfettered reason are closer to the concepts needed to engage in deliberation. This suggests that

---

[18] *NDMR*, 283–4.

[19] I offer the remarks in this paragraph as an interpretation of Grisez et al., "Practical Principles, Moral Truth and Ultimate Ends," 128: "This formulation focuses on the principle of morality insofar as it is a principle of moral goodness which actualizes moral truth."

willing towards integral human fulfillment is of secondary importance for guiding choices.

Second, this formulation directs us to consider an *ideal* which is thought of as willed, at least hypothetically, and against which our actual choices and intentional actions are to be compared. That ideal provides a sketch of what the fruits of morally good choices would be in the community in which all the fulfillment by rational creatures in all basic goods could unfold. But that ideal does not indicate what actual goals one could pursue to realize moral goodness in one's own choosing. For an ideal is not a goal: ideals can be wished for or wanted but only goals are intended. Moreover, this particular moral ideal is not one a person alone or in cooperating with other human beings could choose to realize. The coming to be of a complete community in which integral human fulfill-ment obtains is surely beyond human power to realize, although as Grisez has shown,[20] God has set up conditions that would allow human beings to cooperate in working for a community very much like that.

In other words, this formulation of the basic principle does point to the fruits of morality as they would unfold on a global scale, but it does not point to the fruits of morality that a person can seek to realize in his or her life. Those fruits must be realized in goals a person can choose to realize, not in ideals.

There are moral goals. A person can aim to be and can choose to be conscientious and responsible in some matter, or in many, or to shape his or her personality so as to be habitually conscientious in all the choices to be faced. That often takes self-denial and discipline; these are definite means taken for real goals that instantiate human goods. Similarly, one can aim to remain or become a steady, fair-minded participant in civic society, and in other communities. And one can aim to cooperate with God and avoid sinning. The goals pursued in these choices are obviously moral goals. And the goods they instantiate, foster, or protect are basic human goods. Human beings are fulfilled by the relationships established in morally upright choices to conform to practical reason, to interact reasonably with other people, and to cooperate with God. These are what Finnis has called "reflexive goods," reflexive because they include choice within the definition of the good.[21]

The intended goals of these actions might be hard exactly to pinpoint and individu-ate but they are doubtless genuine goals one pursues by choosing certain actions one thinks can contribute to achieving and protecting them, just as staying healthy is a long standing goal or related set of goals pursued and protected by many actions over time.

Moral goodness is not in itself ideal; it obtains when people choose in accord with the integral directiveness of practical reason. The import of that directiveness can

---

[20] Grisez, "The True Ultimate End of Human Beings."

[21] See for example, Grisez et al., "Practical Principles, Moral Truth and Ultimate Ends," 108. There are at least three such goods: *sociality* is partially constituted by choices in which we relate to others; *religion* similarly is constituted by making choices that constitute what we can do about our relationship to God; and *practical reasonableness* or conscientiousness is constituted by choices human beings make about the elements of the self—judgment, feelings and motivations, and choices. All of these goods are harmonies between elements including choices; each allows for the harmony to be realized more or less adequately and in rather different ways.

certainly be illuminated by reference to a morally ideal community. But the realization of the moral goodness comes precisely in choosing rationally, and in the proper fruits of such choices. Those fruits are realized in moral goals—the future selves we realize by aiming to be conscientious, just, and pious in pursuing the other basic human goods. Since these moral goals instantiate basic human goods, the motivation which ideals as such cannot provide is fully in place. We can be motivated to respond to the integral directiveness of practical reason because we can judge, for example, that the fulfillment anticipated when we organize the elements of our very selves, by harmonizing our feelings and choices under the stable and satisfying direction of reason, instantiates a basic human good. It seems to me, therefore, that Finnis's discussion of the good of practical reasonableness and the other reflexive goods,[22] draws our attention more directly and effectively towards the reality of moral goodness than the ideal formulation of willing integral human fulfillment could.

Bibliography

Anscombe, G.E.M. (2000) *Intention: Second Edition* (Cambridge, MA: Harvard University Press).

Aquinas, St. Thomas, (1947) Literally translated by the Fathers of the English Dominican Province, *Summa Theologica* Volume One (New York: Benziger Bros).

Grisez, Germain, Joseph Boyle, and John Finnis, "Practical Principles, Moral Truth and Ultimate Ends," *The American Journal of Jurisprudence* 32 (1987), 99–151.

Grisez, Germain (1997) "Appendix I: Human Acts and Moral Judgments," in *The Way of the Lord Jesus, Volume 3: Difficult Moral Questions* (Chicago, IL: Franciscan Press), 861–9.

Grisez, Germain, "The True Ultimate End of Human Beings: The Kingdom, Not God Alone," *Theological Studies* 69 (2008), 38–61.

---

[22] See *NLNR*, 88–90.

5

What is Natural Law Like?

Jeremy Waldron

I

"The State of Nature," said John Locke, "has a Law of Nature to govern it, which obliges every one."[1] But what is "a law of nature"? How would we tell, in the state of nature, that there was a natural *law* as opposed to something else—like positive law, a set of customs, natural morality, natural ethics, a set of natural inclinations, the truth of certain prudential calculations, a widespread but perhaps false belief in some transcendent law, the voice of God, or just a natural disposition on the part of some people to make sonorous objective-sounding pronouncements? What form should we expect natural law to take in our apprehension of it? To what should we be attentive, if we want to figure out whether a claim like that of John Locke at the beginning of this paragraph is true?

Presumably, we should expect natural law to be law-like. It should be *like law*. We already have the experience of our lives and our dealings with others being ruled, governed, and ordered forcefully by law—positive law mostly. Natural law should manifest itself as something capable of ordering our actions and interactions in something like the way that positive law orders our actions and interactions. Otherwise we should not call it "law." I say it should be *something* like positive law, not exactly like it. If it were exactly like it, we would hardly need a separate category. The experience of being governed, ruled, and ordered by natural law should add to our repertoire of being governed, ruled, and ordered by law, not simply imitate existing items in that repertoire. And maybe we have to keep faith with the assertion of natural law thinkers from Aquinas to Locke that there is also something inadequate about being ruled by natural law (something missing, like determinate rules) compared with being ruled by human law,[2] which of means of course that the former cannot be quite like the latter. Anyway, our experience of being governed, ruled, and ordered by positive law is not singular but diverse—there is for example, our experience of municipal law, international law, and the law of nations; and within the domain of municipal law we have experience of such diverse elements as customary law, statute law, constitutional law, common law, rules, standards, principles, doctrines, and precedents—and there is a question which of these experiences we should expect our experience of natural law to be like.

I shall consider in a moment the various things that might be meant by saying that natural law must be rather like municipal law. That discussion will include a

---

[1] Locke, *Two Treatises*, 271 (II, §6).
[2] See Aquinas, *Summa Theologiae*, I–II, Q. 91, Art. 3 and Q. 95, Art. 1; Locke, *Two Treatises*, 350–2 (II, §§ 123–7).

provocative claim to the effect that natural law would have to present itself as something distinct from natural morality or natural ethics (if there are such things). It would have to contain something like the legal positivist's separation thesis, though in this case the thesis would be motivated in a rather different way.

My discussion will raise some questions concerning the account given by John Finnis in *Natural Law and Natural Rights*. In this essay, I am going to suggest that Finnis has not really given us a theory of natural law at all—certainly not a theory of natural law considered as a body of law that might order our affairs in a state of nature. Indeed I am not even sure that he believes in natural law *qua* law, i.e. as something that is capable of fulfilling the governance functions of law in the absence of positive institutions.[3] Let me explain.

One of the things that was intriguing but also in a way disconcerting about Finnis's book was that his account of what he called "natural law" presented itself, in the first instance, in the form of a well worked out moral and ethical theory, with lists of basic human goods (there are apparently seven of them) and eight principles of practical reason. Chapters III through V of his book, discussing all this, were fine exercises in moral and ethical theory. But what was presented there did not seem much like law. In an early review, Philip Soper wondered about the appropriateness of accepting Finnis's presentation of what is, in substance, just a practical theory of objective human good as a theory of natural law.

> Now there is nothing in a name per se, and Finnis certainly has historical support for using the term "natural law" so broadly that it includes almost any objective moral theory. Still, it is somewhat curious to realize that a group as diverse as Aquinas, Kant, and Bentham can all be viewed as "natural law" theorists. Why does he not simply call his theory a "moral theory"?[4]

In what follows I will try to flesh out Soper's concern. I will not deny that Finnis's work in *Natural Law and Natural Rights* is a valuable contribution to jurisprudence and practical philosophy. But I will try to show that there is a further question worth asking—the question intimated in my title—to whose answer Finnis's book does not actually make much of a contribution.

In undertaking this project I want to distinguish between an answer to my question—what is natural law like?—and a contribution to the modern debate about legal positivism. We teach our students that the great divide in jurisprudence is between positivism and natural law. But we can be more precise than that. The great divide is between positivist accounts of positive law and non-positivist accounts of positive law. The latter—or some of the latter—are sometimes called theories of natural law, but it is not their purpose to say much about natural law as such. They are mainly "natural-law" accounts of positive law. I think Finnis's account in Chapters I, IX, and X of *Natural Law and Natural Rights* is the best "natural-law" account of positive law that we have. When asked what natural law amounts to, the proponents of these anti-positivist theories will usually produce a set of moral criteria for evaluating positive law. Of

---

[3] See *CEJF* I.13, 200, for a distinctive understanding of "law" in the phrase "natural law."
[4] Soper, "Legal Theory and the Problem of Definition," 1174–5.

course the positivist can do the same. The difference is that the "natural-law" theorists will insist that their moral criteria have an internal relation to the concept of law, so that—with various qualifications and nuances—the identification of something as law is called into question if it does not satisfy these criteria. All this is intriguing and important. But a "natural-law" theory of positive law of this kind is not itself a theory of natural law. And a well worked out moral theory, however objective it is, is not itself a theory of natural law. Nor, in my view, does something which is just a combination of the two amount to a theory of natural law. So let us focus for a while on natural law itself, undistracted by debates about positivism. What would natural law have to be like, if it were to be available as a basis for ordering human affairs in a state of nature?

II

Natural law must be law-like. It must be the sort of thing that can order human affairs in the forceful way law does. That means, *first*, that natural law has to be deontic: that is, it would present itself in the first instance as a set of requirements or prohibitions, as opposed to a set of values, reasons, or just rather good ideas. And, *second*, its deontic dictates would have to be understood as in some sense enforceable, that is, it would have to be thought not inappropriate for coercion to be used to uphold them. Between them, these first two conditions embody what we might call the "forcefulness" of natural law. *Third*, in order to operate in anything approaching a law-like manner, natural law requirements and prohibitions would also have to be complemented by ancillary principles of various sorts. *Fourth*, natural law, like all law, would have to be separable from ethics and morality, even from objective ethics and morality. And, *fifth*, natural law would have to be subject to some requirement of shared recognition; like any body of law, natural law has to work among and between individuals, not just upon individual conduct considered solipsistically.

With the possible exception of the first two points about forcefulness, these propositions will strike many jurists as odd. The fourth (*separability*) and the fifth (*shared recognition*) seem to require as criteria for the existence of natural law conditions that are more appropriately regarded as criteria for the existence of positive law. And the third proposition (*ancillary principles*) seems to attribute to natural law itself what many regard as the function of positive law in a natural law theory, the function that natural law traditionalists call *determinatio*.[5] These reactions are understandable. But I hope to be able to show that we should rethink them in our attempt to grasp how something appropriately described as natural law can actually present itself to large numbers of humans and operate as law among them.

A. Deontic character

Law governs human affairs by—among other things—identifying certain actions as forbidden and others as required. This is not all that law does—we shall consider some

---

[5] See Aquinas, *Summa Theologiae*, I–II, Q.95, Art. 2, 59–60; and *NLNR*, 284.

other norms that it has to comprise under heading C—but the designation of duties, positive and negative, is surely a primal function of law. So this is one of the things natural law must be like. To understand, or be acquainted with it is to grasp it as imposing requirements and prohibitions.

What distinguishes this deontic element? It is a matter of normative form: requirements and prohibitions have a particular normativity. Now, any operation of practical reason is normative. But normativity comes in different shapes and sizes. The normativity of a value-statement is not the same as the normativity of a piece of advice, and neither is the same as the normativity of a rule. It is the latter sort of normativity that we associate with law—peremptory normativity that cuts through the leisurely consideration of reasons for and against a given course of action by indicating sharply to us that an action is simply required, or that an action is simply forbidden.[6] We sometimes use the phrase "guiding action" to refer to law's normativity.[7] But again, there are all sorts of ways of guiding action. Telling a friend that one conductor's recording of a given symphony is better than another conductor's recording is a way of guiding action (e.g. CD-buying actions), but it is not like the action-guidingness of law.[8] Law guides action by requiring that certain things be done rather than just commending them to us and it guides action by prohibiting certain things, rather than merely explaining why they may not be a good idea. Its "guidance" is peremptory and direct. Of course legal requirements are often complicated, hedged around with conditions and exceptions. But these do not dilute the force of a requirement's directiveness; they just focus the incidence of the requirement.

Various terms are used in the natural law tradition to capture this deontic element. Aquinas tells us that "[l]aw is a certain rule and measure of acts, whereby man is induced to act or is restrained from acting."[9] This veers close to the language of force, which we will address below under heading B. In principle, directive normativity is distinct from that: it is the idea of something being compulsory as opposed to physically compelled. Aquinas also uses the language of "imposition"[10]—"a law is imposed...by way of a rule or measure"—and that suggests something like a command theory, with "required" and "forbidden" being understood in terms of affirmative and negative commandments imposed from above. In the case of natural law, we should be careful about this, so as not to prejudge its relation to any sort of voluntarism or Divine Command theory. Those who associate natural law with nature or reason may want to hold on to its deontic character without necessarily committing themselves to the model of a personal law-giver. G.E.M. Anscombe famously questioned whether it was possible to do this,[11] but some philosophers have suggested that we can proceed with "required" and "forbidden" by analogy with the laws of logic and

---

    [6] See the discussion of mandatory reasons in Raz, *Practical Reason and Norms*, 73–84.

    [7] Hart, *The Concept of Law*, 40; Coleman, *The Practice of Principle*, 118.

    [8] For the relation between evaluations and prescriptions, see Hare, *The Language of Morals*, Ch. VIII.

    [9] Aquinas, *Summa Theologiae*, I–II, Q.90, Art. 1, 12.

    [10] Aquinas, *Summa Theologiae*, I–II, Q.93, Art. 6, 43. Aquinas uses a striking metaphor to capture the sense in which we are burdened by the law: "A man is said to be under the law through being pinned down thereby against his will."

    [11] Anscombe, "Modern Moral Philosophy," 6. See also the observations on "directiveness" in *CEJF* V.3, 58 ff. and *CEJF* II, 74–5.

mathematics.[12] The distinction seems always precarious in the natural law tradition. Finnis quotes a passage from Hugo Grotius, where the latter uses the language of "Moral Necessity" to characterize the deontic force of law.[13] But is this really analogous to the logical sense of necessity? Grotius contrasts "Moral Necessity" with "Moral Deformity" and he goes on immediately to associate both with "Suitableness or Unsuitableness to a reasonable Nature, and consequently . . . [being] either forbidden or commanded by God."[14]

Years ago there was a debate about the interpretation of Thomas Hobbes's *Leviathan*, and in particular the status of the principles described both as principles of natural law and as "Conclusions, or Theoremes concerning what conduceth to the conservation and defence" of those to whom they apply.[15] A.E. Taylor and Howard Warrender both insisted that Hobbes's laws of nature did possess the appropriate deontic force.[16] In furtherance of the Taylor/Warrender thesis, perhaps we can also say that there is a distinction between the deontic force of a norm and the considerations on which it is based and by reference to which it is justified. Even if the considerations are prudential, the norm that they support can still be something that requires certain actions or prohibits others.

It is of course an open question whether laws should be understood as distinct from, and as applicable without consideration of, the reasons that justify them. Since the time of Plato it has been suggested that laws are best promulgated along with a statement of the reasons that support them.[17] With positive law, enacted in a large legislature, that may be hard to do: statutes may represent what Cass Sunstein has called "incompletely theorized agreements," in the sense that their passage does not presuppose consensus (even among a majority) about the reasons for their enactment.[18] But in the case of natural law, maybe these considerations do not apply. Perhaps it makes no sense to think of the deontic content of the law as discontinuous from its justification. To have one is to have the other, and that may be the reason that what John Finnis calls his account of natural law appears to involve an entire moral theory, not just a set of peremptory "Thou shalt nots."

I am not sure. On the one hand, even in a municipal legal system some legal norms (such as Dworkinian principles) are more or less continuous with the reasons that support them.[19] On the other hand, if this point is supposed to apply to natural law, it may be dependent on too-rationalistic an account of the latter. True, some theorists in this tradition identify natural law with reason: Locke is an example.[20] But others, like

---

[12] See, e.g., Kagan, "Defending Options," 344–5.

[13] Grotius, *The Rights of War and Peace*, 150 (Bk. I, Ch. 1, §x), quoted in *NLNR*, 44.

[14] Grotius, *The Rights of War and Peace*, 151 (Bk. I, Ch. 1, §x).

[15] Hobbes, *Leviathan*, 111 (Ch. XV).

[16] See Taylor, "The Ethical Doctrine of Hobbes," and Warrender, *The Political Philosophy of Hobbes*.

[17] See Plato, *The Laws*, 106 ff. (Bk. IV, 719c ff.).

[18] See Sunstein, "Incompletely Theorized Agreements"; and also Waldron, "Legislation by Assembly," 531–3.

[19] See Dworkin, *Taking Rights Seriously*, 24–8.

[20] Thus the quotation from Locke that begins this essay continues: "and *Reason, which is that Law*, teaches all Mankind, who will but consult it, that . . . no one ought to harm another in his Life, Health, Liberty or Possessions" (Locke, *Two Treatises*, 271 (II, §6)), my emphasis.

Aquinas, associate it with inclinations,[21] without insisting as strictly as Locke does, for example, that all human inclinations must be scrutinized and rationalized by reason before they can safely be regarded as natural law.[22] In the case of inclinations, there *is* likely to be a discontinuity between our apprehension of what we are inclined to do and our apprehension of why we are inclined to do it.

To sum up: we can acknowledge, I think, that law (and therefore natural law) need not be *just* a set of peremptory requirements and prohibitions. It may include standards and principles as well as rules, and perhaps policies and goals as well, in addition to the ancillary norms that we will consider under heading C. It is just conceivable, then, that the category of law could be stretched generously enough to include a body of values and principles of practical reason of the sort that Finnis outlines in Chapters III through V of *Natural Law and Natural Rights*. But to be understood as law and to be capable of doing the work law is supposed to do, a normative theory must prominently comprise at least some deontic requirements and prohibitions. I have no doubt that Finnis can eke out one or two from his discussion of "Practical Reasonableness" in Chapter V.[23] So it may seem that his account of natural law touches all the bases that are required if something is to be an account of law. But actually I do not think this is his intention. Finnis's aim in Chapters III through V of his book is not to imitate the complexity of law as a body of variously shaped norms but rather to present a full-blown complex moral and ethical theory, which can then be made available as an immanent standard for defining and evaluating human law.

B. Enforceability

It has long been considered part of law's inherent character that it be enforceable. Though this is distinct from its deontic forcefulness, the two are connected. To count as enforceable, a body of law must contain norms that are sufficiently sharply directive to be amenable to the decisive use of force and sanctions. This can hardly be the case if all natural law consists of is an array of reasons which do not generate clearly delineated directives.

What does enforceability amount to? It may refer mostly to the availability of coercive practices or institutions. But the sense that concerns us right now is the sense of its being appropriate, or at least not inappropriate, to uphold a given norm with force. This may be something we can figure out: whether enforcement resources are actually available or not. For example, John Locke argued in *A Letter Concerning Toleration* that matters of religious belief are inherently unenforceable in this sense, because there is nothing that force or sanctions can secure in the way of the requisite sincere belief.[24]

---

[21] Aquinas, *Summa Theologiae*, I–II, Q.91, Art. 2, 20.

[22] See Locke, *Essay Concerning Human Understanding*, Bk. I, Ch. 3, §§3 and 13; and the remarkable application of this discipline to the instinct of self-preservation in Locke, *Two Treatises*, 204–5 (I, §86).

[23] *NLNR*, 118.

[24] Locke, *Letter Concerning Toleration*, 18–20. See also Waldron, "Locke, Toleration and the Rationality of Persecution," in Waldron, *Liberal Rights*, 88.

Aquinas also invokes some considerations that seem to go to this issue of enforceability. In his discussion of human law, he suggests that it may not be appropriate to enforce all virtues, but to prohibit only "the more grievous vices from which it is possible for the majority to abstain and chiefly those that are to the hurt of others."[25] In many areas, he says, legal enforcement might operate too abruptly (in a curious metaphor he compares it to nose-blowing that brings out blood), whereas people need to be led to virtue "not suddenly but gradually."[26]

The idea that there is an enforcement dimension to the rule of natural law quite apart from human institutions is something we know best from the work of John Locke. In Locke's view, "the Law of Nature would, as all other Laws that concern Men in this World be in vain, if there were no body that in the State of Nature had a Power to Execute that Law, and thereby preserve the innocent and restrain offenders."[27] In the absence of institutions, Locke maintains that natural law is enforceable by any individual. Enforcement is partly a matter of a right to resist and seek reparations for violations that concern oneself, but it also includes a more general right to punish wrongdoers on account of the danger they pose to all mankind.[28] Finnis observes quite rightly that "there is no absolute 'natural' measure of due punishment," but he figures that there might emerge at the level of natural-law thinking "a rough-and-ready . . . 'scale' of relatively appropriate [punitive] responses."[29] And this seems to be what Locke has in mind too. Though he believed it was one of the functions of man-made law to annex known penalties to the laws of nature, he believed that even in the absence of positive institutions it was possible for an individual to think more or less carefully and "soberly" about the amount of punishment that would be appropriate.[30]

So, when we ask what the law of nature is like, we must expect it to contain not just a set of deontic norms, but norms that it makes sense to enforce and norms concerning which we can imagine serious, sober, and reasonably conclusive thought about appropriate punishment for violations.

C. Ancillary principles

As we have just seen, law that requires certain things of free beings and prohibits certain other things must be in a position to confront violations of these directives. In regard to municipal law, we think of this as the task of institutions like courts and police forces. Now, the point of thinking about natural law is to contemplate the absence of such institutions. This does not mean, however, that natural law must lack any principles for dealing with wrong-doing; it means rather that we must be able to distinguish in thought between such principles and the institutions which, in our municipal experience, embody them.

---

[25] Aquinas, *Summa Theologiae*, Q.96, Art. 2, 67.
[26] Aquinas, *Summa Theologiae*, Q.96, Art. 2, 68.
[27] Locke, *Two Treatises*, 271 (II, §7).
[28] Locke, *Two Treatises*, 272–6 (II, §§8–13). [29] *NLNR*, 264.
[30] Locke, *Two Treatises*, 358 (II, §135) on human laws annexing known penalties, and 273 (II, §9) on judging soberly about punishment in the state of nature.

So we can imagine not only principles of punishment, but also principles of culpability, excuse, justification, and mitigation. Just as a person is not culpable in positive law in respect of a killing if he lacked the necessary *mens rea*, so something similar would have to be said about similar situations from the point of view of natural law. And natural law would have to include principles that enabled us to make sense of this.

Equally, if there are disputes or conflicts about wrong action—disputes about who did what or whether what was done was really a violation—there would have to be principles governing the determination of guilt or liability. Again, we think of these as principles for courtrooms, and talk of natural law envisages a world without courtrooms. But that is not the same as a world without the principles that are applied in courtrooms. The phrase "natural justice" is sometimes used to refer to rudimentary principles of due process—"*Audi alteram partem*," "*Nemo iudex in sua causa*," etc.— that are to be observed in any setting where someone's interest or moral position or standing is being, in any sense, adjudicated. The term "natural" in "natural justice" suggests that we may use it also to refer to the quasi-procedural constraints that we would expect to see working in people's accusatory dealings with one another even in an institutional vacuum.

It is tempting to say that these matters are too "technical" to be associated with natural law, and that they have to be regarded as artifacts of positive law, supplementing natural law by way of the process that natural law traditionalists call *determinatio*. Aquinas says that *determinatio* is similar to the process "whereby, in the arts, general forms are particularized as to details: thus [by analogy] the craftsman needs to determine the general form of a house to some particular shape."[31] In law, common examples include the specification of punishments, the settling of numerical elements in rules (like speed limits), the elaboration of property in terms of precisely surveyed boundaries, as well as the establishment of norms of culpability and procedure of the kind we have just been considering.[32] This is all thought to be a matter of positive law-giving, not a characteristic of the rule of natural law.

But is it really true that natural law reaches into these matters only in a shallow way, and that positive law has to take up all the burden? At least some norms of this character present themselves as products of reason. The inherent unfairness of condemning someone before hearing both sides of the story, the wrongness of blaming someone for something that he did not intend and could not have helped—these are familiar intuitions that are no doubt given very specific form in actually existing legal systems, but whose basic elements must be assumed to characterize pre-institutional thought as well. Indeed, some of these principles are also characteristic of moral thought and may be associated with some of the reactive attitudes that P.F. Strawson argued were important for our dealings with one another.[33] The phrase "moral due process" hardly rolls off the tongue; but we understand naturally enough what it means when we begin engaging in the process of condemning or denouncing people for moral

---

[31] Aquinas, *Summa Theologiae*, I–II, Q.95, Art. 2, 59. See also *NLNR*, 284.
[32] For discussion, see Waldron, "Torture, Suicide, and *Determinatio*."
[33] Strawson, *Freedom and Resentment*, 6–7.

failings. I do not mean to identify natural law and morality; but I want to suggest that natural law, just like morality, can go a considerable distance in this regard without help from positive law.

Writers in the natural law tradition sometimes exaggerate the difference between the apprehension of basic deontic principles, and the kind of thinking required to give these the determinate form of human law. The difference is primarily one of detail and complexity; it is not, as Aquinas and (following Aquinas) Robert George suggest, a difference between rationally constrained thinking and artistic choice: Aquinas misleads us, I think, with his architecture analogy.[34] Aquinas is on firmer ground when he suggests that there might be a greater expectation of difficulty and controversy when reasoning on these matters of detail than on the basics of natural law.[35] But that certainly does not mean that the matters of detail can be settled simply by an exercise of creative will.

D. Separability from ethics and morality

I mentioned earlier my conviction that if there is natural law, it will present itself as something distinct from ethics and morality in a state of nature. I said this is likely to seem quite implausible to many jurists. The idea of a separation between law and morality is usually associated with legal positivism and, to those who are familiar with this association, it will seem odd to present it as an aspect of what natural law must be like. Since the *denial* of the separation of law and morality is definitive of what many people regard as natural-law jurisprudence, the idea of citing this as one of the key features of natural law will seem almost incoherent. So let me try to explain.

Modern legal positivism is associated with two separability theses, not just one, and it may be helpful to start with the difference between them. On the one hand, there is the definitive separation between positive law and critical morality insisted upon by H.L.A. Hart and others: "We shall take Legal Positivism to mean the simple contention that it is in no sense a necessary truth that laws reproduce or satisfy certain demands of morality, though in fact they have often done so."[36] On the other hand, there is an insistence, also found in Hart's work, on a separation between positive law and *positive* morality.[37] The norms that flourish in the conventional morality of a society are not the same as its positive laws, though of course there is likely to be some contingent match-up between some of them. (One of the key distinctions in Hart's account of the difference between positive law and positive morality has to do with the forms of "pressure" that are used to sustain the respective systems. Moral pressure, says Hart, is exerted not through threats of punishment but by appeals to common values.[38])

---

[34] See George, "Natural Law," 189: "Like the architect, the lawmaker will in many domains exercise a considerable measure of creative freedom in working from a grasp of basic practical principles . . . Through his exercise of creative freedom, he will craft concrete schemes of regulation aimed at coordinating conduct for the sake of the all-around well-being of the community—that is, the common good."

[35] Aquinas, *Summa Theologiae*, I–II, Q.94, Art. 4, 51.

[36] Hart, *The Concept of Law*, 185–6. For a sophisticated attempt to dissociate legal positivism from some versions of a separation thesis: see Coleman, "The Architecture of Jurisprudence," 11–33.

[37] Hart, *The Concept of Law*, 169–80.　　　[38] Hart, *The Concept of Law*, 179–80.

Someone who rejects the first of these separations need not reject the second. A "natural-law" critic of positivism might insist that, in Hart's words, "there are certain principles of human conduct, awaiting discovery by human reason, with which man-made law must conform if it is to be valid."[39] But that critic might still acknowledge that man-made law (so understood) has functions to perform which separate it, in its structure and content, from man-made morality and man-made ethics. Systems of ethics are designed to address matters of personal virtue that it may be quite inappropriate for positive law to address. And systems of morality, even though they do address other-regarding actions, have it as their function to embody *all* the ways in which a given intention or action or relationship can be evaluated. Laws, by contrast, focus on aspects of evaluation that have to do with forcefully ruling certain acts in as required or ruling them out as unacceptable.

I have been talking about what a natural law theorist might make of a distinction between man-made law and man-made morality, and I have argued that there is no reason why he should not endorse it. However, the thesis I am most concerned with is the separability of natural law from objective or critical morality. This involves a separation among various domains of objective normativity. The idea of distinguishing such domains is not unfamiliar. For example, we may think of ethics as something distinct from morality, even when both are understood in the objective sense. Ethics, we might say, addresses matters of personal value and virtue, whereas morality addresses other-regarding issues. If we draw this distinction, we might then go on to say that the domain of natural law is mostly confined to moral issues; it may not cover all issues of objective morality; and it certainly does not cover the issues dealt with in ethics. At least we can *imagine* a natural lawyer saying that; others might have a more extensive agenda in mind. I am unsure whether the position I have just outlined is different from that of the *Summa Theologiae*. Aquinas asks whether all acts of virtue are prescribed by natural law. He replies that they are, but only because he thinks a common-good or other-regarding account can be given of all virtues.[40] If it cannot, then the tendency of his argument is to separate natural law from the objective truth about self-regarding virtues.

What about the relation between natural law and objective morality, understood as including mostly other-regarding concerns? We might say that the function of objective morality is to embody all the ways in which other-regarding actions and relationships can be evaluated, whereas natural law necessarily embodies the sort of normativity that involves peremptorily ruling some in as required and others out as unacceptable. (Again this is a distinction between different kinds of normativity, drawn without departing from the realm of moral objectivity.) Now of course, morality may also comprise norms that have a law-like logic: Kant, for example, presents some of morality's most important norms as "imperatives."[41] But even in a Kantian theory there are other modes of evaluation that do not work in this way—duties to oneself,

---

[39] Hart, *The Concept of Law*, 186.
[40] Aquinas, *Summa Theologiae*, I–II, Q.94, Art. 3, 49. But compare Q.96, Art. 3, 69.
[41] Kant, *Groundwork*, 24 ff. (4: 413 ff.).

imperfect duties, duties of love, and so on.[42] And non-Kantian theories may center themselves primarily on value and virtue, which are difficult to render in the language that matches the deontic concerns of law. And even when the commands of morality or ethics *are* represented in deontic form, they may still need to be separated from natural law. Thus Kant draws a sharp distinction between domains of duty which affect external action and are not oriented in the first instance to the quality of a person's willing, and domains of action which are concerned primarily with the will's orientation to duty itself.[43]

We need not think of this distinction between natural law and objective morality as a comprehensive separation. Perhaps objective morality is the more inclusive category and natural law is a subset of it, distinguished by the features of forcefulness that we have considered under headings A and B. This still means natural law is separable in thought from morality, even if there is some overlap. Imagining rule by natural law, then, is not the same as imagining the undifferentiated rule of objective morality.

E. Shared recognition

A world ruled by natural law is a world in which large numbers of us govern our actions and interactions according to forceful norms that exist independently of human institutions. The plurality of the first-person reference here is crucial. Natural law is not something that just governs an individual life, like a code of personal piety. It rules *us*; it orders what *we* do to and with *one another*; therefore it must be something we share and know that we share.

True, some natural law norms can intelligibly be apprehended and applied by one person, irrespective of what others think and do. The natural law prohibiting killing is like that: I do not need to know anything about what you have figured out in order to figure that it is wrong for me to kill another human being. But it is surprising how few norms can operate in this individualized way. Even with regard to a norm that can in principle be applied individualistically, like the rule against killing, there is a further question about whether punishing someone for a killing can be done simply on the basis of the punisher's own individual apprehension of the killing's wrongness. The theory of punishment embodied in natural law may tell us that punishment cannot do its work, by way of deterrence or retribution, unless knowledge of the wrongness of the conduct being punished is shared between punisher, punishee, and onlookers. More abstractly, we may say that it is often the function of law to coordinate actions and understandings. In *Natural Law and Natural Rights*, John Finnis suggests that the coordination of important matters left unspecified by natural law is one of the functions of human authority.[44] I am sure he is right, but we should not infer that natural law itself does not do any coordinating. Certainly—to take one well-known instance–coordination is part of what's required for natural law rules of property and it

---

[42] See, e.g., Kant, *The Metaphysics of Morals*, 214 ff. (6: 417 ff.) duties to oneself, 246 ff. (6: 452 ff.) imperfect duties, and 243 ff. (6: 448 ff.) duties of love.
[43] See Kant, *The Metaphysics of Morals*, 45 ff. (6: 218 ff.) for this distinction.
[44] *NLNR*, Ch. IX.

will also be important for promises and agreements of all kinds. So we have to imagine that a state of affairs ordered by natural law will be a state of affairs in which people know that it is so ordered and are in a position to arrive at a shared understanding of the principles that apply.

In systems of positive law, we are accustomed to the idea of rules of recognition—secondary rules which, in H.L.A. Hart's formulation, specify "some feature or features possession of which by a suggested rule is taken as a conclusive affirmative indication that it is a rule of the group to be supported by the social pressure it exerts."[45] For example, a rule of recognition may specify certain source-based criteria, such as publication in a legislative gazette.[46] But this sort of recognition is out of the question in the case of natural law.

Any law, says Aquinas, obtains its proper binding force by being "applied to the men who have to be ruled by it." Such application, he says, "is made by its being notified to them by promulgation."[47] But how? How do people find out what the natural law is? One possibility is that we all just find ourselves in possession of beliefs about natural law. The first question Aquinas asks on the subject is "Is there a Natural Law *in* Us?"[48] and he suggests that "[t]he natural law is promulgated by the very fact that God instilled it into men's minds so as to be known by them naturally."[49] However, his considered theory is much more sophisticated. It is partly a theory of inclinations resting on an Aristotelian-style teleology, partly a vague naturalism, and partly a matter of reasoning—"the light of natural reason, whereby we discern what is good and what is evil, which is the function of the natural law."[50] Aquinas reconciles this rationalist account with his inclinations account by saying that "there is in man an inclination to good, according to the nature of his reason, [and] . . . a natural inclination to know the truth."[51] Reasoning here involves the apprehension of things that are self-evident, which does not mean that they are obvious: "some propositions are self-evident only to the wise."[52]

For our purposes, the crucial thing is that knowledge of the law of nature must be available as something shared by all who are under it. It must, as Aquinas puts it, be "apprehended universally,"[53] not just in the sense that there is a line of reasoning available (like a book in the library) to each person, but in the sense that it is pretty evident to each that all or most will come up with roughly the same conclusions. This may involve deference to "the wise" in some cases, but the appropriateness of such deference must also be shared knowledge; and in any case the reasoning that natural law involves cannot be abstruse to the point of esoteric. Of course, that some proposition is accessible only by the most esoteric reasoning is not itself incompatible with its being objectively true. But it is incompatible with its operating as law. The truths of

---

[45] Hart, *The Concept of Law*, 94.
[46] Hart, *The Concept of Law*, 94–5, 250–4, and 263–4.
[47] Aquinas, *Summa Theologiae*, I–II, Q.90, Art. 4, 17.
[48] Aquinas, *Summa Theologiae*, I–II, Q.91, Art. 2, 19 (my emphasis).
[49] Aquinas, *Summa Theologiae*, I–II, Q.90, Art. 4, 17.
[50] Aquinas, *Summa Theologiae*, I–II, Q.94, Art. 2, 47–8, and Q.91, Art. 2, 20.
[51] Aquinas, *Summa Theologiae*, I–II, Q.94, Art. 2, 48.
[52] Aquinas, *Summa Theologiae*, I–II, Q.94, Art. 2, 47–8. (Cf. Finnis on self-evidence in *NLNR*, 67 ff.)
[53] Aquinas, *Summa Theologiae*, I–II, Q.94, Art. 2, 48.

natural law must be (and be known to be) available to all, either directly or by relatively short and straightforward chains of indirect deference.

Esoterism is one hazard. Intractable disagreement is another. As I have argued elsewhere, the fact that some proposition is objectively true is not incompatible with there being endemic controversy among mankind about its objective truth.[54] If Aquinas is wrong about the self-evidence of natural law propositions or wrong about the degree of deference that is required to convince people of their self-evidence, then different people may accept different norms that are at odds with one another, and different wise men may try to convince people of different conclusions so far as the chains of self-evident reasoning available only to them are concerned.

What are we to think of these disagreements? Should we accept that they are in some sense reasonable?[55] Natural law theorists usually balk at this point. John Locke insisted that controversies that arise concerning the content of natural law are mainly the result of "Men being biased by their Interest, as well as ignorant for want of study of it."[56] And John Finnis holds that on important matters of objective morality,

> differing opinions can only be rooted in ignorance or some sub-rational influence, and it is mistaken...to say that there is more than one..."perfectly reasonable" belief. If by "perfectly reasonable" though erroneous belief Rawls means a belief which is held without subjective moral fault in respect of the forming of it, I would say that that is an important category of de facto beliefs but one which would better be called..."inculpably erroneous," blamelessly mistaken or, in one traditional idiom, "invincibly ignorant."[57]

Fortunately we do not have to settle this issue here. Whether we call it reasonable or unreasonable error, the fact is that any theory of natural law must address the prospect of its imperfect promulgation, so far as people's actual reasoning is concerned. Now, so long as natural law is identified, Finnis-style, with comprehensive moral theory, the problem might not be acute, for the idea of a moral theory does not presuppose this notion of something's being promulgated in a way that ensures its being shared among the lives that it governs. But natural law *qua* law *does* have such a presupposition.

What, then, is to be said about the prospect of dissensus? Locke veers between two views. One is that absolute unanimity is not necessary: after all, many positive law systems are obscure, embodying as they do "the Phancies and intricate Contrivances of Men, following contrary and hidden interests put into Words."[58] The other is that a situation of dissensus indicates that natural law really cannot do the work it is supposed to do and that it needs to be superseded by "an established, settled, known law, received and allowed by common consent to be the standard of right and wrong."[59] Before embracing that possibility, however, there is one last move that can be tried.

---

[54] Waldron, "The Irrelevance of Moral Objectivity," 158. See also Waldron, *Law and Disagreement*, 164 ff.
[55] Compare Rawls, *Political Liberalism*, 55 ff. on reasonable disagreement and the burdens of judgment.
[56] Locke, *Two Treatises*, 351 (II, §124). But for hints of a more generous view in Locke, see Waldron, *The Dignity of Legislation*, 73–80.
[57] *CJEF* I.16, 265.   [58] Locke, *Two Treatises*, 275 (II, §12).
[59] Locke, *Two Treatises*, 351 (II, §124).

I said earlier that Aquinas envisages some people deferring to the reasoning of others, notably "the wise" on matters of natural law.[60] In this spirit, we might include, among the sources of natural law's promulgation, the tradition of natural law thinking. Now, Finnis's book might be read as hostile to this in its insistence early on that its topic is natural law itself, not the history of opinions, theories, and doctrines about natural law.[61] But one can accept this without isolating oneself from the work of others, provided one accepts the fallibility of various sources. And Finnis himself cites Thomas Aquinas and numerous others in exactly this spirit.[62]

There may also be other modes of deference. Some early modern thinkers suggested that we might tentatively equate natural law with *ius gentium*, the law of nations, based on the experience of mankind. I have argued elsewhere that this was Alberico Gentili's view.[63] According to Gentili,

> the law of nations is that which is in use among all the nations of men, which native reason has established among all human beings, and which is equally observed by all mankind. Such a law is natural law. "The agreement of all nations about a matter must be regarded as a law of nature."[64]

Certainly one has to be careful with Gentili's "equation." On his account, we find out about the law of nations by studying history (sacred and profane) and listening to travelers' tales; by these means we try to ascertain what all nations agree upon (in a suitably loose sense of "all").[65] But of course natural law is emphatically not a consensus-concept. We should use the idea of consensus only in respect of this business of promulgation. And even there we should accept its fallibility. Still, human fallibility applies also to all of the other sources of human knowledge that are cited in the natural law tradition, including reflection upon one's inclinations, trust in one's own reasoning, and deference to the wise. Strictly speaking none of these can be identified with natural law, because some of our inclinations are bad, any of them can be mischaracterized, our reason is fallible, and wise men are not always as smart as they think they are or as they are reputed to be.

III

I began with a quotation from John Locke about the role of natural law in a state of nature, and I have been trying to figure out, in his company and that of other natural law theorists, what people's experience of natural law and of having their affairs ordered by natural law might be like in that condition.

I have said that for natural law to exist, people would have to be able to arrive at some common sense of forceful norms requiring or prohibiting certain things, distinct from mere moral or ethical judgment, and accompanied by the sort of ancillary

---

[60] Aquinas, *Summa Theologiae*, I–II, Q.94, Art. 2, 48.
[61] *NLNR*, 24.   [62] *NLNR*, 28–30.
[63] Waldron, "*Ius Gentium*," 283.
[64] Gentili, *De Iure Belli Libri Tres*, 10 (Bk. I, Ch. 1). The quotation at the end is from Cicero, *Tusculan Disputations*, Bk. I, Ch. 13, §30.
[65] Gentili, *De Iure Belli Libri Tres*, 13.

principles that would enable the primary norms to operate decisively in human affairs. All that would have to be inferred as common knowledge through people's reasoned reflections on their own nature, supplemented by their awareness of the results of similar reflections by others. I emphasized at the end of section II the collective, civilizational aspect of this common knowledge in contrast to solitary Cartesian philosophical conceptions of natural law reasoning. Whatever our mode of access to natural law, it will be tentative and fallible. From a human point of view, we can only be governed by what we *think* is natural law. God's rule in the world aside, that is all natural law can be so far as our actions and interactions on earth are concerned.

In a way this generates something like an idea of *the positive presence of natural law among us*. What governs us in the name of natural law is a set of human propositions, commonly recognized as purporting and perhaps succeeding in capturing laws that apply objectively to us in the absence of human institutions. This conception does not, I think, blur the distinction between natural law and positive law. Positive law is institutional, but the rule of natural law that I am imagining is not. Positive law is understood to be changeable at human hands; natural law is not, though of course our understandings of natural law can change.[66] Positive law often has canonical formulations (in statutory and constitutional texts); natural law never does. Positive law can be understood to command things that are decisively wrong; natural law cannot, even in spite of our arguments under heading D about its separation from morality. These differences matter. But they should not lead us to neglect the importance of the positive presence among humans of (what they think are) natural laws.

What is the importance of all this? In one of his essays John Finnis denies that "the typical natural law theory" is "concerned with any alleged 'state of nature'... prior to... the formation of... states or political communities."[67] He is almost right. With one exception that I will outline in a moment, we are not *now* concerned with the governance of a state of nature. Our interest in natural law jurisprudence is primarily in its bearing upon our understanding of positive law (and our criticisms of legal positivism). But it would be unfortunate if our only interest in natural law were in the use of moral criteria to distinguish central from non-central cases of positive legal validity. I think it is helpful also to deepen our sense of the connection between natural law and positive law by understanding ways in which the one developed into the other. Aquinas's notions of derivation and *determinatio* offer some help in this regard. But it also helps to consider, as I have done here, the positive presence of natural law here on earth among us.

Then there is the question of law in the international realm. (This is the exception I mentioned a moment ago.) I came to these issues by considering the proposition that one finds in the work of the founders of modern international law—Gentili, Grotius, and Vattel[68]—and also in the work of early modern contract theorists like Hobbes

---

[66] I develop this point in Waldron, *The Rule of Law and the Measure of Property*, Ch. III.

[67] *CEJF* I.13, 200. I guess this must be read alongside Finnis's puzzling dismissal of the work of John Locke as a "crude attack" on natural law: see *NLNR*, 425. (I cannot believe that Finnis's critique is directed at Locke's *Two Treatises*.)

[68] See Gentili, *De Iure Belli Libri Tres*, 10 (Bk. I, Ch. 1); Grotius, *The Rights of War and Peace*, 75–107 (Preliminary discourse); and Vattel, *The Law of Nations*, 68–9 (Preliminaries, §5).

and Locke[69]—that the international realm is a state of nature and that relations among sovereigns are governed by natural law. Something like this view is still held by certain international jurists, though others disparage it.[70] Those who hold it believe some of the most important work in the international realm (the recognition of *ius cogens* norms, for example) is done under the auspices of natural law principles.[71] I have been skeptical about this,[72] but it seemed still worth exploring. And I believe an analysis like the one advanced here might be helpful in thinking about *ius cogens* norms. Some international lawyers demur. According to Martti Koskenniemi,

> [a] norm is *jus cogens*...not because it was so decreed by God, or because according to this or that theory it is necessary for the survival of the human species. It is *jus cogens* if and inasmuch as, to quote Article 53 of the Vienna Convention on the Law of Treaties, it "is a norm accepted and recognised by the international community of States as a whole."[73]

But if what I have said here is correct, particularly under heading E in section II,, then we should be careful about drawing too sharp a contrast between natural law and laws acknowledged and recognized by the sovereigns of the world. Acknowledgment and recognition, I have argued, does not make something a natural law. But natural law cannot do its work on earth unless it is acknowledged and recognized, and we should be wary about consigning to the positive law side of the ledger everything that is acknowledged and recognized on earth as law simply by virtue of the all-too-human fallibility of its acknowledgment and recognition.

Bibliography

Anscombe, G.E.M. (1958), "Modern Moral Philosophy," *Philosophy* 33, 1–19.

Aquinas, Thomas (1988), *Summa Theologiae*, in Saint Thomas Aquinas, *On Law Morality and Politics*, ed. William Baumgarth and Richard Regan (Indianapolis, Hackett Publishing Company).

Coleman, Jules (2003), *The Practice of Principle: In Defense of a Pragmatist Approach to Legal Theory* (New York, Oxford University Press).

Coleman, Jules (2011), "The Architecture of Jurisprudence," *Yale Law Journal* 121, 2–80.

Dworkin, Ronald (1977), *Taking Rights Seriously*, Revised Edition (London, Duckworth).

Gentili, Alberico (1933), *De Iure Belli Libri Tres*, trans. J.C. Rolfe (Oxford, Oxford University Press).

George, Robert (2008), "Natural Law," *Harvard Journal of Law and Public Policy*, 31, 171–96.

Grotius, Hugo (2005), *The Rights of War and Peace*, Book I, ed. Richard Tuck (Indianapolis, Liberty Fund).

Hare, R.M. (1952), *The Language of Morals* (Oxford, Clarendon Press).

Hart, H.L.A. (1994), *The Concept of Law*, Second edition, ed. Penelope Bullock and Joseph Raz (Oxford, Clarendon Press).

Hobbes, Thomas (1996), *Leviathan*, ed. Richard Tuck (Cambridge, Cambridge University Press).

---

[69] See Locke, *Two Treatises*, 276 (II, §14) and Hobbes, *Leviathan*, 90 (Ch. XIII) and 244 (Ch. XXX).

[70] See Lauterpacht, "The Grotian Tradition in International Law," 22–3. For an opposing view, see Oppenheim, *International Law*, 92.

[71] See O'Connell, *The Power and Purpose of International Law.*

[72] Cf. Waldron, "A Religious View of the Foundations of International Law."

[73] Koskenniemi, "International Law in a Post-Realist Era," 3.

Kagan, Shelly (1994), "Defending Options," *Ethics* 104, 333–51.

Kant, Immanuel (1991), *Groundwork of the Metaphysics of Morals*, ed. Mary Gregor (Cambridge, Cambridge University Press).

Kant, Immanuel (1991a), *The Metaphysics of Morals*, ed. Mary Gregor (Cambridge, Cambridge University Press).

Koskenniemi, Martti (1995), "International Law in a Post-Realist Era," *Australian Year Book of International Law* 16, 1–19.

Lauterpacht, Hersch (1946), "The Grotian Tradition in International Law," *British Yearbook of International Law* 23, 1–53.

Locke, John (1950), *A Letter Concerning Toleration*, ed. Patrick Romanell (Upper Saddle River, NJ, Prentice-Hall).

Locke, John (1971), *An Essay Concerning Human Understanding*, ed. P.H. Nidditch (Oxford, Clarendon Press).

Locke, John (1988), *Two Treatises of Government*, ed. Peter Laslett (Cambridge, Cambridge University Press).

O'Connell, Mary-Ellen (2008), *The Power and Purpose of International Law: Insights from the Theory and Practice of Enforcement* (New York, Oxford University Press).

Oppenheim, Lassa (1996), *International Law*, 9th edition, ed. Robert Jennings and Arthur Watts (London, Longman's).

Plato (1998), *The Laws*, trans. Thomas Pangle (Chicago, University of Chicago Press).

Rawls, John (1993), *Political Liberalism* (New York, Columbia University Press).

Raz, Joseph (1990), *Practical Reason and Norms* (Oxford, Oxford University Press).

Soper, Philip (1983), "Legal Theory and the Problem of Definition," *University of Chicago Law Review* 50, 1170–200.

Strawson, P.F. (1974), *Freedom and Resentment, and Other Essays* (London, Routledge).

Sunstein, Cass (1995), "Incompletely Theorized Agreements," *Harvard Law Review* 108, 1733–72.

Taylor, A.E. (1938), "The Ethical Doctrine of Hobbes," *Philosophy* 13, 406–24.

Vattel, Emer de (2008), *The Law of Nations*, ed. Bela Kapossy and Richard Whatmore (Indianapolis, Liberty Press).

Waldron, Jeremy (1988), "Locke, Toleration and the Rationality of Persecution," in Susan Mendus (ed.) *Justifying Toleration: Conceptual and Historical Perspectives* (Cambridge, Cambridge University Press), 61–86.

Waldron, Jeremy (1992), "The Irrelevance of Moral Objectivity," in Robert George (ed.) *Natural Law Theory: Contemporary Essays* (Oxford: Clarendon Press), 158–87.

Waldron, Jeremy (1993), *Liberal Rights: Collected Papers 1981–91* (Cambridge, Cambridge University Press).

Waldron, Jeremy (1999), *The Dignity of Legislation* (Cambridge, Cambridge University Press).

Waldron, Jeremy (1999a), *Law and Disagreement* (Oxford, Clarendon Press).

Waldron, Jeremy (2000), "Legislation by Assembly," *Loyola Law Review* 46, 507–34.

Waldron, Jeremy (2010), "Torture, Suicide, and *Determinatio*" (The 2010 Natural Law Lecture), *American Journal of Jurisprudence* 55, 1–29.

Waldron, Jeremy (2011), "A Religious View of the Foundations of International Law" (The Charles E. Test Lectures at Princeton University, 2011, NYU School of Law, Public Law Research Paper No. 11–29), available at <http://ssrn.com/abstract=1823702>.

Waldron, Jeremy (2011a), "*Ius Gentium*: A Defense of Gentili's Equation of the Law of Nations and the Law of Nature," in Benedict Kingsbury and Benjamin Straumann (eds) *The Roman Foundations of the Law of Nations: Alberico Gentili and the Justice of Empire* (Oxford, Oxford University Press), 283–96.

Waldron, Jeremy (2012), *The Rule of Law and the Measure of Property: The 2011 Hamlyn Lectures* (Cambridge, Cambridge University Press).

Warrender, Howard (1957), *The Political Philosophy of Hobbes: His Theory of Obligation* (Oxford, Clarendon Press).

INTENTIONS IN ACTION

6

Intention and Side Effects
John Finnis and Elizabeth Anscombe*

Luke Gormally

In a recent essay reviewing two posthumously published collections of papers by Elizabeth Anscombe,[1] John Finnis displays both a profound and strongly positive appreciation of her intellectual achievement. Prominent, however, among the reservations he has about her work is what he takes to be her failure in her 'ethics-oriented analysis' to remain faithful to 'the act-analysis (intention-analysis) employed in her non-ethical writings'.[2] This is a criticism he first forcefully expressed in 1991 with reference to Anscombe's 1982 paper 'Action, Intention and "Double Effect"'.[3] His 1991 paper 'Intention and Side Effects'[4] rather implies that his own ethical analyses are faithful to the understanding of intentional action she developed in her 1957 monograph *Intention*[5] while alleging that she had failed to maintain in at least some of her later writings on ethical issues that understanding of intention. In these writings she is said to identify intention by reference to the cause-effect sequence that might be transparent to an observer rather than by reference to the practical reasoning of the agent.

It is a bold claim that Anscombe lost her intellectual grip on her own pioneering work in action theory, especially when reflection on it continued to engage her and when only three years prior to the paper Finnis impugns she published a detailed corrective to various misinterpretations of her use of the phrase 'under a description' which is central to *Intention*.[6] In any case, I think it can be shown that Finnis's own

---

* The following paper in honour of John Finnis has been written in the spirit of an observation by Mary Geach about the writings of her mother, Elizabeth Anscombe: 'The difference between a philosopher, as we in the West understand that word, and a sage who is giving of his wisdom, is this: that the way to show respect for a sage is to accept his teaching, but the way to respect the philosopher is to argue.' (From Geach's 'Introduction' to *Human Life, Action and Ethics. Essays by G E M Anscombe*, xxi.) I am conscious of an immense debt to John Finnis in my own modest labours in the field of bioethics for his exemplary dedication to the pursuit of truth, the outstanding quality of his scholarship, and the generous and invaluable help and support he has given to me over more than three decades.

[1] Finnis, 'Anscombe's Essays'; part is to be found in *CEJF* II.3, and parts in *CEJF* V.23 and V.9. The part referred to here is in *CEJF* II.3, 69–78.

[2] *CEJF* II.3, 77.

[3] Anscombe, 'Action, Intention and "Double Effect"'.

[4] *CEJF* II.10, 173–97.

[5] Anscombe, *Intention* (Second Edition). An endnote to the republication of 'Direct and Indirect in Action' [originally published in 2001, and of which the co-authors are Germain Grisez and Joseph Boyle] in *CEJF* II.13, 268 refers to *Intention* as 'a book whose approach we follow rigorously'.

[6] Anscombe, 'Under a Description'.

action analysis cannot claim fidelity to *Intention* because

(i)   it relies on an assumption which has no demonstrable place in Anscombe's action theory and is indeed quite alien to her thought, and

(ii) is selective in what it takes from *Intention* and inadequately meets *Intention*'s requirement for control on the truthfulness of an agent's act descriptions.

Furthermore, I shall argue that Finnis's claim about Anscombe's ethical analyses is based on misunderstandings and that there is a case for saying that the understanding of intention on which they are based is consistent with the understanding of intention advanced in *Intention*. What divides Anscombe and Finnis is morally significant since, both holding that there are exceptionless prohibitions of certain kinds of intentional acts, their differences over the scope of intention lead to different conclusions about what in certain cases falls under those prohibitions. This essay concentrates primarily on the interpretation of Anscombe on act analysis rather than the associated ethical issues.

In what follows I

(1)   offer an account, mostly in his own words, of how John Finnis distinguishes side effects from what is intended in action, illustrate how he applies the distinction in what has become a test case for his position, and highlight the assumption which underpins the way he draws the distinction;

(2)   look at what Elizabeth Anscombe has to say about the test case and what Finnis has to say by way of criticism of her ethical analysis;

(3)   argue that Finnis's criticism overlooks considerations central to *Intention* that go some way towards explaining Anscombe's ethical analyses; and

(4)   apply, by way of illustrating their differences, what I take to be Anscombe's understanding of the scope of intention to a small number of types of case discussed by Finnis in his writings.

I. Finnis on Intention and Side Effects

John Finnis has a usefully compendious statement of his position in a 1991 paper largely devoted to the interpretation of Aquinas:

What consequences, results, outcomes of one's choosing and doing are to be judged intended and what are to be judged side effects (*praeter intentionem*) is not to be determined by considering which consequences were foreseen or foreseeable and which not, which were physically immediate ('directly caused') and which not, which are treated by convention and common speech as part of the action and which not. It is settled simply by considering why one is doing what one is doing, counting as within the proposal one has adopted by choice everything which one wants for its own sake or for the sake of what one wants for its own sake, and describing each and every aspect of the behaviour just as, and to the extent that, it is described in the practical reasoning which identifies its point.[7]

------

[7] *CEJF* II.9, 171.

The terms of one's proposal include what one judges to be choiceworthy as needed means to secure one's end under the description which identifies its desirability:

> ...one's intention is defined by one's practical reason in terms of the desirability characterisation under which one wills the end and the description under which one judges one's chosen means appropriate to that end.[8]

This understanding of the scope of intention means that side effects of a course of action are to be understood as

> ...states of affairs which one foresees will result from carrying out one's plan or proposal, *but which one does not need or want* as part of one's way of bringing about what one plans or proposes to bring about...[9]

A critical illustration of what Finnis reckons 'one does not need or want as part of one's way of bringing about what one plans' is provided by his discussion of craniotomy in cases of obstructed labour[10]:

> ...a surgeon who performed a craniotomy and could soundly analyse the action, resisting the undue influence of physical and causal factors that would dominate the perception of observers, could rightly say 'No way do I intend to kill the baby' and 'It is no part of my purpose to kill the baby'.[11]

All that is strictly needed to relieve the obstruction, it is reasoned, is an alteration in the dimensions of the child's head. The fact that the form that this alteration takes is that of emptying the contents of the skull and crushing it should not be taken as necessarily defining the significance of what one is doing—what one is intending. For it is *qua* 'altering the dimensions of the child's head' that the means are '*choiceworthy*'. It is acknowledged that the chosen means are lethal but it is assumed that one's actual choice of means can be defined in terms of what is *conceivably possible*. The assumption that the specification of an agent's *actual* choices may be articulated in terms of what is merely conceivably possible untethers practical reasoning from its necessary relationship to the actually possible. This is the assumption which finds no support in *Intention*. For Anscombe, agents can intend performances that are actually possible (what is possible falling as it does within the constraints of the actual) not performances that are merely conceivably possible. That Finnis seeks to specify the identity of the surgeon's act by reference to practical reasoning in terms of what is *conceivably* possible is confirmed by the following:

> Though a craniotomy...in which the contents of the skull are emptied so that it can be crushed, is not a procedure that could be done to help *the baby*, there could be a form of craniotomy in which, though the usual outcome is the death of the baby, the

---

[8] *CEJF* II.10, 189.   [9] *CEJF* II.8, 143. Emphasis added.

[10] Craniotomy in obstetric emergencies is sometimes referred to as if it were a thing of the past. It is a procedure which is not infrequently employed in countries where health care services are seriously under-resourced. See, for example, Duffy, 'Obstetric Haemorrhage in Gimbie, Ethiopia', recording eight cases of 'destructive craniotomy-aided vaginal delivery' in an audit of 595 consecutive deliveries in Gimbie Hospital in 2005.

[11] *CEJF* II.13, 251.

surgeon nevertheless hopes that cutting and squeezing the skull without emptying its contents will not result in the baby's death. This too is a sign that the fact that the craniotomy normally results in the baby's death does not suffice to settle what is or is not the object and therefore the moral species of the act.[12]

II. Elizabeth Anscombe on Craniotomy and Finnis's Criticism of Her Type of Ethical Analysis

As far as I am aware there is no discussion of craniotomy in Anscombe's published writings. However, in organising and archiving her papers I came across a single hand-written sheet which bears on the procedure.[13] It well illustrates how contrary Anscombe's position is to the assumption which informs Finnis's action theory. The text reads in its entirety as follows:

'Certainty' comes into the question whether doing this is *eo ipso* doing that.

E.g. shooting an arrow is not *eo ipso* transfixing a man, so you might shoot an arrow in a certain direction for a certain purpose without having to be *eo ipso* intentionally transfixing a man. But there might be *danger* that you would transfix a man; and then the question of your accusability in that matter, if a man got transfixed, would be determined by the gravity of the *need* to shoot the arrow in that direction, weighed against the greatness of the risk and the gravity of what it is a risk of.

But if your purpose in shooting the arrow is one that can only be attained *by transfixing* a man, so that transfixing a man is your means to the accomplishment of the purpose, *then* you could not argue that you were only *transfixing* him with the arrow, not damaging him with the arrow, on the ground that your purpose would be attained by transfixing without damage, were that possible. For *if* transfixing a man with an arrow is certainly damaging him, and *if* you may absolutely not try to damage him, you may not try to transfix him.

Thus the question is not: 'may I do so-and-so with my hands?' but 'may I cut off the child's head?' Thus in one way certainty of upshot is not what is in question. For the question is: what is the agent trying to do? In the case of the shooting the answer is: to transfix the man (let us suppose). And this may not be a *certain* result of 'the way he moves his hands'. Similarly, then, for the surgeon: the relevant immediacy is not that between how he moves his hands and the child's death, but between what he is trying to do *in* moving his hands and the child's death.

Certainly sometimes—no, very often—omissions are blameworthy but not when what is omitted is itself a great wrong (injury). And that is how one 'gives moral significance' to the distinctions employed; to kill an innocent person is to commit a very great injustice against him, to wrong him gravely. Life is not like property, something one's right to which lapses in face of another's need. To let another person die *may* sometimes be an injustice to him, if you could do something to save him; to kill him deliberately when he is neither aggressor nor criminal is certainly so; therefore if that is the only way of saving someone else, it is no injustice to that other to let him die, however bitterly he and others may feel about it.

---

[12] *CEJF* II.13, 252.   [13] Anscombe, Unpublished manuscript.

Doubtless this text would invite the criticism John Finnis has of the role the notion of 'immediacy of effect' plays in Anscombe's ethical analyses. The specific target of his criticism is a text from her paper 'Action, Intention and "Double Effect"'[14] in which she discusses the options open to a group of potholers trapped in a cave because a fat companion has got stuck in the exit; they are in danger of drowning because of rising waters in the cave. She envisages two scenarios:

> in one he can be blown up; in the other, a rock *can* be moved to open another escape route, but it will crush his head. He will be killed by it ... As I have described the case, we are only given that moving the rock will crush the pot-holer's head. This might be a result so immediate that the action could not be called 'taking the risk that that would happen'. If so, then it is at best a dubious business to say 'We don't intend that result' ... a ground for saying you can intend to move the rock and not intend to crush the head is that you might not know that in moving the rock you would crush his head. That is true, we may suppose; ... But if you *do* know, then where the crushing is immediate you cannot pretend not to intend it if you are willing to move the rock.[15]

Finnis has a number of criticisms to make of Anscombe's discussion of this case but his key one is:

> I think this attempt to distinguish the intended from the unintended by reference to sheer physical 'immediacy' of cause and effect is unsound, a confusion of categories, an elision of human behaviour with human action.

He sees Anscombe in her ethical analysis as having abandoned the standpoint of the acting person and the understanding of intentional action in terms of the practical reasoning of the acting person, and having replaced it with the observational standpoint of someone identifying what is intended by reference to observable efficient causal behaviour. What he thinks of her as having abandoned he explains by reference to her analysis of the variant version of the man in *Intention* who is knowingly pumping poisoned water to supply water to a house. In this alternative scenario he is not doing it because he seeks to poison the inhabitants but only to earn his pay 'by doing his usual job'. On which Anscombe commented:

> In that case, although he knows concerning an intentional action of his—for it, namely replenishing the house water-supply, is intentional by our criteria—that it is *also* an act of replenishing the house water-supply with *poisoned* water, it would be incorrect by our criteria, to say that his act of replenishing the house supply with poisoned water was intentional. And I do not doubt the correctness of the conclusion; it seems to show that our criteria are rather good.[16]

Finnis's comment on this is:

> Notice how fine-grained is the analysis which Anscombe accepted as correct: not merely that the poisoning of the inhabitants—which is not physically 'immediate'—is

---

[14] Anscombe, 'Action, Intention and "Double Effect"'.
[15] Anscombe, 'Action, Intention and "Double Effect"', 221, 223, 224.
[16] Anscombe, *Intention* (Second Edition), 42.

not intentional, but that the *replenishing of the house water-supply with poisoned water* is not intentional (because that the water be poisoned is not part of the pumper's proposal, viz. to do his usual job of replenishing the water supply). Nothing could be more 'immediate' than the known presence of the poison in the water supply: as *behaviour*, replenishing the water supply with water *just is*, in this case, replenishing it with poisoned water. Yet the criteria for a sound analysis of intention(ality) and thus of *action* require that we distinguish knowingly pumping in poisoned water from intentionally pumping in poisoned water... That the water supply be poisoned was, for this man on this occasion, a side effect.[17]

Following her analysis of the example of the man who, asked why he pumped what he knew to be poisoned water, answers 'I wanted my pay and just did my usual job', Anscombe in the same section of *Intention* goes on to discuss the truthfulness of an agent's reply to 'why' questions about his behaviour; the fact that the agent is in a privileged position in identifying his intentions does not mean that his answers are uncheckable for their truthfulness. '[B]ut what sort of control of truthfulness can be established here?' she asks.

> The answer to this has to be: there can be a certain amount of control of the truthfulness of the answer. For example, in the case of the man who didn't care tuppence [about whether the inhabitants of the house got poisoned], part of the account we imagined him giving was that he just went on doing his usual job. It is therefore necessary that it should be his usual job if his answer is to be acceptable.[18]

Anscombe's analysis of what the man intended clearly assumes that it was not part of the man's *understanding* of his job description that he was responsible for the quality of the water he was to pump; the scenario has him taking his job to be that of pumping whatever water happened to be there. It has been argued[19] that Anscombe overlooked the fact that she had offered a more determinate description of the man's job when she described it as that of 'pumping water into the cistern which supplies the drinking water of the house'.[20] If one were to infer from this wording (which she does not) that it is integral to the man's job description that he ensure the water is drinkable, then he could not be taken to be speaking *truthfully* in saying 'I just did my usual job to get my pay', since he would have been obliged to refrain from pumping poisoned water. On this account, his aim of getting his pay would have involved him in *giving the impression* of doing his usual job by adopting the proposal to pump poisoned water, i.e. by *intentionally* pumping poisoned water.

The general claim that follows from Anscombe's observation that 'it is ... necessary that it should be his usual job if his answer is to be acceptable', is that the character of the role an agent is playing can serve as a check on the truthfulness of avowals of intention, and the more determinate that role the more specific the checks can be.

---

[17] *CEJF* II.10, 192–3.   [18] Anscombe, *Intention* (Second Edition), 43.
[19] O'Brien, *Practical Necessity*, Ch. 4.   [20] Anscombe, *Intention* (Second Edition), 37.

III. Anscombe's *Intention* and Ethical Analysis

There are two key questions raised by Finnis's critique of Anscombe:

(i) What sort of knowledge of 'immediacy of effects' does she have in mind when she discusses whether or not it is determinative of a person's intentions and for what reasons might it be determinative?

(ii) Is Finnis's account of the specification of intention consistent with what Anscombe has to say about controlling for the truthfulness of declarations of intention?

A. Knowledge of immediacy of effects

Finnis construes Anscombe's later references to knowledge of 'immediacy of effects' as instances of observational knowledge—he accuses her of adopting the standpoint of the observer of efficient causal behaviour in identifying an agent's intentions. But this, I suggest, is seriously to misunderstand her. The knowledge Anscombe had in mind is the specific kind of non-observational practical knowledge which is 'the cause of what it understands'[21] (extensively discussed in *Intention*) which an agent has of his intentions in virtue of his practical reasoning about means and ends. 'It is the agent's knowledge of what he is doing that gives the descriptions under which what is going on is the execution of intention.'[22] Those descriptions are acknowledged by an agent as descriptions of what he is intentionally doing when he acknowledges the applicability to them of a certain kind of 'Why?' question ('Why are you doing X?'). Answers to 'Why?' questions will display a pattern which exhibits the internal teleological structure of action; Anscombe speaks of an A-B-C-D pattern in the case of the man pumping water to fill a cistern supplying drinking water to a house. In the first scenario she discusses, his intention is to poison the inhabitants of the house. 'A' will be the initial description of the exercise of a power or skill by the agent (in this case 'moving his arm up and down with his fingers round the pump handle') and 'B' (operating the pump) yields an explanation for why the agent is doing 'A' thereby providing a further description of what he is up to, and the answer 'C' (replenishing the water supply) in response to a Why? question about 'B' yields a further elucidatory description of what the agent is up to, and so on till one arrives at an answer giving a description providing the purpose of the pumping exercise (poisoning the inhabitants of the house, in this scenario). The final answer identifies the *intention with which* the agent is acting; the intermediate descriptions identify the *means* which have the character of being *intentional*. The description of the means identifies 'How' one's purpose is achieved.[23]

As Anscombe repeatedly says in her writings, what a person is doing admits of more than one description under which it is intentional; specifically, an agent cannot confine

---

[21] Anscombe, *Intention* (Second Edition), 87, quoting Aquinas, *Summa Theologiae*, 1a 2ae, q.3, a.5, obj.1.

[22] Anscombe, *Intention* (Second Edition), 87.   [23] Anscombe, *Intention* (Second Edition), 45–7.

his answer to a description of the *intention with which he is acting*; he must also acknowledge as intentional those descriptions which identify his chosen means.

When Anscombe said in her 1982 paper on 'Action, Intention and "Double Effect"'

> Circumstances, and the immediate facts about the means you are choosing to your ends, dictate what descriptions of your intention you must admit. Nota bene that here 'intention' relates to the intentionalness of the action you are performing as means.[24]

her remarks echo what she has to say in *Intention* about the description of means in the light of circumstances as answering the question 'How?' about the achievement of one's end.[25]

For what reasons might consideration of 'immediacy' of effects lead an agent in his practical reasoning to the recognition that they fall within the scope of intention? If we consider the two texts already cited in which Anscombe counts the immediacy of an effect as falling within the scope of intention it will emerge that she can reasonably be construed as having had two kinds of reason for doing so.

The first text, on craniotomy, begins with the statement 'Certainty comes into the question whether doing this is *eo ipso* doing that.' Then she adds later: '. . . certainty of upshot is not what is in question. For the question is: what is the agent trying to do?' The wording surely makes it clear that it is a question which looks for an answer in terms of the practical reasoning of the agent. But that practical reasoning is constrained by 'circumstances and immediate facts about the means [one is] choosing'. Just as a person who aims to transfix a man as a means to the accomplishment of his purpose cannot say that he only aims to transfix him with the arrow, not damage him with the arrow, 'on the ground that [his] purpose would be attained by transfixing without damage, were that possible'; so the surgeon planning to perform a craniotomy cannot say 'I only aim to alter the dimensions of the child's head', on the grounds that that would be sufficient for his purpose, were it possible, when the form of his planned means is emptying the child's skull and crushing it and tearing it off. It would be part of the practical knowledge a surgeon had of his intentions that he aimed to kill the child, for to act as he planned to act is, as Anscombe puts it, *eo ipso*, to kill. By *eo ipso* I take Anscombe to mean in this case that the surgeon's chosen course of action is *in itself* a form of killing—not that the causation of death is a 'downstream' effect of what he proposes to do. Because killing belongs to the character of what the agent is 'trying to do' *under the description under which he is trying to do it* he enjoys a practical certainty that he intends to kill.

The craniotomy case offers a clear example of what Anscombe had in mind when she said 'Circumstances, and the immediate facts about the means you are choosing to your ends, dictate what descriptions of your intention you must admit'. The circumstance that the child is stuck in the birth canal makes a particular way of proceeding—'emptying the child's skull and crushing it'—*choiceworthy* for the surgeon who understands it to be a practical necessity. It enters into his practical reasoning under that description as the way of relieving the obstruction. But to so proceed just is to kill: it is

[24] Anscombe, 'Action, Intention and "Double Effect"', 223.
[25] Anscombe, *Intention* (Second Edition), 45–7.

in the nature of the procedure that it is lethal. It is true that it is not precisely *qua* act of killing but rather *qua* act of rendering the child's body removable from the birth canal that 'emptying the child's skull and crushing it' serves the purpose of saving the mother's life. But the surgeon's chosen way of rendering the child's body removable from the birth canal just is a form of killing. Circumstances can constrain one to choose a kind of performance which fails to answer to the description of what ideally one 'needs and wants'.

A surgeon giving a truthful, clear-headed account of what he is intentionally doing would not allow himself to be confused by the fact that he did not desire the death of the child—for he had chosen an intrinsically lethal way of proceeding in order to save the life of the mother—nor would he allow himself to be distracted by thoughts of possible worlds in which entities had different constitutions from the world in which he was obliged to act or in which it was open to him to employ different but, in reality, unavailable procedures.

John Finnis's objection to the contention that 'doing X just is doing Y' is that 'what is *being done* . . . is settled by what one chose, *under the description that made it attractive to choice*'.[26] But here the conception of what makes a means attractive to choice is unconstrained by immediate facts about what one has to choose to do if one is to secure one's end; it is conceived, rather, in terms of what 'one wants and needs', where these can be formulated in terms of what one could confine oneself to doing in some conceivable world. Anscombe's text on craniotomy should be seen as directly critical of this conception of practical reasoning: what one chooses as means *is constrained* by the specific circumstances in which one is acting.[27]

Finnis considers that it would be open to a surgeon performing (or proposing to perform) a craniotomy to think of the death of the child as a side effect of the procedure. In *Intention* Anscombe wrote:

> Something is voluntary though not intentional if it is the antecedently known concomitant result of one's intentional action, so that one could have prevented it if one would have given up the action; but it is not intentional: one rejects the question 'Why?' in its connexion.[28]

In craniotomy the death of the child is not a concomitant result of evacuating the contents of the baby's skull and then crushing and tearing off the baby's head: those actions are constitutive of killing the child.[29] No way could a surgeon reject the applicability to what he was doing of the question 'Why are you killing (or proposing to kill) the child?' He could only say 'I've no other way of choosing to proceed in the

---

[26] *CEJF* II.10, 191.

[27] It seems clear from the wording of the text on craniotomy that Anscombe's critical target is precisely the conception of chosen means defended by Finnis.

[28] Anscombe, *Intention* (Second Edition), 89.

[29] Matthew O'Brien drew my attention to the point made very clearly in Anscombe's 'Under a Description', that the conceptual separability of certain act descriptions generally does not prevent them having identical reference in concrete cases. To think otherwise is to mistakenly treat act descriptions as if they were singular terms referring to individual actions rather than predicates.

circumstances if I am to save the mother's life'. The applicability of that 'Why' question is, according to *Intention*, a mark of intention.

So one kind of reason why an 'immediate effect' Y of doing X would fall within the scope of intention is that doing X would *eo ipso* be a case of doing Y, i.e. it would be in the very nature or character of a doing of X that it would be a doing of Y.

Anscombe's discussion of the case of the stuck potholer, which occasioned Finnis's criticism of her, can be seen as offering a second type of reason why an immediate effect may be judged to fall within the scope of an agent's intention. The discussion is somewhat confusing. At one point she writes:

> ... someone might say of moving the rock and crushing his head: 'Isn't that direct killing too?' The point of not calling it direct was that it isn't his being crushed that gives the escape route—and so his being crushed is something you don't *intend*.[30]

And in the following paragraph she distinguishes the category of 'immediacy' from 'what is intended', and goes on (on the following page) to speak of those who, though they would refuse to blow up the stuck potholer, would move the rock, as 'shewing themselves [to be] people who will reject any policy making the death of innocent people a means to an end'. But she then immediately speaks of moving the rock as

> *perhaps* ... not excluded on the score of being intentional killing. We have to say 'perhaps' because of the possible *closeness of the result*. As I have described the case, we are only given that moving the rock will crush the pot-holer's head. This might be a result so *immediate* that the action could not be called 'taking the risk that it would happen'. If so, then it is a dubious business to say 'We don't intend the result'. At most, it is not part of the aim, in securing the opening, that the man's head should be crushed ... But if you do know [that in moving the rock you would crush his head], then where the crushing is *immediate* you cannot pretend not to intend it if you are willing to move the rock.[31]

The phrasing 'At most, it is not part of the aim . . .' gives the clue, implying as it does that it *could* be part of the aim. In this scenario it is not the case that rock-removing is under that description *eo ipso* head-crushing. But it could be intentionally head-crushing if the agent knows that circumstances are such that he will certainly be *required* to crush the fat man's head *in* removing the rock. In this scenario, then, you would not be in a position to say that head-crushing is not required by rock-removing; head-crushing is part of what is required to create an exit. You know that if you are not willing to choose to act in a way which will, as chosen in view of the circumstances, crush the fat man's head then you will not secure an escape route. Head-crushing is not a concomitant effect which does not directly serve one's purpose. So what I take to be Anscombe's analysis of this scenario, which Finnis takes to exemplify her lapsation from intention analysis, envisages an 'immediate effect' as an effect which the agent has to think of—because of the circumstances which confront him in his practical reasoning—as an inseparable part of his chosen means if he is to secure his end.

---

[30] Anscombe, 'Action, Intention and "Double Effect"', 221.
[31] Anscombe, 'Action, Intention and "Double Effect"', 222–3, 224. Emphases added.

What this construal of Anscombe's treatment of this example again brings out is the clear distinction between *her* understanding and Finnis's of 'what description of your intention you must admit' in your practical reasoning about your means to your end. For Finnis, what is determinative of the description of one's intended means is one's purpose in acting such that what is to count as a means in one's practical thinking is delimited by what is needed to secure one's purpose and where the conception of what is needed may be framed in terms of merely conceivable possibilities. By contrast, for Anscombe practical thinking about means has to count as determinative of one's means, what one has to aim to do in the circumstances in which one is obliged to act. It is no use saying 'I do not need or want to crush the fat man's head for the satisfaction of my proposal in acting' if the concrete circumstances are such that I am required to crush his head as an inseparable part of my chosen means of securing an exit.

Certainty, then, that an 'immediate effect' of what one proposes to do is intended may arise in the practical reasoning of an agent *either* from the recognition that the description under which he proposes to act identifies a type of action constitutive of bringing about that effect (doing X is *eo ipso* doing Y),[32] *or* from the recognition that circumstances make bringing about the effect a contingently inseparable part of one's chosen means since it is inseparable from what one is aiming to do if one is to achieve one's end.

There are effects of chosen courses of action which one might be inclined to call 'immediate' but which are not integral to one's means to one's ends because one is not committed to bringing them about intentionally for either of the kinds of reasons I have identified as implicit in Anscombe's texts. These are what Anscombe calls concomitant or side effects. Whether what she refers to as an 'immediate effect' counts as an intended effect or a side effect is to be decided along the lines that I think Anscombe's examples indicate. One should not suppress from the identification of one's means any description which identifies effects integral to one's chosen means. It should be carefully noted that the *certainty* about 'immediacy of effects' of which Anscombe speaks is the certainty of the agent in his practical reasoning that they are integral to what he is aiming at in the circumstances in which he is proposing to act. As she says about the surgeon in the craniotomy case: 'the relevant immediacy is . . . between what he is trying to do *in* moving his hands and the child's death'.

B. 'Intention' and the truthfulness of declarations of intention

There is more at issue in Finnis's criticism of Anscombe than the character of the knowledge into which consideration of 'immediacy of effect' enters: practical or observational. As we have seen, Anscombe, in *Intention*, also discusses control of the truthfulness of an agent's account of his practical reasoning. Finnis's conception of practical reasoning seems to offer an unduly limited kind of control for truthfulness.

---

[32] This kind of effect is to be distinguished from a 'downstream' effect which follows from the nature of one's chosen action, for such effects may not enter into one's practical reasoning about one's means to one's end.

Consider his understanding of side effects as

> ...states of affairs which one foresees will result from carrying out one's plan or proposal, *but which one does not need or want* as part of one's way of bringing about what one plans or proposes to bring about...[33]

If there are cases in which one is allowed to determine 'what one does not need or want' by specifying what is merely *conceivably possible* then the specification of what is intended is in those cases resistant to reality checks for truthfulness. Finnis's account of intention certainly allows for convicting an agent of lying or self-deception in his avowals of what he intends; but one would do so on the basis of an honest account of the agent's own practical reasoning. Lying or self-deception is not the issue raised by avowals of intention when the specification of intention is determined solely by what the agent counts within the proposal he has adopted by choice[34] and that proposal may be phrased in terms of what is merely conceivably possible.

Though the agent's standpoint is not the observer's standpoint, if what the agent said he intended in acting did not normally find confirmation in what appeared to the observer to be the agent's intentions, the agent's declarations of his intentions would be unintelligible, and uncheckable, therefore, for truthfulness. An observer must be able to make sense of what an agent says his intentions are. As Anscombe says:

> In order to make sense of 'I do P with a view to Q', we must see how the future state of affairs Q is supposed to be a possible later stage in proceedings of which the action P is an earlier stage...A man's intention in acting is not so private and interior a thing that he has absolute authority in saying *what* it is—as he has absolute authority in saying *what* he dreamt. (If what a man says he dreamed does not make sense, that doesn't mean that his saying he dreamed it does not make sense.)[35]

Control for truthfulness depends on constraints on practical reasoning. I have already distinguished the kinds of constraints that arise on Anscombe's account from knowledge of the nature of what one is doing given the description under which one chooses to do it, from knowledge of the physical circumstances which confront an agent and thereby constrain the character of choice, and from knowledge of the role one is exercising in one's choices, a role which specifies the teleology of acquired skills appropriate to a role; to which one should add knowledge of the function of formal acts required by a role. Knowledge of such constraints can ground checks on the truthfulness of declarations of intention.

IV. Distinguishing Intention and Side Effects in Some Types of Case

In this section I briefly discuss the application of Anscombe's approach (as I have interpreted it) to distinguishing side effects from what is intended in a number of types of case analysed by John Finnis. There are no doubt many types of case on which their views would coincide. But Finnis's construal of her references to 'immediacy of effects' as a lapsation into a spectatorial cause-effect analysis of human behaviour fails to

---

[33] *CEJF* II.8, 143.   [34] See *CEJF* II.9, 171.   [35] Anscombe, *Intention* (Second Edition), 36.

recognise that quite good sense can be made of those references to 'immediacy of effects' if one sees that she envisages consideration of them as entering into the practical reasoning of the agent and as relevant to his practical knowledge of what he is intentionally doing or proposes to do.

A. The case of the castrating farmer

Here is Finnis's presentation of the case:

> A farmer castrates male calves in order to change their hormonal constitution and thereby make them fat and manageable. He accepts that this will make them sterile, and if he did not find it more profitable to fatten and calm them all he would keep some unsterilized for breeding (instead of hiring bulls for breeding in season). Nothing in the behaviour he does perform differentiates *sterilizing the calves by castrating them* from *fattening and calming them by castrating them*. But the proposal to fatten is quite distinct from any proposal to sterilize. So although the *performance* is sterilizing (as anyone would say who just looks at the performance and its physical effects), any question as to what is included in the farmer's proposal is not settled by reference to his behaviour. Indeed, since sterilizing (achieving a state of infertility) is for the farmer neither end (purpose) nor means, it is not included in the proposal he adopts, is not what he chooses, and for the purposes of an account of human action is not what he is *doing*.[36]

i. Comment

The farmer's chosen means is castration. Sterilisation is not a contingent side effect of the nature of the activity in which he chooses to engage precisely to achieve his ends. To be castrated is *eo ipso* to be sterilised and as such would presumably be counted by Anscombe as intended by the farmer, even if, *per impossibile*, he would happily do without bringing it about.

B. The case of the stuttering witness

Finnis's presentation of the case:

> A woman has decided to give testimony at her brother's trial, although she is acutely conscious of her uncontrollable stutter. Her purpose is to help her brother get justice, her means of helping is giving evidence, and a side effect is publicly stuttering. This side effect is an inseparable part of the woman's performance; her speaking is always stuttering. But that side effect is unwanted in itself; indeed, it is a side effect that obstructs her purpose in testifying … Stuttering is not included in her intentions. She chooses and tries to *speak* as well as she can. She does not choose to stutter.[37]

---

[36] *CEJF* II.13, 237–8.   [37] *CEJF* II.13, 237.

i. Comment

No doubt what motivated choice of this example was interest in showing that the 'immediacy of the effect' of a performance—in this case the inseparability of the effect—is not a ground for regarding it as intended. Would it be regarded as intended on the interpretation I have given to the ways Anscombe invokes the notion of 'immediacy of effect'? A choice to testify is not *eo ipso* a choice to stutter. But would the circumstance that her speaking is inseparably ('uncontrollably') an act of stuttering mean that in intending to give spoken testimony she intended to stutter? What she aims to do is to make intelligible utterances, and it is under the description 'making intelligible utterances' that her performance is a chosen means to her end of giving testimony in favour of her brother. In so far as the stuttering diminishes the efficaciousness of her performance it is not part of what she chooses as her means to her end. This is unlike the potholer case in which crushing the fat man's head is envisaged as part of the means of securing the exit from the cave, and had to be chosen as such.

C. The case of the conjoined twins

Conjoined twins come in many different conditions, ranging from twins who each enjoy a complete set of adequately functioning vital organs to those who share a single set of vital organs. John Finnis characterises the case he has discussed in the following way:

> [the twins] share vital organs in such a way that (a) unless they are separated both will die because these organs cannot sustain both children, (b) the separation will result in the more or less immediate death of the twin who is separated from the vital organs necessary to the survival of each twin, and (c) the other stronger twin is reasonably expected to survive the operation indefinitely.[38]

The specific case to which this characterisation is intended to apply was one in which the twins each had her own vital organs, but the weaker twin had a heart that was only 10% functional and was maintained by the functioning of the stronger twin's heart in virtue of the fact that they had a conjoined circulatory system. It was accepted that continuation in that condition would lead to the eventual death of both twins because the stronger twin's heart could not bear the burden of sustaining two bodies. So separation to save the stronger twin was proposed (and in fact carried out).

One objection advanced against the procedure was that it involved the intentional non-beneficial mutilation of the weaker twin. About which Finnis remarks: 'That contention is inconsistent with the understanding of intention expounded in these [i.e. his and colleagues'] essays.'[39] He argues that as shooting in self-defence with the result that one kills may be construed as not intentionally killing, so mutilating a body that directly threatens the life of another body should not be construed as intentional mutilation. It is possible for A to shoot with lethal effect B who threatens his life but without the intention of killing him. But if A shoots precisely to put an end to B's life as

---

[38] *CEJF* II.13, 266–7.   [39] *CEJF* II.13, 266–7.

a means of preserving his own life then he shoots with the intention of killing B. Securing the death of B is the chosen means of self-defence. The ethical issue then is whether intentionally killing in those circumstances is justified. Similarly, if one cuts into the body of M conjoined to the body of J to benefit J then Anscombe would surely have argued that you are intentionally mutilating M: that is your chosen means of benefiting J. The ethical issue then would be whether in such circumstances intentional mutilation is justified.

V. Conclusion

Intention was a pioneering work in action theory which Anscombe saw as part of the work on topics in philosophical psychology which she thought a necessary preliminary to work in ethics. Its acquired status as a classic and its characteristic compactness mean that it is today increasingly the subject of exegetical debates.[40] In this essay I have argued that John Finnis's exegesis of what *Intention* has to say about the specification of intention cannot claim 'rigorous' fidelity to the insights of that volume, and that he is mistaken in holding that Anscombe departed from its insights when she talked of 'immediate effects' of action as falling within the scope of intention. That talk can be seen to refer to considerations which enter into the practical reasoning of an agent in ways that define his intentions. The view that it does certainly poses challenges to John Finnis's ethical theory if his ethical analyses are to claim consistency with her action theory. There is no reason to think that Anscombe would have thought it appropriate to meet such challenges by having ethical theory determine the character of one's action theory.[41]

Bibliography

Anscombe, G.E.M. (n.d.), Unpublished manuscript, without title.
Anscombe, G.E.M. ([1957] 1963), *Intention*, Second Edition (Oxford: Blackwell).
Anscombe, G.E.M. (1979), 'Under a Description', *Nous* 13; reprinted in *The Collected Philosophical Papers of G E M Anscombe*, vol.2, *Metaphysics and the Philosophy of Mind* (Oxford: Blackwell, 1981; Minneapolis: University of Minnesota Press), 208–19.
Anscombe, G.E.M. (1982), 'Action, Intention and "Double Effect"', Proceedings of the American Catholic Philosophical Association; reprinted in Mary Geach, and Luke Gormally (eds) (2005), *Human Life, Action and Ethics. Essays by G E M Anscombe* (Exeter, UK & Charlottesville, VA: Imprint Academic), 207–26.
Duffy, Shane (2007), 'Obstetric Haemorrhage in Gimbie, Ethiopia', *The Obstetrician and Gynaecologist* 9: 121–6.
Finnis, John (2009), 'Anscombe's Essays', *National Catholic Bioethics Quarterly* 9/1: 199–207.

---

[40] See, for example, Ford et al., *Essays on Anscombe's Intention*; and Teichmann, *The Philosophy of Elizabeth Anscombe*. There is much that is highly relevant in O'Brien, *Practical Necessity*.

[41] I am grateful for critical and constructive comments on an early draft of this essay to Joseph Boyle, Stephen Brock, Kevin Flannery, Mary Geach, Rebecca Gormally, and Matthew O'Brien. I am particularly grateful for the strongly dissenting criticisms of Joseph Boyle and the extensive constructive proposals of Matthew O'Brien. A penultimate draft of the essay was shown to Anselm Müller and Roger Teichmann to whose very perceptive comments I am much indebted. None of these friendly critics should be taken to endorse all I say. I owe a longer-standing debt to provocations to thought from Mary Geach.

Finnis, John (2011), *CEJF* II.3: 'Anscombe on Spirit and Intention', in John Finnis, *Intention and Identity. Collected Essays: Volume II* (Oxford: Oxford University Press), 69–78.

Finnis, John (2011), *CEJF* II.8: 'Human Acts', in John Finnis, *Intention and Identity. Collected Essays: Volume II* (Oxford: Oxford University Press), 133–51.

Finnis, John (2011), *CEJF* II.9: 'Intentions and Objects', in John Finnis, *Intention and Identity. Collected Essays: Volume II* (Oxford: Oxford University Press), 152–72.

Finnis, John (2011), *CEJF* II.10: 'Intention and Side Effects', in John Finnis, *Intention and Identity. Collected Essays: Volume II* (Oxford: Oxford University Press), 173–97.

Finnis, John (2011), *CEJF* V.9: 'Historical Consciousness and Theological Foundations', in John Finnis, *Religion and Public Reason. Collected Essays: Volume V* (Oxford: Oxford University Press), 139–69.

Finnis, John (2011), *CEJF* V.23: 'On Retranslating *Humanae Vitae*', in John Finnis, *Religion and Public Reason. Collected Essays: Volume V* (Oxford: Oxford University Press), 344–67.

Ford, Anton, Jennifer Hornsby, and Frederick Stoutland (eds) (2011), *Essays on Anscombe's Intention* (Cambridge, MA & London, UK: HUP).

Geach, Mary, and Luke Gormally (eds) (2005), *Human Life, Action and Ethics. Essays by G E M Anscombe* (Exeter, UK & Charlottesville, VA: Imprint Academic).

O'Brien, Matthew (2011), *Practical Necessity: A Study in Ethics, Law and Human Action* (dissertation, University of Texas at Austin), available at <http://catalog.lib.utexas.edu/record=b7762103-S29>.

Teichmann, Roger (2008), *The Philosophy of Elizabeth Anscombe* (Oxford: Oxford University Press).

7

Intention and Side Effects: the *Mens Rea* for Murder

Anthony Kenny

Jeremy Bentham, in his *Principles of Morals and Legislation*, offered a detailed analysis of human actions and their consequences. In particular he offered a precise and novel definition of the concept of *intention*. The most important feature of this was a distinction between direct and oblique intention. The consequence of an action, he said, may be either directly intentional ("when the prospect of producing it constituted one of the links in the chain of causes by which the person was determined to act") or obliquely intentional (when the consequence was foreseen as likely, but the prospect of producing it formed no link in the determining chain).[1]

The effect of Bentham's innovation was to define intention itself in purely cognitive, rather than volitional terms: to find out what a person intended you needed only to ascertain what she knew, not what she wanted. What she wanted was relevant only to the sub-class of intentionality involved, direct or oblique. An act was unintentional only if its upshot was quite unforeseen; it is thus that "you may intend to touch a man without intending to hurt him; and yet, as the consequences turn out, you may chance to hurt him."[2] The cognitive slant that Bentham gives to intention was of great importance, since for him intention—understood as foresight of consequences—was a key criterion for the moral and legal evaluation of actions.

The Benthamite definition of "intention" is far removed from common usage. In ordinary language we are only said to intend B by doing A if we do A *in order* to bring about B: the mere knowledge that B is the natural effect of A is not sufficient. If I drink too heavily I know I will get a hangover, but I do not drink in order to get a hangover. A father gets up at night to get a drink of water; he knows he may wake the baby, but he does not get up in order to wake the baby. When the Protestant martyr Latimer refused to recant, he knew that he would be burnt as a heretic; but he did not refuse in order to be burnt. None of these is a case of doing A for the sake of B, and in no case is the consequence intended. In the ordinary sense of the word, one intends only what one wants either as an end in itself or as a means to some wanted end.

By the middle of the last century, however, the Benthamite concept of intention had secured a dominant position in the thinking of legal academic writers and in the

---

[1] Bentham, *The Principles of Morals and Legislation*, Ch. VIII, section VI.
[2] Bentham, *The Principles of Morals and Legislation*, Ch. VIII, section II.

judgments of the courts. H.L.A. Hart wrote that

> for the law a foreseen outcome is enough, even if it was unwanted by the agent... the law does not require in such cases that the outcome should have been something intended in the sense that the accused set out to achieve it, either as a means or an end, and here the law diverges from what is ordinarily meant by expressions like "he intentionally killed those men."[3]

Hart relied on the 1868 case *R v. Desmond, Barrett and Others*. Barrett dynamited a prison wall in order to liberate two Fenians; the plot failed, but the explosion killed some persons living nearby. It was not contended that it was part of Barrett's purpose, either as a means or an end, to cause death or injury; but the Lord Chief Justice summed up: it is murder "if a man did an act not with the purpose of taking life but with the knowledge or belief that life was likely to be sacrificed by it."[4]

The courts no less than academic lawyers operated with a cognitive interpretation of intention: but there was uncertainty about what degree of awareness of consequences was necessary in order to make them intentional. Was it certainty, and only certainty, or would mere foresight of consequences as highly probable suffice to constitute intention?

The issue was widened by the case of *Smith* in 1961 in which the accused, an escaping thief, shook off his car a policeman who was then run over and killed. The case caused controversy because the House of Lords, restoring a verdict of murder that had been quashed on appeal, decided that an accused must be taken to intend those consequences of his actions that a reasonable man would have foreseen, even if he did not himself foresee them.[5]

At no point of the proceedings was it questioned that Smith intended whatever Smith himself foresaw. However, dissatisfaction with the objective test proposed by the House of Lords led to the Law Commission proposing a reform of the law. This suggested that no court or jury should be bound to infer that a man intended or foresaw the natural and probable consequence of his actions. It also recommended that killing should not amount to murder unless done with intent to kill; a man has such intent "if he means his actions to kill, or if he is willing for his actions, though meant for another purpose, to kill in accomplishing that purpose."[6]

The first but not the second of these recommendations was embodied in the Criminal Justice Act of 1967. If the second recommendation had been accepted, death which was obliquely intentional would still count as murder: for if one fails to desist from a course of action one knows is likely to cause death, then one is willing for one's actions to kill.

In the case of *Hyam v. D.P.P* [1975] AC 55 the accused was a woman who had set fire to the house of a rival in love and left the house burning with the effect that her rival's two daughters died. The jury were told that the accused was guilty of murder if she had intended to do serious bodily harm, and that the prosecution had proved the necessary intent if the jury were satisfied that when she had set fire to the house she had known that it was highly probable that the fire would cause such harm. The jury convicted, and

---

[3] Hart, *Punishment and Responsibility*, 120.
[4] *The Times*, 28 April 1868.   [5] *DPP v. Smith* [1961] AC 290.
[6] Law Commission Report No. 10 ("Imputed Criminal Intent") HMSO, 1967.

the accused's appeal was dismissed both by the Court of Appeal and by the House of Lords. The Lords' decision was given by majority of three to two, and the reasons given by the three majority judges were based on three different theories of the malice aforethought required for murder.

The variety of *rationes decidendi* offered in *Hyam* left the law of homicide in a confused state. Was intent to cause grievous bodily harm sufficient to constitute malice aforethought in murder? Two of the law lords denied this. Was knowledge that certain consequences were highly probable sufficient to constitute intent? The Lord Chancellor, Lord Hailsham, called this into question.

John Finnis, in a paper of 1991, *Intention and Side Effects*[7] claimed that the confusion concerning intention in the English law of homicide had been cleared up by a number of decisions subsequent to *Hyam*. In recent cases, he wrote, the courts had made a sharp distinction between intention and foresight: the fact that one foresees a certain result as likely or even certain to follow from one's action(s) does not entail that one intends that result. The cases which he cited as exhibiting this new understanding of intent were *R v. Moloney* [1985] AC 905 and *R v. Hancock and Shankland* [1986] AC 455.

Lord Bridge, in *Moloney*, stated "The golden rule should be that when directing a jury on the mental element necessary in a crime of specific intent, the judge should avoid any elaboration or paraphrase of what is meant by intent, and leave it to the jury's good sense to decide whether the accused acted with the necessary intent, unless the judge is convinced that, on the facts and having regard to the way the case has been presented to the jury in evidence and argument, some further explanation or elaboration is strictly necessary to avoid misunderstanding."[8] This implies that "intent" should be given its ordinary, and not its Benthamite, meaning.

Moreover, in the same case, the House of Lords approved the judgment of the Court of Criminal Appeal in *R v. Steane* [1947] KB 997 (CA), a case which concerned a man who had assisted the enemy in order to prevent his family being sent to a concentration camp. He was acquitted of the crime of doing an act likely to assist the enemy with the intention of assisting the enemy, on the grounds that the assistance to the enemy was merely foreseen and in no way desired. Finnis, in his article, took the approval of *Steane* in *Moloney* as evidence that the House of Lords rejected the doctrine of oblique intention.

Again, in *Hancock and Shankland* a clear distinction was made between foresight and intention. Lord Scarman said "the greater the probability of a consequence the more likely it is the consequence was foreseen and ... if that consequence was foreseen, the greater probability is that the consequence was intended ... the probability, however high, of a consequence is only a factor." Thus a jury may, but need not, argue from foresight to intent.[9]

---

[7] Reprinted, with new endnotes, as *CEJF* II.10.
[8] *R v. Moloney* [1958] AC 905 at 926.
[9] *R v. Hancock and Shankland* [1986] AC 455 at 473–4.

Finnis, in his article, applauded this "new English judicial understanding of intention" which he hoped had placed the law of homicide onto a sound track. The subsequent history of the law has shown that his optimism was misplaced.

Lord Bridge had said that there could be exceptional cases where a special definition of "intent" might be necessary. In *R v. Nedrick* [1986] 1 WLR 1025 Lord Lane CJ said that in such cases the jury should be directed not to infer the necessary intention unless they felt sure that the accused knew that death or serious bodily harm was a virtual certainty. The reference to "virtual certainty" was ominous: but Lord Lane did not say that in such cases the jury *must* infer the necessary intention.

But already, in the very judgment in *Moloney* on which Finnis based his optimism, Lord Bridge had invited us to imagine a man who, to escape pursuit, boarded the first plane leaving Heathrow, which as it happened, was flying to Manchester, a place where he had no desire to be. Did he intend to go to Manchester? Yes, said Lord Bridge "By boarding the Manchester plane, the man conclusively demonstrates his intention to go there, because it is a moral certainty that that is where he will arrive."[10]

What showed conclusively that the courts were not following the path that Finnis desired was the case of *R v. Woollin* [1999] AC 82. Woollin killed his three-month-old son by throwing him onto a hard surface in a rage. He was found guilty of murder, the judge having told the jury to convict if they were satisfied that he had realized there was a substantial risk that the child would suffer serious harm. Woollin took an appeal to the House of Lords, where he was successful and the verdict was changed to manslaughter.

The appeal was allowed because it was held that the judge had departed from the direction in *Nedrick* by extending the scope of *mens rea* to include awareness of substantial risk as well as virtual certainty of death ensuing. But the court's interpretation of the *Nedrick* direction, as presented by Lord Steyn, was that a result foreseen as virtually certain actually amounts to an intended result. "[O]ver a period of 12 years since *Nedrick*," he said, "the test of foresight of virtual certainty has apparently caused no practical difficulties. It is simple and clear."[11]

So once again the law is in a state of confusion about the nature of the intent that constitutes the *mens rea* of homicide. If we accept the direction in *Moloney* that the word is to be given its ordinary meaning, it does not include foresight, however certain. If we accept the direction in *Nedrick*, in the sense expounded in *Woollin*, then virtual certainty does indeed amount to intention.

Academic discussion of intention in homicide has focused on a number of difficult cases, of the kind that were envisaged in *Nedrick* as involving the need to offer the jury special clarification of the concept. A man throws his baby from the top of a high burning building to save him from being burnt to death, and the child is killed in the fall. As the only way to save his patient's life, a surgeon undertakes an operation with a minimal chance of success, and the patient dies under the knife. A terrorist plants a bomb in order to blow up an electricity pylon in an isolated situation: a bomb disposal

---

[10] *R v. Moloney* [1985] AC 905 at 926. In an endnote to the reprint of the 1991 paper in Volume II of his collected essays (*Intention and Identity*), 196, Finnis acknowledges that he had misrepresented *Moloney*.
[11] *R v. Woollin* [1999] AC 82 at 94.

expert is killed while trying to defuse it. A surgeon (a different one this time) removes a patient's heart in order to transplant it into his own wife, who would otherwise die. A third surgeon removes a heart merely in order to add it to his stock of hearts to be used for experimental purposes. In which of these instances do we have a case of murder?[12]

Most notorious is the case ("invented by Glanville Williams and everywhere repeated", as Finnis says[13]) of a man who blows up an aircraft in flight in order to collect the cargo insurance, thereby killing the pilot. Finnis has been almost alone in denying that such an act would involve any intention to kill.[14] But a scenario that is sadly less fanciful may be thought to give plausibility to his view. Many people believe that it would have been right to shoot down one of the hijacked planes with innocent hostages on board that was about to attack the Twin Towers in New York on 11 September 2001. US Air Force pilots are now under orders to shoot down hijacked planes posing similar threats. If a pilot did so, would he be guilty of the war crime of deliberately killing non-combatants?

In conformity with his judgment about the Glanville Williams case, Finnis would say that none of these cases involved any intent to kill. I would agree with him in the first three cases, and would count none of them as murder, though a verdict of manslaughter would very likely be appropriate in the third case. But what of the fourth and fifth cases: does not the deliberate removal of a person's heart establish intent to kill?

That Finnis would give a negative answer is suggested by the discussion of craniotomy in the article "'Direct' and 'Indirect' in Action" which he wrote with Germain Grisez and Joseph Boyle and which was published in *The Thomist* in 2001.[15] Craniotomy is a procedure which is, or was, sometimes used when a baby's head was too large to allow normal delivery in childbirth. The surgeon would use an instrument to crush the baby's head, perhaps after emptying its skull, so as to allow the child's removal from the birth canal. Finnis argues that craniotomy is not direct killing of the innocent and therefore does not, as abortion does, fall under the absolute prohibition of such killing. He writes: "A surgeon who performed a craniotomy ... could rightly say 'No way do I intend to kill the baby' and 'It is no part of my purpose to kill the baby.'"[16]

The sentences that Finnis puts into the surgeon's mouth are uncomfortably reminiscent of the practice of "directing the intention" that was satirized by Blaise Pascal in his attack on the laxity which, he alleged, Jesuit confessors encouraged in their clients. The imaginary Jesuit in his book says "Our method of direction consists in proposing to oneself, as the end of one's actions, a permitted object. So far as we can we turn men away from forbidden things, but when we cannot prevent the action at least we purify the action." Thus, for instance, it is allowable to kill a man in return for an insult, even

---

[12] These cases are helpfully discussed in the fourth edition of Jonathan Herring's textbook of *Criminal Law*, 179.

[13] *CEJF*, II.10, 184.

[14] In an article of 1977, which Finnis cites, I express agreement with him that in the Glanville Williams case there is no direct intention to kill or endanger life; it should, however, amount to murder because there is a direct intention to bring about a state of affairs of which death is known to be a certain consequence (Kenny, "Intention and *Mens Rea* in murder," 173).

[15] It is reprinted as *CEJF* II.13.   [16] *CEJF* II.13, 251.

though the Bible tells us not to return evil for evil. "All you have to do is to turn your intention from the desire for vengeance, which is criminal, to the desire to defend one's honor, which is permitted". Dueling is prohibited, but if one is challenged one may turn up at the place designated, not with the intention of fighting a duel, but to avoid being thought a coward; and then, if threatened by one's opponent, one may of course kill him in self-defense.[17]

Such direction of intention, obviously enough, is simply a performance in the imagination which has little to do with genuine intention, which is expressed in the means one chooses to one's ends. It was this doctrine, and Pascal's attack on it, which brought into disrepute the doctrine of double effect, according to which there is an important moral distinction between the intended and unintended effects of one's action. The theory of double effect is a respectable and indeed necessary part of ethics: but if combined with the practice of direction of intention, it becomes no more than a hypocritical cloak for the justification of the means by the end.

In this context Finnis discusses the imaginary case, proposed by Anscombe, in which a fat man wedged in a hole is blocking the escape of cave explorers threatened by rising waters. It would not be permissible, she held, to make an exit by moving a rock whose movement would crush the fat man's head. "At this point," she says, "the Doctrine of Double Effect helps itself to an absurd device, of choosing a description under which the action is intentional, and giving the action under that description as *the* intentional act. 'I am moving what blocks that egress' or 'I am removing a rock which is in the way.'"[18]

If you know that the crushing of the potholer's head is the immediate effect of moving the rock, Anscombe claims, you cannot pretend not to intend it if you are willing to move the rock. Finnis disagrees: however immediate an effect the fat potholer's death may be, the person moving the rock, he maintains, can claim not to intend to kill. He rejects the idea that this denial must be a case of some inner act of direction of intention. The description under which what is done is intended is not something chosen as a device. "[I]t is settled by one's practical reasoning as an agent, by the intelligible benefit one seeks and the means one chooses under the description which promises to yield that benefit".[19] But surely focusing on the description that promises to yield that benefit—rather than the other descriptions indicating the impermissibility of the means—is precisely what constitutes "direction of intention."

Finnis defends his position by saying[20] that in morally evaluating human actions one must identify the action to be evaluated from the perspective of the acting person rather than from the perspective of an observer. It is wrong to consider actions, behavior, and outcomes from the outside, giving primary or exclusive attention to causal relationships. But this contrast which Finnis draws between the first-person perspective and the realm of cause and effect is deceptive.

First of all, practical reasoning does not operate in isolation from the causal order. If I do A in order to bring about B it is precisely because I think that B will be an effect

---

[17] Pascal, *Lettres Provinciales, Lettre Septième.*
[18] Anscombe, "Action, Intention, and 'Double Effect,'" 23.
[19] *CEJF*, II, 190.   [20] *CEJF*, II.13, 243.

caused by my doing A. Second, it is wrong to attribute to a human agent a privileged first-person authority in the description of the action of his that is up for moral evaluation. In fact others may know better than I do what I am up to. It is true that in moral evaluation it is the individual's intention that matters, not the beliefs of others about what he is doing; but the individual does not necessarily have the last word on what his own intention is.

The alternative to giving first-person privilege in the matter of intention is not a simple study of objective causal chains. What provides the criteria for a person's genuine intentions is his actual and hypothetical behavior. X's actions, let us say, bring about both B and C as effects. X tells us that he is doing A for the sake of B, and not for the sake of C. But suppose doing A continues to produce B but no longer C—what do we conclude if X then desists from doing A?

Finnis does indeed realize that a person may not have indefeasible authority in describing his own intentions. In a different context he offers the following example.

> A commander orders the instant destruction of a city by nuclear bombing, in order to shock the adversary out of the war or to deter escalation by the adversary. The targeters select some purely military installation in the city as their aim point, and tell themselves that what they intend is the destruction of that target "all else is side-effect." But they merely deceive themselves.[21]

This consideration shows that what people tell themselves is not decisive about what their intention genuinely is. But the sharp distinction that Finnis elsewhere makes between the perspective of the active agent and the cause-effect sequence does not seem to leave room for people to be wrong about their own intentions in this manner.

One way to test whether a consequence of a person's action is intentional or not is to put a question to the agent. Suppose the expected consequence had not come about, would you be pleased or sorry? Would you have succeeded or failed in your project? Someone who intends his actions to kill a victim will be disappointed, and will have failed, if the victim survives. But someone who is creating a danger to life for a different purpose—Smith, for instance, zigzagging his car to shake off the policeman who was preventing his escape—will be relieved, rather than disappointed, if his escape tactics prove not to be lethal. This test, I believe, is applicable even when the probability is very high of death being the consequence of one's action. I agree, therefore, with Finnis that even virtual certainty of an outcome does not amount to intention.

However, I think that the failure test does not apply if the failure to kill could only be as a result of a miracle. The "virtual certainty" that a passenger will reach Manchester if he boards a plane scheduled to fly there demands an act of faith in the reliability of airline schedules, and a discounting of the possibility of being re-routed to Leeds. This is something very different from a surgeon's knowledge that if he removes a heart without replacing it his patient will die. If he does so, whether to save the life of his ailing wife, or for purposes of scientific experimentation, it does not lie in his mouth to say that he did not intend death because he would have been perfectly happy if his victim had continued to live without a heart.

---

[21] *CEJF*, II, 180.

It is possible, therefore, to reject the identification of intention with virtual certainty, without adopting the excessively narrow definition of intention that Finnis espouses.

Like Finnis, however, I find unsatisfactory the state of the English law of homicide after *Woollin*. What would be a more satisfactory statement of the *mens rea* for murder? It is sometimes said—e.g. by the Law Commission in 1967—that the essential element in murder should be willingness to kill.[22] But "willingness to kill" may amount to no more than more foresight of the likelihood of death: for if a man foresees death as a likely result of his actions, but thus does not therefore desist from his actions, he is willing for them to kill. This fact shows that there is certain artificiality in the sharp distinction between cognitive and volitional elements in *mens rea* that our discussion has up to this point assumed.

Some years ago, following a line of thought developed by Lord Hailsham in *Hyam*, I proposed that murder should be definable as doing an act that causes death with the intent either to kill or to create a serious risk of death: the intent in each case to be direct.[23] The intent to kill should be taken to include the (direct) intent to bring about a state of affairs from which one knows death will certainly follow. This still seems to me a sound proposal, but I would now wish to expand the last clause to "from which one knows that, short of a miracle, death will certainly follow."

Such a definition would allow the difficult cases to be decided in the way in which (to me at least) seems intuitively correct. The surgeon who undertakes a risky operation for the benefit of his patient will lack malice aforethought because he has no direct intention of killing or endangering him, and will indeed welcome any measure that reduces the danger. The experimental surgeon and the uxorious surgeon will both be guilty because their victims cannot survive without a miracle. The man who blows up the plane for the insurance on the cargo, whether or not he directly intends to kill or endanger the life of the pilot, does directly intend to bring about a state of affairs of which he knows death is the certain consequence. The father who throws his baby out of a burning building will not be guilty of murder, even though the baby dies, because there are sufficient cases on record of people surviving falls from heights to show that it would not have taken a miracle for him to survive. The terrorist should be held guilty of manslaughter not murder (as remarked by Lord Steyn in *Woollin*).[24]

A more difficult case is the shooting down of a hijacked plane full of innocent passengers. Is it possible to distinguish this from the destruction of a cargo plane to claim the insurance? I believe that it is. Hijackers aiming a plane at a skyscraper are *hostes humani generis* who present a legitimate target, and USAF pilots are authorized by a competent authority to use lethal force against them. The deaths of the passengers, even though they are, bar a miracle, certain, can be regarded as side effects of the legitimate military action in the same way as unintended civilian casualties of an air attack on a military target. Since the number of deaths to be avoided by preventing a repeat of 9/11 will be enormous, the issue of proportionality does not arise.

---

[22] Law Commission Report No. 20 (Imputed Criminal Intent), HMSO. Compare the remark of Keene LJ in *Hales* [2005] EWCA Crim 1118 that if someone is "prepared to kill in order to escape" he intends to kill.
[23] Kenny, *Will, Freedom and Power*, 67–8.
[24] [1999] AC 82 at 94.

The case I find most difficult of all is *Re A(Children)(Conjoined Twins: Medical Treatment)* [2001] Fam 147. Surgeons proposed to separate conjoined twins who shared organs that were insufficient to sustain both of them: the separation would give reasonable hope of the survival of the stronger twin, but would result in the more or less immediate death of the weaker one. By the definition of murder proposed above, the separation would count as murder unless some further consideration could be adduced in justification. By a different route, therefore, I reluctantly arrive at the conclusion which Ward and Brooke LLJ reached in this case by following the *Woollin* direction: the surgeons had a "murderous intent."[25]

Bibliography

Anscombe, G.E.M. (1982) "Action, Intention, and 'Double Effect,'" *Proceedings of the American Catholic Association.*

Bentham, *The Principles of Morals and Legislation.*

Hart, H.L.A. (1968) *Punishment and Responsibility* (Oxford: OUP).

Herring, Jonathan (2010) *Criminal Law*, Fourth Edition (Oxford: OUP).

Kenny, Anthony (1975) *Will, Freedom and Power* (Oxford: Blackwell).

Kenny, Anthony (1977) "Intention and *Mens Rea* in murder," in P.M.S. Hacker and J. Raz (ed.), *Law, Morality and Society* (Oxford: OUP).

Pascal, Blaise, *Lettres Provinciales, Lettre Septième.*

---

[25] In order to justify the separation, and dismiss the appeal against it, Lords Justices Ward and Brooke invoked a doctrine of necessity. I confess that I am uncomfortable with this doctrine; but that would be a matter for a different essay.

8

John Finnis on Thomas Aquinas on Human Action

Kevin L. Flannery SJ

After seven centuries of interpretation, a common—if not terribly profound—reaction to those who put forward theories as Thomistic is to say that the writings of Thomas Aquinas accept of various interpretations and to leave the matter there, suggesting thereby that one can simply take one's pick: the various interpretations are all equally respectable. Neither John Finnis nor the present writer is party to this attitude. While acknowledging the possibility of a change of position over Aquinas's relatively brief intellectual career, we both believe that it is usually possible to determine what he holds on a particular issue that interests him, especially (but not only) when it is a matter of studying a single work or works written within a few years of each other.

We both also realize that interpreting an author as rich and as precise as Aquinas is not only a difficult task but one that is chock full of occasions for error and self-deception. Although there are interpreters of Aquinas even in our own day who have achieved a familiarity with his way of thinking that greatly reduces the incidence of misinterpretation, the rest of us—and indeed even they—must acknowledge that returning to a text even after a few hours, perhaps in the meantime having read other texts or consulted other scholars, one often sees that previously one was putting upon an argument a construction not intended by the Angelic Doctor. Acknowledging in this way the possibility of misinterpretation is the very opposite of the thesis that various interpretations are equally respectable, for it is to acknowledge that there is a standard against which any interpretation can be measured and possibly rejected: the text in question, properly understood.

I do think that Finnis has misinterpreted Aquinas's theory of human action and in particular his understanding of the object of the human act and its bearing upon the intention with which an agent acts. I offer, however, my criticism of Finnis's interpretation as a friend and as a colleague in the continuing effort, by us and by others, to understand Aquinas correctly and to apply his ideas to contemporary problems. The contemporary importance of this common enterprise is apparent, given that the church has associated itself so closely with the thought of Thomas Aquinas, in particular with respect to the nature and structure of human action.

Most of the texts to be examined here are cited by Finnis in an essay originally entitled 'Object and intention in moral judgments according to St. Thomas Aquinas'. In the second volume of Finnis's *Collected Essays* (*CEJF* II.9), it is given the title 'Intentions and objects' and is one of seven essays making up that volume's 'Part Three: Acts and Intentions'. In the introduction to the volume, Finnis describes this essay as 'fundamental for almost everything else in this part'.[1] It will serve, therefore, as a framework for the present essay, although use will be made also of other works by Finnis. I begin, therefore, with a quick summary of Finnis's interpretation of Aquinas's action theory, with a special emphasis on 'Intentions and objects.'

I. A Summary of Finnis's Theory

Finnis characterizes the approach he opposes as one in which intention is conceived of as 'a distinct content of consciousness' that one might direct toward or away from aspects of one's chosen behaviour, thereby allowing one to adopt means usually considered immoral, on the grounds that one's intention is good. As a corrective to this mistaken approach, Finnis says near the beginning of 'Intentions and objects' that he will focus on two 'controlling elements' in Aquinas's theory:

> (1) in choosing, one not only intends as one's end some intelligible benefit, but also *prefers* one proposal offering such benefit to one or more alternative available pro-posals offering the same or some other intelligible benefit; (2) in choosing means (adopting one proposal for the sake of its intelligible benefit), one not only *constitutes that means as the (proximate) end* for any technique, procedure or performance one may use to do or carry out one's choice, but also *settles the end (the benefit) one intends.*[2]

In order to understand these controlling elements, it is necessary to understand what Finnis means by two key terms. The first is 'choice.' Finnis states in the opening sentence of the essay that 'Intention is of end, choice is of means.' Bearing in mind that 'intention' refers to the proper act of the will, which is for the end, this statement corresponds, more or less, to what Aristotle says in *Nicomachean Ethics* 3.2.1111b26–27: 'will is of the end, choice is of those things that are for the end'.[3] One of Finnis's points in (2) is that there is a mutual and interactive relationship between intention and choice, so that, even though it is true that choice is of the 'means', that choice is an act of the will not separate from the act of the will with respect to the end (the intention).

The second term is 'proposal'. A proposal is closely associated with choice, for to choose is to adopt a proposal in preference to another (or others), as in controlling element (1).[4] A proposal will not be involved in cases in which just one option is of any interest at all:

> For example, a traveller spontaneously responding to nature's call may follow signs towards a toilet. Common speech, attending to the fact that he is pursuing an intelli-gently guided causal process, will say he is acting intentionally (and 'rationally'). But

---

[1] *CEJF* II Introduction 14.

[2] *CEJF* II.9, 153. Emphases in all quotations are in the original, unless otherwise indicated.

[3] *ST* 1–2.13.4c. At 13.3 *sed contra*, Aquinas attributes the quotation to Aristotle. Some contemporary scholars will object to translating Aristotle's *boulēsis* as 'will', but the English translation offered here is of the Latin that Aquinas was reading: *voluntas est finis, electio autem eorum quae sunt ad finem.* When speaking of choice, Aquinas does not speak of means (*modus* or *modi*) but uses the much more open-ended Aristotelian expression, 'things that are for the end'.

[4] *CEJF* II.11, 198–9.

his actions, insofar as they are spontaneous (rather than deliberately chosen by him for a reason, in preference to some rationally appealing alternative such as catching his plane), do not instantiate choice and intention in their focal senses and should not be confused with rationally motivated action; he is not acting for a reason . . .[5]

A proposal will also not include things that Finnis regards as 'side effects', such as wearing away the leather on one's shoes as one walks to the store but also the killing of a baby whose skull is crushed by a doctor in an effort to save the life of its mother.[6] The term 'proposal' is also primarily to be associated with the will rather than with the intellect, although Finnis does not deny that intellect (or reason) also plays an important role in a proposal.

In section I of 'Intentions and objects', Finnis considers 'a schema of 12 terms signifying a sequence of psychological acts involved in willing and doing something',[7] which he calls the 'neo-scholastic schema'.[8] He takes particular issue with the ordering of certain stages in this schema, maintaining that it shows that these commentators did not appreciate the importance of choice in Aquinas's action theory—choice, that is, among (or between) proposals.

In section II of 'Intentions and objects', Finnis discusses the nature of means, maintaining first of all that 'choice is of human actions' and so means (the objects of choice) are human actions. A consequence of this would be that 'technical means', including instruments and procedures that 'could in principle be replicated by machines or other devices', are not means 'in the sense intended when we say that choice is of means'. This exclusion of technical means from the realm of human action is closely connected with Finnis's concept of a proposal, such as would allow him to exclude from the same realm the procedure that kills the baby whose skull is crushed in the effort to save the life of its mother. But, as Finnis acknowledges, this thesis is also connected with his elaboration of remarks, found at the beginning of Aquinas's commentary on the *Nicomachean Ethics*, about the four orders or types of science. He does not go into this matter at any length in 'Intentions and objects' but rather (or especially) in *Aquinas*.[9]

In the same section of 'Intentions and objects,' Finnis also argues—indeed, shows— that 'to the extent that some prior activity empowers one to carry out [some] means, that means stands to that prior action as end stands to means'. This concept of 'nested ends', is bound up with controlling element (2), for it not only gives Finnis a basis for arguing that choice and intention are mutually dependent but also that the choice (or proposal) to adopt certain means 'constitutes that means as the (proximate) end for any technique'. This in turn is bound up with the notion that technical means, qua technical means, are not within the realm of human action.

---

[5] *CEJF* II.10, 179; at this point, Finnis refers to the 'strict sense' of 'acting for a reason', set out later in the concluding section of the same essay.
[6] *CEJF* II.13, 255.　　　[7] *CEJF* II.9, 152.
[8] The schema is presented below.
[9] In the index of *Aquinas*, see the long list of references under the entry 'four types of order/science/ theory'. Below, I consider the four orders, as they are presented in *Aquinas*.

In section III of 'Intentions and objects', Finnis takes up the thorny issue of the object, which, according to Aquinas, specifies the moral act. As part of his explanation of how he understands the object, Finnis introduces the standard distinction between the *per se* and the *per accidens*, associating the former (in the moral realm) with what is intended: '. . . for moral assessment and judgment, the act is what it is just as it is *per se*, that is, just as it is intended, under the description it has in the proposal which the agent adopts by choice . . .' He also quotes a passage in which Aquinas says that an action receives its species from its *per se* object and 'not from what is only incidentally [*per accidens*] its object', which is *praeter intentionem* or 'outside the intention'.[10] The position defended in this section is, therefore, that the object that specifies the moral act is the proposal adopted by choice: anything excluded from the proposal is excluded also from the object and from the specification of the act.

II. The Neo-scholastic Schema

It will be useful to have the neo-scholastic 12-stage schema before us:[11]

Intelligence	Will
Concerning the end	
1. Simple understanding	2. Simple volition
3. Judgment: end is attainable	4. Intention
Concerning the means	
5. Deliberation (*consilium*)	6. Consent (*consensus*)
7. Judgment on means (*sententia/iudicium*)	8. Choice (*electio*)
Executing the choice	
9. Direction (*imperium/praeceptum*)	10. Application (*usus*)
11. Application of intelligence in executing choice	12. Enjoyment (*fruitio*)

As already indicated, Finnis's central criticism of this schema is that it was used by certain neo-scholastics to eliminate true choice; they designed the schema, he says, 'as if deliberation must conclude to only one acceptable means, that is, as if the role of choice were really played by practical reasoning and judgment'.[12] This 'defiance of Aquinas's account' they effected by placing judgment on means (*iudicium*) between consent

---

[10] *ST* 2–2.59.2c. The quoted passages are from Finnis's translation (*CEJF* II.9, 162).

[11] This schema is found in *CEJF* II.9, 154. A similar but more articulated schema is found in *Aquinas*, 71.

[12] *CEJF* II.9, 156.

(*consensus*) and *electio* (choice). This does not mean, however, that Finnis would change this ordering. He says in a note that 'I am not suggesting that *iudicium* should be removed from its place immediately "prior to" *electio*'.[13] He then cites favourably the interpretation by Reginald Garrigou-Lagrange of a thesis approved in 1914 by the Vatican's *Congregatio Studiorum*. The thesis concludes with the words: 'choice . . . follows the last practical judgment, but that it *is* the last, this the will effects'.[14] So, according to this interpretation, *iudicium* and *electio* interact with one another: a decision in favour of one possible means to the end has not already been made when an action arrives at stage 8 (*electio*).

Moreover, according to Finnis, for this joint activity of *iudicium* and *electio* to be the essential part of human action that it is, *consensus* (stage 6) must involve at least two options; otherwise there would be no choice.

> Any deliberation which ends in *choice* must have yielded, not one judgment affirming the choiceworthiness of an option awaiting adoption by the will, but (at least) *two* judgments. (One of these judgments may be no more than: there is reason not to act on the other.) And there is need for choice because one responds to the attraction— the different attractions—of the respective alternative options which one judges to be, each in its own way, a suitable way of doing or getting or carrying on something one is interested in. Each of those options, those *eligibilia*, arouses in one that form of willingness which St Thomas calls *consensus*.[15]

Notable here is Finnis's insistence not only that *consensus* presents more than one option but that each of these is attractive. A page later, Finnis will say that choice demands that matters not be settled at the stage of *consensus*. 'There is a practical judgment or judgments affirming the suitability of an option or options eventually rejected. And there is an interest in (*consensus* to) an option or options which one does not adopt, make one's own, act upon.'

There are a number of issues connected with what Finnis says about the neo-scholastic schema, but two merit at least some attention here. First of all, Finnis provides no evidence that any interpreter of Aquinas (neo-scholastic or otherwise) ever placed *iudicium* between *consensus* and *electio* for the reasons he gives. That is, he cites no such interpreter who defies the plain sense of the word *electio*—not to mention Aquinas's statement to the contrary (see, for instance, *ST* 1–2.13.2c)—by maintaining that, when any action arrives at the stage of *electio*, matters have already been decided. In a note, Finnis does mention as setting out the schema three fairly recent authors, but none of them holds the position he describes.[16]

If an author claiming to be interpreting Aquinas were to deny that *electio* regards options, that would indeed be controversial and worthy of refutation; but it is rather

---

[13] *CEJF* II.9, 155, n. 7.

[14] *Sequitur . . . electio iudicium practicum ultimum; at quod sit ultimum, voluntas efficit* (AAS 6 (1914) 386). The emphasis is in my translation, although the syntax of the Latin seems to call for it. Garrigou-Lagrange discusses this thesis in Garrigou-Lagrange (1951), 253–4.

[15] *CEJF* II.9, 155.

[16] The three authors are Servais Pinckaers, Thomas Gilby, and Tito Centi (*CEJF* II.9, 154, n. 5). For Pinckaers, see Pinckaers and Gardeil, *Saint Thomas d'Aquin, Somme théologique*, 423. For Gilby, see Gilby, *St. Thomas Aquinas, Summa theologiae*, 216. For Centi, see Centi, *S. Tommaso d'Aquino, La somma teologica*, 172. Finnis acknowledges that Centi has 'reservations' regarding the schema.

Finnis's position that is controversial—the position, that is, that in human action there *must* always be plural options that are attractive, suitable, and practically interesting. This is the second issue that merits our attention. The third objection in *ST* 1–2.15.3 argues that *consensus* cannot be of that which is for the end since then *consensus* would be the same as *electio* and John of Damascus says that they are not.[17] Aquinas's answer is that sometimes and in a certain sense they *are* the same thing: 'But if there is only one [thing leading to the end] that pleases, *consensus* and *electio* do not differ in reality but only in our way of looking at them, so that it is called *consensus* in as much as [the one thing] pleases with a view to action, but *electio* in as much as it is preferred to the things that do not please.'

It is true that here at the very end of his response, Aquinas appears to make a concession to the suggestion that the case of the one option involves a choice (that is, an *electio*, as at stage 8). But that which is called here both *consensus* and *electio* is essentially *consensus* and only derivatively *electio*. One readily accepts the idea that an *electio* involves *consensus*; one balks at the unqualified assertion that *consensus* necessarily involves *electio*—in the sense of a choice among desirable options—since the things that do not meet with *consensus* do not do so precisely because they do not please. A human act does not require such a choice; it can be simply seeing (being presented with) a thing to be pursued and consenting. Consent is a favourable assessment of—a *sententia* regarding—what is set before a person by judgment.[18] If just one thing is set before the person, he can assess it favourably all the same. It would appear, then, that much more important than choice (in the sense of making a selection among options) is apprehending that one has been presented with an object and going toward it.[19]

ST 1–2.15.3 ad 3 is a problem for Finnis since he makes proposals so central to his theory and a proposal is an activity of choosing among options that are attractive,

[17] The passage in John of Damascus—which in fact determines a number of the 'stages' in Aquinas's analysis of the human act—reads as follows: ' "Counsel [*consilium*] is an enquiring appetite coming about with regard to those things that are up to us" [Maximus Confessor, *Patrologia graeca* 91.16B]. One counsels whether one ought to go through with something or no. Then one judges what is best, and this is called judgment [*iudicium*]; then one becomes disposed toward [*disponit*] and greets with affection [*amat*] that which was judged by counsel, and this is called positive assessment [*sententia*]. For if one judges but is not disposed toward that which is judged, that is, if one does not greet it with affection, it is not called positive assessment [*sententia*]. Then, after the disposition, there is choice [*electio*]; "choice", however, is to choose with respect to two things set before one [*praeiacentibus*] and to opt for this one rather than the other.' The Latin can be found in Buytaert, *Saint John Damascene, De fide orthodoxa*, Ch. 36, lines 91–8; the corresponding Greek can be found in the work entitled *Expositio fidei* in v.2 of Kotter, *Die Schriften des Johannes von Damaskos*, Ch. 36, lines 75–82. The word *consensus* does not appear in this passage, but 'becoming disposed toward' and 'greeting with affection' together constitute the equivalent. The Greek word corresponding to the Latin *amat* is *agapai* (from *agapaō*). (The first definition for *agapaō* given by the Liddell-Scott-Jones Greek-English Lexicon is 'greet with affection'.) The Greek word corresponding to the Latin *praeiacentibus* is *prokeimenōn* (from *prokeimai*). Below we shall see the importance of this latter concept.

[18] See note 17.

[19] That the will is free even in such instances is stated at *ST* 1.82.1c: 'Necessity, however, with respect to the end is not repugnant to the will, when it is not possible to arrive at the end except in one way: for instance, from the will to cross the sea there comes about in the will the necessity of willing a ship.' Also important here is the concept of particular (as opposed to universal) judgments and the distinction between liberty of exercise and liberty of specification—on which topics see Aquinas's *Quaestiones disputatae de malo* 6, *passim*.

suitable, and practically interesting. In the case of *consensus* under consideration, however, there is just one acceptable 'thing leading to the end'. It is true that occasionally Finnis speaks in a way that, apart from a certain verbal inconsistency, might be considered unexceptionable. At one point, for instance, he says that the case in which one finds many things leading to the end is the 'standard case', that in which 'only one possible course of action is attractive is perhaps rather rare'[20]; and at another point he speaks of a human act in which 'one chooses (or perhaps spontaneously decides, by *consensus* without need for choice)'.[21] But his willingness to speak in this way depends on his misinterpretation of *ST* 1-2.15.3 ad 3, that is, his position that even consent to one option involves a choice between attractive options.

III. The Nature of Means

As mentioned, Finnis goes on in section II of 'Intentions and objects' to discuss the nature of means to an end, developing the first clause of controlling element (2), according to which (as he says here) 'in choosing means one constitutes that means as the (proximate) end for any technique, procedure, or performance used to do or carry out that choice'.[22] One notices here that the means chosen would not be the technique (procedure or performance) itself; rather the means becomes (is 'constituted' as) the proximate end *of* the technique. This does not correspond to normal speech where it is perfectly legitimate to say, for instance, that 'my means of extracting the organ will be the technique developed by my colleague here'; but Finnis bases his thesis on a remark in Aquinas.

> In discussing intention and choice, Aquinas makes clear that the means referred to when we say that choice is of means are human actions: *electio semper est humanorum actuum* [*ST* 1-2.13.4]. Technical 'means', viz. implements, instruments, devices, systems and 'procedures' as such (that is, just insofar as they could in principle be replicated by machines or other devices), are not means in the sense intended when we say that choice is of means. Rather, technical means are means in a derivative, participative sense, insofar as they are used in the acting which is the (carrying out of) means properly so called.[23]

ST 1-2.13.4, however, does not support Finnis's thesis. The question posed there is whether choice is 'only of those things done by us', or, as Aquinas puts it just before introducing objections, whether choice is 'only *with respect to* human acts' [*solum respectu humanorum actuum*]'. He begins his reply by saying that we must treat things chosen as we treat ends.

> An end is either an action or some thing [*res aliqua*], and when some thing is the end it is necessary that some human action intervene, either in as much as a man brings about that thing [*illam rem*] which is the end, as when a doctor brings about health, which is his end (so that to bring about health is called the end of the doctor), or in as

[20] *CEJF* II.9, 156, n. 13.   [21] *CEJF* II.9, 157.
[22] *CEJF* II.9, 159.   [23] *CEJF* II.9, 159.

much as a man in some way uses or enjoys the thing which is the end, as when the end for a miser is money, or the possession of money.

Notable here is that, in the second case considered (where the end is a thing [*res*]), the thing (the object) is not the human action; the human action rather 'intervenes'. For this reason Aquinas says that 'to bring about health is *called* the end of the doctor'; the argument itself, however, presumes that strictly speaking the end is *res aliqua* (for example, health). One also notes that the human action that intervenes is whatever the doctor does in order to bring the patient to health. This would certainly include technical means and procedures.

Aquinas goes on to apply these ideas to 'that which is for the end', saying again that this might be either an action 'or some thing, provided some action intervenes through which the man brings about that which is for the end or uses it'. He adds then in conclusion: 'And it is *in this way*, that choice is always of human acts' [*Et per hunc modum electio semper est humanorum actuum*]. So, Aquinas's assertion that 'choice is always of human acts' is a limited one: choice is of human acts in the sense that that which is for the end is always part of a human act. He does not, as Finnis would have it, exclude 'implements, instruments, devices, systems and "procedures"' as the objects of choice.

Aquinas's basic approach comes, in fact, from Aristotle, who, in his *Physics*, speaks of objects as things or states of affairs but then qualifies this, saying that a full understanding of objects requires that we understand also the context within which they serve as objects.[24] When an object is the object of a human act (such as are often used in *Physics* as examples of movements), that context includes knowledge of what one is doing and the intention one has when doing it.

IV. The Four Orders

This is an opportune moment to consider Aquinas's treatment of the four orders, for it is at this point in 'Intentions and objects'[25] that Finnis refers us to that treatment. The four orders, Finnis tells us, are 'irreducibly distinct'.[26] But does Aquinas hold that they are distinct in quite the sense Finnis suggests? In the sense, that is, that would separate the fourth order ('of things used or made') from the third ('of human acts precisely as chosen')?[27]

Aquinas's presentation of the four orders comes near the beginning of the first *lectio* of the first book of his commentary on the *Nicomachean Ethics*.[28] Some 50 lines after his treatment of the four orders and in the same *lectio*, following his usual methodology, he identifies various divisions within the text to be commented upon.[29] Regarding the piece that reads in full, 'Since there are many actions, crafts, and teachings, there are also many ends—the end of the medical craft being health, that

---

[24] Aristotle, *Physics* 5.1.224b7–8, but then 5.4.227b14–29. On these matters, see Flannery, *Action and Character According to Aristotle*, Chs 2 and 4.
[25] *CEJF* II.9, 159, n. 24.   [26] *Aquinas*, 21.
[27] *CEJF* II.9, 159, n. 24.   [28] *In Eth.* 1.1.
[29] Aristotle, *NE* 1.1.1094a1–18.

of shipbuilding a ship, that of strategy victory, that of economics wealth',[30] Aquinas remarks that it has to do with the 'relation of human acts to an end' (*habitudinem humanorum actuum ad finem*).[31] So, even before getting to the passage that most interests us, it is apparent that Aquinas regards crafts such as medicine and shipbuilding—which belong to the fourth order—as human acts.

A few lines later,[32] he begins his comment upon the opening two lines of *NE*, where Aristotle writes: 'Every craft and every teaching, and similarly [every] act and choice appears to desire some good.'[33] Aquinas understands his task to be to explain the presence here of the four terms 'craft' [*ars*], 'teaching' [*doctrina*], 'act' [*actus*], and 'choice' [*electio*]. He does so in the following passage (which I have divided into four paragraphs for easier reference):

> Regarding the first division [*NE* 1.1.1094a1-3], one ought to consider that the principles of human acts are two: intellect (or reason) and appetite, which are the moving principles, as is said in *De anima* 3 [10.433a9].
>
> Considered in intellect or reason is the speculative and the practical; in rational appetite, choice and execution. All of these are ordered toward some good as towards an end, for the true is the end of speculation.
>
> So, with respect to speculative intellect, [Aristotle] mentions teaching, by means of which knowledge is transmitted from teacher to student; but with respect to practical intellect, he mentions craft, which is right reckoning regarding things to be made, as is said in *Nicomachean Ethics* 6.[34] With respect to the act of the appetitive intellect, he mentions choice; but with respect to execution, he mentions act.
>
> He makes no mention of prudence, which, like craft, is in practical reason, for choice is directed properly through prudence. He says, therefore, that each of these clearly desires some good as an end.[35]

In the first paragraph, Aquinas says that human acts are human acts in so far as they depend upon two principles, intellect (or reason) and appetite. He refers to *De anima* 3.10, where, as he is well aware, Aristotle indicates that will is an appetite, that is, a rational appetite. One notes that both principles—including intellect—are described as 'moving principles'. Eventually the first two of the four terms—'craft' and 'teaching'— will be assigned to intellect; the other two—'act' and 'choice'—to rational appetite. All of them, however, even within the practical realm, fall under intellect, which 'picks up' the end (or ends) for the human person who acts. As Aristotle says in *De anima* 3.10 (433a17–23), the thing desired, the *appetibile*, moves the intellect, which is bound up with appetite. The moving principles are moving principles only in so far as they encounter things desired.

---

[30]   Aristotle, *NE* 1.1.1094a6–9.   [31] *In Eth.* 1.1.118–119.   [32] *In Eth.* 1.1.128.
[33]   Aristotle, *NE* 1.1.1094a1–2. The Latin Aquinas was reading would be: *Omnis ars et omnis doctrina, similiter autem et actus et electio bonum quoddam appetere videtur.* Since, when interpreting Aristotle, Aquinas is always dealing with a Latin, and not a Greek, text, I will not be giving Greek equivalents for the terms that Aquinas employs.
[34]   The Leonine edition cites Aristotle, *NE* 6.3.1140a6–10, noting, however, that even there this precise idea is not to be found.
[35] *In Eth.* 1.1 ll.128–147.

In the second paragraph, Aquinas divides each of the two moving principles into two, immediately associating the second pair with the third and fourth terms: action and choice. That is, intellect is divided into speculative and practical, while rational appetite is divided into 'choice' and 'execution.' (In paragraph three, he will identify 'execution' as 'act'.) But although Aquinas puts 'choice' and 'execution' under appetite, he also points to their connection with intellect: 'All of these', he says—that is, reason, both speculative and practical, choice and execution—'are ordered toward some good as towards an end, for the true is the end of speculation'. The *appetibile* moves the intellect as a good.

In the third paragraph, Aquinas turns his attention more directly to intellect and its two divisions, associating the first two terms (teaching and craft) with the speculative and the practical, respectively. But again nothing is ever wholly withdrawn from the influence of any principle. The term 'teaching' is referred to speculative intellect, although even this involves human action: 'knowledge is transmitted from teacher to student'. 'Craft' is referred to practical intellect, which is, certainly, less speculative than teaching but is still described by Aquinas as 'right reckoning' ('recta ratio'). 'Choice' is referred to the act of rational appetite, which he calls here—not by accident—appetitive *intellect*, while 'act' is identified as the act's execution.[36] Since this falls under 'appetitive intellect' (or rational appetite), it too has a 'speculative' aspect—which is to say no more than that it too 'desires' some good as an end.

Aquinas does not offer an explanation of why Aristotle does not mention prudence (*phronēsis*); he says only that it directs choice, in the manner of a craft.[37] This too, however, amounts to a combining of the speculative and the practical, the intellective and the appetitive. Prudence is an intellectual virtue,[38] but it is said here to be like a craft. And prudence directs choice, which has previously been put under rational appetite.

Although none of this contradicts the idea that the four orders are distinct—what it is to be a human act is distinct from what it is to be, for instance, a technical process—the quoted passage is difficult to reconcile with any suggestion that the four orders, and in particular the third and the fourth, are 'irreducibly distinct', as Finnis maintains.[39] Not only does Aquinas say that 'actions, crafts, and teachings'[40] all belong to the category of human acts, but he also expends considerable ingenuity in order to connect not only teaching, act, and choice, but also craft to the moving principles of human action.

---

[36] On 'execution', see, for instance, *ST* 1–2.15.2 ad 2; 16.1 obi.2; 16.4 obi.1.

[37] *Summa contra gentiles* 3.78.5 (§2539). On prudence as directive, see *CEJF* I.11; see also Irwin, *The Development of Ethics*, 582. See also Aristotle, *NE* 6.10.1143a8–10, *Eudemian Ethics* 8.3.1249b14–15. Gauthier points also to *Magna Moralia* 1.34.1197a13–15, b22–24. Given Aristotle's various remarks, the author of that work, says Gauthier, was right to conclude that prudence directs 'decisions' (*prohaireseis*) (Gauthier, 'Saint Maxime le Confesseur et la psychologie de l'acte humain', 62, 85–8, especially n. 127).

[38] Aristotle, *NE* 6.3.1139b15–17.

[39] *Aquinas*, 21. In note 5, Finnis cites a number of texts where Aquinas discusses the term (*diversus*) which he (Finnis) understands as meaning 'distinct'. 'Diverse', says Finnis, 'means the very opposite of "same", in as many senses as there are of 'same' . . . and is appropriately used of things which differ from each other essentially . . . and/or in their way of originating . . .'

[40] Aristotle, *NE* 1.1.1094a6–7.

V. The Nature of Objects

As we have seen, in controlling element (2) Finnis maintains that between the choice of means, which is the adoption of a proposal for the sake of an intelligible benefit, and the end (the benefit one intends) the relationship is very close. A consequence of this is that, in the analysis of particular human acts, only that which is within this relational area— this line of intelligibility between the end and the means and back again—has an immediate bearing upon the moral character of the act, although other factors can affect this character as circumstances. Or, in other (more technical) words, only that which is intended *per se* (either as a means or an end) contributes to the act's species; everything else is *per accidens* or (equivalently) *praeter intentionem* (beside the intention).[41]

This thesis has an immediate bearing upon how Finnis conceives of the object, which Aquinas says gives an act its species. Whereas Aquinas, adhering to the theory set out in *De an.* 3.10, understands the object as something presented to the intellect (which is inseparable from rational appetite) as an *appetibile* (or desirable thing),[42] Finnis understands it as a *proposal*: as something coming from the agent.

A place in which one can see Finnis reading Aquinas in this way appears in the essay found now just before 'Intentions and objects' in the *Collected Essays* (*CEJF* II.8). There he writes, 'To choose is essentially to *adopt a plan or proposal* which one has devised and put to oneself in one's practical reasoning and deliberation on the merits of alternative options, i.e. plans or proposals'.[43] In a note appended at this point, Finnis cites two texts in support of this thesis, the first of which mentions the object and employs the word *propono*. The note now reads as follows (the words in square brackets being found only in the *Collected Essays* version):

> *Objectum voluntatis est id quod* proponitur *a ratione* ['one's will's object is what is proposed', reasonably or unreasonably, rightly or wrongly 'by one's reason']: *ST* 1–2.19.5c; *actus dicuntur humani, inquantum procedunt a voluntate deliberata*: *ST* 1–2.1.3c.[44] [*proponitur* = is proposed; *propositum* = that which has been proposed—a proposal.][45]

All of the bracketed material pertains to the first text (1–2.19.5c) rather than the second (1–2.1.3c). Translating *Objectum . . . ratione* as 'one's will's object is what is proposed by one's reason' is fair enough, although speaking of 'one's reason' makes it sound as if one is making the proposal to oneself by means of one's reason. And indeed this is what comes out in the second bracketed remark (or equation): '*proponitur* = is proposed; *propositum* = that which has been proposed—a proposal'. This begins well enough with

---

[41] Finnis acknowledges that Aquinas says that circumstances which are *praeter intentionem* can specify acts (*ST* 1–2.18.4, 10), but he sees this as 'a source of confusion' (*CEJF* II.9, 164, n. 43; also 168, n. 49).

[42] We encountered the same Aristotelian concept in the passage from *De fide orthodoxa* examined above, where John of Damascus speaks of choosing between things 'set before one' [*praeiacentibus*]. See note 17.

[43] *CEJF* II.8, 142–3.

[44] 'Acts are called human in as much as they proceed from the will.' The passage continues: 'But the object of the will is a good or an end' (*ST* 1–2.1.3c).

[45] *CEJF* II.8, 143, n. 14.

something *proposed* (and received passively) but finishes with a *proposal* (something 'which one has devised and put to oneself'[46]). There is nothing in the cited passages that would support this shift from *propositum* to proposal.

One encounters a similar reading in a note in 'Intentions and objects'. In the note, Finnis is considering Aquinas's criticism of how presumably Peter Lombard would analyse an act of forging a document (a testament) in order to have money to give to the poor. The question asked in the pertinent article is, 'Whether an action is to be judged good or bad simply by looking to the will.' Finnis writes:

> Such acts, says Aquinas, *are* wrongful by reason of the acting person's will. There need be nothing wrong with his *intentio* or *voluntas intendens*, his ultimate motivating purpose (*finis ultimus*), e.g. to give money to the poor. What is wrongful is, rather, his choice, his *electio* or *voluntas eligens*, his immediate purpose (*obiectus proximus* or *finis proximus*) e.g. to forge this testament: *Sent.* 2.40.1.2.[47]

Most of the Latin terms employed in this note come from Aquinas's answer to the article's third objection, which puts forward a position that looks only to the object—the word used is *obiectum*—of the intending will [*voluntas intendens*]. Aquinas replies:

> With respect to the third objection, it must be said that the goodness of something requires not only the goodness of the final end towards which the intending will [*voluntas intendens*] looks but also the goodness of the proximate end [*finis proximi*] towards which the choosing will [*voluntas eligens*] looks; and so, it does not follow that the goodness of the intending will suffices for the goodness of the act [*Sent.* 2.40.1.2 ad 3].

At variance with what Finnis says in his note, Aquinas is not saying that what makes the difference 'is, rather, [the agent's] choice, his *electio* or *voluntas eligens*, his immediate purpose (*obiectus proximus* or *finis proximus*)'. Aquinas is speaking here about just one act of the will, under two aspects: as (1) intending and therefore bearing upon the ultimate end and as (2) choosing and therefore bearing upon what he usually calls simply the *objectum* but here calls the *obiectum proximum*, 'which is ordered toward the ultimate end'.[48] What makes the act of the will wrong is this *obiectum proximum*, the *finis proximus*.[49] The expression employed by Finnis, *obiectus proximus*, which might indeed be translated 'immediate purpose' (or even 'immediate proposal') never appears in *Sent.* 2.40.1.2. In fact, the word *obiectus* (the fourth declension noun), as opposed to *obiectum* (the passive participle of *obicio*) never

---

[46] *CEJF* II.8, 142.

[47] The reference that Finnis actually gives is '*Sent.* II d.40 q.2' (*CEJF* II.9, 165, n. 44). In fact, there is no q.2 in *Sent.* II d.40, which contains only one question. Finnis ought to have followed the method of citation he employs in the subsequent note, where he refers to '*Sent.* II d.40 q.1 a.1c'.

[48] *Sent.* 2.40.1.2c; see also *ST* 1–2.20.3c: '. . . the interior act of the will and the exterior act, as they are considered within the realm of the moral, are one act'.

[49] In *ST* 1–2.20.2c, Aquinas says that the goodness or badness of the exterior act can come either from its ordering toward the will (as when even an act of giving alms is bad because it is done for vainglory) or from the appropriate (or inappropriate) matter or the circumstances of the exterior act (as when an act of altruism is bad because it involves *stealing* from someone in order to give to another in need). In cases such as the latter, says Aquinas, the goodness or badness 'depends upon reason—and it is upon this [that is, reason] that the goodness [or badness] of the will depends, in so far as it [the will] looks toward it'.

appears in Aquinas's works.[50] The *finis proximus* is certainly not an *obiectus proximus*. Finnis discusses the same article from the *Sentences* commentary elsewhere, and in both places he speaks not of an *obiectus proximus* but of the *obiectum proximum*; the fact, however, that in 'Intentions and objects' he uses the expression *obiectus proximus* is revealing.[51] Finnis does understand the object of the external act (the *finis proximus* of the act) to be a proposal, an *obiectus*; Aquinas would never have said such a thing.

At one point Finnis cites the one article that (probably) most goes against his theory—*ST* 1-2.20.1, in which it is asked whether the goodness or badness of an action is present first in the act of the will or rather in the exterior act—but again he misinterprets it. In the course of an argument to the effect that 'acts are morally significant and are morally assessed in terms of their type, their intrinsic character, just insofar as they are willed'[52], Finnis quotes a piece of *ST* 1-2.20.1 ad 1, as follows: 'The exterior act is the object of the will, *in as much as it is proposed to the will by reason as some good apprehended and ordered by reason*, and *thus* is prior to the act of the will'.[53] This quotation itself would seem to go against his thesis (for the first emphasized portion says that a good is proposed *to* the will), but Finnis understands it as limiting the sense in which the good of the exterior act is prior to the act of the will: that is the reason for the emphasized 'thus' (which translates *sic*).

It is true that the article does limit the sense in which 'goodness or badness is present in the exterior act prior to its presence in the act of the will' (as the objections of *ST* 1-2.20.1 go on to argue), but it does not do this in any sense that helps Finnis. In order to understand why, it is necessary first of all to know that Finnis has left a crucial word out of the above quotation: the last section should read, 'and thus [the exterior act] is prior to *the good* of the act of the will' (my emphasis).[54] Not only does Aquinas hold that some good thing serves as the object of the exterior act, but there is also a good presented to the will (the intending will) as *its* object.

Aquinas's argument in the body of the article is that, if one attends to the goodness of the exterior act as it presented to the will, that is, as its object, that goodness is prior to the good pertaining to the act of the will. But if one attends to the same not *as* an object but as a deed to be performed, the goodness of the exterior act 'follows the goodness of will, which is its principle'. Or, as he says in *ST* 1-2.20.1 ad 1 (now quoted in full):

> The exterior act is the object of the will, in as much as it is proposed to the will by reason as some good apprehended and ordered by reason, and thus is prior to the good of the act of the will. In as much, however, as this is present in the performance of the deed, it is an effect of the will and follows the will.

[50] The word does appear in one work—*De demonstratione*—sometimes included in the corpus but which is of dubious authenticity. The signification of the word is entirely different, however: *Omne corpus naturale illuminatum a sole, privatum luce a terrae obiectu, deficit* (Spiazzi, S. *Thomae Aquinatis, Opuscula philosophica*, §630).
[51] Finnis discusses *Sent.* 2.40.1.2 in the essay now entitled '"Direct" and "indirect" in action' (*CEJF* II.13), in *Aquinas*, 165–6, and in *MA*, 65–7.
[52] *CEJF* II.9, 165.   [53] *CEJF* II.9, 166 n. 46.
[54] In *CEJF* II.9, 166, n. 46, Finnis quotes the Latin, but as follows (including his emphases): *actus exterior est obiectum voluntatis*, inquantum proponitur voluntati a ratione ut quoddam bonum apprehensum et ordinatum per rationem: *et sic est prius quam actus voluntatis*. The last phrase should be *et sic est prius quam* bonum *actus voluntatis* [my emphasis].

The thing to note here is that in *both* cases—the good of the exterior act and the good of the interior act of the will—these object (or goods) are presented *to* the agent. Aquinas states this explicitly in the case of the exterior act: 'the goodness or badness which, as itself, the exterior act has on account of the appropriate matter and appropriate circumstances, *is not derived from the will* but rather from reason'.[55] But it is apparent also, from Aquinas's frequent use of *De anima* 3.10, that he recognizes that the principle or starting point of the will is distinct from the will itself. Aristotle says there, 'Every appetite is *for* something, since that for which it is an appetite, this is the starting point of practical reasoning.'[56] Commenting upon this remark, Aquinas says: 'It is apparent that every appetite is for something, for it is nonsense to say that someone desires for the sake of desiring, since desiring is a certain motion tending towards another thing.'[57]

VI. Conclusion

I conclude, therefore, that Finnis's interpretation of Thomas Aquinas's theory of human action is incorrect. Among other things, it does not square with what Aquinas says about the nature of *consensus* in the case in which the latter consists of the favourable assessment of a single option. It misinterprets Aquinas's remarks in *Summa theologiae* 1–2.13.4 about the connection between human acts and their objects. It puts a construction upon Aquinas's remarks about the 'four orders' in his commentary on the *Nicomachean Ethics* that is incompatible with remarks coming a few lines later in the same commentary. It finds a particular understanding of the moral object (as proposal) in Aquinas's commentary on Peter Lombard's *Sentences*, that is, in *Sent.* 2.40.1.2 ad 3, a passage that will not bear this reading. And, finally, it misinterprets *Summa theologiae* 1–2.20.1 in a way that overlooks Aquinas's position that the object of an act is not the agent's own proposal but is presented rather to the agent by way of his own intellect.[58]

Bibliography

Aquinas, Thomas (1961–67), *Summa Contra Gentiles* (Turin/Rome: Marietti).
Aquinas, Thomas (1969), *Opera Omnia: Vol. 47. Sententia libri Ethicorum* (Rome: Commissio Leonina).

[55] *ST* 1–2.20.1c, my emphasis. The words 'on account of the appropriate matter and appropriate circumstances' translate *propter debitam materiam et debitas circumstantias*, which remark refers to the two ways in which the object of the external act might be bad: *ST* 1–2.18.2, 3, and 5. See Aquinas, *Quaestiones disputatae de malo* 2.3c.

[56] *De an.* 3.10.433a15–16: *Et appetitus propter aliquid omnis est; cuius enim appetitus, hoc principium practici intellectus*... Key places where Thomas cites *De an.* 3.10 would include: *ST* 1.19.2, 1.80.2, 1–2.26.2; Aquinas, *Quaestiones disputatae de veritate* 25.1; Aquinas, *Quaestiones disputatae de malo* 6.

[57] *Et manifestum est, quod omnis appetitus est propter aliquid (stultum enim est dicere, quod aliquis appetat propter appetere, nam appetere est quidam motus in aliud tendens)* (*in De an.* 3.9.50–53).

[58] For their help with this essay, I thank Fr. Stephen Brock and John O'Callaghan. I also thank John Finnis for sending me to the text of Thomas Aquinas—not for the first time—with some fascinating and important questions.

Aquinas, Thomas (1970–76), *Opera Omnia: Vol.22. Quaestiones disputatae de veritate* (Rome: Commissio Leonina).

Aquinas, Thomas (1982), *Opera Omnia: Vol.23. Quaestiones disputatae de malo* (Rome: Commissio Leonina; Louvain: Librairie Philosophique J. Vrin).

{Aristotle} (1883), *Magna moralia* (Leipzig: Teubner).

Aristotle (1894), *Ethica Nicomachea* (Oxford: Clarendon).

Aristotle (1950), *Physica* (Oxford: Clarendon).

Aristotle (1956), *De anima* (Oxford: Clarendon).

Aristotle (1991), *Ethica Eudemia* (Oxford: Clarendon).

Buytaert, E.M.M. (ed.) (1955), *Saint John Damascene, De fide orthodoxa: Versions of Burgundio and Cerbanus* (St. Bonaventure, NY: Franciscan Institute; Louvain: Nauwelaerts; Paderborn: Schöningh).

Centi, T.S. (ed. & trans.) (1959), *S. Tommaso d'Aquino, La somma teologica: Vol. 8. La beatitudine, gli atti umani (I-II qq.1–21)* (Florence: Salani).

Finnis, J. (1991), *Moral Absolutes: Tradition, Revision and Truth* (Washington, DC: Catholic University of America Press).

Finnis, J. (1998), *Aquinas: Moral, Political and Legal Theory* (Oxford: Oxford University Press).

Finnis, J. [II.13] (2011), ' "Direct" and "indirect" in action', in *Intention and Identity: Collected Essays, Volume II* (Oxford: Oxford University Press), 235–68.

Finnis, J. [II.8] (2011), 'Human acts', in *Intention and Identity: Collected Essays, Volume II* (Oxford: Oxford University Press), 133–51.

Finnis, J. [II.10] (2011), 'Intention and side effects', in *Intention and Identity: Collected Essays, Volume II* (Oxford: Oxford University Press), 173–97.

Finnis, J. [II.11] (2011), 'Intention in tort law', in *Intention and Identity: Collected Essays, Volume II* (Oxford: Oxford University Press), 198–219.

Finnis, J. [II.9] (2011), 'Intentions and objects', in *Intention and Identity: Collected Essays, Volume II* (Oxford: Oxford University Press), 152–72.

Finnis, J. [I.11] (2011), 'Prudence about ends', in *Reason in Action: Collected Essays, Volume I* (Oxford: Oxford University Press), 173–86.

Flannery, K.L. (forthcoming), *Action and Character According to Aristotle: The Logic of the Moral Life* (Washington, DC: Catholic University of America Press).

Garrigou-Lagrange, R. (1951), *De beatitudine, de actibus humanis et habitibus: Commentarius in Summam Theologicam S. Thomae I^a II^ae qq.1–54* (Turin: L.I.C.E.-R. Berruti).

Gauthier, R.-A. (1954), 'Saint Maxime le Confesseur et la psychologie de l'acte humain', *Recherches de Théologie Ancienne et Médiévale* 21: 51–100.

Gilby, T. (ed. & trans.) (1970), *St. Thomas Aquinas, Summa Theologiae: Vol. 17. Psychology of Human Acts (1a2ae. 6–17)* (London; New York: Blackfriars in conjunction with Eyre & Spottiswoode/McGraw-Hill).

Irwin, T. (2007), *The Development of Ethics: A Historical and Critical Study (Volume I, from Socrates to the Reformation)* (Oxford; New York: OUP).

Kotter, P.B. (ed.) (1973), *Die Schriften des Johannes von Damaskos: Expositio fidei* (vol. 2), Patristische Texte und Studien, vol. 12 (Berlin: De Gruyter).

Pinckaers, S. (ed.) and Gardeil, H.-D. (trans.) (1962), *Saint Thomas d'Aquin, Somme théologique: Les actes humains (tome premier, 1^a–2^a, questions 6–17)* (Rome: Tournai; Paris: Desclée).

Spiazzi, R. (ed.) (1954), *S. Thomae Aquinatis, Opuscula philosophica.* Turin; Rome: Marietti.

9

On Moral Philosophy and Kinds
of Human Actions*

Cristóbal Orrego

Elizabeth Anscombe offered an allegedly non-moral elucidation of human action in *Intention*.[1] She contended, besides, 'that it is not profitable for us at present to do moral philosophy; that should be laid aside at any rate until we have an adequate philosophy of psychology, in which we are conspicuously lacking'.[2]

Anscombe asserted that we cannot even begin to give an explanation of 'how an unjust man is a bad man, or an unjust action a bad one (...) until we are equipped with a sound philosophy of psychology'.[3] For 'the proof that an unjust man is a bad man would require a positive account of justice as a "virtue"',[4] and '[t]his part of the subject-matter of ethics is, however, completely closed to us until we have an account of what *type of characteristic* a virtue is (...) and how it relates to the actions in which it is instanced'.[5] This is 'a problem, not of ethics, but of conceptual analysis'.[6] 'For this', she added, 'we certainly need an account at least of what a human action is at all, and how its description as "doing such-and-such" is affected by its motive and by the intention or intentions in it; and for this an account of such concepts is required'.[7]

After more than 50 years, perhaps we need rather a 'sound *moral* philosophy' in order to answer the basic questions of present-day non-moral philosophy of action. For the difference between two ways of approaching the conceptual elucidation of human actions lies fundamentally in whether or not one presupposes a moral point of view. One of these approaches aims at describing the causal relations between events that ensue in a bodily movement. According to this approach, not only the external descriptions of bodily movements but also the internal *reasons* of the agent are interpreted as events in the causal chain of events that *produce* the action. The other approach considers the process of acting from the point of view of the agent, who deliberates about what to do in order to achieve his end, and then chooses and does something as a means. This *something done* can be described as from without or as

* The National Commission for Scientific and Technological Research of the Republic of Chile (CONICYT) made possible this contribution through the Research project FONDECYT N. 1080680 and a scholarship for a postdoctoral research stay in Oxford (Beca Chile 2009–10, Folio 74090009).

[1] Anscombe, *Intention*, 45 (para. 25).
[2] Anscombe, 'Modern Moral Philosophy', 169.
[3] Anscombe, 'Modern Moral Philosophy', 174.
[4] Anscombe, 'Modern Moral Philosophy', 174.
[5] Anscombe, 'Modern Moral Philosophy', 174.
[6] Anscombe, 'Modern Moral Philosophy', 174.
[7] Anscombe, 'Modern Moral Philosophy', 174.

from within the agent. Many true descriptions of the action 'from without' may be beside the purpose of the agent, or against it, or even unknown to him. A typical example is that of a man who turns on the light *in order to* illuminate his room (intentional action), which also alerts a burglar (true description of the action from the point of view of its external effect). Some of the questions in the philosophy of action mean something different depending on whether we adopt one approach or the other. For example: What is a human action? Is the event stemming from a human agent a single action under several descriptions or several actions, one for each true description of the event? Which are the relevant descriptions of an action as *intentional*? What are the relations between the several relevant descriptions? What constitutes a kind of action as such, i.e. as essentially different from other kinds of actions considered in general?

I do not mean to address these and similar questions. I rather wish to show that to answer them before entering the disputed field of ethics is a misleading proposal. We can follow the path of describing movements in sub-rational beings, and we shall arrive at some sort of descriptive physics and biology. The nature of the explanation does not change just because the actions stem from human beings, because the causal approach is fitting for a description of humanly caused events considered in the first order of reality only.[8] On the contrary, when we analyse actions from the point of view of agents who have spiritual capacities, these actions are already in the third order of reality, i.e. in the order of free choice, which is the subject matter of moral philosophy. They cannot be thought of as human acts—i.e. as more than just physical events—apart from the order that reason introduces in the acts of the will. I shall try to prove this relying on John Finnis and Elizabeth Anscombe, and on some illuminating disagreements between them.

Finnis recalls Aquinas's 'epistemological principle'[9] according to which the nature of something is understood by understanding its capacities, and those capacities are understood by understanding their acts, and those acts are understood by understanding their objects.[10] The external behaviour is not understood as a human act when it is described from the point of view of its physical structure alone, because its specific nature or identity depends on the object or objective sought by the agent. The question *what is done* cannot be answered apart from the question *why* the agent performs the external deed,[11] since the object is the end or purpose that attracts the will, i.e. the *reason* that moves the human capacity to respond to the good known by the intellect. After a detailed exposition of Aquinas's explanation of the several analytically distinct stages of interaction between reason and will in human action,[12] Finnis draws the conclusion of the 'epistemological principle'. We start by understanding the goods and ends that are objects of actions; then we understand the capacities that are 'fulfilled by action which participates in and realizes those goods';[13] and finally we acquire a 'deep understanding of human nature'.[14] Finnis is not talking about morally good actions, since the objects of morally evil actions *are also goods* presented by reason as in some way fulfilling. They are called *apparent goods* because real goods are those in

---

[8] On the four orders, see e.g. *Aquinas*, 20–3.
[9] *Aquinas*, 29.   [10] *Aquinas*, 29.   [11] *Aquinas*, 31–2.
[12] *Aquinas*, 62–90.   [13] *Aquinas*, 91.   [14] *Aquinas*, 91.

conformity with right reason. The morally good actions are those directed by practical reasonableness towards our integral human fulfilment, in agreement with the principles and rules of right reason.[15] Now, these true principles of right reason allow a true understanding of human affairs, because human affairs are really as they seem to the virtuous person who lives in agreement with those principles.[16] Therefore the understanding of morally good actions, through the understanding of morally good objects and ends, allows us to understand human capacities as they really are and human nature as it really is.

Anscombe's suggestion was, then, inadequate. She contended, as we have seen, that we cannot even begin to tackle the ethical issues until we have 'a sound philosophy of psychology'.[17] Several concepts such as 'action', 'intention', 'pleasure', 'wanting', and others, 'need investigating simply as part of the philosophy of psychology',[18] while *banishing ethics totally* from our minds'.[19] 'Eventually it might be possible to advance to considering the concept of virtue; with which, I suppose, we should be beginning some sort of study of ethics'.[20] My objection is that even the 'conceptual analysis' and the 'philosophy of psychology' about realities such as action, intention, pleasure, etc., considered *qua* human realities, *presuppose rather than precede* our practical experience and the reflexive explanations of moral philosophy.

Some of Anscombe's concerns are appropriate to show the need for a sound philosophy of morals before we even start to develop a sound theory of action. I do not mean just to *label* the same analysis with different words, but to take seriously the need to adopt a practical point of view—even, more precisely, the moral point of view of the wise person—simply in order to see things as they really are when their description as such-and-such affects our moral reasoning.

First we have the issue of 'what type of characteristic a virtue is'.[21] Is a non-moral psychology of 'virtue', a purely 'conceptual analysis' of it, possible? It seems not. For the description of the virtues—even the psychological, non-evaluative description of the traits of character associated with the virtues—presupposes the moral distinction between virtue and vice. One might think that it should be possible to describe, without relying on any moral distinction, the common genus of virtues and vices: the operative habits. That sort of description, however, would not get us too far in the field of descriptive psychology, because the generic concept of habit does not reveal the most important effects of habits in human capacities; it tells us only that the human capacity is more inclined to act in a certain way. The differences which are relevant even for descriptive sciences—for experimental psychology, but even more for descriptive or non-ethical 'philosophy of psychology'—are determined according to an evaluative criterion of relevance.[22] In the case of human habits the most relevant distinction is that between good and evil. Between virtuous and vicious there is no psychological

---

[15] *Aquinas*, 104–10, 118–29, 314–19.   [16] *Aquinas*, 48–51.
[17] Anscombe, 'Modern Moral Philosophy', 169.
[18] Anscombe, 'Modern Moral Philosophy', 188.
[19] Anscombe, 'Modern Moral Philosophy', 188. Italics in the original.
[20] Anscombe, 'Modern Moral Philosophy', 188.
[21] Anscombe, 'Modern Moral Philosophy', 174.
[22] *NLNR*, 3–22; *Aquinas*, 47–51.

parallelism and no common ground of morally neutral description. There is rather a *continuum* of psycho-moral paradigms from the virtuous to the vicious person. The *virtuous* person exhibits strength of character, true practical knowledge of the principles of right action and their most difficult applications, and readiness and joy in doing good actions. The *continent* person still possesses true knowledge of principles, but feels the weakness of his will; eventually he does the right action in spite of the interior difficulty and resistance in the appetite. The *incontinent* person knows the good action and even *wishes* to do it, but he eventually does the evil action, overcome by the weakness of his will (*akrasia*). Finally, the *vicious* or *wicked* person believes that what is evil is really good; his reasoning from first principles does not reach the right conclusions concerning good actions in those matters in which he is vicious; his character has been corrupted by his evil actions, and his reason and will are deformed even as radical capacities for acting as a human being.[23] So it seems to me impossible to describe, analyze or otherwise explain what type of characteristic the virtues are in human beings if we leave aside the *prior* ethical distinctions—and the correct ones—between what is morally good and morally bad.

Second, we have Anscombe's concern for 'an account at least of what a human action is at all, and how its description as "doing such-and-such" is affected by its motive and by the intention or intentions in it'.[24] She said that 'for this an account of such concepts is required',[25] and in truth she herself had provided, a year before, her own brilliant account of intentional action. *Intention* was offered with the explicit intention of not doing moral philosophy.[26] She proposes the story of the man who moves his arm up and down, pumps poisoned water, replenishes the cistern of a house, where the chiefs of a party, who are engaged in exterminating the Jews and perhaps provoking a world war, will drink the water and will be poisoned little by little, so that it is calculated that they will die and some good men will get into power and govern well.[27] In one of the variants of the story, the man is just *doing his usual job*—to replenish the cistern to get his pay—knowing that the water has been poisoned. In another version, the man is *hired* to pump the water, and he is aware of the fact that the water has been poisoned. Her analysis is so 'fine-grained'[28] that she thinks that the man does not pump *poisoned* water intentionally *in the first version* of the case; but he does so *in the second*, for he accepts a commission to do the action for which he has been hired, an action which includes in its description—as part of its object—the water being poisoned.

Anscombe says that 'the interest of the intention of the man' in these cases 'is certainly not an ethical or legal interest' because even if what the man says were true—that his action is not intentional under the description 'to pump *poisoned* water'—'that will not absolve him of the guilt of murder!'[29] I understand that she did not mean that

---

[23] *NE* VII and *In Eth.* ad loc; also, on errors about first principles, *Aquinas*, 100–1.
[24] Anscombe, 'Modern Moral Philosophy', 174.
[25] Anscombe, 'Modern Moral Philosophy', 174.
[26] Anscombe, *Intention*, 45 (para. 25). On page 76 (para. 39) she speaks of 'ethics, if there is such a science'.
[27] Anscombe, *Intention*, 37 (para. 23).   [28] *CEJF* II.10, 192.
[29] Anscombe, *Intention*, 45 (para. 25).

the distinction was not interesting for legal or moral purposes in an absolute way, since—as Finnis objects—law and ethics cannot be 'indifferent to such true and interesting distinctions',[30] and she is certainly aware of that interest in her ethical writings. She only means her interest *here*, in the context of *Intention*, which is only to elucidate intentional action from the point of view of a non-ethical 'philosophical psychology', by means of the link between intentionality and 'a response to our special question "Why?"'.[31] Her claim, however, that she *can* have such non-ethical interest seems to me unwarranted. An ethical interest moves her to focus on the distinction intentional/non-intentional in the first place. Besides, she can only draw the distinction itself from the point of view of the agent *qua* moral agent. For the question arises whether the special question 'Why?'—which detects intention and relevant descriptions of actions by reference to the agent's purposes—can be detached from its meaning in the fully human context of *praxis* or moral action. Furthermore, the *examples* that she proposes have a special force precisely because they include a particular moral issue, e.g. that of the relationship between moving one's arm and killing bad people in order to 'save the Jews' or 'to get the Kingdom of Heaven on Earth'. Next, the most remarkable and strategic thesis in *Intention* is defended in a clear ethical context. She introduces *a break in the chain of act-descriptions* that apply to a single act that falls under several descriptions in order to determine which of those descriptions can be applied to the act as intentional.[32] She says that the description 'the man is poisoning the inhabitants' is a description of his action as intentional, while none of the *further* answers to the question 'why are you poisoning the inhabitants?' (e.g. 'to save the Jews, to put in the good men, to get the Kingdom of Heaven on Earth') can provide the description of the action as intentional. For, in her view, any further description of the sort 'is not such that we can now say: he is saving the Jews, he is getting the Kingdom of Heaven, he is putting in the good ones'.[33] Of course, she does *not* say that the agent has no intention to do those things in the future; only that those present intentions do not define the present action, i.e. this action now is not intentional under those descriptions of further ends. The truth of this assertion, however, depends on how 'fine-grained' the distinction between intentional and non-intentional is. Perhaps the action of the man who does his usual job or is hired to pump the (poisoned) water cannot be characterized by the purpose of saving the Jews, etc., since that specific effect is not a reason for him to act: it is not an end or purpose of his. We cannot say the same, however, about the man who has poisoned the water or has planned a whole set of actions, starting from poisoning the water, *in order to* save the Jews, etc. Despite the fact that the realization of these further ends requires new actions, to be done in the future, the agent is doing *now* whatever is the last end—the answer to our special question 'Why?'—of his *present* individual action. That is the way in which Aquinas unifies different singular actions in a single moral action.[34] This is the way in which he can explain that when one is walking to the cupboard one is getting healthy[35] or that a

---

[30] *CEJF* II.10, 193.   [31] Anscombe, *Intention*, 45 (para. 25 *in fine*).
[32] Anscombe, *Intention*, 37–41 (para. 23).
[33] Anscombe, *Intention*, 40 (para. 23). See also Anscombe, *Intention*, 38–9 (para. 23).
[34] *ST* I-II, q. 1 a. 3; q. 20 a. 3 ad 1; q. 17 a. 4; q. 18 a. 7.   [35] *Aquinas*, 31–2.

soldier who is obeying his commander's orders, and fighting on the ground, is winning the war as a part of a complex group action.[36] It is not clear to me how Anscombe can justify the break of the chain of act-descriptions, whose intentional character depends on being an acceptable answer to the question 'Why?' For at some point she seems to hold that the intentional action as such cannot be defined or specified by 'intentions with which' it is done when those intentions are not wholly realized in or by the present intentional action, as is the case when they depend upon the intervention of additional actions, and particularly when some of these actions should be done by other agents;[37] but in another context she seems to say that 'the chain of "Why's" comes to an end' when the agent gives a 'desirability-characterisation' that can be very remote from the present action, such as pleasure or health.[38] In any case, even if the chain of act-descriptions related as means and ends is broken, this is irrelevant according to Aquinas's view about the specification of the moral unity of a human action as chosen with some proximate end or object and some further intention or intentions. For a human act may comprise in a single moral unity many different actions. The fact that Anscombe proposes to break the chain of act-descriptions at some point is a key idea in need of an explanation. I propose the following. She is just transposing into a descriptive, non-moral 'philosophy of psychology', the classical *moral* refusal to allow an evil action to be characterized as a kind of good action by virtue of the further ends of the agent. In fact, *Intention* as a whole can be read as a nuanced exploration and development of the scholastic doctrine of the *fontes moralitatis*: object, end, and circumstances.[39] Contrariwise, perhaps some proportionalists have erred in their action theory because of their prior errors on moral matters. Their defective understanding of the way in which human goods and evils can be known, assessed, compared, and realized in action (i.e. as moral goods and evils) seems to be itself a moral error, which depends on a previous wish to rationalize some specific kinds of actions.[40] I do not say that Anscombe and proportionalists are on the same footing, just rationalizing their moral convictions and producing ad hoc, arbitrary, deceitfully 'descriptive' theories of action suitable to support their ethical theories. On the contrary, I think that a true descriptive theory of action is needed to back up any sound ethics, both in its general part and in its application to specific moral issues. However, we cannot *discover* and *explain* that true 'philosophy of psychology' if we do not know already our moral reality, without distortions stemming from vices and passions; or if we do not understand from within our free, moral actions, which are necessarily morally good or evil; or if we cannot see the descriptions and explanations of actions *qua* human as just a part of our self-understanding as men and women *qua* moral agents. Hence proportionalists adhere to a false theory of action *because* they hold prior false and evil views about human good and the rectitude of the will in freely chosen actions. Their 'philosophy of action' is mere rationalization. On the other hand, Anscombe—in agreement with classical philosophy—adheres to a generally true philosophy of action

---

[36] *Aquinas*, 32–4.   [37] Anscombe, *Intention*, 33–41 (paras. 21–23).
[38] Anscombe, *Intention*, 70–6 (paras. 37–9).
[39] Torralba, *Acción Intencional*, reorganizes her thought precisely on those lines.
[40] *CEJF* II.8, 143–8; II.13, 265; II.9, 152–3; *Aquinas* 163–70; *MA*, passim.

because she previously holds a true ethics, and is moved by it to defend traditional mores against sophisms.

Third, let us consider Anscombe's proposal *to relate* act-descriptions to genera of virtues and vices, avoiding at the same time *defining*—as a matter of linguistic meaning—those act-descriptions and those virtues and vices as *morally right or morally wrong*.[41] For to incorporate the moral appraisal as a part of the act-description itself, *before* proving that it falls under a generic virtue or vice, would render any subsequent moral evaluation a mere tautology; and to incorporate the moral appraisal as a part of the definition of a type of virtue (or vice) as a psychological characteristic, *before* proving that that virtue (or vice) makes a man good (or evil) *qua* man, would also render any subsequent moral evaluation of the virtue (or vice) a mere tautology. In other words, it must be possible to describe specific kinds of human acts and human habits (virtues and vices) in such a way that the question about their moral goodness or badness remains open and therefore meaningful. The conclusion of the argument should have the last word on the classification of any act as good or evil, and of any habit as good/virtuous or evil/vicious. If we prove that the concepts of virtue and vice include moral goodness or badness, then to prove that a given habit is morally good or bad amounts to proving that it is a virtue or a vice. This does not mean, however, that the goodness or badness of the virtue or vice is a part of its description. For we can always ask whether such-and-such a habit, which until now has been considered a virtue, and has therefore a good-sounding name, is indeed morally good and hence really a virtue. What has been said about actions and habits (virtues or vices) is obvious when one considers some acts, virtues, and vices, in a time of cultural change, when they start to be valued contrariwise. Then it is not nonsense to ask whether humility or obedience or chastity are indeed virtues; or whether ambition or lust or hypocrisy or cynicism are indeed vices; or whether praying or organ donation or dissection of human corpses or enslavement of prisoners or usury or fox hunting or sodomy or abortion or euthanasia or lying or torture are morally good or bad human acts.

In addressing this concern, Anscombe defends two contentions of great significance for her discussion of consequentialism: (i) that the then available 'philosophy of psychology' was unable to provide the concepts and analytical tools needed to do moral philosophy in a profitable way; and (ii) that the force of the 'moral' ought and obligation is linked to a '*law* conception of ethics',[42] which assumed the existence of a divine law, but that 'no longer generally survives';[43] and therefore we should avoid using related terms such as '*morally* ought', '*morally* wrong', and the like.[44] The combination of these two theses is apt to neutralize two tenets of consequentialism. The first one is that the *intention*, which in pre-modern ethics defined the 'act itself' for the purpose of its first and essential moral evaluation, includes all foreseeable consequences. This is an error which Anscombe thought 'no one would be found to defend'[45]

---

[41] Anscombe, 'Modern Moral Philosophy', 174.
[42] Anscombe, 'Modern Moral Philosophy', 175, 176.
[43] Anscombe, 'Modern Moral Philosophy', 169.
[44] Anscombe, 'Modern Moral Philosophy', 169, 75–177, 190–4.
[45] Anscombe, 'Modern Moral Philosophy', 183.

then, in 1958; but which Sidgwick used 'to put forward an ethical thesis which would now be accepted by many people: the thesis that it does not make any difference to a man's responsibility for something that he foresaw, that he felt no desire for it, either as an end or as a means to an end'.[46] Since 1958 many have come to include merely foreseen effects in what is intentional, or at least to reject the moral relevance of the psychological distinction intended/foreseen; and this seems to corroborate the relative priority of ethics over action theory, because both non-moral theses are motivated by the need to reach— through either way—the ethical conclusion about moral and legal responsibility. The second consequentialist contention is that one can speak meaningfully of a definite notion of 'morally ought', and 'retain the psychological force of the term' (i.e. the force of a divine command, albeit in a godless world!), but with 'an alternative (very fishy) content':[47] one which allows talk of acts that are an 'intentional killing of the innocent', 'adultery', 'treachery', etc., or even acts that are 'untruthful', 'unchaste', 'unjust', but not on that account 'morally wrong' but rather 'morally permissible' or even 'morally right' or 'morally obligatory' on account of further aims, motives, circumstances, and, especially, consequences. Suppose that Anscombe had managed to convince her fellow moral philosophers that '[i]t would be a great improvement if, instead of "morally wrong," one always named a genus such as "untruthful," "unchaste," "unjust."';[48] and that '[w]e should no longer ask whether doing something was "wrong," passing directly from some description of an action to this notion; we should ask whether, e.g., it was unjust; and the answer would sometimes be clear at once'.[49] Had she been successful, a discussion *could not even begin* about whether or not a particular action, agreed to be unjust or unchaste, could be permissible or morally right or obligatory on account of its consequences or further ends. For Anscombe assumes that a 'sound philosophy of psychology' can prove how a virtue is a characteristic of such a kind that it makes a man good *qua* man, so that no action contrary to virtue may be permissible.[50] The same 'sound' theory of action should not, of course, include all the foreseeable consequences *within the intention that defines an action* for the purpose of its *description* as just or unjust, chaste or unchaste, or as of any kind of virtue or vice. For if all the foreseeable consequences were part of the intention which defines the kind of action, then the disagreement about whether or not an act in a particular situation is 'morally wrong' would just be transformed into a disagreement about whether or not the act falls, according to the circumstances and consequences, under the general genus of just or unjust, etc.

These are not merely verbal disagreements. According to Anscombe, 'the best known English academic moral philosophers'[51] defend some form of '*consequentialism*',[52] i.e. 'a philosophy according to which, e.g., it is not possible to hold that it cannot be right to kill the innocent as a means to any end whatsoever and that someone who

[46] Anscombe, 'Modern Moral Philosophy', 183.
[47] Anscombe, 'Modern Moral Philosophy', 179.
[48] Anscombe, 'Modern Moral Philosophy', 180.
[49] Anscombe, 'Modern Moral Philosophy', 180.
[50] Anscombe, 'Modern Moral Philosophy', 174.
[51] Anscombe, 'Modern Moral Philosophy', 181.
[52] Anscombe, 'Modern Moral Philosophy', 184.

thinks otherwise is in error'.[53] The great incompatibility between this consequentialism and the whole moral tradition preceding it can be shown by understanding how acts are morally specified, because 'it has been characteristic of [the Hebrew-Christian] ethic to teach that there are *certain things forbidden* whatever *consequences* threaten';[54] and some of these forbidden actions are described in words that do not imply their moral evaluation: 'choosing to kill the innocent for any purpose, however good', 'vicarious punishment', 'treachery', 'idolatry', 'sodomy', 'adultery', and 'making a false profession of faith'.[55] Anscombe identifies the precise issue between classical ethics and English modern moral philosophy in terms of an insurmountable disagreement about the way in which the descriptions of some types of actions settle the question of their goodness or badness, because right reason identifies those act-types as in themselves good or evil. 'The prohibition of *certain things* simply in virtue of their *description as such-and-such identifiable kinds of action*, regardless of any further consequences',[56] presupposes both the importance of, and the right answer to, the problem of action specification. Is the right answer to this problem to be found, however, in a non-moral action theory or rather in a *straightforward ethical distinction* between good and evil as the basic specifications of actions *qua* human? Let us recall the first and second of Anscombe's concerns considered above: (i) 'what *type of characteristic* a virtue is (...) and how it relates to the actions in which it is instanced',[57] and (ii) 'what a human action is at all, and how its description as "doing such-and-such" is affected by its motive and by the intention or intentions in it'.[58] Let us look at them now in the light of her observation that 'it is pretty well taken for obvious among [the modern moral philosophers] that a prohibition such as that on murder does not operate in face of some consequences. But of course the strictness of the prohibition has as its point *that you are not to be tempted by fear or hope of consequences*'.[59] The non-evaluative descriptions of the act-types certainly precede their moral evaluation; nevertheless, those descriptions presuppose the constitution of the act-types in the order of morality, because they are the descriptions of human acts *qua* human.[60] This means that human reason *stops* in a given description of a kind of human act—considered *qua* human, as intentional action—in order to evaluate it as good or evil or indifferent, and thereafter, in a few but strategic cases, to pronounce an absolute prohibition upon it (a 'moral absolute');[61] but right reason *stops* there, and defines 'such-and-such' act-description as a determinate kind of action, precisely after finding it morally good or evil. Human reason *stops* in an act-description to define it as a determined kind of action *qua* human (i.e. a moral kind of action) precisely *because* that act-description is *per se* good, indifferent or evil; and human reason realizes that. Otherwise it would be a strange coincidence that some *morally neutral* descriptions of

[53] Anscombe, 'Modern Moral Philosophy', 181.
[54] Anscombe, 'Modern Moral Philosophy', 181. The first italics are mine.
[55] Anscombe, 'Modern Moral Philosophy', 181.
[56] Anscombe, 'Modern Moral Philosophy', 181–2. My italics.
[57] Anscombe, 'Modern Moral Philosophy', 174.
[58] Anscombe, 'Modern Moral Philosophy', 174.
[59] Anscombe, 'Modern Moral Philosophy', 182.
[60] *Aquinas*, 20–3; *NLNR*, 457.   [61] *Aquinas*, 164–5.

human acts were at the same time the content of kinds of actions *per se* morally evil or morally good. The description is morally neutral only in the sense that the words do not imply, as a matter of linguistic definition, any moral evaluation; but the act-type is *per se* good or evil, which means that we know its moral kind and character only after the process of moral evaluation, while at the same time the kind of action is good or evil regardless of our moral evaluation. The link between the *morally neutral* or 'factual'[62] descriptions of kinds of intentional actions and habits—for the purpose of their *subsequent* moral evaluation—and the *consequential* classification of the kinds of human actions and habits *qua* human according to that *prior moral evaluation*, shows that the elucidation of human actions cannot start from a merely non-ethical or pre-moral point of view. The specification of human acts *qua* human includes, *in a non-tautological way*, their being *per se* morally good or evil or indifferent.[63]

Let us explore further, then, the specification of human actions. The problem is twofold: (i) to *individuate* a particular action as an instance of a generic kind (or as an instance of two or more kinds of actions, when a single action has several species), and (ii) to *define* different kinds of actions in the abstract, as generic act-descriptions, so that each act-description is something meaningful in itself *qua* human action, and, in a relevant way, different from other kinds of actions. These are two sides of the same coin, which I present in a simplified way. For things are more complicated. Between the most generic act-description and the particular human act that instantiates it there are many abstract act-descriptions that are more specific and equally instantiated by the individual action. For example, Paul withdraws money from his bank account to buy two tickets for the cinema, to invite his girlfriend, to ask her to marry him, to marry her and hopefully have many children, and for them all to be happy for evermore. The individual human act is chosen under several descriptions, which are intentional from the first to the last; but there are some 'hidden' act-descriptions, which are objective characteristics of the act that apply to it precisely in virtue of being such-and-such an intentional action; e.g., that Paul's act was an act of *reclaiming his deposit*, an act of justice, in order to do another kind of act of justice (a contract: buying and paying for the tickets), in order to do an act of friendship that he had done before (to invite his girlfriend to the cinema), in order to do—for the first time in his life—a specific act of commitment (to propose marriage), in order to do other types of acts of justice, faithfulness, chastity, etc. (to actually marry her and to have many children), in order to be and make others happy in that way of life—and this is the last, very generic characterization of what he was doing or trying to do while withdrawing money from the bank. So we can look at the specification of the human act from the top of the most generic true characterization of an action—which is intentional under that very description—to the bottom of the most specific characterization of the individual action—which is intentional as well under that very particular characterization; or, the other way round, down from the most proximate and specific description of the individual action, whose character we wish to describe or understand, up to its most

---

[62] Anscombe, 'Modern Moral Philosophy', 174.
[63] Aquinas, *De Malo* q. 2 aa. 4 and 5.

general characteristic (or the most generic act-description which is instantiated in the particular action).

These two interrelated problems—the *individuation of actions* as falling under general act-descriptions and the *definition of kinds of actions* according to relevant descriptions that can be instantiated in many particular human acts—are clearly seen by John Finnis. When he defends the requirement of practical reasonableness to respect every basic good in every act, and therefore the absolute prohibition of certain kinds of acts and the existence of some 'absolute human rights', he says: 'Obviously, the principal problem in considering the implications of this requirement is the problem of individuating and characterizing actions, to determine what is one complete act-that-itself-does-nothing-but-damage-a-basic-good'.[64] In the first edition of *Natural Law and Natural Rights*, Finnis captures the classical thesis of the specification of human action by 'intention'.[65] In the following decades he provides a

> clearer understanding of intention, as the adoption of a proposal for action, by choice, such that what is included in one's intention—and defines one's action—is (just) the whole set of ends and means which make the proposal attractive to one as an immediate option, under the description of ends and means which makes them seem as a set choiceworthy and to be chosen by me here and now.[66]

In different contexts, Finnis is interested mainly in the correct characterization of what the agent is doing, which depends on the contents of the means and ends chosen or intended precisely under the descriptions that make them intelligible and attractive for the agent.[67] According to whether or not these act-descriptions correspond to types of actions that are morally good or evil, right or wrong, practical wisdom will permit, command, or forbid them. For example, the debate about craniotomy is intricate precisely because it is not easy to describe the action with precision in order to judge whether or not it falls under the description of 'directly killing the innocent'.[68] Something similar can be said about the disagreements on capital punishment, on sterilization and other interventions to prevent conception in some contexts of non-voluntary sexual intercourse, on voting in favour of statutes that include unjust provisions, etc. This concern for the correct characterization of the action in a value-free description, for the purpose of its subsequent evaluation, corresponds to the first aspect of the problem of the specification of action, i.e. to the individuation of action as falling under a general description.

The second aspect of the problem is how to distinguish between kinds of actions *in general*, and between more and less generic kinds. This is even more problematic. Finnis focusses on the kinds of actions that correspond to the most specific or basic descriptions of actions, which do not include any moral evaluation in the description itself; e.g., torture, sodomy, adultery, murder, lying, theft. (Notice that he is aware that the moral evaluation and condemnation of those kinds of actions *flows backward* into

---

[64] *NLNR*, 122.   [65] *NLNR*, 122.   [66] *NLNR*, 454, and *CEJF* II.11, 198–9.
[67] *Aquinas*, 62–6; *CEJF* II.9, 153, 165.   [68] See the discussion in *CEJF* II.13, 249–56.

the common meaning of the word.[69]) He considers confusing, however, what Aquinas says about the specification of *more generic kinds of actions*, which seem to have names that imply a moral evaluation, such as 'just' and 'unjust', 'right' and 'wrong', 'morally good' and 'morally evil'.[70] Finnis thinks that Aquinas 'is willing to identify or specify acts by reference to morally relevant circumstances which are *praeter intentionem* and thus in a sense is willing to treat good and bad, right and wrong, virtue and vice, as if they were somehow categories *specifying* acts within the moral order', and this is 'a source of confusion'.[71] He also thinks that the organization of the *Summa Theologiae* according to the classification of virtues 'was understandable' but 'can obscure morality's foundations', because in deliberation one needs 'to understand what reason requires, what acts are consistent with pursuing human goods and avoiding evil'. Virtues are 'the consequences of resolving such issues rightly'. So the classification of virtues, which are 'aspects of character', is not a classification 'of the goods to which rational acts are directed, nor of types of act, nor of practical reason's norms'.[72] So it seems that Finnis does not see the connection between non-evaluative descriptions of human acts in their most specific kinds, such as murder or fornication, and the similarly *non-evaluative* characterizations of human acts in their more generic kinds, such as just or unjust and chaste or lustful. By contrast, Anscombe appears to think that only the descriptions '*morally* good' and '*morally* evil' lead to confusion. For she says that all of the other 'descriptions' may be used as *non-evaluative*: 'So far, in spite of their strong associations, I conceive "bilking," "injustice" and "dishonesty" *in a merely "factual" way*'.[73] She, like Finnis, considers as non-evaluative the most specific act-description; but then she contends that the same holds true for the more general act-descriptions, however strange it might sound: 'That I can do this for "bilking" is *obvious enough*; "justice" I have no idea how to define, except that its sphere is that of actions which relate to someone else, but "injustice," its defect, can for the moment be offered as a generic name covering various species. E.g.: "bilking," "theft" (which is relative to whatever property institutions exist), "slander," "adultery," "punishment of the innocent."'.[74]

Confronting this paradox, reflected in the disagreement between Anscombe and Finnis, I think that Aquinas's statements on the distinctions among different kinds of actions in general, following the classification of human habits according to their objects, are not a source of confusion. On the contrary, they clarify how it is that all good or evil actions, which have *in common* their being in agreement with or against the precepts of natural law (i.e. human reason), can be classified in different kinds of human actions according to their objects.[75] His theory of the specification of actions by their intended objects, which Finnis follows so closely *only* in relation to the most specific act-descriptions, is consistently applied to the specification of actions by more generic descriptions of kinds of virtues and vices, and even by the most generic

---

[69] *MA*, 37.   [70] *CEJF* II.9, 164.

[71] *CEJF* II.9, 164. He cites *ST* I-II, q. 18 aa. 4 [5] and 10.

[72] *Aquinas*, 187.

[73] Anscombe, 'Modern Moral Philosophy', 174. My emphasis.

[74] Anscombe, 'Modern Moral Philosophy', 174. My emphasis.

[75] *De Malo*, q. 2 a. 6.

description of good and evil. For good and evil actions, and virtues and vices, are also specified by *per se* distinctions of objects.[76] Aquinas is not begging the question of the moral goodness or badness of act-descriptions such as 'virtuous', 'vicious', 'right', 'wrong', 'just', 'unjust', 'brave', 'coward', 'chaste', 'unchaste', etc. For these act-descriptions are only *apparently* value-laden as a matter of linguistic definitions; or we may say that 'their strong associations'[77] are compatible with their 'factual' or descriptive meaning, or that their moral connotations are the historical and cultural effect of traditional moral evaluations that *flow backward into their common meanings or working definitions.*[78] Aquinas is even *worse*—more striking—than Anscombe, because he does not even beg the question of the *goodness* of *morally good* types of actions, or the *badness* of *morally evil* types of actions. For not even the most general division of kinds of human actions *qua* human—i.e., the distinction between *morally good* and *morally evil*—is self-evident.[79] The distinction between moral good and evil does not include *in the meaning of the words*, before the demonstration, the conclusions (i) that what is morally good is good *simpliciter* (and therefore better than just pre-moral good, and preferable to what is morally evil), and (ii) that what is morally evil is bad *simpliciter* (and therefore worse than just pre-moral or physical evil, and not-preferable to what is morally good), and (iii) that the difference between moral good and moral evil *is* the essential distinction between types of human acts *qua* human.

This thesis can be traced back to Plato and Aristotle, but only Aquinas articulates it from top to bottom: from the most general specifications of human acts to their most particular instantiations in very specific kinds of acts. For want of space, I leave aside the treatment of the issue by Plato and Aristotle. Suffice it to say that one should focus first on the *questions* confronted by Plato and Aristotle, and only thereafter on their answers. For the most illuminating fact is that those questions had sense.[80] I must rest content with suggesting the following summary of Aquinas's more systematic position. This scheme makes sense of Aquinas's organization of moral theology because it allows him to prove *step by step* which types of acts are really conducive to happiness (*beatitudo*), and therefore good, and which are only *apparent* goods, possible objects of choice because in some respect they seem to lead to happiness (*beatitudo*).

First, then, Aquinas looks at the whole set of acts that in whatever way can be described as 'done by human beings'.[81] Among these, some are properly *human*—i.e. voluntary—and others are *not properly human*: these can be called 'of the human being' because a human being materially produces them, but they do not proceed from his or

---

[76] *ST* I-II, q. 54 aa. 2 and 3; q. 60 aa. 1 and 5; q. 72 a. 1; etc.

[77] Anscombe, 'Modern Moral Philosophy', 174.

[78] *MA*, 37.

[79] This thesis is implicit in Finnis's analysis of the relationship between self-evident first practical principles—whose objects are non-moral goods—and derivative moral principles about the goodness and badness of human actions. For that analysis entails that the goodness and badness of moral goods—i.e. that some human acts are indeed good or evil *qua* human (*ST* I-II, q. 18, a. 1), and hence to be done or avoided—ought to be proved rationally: secondary precepts of natural law are not self-evident for all. See *Aquinas*, 79–90, in relation to *Aquinas*, 123–9.

[80] See, for example, Plato, *Euthyphro* and *Gorgias*; Aristotle, *Rhetoric* I, 1374a1–15; *Topics* IV, 5: 126a35; *NE* II, 6: 1107a9–10; *Eudemian Ethics* II, 3: 1221b20–26.

[81] *ST* I-II, q. 1 a. 1c.

her rational deliberation.[82] This first classification, albeit trivial in appearance, is crucial against those who think that the specification of human actions *qua* human may be done just at the level of their physical or pre-moral being (*in genere naturae*) or that the human act *in genere moris* can be described just as its description *in genere naturae* plus a moral evaluation.[83] Not at all. The first and basic division of actions caused by human beings *leaves out* all acts *in genere naturae* for the purpose of further specifications and classifications of human acts *qua* human. Acts 'of men' as such cannot be classified as species of 'human acts' (i.e. *qua* human). This would be as illogical as classifying, in the first order of reality, types of minerals as sub-species of living beings! For this reason, a distinction *in genere naturae* is *altogether irrelevant* to establishing a distinction *in genere moris*. Only those circumstances of the human act that are meaningful for the rational deliberation of the agent can be relevant for the definition of a kind of act within the moral realm, since an act is human—belongs to the *genus moris*—precisely as deliberately willed under a rationally understood description.

Second, Aquinas shows that *all* human acts share the same most generic kind, precisely that of being 'properly of the human being as human being'.[84] The defining characteristic of this genus is that these kinds of acts are done—chosen, intended—for the sake of the same object under the most general description: as an end and good understood by reason.[85] Because 'voluntary actions receive their species from the end',[86] whether morally good or evil,[87] they receive their genus from the last end, which is common to all the actions.[88] For all the things that can be desired by the will, regardless of their moral goodness, belong to a single genus.[89] So the supreme genus of all human acts *qua* human is *not* the moral good but the perfect human good and happiness as such, before any specification of actions as morally good or evil.

Third, Aquinas enquires as to the essential *division* or most generic species that divide all human acts *qua* human (i.e. moral), and also all human passions considered *in genere moris* (i.e. as they are under the power of reason and will).[90] He tries to prove that the most generic species of human acts are 'morally good',[91] 'morally evil',[92] and 'morally indifferent',[93] in so far as being according to reason or against reason are essential differences from the point of view of the principle of human acts, which is reason and will.[94] His arguments are irrelevant to my argument. What is relevant here is that he *sees the need* to demonstrate that the specification of human acts *qua* human at the most general level depends on the essential distinction between morally good, indifferent, and evil. All other specifications of human acts will be subdivisions of morally good and evil. Next he establishes that the consequence of the specification of any act as morally good or evil is that it is right or wrong/sinful, and laudable or guilty, and worthy of a positive or negative retribution (reward or punishment) from others

---

[82] *ST* I-II, q. 1 a. 1 ad 2 and ad 3.
[83] Finnis refutes this confusion at *CEJF* II.9, 164–5.
[84] *ST* I-II, q. 1 a. 1c.   [85] *ST* I-II, q. 1 a. 1c; and also q. 1 a. 2c.
[86] *ST* I-II, q. 1 a. 5c and q. 1 a. 3c.
[87] *ST* I-II, q. 18 aa. 1, 2, 4, 5 and 6.
[88] *ST* I-II, q. 1 a. 5c.   [89] *ST* I-II, q. 1 a. 5c.
[90] *ST* I-II, q. 24, in particular aa. 1 and 4.
[91] *ST* I-II, q. 18 aa. 2 and 5.   [92] *ST* I-II, q. 18 aa. 2 and 5.   [93] *ST* I-II, q. 18 a. 8.
[94] *ST* I-II, q. 1 aa. 1 and 3; q. 18 aa. 5 and 10; q. 19 aa. 1 and 3; but see also q. 19, a. 4.

and from God.[95] Hence the knowledge of the specification of human acts under some morally good or evil species constitutes the most important piece of information, so to speak, when one deliberates about what to do or not to do.

Fourth, and last, Aquinas organizes the rest of the moral part of his *Summa Theologiae* as a grand attempt to prove rationally which are the more specific genera of human acts under the most generic divisions as good and evil. He tries to prove that the essential distinction among habits is between good and evil, which in the case of human habits means *according to or against reason*.[96] Then he proves that human virtue is good,[97] and that it is the *common genus* of specific virtues.[98] The fact that he *has to prove rationally* that virtues in general are good, and that some specific habits are virtues, is consistent with Finnis's thesis of the priority of natural law (i.e. principles, rules, norms of reason) over the virtues (i.e. the dispositions of character towards doing what is good),[99] because in order to prove that some act-description is good or evil— whether the act-description is very specific, such as restitution or murder, or more generic, such as just or unjust—one has to show that that sort of act is in agreement with or against reason (i.e. natural law). This is, however, only one side of the coin.

The other side is that the classification of kinds of act-descriptions, precisely because it depends on reason's knowledge of relevant *differences* in moral objects,[100] is the key strategy and the architectonic or organizing principle of further attempts to show that more specific kinds are morally good or evil in so far as each one of them falls under a more generic kind whose goodness or badness *has already been demonstrated*. There-fore Aquinas distinguishes the different species of virtues according to the more generic objects of reason,[101] and the species within the species, etc.,[102] until he reaches the most specific descriptions of human acts under specific virtues: e.g., under the species of justice or similar virtues we find restitution,[103] obeying superiors,[104] expressing grati-tude,[105] etc. The same he does with vices. First he tries to prove that they are bad in general;[106] then he distinguishes species of vices, and species within species (usually after dealing with each species of virtue), until he reaches the most specific descriptions of vicious acts under specific vices: e.g., under the species of injustice we have *killing the innocent*—but not *killing the sinner* by public authority—,[107] suicide,[108] theft,[109] etc.

In order to demonstrate that a human act is good or evil *per se*, because of its most specific kind, Aquinas describes the kind of act as a species of some virtue or vice whose morality has already been proved. For in order to prove that an act is in conformity with or against reason one must show how it favours some basic good or some end of the virtues,[110] or how it harms them *in a special way*, due to a particular goodness or

---

[95] *ST* I-II, q. 21.   [96] *ST* I-II, q. 54 a. 3.

[97] *ST* I-II, q. 55 a. 3.   [98] *ST* I-II, q. 55 a. 4c.

[99] *Aquinas*, 163–70, 138–40, 187–8.

[100] *ST* I-II, q. 18 a. 10 and q. 19 a. 1.

[101] *ST* I–II, q.58, q. 60, q. 61 aa. 2 and 3, q. 71 a. 1, q. 72 a. 1; but see q. 94 a. 3.

[102] *ST* II-II, *proemium*, and then see the scheme of II-II in general.

[103] *ST* II-II, q. 62 a. 1.   [104] *ST* II-II, q. 104 aa. 1 and 2.

[105] *ST* II-II, q. 106 a. 1.   [106] *ST* II-II, q. 71 aa. 1, 2 and 3.

[107] *ST* II-II, q. 64 aa. 2, 3 and 6.   [108] *ST* II-II, q. 64 a. 5 ad 1.

[109] *ST* II-II, q. 66 aa. 4 and 5.

[110] *Aquinas*, 79 n 92, 86, 98–99 n *r*, 99–100 n *t*, 124 n 103.

badness of its moral object. A human act is licit or illicit, right or wrong, because it is morally good or evil; but it is morally good or evil not just in a general way, but due to a special conformity or contrariety to human reason, i.e. *because* of its object being in a particular way and in relation to some specific matter in line with right reason or against it: just or unjust, chaste or unchaste, etc. To prove this is to prove that its specific description falls under a more generic species, the goodness or badness of which has already been clarified. And this seems to confirm, at last, that in order to describe a human act *qua* human, and thereafter to define its kind or species as essentially different from other kinds or species, we need to demonstrate its moral worth and the special way in which it is morally good or evil. We cannot stop at relevant descriptions and propose relevant explanations of human acts from outside the field of ethics.

Bibliography

Anscombe, G.E.M. ([1958] 2005), 'Modern Moral Philosophy', in *Human Life, Action and Ethics. Essays by G.E.M. Anscombe* (eds Mary Geach and Luke Gormally) (Exeter: Imprint Academic), 169–94.

Anscombe, G.E.M. ([1957] 1985), *Intention* (Oxford: Blackwell; HUP).

Aquinas, Thomas (1269–71), *Quaestiones disputatae De Malo* (*De Malo*: Disputed [Debated] Questions on Evil), in *Opera Omnia Sancti Thomae Aquinatis Doctoris Angelici* (Leonine Edition) vol. 23.

Aquinas, Sententia Libri Ethicorum [*In Eth.*—Commentary on *NE*] (ed. Gauthier) (1969).

Torralba, J.M. (2005), *Acción Intencional y Razonamiento Práctico según G.E.M. Anscombe* (Pamplona: Eunsa).

JUSTICE, RIGHTS, AND WRONGDOING

10

Finnis on Justice

John Gardner

I. Justice as a Virtue of Character

> Because one's pursuit of fulfilment would be unreasonable and self-mutilating if it
> were indifferent to friendship and to the worth of the instantiation of human goods in
> the lives of other people, one needs look to getting order into one's relations with one's
> fellows, one's communities. The name for that order, *and* for one's constant concern
> for it, is justice.[1]

We will have occasion, in what follows, to engage critically with some ideas in the first
sentence of this passage. But we begin with the second. Justice, for John Finnis as for
me, names two things. It names a virtue of character (a 'constant concern') and a state
of affairs (an 'order [in] one's relations' that one 'look[s] to getting').[2] Clearly, the two
are logically related. The constant concern, in Finnis's formulation, is a concern for the
order. Does this mean that the order has logical priority over the concern? Does it
entail that the just state of affairs can be characterised independently of the virtue of
character, and that the virtue is to be understood derivatively as the virtue of one who
cares about the existence of that (independently specified) state of affairs?

No. It is consistent with what Finnis says here that the just state of affairs is to be
understood as the state of affairs in which all just actions have been performed, and that
just actions are to be identified in turn as those which a just person—a person with the
relevant 'constant concern'—would be disposed to perform. It does not follow (I hasten
to add) that justice, as a state of affairs, can be attained only by just people. The
connection between the state of affairs and the virtue of character could be more
indirect than that. Quite possibly it goes like this. First one identifies the constant
concern of just people, what it is they care about *qua* just. From that one can identify
certain actions as just even if they are not performed by just people, because they are
the actions that just people would be disposed to perform. Then a just state of affairs
can be thought of as one in which those very actions have been performed, whether by
just people or not. Or perhaps we would prefer to call that a *not unjust* state of affairs,
reserving the title of a just state of affairs for the rarer case in which injustice was
avoided by people manifesting the virtue of justice. Either way, it is the virtue that is in
the logical driving seat.

---

[1] *CEJF* I.2, 47. Emphasis in original.
[2] Finnis famously resists the portrayal of practical rationality as the pursuit of 'states of affairs', See *FoE*,
112–20. But he uses the offending expression in a technical sense that associates it with an 'eventist' (or
loosely consequentialist) moral outlook. I use it less technically to mean the state of (my, your, our, and
hence the world's) affairs, which includes the condition of (my, your, our) relationships, roles, and projects.

Let me address a couple of possible objections to this way of thinking about justice. First, as Finnis rightly insists, the only actions that exhibit the virtue of their agents are justified actions or (synonymously) reasonable actions.[3] Contrary to the exotic teachings of some 'virtue ethicists', however, actions are not reasonable because they are virtuous. On the contrary: actions are virtuous because they are reasonable. Their reasonableness is independently determined; it resides in the fact that they are performed for one or more undefeated reasons—not just reasons thought by the agent to be undefeated, but reasons truly undefeated. This independently determined fact of the action's reasonableness (together with some other facts about the agent) makes its performance virtuous. So surely the independently determined fact of the action's justice (together with some other facts about the agent) is likewise what makes an action that of a just person? That does not follow. Often, there are multiple undefeated reasons for performing one and the same action, and people with different virtues of character perform that action for different undefeated reasons. As people with different virtues, they have (in Finnis's terminology) different 'constant concerns', or (as I prefer to put it) different rational priorities.[4] Our question is: Granted that a certain action is reasonable, what makes it just? What gives it that special mode, key, shading, or flavour, of reasonableness? A good answer, I am suggesting, invokes the constant concerns of the just person. The action is just because (in that) at least one of the undefeated reasons for its performance is a reason of the kind that just people, in particular, care about. So just people would be disposed to perform it. That makes it such that its performance is capable of contributing constitutively to justice, now understood as a state of affairs.

A different kind of objection: If we understand justice as a state of affairs only by thinking about justice as a virtue of character, we leave no logical space for justice or injustice that is not the work of some agent. Justice and injustice must be *done*. They cannot reside in any pattern of holdings or advantages, defined independently of what anybody did to create or sustain it. And that surely makes an oxymoron of familiar ideas such as 'social justice' and 'global justice', and if not an oxymoron then at least a mockery of 'distributive justice' as many now understand it? F.A. Hayek famously relished that conclusion.[5] But one need not follow him, either in relishing it or in drawing it. Justice may, as John Rawls emphasised, be a virtue of social institutions as well as of natural persons.[6] Moreover, omissions as well as interventions, and either of them accidental as well as intentional, are among the ways in which agents, natural or institutional, may exhibit their justice. Finnis agrees that there may be 'a failure of justice, by act or omission'.[7] And of social justice he is consequently able to write, in non-Hayekian vein:

> [S]ocial justice, occupying the place of Aristotle's and Aquinas's general/legal justice, clearly has the character attributed to the latter by Aquinas..., namely that social/general/legal justice is centrally a virtue of the ruler(s)...It is a concern of the citizen

---

[3] E.g. *CEJF* III.4, 76.
[4] See Gardner, 'The Virtue of Justice and the Character of Law'.
[5] Hayek, *Law, Legislation, and Liberty*, Ch. 9.
[6] Rawls, *A Theory of Justice*, 3.   [7] *NLNR*, 165.

only insofar as citizens have the character [role?] ascribed to them (in the central case of citizenship) by Aristotle: participants in governing, ie in ruling.[8]

Do these remarks also associate Finnis with my suggested way of thinking about justice, according to which what counts as a just 'order' depends on what count as the 'constant concerns' of just people? I am not so sure. He certainly laments, in his recent postscript to *Natural Law and Natural Rights*, that while

> 'justice as a quality of character' is the subject of the sentence that wraps up sec. VII.2, the opportunity is missed to reflect a little, somewhere in the chapter, on the fact that the classic definition picks out a *virtue—constans et perpetua voluntas* jus suum cuique tribuere.[9]

But maybe he regards this as only a matter of emphasis, not of logical priority. Whatever Finnis's position on the matter, I will be focusing attention here primarily on justice as a virtue of character. That is because my main aim is to contrast Finnis's account of the just person's 'constant concerns', her distinctive rational priorities, with a rival account that I tend to favour.

II. Justice, Wide and Narrow

I face a preliminary problem in structuring my disagreement with Finnis. The language of justice, notes Aristotle, is sometimes used in a wide sense. Justice in this sense 'is not a part of virtue but is co-extensive with virtue... in so far as [virtue] has respect to one's neighbour'.[10] Justice in the wide sense, in other words, is the other-regarding part of ethics, for which the label 'morality' is nowadays sometimes reserved. In this sense it is just to be diligent, honest, trustworthy, reliable, considerate, loyal, and humane— towards others. And in this sense there is no contrast between justice and charity, or between justice and mercy, or between justice and generosity, for they too are virtues capable of being exhibited in one's treatment of others.

Justice in this all-encompassing sense is to be contrasted, says Aristotle, with 'justice in the sense in which it is a *part* of virtue', or one virtue of character among others.[11] In this narrower sense, being impeccably just does not entail being impeccably loyal, honest, humane, diligent, considerate, and so forth, even in one's treatment of others. And being impeccably just may even entail that one is less than impeccably charitable or merciful. In this sense justice is but one virtue among many, competing with the others to constitute our rational priorities, and thus to determine which justified action, when there is more than one available justified action, we are most disposed to perform.

Like Aristotle, I am primarily interested in understanding justice in the narrow sense, justice as one virtue of character among many. But it is not entirely clear whether Finnis is interested in the same thing, for he declines to maintain the Aristotelian distinction between justice in the wide sense and justice in the narrow sense. True, he

---

[8] *NLNR* 2nd ed., 462.   [9] *NLNR* 2nd ed., 460.
[10] Aristotle, *Nicomachean Ethics*, 1130ª9–13.
[11] Aristotle, *Nicomachean Ethics*, 1130ª15.

distinguishes prominently between 'general justice' and 'particular justice', but that turns out to be a different contrast.[12] As Finnis and Aristotle agree, the 'constant concerns' of the just person can conveniently be divided up. In *Natural Law and Natural Rights* Finnis, following Aquinas, divides them ('exhaustive[ly]') into 'distributive' and 'commutative' concerns.[13] Distributive and commutative justice are then presented as the two species of justice, the two particular forms that general justice may take. But this leaves open whether 'general justice' itself is justice in the wide sense or justice in the narrow sense. Finnis says: no need to distinguish the two. Indeed, he seeks a unity or reintegration of the two senses, putting to rest what he regards as a 'technical distinction' that Aristotle 'wanted to introduce into academic discourse' for want, he says, of adequate conceptual resources to avoid it.[14]

This seems to me to be a mistake. There is nothing technical about Aristotle's distinction. Admittedly, one might wonder whether the word 'justice', in modern English, does the same double service that the Greek word δίκαιος does according to Aristotle. Leaving aside a few stock phrases, I do not think it does.[15] But whatever one thinks about this, there is still a nontechnical distinction to be drawn, along Aristotelian lines, between the investigation of *one* virtue of character, with 'constant concerns' that diverge from (whether or not they necessarily rival) those constituting other virtues of character, and an investigation of *all* virtues of character, with all their different 'constant concerns', where these manifest themselves in one's treatment of others. To avoid cross-purposes, we still need to know: which investigation are we conducting when we investigate justice? The first or the second?

In spite of his attempt to dismiss the distinction, I will treat Finnis as pursuing the first investigation. He presents justice as 'a virtue',[16] 'a quality of character'.[17] The singular indefinite article licences us to read him as differentiating justice from other virtues of character. True, we might think that there is a master-virtue that all who exhibit any (other) virtue of character also exhibit. But for Finnis, as for Aristotle, this master virtue is practical wisdom or 'practical reasonableness' as Finnis usually calls it.[18] Acting justly is but one way of exhibiting practical wisdom; acting unjustly is correspondingly but one way of exhibiting a lack of it. Therefore, 'one's personal failings do not all on every occasion implicate one in injustice'.[19] Not even one's personal failings exhibited towards others implicate one, on every occasion, in injustice. There is also meanness, lack of mercy, unkindness, intolerance, disloyalty, and so on. So there is no risk (to return to the quotation with which we opened our discussion) that the 'pursuit of fulfilment' will be 'unreasonable and self-mutilating', 'indifferent to friendship and to the worth of the instantiation of human goods in the lives of other people' *merely* for want of justice. Personally, I prefer that my friends be as kind and patient as can be, even where the price is that they are less than totally just. On the other hand I prefer that the judge that I am appearing before be as just as can be, even if this means that he or she is less than totally kind or patient.

---

[12] *NLNR*, 166.   [13] *NLNR*, 166.   [14] *NLNR*, 165.
[15] Miller, *Social Justice*, 17. A stock phrase: 'the sleep of the just', meaning the sleep of the virtuous. Consider also the word 'justify', which means 'make acceptable', not 'make just'.
[16] *NLNR* 2nd ed., 460.   [17] *NLNR*, 165.   [18] E.g., *FoE*, 70–4.   [19] *NLNR*, 164–5.

In his reintegrated account of justice Finnis combines some aspects of Aristotle's account of justice in the narrow sense with some aspects of Aristotle's account of justice in the wide sense. From the latter he imports the thought, quite alien to the former, that justice and injustice are 'other-directed', meaning that justices and injustices can only be done to others.[20] So the case in which one is said to be doing oneself an injustice, or not being fair to oneself,[21] involves, for Finnis, 'a kind of metaphorical extension' of justice-talk.[22] I see no reason to think that there is either metaphor or extension here. Maybe some virtues of character can only be exhibited towards others. Loyalty and public-spiritedness are possible examples. But one can be just or unjust towards oneself, I think, in much the same way that one can be charitable or uncharitable towards oneself, or honest or dishonest with oneself. It is not even an odd case. A person impeccably manifesting the virtue of justice is neither especially unconcerned for herself nor especially concerned for herself. It is part of her being impeccably just that she gives herself her due precisely as she gives others their due; what concerns her is that people, including her, always get their due.

III. Giving People Their Due

Finnis and I agree that the constant concern of just people, *qua* just people, is to give people their due. But we interpret this differently. For Finnis (under the influence of Justinian as well as Aquinas) 'due' has the following sense or connotation:

> that of *duty*, of what is owed (*debitum*) or due to another, and correspondingly of what that other person has a right to (viz. roughly, to what is his or her 'own' or at least 'due', by right).[23]

You can see here why talk of 'doing oneself justice' has to be sidelined by Finnis. One may owe duties to oneself, but one has no rights against oneself. So if the constant concern of just people is a concern with rights, it is with what is due to *other* people, not with what is due to people full stop. No doubt this is one reason why Finnis says, revisiting the foregoing passage:

> [T]he Roman definition of justice, which I quoted, about giving every man his due, is not wholly adequate.[24]

He also has another problem in mind when he says this. He worries that the person to whom something is due in a given situation is not always the same person to whom our attention first turns when we reflect on the rights that are at stake, and hence the injustices that are possible in that situation. Supplies are stolen, for example, on their

---

[20] *NLNR*, 161.

[21] There is, to my ears, no significant difference between justice and fairness, and so the expression 'justice as fairness', coined by John Rawls, to my ears means 'justice as justice'. So when I speak of a just person I mean the same person who might these days more commonly be described as a 'fair-minded' person. Finnis seems to agree in regarding justice and fairness as essentially equivalent, speaking of 'what is fitting, fair, or just' (*NLNR*, 178), and treating a 'just balance of advantages' as an 'order of fairness' (*NLNR*, 263).

[22] *NLNR*, 161. [23] *NLNR*, 162. [24] *CEJF* III.4, 79.

way to the army; the supplies themselves are due to the soldiers, but the injustice is done, he thinks, first and foremost to the general population who rely on the soldiers for their defence, and who, I suppose he would say, have a collective right to the safe delivery of the supplies even though they do not have a right to the supplies themselves. Any rights of the soldiers to the supplies, and any injustice done to them by non-delivery, is according to Finnis derivative.

I am not sure that I agree with Finnis's verdicts about who has the rights to what in this case. But I do think that his worries about the reconcilability of these verdicts with an understanding of justice as 'giving people their due' are well-founded. To that extent the case alerts us, I think, to a larger dislocation or disorientation in Finnis's under-standing of justice. To bear that claim out, I will split it into two subsidiary claims. First, I will claim, although many things that are due to A, in the sense that concerns just people, are also A's by right, others are not. Second, I will claim, while many things that are A's by right are also due to A, in the sense that concerns just people, others are not. So the sense of 'due' that matters for a sound understanding of justice is not 'owed as of right'. Even 'owed' by itself is, I will suggest, a very misleading reformulation. The legalistic Romans were wrong to associate getting what is due, in the sense that concerns the just person, with the payment of debts or dues.

(a) Due, but not owed as of right. Some of the things that are due to people, in the sense that concerns the just person, are things that those people deserve. I do not suggest that people getting what they deserve is the only or even the main thing that concerns the just person,[25] but it is one thing that concerns him, which does not similarly concern those who possess other virtues.

Consider some unwelcome things that people may deserve: criticism, opprobrium, punishment, misery, hardship, failure. For Finnis, as for most people, it is conceptually awkward to classify any of these as owed as of right to those who deserve them. That is because it is common to all plausible accounts of rights, including Finnis's,[26] that a right is to something that the rightholder either does or should welcome. To be sure, there are aspects of punishment that should be welcomed by the person who is deservedly punished. There is, for example, the implicit acknowledgement that he is a morally responsible agent.[27] But that does not suffice to overcome the conceptual awkwardness of regarding him as having a right to be punished. It is a defining purpose of punishment that, on balance, it be unwelcome to the person punished. Even if punishment has a silver lining, then, it needs on the whole to be a cloud. Besides, the same silver lining is not present in other clouds that people deserve to live under. In what way is deservedly losing one's reputation or one's business—not by way of punishment—an acknowledgement by anyone of one's status as a person, or of any other facts the acknowledgement of which one should welcome? A self-important narcissist or a needy arch-manipulator may deserve to lose all her friends, even if she

---

[25] Compare Campbell, 'Humanity Before Justice', 1, where the stronger claim is made.
[26] *NLNR*, 205.
[27] See Gardner, *Offences and Defences*, 192, for discussion.

does not deserve to be punished.[28] The just person—in this respect very unlike the compassionate or the merciful or the humane person—sees no cause for sympathy when she, meaning the narcissist or arch-manipulator, does lose her friends. Unless there are other respects in which her loss is undue, he is not disposed to remonstrate with her ex-friends, or to set her up with new ones. But that is clearly not because the narcissist or arch-manipulator has a *right* to be abandoned by her friends. It is because she got what she deserved.

The just person, if I am correct here, is concerned that people get what they deserve, never mind whether they also have a right to it. True, the just person also has a matching concern about the avoidance of *un*deserved ills. It is a cause of satisfaction to the just person not only that people deservedly lose their friends, but also that they do not undeservedly lose them. He or she cares not only that people are punished as they deserve to be, but also that they are not punished as they do not deserve to be. It is clearly not conceptually awkward (never mind whether it is morally correct) to think of people as having a right not to suffer ills that they do not deserve. But it strikes me as impossible to admit that people sometimes deserve ills in such a way as to be able to draw a contrast with those who do not deserve them, without in the process regarding the fact that the former people deserve those ills as a positive reason why they should have them. That much seems to me to be built into the very concept of desert.[29] So one cannot, it seems to me, use this shift from getting what is deserved to avoiding what is undeserved to reunite what is due to people, in the sense that matters for the rational priorities of the just person, with what people have a right to get.

Finnis may have a different plan for reuniting deserts and rights. He writes very little about deserts.[30] When he speaks about punishment in his mature work he portrays it as a right of people other than the person punished, a right of others, assembled together in a community, to a kind of rebalancing of the moral books. And he adds that therefore, in his view,

> one merits reward or deserves punishment (which can only be rightly imposed by persons responsible for a community, administering its law) precisely as someone who is (or, like a visitor, is reasonably taken to be) a part of a community.[31]

Here, as with the army supplies, the question 'to whom is this punishment due?' does not readily invite the same answer as the question 'who has a right to it?' The community, for Finnis, has a right that the punishment be delivered to the person to whom it (the punishment itself) is due. In this case there is not even a derivative right owed to that person of the kind that was owed to the soldiers. True, in this situation we would never say that an injustice was done *to* the person deserving punishment if he or

---

[28] Punishment can be deserved only for wrongdoing. One may exhibit numerous vices without being a wrongdoer, and deserve various ills other than punishment when one does. See Hurka, 'Desert: Individual-istic and Holistic', 51ff.

[29] See Gardner and Tanguay-Renaud, 'Desert and Avoidability in Self-Defense'.

[30] They enjoy a mention in the *NLNR* discussion of justice only as a criterion of comparison that may figure in a scheme of distributive justice: *NLNR*, 175. Non-comparative deserts appear to be absent from the scene altogether.

[31] *CEJF* III.12, 175, n. 40.

she went unpunished. But that only goes to show, I think, that while all injustices need to be done, not all injustices need be done to someone. And that in turn is because the things that are due to people, in the sense that concerns the just person, are not only the things that people have a right to. This is not to deny—although I would deny it in a longer discussion—that the rest of us have the collective right that Finnis says we have to see those who deserve it punished. Neither is it to deny—although I would deny it in a longer discussion—that the just person has a constant concern, *qua* just, to see that collective right honoured if it exists. My point is only that, whether or not there is such a right and whether or not the honouring of it sounds in justice, the just person has an independent concern with whether the person punished gets the punishment that he or she deserves (and with the gullible electorate getting the government they deserve, the remiss father getting the relationship with his children that he deserves, the shyster getting the friends he deserves, etc.).

These remarks also hint at a more radical objection to what Finnis says about justice. Not only does reflection on people's 'just deserts' drive a wedge between justice and rights; it also drives a wedge between justice and duties. To see why, consider some more welcome things that people may deserve. A well-behaved child may deserve a treat, a hard-working carer may deserve some respite, a well-run voluntary organisation may deserve public support, a friend who has made an effort may deserve a compliment. As already indicated, to say this much is already to give a reason in favour of giving these things to these beneficiaries. But does it mean that anyone has a duty to give them, rights-based or otherwise? No. Normally, that these things are deserved is just one reason among others for giving them. Even in the eyes of the just person, no wrong (to the deserving, or at all) is done if treats, gifts, concessions, donations, and compliments do not reach those who deserve them. It is a shortfall of conformity with reasons of justice, but not by virtue of that alone an *in*justice, which connotes breach of duty.

To put it another way: the just person has a special concern for people getting (inter alia) what they deserve, but this is consistent with her treating it on occasions as no more than desirable, and perhaps supererogatory, to get it to them. I tend to think that the same is often true of punishment and other ills that are deserved. That ills are deserved is a reason for anyone to mete them out, but that does not make it anyone's duty to mete them out. And that, it seems to me, is also how the just person sees it. For the just person is also practically wise. Her special attention to some reasons rather than others when there are multiple undefeated reasons for action does not lead her to imagine that everything that earns that attention is her, or someone's, duty. If this is right then 'giving people their due' in the sense that is relevant to an understanding of justice has nothing special to do with 'duty' or what is 'owed'. It means something more like: giving people what is appropriate, fitting,[32] apt, or suited to them in their situations, of which giving them what they deserve is a prominent, but certainly not the only, species.

---

[32] Finnis occasionally relates dueness to fittingness, e.g. *NLNR*, 163, 178, 180.

If I am right about this it has radical implications for the way in which justice is sometimes contrasted with charity, generosity, mercy, and so on in modern political theory. A common view is that up to a certain point justice requires actions of us, and after that point they become 'merely' charitable, generous, merciful, benevolent, humane, etc., which is taken to mean that they are not required, or at any rate not a matter of duty. That seems to me to be an entirely misguided picture. There are duties of justice but there are also duties of charity (etc.).[33] There are also ordinary non-mandatory reasons of justice as well as of charity. Just people (and institutions) differ from their charitable counterparts in respect of which reason or reasons they are disposed to act on, when more than one reason is undefeated and hence rationally available to be acted on by a virtuous person. Since duties do not automatically defeat non-duties, this leaves open whether either just or charitable people are always disposed, all things considered, to do their duty or whether they are sometimes disposed to breach it (unlike diligent people, for whom the doing of duty *per se* is a constant concern).

(b) *Owed as of right, but not due.* A complete set of principles of justice, for Finnis, is one that

> includes principles for assessing how one person ought to treat another or how one person has a right to be treated, regardless of whether or not others are being so treated; in my usage, a principle forbidding torture in *all* cases is a principle of justice.[34]

Allow me to leave aside the words 'regardless of whether or not others are being so treated'. It leads one to presume that resistance to Finnis's final remark about torture and justice will be limited to so-called 'strict egalitarians', those who believe that how one person should be treated (in justice) depends on how others are already being, or have already been, treated.[35] I am no strict egalitarian, and I tend to think that there are few valid strictly egalitarian principles. In particular, I do not think that the fact that some people have already been tortured or are about to be tortured supplies any kind of reason, however slight, to torture anyone else. So my resistance to Finnis's final remark about torture and justice has a quite different source.

Imagine someone who has been tortured severely, and who complains of the injustice of it. To my ear this complaint would indicate warped rational priorities. Has the torture perhaps affected its victim's moral compass? What comes across to me, but perhaps not to Finnis, is that this torture victim regards himself as having been wrongly picked out for torture, or as having been exposed to disproportionate torture, or as having been tortured on the wrong ground, or in some other way as having been

---

[33] For more discussion see Gardner, 'The Virtue of Charity and its Foils'.

[34] *NLNR*, 163–4. He thinks this about murder as well as about torture: *CEJF* III.4, 78. My comments below apply, *mutatis mutandis*, in the case of murder too. I do not think that an ordinary murder—by contrast with a death penalty, a revenge killing, or a murder of one who is mistaken for another—is best thought of as an injustice.

[35] On 'strict egalitarianism' so understood, see Raz, *The Morality of Freedom*, Ch. 9; and Parfit 'Equality and Priority'.

unduly tortured. He is complaining about this undueness rather than about the resort to torture as such. Why? What sort of person, reflecting on such extreme inhumanity, quibbles instead about the allocation of it? There are rare cases, to be sure, in which this might be the natural focus. If the only possible way to prevent one person being tortured is to torture another, then there is immediately a live question of who should bear how much of the (*ex hypothesi* unavoidable) torture. In that situation the most pressing moral question is, alas, one of justice. But when, as is usual, there is an unlimited amount of non-torture to go round, focusing on the injustice of a given act of torture suggests the mindset of a childish person, incapable of grasping moral problems except as problems about who gets how much of what and why. Such a person is a justice-fanatic.

I am not suggesting, I hasten to add, that the just person is this justice-fanatic, converting every problem childishly into an allocative one. The just person is also practically wise, and can see when the reasons for doing something are all defeated, such that the question of which undefeated reason one is to act for does not arise. All that I am suggesting is that the just person has nothing much to add to what any other practically wise person has to say on the subject of torture. She has no distinctive take on it *qua* just. Or at any rate, her only distinctive take on it is that she has nothing much to add: she can confirm, in case anyone was wondering, that torture is never deserved, and she can confirm that the question of how to allocate it does not arise except in rare situations of unavoidable torture. The problem of torture is not, in the normal run of things, a problem of justice, one that calls for a specifically just person to sort it out. And that is in spite of the fact that each of us has a right not to be tortured.

It is easy to slip into thinking that every question about rights is an allocative one. After all, a duty that is owed to nobody in particular is not a right-based duty. I have a duty not to despoil a beautiful landscape, or burn an important historical document, even when I am its owner. A duty to whom? To the world, we sometimes say, or to posterity. But it would be better to admit that this duty is just a duty, a duty to nobody, so that no right is involved. That is because talk of rights is implicitly contrastive. It indicates that a duty is owed to one person or group rather than another. If everyone together—the universe of valuers—is the beneficiary of the duty, then who is the other who is not? It is very tempting to think that this implicit contrastiveness in rights-talk already makes rights-talk implicitly allocative. But when I say that a rights-based duty is owed to one person or group rather than another I do not mean that it is owed to one *at the expense of* the other, or *in competition with* the other, or *such that a like duty is not equally owed to the other*, or anything like that. That one person has a right to my ϕing or to my not ψing in her case is often fully consistent with everyone else in the world having a like right to my ϕing or to my not ψing in their cases. If there is plenty of my ϕing or my not ψing to go round, and if the right in question is not a right to some allocation, some quota or measure or share, of my ϕing or not ψing, the extent of which calls for determination, then no allocative question arises for me when I ask whether to ϕ or not ψ in your case.

Surely (you may object) that is because an allocative question was already asked in connection with the right itself, and the answer was already given 'everyone gets the right'? Not so. To be sure, allocative questions arise automatically in connection with some legal and more broadly institutional rights, when we have to decide (the question being open until we do decide) who is going to get them. But we do not need to decide this—in fact there is no room for *deciding* it—in connection with ordinary moral rights. They are held by those who hold them irrespective of what we decide about who is going to hold them. There is therefore nothing up for allocation. And there is a question of justice, I contend, only when something is up for allocation. The distinctive role of the just person is to do the allocating: to determine who is to get how much of what, and why.

For the avoidance of doubt let me stress that all of this is consistent with Finnis's view that, as just people,

> we may be interested in comparing adult's rations with small children's rations as shares of some available supply, or we may be interested in comparing adults' rations with what they need or with what is *fitting* for them to have if they are to remain alive and well, regardless of questions of supply and shares.[36]

Although I have some minor reservations about the examples, I agree with Finnis's main point here. Scarcity of resources always gives rise to questions of justice, but not all questions of justice arise from scarcity of resources, or scarcity of anything.[37] I would add: Not even all questions of *comparative* justice arise from scarcity. There are questions of comparative justice that arise in connection with punishment, for example, even when there is an unlimited amount of punishment, as well as an unlimited amount of non-punishment, to go round. And there are also plentiful non-comparative questions of justice, such as whether a particular punishment (or criticism or reward or compliment or electoral defeat, etc.) is deserved, or whether a particular procedure (e.g. for determining guilt or awarding a license) is fair, irrespective of parity with any other instances or recipients. All of this is included within the ethics of giving people their due, and hence belongs squarely to the distinctive constant concerns of the just person, as I have now explained them.

IV. The Forms of Justice

The contrast that Finnis draws, in *Natural Law and Natural Rights*, between justice in its distributive form and justice in its commutative form seems, in at least some of his formulations,[38] to map onto the contrast between comparative and non-comparative justice. We 'compar[e] adult's rations with children's rations as shares of some available supply' when we are doing distributive justice, whereas the pursuit of

---

[36] *NLNR*, 163.
[37] In 'The Virtue of Justice and the Character of Law' I overemphasised scarcity. What I had in mind was that scarcity forces us to confront some problems as problems of justice when otherwise we might more naturally have seen them through a different lens. However, I came across as denying that they could be problems of justice without scarcity. Thanks to Leslie Green for drawing my attention to the misleading impression I gave.
[38] He formulates the contrast in various ways and not, I think, always consistently. For example, to judge by *NLNR*, 169, n. 10 only strictly egalitarian comparative justice (where the fact that A got an extra ration, now eaten, is a reason why others should get an extra ration too) is distributive; other kinds of comparative justice seem to be classed, by implication, as commutative.

commutative justice does not raise 'questions of supply and shares', but includes (for example) 'comparing adults' rations with what they need or with what is fitting for them to have if they are to remain alive and well, regardless of questions of supply and shares.'

I think both of these are best regarded as not merely allocative but specifically distributive concerns. The first is a comparative distributive concern, the second a non-comparative one. I agree with Finnis, of course, that picking out some of the just person's concerns as somehow distributive ones, to be contrasted with some others that are somehow non-distributive, is 'no more than an analytical convenience'.[39] Yet Finnis's contrast between distributive and commutative justice, inherited from Aquinas, is not very convenient, as Finnis himself has come to recognise. In later work, Finnis wisely abandons what he calls 'Aquinas' unstable classifications of justice',[40] in which the second classification, 'commutative justice', serves as no more than a residual ragbag containing all the many forms of justice that are left behind when distributive justice has been hived off, distributive justice itself having a somewhat mysterious scope.

Should the failure of Aquinas's attempt to subdivide the just person's concerns lead us to abandon all attempts to subdivide them? I do not think so. Here I want to speak up for one scheme of subdivision, Aristotle's, on which Finnis has consistently poured cold water. In his recent postscript he writes:

> Oddly, in the years since the first edition [of *Natural Law and Natural Rights*], Aristotle's discussion of corrective justice has received wide attention and a surprising measure of acceptance from philosophers of law and of common law—surprising because this is a rather weak part of his *Ethics*, since it quite fails to discuss the duties of justice which, if violated, give rise to claims of corrective justice.[41]

This echoes and amplifies an earlier passage:

> The real problem with Aristotle's account is its emphasis on correction, on the remedying of the inequality that arises when one person injures or takes from another, or when one party fulfils his side of a bargain while the other does not. This is certainly one field of problems of justice, but even when added to the field of distributive justice it leaves untouched a wide range of problems. 'Correction' and 'restitution' are notions parasitic on some prior determination of what is to count as a crime, a tort, a binding agreement, etc.[42]

Aristotle's 'leaving untouched a wide range of problems' with 'corrective justice' is the origin, as Finnis goes on to explain, of Aquinas's invention of 'commutative justice' as a more capacious replacement. 'Commutative justice' includes the whole of Aristotelian corrective justice but bundles it together with 'the duties of justice which, if violated, give rise to claims of corrective justice'. The bundling together is undermotivated, since Aristotle never suggests that the distributive-corrective scheme is meant to be

---

[39] *NLNR*, 179.   [40] *Aquinas*, 215.
[41] *NLNR* 2nd ed., 464.   [42] *NLNR*, 178.

exhaustive. But even if the scheme were meant to be exhaustive, the bundling together should still be resisted, and for a quite independent reason.

I have already given some advance notice of that reason. The duties which, if violated, give rise to claims of corrective justice need not be, and often are not, duties of justice at all, so no 'problems of justice' are left 'untouched' by a classificatory scheme that does not pay them any specific attention. They are often duties of (for example) considerateness, loyalty, honesty, humanity, or trustworthiness. Put less elliptically, they are duties that we have for reasons that are of special concern to considerate, loyal, honest, humane, or trustworthy people. Imagine someone who has been ripped off, who has fallen victim, say, to a scam. Suppose that she complains of the injustice of it. As with the torture victim who complains in similar terms, this complaint has some curious connotations. To my ears at least, it suggests that the victim of the scam regards herself as having been wrongly picked out for the scammer's attentions, or as having been subjected to more than her rightful share of scamming, or in some other way as having been *unduly* scammed. She does not, in other words, seem to be focusing attention on the main wrong that was done to her, namely the fact that she was scammed *tout court*. If she wanted to focus attention on that, it would be more natural for her to speak of having been a victim of dishonesty or unscrupulousness. Of course if the victim has to bear the loss while the scammer enjoys the ill-gotten gains, it would be perfectly natural to speak of *that* as an injustice. But it is not an injustice in the original scam. It is an injustice in the aftermath. It is an injustice in the fact that the scam went uncorrected—in other words a corrective injustice in the strict Aristotelian sense. For there to be corrective injustice it is not necessary that an injustice go uncorrected. All that is necessary is that there be an injustice in the non-correction of something, which need not itself be an injustice.

Take, as a slightly trickier example, a case of inconsiderate or careless driving that injures a pedestrian. The careless person is sometimes said to 'fail to take due care' and this may lead one to think of the carelessness as unjust, because undue, to those who are injured by it. But such a failure of allocation is not what the word 'due' is meant to convey here. It is meant to convey that the driver was not taking the care that befits a driver, never mind how he allocated whatever care he did take among other road users. Once again it would be odd, suggestive of an unusual kind of case, for a pedestrian who has been run over to describe this as the doing of an injustice by the driver. That description would suggest that the driver mowed down the victim in a misdirected rage, or was discriminating on improper grounds against certain road users in giving out his care and attention, or something like that. But in the normal case of a driver who is simply not paying enough attention to anyone's safety, including his own, that seems to miss the point. The problem is that the driver is careless or inconsiderate full stop, never mind whether unjustly so. Injustice is soon to be added to the mix, of course, if the pedestrian cannot get the driver or the driver's insurance company to pay up for the loss of earnings that befell him because of the careless driving. But again that injustice is not an injustice in the driving of the car, or even in the running down of the pedestrian. It is injustice in the failure to correct, to repair, to remedy, the damage thereby inflicted. It is a corrective injustice, but not one that lies in the failure to correct an injustice. Rather, it lies in the failure to correct a wrong of carelessness or inconsiderateness, whether or not it is also unjust.

Readers of Aristotle sometimes have trouble understanding how there could ever be reasons of corrective justice that do not simply boil down to reasons of distributive (or otherwise non-corrective) justice. If there is an injustice, let us say a distributive one, then it does not take a reason of corrective justice to tell us to undo it. We should undo it because *ex hypothesi* it is an injustice. If, on the other hand, there is no injustice then there is nothing, so far as justice is concerned, to undo. Either way there is no role for a distinct set of reasons of corrective justice. But the dilemma posed here is a false one. The second horn presupposes, falsely, that the only things in need of correction are injustices, or, to put it another way, that only an allocative wrong, a wrong of failure to give people their due, can give rise to a case for repair of the wrong by the wrongdoer. The just person has no particular eye for wrongdoing. That is not her distinctive department of practical life. But she has a particular eye for the secondary wrongdoing which is the non-correction of wrongdoing. That is always a problem of allocation, a problem of someone's not getting what she is due, and that kind of problem, as I have explained, is what occupies the just person's distinctive department of practical life. Her concern for correction (reparation, restitution, disgorgement) is usefully regarded as a distinct subdepartment because it involves a special kind of allocation that could have an intelligible role in practical life even if there were no other reasons of a distinctively allocative kind for her to attend to. One does not need to understand any other forms of justice in order to understand corrective justice.

Do not rights of corrective justice themselves have to be allocated? And is it not a question of distributive justice how we are going to allocate them? Not always. As we already saw, rights are not always up for allocation. Ordinary moral rights do not need to be allocated by anyone; those who have them, have them by virtue of morality itself without the intervention of an allocator. Allocative questions arise only in connection with some legal and more broadly institutional rights, when we have to decide (the question being open until we do decide) who is going to get them. So in the law, it is true, raising a question of corrective justice normally raises a question of distributive justice about how corrective justice (meaning here a legal right to it) is going to be distributed. Do trespassers get it as well as lawful visitors? Do the intended beneficiaries of a broken contract get it even when they were not parties to the contract? But even in this institutional setting, notice, there is a good deal of 'analytical convenience' in contrasting norms of corrective justice, as Aristotle does, with norms of distributive justice. Without this contrast, it is a lot less easy to distinguish the thing to be allocated (which is a right of corrective justice) from the standard of allocation (which is a standard of distributive justice). True, the rival Aquinas-Finnis classification can boast a like analytical convenience, as Finnis's justly famous discussion of bankruptcy law demonstrates. If I am right, however, this convenience in the Aquinas-Finnis classification is eclipsed by the inconvenience of its including, under the heading of 'commutative justice', many matters that are either matters of distributive justice, or not matters of justice at all but rather matters of humanity, considerateness, honesty, politeness, generosity, etc.

V. Justice in Politics, Justice in Law

I have focused here on questions about justice concerning which Finnis and I disagree, or seem to disagree. Sadly I have left too little space to highlight the many compelling things he says on the subject, several of which have had an abiding influence on me since I first became acquainted with them some 25 years ago. Allow me just to mention, in concluding, two points on which Finnis has done more than any other writer to shape my views.

First, Finnis stands up for the classical view that questions of justice arise first and foremost for each of us as ordinary moral agents, and only derivatively for political authorities and the like. Thus, *contra* Rawls, the question of what makes 'social institutions' just cannot be tackled without first tackling the question of what would make you or me just:

> [W]hat is unjust about large disparities of wealth in a community is not the inequality as such but the fact that (as the inequality suggests) the rich have failed to redistribute that portion of their wealth which could be better used by others for the realization of basic values in their own lives ... Where owners do not perform these duties, or cannot effectively co-ordinate their efforts to perform them, then public authority may rightly help them to perform their duties by devising and implementing schemes of distribution.[43]

These remarks correctly locate the theory of justice in what has now come to be known as the 'perfectionist' view of politics, according to which it is the main task of the authorities to assist us in doing what we ought to be doing anyway, and not (therefore) to stand aloof from questions about what would qualify as living well, fulfilling our potentials, treating each other well, making the most of life, aspiring to excellence, etc.

And yet, as Finnis also says, there may be a special connection between justice and the law, such that justice may strike us as the first virtue of the law, even though it strikes us as only one virtue among many for you and me, and perhaps not the one that we would most treasure among our friends and colleagues and travel agents and so forth. Why is a government department responsible for the workings of the legal system often called a 'Ministry of Justice'? Why are law courts sometimes known as 'courts of justice'? Why is legislation aimed at reform of the criminal process sometimes called a 'Criminal Justice Act'? Why not, for example, a Ministry of Kindness or a court of honesty or a Criminal Diligence Act? Here is a good answer from Finnis:

> [W]hether the subject-matter of [an] act of adjudication be a problem of distributive or commutative justice, the act of adjudication itself is always a matter for distributive justice. For the submission of an issue to the judge itself creates a kind of *common* subject-matter, the *lis inter partes*, which must be allocated between parties, the gain of one party being the loss of the other.[44]

---

[43] *NLNR*, 174 and 173. I have reversed the order of two passages here to create a composite in which Finnis's direction of argument is clearer.

[44] *NLNR*, 179.

The point is that the bringing of a moral question before the courts is a way of guaranteeing its transformation into a question of justice even if there would, outside the courts, have been plenty of other (non-allocative) ways to approach it. If that is right, then we want our judges to be just people above all, even though we would not want our doctors or our social workers or our airline pilots, let alone our friends, to be just above all. I have explored this topic in considerable detail elsewhere, without at the time acknowledging, because without at the time being aware of, my debt to Finnis.[45] His is a way of explaining, without condoning, the late 20th-century tendency to think of justice as a topic for political and legal philosophers rather than for other moral philosophers. It allows us to see why Rawls began where he did, without agreeing that it was the best way to begin. For one may be led to imagine that justice is the first virtue of social institutions in general by taking an overly juridical view of social institutions, by thinking of society as a big law court and the rest of us as parties litigating for our fair shares of some social booty. Finnis does not make this mistake. But he certainly does help us to see how others come to do so.

Bibliography

Aristotle, *Nicomachean Ethics* [no particular edition specified].

Campbell, Tom (1974) 'Humanity Before Justice', *British Journal of Political Science* 4, 1.

Finnis, John (1980) *Natural Law and Natural Rights* (Oxford: Clarendon Press) [cited as *NLNR*].

Finnis, John (1983) *Fundamentals of Ethics* (Oxford: Clarendon Press) [cited as *FoE*].

Finnis, John (1998) *Aquinas: Moral, Political, and Legal Theory* (Oxford: Oxford University Press) [cited as *Aquinas*].

Finnis, John (2011a) *Natural Law and Natural Rights* (2nd ed., Oxford: Oxford University Press) [cited as *NLNR* 2nd ed.].

Finnis, John (2011b) *Reason in Action: Collected Essays of John Finnis Volume I* (Oxford: Oxford University Press) [cited as *CEJF* I].

Finnis, John (2011c) *Human Rights and Common Good: Collected Essays of John Finnis Volume III* (Oxford: Oxford University Press) [cited as *CEJF* III].

Gardner, John (2000a) 'The Virtue of Charity and its Foils', in Charles Mitchell and Sue Moody (eds), *Foundations of Charity* (Oxford: Hart Publishing).

Gardner, John (2000b) 'The Virtue of Justice and the Character of Law', *Current Legal Problems* 53, 1.

Gardner, John (2007) *Offences and Defences: Selected Essays on the Philosophy of Criminal Law* (Oxford: Oxford University Press).

Gardner, John and François Tanguay-Renaud (2011) 'Desert and Avoidability in Self-Defense', *Ethics* 122, 111.

Hayek, Friedrich (1976) *Law, Legislation, and Liberty Volume 2: The Mirage of Social Justice* (London: Routledge and Kegan Paul).

Hurka, Thomas (2003) 'Desert: Individualistic and Holistic', in Serena Olsaretti (ed.), *Desert and Justice* (Oxford: Oxford University Press).

Miller, David (1976) *Social Justice* (Oxford: Clarendon Press).

Parfit, Derek (1997) 'Equality and Priority', *Ratio* 10, 202.

Rawls, John (1971) *A Theory of Justice* (Cambridge, MA: Harvard University Press).

Raz, Joseph (1986) *The Morality of Freedom* (Oxford: Clarendon Press).

---

[45] In Gardner, 'The Virtue of Justice and the Character of Law'.

11

Retributivism in the Spirit of Finnis[*]

Matthew H. Kramer

John Finnis's contributions to the philosophy of criminal law have received somewhat less attention than a number of his other major jurisprudential insights. This essay will highlight the virtues of his work on the central purpose of punishment, by elaborating a version of retributivism that is quite closely similar to his. My arguments are significantly different from those which Finnis presents—for example, I attach no importance whatsoever to the degree of correspondence between my positions and those advocated by Thomas Aquinas or other medieval philosophers—but the upshot of this essay is to underscore the solidity of Finnis's reflections on the moral role of punishment.

At the outset, the limits of my arguments should be stated clearly. This essay does not set out to establish that retributivism of any kind is correct as an overarching justification of punishment, nor does it even set out to establish that the general type of retributivism discussed herein—desert-focused retributivism—is superior to the principal alternative type, which concentrates on vindicating the dignity of victims rather than on offsetting the gains achieved by wrongdoers. Instead, the aim is to show that the best account of punishment within desert-focused retributivism is closely similar to the account propounded by Finnis.

I. An Opening Sketch of Desert-focused Retributivism

Nearly every theory that can correctly be classified as a specimen of retributivism is concerned with the negative deserts of people who have engaged in wrongdoing. Here, however, the epithet "desert-focused" will be reserved for retributivistic theories that devote attention chiefly to the ways in which any malefactors gain through their self-indulgent noncompliance with the legitimate criminal-law mandates of their community. Precisely because a miscreant elevates himself above his fellows and his community when he contravenes just legal requirements in order to satisfy his own impulses and desires, the administration of punishment is necessary to offset the unfair advantage that he has seized. By offsetting that advantage, the punishment reasserts the ideal of human equality which the wrongdoer has implicitly or explicitly denied through his transgression(s). In two respects, the imposition of a sanction brings the offender down to his

 * An abridged version of this essay was presented as a Royal Institute of Philosophy Lecture at the University of Hull in March 2011. I am very grateful to Antony Hatzistavrou for his organization of that event, and to the members of the audience (especially Kimberley Brownlee, Miroslav Imbrisevic, Suzanne Uniacke, and Tony Ward) for their stimulating questions. I presented a slightly revised version of the essay at a seminar in the Cardiff University Philosophy Department in August 2011. I am extremely grateful to Jules Holroyd for organizing my presentation. I am likewise obliged to her, and to Thom Brooks and Christopher Norris, for some perceptive questions.

proper level vis-à-vis the others in his society. First, by subjecting him to material hardships such as the loss of most of his freedoms, it serves in palpable ways to lessen the amenity of his everyday life. Second, it symbolizes the downfall of his effort to place himself above his fellows through his indulgence of his urges while most other people were exercising proper self-restraint, and it thereby conveys to him the impertinence of that effort. Both materially and communicatively, then, a suitable punishment counteracts the disruption of fair social relations that has been brought about by an offender's misdeed(s). It "is the healing of a disorder—precisely an unjust inequality—introduced into a whole community by the wrongdoer's criminal choice and action."[1]

Proponents of this version of retributivism have to specify the nature of the unjust inequality that has been generated by a criminal's misconduct. That is, they have to specify the nature of the unjust gain that has accrued to any wrongdoer simply by dint of his having acted athwart the terms of a morally worthy criminal-law mandate. Clearly, the relevant gain does not consist in one or more of the desiderata that can contingently be acquired through criminal endeavors, such as money or power or land or sexual gratification. Though many instances of criminal activity do endow their perpetrators with such goods, many other instances do not. (Consider, for example, bank robbers who have to abandon their loot as they begin to flee the scene of their dastardly venture.) Likewise, the relevant gain does not consist in feelings of pleasure or satisfaction resulting from the performance of a misdeed. Though many instances of criminal activity do elicit such feelings in their perpetrators, many other instances do not. Desert-focused retributivism aspires to offer a comprehensively applicable account of the grounds for inflicting punishments upon criminals within a liberal-democratic society; that aspiration will obviously go unfulfilled if the grounds adduced are in fact applicable to only some crimes. Hence, desert-focused retributivists who strive for comprehensiveness will need to look beyond the sorts of goods and feelings mentioned above—and so they have.

II. Freedom as the Unjust Gain?

Most problematic is the suggestion that the unjust gain accruing to every criminal resides in the inordinate freedom which he arrogates to himself through his lawbreaking conduct. This line of thought has been most sustainedly developed by George Sher,[2] but it has also won varying degrees of adherence from some other writers.[3] Even Russ Shafer-Landau, who objects to the line of thought, has acquiesced in certain key aspects of it.[4] Nonetheless, we should reject altogether the proposition that every

---

[1] *CEJF* III.12, 173.   [2] Sher, *Desert*, 74–90.

[3] Bradley, "Retribution and the Secondary Aims of Punishment"; Duff, "Auctions, Lotteries, and the Punishment of Attempts," 16–17; *CEJF* III.11, 162; *CEJF* III.12, 175, 176; Markel, "State, Be Not Proud," 430; Markel, "Executing Retributivism," 1186–7; Von Hirsch, "Proportionality in the Philosophy of Punishment," 266, 268.

[4] Shafer-Landau, "The Failure of Retributivism," 293, 302–3; Shafer-Landau, "Retributivism and Desert," 206. Much the same is true of Murphy, "The State's Interest in Retribution," 291. Likewise, Richard Burgh, who takes exception to desert-focused retributivism, nonetheless commits Sher's error in the second of the following two sentences: "According to [Jeffrie] Murphy, the benefit received [by any criminal] is the renouncing of the burden of self-restraint, which a violation of the law entails. I take it that this is a benefit,

violation of a criminal-law mandate bestows upon its perpetrator a quantum of extra freedom.

Sher takes as his point of departure a celebrated essay by Herbert Morris which is in many respects the fountainhead of modern desert-focused retributivism.[5] Under Morris's account of punishment, every criminal is said to have gained an unfair advantage over others by violating some legal requirement(s) within a network of such requirements that are collectively beneficial for everyone. Seeking to build upon this account, Sher has to pin down the nature of the unfair advantage that is said to be conferred by every criminal course of conduct. He submits that that unfair advantage can best be explicated along the following lines: "[A] person who acts wrongly does gain a significant measure of extra liberty: what he gains is freedom from the demands of the prohibition he violates. Because others take that prohibition seriously, they lack a similar liberty. And as the strength of the prohibition increases, so too does the freedom from it which its violation entails." Sher slightly later repeats his view that "the most plausible way of understanding [a wrongdoer's unfair extra benefit] is as an extra measure of freedom from moral restraint," and that a "wrongdoer [through his misconduct] has unfairly gained an extra measure of freedom from moral restraint."[6]

These statements by Sher are unsustainable.[7] Under any tenable conception of freedom, it is not the case that someone who transgresses a legal mandate has thereby acquired freedom from its demands. Were Sher correct, then no violation of a law would ever be a violation, since a wrongdoer would become free of a law's requirements precisely by virtue of having flouted those requirements. Only because a lawbreaker does *not* become free of the demands of a legal mandate when he contravenes them, is his contravention classifiable as such. As David Dolinko pungently observes, "there would be no basis for deciding to punish the wrongdoer if his criminal act had somehow repealed the prohibition it is alleged to violate."[8]

Sher does not improve his position when he focuses his remarks on moral restraints. Indeed, he worsens his position, for he appears to be relying on an assumption that will be briefly challenged later in this essay: namely, the assumption that everybody in a society governed by a reasonably just regime is always under a prima facie moral obligation to comply with the terms of each of the morally justified legal mandates introduced or retained by that regime. At any rate, the chief weakness that besets Sher's argument in application to moral constraints is the same as the weakness that besets the argument in application directly to legal mandates. No defensible conception of freedom would support the claim that someone who breaches a moral restriction has thereby freed herself from that restriction or from any other moral requirement. On the

---

because the offender now has a bit more freedom than those who undertook the burden of obeying the law." Burgh, "Do the Guilty Deserve Punishment?" 209.

[5] Morris, "Persons and Punishment."

[6] Sher, *Desert*, 82, 83, 84.

[7] My criticisms of Sher are prefigured by those in Dolinko, "Some Thoughts about Retributivism," 546–48, and in Dolinko, "Mismeasuring 'Unfair Advantage,'" 499–500. (In the latter work, the immediate target of Dolinko's censure is Michael Davis rather than Sher.) Dolinko's objections to Sher's analysis are recounted—but neither endorsed nor repudiated—in Davis, *Justice in the Shadow of Death*, 259.

[8] Dolinko, "Some Thoughts about Retributivism," 548.

contrary, her breach is a breach exactly because she remains subject to the violated restriction before, during, and after the occurrence of the violation. If Sher's position were correct, then anyone could come to be free from a moral requirement simply by transgressing it, and thus no transgression would ever count as such (since the sheer fact of its having happened would negate its status as a contravention). By murdering some person, anyone could liberate herself from a moral constraint against murdering that person.

The startling implications of Sher's analysis reveal the unsustainability of that analysis. Instead of becoming free from a moral restraint by doing what it forbids, an offender remains subject to that restraint, and she also incurs further moral obligations to remedy the wrong that she has perpetrated. Morally, her overall liberty is lower than before. Hence, the notion that a criminal gains an extra quantum of moral liberty whenever she commits an offense is very far indeed from the truth.

Sher cannot rescue his position by switching to a focus on physical freedom in contrast with deontic freedom.[9] That is, he cannot vindicate his analysis by concentrating on unpreventedness or abilities rather than on permissibility. Suppose that he were to be understood as claiming that a criminal always becomes physically free (that is, physically able) to commit an offense by dint of committing it, and that a criminal thereby acquires something which her law-abiding fellow citizens lack. Both of the theses in this revised claim are false.

Except in special cases, a miscreant who engages in a criminal act at some time t was physically free before t to engage in the specified act at t. Hence, the performance of a misdeed is not typically what endows a miscreant with the physical freedom to perform it; the performance is not typically what removes any physical obstacles to its own occurrence, since those obstacles were already absent. Accordingly, the first thesis in the revised claim posited above—the thesis that a criminal always becomes physically free to commit an offense by dint of committing it—is false.

Also false is the second thesis, and not only because of the falsity of the first thesis. Quite a few people in any society are physically free to engage in numerous modes of conduct that are criminally proscribed therein (even if they might be apprehended pretty quickly thereafter). Some people would of course be more adept than others at performing any of those modes of conduct, but it is certainly not the case that the only people able to perform any of them are the criminals who actually do so. People possess countless physical freedoms—including freedoms to carry out criminally forbidden acts—which they decline to exercise. Thus, the fact that a criminal has been physically free to commit a misdeed of some kind is typically not anything that sets her apart from most of the people in her society who do not commit any such misdeed.[10]

---

[9] "Physical" is not here contrasted with "mental" or "psychological." Rather, the sole contrast is with "deontic" or "normative." Someone is not physically free to ϕ unless she is psychologically capable of ϕ-ing. On the distinction between physical freedom (including psychological freedom) and deontic freedom, see Kramer, *The Quality of Freedom*, 60–75.

[10] The points in this paragraph and the preceding paragraph are missed by Don Scheid when he writes as follows: "By breaking the law, [a criminal] makes for himself opportunities not available to law-abiding persons ... [B]reaking a rule against embezzlement might create an opportunity for gaining an enormous sum of money, while breaking a law against jaywalking only creates the opportunity for realizing a very

Defenders of Sher might contend that the physical liberty newly acquired by any wrongdoer is not the liberty to perpetrate the crime which she actually does perpetrate, but instead some further physical freedom that is engendered by the wrongdoer's exercise of her liberty to carry out the aforementioned crime. Such a retort would be misguided in two respects. First, the acquisition of some further physical liberty through the commission of a criminal misdeed is contingent rather than inevitable. For example, if Joe commits assault and battery against Julia and is then forcibly apprehended straightaway, he will have lost many of his erstwhile freedoms and will not have gained any additional freedoms. Second, even when a criminal does acquire some additional freedom-to-ϕ through his criminal misconduct, numerous law-abiding people in his society might also possess the freedom to ϕ. For instance, if Bruno kills his wife in order to be able to watch a football game on television in peace, the newly acquired freedom-to-watch-the-football-game-in-peace is something that he shares with any number of law-abiding people in his society. Thus, if defenders of Sher were to engage in the maneuver suggested at the outset of this paragraph, they would be failing to specify a way in which every criminal vests herself with some liberty that is not enjoyed by her law-abiding fellow citizens.

Defenders of Sher might try instead to shift the focus from a criminal's particular liberties to her overall liberty. That is, instead of maintaining that every criminal acquires some new freedom-to-ϕ as a result of indulging in misconduct, those defenders might submit that every criminal undergoes an increase in her overall liberty through her misconduct. Any such rejoinder, however, would be a non-starter. After all, there is no guarantee that a criminal will have acquired any new physical freedom-to-ϕ whatsoever as a result of carrying out this or that crime. Under some theories of freedom (such as that espoused by Hillel Steiner),[11] the absence of such a guarantee is itself sufficient to negate any guarantee of an increase in a criminal's overall liberty. Admittedly, under the theory of freedom for which I myself have argued at length elsewhere,[12] the absence of a guarantee of the former type is *per se* not quite sufficient to preclude the existence of a guarantee of the latter type—because, under my theory, an increase in a person's overall freedom can be attributable to the replacement of an instance of unfreedom by a mere inability. In other words, somebody may have become freer overall if a particular inability of hers is no longer due to some action(s) or disposition(s) of some other person(s) but is now due decisively to natural limitations. Nevertheless, the notion that every perpetrator of a crime undergoes that sort of increase in her overall liberty by virtue of indulging in her criminal misconduct is fanciful. The occurrence of such an increase will be rare rather than inevitable. Consequently, an attempt to salvage Sher's argument by construing it as focused on every culprit's *overall* physical freedom—rather than on any *particular* physical freedom(s) of each culprit—will prove unavailing. Sher's argument does not withstand scrutiny when it is assessed in the light of any credible account of liberty.

---

minor convenience of saving a few minutes' walking time." Scheid, "Davis, Unfair Advantage Theory, and Criminal Desert," 393–4.

[11] See Steiner, "How Free."   [12] Kramer, *The Quality of Freedom*.

III. The Price of a License

Michael Davis has been a prominent and astute exponent of desert-focused retributivism since the early 1980s. He has developed a piquant thought-experiment in an attempt to pin down the nature and extent of the unfair advantage that is gained by every criminal through his or her misconduct.[13] However commendably thought-provoking Davis's exposition of the nature and extent of that unfair advantage may be, it is deeply flawed—both in itself and in its relationship with another scheme proposed by Davis for the assignment of punishments to crimes. On a number of points, my queries about his analysis are broadly in line with those of several previous critics.[14]

Davis envisages an auction in which people can bid for licenses to commit various crimes with impunity. The number of licenses for each type of crime is limited to reflect the exigencies of social cohesion. Because the especially serious crimes are more disruptive of such cohesion than are crimes that are less serious, the licenses for each of the former kinds of crimes will generally be fewer than those for each of the latter kinds. "The more serious the crime, the fewer the social order can tolerate, all else equal."[15] People can submit bids for licenses either because they wish to commit the specified crimes or because they wish to lower the incidence of those crimes by buying up the licenses. When all the bids are in, the licenses for each type of crime will have been sold at a price that can be used as a benchmark for the assignment of penalties to offenses. "A penalty is a fair price [for the commission of a crime] only if it corresponds to what a license to do that crime would fetch on the open market." Davis makes clear that the correspondence to which he here refers is a matter of proportionality rather than of commensurateness: "The correspondence is not equality but homology, a relative correspondence. There is, after all, no decisive reason that the society should choose this or that minimum of social order; nor is there any privileged rule for converting dollars into years in prison, lashes of the whip, or the like."[16]

A. A first query

One major weakness in Davis's scenario of the auction is that it has to be supplemented with some extremely dubious assumptions in order to shield it against sundry telling objections. For example, in response to queries about the commission of unlicensed crimes, Davis has to assume either that all such crimes will be punished in the same way

---

[13] Davis, "How to Make the Punishment Fit the Crime," 743–5; Davis, "Harm and Retribution," 258–60; Davis, "Criminal Desert, Harm, and Fairness," 530–1; Davis, *Justice in the Shadow of Death*, 257–80.

[14] Dolinko, "Mismeasuring 'Unfair Advantage'"; Duff, "Auctions, Lotteries, and the Punishment of Attempts," 3–17; Reiman, "Why the Death Penalty Should be Abolished in America," 75–6, 85–6; Ridge, "If the Price is Right"; Scheid, "Davis and the Unfair-advantage Theory of Punishment"; Scheid, "Davis, Unfair Advantage Theory, and Criminal Desert"; Shafer-Landau, "The Failure of Retributivism," 303–4; Shafer-Landau, "Retributivism and Desert," 206–7; Von Hirsch, "Proportionality in the Philosophy of Punishment," 265–8.

[15] Davis, "How to Make the Punishment Fit the Crime," 744.

[16] Davis, "How to Make the Punishment Fit the Crime," 745.

or that no unlicensed crimes of any sort will occur.[17] He disconcertingly explains his assumptions as follows: "The point of the assumptions defining the market is to filter out irrelevant factors. If an argument [by a critic] reveals an irrelevant factor, then I will try to filter it out."[18] When Davis fends off objections to his model by amplifying it with outlandish assumptions, his claim that the objections are concerned with "irrelevant factors" is hardly reassuring. As Dolinko acridly retorts: "Avoiding the punishment one would receive for an unlicensed crime is plainly the most important reason for buying a crime license in the first place. How, then, can Davis treat the differing punishments for unlicensed crimes as mere irrelevancies to be swept away by fiat?"[19]

B. A second query

Another major weakness in the scenario of the auction is that the rankings generated by it do not coincide with any plausible scale of the seriousness of crimes. Davis somewhat blithely asserts that "the demand for licenses is likely to increase with the seriousness of the crime." In parentheses he adds: "If that seems unlikely given moral constraints on potential buyers, ask yourself whether you would prefer to have a license to steal or a license to jaywalk."[20] Even if we were to accept these assertions by Davis entirely on their own terms, we would be well advised to note that they advert only to a likelihood rather than to any firmer correlation between the prices of the licenses and the seriousness of the crimes. What is more, the assertions are not in fact convincing. Consider, for example, instances of murder that involve cannibalism. Such crimes are more serious than ordinary murders, and *a fortiori* they are more serious than acts of grand larceny. Yet the demand for licenses to commit grand larceny will be far, far higher than the demand for licenses to commit murders that involve cannibalism. Thus, even if the latter licenses are substantially fewer in number than are the former, the strong likelihood is that the price for each of the licenses to commit cannibalistic murder will be lower than the price for each of the licenses to commit grand larceny. Accordingly, Davis is committed to the conclusion that the punitive measures imposed for cannibalistic murder should be gentler than the punitive measures imposed for grand larceny.

Davis is committed to a similar conclusion concerning cannibalistic murder versus ordinary murder. (I am assuming that a license to commit cannibalistic murder cannot be employed to gain exemption from punishment for an act of murder that is not followed by the perpetrator's consumption of the flesh of the victim.) Although the demand for licenses to commit ordinary murder might be somewhat lower than the demand for licenses to commit grand larceny, it will still be far higher than the demand for licenses to commit cannibalistic murder. Moreover, the disparity between the number of licenses to commit cannibalistic murder and the number of licenses to commit ordinary murder will be significantly narrower than the disparity between the former number and the number of licenses to commit grand larceny. Consequently,

---

[17] Davis, *Justice in the Shadow of Death*, 272, 279, n. 27.
[18] Davis, *Justice in the Shadow of Death*, 278, n. 27.
[19] Dolinko, "Mismeasuring 'Unfair Advantage,'" 504–5, footnote omitted.
[20] Davis, "How to Make the Punishment Fit the Crime," 744.

the strong likelihood is that the price for each of the licenses to commit ordinary murder will be higher than the price for each of the licenses to commit cannibalistic murder. Davis's version of retributivism thus has to call for the imposition of stiffer penalties in response to each instance of the former crime than in response to each instance of the latter.

The rankings that would emerge from Davis's auction are rendered problematic in further ways by the influence of factors that can weaken the correlation between the prices of licenses and the seriousness of crimes. To discern a principal example of those factors, we should note that the licenses in Davis's auction do not by any means guarantee that the holders thereof will be successful in their nefarious endeavors. In particular, the licenses do not shield the holders from opposition to their pursuit of their misdeeds. As Davis writes:

> A license bought at our auction guarantees only that if the holder commits the appropriate crime and is then captured, tried, convicted, and sentenced, she can hand in the license and be excused from punishment. The license pardons. It does not guarantee success (for example, that a thief will get to keep what she has stolen for more than an instant).[21]

Given that the possession of a license does not exempt its owner from interference with his wrongdoing, the potential purchasers of the licenses will *ceteris paribus* gravitate toward crimes that are less likely to be opposed and thwarted. "All else equal, [a criminal] will prefer 'easy pickings.'"[22]

In any given society, crimes of various types can be stymied (by police officers or by private citizens) more effectively than crimes of other types, and not all the latter crimes are more serious than the former. Insofar as the more serious crimes are among those that can most effectively be halted or disrupted, the consideration adduced in the preceding paragraph will skew Davis's rankings in a perverse direction. To be sure, that consideration will prevail only *ceteris paribus*. Some of the more serious crimes that can quite effectively be thwarted are probably more lucrative for their perpetrators than are some of the less serious crimes that cannot so effectively be countered. In the mind of a rational miscreant who contemplates the commission of one of those former crimes, the greater lucrativeness would partly or fully offset the unappealingness of the greater vulnerability. Nevertheless, not all the perverse skewing of Davis's rankings will be offset in that fashion.

For instance, suppose that bank robberies can effectively be scotched (or, at the very least, can be made extremely perilous for their perpetrators) through the presence of a few armed police officers or security guards in the lobby of each bank. If every bank in some society has introduced such a precaution, then the bids within the hypothetical auction for licenses to commit bank robberies in that society will tend to be very low. Suppose now that, in the same society, the crime of shoplifting is much less easily foiled. Employing the number of plain-clothes detectives required to avert most instances of that latter crime would be prohibitively expensive for any shop. Accordingly, the likelihood of one's being thwarted in one's efforts to steal goods from a shop is markedly lower than the likelihood

[21] Davis, *Justice in the Shadow of Death*, 272.
[22] Davis, *Justice in the Shadow of Death*, 270.

of one's being frustrated in one's efforts to rob money from a bank. Furthermore, even a shoplifter caught in the act does not typically face nearly the same level of danger as a bank robber who is confronted with armed policemen or security guards. Hence, although the proceeds from a successful bank robbery will normally be considerably higher than the proceeds from a successful bout of shoplifting, that disparity can be wholly or largely offset in the minds of aspiring criminals by the other disparities just mentioned (concerning the probability of success and the level of hazard). Thus, with reference to the eminently credible society that is envisaged here, the bids in Davis's auction for licenses to commit bank robberies might well be somewhat lower than the bids for licenses to carry out acts of shoplifting. At any rate, there is a strong likelihood that the former bids will not be much higher (if at all higher) than the latter. Consequently, Davis is committed to the conclusion that the punishments for acts of shoplifting in the envisaged society should be approximately the same as the punishments for bank robberies. Such a conclusion is at odds with the retributivistic principle of proportionality.

What is more, with some slight modifications, this example will reveal a further respect in which Davis's rankings can depart sharply from retributivistic principles. Suppose that, within the limits of the resources at the disposal of the merchants in some society S, the monitoring of customers is insufficient to stymie any act of shoplifting that is performed with at least a minimal degree of dexterity. The probability of success among the potential shoplifters in S is very close to 100%. Therefore, nobody or virtually nobody in S would be disposed to bid anything in a hypothetical auction for licenses to engage in the crime of shoplifting. There is no point to paying for a license of that kind when thefts of items from shops can already be carried out with no negative consequences. In application to S, then, Davis's scenario of the auction generates the conclusion that no penalty should be assigned to the crime of shoplifting. Far from making the punishment fit the crime, Davis has supplied a justificatory procedure that removes the punishment for the crime.

C. A third query

Another major problem, pointed out by most of the previous critics of Davis who were cited near the beginning of my discussion of his work, is that the outcomes of his hypothetical auction do not tally with those of another procedure (a seven-step procedure) which he proposes for the attachment of penalties to crimes. Davis insists that the results of the auction converge with those of his seven-step procedure, but his insistences are unpersuasive. Incongruities between the two procedures complicate his desert-focused version of retributivism, since the seven-step procedure—despite its limitations—is a far more plausible method for assigning punishments to crimes than is the hypothetical auction. With his adoption of the seven-step procedure, Davis adumbrates a more sophisticated understanding of the notion that the object of punitive measures is to remove unfair advantages gained by criminals through their wrongdoing.

He outlines the seven-step procedure as follows:

1. Prepare a list of penalties consisting of those evils (*a*) which no rational person would risk except for some substantial benefit and (*b*) which may be inflicted through the procedures of the criminal law.

2. Strike from the list all inhumane penalties.
3. Type the remaining penalties, rank them within each type, and then combine rankings into a scale.
4. List all crimes.
5. Type the crimes, rank them within each type, and then combine rankings into a scale.
6. Connect the greatest penalty with the greatest crime, the least penalty with the least crime, and the rest accordingly.
7. Thereafter: type and grade new penalties as in step 2 and new crimes as in step 4, and then proceed as above.[23]

As many commentators have pointed out, the paramount problem for Davis is that this procedure does not gauge the same thing that is gauged by his hypothetical auction. Whereas the latter device is supposed to measure the value placed by potential criminals on the avoidance of penalties for the commission of various crimes, the seven-step method focuses on the fearsomeness of various crimes in the eyes of potential victims. Within each category of crimes envisaged by the seven-step procedure, the offenses are to be ranked not according to the benefits which they bestow upon their perpetrators (however measured), but instead according to the assessments of those crimes by the people who might fall prey to them. As Davis writes: "The least crime [within each category] is the one a rational person would prefer to risk (all else equal) given a choice between risking it and risking any other [crime] of that type; the next least is the one a rational person would prefer to risk given a choice between it and any other of that type except the least; and so on."[24] Since there are no reasons to expect that one's ranking of crimes by reference to their fearsomeness in the eyes of potential victims will match (or even come close to matching) one's ranking of crimes by reference to their benefits in the eyes of potential malefactors, there are no reasons to think that Davis's two methods for assigning punishments to crimes will tally. The two sets of rankings will probably converge at some points, of course, but they will diverge at numerous other points. Thus, even if we leave aside all the problems that afflict each set of rankings in isolation, the incongruity between the two sets is a difficulty that confronts anyone who hopes to draw upon Davis's work for guidance in the fixing of punishments.

Davis persistently defends himself against the charge of having presented two procedures that yield dissimilar sets of rankings, as he contends that the procedures will in fact arrive at the same results. However, his arguments on that score are far from compelling. He points out that the licenses for each type of crime in his scenario of the auction are limited in ways that reflect the degree of apprehension felt by members of the public toward each type of crime. Similarly, the licenses can get purchased by people who wish to keep would-be criminals from using them. Moreover, given that a license guarantees only an ultimate pardon rather than success in the commission of a crime, a society with a crime-license auction can still aptly devote more resources to thwarting felonies than to thwarting misdemeanors.[25] In all these ways, the outcomes of the hypothetical auction are shaped by the very anxieties of the public that are taken

---

[23] Davis, "How to Make the Punishment Fit the Crime," 736–7.
[24] Davis, "How to Make the Punishment Fit the Crime," 739.
[25] Davis, *Justice in the Shadow of Death*, 266–73.

squarely into account under the seven-step procedure. Thus, Davis concludes, "our imagined [auction] and the seven-step method each reproduce the structure underlying the other." He confidently exclaims: "Contrary to what critics claimed, we have no reason to expect the two procedures to produce inconsistent results. The two are alternate ways of doing the same thing."[26]

Albeit the factors highlighted by Davis do bring the hypothetical auction closer to the seven-step method, they are not nearly enough to reconcile the results of those two approaches in all contexts. What remains true is that the latter method ranks crimes by reference to their fearsomeness in the eyes of potential victims while the former device ranks crimes partly by reference to their attractiveness in the eyes of potential perpetrators. In a wide range of contexts, then, the two procedures will fail to converge.

Let us contemplate here a somewhat modified version of an example adduced by Don Scheid for a slightly different purpose.[27] Suppose that robbery is feared by the typical person considerably more than is securities fraud, even though the latter type of crime is generally more lucrative and physically less dangerous for its perpetrators. We can suppose that the chances of being stymied are approximately equal between these two kinds of crimes. We can likewise suppose that, in the hypothetical auction, the number of licenses to commit robbery is roughly the same as the number of licenses to commit securities fraud— since the greater fearsomeness of the former crime is counterbalanced by the greater economic costliness of the latter. Thus, in application to these credible circumstances, Davis's seven-step procedure will generate the conclusion that robbery is to be punished more severely than securities fraud, whereas his hypothetical auction will generate the conclusion that securities fraud is to be punished more severely than robbery. Of course, if the specified circumstances were to be tweaked suitably, the seven-step method and the hypothetical auction could be made to tally. However, the point is precisely that the reconcilability of the two procedures will be dependent on the contingencies of various situations. In a wide range of circumstances, the two methods lead to divergent results (and sometimes even to starkly opposed results, as in this paragraph's example).

D. A fourth query

Let us now ponder an even more sweeping objection to Davis's scenario of the auction for crime-licenses. This objection, adeptly pressed by Scheid,[28] contests the very coherence of Davis's scenario by showing that it has to presuppose the schedule of punishments which it is designed to establish. To see why the hypothetical auction is afflicted by vicious circularity, we should attend more closely to what the bidders in the auction are seeking to purchase.

When somebody bids in the auction for a license to commit a crime of some kind, she is endeavoring to acquire a pardon that will enable her to avoid punishment for the perpetration of that crime. (Let us leave aside here the potential victims who bid for licenses in order to prevent villainous people from obtaining them. Any complications

---

[26] Davis, *Justice in the Shadow of Death*, 269.
[27] Scheid, "Davis, Unfair Advantage Theory, and Criminal Desert," 394–5.
[28] Scheid, "Davis, Unfair Advantage Theory, and Criminal Desert," 395–7.

arising from such bids will hardly redound to Davis's benefit.) Thus, in addition to some important ancillary concerns such as the likelihood of one's being thwarted in one's criminality and the danger posed to oneself by one's undertaking of that criminality, two main factors will determine the size of anybody's bid for some license: (1) the favorableness or unfavorableness of her attitude toward committing the type of crime that is covered by the license; and (2) the importance to her of avoiding the sanctions that are attached to that type of crime.

My discussion so far has concentrated solely on the first of those main factors along with the ancillary concerns. That first main factor is indeed of great significance. If somebody is not at all disposed to engage in armed robbery, for example, he will not submit any bid for a license to commit armed robbery. Similarly, if he is only weakly tempted to engage in armed robbery, he will not be willing to pay very much for such a license. Still, weighty though those considerations are in influencing the size of a person's bid, the role of the second main factor enumerated above is also crucial.

Suppose that Marvin is quite strongly attracted to the prospect of carrying out an armed robbery. Before he can informedly submit a bid for a license to commit such a crime, he needs to know the severity of the sanctions that will be avoided through his possession of the license. If the likely term of imprisonment for somebody convicted of armed robbery is one week, then Marvin will be far less strongly disposed to expend large quantities of money on a license than he will if the likely term of imprisonment for somebody so convicted is ten years. Thus, until Marvin knows the magnitude of the penalty from which he will be gaining an exemption through his purchase of a license, he does not have any informed basis for deciding how much to bid. He does not know what he will be buying. A parallel point applies, naturally, to everyone else who is at all inclined to bid for any of the licenses in Davis's auction. Information concerning the sanctions attached to each type of crime must be available to the parties who participate in the auction, if their bids are to be more than groundless conjectures. Without such information, the participants in the auction will not know what they are seeking to purchase.

Accordingly, before the parties in the hypothetical auction can reasonably bid for any crime-licenses, they need to know the sizeableness of the penalties from which those licenses will shield them. What is so problematic for Davis, of course, is that the parties' bids are supposed to serve as the basis for fixing the levels of those penalties. His scenario of the auction, despite its initial plausibility, has turned out to be incoherent.

IV. Self-indulgence

More promising than either Sher's focus on freedom or Davis's scenario of an auction is the proposition that the gain accruing to every criminal by virtue of his or her wrongdoing consists in self-indulgence. Nevertheless, this proposition has to be construed carefully. Understood as a rather facile claim, the proposition is plainly unsustainable and has rightly been derided by critics of retributivism. Understood as a more subtle claim, however, the thesis concerning self-indulgence is the best means of upholding desert-focused retributivism as a credible theory of punishment. To be sure, such a theory is scarcely unproblematic and in particular is incapable of justifying the use of capital punishment (a fact that will not trouble most of the theory's proponents). All the same, it is considerably more powerful as a general theory of punishment than are any of the alternative varieties of desert-focused retributivism. Before we examine the preferable rendering of the thesis about self-indulgence, we should briefly probe the more dubious rendering for which it might be mistaken.

A. A manifestly unsustainable version of the thesis

When desert-focused retributivists contend that the unjust advantage gained by every criminal through his or her wrongdoing is self-indulgence, they might be understood as asserting that every criminal through his or her misconduct has forgone the disagreeable burdens of law-abidance that are borne by everyone else. According to such a thesis, the unfair gain arising from every instance of criminality consists in an escape from the hardships involved in hewing to legal requirements. While other people toil strenuously to comply with those requirements, a criminal indulges himself by laying aside such toil. Unlike his fellow citizens, he does not undertake the hard work of stifling the propensities to which the law forbids him to succumb.

When the proposition about the self-indulgence of criminals is elaborated along these lines, it is highly vulnerable to the sorts of objections that have been raised against it by Richard Burgh and David Dolinko and other critics of retributivism.[29] They have pointed out that the vast majority of people are much less strongly inclined to engage in monstrous crimes such as cannibalistic murder than to undertake far milder crimes such as tax evasion or speeding or shoplifting. For nearly everyone, abstaining from the perpetration of cannibalistic murder is utterly effortless, whereas abstaining from the perpetration of the milder crimes just mentioned is often a matter of conscious self-discipline. Thus, if we were to accept the preceding paragraph's analysis of the unfair advantage that is gained by every criminal through his or her wrongdoing, we would be committed to the conclusion that somebody who performs an act of cannibalistic murder has thereby attained a much smaller unfair advantage than has somebody who drives above the speed limit or who understates his income on his tax return. Ergo, a cannibalistic murderer would deserve a much lighter sentence than would someone convicted of speeding or of tax evasion. Such a conclusion is patently ridiculous, and Burgh and Dolinko are right to dismiss it. If desert-focused retributivism is to be strengthened through its drawing of attention to the self-indulgence of criminals, such a reorientation cannot concentrate on the intensity of people's desires to commit misdeeds of various types.

B. A tenable version of the thesis

Instead of adverting to the greater or lesser intensity of people's proclivities to engage in sundry criminal activities, the advocates of desert-focused retributivism should advert to the gravity of those activities. By so doing, they will be addressing the extent to which

---

[29] Burgh, "Do the Guilty Deserve Punishment?" 207–10; Dolinko, "Some Thoughts about Retributivism," 545–6; Murphy, "The State's Interest in Retribution," 290.

those activities deviate from norms of law-abidingness and non-injuriousness. Subject to some qualifications that will be noted shortly, the extent of the deviation from those norms that is entailed by any given act of criminality is what constitutes the degree of self-indulgence that has been exercised by the culprit who has performed the specified act. The size of the deviation is the size of the unfair gain or advantage which the culprit has acquired simply by virtue of carrying out the crime that he has committed. Whether he has also benefited in other ways—by experiencing some feelings of gratification, for example—is neither here nor there, for the purposes of desert-focused retributivists. Any such additional benefits might appropriately be handled by non-punitive legal proceedings (restitutionary legal proceedings, for instance), but the punishments in a desert-focused system of criminal justice are designed to nullify the unfair gains that are intrinsic to criminal wrongdoing.

When somebody perpetrates a criminal act, he uses his body and other objects or persons in ways that are legally proscribed. His maneuvering of his body and other objects or persons through regions of space is such as to be eschewed by everybody who wants to avoid contravening any legal requirements. By going ahead with such maneuvering despite its being forbidden, a criminal gains something valuable that is not likewise gained by any law-abiding citizen, and he thereby obtains an advantage over all law-abiding citizens. His manipulation of his body and other objects or persons through regions of space is valuable not because he relishes it (though, of course, many criminals do relish what they have done), but precisely because that manipulation of his body and other objects or persons is legally forbidden. Since he has not rendered his conduct legally permissible by securing a change in the law or by purchasing a special exemption from the requirement(s) which he has breached, his employment of his body and other objects or persons through portions of space has temporarily misappropriated those very portions of space. Because law-abiding citizens have not engaged in any similar misappropriations, he has placed himself at an advantage vis-à-vis them. That advantage obtains even if his criminal endeavors are thwarted and come to nought. Regardless of whether he gets and retains any other advantages from those endeavors, the aforementioned misappropriation is what sets him apart from law-abiding citizens and is what renders him liable to punishment. It is the gain intrinsic to every act of criminal wrongdoing.

The extent of that gain is determined not by the sizeableness of the portions of space that have been misappropriated, but by the gravity of the purposes to which they have been put.[30] The more seriously wrong those purposes are, the greater the value of the misappropriation. To see this point, we need to attend to the distinction between offer prices and asking prices. An offer price is the maximal amount that someone is able and willing to pay in order to acquire something, whereas an asking price is the minimum amount that someone would demand in return for transferring something

---

[30] Although I refer to illegitimate purposes here and elsewhere in this discussion, my remarks are not confined to intentional wrongdoing. Criminality impelled by any culpable frame of mind is covered by my discussion.

to somebody else.[31] Among the many other shortcomings in Davis's scenario of the hypothetical auction is his assumption that the offer prices of the bidders for licenses are the dispositive indicators of the value of the unfair advantages that are gained by criminals. Rather, the value of any criminal's misappropriation is determined by its asking price within the society where his crime occurs. In other words, it is determined by the amount that would be demanded by the society in return for allowing the criminal to go ahead. Of course, I am not here suggesting that anything akin to the scenario of the hypothetical auction should be reintroduced with a focus on asking prices rather than offer prices. That scenario suffers from too many major weaknesses to be worth reviving in any form. Instead, the point here resides simply in observing that there is quite a straightforward sense in which the portions of space temporarily misappropriated by a criminal are valuable. Had the criminal temporarily acquired those portions of space for his purposes through some sort of exemption-procuring payment that could meet the society's asking price, the acquisition would have cost him dearly indeed. In exactly that sense, the value of his misappropriation is given by the seriousness of his crime.

Indeed, with the shift from offer prices to asking prices, the version of desert-focused retributivism recounted here is quite close to Davis's seven-step method rather than to his hypothetical auction. On the one hand, *pace* the seven-step method, the objective seriousness of various crimes does not necessarily accord fully with the extent to which those crimes are respectively feared by members of the public. On the other hand, the seriousness will indeed correspond closely (even though not always fully) to the fear. At any rate, what is common to the seven-step procedure and the version of desert-focused retributivism just described is their recognition that the value of a criminal's unfair gain is to be gauged from a societal perspective rather than from the perspective of the criminal.

One notable feature of this reconception of desert-focused retributivism, indeed, is that it clearly differentiates criminal law from tort law by concentrating on the unfairness of any crime toward a society as an overarching unit. Though every crime that victimizes some individual(s) is of course directly harmful and unjust to any such individual(s), the injustice rectified in a desert-focused system of criminal law is that which has been committed against the whole community whose normative protection of the victimized individual(s) has been flouted. When a criminal employs his own body and certain other objects or persons through regions of space in furtherance of his nefarious purposes, he contravenes that normative protection and thus perpetrates an injury against the community as a whole (irrespective of whether he succeeds, even briefly, in realizing his objectives). Punishment rectifies that injury by imposing on the wrongdoer a disadvantage—in the form of imprisonment or some other disciplinary measure—that counterbalances the valuable advantage which he has gained simply by dint of pursuing his criminal purposes. It counterbalances that advantage by resubordinating the criminal's wrongful ends to the community's proper ends.

---

[31] In quite a different context, the offer/asking distinction is explored at length in Kennedy, "Cost-Benefit Analysis of Entitlement Problems," 401–21. I myself have invoked that distinction in a context more closely relevant to the present discussion, in Kramer, *In the Realm of Legal and Moral Philosophy*, 142–3.

Although Finnis intermittently writes as if he were in agreement with Sher's mis-conceived account of the unfair advantage gained by every criminal, his overall exposition of that advantage is in fact along the lines elaborated here.[32] His exposition highlights the egalitarian impetus of desert-focused retributivism, as he affirms that the role of desert-focused punishments is "to maintain a rational order of proportionate equality, or fairness, as between all members of the society."[33] Despite his occasional lapses into Sher's language, Finnis usually makes clear that it is a criminal's self-indulgence—rather than some extra share of freedom supposedly accruing to a criminal—that constitutes the gain which is intrinsic to every offense and which is properly counteracted through punishment. As he writes: "Punishment does not negate the crime, but it does negate, cancel out, the advantage the offender gained in the crime—the advantage not necessarily of loot or psychological satisfaction, but of having pursued one's own purposes even when the law required that one refrain from doing so."[34] By reasserting the priority of a community's moral purposes over the malign purposes of a criminal, punishment restores the fair social arrangements that have been disrupted by the criminal's wrongdoing: "What is done cannot be undone. But punishment rectifies the disturbed pattern of advantages and disad-vantages throughout a community by depriving the convicted criminal of his freedom of choice, proportionately to the degree to which he had exercised his freedom, his personality, in the unlawful act."[35] Hence, the aim of punishment based on desert-focused retributivism lies in "restoring equality between offenders and [the] law-abiding, and cancelling the wrongdoer's unfair profit (advantage over them)."[36]

Again, the restorative role expounded here by Finnis is distinct from the restorative role of awards of damages in tort law. Damages are awarded against tortfeasors to compensate their immediate victims for the harms which those victims have suffered. By contrast, punishments—according to desert-focused retributivists—are imposed upon criminals to repair any serious disruptions of a society's moral order and to uphold the egalitarianism of its social and economic relationships. Though the extent of the harm inflicted by a crime on any immediate victim(s) is a key determinant of the crime's gravity and consequently of the magnitude of its damage to a society's moral order, the punishment imposed in response to a crime is undertaken on behalf of the entire society rather than specifically on behalf of the immediate victim(s). Any such victim V stands to benefit from the subjection of the crime's perpetrator to punitive measures, of course, but the benefit accrues to V in her status as a member of a moral community rather than in her status as an immediate victim. Every other member of the moral community benefits likewise, as the priority of the com-munity's upright purposes over the nefarious purposes of a criminal is reasserted. Far from being a doctrine of revenge, desert-focused retributivism is a doctrine of impersonal justice.

---

[32] *CEJF* III.11; *NLNR*, 262–4; *CEJF* III.12.
[33] *NLNR*, 262.   [34] *CEJF* III.12, 177.
[35] *NLNR*, 263, footnote omitted.   [36] *CEJF* III.12, 177.

C. Some qualifications

If desert-focused retributivism is to partake of any credibility as an account of the worthy purposes of punishment, it has to be qualified in a few important respects. For one thing, its pertinence in application to any given society is dependent in two ways on the realization of liberal-democratic ideals. First, the saliently egalitarian tenor of desert-focused retributivism confines its justificatory reach to liberal-democratic societies. Only in such a society is the ideal of human equality realized sufficiently to render germane the proposition that punitive measures serve to effectuate that very ideal.[37] Only in such a society do the citizens form a moral community of the sort envisaged by desert-focused retributivists when they ascribe to punishment the role of restoring a society's moral order.

Second, desert-focused retributivism as a theory of punishment has to be combined with a suitable liberal-democratic theory of criminalization, if it is to respond adequately to objections that have been raised by critics of retributivism. For example, as Dolinko and Shafer-Landau have separately contended, desert is not in itself the key to legal punishment; somebody can deserve to suffer for his or her misdeeds even though the imposition of legal punishments for those misdeeds would be morally untenable.[38] Suppose that Mark has callously jilted his long-time lover Jane for a younger woman or for some other selfish reason. Although Jane may well feel devastated by her lover's abandonment of her, and although Mark undoubtedly deserves to receive his come-uppance for his unfeeling treatment of her, the subjection of him to criminal penalties for his misbehavior would be morally unsustainable—and not only because his conduct has in fact violated no criminal prohibitions. Even if there were a criminal-law mandate forbidding any callous and selfish rebuffing of one's lover, neither the punishment of Mark nor the punishment of anyone else under that mandate would be morally appropriate. Desert-focused retributivism cannot in itself account for the moral illegitimacy of subjecting Mark or anybody else to punishment under the imagined mandate. To account for that point, a liberal-democratic theory of criminalization is needed. When the laws in a system of governance conform to the prescriptions of such a theory, Dolinko's and Shafer-Landau's worries about the gap between somebody's deserving to suffer and somebody's deserving to undergo legal punishment will have been accommodated and defused. In other words, a necessary condition for the satisfactoriness of desert-focused retributivism as an account of the worthy ends of punishment is that it be conjoined with a liberal-democratic theory of criminalization. Only when it is so conjoined, and only when the notion of negative desert which it invokes is understood to be trained solely on breaches of criminal-law prohibitions, does the doctrine of desert-focused retributivism adequately overcome the problem broached by Dolinko and Shafer-Landau.

A further qualification is needed, however. As elaborated so far, the doctrine of desert-focused retributivism appears to presuppose that everyone within the jurisdiction of a

---

[37] For a suggestion along these lines, see *NLNR*, 263, n. 1.

[38] Dolinko, "Some Thoughts about Retributivism," 542–4; Shafer-Landau, "The Failure of Retributivism," 289–92.

liberal-democratic regime is under a moral obligation to comply with each of the regime's legal mandates in all circumstances to which any such mandate is applicable. Yet, as I have argued elsewhere,[39] there can be circumstances in which somebody does not have any ethical reason at all—much less any moral obligation—to comply with a particular benign legal mandate promulgated by a liberal-democratic regime. Hence, as a justificatory account of the role of punishment, desert-focused retributivism pertains only to situations in which people are indeed under moral obligations to comply with the terms of the benign legal mandates which they contravene.[40] Extended to a situation in which somebody is not under a moral obligation of that kind, desert-focused retributivism would call for the imposition of a punitive measure when no such measure is legitimate. Hence, if this species of retributivism is to retain credibility as a justificatory doctrine, its sphere of application must be delimited in the manner suggested here.

Bibliography

Bradley, Gerard. 1999. "Retribution and the Secondary Aims of Punishment." 44 *American Journal of Jurisprudence* 105–23.

Burgh, Richard. 1982. "Do the Guilty Deserve Punishment?" 79 *Journal of Philosophy* 193–210.

Davis, Michael. 1983. "How to Make the Punishment Fit the Crime." 93 *Ethics* 726–52.

Davis, Michael. 1986. "Harm and Retribution." 15 *Philosophy and Public Affairs* 236–66.

Davis, Michael. 1991. "Criminal Desert, Harm, and Fairness." 25 *Israel Law Review* 524–48.

Davis, Michael. 1996. *Justice in the Shadow of Death*. Lanham, MD: Rowman & Littlefield.

Dolinko, David. 1991. "Some Thoughts about Retributivism." 101 *Ethics* 537–59.

Dolinko, David. 1994. "Mismeasuring 'Unfair Advantage': A Response to Michael Davis." 13 *Law and Philosophy* 493–524.

Duff, R.A. 1990. "Auctions, Lotteries, and the Punishment of Attempts." 9 *Law and Philosophy* 1–37.

Kennedy, Duncan. 1981. "Cost-Benefit Analysis of Entitlement Problems: A Critique." 33 *Stanford Law Review* 387–445.

Kramer, Matthew. 1999a. *In Defense of Legal Positivism*. Oxford: Oxford University Press.

Kramer, Matthew. 1999b. *In the Realm of Legal and Moral Philosophy*. London: Macmillan Press.

Kramer, Matthew. 2003. *The Quality of Freedom*. Oxford: Oxford University Press.

Markel, Dan. 2005. "State, Be Not Proud: A Retributivist Defense of the Commutation of Death Row and the Abolition of the Death Penalty." 40 *Harvard Civil Rights-Civil Liberties Law Review* 407–80.

Markel, Dan. 2009. "Executing Retributivism: *Panetti* and the Future of the Eighth Amendment." 103 *Northwestern University Law Review* 1163–222.

Morris, Herbert. 1968. "Persons and Punishment." 52 *Monist* 475–501.

Murphy, Jeffrie. 1994. "The State's Interest in Retribution." 5 *Journal of Contemporary Legal Issues* 283–98.

Reiman, Jeffrey. 1998. "Why the Death Penalty Should be Abolished in America." In Louis Pojman and Jeffrey Reiman, *The Death Penalty: For and Against*. Lanham, MD: Rowman & Littlefield, pp. 67–132.

---

[39] Kramer, *In Defense of Legal Positivism*, 285–7.

[40] In some contexts, such obligations can obtain simply because noncompliance with the terms of certain benign legal mandates would foster disrespect for the law generally (either on the part of the noncompliant person or on the part of other people). However, it is not the case that violations of such mandates always produce—or are always likely to produce—some effects of that kind or any other detrimental effects.

Ridge, Michael. 2004. "If the Price is Right: Unfair Advantage, Auctions, and Proportionality." 3 *APA Newsletter on Philosophy and Law* 81–6.

Scheid, Don. 1990. "Davis and the Unfair-advantage Theory of Punishment: A Critique." 18 *Philosophical Topics* 143–70.

Scheid, Don. 1995. "Davis, Unfair Advantage Theory, and Criminal Desert." 14 *Law and Philosophy* 375–409.

Shafer-Landau, Russ. 1996. "The Failure of Retributivism." 82 *Philosophical Studies* 289–316.

Shafer-Landau, Russ. 2000. "Retributivism and Desert." 81 *Pacific Philosophical Quarterly* 189–214.

Sher, George. 1987. *Desert*. Princeton, NJ: Princeton University Press.

Steiner, Hillel. 1983. "How Free: Computing Personal Liberty." In A. Phillips-Griffiths (ed.), *Of Liberty*. Cambridge: Cambridge University Press, pp. 73–89.

Von Hirsch, Andrew. 1990. "Proportionality in the Philosophy of Punishment: From 'Why Punish?' to 'How Much?'" 1 *Criminal Law Forum* 259–90.

12

The Nature of Limited Government

*Leslie Green**

I. Thoreau's Motto

Henry David Thoreau said he endorsed the motto, 'That government is best which governs least.'[1] Before we could decide whether to join him we would have to know what the motto means. What would it be for a government to 'govern least'? That cannot refer to the amount of governing it does. A minimal state, on the usual view, enforces contracts without regard to their terms, for example, it enforces exploitive and unfair contracts along with the others, provided only the deals were free and informed. But to enforce both unfair and fair contracts does not involve less governing than it does to enforce fair ones only. Or again, some who declare themselves opposed to government interference think people should have the right not be insured against ill-health or poverty in old age. Securing that right may require a lot of government activity, for example, in preventing executives or legislatures from insuring people or imposing obligations of self-insurance, or in limiting the power of collective agreements to impose them on dissenting union members. Think what you like about the merits of such policies, there is no doubt that enforcing contracts, voiding provisions of collective agreements, and striking down legislation are ways of governing, and of governing fairly vigorously.

Nor do we get a better handle on limited government if we turn to the considerations Thoreau offers in favour of his motto. He says, 'Government is at best but an expedient but most governments are usually, and all governments are sometimes, inexpedient.'[2] If that were true it would not argue in favour of limitations on government. After all, if a government is *usually* inexpedient—if its actions are generally pointless, unwise, or unjust—then it should not be trying to govern in some special way ('minimally'), it should not be governing at all. Comprehensive failure at its tasks undermines the legitimacy of a state across the board: a government that persistently gets things wrong should stand aside. As Thoreau says, all governments sometimes do things that are inexpedient. But it is unclear what that establishes. It does not show that they could do better by backing off. The income tax systems of all modern states contain significant unfairness; it does not follow that by not enforcing the tax code or by abolishing income tax we would improve things.

* I thank Denise Réaume for criticism of an earlier draft of this essay, and I thank John Finnis for many years of example, instruction, and disagreement.
[1] Thoreau, 'Civil Disobedience', 224.
[2] Thoreau, 'Civil Disobedience', 224.

It is true that if a government is doing a particular inexpedient thing then to stop doing that thing stops *that* inexpediency (as done by them, on that occasion). But stopping may cause a new inexpediency, or may allow others to cause one, and these may be worse than the inexpediency we stopped. The underlying point is put well by John Finnis:

> Being 'limited' is only to a limited extent a desirable characteristic of government anyway: bad and powerful people and groups want government limited so that they can bully and exploit the weak, or simply enjoy their wealth untroubled by care for others. So 'limited' cannot be a framework term like 'just'.[3]

The key idea here is both correct and important. There is a difference between the idea of justice and the idea of limited government: A government that becomes more just necessarily becomes, as far as justice goes, a better government.[4] A government that becomes more limited does not necessarily become a better government in any morally relevant way. That depends on what its limitations are.

In the liberal tradition limited government is an ideal. This shows that the limits in question are not quantitative—it is not simply the idea of a government that is, by some metric or other, inactive. It is an ideal defined by certain *kinds* of governance. Here, I explore some of its aspects. I am not going defend a substantive view about proper state action—I will not examine how far governments should regulate the banks or the personal lives of their subjects, or whether they should intervene in the affairs of foreign countries. When it is useful to have some examples, I will draw on what are, I hope, uncontroversial ones. My interests are structural: What is the source of the relevant limits on government—are they practical, principled, or some combination of the two? What is their stringency—are there 'absolute' limits to government activity and if so, what is their basis? How, if at all, could a case be made for having spheres of activity free from political regulation? Much of what I have to say should, I hope, sound familiar, for I am trying to articulate some aspects of a familiar tradition. I conclude with a few thoughts about the relationship between that tradition and another one that is sometimes called 'natural law' theory.

II. Aspects of a Political Tradition

Not all limits on government belong to the liberal tradition of 'limited government'. Let's start by noticing some that are more generic, before identifying two that are more or less indigenous to it.

A doctrine of limited government is part of the theory of political legitimacy. It maintains that the authority of states is legitimate only when it keeps within bounds. Here, 'legitimacy' has its full-blooded normative sense, meaning rule that is morally justified, and not merely its juridical sense of 'legally valid' or its sociological sense of 'widely accepted'. The law may permit government that is atrociously immoral; the

---

[3] *CEJF* III.5, 83.
[4] I say 'as far as justice goes' because justice should sometimes be sacrificed to other virtues in politics, such as humanity or generosity.

people may unquestioningly approve it. Limited government is therefore not the same as either constitutionalism or democracy, even if it is a common hope that these are not only mutually compatible, but also mutually supporting.

All that is correct as far as it goes, but the idea that the authority of states has moral limits is common to most political philosophies and does not pick out what is distinctive in limited government. Almost everyone—Thomas Hobbes—holds that political authority is subject to limitation. This is because whatever considerations are taken to justify authority may fail to apply and, where they do, government should not act authoritatively.

It is tempting to say that limited government is distinguished by its advocacy of principled, not merely practical, limits on authority. This distinction is a blurry one, however. Some writers use 'practical' to refer neutrally to de facto limitations on political power, things governments cannot manage to pull off, or cannot get away with. John Stanton-Ife treats as 'practical' limitations any normative limitations that do not depend on what John Rawls and his followers call 'public' reason.[5] This would make all instrumental or efficiency based limits on government 'practical'. I tend to think the distinction is not very helpful, because it is a feature of the sort of activity that constitutes governing that de facto limitations are normatively relevant. Governing is an activity that is subject to a success condition: you should not undertake it unless you have a reasonable chance of doing so successfully. In this way governing is different from playing the flute or cricket, which can be done for fun, or to pass time, no matter how badly you play. But many people depend on the activities of governments: they can be helped or harmed by them, and that being so, governing that is likely to fail at its aims, or backfire, or be disastrously inefficient is not just impractical, it is unprincipled, for it violates a principle to which all governments should conform. It is unprincipled for government to be impractical.

Many important limitations on government flow from this consideration. Take the principle of effectiveness: government should not act where it cannot do so effectively. No limitation on state action is more wide-ranging. It is the kernel of good sense in Thoreau's slogan. But it is not the key to the limited-government tradition. That tradition is concerned with limits that either have a different foundation or, if ultimately founded in effectiveness, coalesce into principles that are referred to and used independently of it. It is one thing to hold, with Aquinas, that prostitution should be tolerated because 'If you do away with harlots, the world will be convulsed with lust.'[6] It is another thing to hold that the state has no business regulating consensual sexual activity among adults. The second sort of argument, and not the first, is a marker of limited government, and that is the sort of view I am trying to epitomize here.

So this is not an analysis of the concept of limits on government: the bar on ineffective action is a limit. We are not analysing a concept that has a clear structure; we are dealing with a loose but recognizable political tradition that treats certain kinds of limits as especially important. It is a tradition concerned to identify constraints that lie upstream of any argument to justify authority, and not just with the

---

[5] Stanton-Ife, 'The Limits of Law'.
[6] *ST* II-II, q 10 a 11 (He is here quoting Augustine, *De Ordine* 11.4).

gaps in political authority that lie downstream of a justification, in the areas where it fails to hold. The most important upstream constraints are these:

(1) Protected Sphere: Certain decisions and activities are to be reserved for individuals and groups, especially those that involve matters important to their moral independence and autonomy. These are protected by familiar individual and collective rights, but not only by them. They are also protected more diffusely by political support for an atmosphere of toleration, especially the toleration of social difference, which supplements and secures rights to shape one's own life.

(2) Restricted Means: Even when the government acts to regulate matters outside the protected sphere, it should do so through certain modalities only. It should govern (mainly) through law and when it does so it should control law-making by the cluster of ideals we call 'the rule of law': its laws should be such that they can actually be followed by their subjects. Hence, they must be knowable, clear, consistent, prospective, and so forth. And, relatedly, law should address its subjects as responsible agents who are capable of conforming to its directives, not merely as patients who need to be incentivized this way or that by coercive force. Limited governments use coercive means sparingly, and mostly for purposes of giving assurance rather than providing motivation.

Although those constraints are, over a range, mutually supporting, they are essentially independent of each other. No doubt there are certain rights that government under the rule of law will not violate (for instance, the right to have a fair opportunity to conform to the law, or to be treated just as anyone similarly situated would be treated). But gross invasions of personal liberty can be effected by laws that are general, clear, prospective, and so forth. And an overweening concern for legality in government may interfere with the protection of other rights. There are remedies for wrongful injury that are adequate only when retrospective in character. There are fundamental human interests that can be protected only by rights whose formulations are bound to be vague (e.g. a right to 'equal protection' of the law, a right to 'dignity').

Two further points. First, in speaking of these as 'upstream constraints'—with its possible flavour of deontological 'side-constraints'—it may seem I have turned my back on instrumental justifications of political authority. Not so. The idea is that in a view of government limited by a protected sphere and the rule of law any instrumental justifications must work within those constraints. There are certainly instrumental justifications for some kinds of political authority. For example, there are what I have elsewhere called 'task-efficacy' considerations: the state has some morally urgent tasks to perform, and it is well-placed to perform them if people take its requirements as binding.[7] The two constraints help specify the relevant tasks and the ways they may and may not be performed. Moreover, the existence of upstream constraints does not exclude the possibility that there are deeper instrumental arguments in favour of the constraints themselves: I shall give an example of one below.

---

[7] See Green, 'The Duty to Govern'. I do not think a task-efficacy argument can ground all of the permissible regulatory authority of the state, nor do I think that it is sufficient to establish a general duty to obey the law, but I cannot go into that here.

Second, I have framed the constraints as if they are both matters of law, and thus as if the idea of limited government is the idea of *legally* limited government. For most purposes that is a fair working assumption. But there are no doubt exceptions, and the extent to which the limits need to be realized through law (as opposed to social custom or convention) let alone through any particular legal institutions (such as bills of rights, specialized courts, judicial review, etc.) is a variable matter. It depends on whether we are trying to establish limited government afresh, say, after revolution or conquest or the collapse of a traditional society, or whether we are trying to sustain a form of government that has evolved in a stable political culture. The rule of law may some-times need explicit constitutional devices, for example, a separation of powers, or specific legal remedies against secret, vague, or retrospective laws. At other times the culture of legality may be sufficiently pervasive that the ordinary operations of govern-ment are likely to conform to it anyway.

III. Exceptionless Limitations

So limited government is an ideal according to which political authority ought to respect the protected sphere and ought to be subject to the rule of law. It may seem I have missed something important. Is it not also part of this tradition that these limits on government are, if not utterly inviolable, then at least very stringent? And if it is, does that not commit us to certain moral assumptions, for instance, that there are absolute rights? I think it is more complex than that.

To begin with, it follows from what I said about the relationship between the rule of law and the protected sphere that the requirement of legality cannot be absolute—that would lead us to violate the protected sphere if the law required it. An elementary idea of the rule of law is that the law is to be applied and obeyed. But '*dura lex, sed lex*' is a poor motto for anyone who also cares about moral rights. In any case, the rule of law is a multi-factor ideal and its various elements may conflict with each other. Laws should be prospective and clear; they should also be stable over time. Some are so retroactive or vague that they should be changed. That will bring instability. It does, however, seem plausible to think that there may be 'unconditional, exceptionless limitations on government'[8] with respect to the protected sphere, as Finnis thinks there are with respect to inviolable rights, including those protected by the following injunctions: 'no intentional killing of the innocent, no rape, no lies, no non-penal enslavement'.[9]

Finnis's case for such unconditional limitations on government rests on his thinking that they track absolute moral requirements, together with the view that governments are not entitled to any exemption from them: there is no '*raison d'état*' that can license serious evil. Of course, this will not be a matter of simply mapping moral absolutes onto legal duties or disabilities. The former need to be made determinate. If there is to be an absolute ban on 'torture' or on the establishment of 'religion', we will need

---

[8] *CEJF* III.5, 86.
[9] *CEJF* III.5, 85. But does the ban only on 'non-penal enslavement' allow an implicit exception? Sexual assault is also widespread in our prisons, and officials often turn a blind eye to it. But we would not say there is to be no 'non-penal rape'.

working definitions of 'torture' or 'religion' and that notoriously opens the door to deliberate manipulation, and also to the milder vice of formalism, with or without the kind of self-deception that often papers it over. We can certainly put on a show of applying an absolute norm that says 'Congress shall pass *no law* abridging freedom of speech', but only under the cover of maintaining that fraud, libel, incitement, obscenity, and so on are not really 'speech' at all. Sometimes fictive absolutisms are harmless—free speech absolutism probably is, since no one takes it seriously anyway—but they can also be morally distracting. Consider Aquinas's attempt to preserve the absolute form of the directive, 'Thou shalt not steal.' Aquinas acknowledges that necessity gives people a moral claim on other's property. He allows that if someone is in manifest and dire need and cannot otherwise survive, 'then it is lawful for a man to succour his own need by means of another's property, by taking it either openly or secretly, *nor is this properly speaking theft or robbery*'.[10] The substantive judgment is correct, but it is hard to resist the feeling that we are witnessing what Mill calls a 'useful accommodation of language' that merely keeps up the appearance of indefeasibility.[11]

This is not the place to test the credentials of putatively absolute moral norms. I want to suggest, however, that the justification for absolute constraints on government, including absolute constitutional constraints, does not depend on them. There can be reasons to promulgate, and attempt to conform to, an absolute norm even if the reasons that justify having a norm in that field are defeasible. We may conform better to underlying (defeasible) reasons if we treat certain norms as indefeasible,[12] and a good way to encourage treating them as indefeasible is for them to be promulgated in absolute form. 'No smoking' is the right categorical imperative to have in various circumstances; but it would be silly to think that the underlying reasons to avoid exposing others to smoke are absolute in force: pleasure to the smoker can outweigh trivial risks to the bystander. The absolute ban, however, protects us from the common errors of judgment, temptations of selfishness, etc. that would make 'Smoking permitted when reasonable' a poor norm to have. In addition to any 'natural' absolutes, then, there can also be 'artificial' absolutes in limited government. Indeed, because of the need for determination of moral norms, every natural absolute will be supported by an artificial one.

This helps us see what is wrong with Patrick Devlin's case *against* absolute constraints in the protected sphere. J.S. Mill, one the greatest defenders of limited government, said the harm principle is 'entitled to govern absolutely the dealings of society with the individual in the way of compulsion and control'[13]: the only valid reason for interfering with someone's liberty is that his action is harmful to others. The UK Wolfenden Report drew on similar ideas in defence of the view that there must be 'a

---

[10] *ST* II-II, q 66 a 7. See also *ST* II-II, q 64 a 6: A judge who has no alternative but to order the execution of an innocent man whom he knows to be convicted by lying testimony does not breach the absolute prohibition on killing the innocent because 'it is not he that puts the innocent man to death but they who stated him to be guilty'.

[11] Mill, *Utilitarianism*, Ch. 5.

[12] For a related sort of two-level argument in favour of binding (but in this case not absolute) norms, see Raz, *Practical Reason and Norms*, 58–62.

[13] Mill, *On Liberty*, Ch. 1, emphasis added.

realm of private morality and immorality which is, in brief and crude terms, not the law's business'.[14] Why is that 'brief and crude'? Just on its own, it does not tell us why something is 'not the law's business'—the phrase is no more illuminating than Locke's suggestion that law is limited to preserving our 'civil interests'. The Report takes there to be spheres of conduct that, of their nature, lie beyond coercive regulation of the criminal sort. To this Devlin objects. Many of his complaints—that sexual non-conformity will cause social disintegration, for example—are comically weak. But he has better arguments and better examples. If we consider, say, private drunkenness (which he counts as immorality) it is easier to see how he could come to his scepticism about absolute constraints. I will try to put a sensible spin on his argument by emphasizing certain words in the following well-known passage. Devlin writes,

> [I]t is not possible to set *theoretical* limits to the power of the State to legislate against immorality. It is not possible to settle *in advance* exceptions to the general rule or to define inflexibly *areas* of morality into which the law is in *no circumstances* to be allowed to enter.[15]

With those emphases added the passage sounds less like an attack on Mill's case for individual liberty and more like a plea for a policy that is sensitive to empirical evidence (not one settled on *theoretical* grounds, or *in advance*) and one that is open to the *possibility* that the proper scope of legal regulation should not track large *areas* of conduct (e.g. 'private' conduct) but should instead be more fine-grained.

Devlin may be correct in thinking there are no a priori grounds for supposing that 'private' conduct should be absolutely free from coercive regulation. 'Private conduct' is, after all, a very broad category. But when friends of limited government speak of a protected sphere, they mean to pick out what is in fact an amalgam of narrower spheres—a zone made up of particular liberties, not liberty as such. For example, most liberals assume that the state has 'no business' prohibiting religious activity, even when it is vicious, at least among truly consenting adults acting in private. (Things get murkier when we consider how the state should respond to parental coercion of minor children on religious grounds, or to religions parading their rituals in public view.) Yet here too we can quickly generate Devlin-style objections: Can we know in advance that this is a wise policy? Religions are inventive. Who knows what fresh falsehood will be declared infallibly correct: can we really bear more superstition? Private religious conduct can be socially risky. It may be fine for some people to spend four hours each day in prayer or mediation, but what would happen to the economy if everyone did that? What if it were eight hours? Yet we have no algorithm that will generate and decide all such cases in advance. Does it follow, then, that there are no limits on the state's authority to regulate religion?

It does not. The considerations just set out bear on the underlying moral reasons. Even if reasons for religious freedom are defeasible in view of such possible risks to individuals and society, it does not follow that our general policy towards it should be

---

[14] UK Committee on Homosexual Offences and Prostitution, *Report of the Committee on Homosexual Offences and Prostitution*, para. 61.
[15] Devlin, *The Enforcement of Morals*, 12–13.

equally defeasible. There may even be sound reasons for having an exceptionless norm, say of the form, 'Congress shall make no law respecting an establishment of religion, or prohibiting the free exercise thereof…' The case for that need not be one deduced in advance from first principles, but argued in light of centuries of experience of the disasters caused by hatred, prejudice, and blindness with respect to others' religious convictions or lack of them. An absolute disability may be the right prophylactic. Admittedly, I have not proven it. But in opening up space between the character of underlying moral reasons and the character of the constitutional and other norms that ought to constrain government, we can see how solid boundaries around a protected sphere may be built up, bit by bit, even in the face of Devlin's scepticism.

IV. Civil Society and the State

Are there other ways to defend stringent limits on government, ones that do not depend on either proving that there are absolute moral constraints, or by establishing the prophylactic value of positive constraints? I will now set out, and reject, one proposed by John Finnis. It is based not on the familiar considerations that go to define a protected sphere, or on the weaker restrictions on modalities of governance that we get from the rule of law, but on claims about the nature of value itself. The key idea is that many associations of civil society—things like families, friendships, churches, universities, or partnerships—instantiate goods that political life does not. The state is an instrument, a means; the associations of civil society involve intrinsically good ends. That being so, governments should let them be.

That contrasts with a line of thought we find in some ancient writers, especially Aristotle. At the beginning of the *Politics* he says, 'if all communities aim at some good, the state or political community, which is the highest of all, and which embraces all the rest, aims at good in a greater degree than any other, and at the highest good'.[16] This is an influential idea. Even Aquinas sometimes treats it as correct.[17] But does every political community really aim at the highest good or even, more plausibly, at what its members *take to be* the highest good? Aristotle's remark does not establish it. The all-embracing character of political communities may show that they aim at something that is, or is taken to be, good for all the subordinate communities they govern, a kind of generic or basic good, but that does not prove it to be the highest good. It could even be the lowest common denominator.

Those who share Aristotle's enthusiasm for political community need not do so on the above grounds. They may accept a substantive thesis about human flourishing: that it is only in the political realm that people can act upon the grand stage their humanity deserves, only there that they can transcend petty differences and free themselves of the dreary necessities of family and household life. That thesis, in stronger or weaker versions, left a mark not only on classical writers but also on Rousseau, Hegel, and many others. The thesis is not necessarily inimical to limited government, but it is shaped by an ideal that is, we might say, coming from a different place. There are

---

[16] Aristotle, *Politics*, Bk I, Ch. 1 (Jowett trans.).   [17] E.g. *ST* I-II, q 90 a 1.

reasons for hesitating about it. Its rather dim view of all private life is hard to credit. A life primarily organized around family, friends, and fellowship may not be for everyone, but it seems enough for many, including many who have other options. Surely the matter turns on individual needs and temperaments? And the civic republican ideal rests on a view of political life that is, to put it mildly, romantic. Politics in modern mass-societies does not have much in common with life in the Athenian *polis*. Most of us who decide to participate in politics are less like titans strutting across the stage than like the audience at a stadium pop concert, participating by deciding whether to dance along, and for whom to clap.

None of this is to deny that states are massively important institutions with urgent tasks to perform. Finnis acknowledges this. As he puts it in *Natural Law and Natural Rights*, these amount to nothing less than a duty 'to secure the whole ensemble of material and other conditions, including forms of collaboration, that tend to favour, facilitate and foster the realization by each individual of his or her personal development'.[18] But as important as that is, the goods political life achieves are, he says, 'not basic, intrinsic, or constitutive, but rather, instrumental'.[19] In this respect they are held to differ from the common goods associated with smaller communities of civil society such as human friendship, married life, or religious association. Their goods are basically and intrinsically valuable. This suggests to Finnis the following principle of government:

> regulation of these associations should never (in the case of associations with a non-instrumental common good)...be intended to take over the formation, direction, or management of these personal initiatives and personal associations.[20]

The task of government, as large and important as it is, must always respect this limit, for government is but an instrument. Let me call that the 'instrumentality' principle. It directs the state to allow these organizations to do their own thing, at any rate 'in ways consistent with other aspects of the common good of the political community'.[21]

I will assume that, even taking into account that restriction, the instrumentality principle is meant to be stringent and that it is meant to supplement whatever restrictions follow from the existence of the protected sphere itself. Government should *never* aim to take over the 'formation, direction or management' of social groups. That will certainly ban interference with what we might call the internal aspects of an associational group (its membership criteria, its authority over its members). And it is likely also to prohibit direction of their relationships with other groups. Some churches may declare others heretical, they may compete for the loyalties of the same people, they may set conditions on their ecumenical activities, and the principle entails that they should be free to do all these things more or less as they see fit, because they are institutions with intrinsic goods, whereas the state is an institution (or more exactly a set of institutions) of instrumental good only.

Now, it is easy to think of weaker principles that will take us some way towards the conclusion that the state should respect the institutions of civil society. There is the

---

[18] *NLNR*, 147. I explored difficulties with this idea of the common good, and the tensions between it and Finnis's defence of legal authority, in Green, 'Law, Co-ordination and the Common Good'.
[19] *CEJF* III.5, 87.   [20] *CEJF* III.5, 90.   [21] *CEJF* III.5, 90.

principle of effectiveness: government should not try to do what it cannot accomplish. There is the principle of efficiency: government should not do what others can do better. And there is the principle of subsidiarity: higher-level organizations should not do what lower-level organizations can do adequately. But none of these will secure limits as stringent as what we have in the instrumentality principle: they will limit governmental control of some of the associations of civil society in some cases and in some respects, but not absolutely and generically. Not even the most stringent of these—subsidiarity—will do that. (Sometimes lower-level organizations *cannot* adequately do important activities; some levels of government are *closer* to the relevant people than are culturally and geographically remote religious hierarchies.) Moreover, none of them has any need for the centrepiece of the instrumentality argument: the idea that civil society organizations are unique in having a non-instrumental common good. And, with the possible exception of subsidiarity, they are all what I have been calling 'downstream' limits on authority.[22]

The instrumentality principle is different from, and more stringent than, any of these. Should we add it to our list of principles of limited government? I doubt it. Let us begin with some clarifications about value itself.[23] Assume that the communal and cooperative goods of civil society are intrinsically good. It does not follow that they are *very* good. A pretty stone on a beach is intrinsically valuable, but not very valuable. On the other hand, even if political cooperation is only of instrumental value, it does not follow that it is of little value. On the contrary, it is of *enormous* value: owing to the special regulatory capacity of the state it can promote many valuable ends. Indeed, it is of such great instrumental value that it would be misleading to describe it as a 'mere' means.[24] Something is of intrinsic value provided it is of value for its own sake and not just for the sake of some other valuable thing to which it is a means. What is of intrinsic value need not be inexplicably valuable. It is hard to make sense of the intrinsic value of married life if it is not of value *to*, or *for*, the married couple. (Which does not make it an instrument of some kind.) If we need to choose between an intrinsic good and an instrumental good, we may have reason to choose the latter. The intrinsic beauty of my antique window frame will be spoiled by boring a hole in it and putting a wire through it. On the other hand the internet connection that can then enter, though only an instrument, is an extremely valuable one, worth having in spite of the loss. With respect to human associations, the gain and loss of regulation can accrue to different people. If the government forces an all-male Junior Chamber of Commerce to admit women

---

[22] We cannot classify the subsidiarity principle independently of the justification for it. Often, it is a rule of thumb in the service of effectiveness. But if it were a rule of thumb aimed at securing a protected sphere based on rights then it would be an 'upstream' limit.

[23] For more detail on instrumental values and law see Green, 'Law as a Means'.

[24] There is a parallel here to a tiresome argument in contemporary political philosophy that insists, correctly, that economic equality is not intrinsically valuable and then infers, wrongly, that it is a 'mere means'. There is nothing 'mere' about a state of affairs that is humanly necessary for fair opportunities, social mobility, and public health. Indeed, that is why political ideologies often fly under the colours of their characteristic means. 'Egalitarians' are not those who favour *equality* as an end; they are those who think *equalizing* is an essential means to their ends. 'Conservatives' are not those who favour *the conserved* as an end; they are those who think *conserving* is an essential means to their ends. (The notable exceptions are 'liberals' who do favour liberty, and often as an end.)

members it may spoil the special and intrinsic common good of an all-boys club. Still, the great and wider instrumental good of reducing sexism and supporting young women entrepreneurs will be worth it.[25]

Second, state direction of social groups need not spoil their intrinsically valuable common goods. A loving association between parents and their children is a common good of non-instrumental value. The state can support it by facilitating the association; for example, by giving parents child-support payments. But it can also support it by overt direction: it can prohibit parents from disciplining their children in certain ways; it can require parents to support their minor children; it can back these up with criminal penalties. It would be a mistake to think that direction must destroy parental love: most parents will in any case not want to hurt their children and will want to support them when they can. The directive that intrudes in the family does not change the normal motivations; it surrounds them with an assurance scheme in which they are more likely to be, and to be known to be, secure.

Third, the reasons for thinking that the common goods of associations can produce intrinsic value are generally also reasons for thinking that they can produce intrinsic *disvalue*—things bad in themselves. Social solidarity and mutual understanding are intrinsically good; divisiveness and incomprehension are intrinsically bad. Churches and families are excellent at producing both. Even if government is merely an instrument, why should it never direct such groups so as to secure more of the intrinsic value and less of the intrinsic disvalue? Why should it not, for example, try to make religions less intolerant of each other, or less intolerant of their dissident members?[26] Any attempt would of course be subject to the principles of effectiveness and efficiency. But even if the state cannot effectively secure intrinsic goods it may nonetheless be able effectively to reduce the intrinsic bads. Its capacities may be asymmetrically effective.

The final point is a different one. I have so far been assuming, for sake of argument, that the common goods that governments can realize *are* of instrumental value only and that there is therefore a categorical difference between the state and civil society. I know of no reason to believe that. Although intrinsic and instrumental values are categorically different, they are not incompatible. Something that is intrinsically valuable may also be instrumentally valuable: a pretty stone can make a useful door-stop. It is also common for things of great instrumental value to take on non-instrumental value, because their instrumentality often makes them central to human life and culture. It is of immense instrumental value for an animal to be able to reason or feel pain, and partly because of that these become constituents of (not means to) moral status. Political organizations are of great instrumental value—that point is not in dispute. As such, they are one of the central sites of communal attachments in the modern world. I noted above that this does not make them in any way primary, nor does it show that anyone's life is shallow or incomplete without them. But the forms of cooperation that inhere in politics, and the identities and loyalties they inspire, can be valuable in themselves, and not as means only. So there are intrinsic goods on both

---

[25] I am not assuming that they are commensurable values. I am assuming that it is not wrong to prefer the instrumental good of reducing sexism to the intrinsic good of clubbiness.

[26] See Green, 'Internal Minorities and their Rights'.

sides of the equation, and that undercuts any general reason for thinking that the state should always defer to civil society.

V. Intrinsic Goods and Institutions: An Example

I now want to look more closely at the objects of regulation themselves, at those institutions of civil society that are thought to be closely bound up with intrinsic and basic goods. Again, I think the picture is more complex than the instrumentality principle takes for granted.

Suppose that knowledge, or the pursuit of knowledge, is basically and intrinsically good. Acquiring knowledge is not a solitary activity. Everyone relies on resources, equipment, and techniques someone else developed; testing hypotheses and replicating results is a collective endeavour; certain criteria of correctness in measurement and argument are inherently public. So even if knowledge or its pursuit is not precisely a 'common good' it has aspects of social production and consumption that make similar reasoning apply to it. Importantly, knowledge is sought in associations, and these can have institutional existence. Universities are institutions engaged in the pursuit of knowledge—that is among their constitutive aims. If we assume that government is primarily instrumental, would it follow that the instrument should never interfere with universities, or never take on their formation, direction or management?[27] In the last section, we found some reasons to doubt that form of argument. Here is another.

If we think the activities that constitute universities instantiate knowledge, we might think of a picture that looks something like this: where '≈' indicates the relation of instantiation, and '⇓' the relation of drawing instrumental support from the institution below.

$$\text{Universities} \approx \text{Knowledge}$$
$$\Downarrow$$
$$\text{State}$$

The instrumentality principle is thus expected to shelter universities from the state because the latter should facilitate knowledge, whereas knowledge is an intrinsic and communal good and universities instantiate it.

But is this picture correct? Remember what universities actually are: institutions of students, teachers, and staff, working under statutes, bylaws, contracts, codes, etc., created and administered by their boards, administrations, and so on. Of course they are not universities if pursuit of knowledge is not among their aims. But to aim is not to succeed. That complex apparatus may serve knowledge well or poorly. Some universities pursue knowledge sufficiently to count as members of the kind while thoroughly subordinating it to other things that matter more to them: profits, or prophets. So the contribution of universities to knowledge is *itself* instrumental. They sometimes pursue it well, sometimes poorly, and how well they do depends on many things, including

---

[27] For simplicity, I will assume that the universities in question are not simply departments of the state that it is entitled to control on other grounds.

their values and institutional structures. This suggests that a better picture of the relationships in play looks something like this:

Knowledge
⇓
Universities
⇓
State

If that is right we have two instrumental relationships to think through, not one. Suppose that universities vis-à-vis the still-smaller associations (teachers and students, research groups, etc.) directly engaged in producing knowledge are subject to the instrumentality principle: they too should facilitate and serve but not take over their direction or management. This might ground various principles of university governance; for instance, that they should protect the academic freedom of teachers and students. What would that entail for the lower relationship, the control of the state over the universities?

Again, there are the downstream principles limiting all government: effectiveness, efficiency, and subsidiarity will place limits on the right of governments to control universities. There may be upstream principles located in the protected sphere or flowing from law's restricted means. But our question is whether the instrumentality principle adds *another* firm limit. Bracketing the worries set out in Section V, we can now see another reason for doubting that. Because universities *themselves* stand primarily in an instrumental relation to knowledge (and also to other goods for the sake of which universities exist) it becomes a live question whether the state can improve that by intervention and direction of one kind or another. For it is not only forces external to the university that can derail the pursuit of knowledge: the institution can do it on its own, by poor governance, financial mismanagement, attacks on academic freedom, etc. If so, it is possible that well-crafted public policies could make things better, knowledge-wise. The state could subject universities to a regime requiring that they respect freedom of speech, or of association, or non-discrimination, or transparency in governance. It could legitimately do all of this because, even if the instrumentality principle were sound, it does not apply to one instrument's governance of another instrument.

That is just one example, though one is enough for us to reject the instrumentality principle. But there are other similar examples among the associations that Finnis mentions. Take marriage. The non-instrumental common good of marriage is really a common good of marital life, not of the social institution of marriage. The extent to which that institution serves that common good is variable: the institution is an instrument to be judged by how well it serves the relationship. There is therefore no intrinsic-good-based reason to think that the state should generally refrain from directing and shaping the social institution: on the contrary, that is precisely what marriage law should do. Religion is perhaps a borderline case. Here, we may have something much closer to the first picture above, where religious institutions instantiate, and do not merely serve, whatever common goods there are to religion. But even here we can imagine some space between them. We can capture it in a stipulation: we could say that the common good is an aspect of the *communion*, and the extent to which *churches* serve it is largely an instrumental question, so that whether state regulation of churches is permissible on these grounds remains, even here, an open question.

VI. Truth, Fallibility and Politics

I turn, now, to a final point. In the original title of the essay I discussed above, Finnis posed a question: 'Is Natural Law Theory Compatible with Limited Government?' The answer is obvious. Of course it is. One of the most influential theories of limited government in our tradition, John Locke's *Second Treatise*, is a natural law theory. So why did anyone ever doubt that a natural lawyer could endorse limitations on state power? In concluding, let me try to shed some light on that.

Legal philosophy is a swampland of homonyms and *faux amis*, and 'natural law' is one of its soggy spots. Two distinct (though historically related) theories are described as 'natural law' views. One is a doctrine in general jurisprudence about the nature of law. Among its central features is a claim to the effect that law and morality are intimately connected.[28] There are many variants of this thesis, everything from the suggestion that legal systems have a constitutive moral aim, through views according to which 'legal system' is a moral category like 'justice' and not a social category like 'market', to the claim that there are laws that are not social artefacts at all: laws that no one (or no human) made. As general jurisprudence, natural law has no bearing on the issue of limited government or any other theory of legislation. This is not because jurisprudence is value-neutral (something natural law jurists dispute). It is because a theory about the conceptual *relations between* morality and law is compatible with any proposed moral constraints on law-making. If some laws are not artefacts—if they are *not* made at all—then moral principles about how we should make laws do not apply to them. If laws *are* made, but do not count as first-rate, full-blooded laws unless made according to certain moral principles, then an attempt to make them other ways will misfire and it will be a conceptual error to classify the result as law (or as law in its central case, or law in its best light). General jurisprudence itself only warns us off the misclassification, it does not warn us off the moral error that leads to the misfire.

That brings us to the second of the homonyms, and it is the one relevant here. This 'natural law' is a theory, not about the relations between law and morality, but about morality itself. For much of the early modern era its distinctive features included the two that give it its name: the idea that morality is somehow rooted in *nature* (including 'the nature of things' and 'human nature') and that morality is in some respects significantly *law*-like. Humean and Kantian objections did a lot to problematize the first idea, and it is now rare to find any moralists purporting to 'derive' moral claims from propositions about nature alone. And the idea that moral requirements are relevantly like laws—something Locke took for granted—became unsettled by doubts

---

[28] This must, however, amount to more than the bare idea that there is 'a necessary connection' between law and morality. Contrary to what some think, that is not a distinctive natural law thesis: Green 'Positivism and the Inseparability of Law and Morals'.

about whether there is a moral law-giver.[29] But if we subtract both 'nature' and 'law' from 'natural law', what is left? Perhaps the definition Finnis offers: 'Natural Law theory is nothing other than the account of all the reasons-for-action which people ought to be able to accept, precisely because these are good, valid and sound as reasons.'[30] That is a very ecumenical definition. It makes Jeremy Bentham a natural law moralist, for he, too, offers an account of all the reasons people ought to be able to accept as valid, and he thinks law should conform to them. Indeed, it is not clear who the definition excludes, except moral sceptics. This is not an objection. It is not as if the idea of natural law were anchored in common moral thought, the way the ideas of honesty or kindness or justice are. 'Natural law' is a philosophical and theological term shaped by theoretical reflection and open to being re-shaped by it however seems useful. But if all non-sceptical moralities are 'natural law' then there is no case to answer as far as its compatibility with ideals of limited government is concerned. Moral scepticism is neither sufficient nor necessary for a commitment to liberty, and there are certain kinds of commitment to liberty with which it is incompatible.

Finnis's question presupposes there is a suspicion that natural law moralities tend to be bossy. What might the sources of that suspicion be? One is a worry about their attachment to classical ideals alleged to give insufficient weight to human liberty and individuality. That was the charge that Mill laid against Graeco-Roman political morality:

> The ancient commonwealths thought themselves entitled to practise, and the ancient philosophers countenanced, the regulation of every part of private conduct by public authority, on the ground that the State had a deep interest in the whole bodily and mental discipline of every one of its citizens . . .[31]

I do not want to deny that elements of the Graeco-Roman view entered some natural law moralities. But most modern natural law moralists have shed that view, and it is not what gives people pause today. I gave a couple of reasons, above, for doubting Aristotle's view that politics involves the highest good. Finnis doubts it, too. He tells us 'integral human fulfillment is nothing less than the fulfillment of all human persons in all communities (in principle) and cannot be achieved in any community short of the heavenly kingdom', a community that, although it cannot be envisaged by unaided reason, has been presented to us by divine revelation, and whose superiority to the political community is also something 'philosophical reflection has confirmed'.[32]

Suppose you read that the Natural Law Party now has five reliable votes in the Supreme Court or has just swept Parliament. Do you worry that a tsunami of civic republicanism is about to hit? I doubt it. The fear is more likely to be that we are in for a loss of liberty in personal life, especially in sexual conduct, that discrimination on grounds of sex and sexual orientation will get a lot worse, and that our criminal justice system will take on a hard, retributive character. That is, the distrust of natural law morality has less to do with a fear of public morality than with a fear of the morality it

---

[29] Though this did not erode all juridical concepts in morality. See Anscombe, 'Modern Moral Philosophy'.
[30] *CEJF* III.5, 10–11.   [31] Mill, *On Liberty*, Ch. 1.   [32] *CEJF* III.5, 92.

will make public. To speak bluntly, the worry is that the values it wants to see in the public sphere are anti-liberal and anti-humanist (not just ante-liberal and ante-humanist). Maybe that is a bad rap. Still, it *is* the rap.[33]

Why worry, though, given that there are resources within the natural law tradition to justify staying its hand in legislating its own view about the good life? Some may worry that its interpretation of the restraints is too narrow—that it will restrict grosser forms of criminalization but will be indifferent to, or even enthusiastic about, official nagging of, or discrimination against, those whose lives it deplores. Some can know how to tolerate, though only narrowly and grudgingly.[34] And even if its principles of restraint are robust, it seems likely that, for social diversity and personal liberty to really thrive, these restraints will be *called on* a lot more often. The more censorious judgments a morality is prepared to make about people's tastes, habits, and convictions the more work its doctrine of limited government will have to do.

There is also a second point. Some people get uneasy about the heavy weather made in certain natural law traditions about moral 'objectivity'. They should not. If moral propositions are straightforwardly true or false, or if correct moral standards are mind-independent, or whatever it is that is supposed to make them 'objective', it is still a further question what these propositions *are* and thus whether they license a broad or narrow ambit for government interference. But perhaps there is something anxiety-provoking in the epistemological corner. It is one thing to believe moral truths are objective; it is another to suppose that one already knows what they are and to govern confidently on the basis of that knowledge. I am not here making a Rawlsian point about the inevitability of evaluative disagreement, nor am I endorsing a kind of abstentionist or proceduralist response to it. Even if we have consensus on moral propositions we must acknowledge that, if it is possible *to be* wrong about them, it is also possible *that we are* wrong about them. So the fear is that, 'while every one well knows himself to be fallible, few think it necessary to take any precautions against their own fallibility...'[35]

Now, fallibilism is not scepticism, so it is not committed to anything a moral objectivist should deny. Nor is it the view that with respect to every matter we are just as likely to be wrong as to be right. It is the view that we may be wrong about matters of fact and even about things that we think 'philosophical reflection has confirmed'.[36] We want any theory of limited government not only to be consistent with fallibility, but to plan actively for it.

First, we need *error-detection* mechanisms. The arguments Mill makes in Chapter 2 of *On Liberty*, in support of freedom of speech and opinion, draw heavily on the idea that we need not only access to such information as is already around, but also that we need to seek more of it, to systematically and regularly expose our ideas to contestation. Rights of free speech are thus an important part of the protected sphere not just

---

[33] For a pretty full charge sheet, see Bamforth and Richards, *Patriarchal Religion, Sexuality, and Gender.*

[34] Cf. Green, 'On Being Tolerated'.

[35] Mill, *On Liberty*, Ch. 2. Of course, some natural lawyers do think that there are people who can be infallible, though they do not normally defend infallibility on grounds of natural law. See Tierney, *Origins of Papal Infallibility, 1150–1350.*

[36] *CEJF* III.5, 92.

because of the important role they play in individual moral independence—in making up our minds for ourselves—but because they are a hedge against fallibility.

Second, we need *error-reduction* mechanisms. We not only know that we are fallible, we have reason to believe that in certain areas governments are especially likely to fall into error. That is why Mill says that 'the strongest of all the arguments against the interference of the public with purely personal conduct, is that when it does interfere, the odds are that it interferes wrongly, and in the wrong place'.[37] He is not a sceptic about assessing this conduct—he knows that people make a hash of their personal lives; they love the wrong people, read the wrong books, worship the wrong things—but the odds that public policy can reliably improve things for them are poor. In important areas of life—especially in matters of belief, sex, and friendship, there are chasms of incomprehension that make it difficult to know *what it is like* to be in another person's position, and thus difficult to have any accurate appreciation of the effects that one's proposed policy may have on him.

Finally, we need *error-correction* policies. From time to time it will turn out that we were tragically wrong either about the ends of life or about the means to them. So we need to avoid ratchet-like institutions that turn inevitable errors into incorrigible ones. All of the devices that allow us to revise and revisit are important here, from responsible government to mechanisms for review and second thought.

The sort of provisions we need to make for fallibility also contribute to the doctrine of limited government. They help explain parts of the protected sphere; they give further reasons for restricting the means through which we govern. When enthusiasms for public morality and objective values turn feverish, they are an antipyretic that brings the temperature back down.

Bibliography

Anscombe, G.E.M. (1958) 'Modern Moral Philosophy', *Philosophy* 33, 1–19.

Aristotle (1943) *Politics*, trans Benjamin Jowett (New York: Modern Library).

Bamforth, Nicholas and David A.J. Richards (2007) *Patriarchal Religion, Sexuality, and Gender: A Critique of New Natural Law* (Cambridge: Cambridge University Press).

Devlin, Patrick (1965) *The Enforcement of Morals* (Oxford: Oxford University Press).

Finnis, John (1996) 'Is Natural Law Theory Compatible with Limited Government?', in Robert P. George (ed.), *Natural Law, Liberalism, and Morality* (Oxford: Oxford University Press), 1–19.

Finnis, John (2011) 'Limited Government', in *Human Rights and the Common Good: Collected Essays Vol. III* (Oxford: Oxford University Press), 83–106.

Green, Leslie (1983) 'Law, Co-ordination and the Common Good', *Oxford Journal of Legal Studies* 3, 299–324.

Green, Leslie (1995) 'Internal Minorities and their Rights', in Will Kymlicka (ed.), *Rights of Cultural Minorities* (Oxford: Oxford University Press), 257–72.

Green, Leslie (2007) 'The Duty to Govern', *Legal Theory* 13, 165–85.

Green, Leslie (2008a) 'On Being Tolerated', in Matthew Kramer, Claire Grant, Ben Colburn and Antony Hatzistavrou (eds), *The Legacy of H.L.A. Hart: Legal, Political and Moral Philosophy* (Oxford: Oxford University Press), 277–97.

---

[37] Mill, *On Liberty*, Ch. 4.

Green, Leslie (2008b) 'Positivism and the Inseparability of Law and Morals', *New York University Law Review* 83, 1035–58.

Green, Leslie (2010) 'Law as a Means', in Peter Cain (ed.), *The Hart-Fuller Debate in the Twenty-First Century* (Oxford: Hart Publishing), 169–88.

Locke, John (1988 [1689]) *Two Treatises of Government*, ed. Peter Laslett (Cambridge: Cambridge University Press).

Mill, John Stuart (2003 [1849]) *Utilitarianism, and On Liberty*, M. Warnock (ed.) (Oxford: Blackwell).

Raz, Joseph (1999 [1979]) *Practical Reason and Norms*, 2nd ed. (Oxford: Oxford University Press).

Stanton-Ife, John (2008) 'The Limits of Law', in Edward N. Zalta (ed.), *The Stanford Encyclopedia of Philosophy (Winter 2008 Edition)*, <http://plato.stanford.edu/archives/win2008/entries/law-limits/>.

Thoreau, Henry David (1966 [1849]) 'Civil Disobedience', in *Walden and Civil Disobedience* (New York: W.W. Norton).

Tierney, Brian (1972) *Origins of Papal Infallibility, 1150–1350* (Leiden: Brill).

United Kingdom Committee on Homosexual Offences and Prostitution (1957) *Report of the Committee on Homosexual Offences and Prostitution* (London: Her Majesty's Stationery Office).

13

Pure Perfectionism and the Limits of Paternalism

Christopher Tollefsen

Perfectionism as a political theory holds that the state should not be neutral about worthwhile forms of life, nor should it exclude moral ideals, or considerations about the good from deliberation about legislation or constitutional essentials. Rather, in making decisions about what activities and forms of life to protect, promote, discourage, or exclude, the state may, and sometimes must, take into account the moral worth of those activities and forms of life, and the ways in which they may, or may not, conduce to a flourishing life.[1] Perfectionism is not thereby an illiberal doctrine; John Finnis and Joseph Raz, for example, have notably provided robust, albeit different, accounts of the importance of political liberty and personal autonomy within a perfectionist framework.[2]

Perfectionism is opposed by various anti-perfectionist forms of liberalism that accept some version or other of what Finnis has called the *neutrality principle*.[3] Adherents to the neutrality principle typically believe that the very project of incorporating substantive moral judgments into the work of legislating, of whatever sort, is compromised by a lack of respect for persons inherent in the project. For Rawls, the demand for neutrality emerges from his 'principle of legitimacy': 'Our exercise of political power is fully proper only when it is exercised in accordance with a constitution the essentials of which all citizens as free and equal may reasonably be expected to endorse in the light of principles and ideals acceptable to their common human reason.'[4] Excluded from these acceptable sources are principles based on comprehensive doctrines or conceptions of the good.

Similarly, Ronald Dworkin argues that neutrality is required by a norm requiring that governments show 'equal concern and respect' for their citizens; such concern and respect are incompatible, thinks Dworkin, with constraints or sacrifices required by government on its citizens for the sake of a favoured conception of the good. Finnis has called this Dworkin's 'argument from contempt',[5] and has noted that Dworkin later supplements the argument from contempt with an argument that takes majority-

---

[1] See, for a paradigmatic statement of a perfectionist theory, Finnis, *NLNR*. Robert P. George further articulates various perfectionist themes in George, *Making Men Moral*.

[2] See Raz, *The Morality of Freedom*, as well as *NLNR*. For Finnis, both political and personal liberty are important conditions for the possibility, in personal and social life, of human flourishing, as I show below, in the text. Yet Finnis's point is well taken that 'liberal' is not, just in itself, a proper term of commendation, as are 'reasonable, sound, true, appropriate, decent, just, and fair' (*CEJF* V.5, 104).

[3] See *CEJF* III.2, 48.   [4] Rawls, *Political Liberalism*, 137.

[5] *CEJF* II.6, 109; see Dworkin, *Taking Rights Seriously*. Later, Dworkin argues that imposition of a favoured conception of the good is incompatible with a citizen's 'sense of his [own] equal worth' (Dworkin, *A Matter of Principle*, 205).

enacted and restrictive legislation as having for its '*reason* and *justification*... the sheer fact that they hold the moral opinion that they do'.[6]

With the principle of neutrality in hand, liberal theorists then may propose various principles of exclusion designed to ensure that comprehensive or non-neutral understandings of the good are ruled out in the appropriate ways. So Rawls proposes a model of 'public reason' according to which one may argue, in proposing constitutional essentials and matters of basic justice (other liberal thinkers are more expansive), only from premises that all citizens 'may reasonably be expected to endorse',[7] and Dworkin proposes various screening or filtering processes.[8] As Finnis notes, the 'whole point' of this dialectic is 'to rule out as illegitimate, in a certain context, certain principles and ideals and in general *theses*, even though they are or may well be true—that is, to rule them out on grounds completely distinct from their falsity...'[9]

Over a range of his work, Finnis has developed a set of related arguments against these forms of exclusion, and against the demand for neutrality. Three such arguments are central to Finnis's work. The first is that the attempt to structure civil and reasonable public deliberation through Rawlsian public reason is self-defeating: Rawlsian public reason and political requirements of neutrality are themselves uncivil, unreasonable, and non-neutral, by virtue of arbitrarily restricting public deliberation and excluding appeals to the truth on important matters 'where people's fundamental human rights are at stake'.[10] So liberal exclusions of the sort generated by Rawlsian public reason are, ultimately, unjust.

A second argument goes to the heart of Finnis's moral, political, and legal-theoretic methodology. The standpoint for thinking about 'constitutional essentials', and matters of 'basic justice' is the standpoint of *unrestricted* practical reasoning, the standpoint of agents, thinking now together, because bound by common needs and goods essential for human flourishing, and deliberating about how they may most reasonably shape their common lives. Such deliberation cannot go well unless open to the full range of goods essential to human well-being, and it will inevitably be stunted by misunderstandings or willful neglect of such goods, or hostility or inattentiveness to such goods.[11]

Finnis's third argument responds directly to the argument from contempt. Briefly, it need show no contempt at all to encourage worthwhile activities, and discourage their opposite, since worthwhile activities contribute to genuine human flourishing, and base activities diminish the possibility of such flourishing. I will address the contempt argument at greater length below, for it returns in the discussion of a different principle, more tightly focused than the neutrality principle, which forms common ground between anti-perfectionist theorists and some, but not all, perfectionist thinkers.

---

[6] *CEJF* II.6, 111. For further discussion, see George, *Making Men Moral*; and Yowell, 'A Critical Examination of Dworkin's Theory of Rights'.

[7] Rawls, *Political Liberalism*, 137.

[8] See the extensive discussion in Yowell, 'A Critical Examination of Dworkin's Theory of Rights', for details of Dworkin's thought here.

[9] *CEJF* I.16, 259.   [10] *CEJF* I.16, 263.

[11] The path taken by such thinking when it goes well will be a focus of later parts of this essay.

In 'Duties to Oneself in Kant', Finnis distinguishes the neutrality principle from the *harm* principle, which he describes thus: 'the state has no right to use coercion directly or indirectly to discourage conduct not harmful to persons other than those who consent to engage in it'.[12] The two principles are clearly not the same: one could reject the neutrality principle while accepting (some version of) the harm principle (though rejecting the harm principle requires rejecting the neutrality principle). For liberal theorists, it is true, the ground for accepting the harm principle is often closely connected with that for accepting the neutrality principle: if non-neutrality shows a lack of respect just as such, then so, *a fortiori*, does coercion for non-neutral reasons. But one could deny that non-neutrality as such is disrespectful (thus rejecting in its broadest form the argument from contempt), yet hold that coercion *does* show disrespect. Joseph Raz, for example, argues in just such a way.

Finnis, as we will see, rejects Raz's reasoning here. Yet he does come to accept and defend the harm principle even while rejecting the neutrality principle. Finnis frames his acceptance of the harm principle as a rejection of *pure paternalism*, the view that the state can, in bringing to bear its coercive force, legislate, in some cases at least, with a view *only* to the moral character of its citizens.

Finnis's rejection of pure paternalism has been questioned by Robert P. George. Like Finnis, George rejects Raz's claim that coercive paternalism necessarily is disrespectful. We may see this disagreement, between Finnis and George, on the one hand, and Raz, on the other, as a disagreement within perfectionism about the legitimacy of certain *means* to an end: is the use of *coercion* to influence behaviour for the good morally problematic? George and Finnis agree that it is not. But the disagreement between George and Finnis should be seen, I believe, as a disagreement about the *ends* of the state: is the moral character of its citizens, just as such, a matter that falls within the scope of the political common good, i.e., that aspect of the more general common good of a society over which the state has authority?

In this essay I argue, with Finnis and George, that coercion is not itself the problem; however, I argue with Finnis that the political common good does not include the moral character of citizens as such. As Finnis writes, in correcting Hart's misunderstandings of the 'idea of *enforcing morality as such*'[13] in the natural law tradition, penalization is authorized 'only when the act has a public character and jeopardizes public order or public morality or the rights of others'.[14]

I. Political Authority

According to one possible form of perfectionism, the state exists to bring its citizens to complete flourishing. Classically, that complete flourishing includes both the recognition and adequate pursuit of the final end of human beings, understood, in the Christian tradition, as including a relationship with the divine, and, because it is either partly constitutive of, or instrumentally necessary for, the achievement of that final end, possession of all-round virtue.

---

[12] *CEJF* III.2, 48.   [13] *CEJF* IV.11, 269.   [14] *CEJF* IV.11, 270.

For a state to embrace such an end amongst its ultimate purposes would result in a quite extensive form of paternalism, that is, for legislating moral norms precisely because of the harm that would be done to himself by an agent's acting immorally. The corruption brought about by immorality would be directly contrary to the agent's final end, and hence to the proper end of the state. It would thus be within the authority of the state to legislate against such immorality, and to promote upright moral character in other ways as well.

Such a robust perfectionism might seem to threaten religious liberty. Without endorsing it, John Finnis identifies the gist of a 'quick reading' of Aquinas' *De Regno* as the view that government should command whatever leads people toward their ultimate (heavenly) end, forbid whatever deflects them from it, and coercively deter people from evil-doing and induce them to decent conduct'.[15] If government has for its purpose the leading of its citizenry towards a heavenly end, and this can only, or best, be achieved by worship of the right sort, then the state might well suppress false forms of worship, and command true forms.

Few perfectionist theorists would accept these claims today, for heavenly fulfillment is thought to be a good outside the authority of the state even by those who think that the moral character of citizens just as such is within the scope of state authority.[16] Yet such an 'immanent' perfectionist politics could still allow or require a quite extensive paternalism were it to hold that the state may or must promote the complete all around virtue that is constitutive of imperfect, human, temporal fulfillment. Such a state would be within the scope of its authority were it to forbid some activity precisely on the grounds of its morally corrupting character, insofar as this corruption blocked an agent's approach to overall flourishing.

In addition to this principled, religious, restriction on the scope of pure paternalist perfectionism, most paternalists acknowledge prudential limits to paternalistic legislation. The regulation of some vices might be so time-consuming, or involve such expense or invasion of legitimate privacy, that it would be better for the state to refrain from the enforcement of morality in such cases. Finally, the reflexive character of morality—the fact that only an agent who *chooses* morally is morally upright—creates limits on what the state can effectively do; while the state, on most strongly paternalist accounts, can forbid self-regarding *actions*, it cannot penetrate to the interior will of the person and compel upright *choosing*. Apart from caveats concerning transcendent ends, and practical possibilities, though, the scope of the moral and the scope of the legislatively permissible in a perfectionism that embraced pure paternalism would appear to be co-extensive.[17]

---

[15] *CEJF* III.5, 91.

[16] The Second Vatican Council expresses this transcendence in its *Declaration on Religious Freedom (Dignitatis humanae)*: 'The religious acts whereby people, by their personal judgments, privately or publicly direct their lives to God transcend by their very nature the order of earthly and temporal affairs. The civil power therefore, whose proper responsibility is to attend to the *temporal* common good, ought indeed to recognize and favor the religious life of the citizenry, but must be said to exceed its limits if it presume to direct or inhibit religious acts' (*Dignitatis humanae*, 4; the translation is from *CEJF* V.4, 92, and emphasizes, as the Vatican's English translation does not, that the *bonum commune* is *temporale*, temporal).

[17] Hadley Arkes, for example, writes: 'To say that "X is wrong"—and not merely unpleasant or distasteful—is to say that people, more generally or universally, should refrain from the "doing of X". It is to say

Finnis has been extremely important both in advancing an interpretive argument regarding St. Thomas Aquinas, which moves his position away from the stereotype depicted above, and in beginning to clarify the principled objections to the stereotype that are available to perfectionism. Rather than replicate Finnis's interpretations and arguments, I will give a brief argument in favour of a more limited view of perfectionism that owes much to Finnis.[18] (I am not, here, concerned with any exegetical questions about Aquinas.[19])

The core of the argument concerns the reasons that persons join together in society, and eventually political society. Individuals just on their own clearly are insufficient for their own flourishing: they require friends, marriage requires a spouse, and even substantive goods such as knowledge and aesthetic experience which can in principle be pursued on one's own will suffer in the absence of cooperation and the generation through time of social forms and practices aimed at pursuit of these goods. So a flourishing human life is necessarily communal in various respects. It requires families, networks of friends, and cooperative social structures for the pursuit of goods. Pursuit of the good of religion too is typically communal, and, in developed forms with traditions of revelation, awareness of the full range of options of understanding and worship requires access to the tradition in the form, e.g., of an established church whose members are in communion with one another. In all these ways the inadequacy of individuals for human flourishing is answered by the pursuit of social goods, and the establishment of social institutions that serve both individual and social goods.

Each such community, we should note, properly has its own *common* good—a shared point, commitment to which binds a multiplicity of agents (even as few as two) into some one reality—a community. In a robust friendship, that shared point just is the mutual willing and pursuit of the good for and with each other; in less robust forms of friendship, the good might be the conditions necessary for each participant to be empowered to achieve his or her more or less independently construed good (a business friendship); or it might be the shared activity itself, and the enjoyment taken from that activity (a friendship of play). Each of the cooperative social structures described in the previous paragraph is *a* community, with its own shared point, its own common good.

But such cooperative social structures—groups, as I shall call them—(a) cannot coordinate themselves in relation to other groups in the absence of a common authority; nor (b) can they, absent such coordinative authority, provide for a common defence against outsiders; nor (c) can they justly—i.e., fairly and efficiently—address offenses against persons and groups committed by insiders; nor (d) can they fairly and adequately care for those who, by disability or other disadvantage, will not be cared for by individuals or groups, whether that is because of a default by some individuals or

---

that people may *justly be restrained* from the "doing of X"; and if they cannot be restrained in advance, they may be justly punished for the doing of a wrong' (Arkes, *Beyond the Constitution*, 184).

[18] Finnis's most developed statements of both his interpretation of Aquinas and his views of the limited nature of what he calls the political common good are to be found in his *Aquinas*, Ch. VII.

[19] The most sustained challenges to Finnis's interpretation of Aquinas come from Dewan, 'St. Thomas, John Finnis, and the Political Common Good', and Pakaluk, 'Is the Common Good of Political Society Limited and Instrumental?'

groups on their existing obligations, or because death, disaster, or other bad fortune has left such individuals without obvious sources of care.[20]

For these reasons, individuals and groups require a coordinating authority. This authority may come to exist simply because some person or group has taken upon themselves the responsibilities of authority and are in fact followed; there is no myth of consent undergirding the picture. But there are clearly forms of authority more and less adequate to the initial needs, and to the condition of the persons with those needs. The authority must, for example, use the coercive force of the sword, and make judgments regarding the good and bad, right and wrong, guilty and innocent within the overlapping set of societies. Such power may be used arbitrarily or selfishly. So an ideal of authority can develop in which the agents of authority are themselves governed by the impersonal authority of law, and, even further, in which those agents are at the same time, both authorities *and* subjects, who take their turn ruling and being ruled.

We are here quite close to the ideals of liberal democratic politics. But those ideals, it is worth noting, insofar as they are liberal and democratic, enter into the picture later than the need for political authority just as such. The needs that govern the creation of political authority are the needs of all human beings within the set of overlapping communities, including those who are proximate, but for whatever contingent reason not currently cared for by some particular community. We could call these needs *human needs*, or *needs of flourishing*; such needs are at the foundation of the natural law account of political authority.

The ideals of liberal democracy, and of democratic citizenship, on the other hand, are not foundational needs for political authority, but a constraint on how that authority most reasonably should be constituted. There is a need for such constraints, and for a democratic mode of politics; but it is a *need of citizenship*.

Somewhere in between these needs—the needs of flourishing, and the need of citizenship, though closer to the first than the second—is the *need for law*. In several places, Finnis has detailed how the impersonal and general character of the law, and the procedural safeguards of constitutional government, protect persons against both deliberate injustice—against, e.g., tyranny and despotism—and unintended injustice—of the form inevitable when judgments are rendered by authorities in a one-off, random, or arbitrary manner.[21] The rule of law, and not of men, is a stronger necessity than the shared rule of a democratic citizenry, however important that is; Finnis characterizes the need for law as a rational necessity—the law is *essential* for the pursuit of the human good. As Finnis notes in the opening sentence of *Natural Law and Natural Rights*: 'There are human goods that can be secured only through the institutions of human law, and requirements of practical reasonableness that only those institutions can satisfy'.[22]

Built into this picture is already one type of limit to the perfectionist state, namely a limit on personal authority in favour of the impersonal authority of law; I shall return

---

[20] Thus Finnis, following Aquinas, summarizes the constitutive elements of the good of the political community as justice and peace (*Aquinas*, 227). For a more detailed account of these four needs, see Tollefsen, 'Disability and Social Justice', from which the following two paragraphs are adapted.

[21] E.g. *Aquinas*, Ch. VIII.   [22] *NLNR*, 3.

to this in the next section.[23] But further limits are apparent: the state exists largely to further the pursuit by individuals and sub-political groups of their flourishing, and it does this by providing conditions under which such flourishing may safely and effectively be pursued. The state is thus doubly instrumental: it is not itself an end, and it provides, for the most part, only instrumentalities, such as coordination and protection, that aid in the pursuit of human well-being at sub-political levels. So Finnis's instrumentalism about the political common good could additionally be opposed by a form of perfectionism that holds that human flourishing is specifically political—i.e., bound up constitutively with existence in a *polis*[24]; his view is also opposed by the earlier described forms of perfectionism which hold that the state is not limited merely to the provision of instrumentalities relative to human flourishing, but may take a direct interest in the condition of its citizens' souls, i.e., whether those citizens are virtuous or not, since virtue is constitutive of the end of man.

Nevertheless, Finnis's instrumentalism about the political common good is clearly perfectionist in at least three important ways. First, the state is not neutral as regards what forms of life and activities are genuinely worthwhile; the state need not provide instrumentalities suitable for worthless forms of life, such as a life of constant intoxication, or for depraved activities, such as indulgence in pornography; and the state may refuse such provisions precisely because of the worthlessness or depravity of such forms of life and activities. Moreover, Finnis has argued that the state should support religion, although not in ways that would transcend its authority.[25]

Second, while the relationships constitutive of the political do not introduce any *new* basic good, and while political society should not be considered a *pre-eminent* form of any good, nevertheless, a political realm, and a realm of persons under law, is an ordered relationship of wills in pursuit of a common end, and thus constitutes a form of friendship—political friendship, we could call it, since it is neither quite the same as a business friendship, a friendship of play, nor a friendship of virtue. This too, it seems to me, is a perfectionist element in Finnis's view.

Finally, Finnis's *liberalism* is itself ultimately understood in a perfectionist manner and contributes to his perfectionist account: human flourishing, both individually, and in the various communities of which the community of overlapping communities is comprised, requires the active self-constitution of the agents who make up these communities. Threats to that self-constitution make political society and the law a rational necessity as a *subsidium*, a help; but that self-constitution is hardly protected by a state that does not accord sufficient liberty to its citizens for them to *be* active self-constituters. This account of freedom within the confines of Finnis's work seems to me different from contemporary liberal accounts, which are often predicated on a

---

[23] A second kind of limit, common to proponents of natural law philosophy, is found in those absolute negative moral norms, violation of which the state can never rightly require or engage in; see *CEJF* III.5.

[24] As for example the view put forth in Dewan, 'St Thomas, John Finnis, and the Political Common Good'.

[25] See the distinction, in footnote 16, made in *Dignitatis humanae* between forms of treatment that show religion favour, and forms of treatment that transcend political authority. Taking religion to be a good worthy of being shown favour is a paradigmatically perfectionist approach; for Finnis's thoughts on religion and the state, see *CEJF* V.4.

scepticism or relativism about human goods; it also contributes in positive ways to his account of private property, which goes beyond the somewhat pessimistic justification offered by St. Thomas Aquinas to a recognition that a scheme of private property provides important opportunities for flourishing not available in more communal regimes.[26]

II. Means

I shall argue in the next section that the state is limited in the scope of its legislation to (a) interpersonal matters, and (b) external actions, in virtue of the form of perfectionism just described.[27] This will enable an interpretation of Mill's harm principle as primarily concerned with the appropriate *ends* of state legislation. But before turning to this implication of the limited scope of the perfectionist state, I look first at a dispute between Raz, on the one hand, and George and Finnis, on the other, over the permissible use of coercion for paternalistic purposes. This dispute primarily concerns the means it is permissible for the state to use in pursuit of its perfectionist ends; yet it naturally leads, as I shall show, to questions about the legitimate ends of state action.

In *On Liberty*, Mill identifies the 'very simple principle' that should 'govern absolutely' society:

> That principle is, that the sole end for which mankind are warranted, individually or collectively, in interfering with the liberty of action of any of their number, is self-protection. That the only purpose for which power can be rightfully exercised over any member of a civilized community, against his will, is to prevent harm to others. His own good, either physical or moral, is not sufficient warrant. He cannot rightfully be compelled to do or forbear because it will be better for him to do so, because it will make him happier, because, in the opinion of others, to do so would be wise, or even right . . . The only part of the conduct of anyone, for which he is amenable to society, is that which concerns others. In the part which merely concerns himself, his independence is, of right, absolute. Over himself, over his own body and mind, the individual is sovereign.[28]

Like Mill, Raz argues that state may use coercion to prevent harm. Raz understands 'harm' sufficiently broadly that the state can, say, impose a redistributive tax scheme, or use public funds for the provision of education and transportation services; by providing what is 'owed' to the recipients of such aid, the state prevents harm, even when non-action would not have left such recipients worse off than they otherwise would have been. Moreover, Raz believes that it is the 'function of government to promote morality',[29] and that government should 'create morally valuable opportunities and . . . eliminate morally

---

[26] I expand on this point in Tollefsen, 'Freedom and Equality in Market Exchange'.

[27] This point has been stressed by Finnis in recent work: '. . . law must be directed to the *common* good, is subject to equitable override, [and] must not go outside the domain of justice, which is *external* acts affecting *other* people' (*CEJF* IV.1, 31). This seems to represent a departure from earlier claims denying the legitimacy not just of the neutrality principle, but also of the harm principle, in *CEJF* III.2.

[28] Mill, *On Liberty*, 19.

[29] Raz, *The Morality of Freedom*, 415.

repugnant ones'.[30] But, despite these clearly perfectionist claims, Raz agrees with Mill that the state cannot, in service even of genuinely moral ends, coerce citizens as regards actions that, while morally repugnant, harm no other person. Raz gives two reasons for this:

> First, it violates the condition of independence and expresses a relation of domination and an attitude of disrespect for the coerced individual. Second, coercion by criminal penalties is a global and indiscriminate invasion of autonomy.[31]

Both of Raz's reasons here are problematic. First, it is deeply unclear why coercion of an individual to refrain from doing something of no benefit to that individual expresses an attitude of disrespect or domination. On Raz's own view, exercises of autonomy in pursuit of morally worthless options have no value as exercises of autonomy just as such. It is not too big a step from this to the claim that an agent who willingly chooses wrongly in fact harms himself, for he thereby misses opportunities to pursue worth-while options (thus, he is worse off than he otherwise would have been), and he habituates himself to worthless options. So preventing the agent from engaging in such options seems to show, not disrespect, but precisely respect to the agent as a person capable of human flourishing, and even to prevent harm.[32]

Something like this possibility, in fact, lurks in Raz's own discussion, generating barely concealed tensions. In the midst of his argument against coercion in regards to self-regarding immoralities, Raz acknowledges that his view 'can justify restricting the autonomy of one person for the sake of the greater autonomy of others *or even of that person himself in the future*'.[33] But Raz then immediately denies that the free pursuit of morally repugnant options detracts from an individual's autonomy.

It seems to me, however, that in any case which one might seriously propose as a candidate for paternalistic legislation on grounds of the immorality of the agent's self-regarding or consensual action, Raz's claim about the pursuit of repugnant options having no effect on an agent's autonomy is quite implausible. Free choice of any option, whether morally upright or not, tends to have the effect of disposing an agent to further choice of that, and similar, options. The eventually formed and settled dispositions do not remove the possibility of free choice in the future—upright agents can go on to choose immorally, and wastrels and scoundrels can turn their lives around. So, from one perspective, we might wish to agree with Raz that, in a deep metaphysical sense, the wrongdoer's future autonomy is not threatened by his immoral actions. But from a commonsense perspective, the perfectionist paternalist could surely argue that self-regarding immoralities are a threat to autonomy; thus, the argument that such pater-nalism would in fact show respect to the wrongdoer by preventing harm is strengthened, rather than the reverse.

Raz may perhaps, in his 'disrespect' objection, be gesturing at a different difficulty, one apparent just under the surface of the discussion of the need for law. We could put

---

[30] Raz, *The Morality of Freedom*, 417.
[31] Raz, *The Morality of Freedom*, 418.
[32] See George, *Making Men Moral*, 185. Finnis has made a similar claim on many occasions, often in response to Dworkin's anti-perfectionist claims. See, e.g., *CEJF* II.6, 109; and *CEJF* III.2, 52.
[33] Raz, *The Morality of Freedom*, 419, emphasis mine.

it in the form of a question: how is it that one man can stand in authority over another? Is there not something inappropriate about this given (a) the natural equality of persons; and (b), in conjunction with (a), given that an authority must stand in *judgment* over others, and, finally (c) given that the authority must also be able to exercise coercive power over his subjects? But this is not a problem particular to morals legislation but to *all* uses of judgment and the sword, and the answer, where morals legislation is concerned, is surely the same answer as in other cases: for one man to have such power can surely tempt him to domination and disrespect of those over which he has power; and this provides strong justification for that power to be invested in the impersonal and general standards of the law, standards that require men for their enforcement, but men operating not as men, but as functionaries of that impersonal law.[34]

Finally, Raz may, as George suggests, be focusing on the harm that punishment would bring to the offender against morals legislation. But on a retributivist account of punishment, punishment actually restores an order of wills that is constitutive of the common good, and 'though it may harm certain interests of the person punished, it is *in itself* a good'.[35] No contempt for the person need be expressed in this at all.[36]

Nor is Raz's second objection strong. There is some bluntness to the law, here as elsewhere. But this, as George points out, is a prudential consideration, and not a principled reason to oppose paternalistic morals legislation.[37] The upshot appears to be that, as far as perfectionism is concerned, the use of coercion in pursuit of the ends the state may legitimately promote does not appear to be as such an illicit means, nor do considerations about the use of force as such deliver a verdict on the limits to state paternalism (of course, prudential considerations about means still remain important).

The Raz-George-Finnis disagreement concerning the harm principle turns centrally on the question of means—is the use of coercion by the state somehow a specially problematic means where *only* the moral well-being of the coerced agent is at stake? Raz's objections to coercion do not, it seems to me, take up in a principled way the question of the legitimate ends of the state: do those ends include the moral well-being of the citizen just as such? But that question surely cries out to be answered at precisely this juncture.

Here, though, we find a new division within perfectionism on the subject of the harm principle, this time between George, on the one hand, and Finnis, on the other. For Finnis holds that recognition of the limited and instrumental nature of the state means that, as George summarizes his position, 'law and the state exceed their just authority—thus violating a principle of justice—when they go beyond the protection of the public moral environment and criminalize "even secret and truly consensual adult acts of vice"'.[38] But, says George in response, 'it does not follow, or so it seems to me, from the

---

[34] This response can be extended to a claim that Raz makes about coercion. He claims that in our society, coercion possesses, by convention, a symbolic quality expressive of disrespect. But one might equally claim that the law, and coercion carried out by means of law, possesses the opposite symbolic quality.

[35] George, *Making Men Moral*, 187.

[36] See, regarding retribution more generally, *CEJF* III.12.

[37] George, *Making Men Moral*, 187–8.

[38] George, 'The Concept of Public Morality', 107; the internal quotation is from *CEJF* III.5, 93.

instrumental nature of the political common good that moral paternalism, where it can be effective, is beyond the scope of that good'.[39] And so George, unlike Finnis, appears to hold that the only legitimate limits on legislation where self-regarding immoralities are concerned are prudential, not principled.

In the following section, I attempt to provide an argument for Finnis's position, starting from the description of the state given earlier, and concluding that there are indeed principled limits to the state's ability to legislate morality, limits that provide an interpretation of Mill's harm principle.

III. Ends

George's objection to Finnis is that the instrumental nature of the state alone does not show that morals legislation as such—e.g., in cases of merely self-regarding immorality—is impermissible. The state's instrumental nature presupposes ends towards which the state is instrumental; and, depending on the nature of these ends, it might be that some function of the state required it to legislate morality just as such. What is essential is the nature of the ends to which the state is instrumental. Here we should reconsider the fourfold purposes for which individuals, and the groups they constitute, are not self-sufficient: coordination amongst groups; defence against outsiders; defence and punishment against internal threats; and provision of care for those who are unable to care for themselves and cannot rely upon others who are obliged to care for them.

It is important to note that the need for a state—for political authority—arises at precisely the point at which individuals *and* social groups are no longer capable of adequately pursuing their well-being, and *this* inadequacy arises for the following reason: the inability of the overlapping groups effectively and fairly to coordinate and protect their common life. It is to this inability that the state, as it were, speaks; otherwise, it oversteps its proper authority.[40]

Consider the difference, then, between an agent contemplating the telling of a lie, and an agent being lied to. While in some contexts, such as those governing medicine or advertising, it might be appropriate or obligatory for the state to legislate concerning the truthfulness of some communication, this emerges from a lack of self-sufficiency only where the one lied to is concerned; that agent cannot effectively protect himself, nor can other interested parties fairly and effectively prohibit the act in question, investigate a breach, and try and punish offenders. Only political authority, and, indeed, the authority of agents operating under the law, can so act. But in the case of the agent considering lying, it is, at that moment, entirely within his power to do the right thing (even when, as earlier discussed, the agent has habituated himself to dishonesty). Accordingly, even if truth-telling (and, more generally, the virtue of

---

[39] George, 'The Concept of Public Morality', 109.

[40] The inability should be construed fairly broadly, however. In the modern age, for technological, financial, communicative, and geographical reasons, the ability of persons to *coordinate* their pursuit of certain essential tasks, like the promotion of scientific research, or the provision of health care, might require, to be reasonably efficient, the aid of the state. Such assistance should not be ruled out on grounds that the *benefits* the state promotes in these cases, knowledge and health, are not to be found among the fourfold purposes for which the state exists; it is the coordination for which the state is essential here.

honesty) is constitutive of the well-being of an agent, it is not as such a legitimate concern of the state for it is a matter over which agents are self-empowered. But where one agent's lies pose a sufficient threat to the potential well-being of another, and where the victim, and other private individuals and groups, are incapable of determining easily and accurately the truth of the matter, then the state legitimately concerns itself with honesty in communication.

It follows, of course, that across many contexts, the state will concern itself with actions that are immoral and degenerative of an agent's character, such as dishonesty. But in each case, the justification is centered on the interpersonal nature of the act and its threat to others, not the moral threat to the agent himself. Consider, for example, the problem of pornography. A public culture in which pornography abounds is properly a concern of the state not because of the choices of individual adult consumers of pornography who are, we will assume, morally capable of desisting, but because of the effects such a culture has on the lives of parents in families who are trying to raise children who will make the appropriate choices regarding pornography, and of adults who wish to live relatively free of the temptations and distractions afforded by omnipresent pornography, and of children and spouses who will be worse off for the harm that use of pornography creates for marriages. The capacity of these agents to live well—to make upright and effective self-constituting choices—is threatened by the choices of others, even if the former agents themselves wish to make entirely upright choices.

But an agent who, say, manufactured and consumed his own pornography in private would, while doing great harm to himself (including harm to his autonomy), be posing no threat to the attempts of others to lead upright lives. He would pose, in other words, no interpersonal threat. And this would be true even if the one person became two, manufacturing and consuming their pornography together, for they would pose no threat to those trying to lead upright lives. Even where multiple agents are engaged in consensual but immoral activities, so long as those activities are walled off from the rest of society's attempts at flourishing they are not, in the relevant sense, interpersonal— these mutually consenting agents do each other no injustice. At the same time, the agent or agents engaged in truly consensual and private vice should be assumed to be self-sufficient as regards the respect in which they are suffering harm; what is required for them to turn towards human flourishing bears upon their own choices.

The point may be made in a slightly different way. George's complaint against Finnis is that it is not clear why the *instrumental* nature of the state should militate against paternalism. But an instrument is a means to some end not otherwise attainable (or easily attainable). We need a hammer in order to join otherwise detached objects with nails. So if the state is an instrument, it addresses some need, some purpose that would otherwise not be attainable; it would address, in other words, some respect in which persons were insufficient for their own flourishing. But as regards their choices, persons *are* self-sufficient: they have sovereignty over their choices, right or wrong, that does not require the assistance of the state just as such. But, of course, individuals are not self-sufficient as regards the choices other agents make. So while it oversteps the limits of the state to coerce a citizen's choices for his own sake, it does not overstep the limits in coercing such choices for the sake of another. We can summarize the point: the state can only concern itself with properly interpersonal matters.

Finnis holds not only that the state must concern itself only with interpersonal actions, but also only with *external* actions; this too I think is defensible. Every agent, in order genuinely to live a flourishing life, requires an upright and integrated inner character: each must make the right choices, act upon those choices, and so structure his or her passions that those choices and actions are not sources of pain, nor are there constant temptations and inducements contrary to those choices and actions. More-over, in certain respects, agents are not self-sufficient as regards the effort to achieve such a character: children require parents, adults require friends and counsellors, and all agents find it helpful to achieve such integrity that they live in a generally upright environment. Still, this interior uprightness is ultimately a matter of the agent's choices and orientation of will. It cannot be imposed upon anyone, nor can anyone be *made* upright, or coerced, into uprightness.

What people can be made, or coerced, to do is merely what is external to their will (or their will can be broken, as by torture). This itself would suffice to limit the state's scope of action to the external: the state cannot make anyone just. Indeed, Finnis and George agree on this: George no more thinks that the state could make an agent virtuous than Finnis.

But George does think that the state can be *concerned* with this interior disposition of the agent in a way that Finnis does not, and can legislate actions with a view precisely to that interiority. George writes that where morals legislation prevents an agent from doing some immoral act, 'the immoral actors themselves are benefited, whether the acts from which they were deterred would have harmed others *or only themselves*'.[41] George does not seem here to be considering laws that prevent self-harm only as a side effect, but laws properly targeted at moral self-harm. The state's ends for George thus appear to include the internal virtue of its citizens, even though the permissible means available to the state are external only (moral action being reflexive, i.e., requiring a choice to be real, the state cannot just as such make an agent do the moral action). By contrast, on the view described above, the very needs for which the state exists are external needs only: matters of actions to be done or refrained from regardless of the motives of the agents precisely because they bear negatively upon others.

There is a deep connection between the interpersonality requirement and the externality requirement. For it is what you do or do not do that is a threat to me and my ability to flourish, not your motivation in so doing. Your character just as such does not affect me, save insofar as that character finds expression in action. So, as Finnis points out,[42] a cowardly character can become a concern of the state insofar as it issues in, e.g., cowardly actions on the battlefield; so too, a character of inadequately integrated sexual desire is of concern insofar as persons with that character tend to fail as spouses and parents, the social consequences of which are severe. But the state's concern is still with that character insofar as it is manifested in interpersonal and exterior actions.

---

[41] George, *Making Men Moral*, 226–7.   [42] *Aquinas*, 225.

To perfectionists, the claims that the state's concern is not with the overall flourishing, or the character of its citizens, or that the interiority of the person constitutes a principled, rather than a prudential, limit on the state's concern, will perhaps seem overly stark. This is a worry that should be addressed. In the ways that I have outlined, the stark claims are true: the needs for which the state provides a *subsidium*, a help, do not extend to the interiority of the person; interiority is thus a principled limit on the state's authority, and not just a matter of practical concern insofar as the state wishes not to legislate in inevitably inadequate ways. Nor do those needs extend to the complete and full flourishing of the state's citizens. Yet those needs—the needs for which the state is necessary—are needs only because they are essential to the genuine and full flourishing of human persons, for whose sake the state, and the law, exists. So it is true to say that the state exists *for the sake of* the complete flourishing of its citizens, including the interior personal integrity and uprightness that is essential to that flourishing, even while it is also true to say that the proximate ends for which the state exists, and which it instrumentally serves, *do not include* the complete flourishing of its citizens, including the interior personal integrity and uprightness that is essential to that flourishing. It is in holding both these thoughts together that perfectionism can chart a middle path between a more robust 'pure' paternalism, and the mutual insurance view of the state that both Finnis and Aristotle deride.

Exteriority and interpersonality thus flow from the instrumental nature of the state given the (proximate) ends to which it is instrumental. And this generates a perfectionist endorsement of Mill's harm principle: that 'the only purpose for which power can be rightfully exercised over any member of a civilized community, against his will, is to prevent harm to others'.[43] This principle need not be read as anti-perfectionist, for harm can be understood broadly and richly as determined by a substantive understanding of human goods. Nor need it be read as prohibiting some forms of morals legislation for the sake of heading off adverse social consequences on grounds that coercion as such is somehow disrespectful. But it does point to the origins of the need for the state, in the lack of self-sufficiency of individuals and groups in pursuing their well-being, and to the limits of the state that are a consequence of those origins. A perfectionist political theory that begins from that starting point thus does end, as Finnis claims Aquinas ends, at a position 'not readily distinguishable from the "grand simple principle"... of John Stuart Mill's *On Liberty*'.[44]

Bibliography

Arkes, Hadley (1992), *Beyond the Constitution* (Princeton, NJ: Princeton University Press).

Dewan, Lawrence (2000), 'St. Thomas, John Finnis, and the Political Good', *The Thomist* 64: 337–74.

Dworkin, Ronald (1977, 1978), *Taking Rights Seriously* (rev. edn with reply to critics) (Cambridge, MA: Harvard University Press).

Dworkin, Ronald (1985), *A Matter of Principle* (Cambridge, MA: Harvard University Press).

Finnis, John (1980; 2011), *Natural Law and Natural Rights* (Oxford: Oxford University Press).

---

[43] Mill, *On Liberty*, 19.   [44] *Aquinas*, 228.

Finnis, John (1987), 'Duties to Oneself in Kant', in *Collected Essays: Volume III*, 47–71.

Finnis, John (1996), 'Limited Government', in *Collected Essays: Volume III*, 83–106.

Finnis, John (1998a), *Aquinas: Moral, Political and Legal Theory* (Oxford: Oxford University Press).

Finnis, John (1998b), '"Public Reason" and Moral Debate', in *Collected Essays: Volume I*, 256–76.

Finnis, John (1999), 'Retribution: Punishment's Formative Aim', in *Collected Essays: Volume III*, 167–79.

Finnis, John (2003), 'Describing Law Normatively', in *Collected Essays: Volume IV*, 23–45.

Finnis, John (2006), 'Religion and State', in *Collected Essays: Volume V*, 80–102.

Finnis, John (2009), 'Hart as a Political Philosopher', in *Collected Essays: Volume IV*, 257–79.

Finnis, John (2011a), *Collected Essays: Volume I, Reason in Action* (Oxford: Oxford University Press).

Finnis, John (2011b), *Collected Essays: Volume II, Intention and Identity* (Oxford: Oxford University Press).

Finnis, John (2011c), *Collected Essays: Volume III, Human Rights and Common Good* (Oxford: Oxford University Press).

Finnis, John (2011d), *Collected Essays: Volume IV, Philosophy of Law* (Oxford: Oxford University Press).

Finnis, John (2011e), *Collected Essays: Volume V, Religion and Public Reasons* (Oxford: Oxford University Press).

Finnis, John (2011f), 'Law, Universality, and Social Identity', in *Collected Essays: Volume II*, 100–21.

Finnis, John (2011g), 'Political Neutrality and Religious Arguments', in *Collected Essays: Volume V*, 103–12.

George, Robert P. (1993), *Making Men Moral: Civil Liberties and Public Morality* (Oxford: Oxford University Press).

George, Robert P. (2001), 'The Concept of Public Morality', in *The Clash of Orthodoxies: Law, Religion and Morality in Crisis* (Wilmington, DE: ISI Books).

Mill, J.S. ([1856] 2011), *On Liberty* (Hollywood, FL: Simon and Brown).

Pakaluk, Michael (2001), 'Is the Common Good of Political Society Limited and Instrumental?', *The Review of Metaphysics* 55: 57–94.

Rawls, John ([1993] 1996), *Political Liberalism* (New York: Columbia University Press).

Raz, Joseph (1986), *The Morality of Freedom* (Oxford: Oxford University Press).

Tollefsen, Christopher (2009), 'Disability and Social Justice', in Chris Ralston and Justin Ho (eds), *Philosophical Perspectives on Disability* (Dordrecht: Springer), 211–27.

Tollefsen, Christopher (2010), 'Freedom and Equality in Market Exchange: Some Natural Law Reflections', *Harvard Journal of Law and Public Policy* 33: 487–94.

Yowell, Paul (2007), 'A Critical Examination of Dworkin's Theory of Rights', *American Journal of Jurisprudence* 52: 93–137.

14

'Lawful Mercy' in *Measure for Measure*

Jacqueline Tasioulas and John Tasioulas

John Finnis's writings on punishment are characterized by a retributivist pluralism: retributive justice is essential and fundamental to the justification of punishment, but other values also play an important justificatory role, both with regard to the institution in general and to particular decisions made within it, such as sentences passed by judges.[1] As to the first prong of the thesis, Finnis characterizes the sphere of justice in general in terms of the following three features: it is *other-directed*, taking as its subject matter our relations and dealings with other people; it concerns duties towards those others regarding which they possess counterpart *rights*; and it gives expression to some norm of *equality* in interpersonal relations.[2] Retributive justice, as a specific norm of justice, grounds an obligatory punitive response to certain rights violations. On Finnis's view, punishment vindicates the rights of the law-abiding members of the community who have been unfairly taken advantage of by the offender's wrongful indulgence of his will. He is considerably sketchier about the non-(retributive) justice values—aspects of the public good of which the law properly takes heed—that play a role regarding the justification of punishment.[3] But they seem to include considerations relating to the deterrence or non-deterrence of further criminal behaviour through the infliction of punishment. In line with this sketchiness, he nowhere engages in an extended discussion of the value that many believe has a prominent role in deliberation about punishment, albeit one parasitic on retributive justice, i.e. mercy. On a standard interpretation, mercy is a matter of imperfect obligation, not something to which its beneficiary has a right, hence it falls outside the sphere of justice. The apparent absence of mercy from Finnis's discussion is all the more notable given that two of his intellectual heroes, Aquinas and Shakespeare, both accord it great significance. For Aquinas, mercy is the highest of all virtues insofar as they relate to how we should treat our fellow human beings.[4] For Shakespeare, it is a dominant theme in a number of plays, most notably *The Merchant of Venice* and *Measure for Measure*.[5] In this essay, we offer a reading of the latter play in the broad spirit of retributivist pluralism.

* * *

---

[1] This twin thesis finds expression, as early as 1968, in a review of H.L.A. Hart's *Punishment and Responsibility*: 'What he [Hart] never explains is why it should not be an aim of punishment to restore the order of justice, by getting the criminal to pay a price for the ill-gotten satisfactions he obtained in indulging his will to injure and in preferring his will to the will of society—satisfactions which his law-abiding fellows have denied themselves. (Moreover, Hart does not explain why there should be only one aim of punishment, not several: there is something suspiciously rigid about his differentiation between Definition, General Justifying Aim (singular), and Distribution.)', *CEJF* III.10, 158–9.

[2] *NLNR*, 161–3.   [3] *CEJF* III.10, 164–5.   [4] *ST* II-II, q.30, a.4.

[5] On the Thomistic background to Shakespeare's engagement with mercy, see the interesting and provocative discussion in Parker, *The Slave of Life*.

The interpretative challenge posed by *Measure for Measure* is an unusually difficult one. Coleridge famously called it a 'horrible' play, its comedy 'disgusting'.[6] More recently, and less damningly, Kermode describes it as a 'muddle', at least from the second half onwards: an unsuccessful attempt at overlaying the logic of comedy on an essentially tragic theme.[7] As such, it is a 'problem play', a term that is apt not simply because of the vagaries of its genre, but because at its heart lies a problem, or even series of problems. It is, as the title's biblical echo implies, a play about justice; but it is also a play about mercy, and we are compelled in the course of events to attend to the complex relationship between the two ideas. Set in the court of Vienna, the play presents us with government officials, executioners, bawds, and criminals, among whom is a young man sentenced to death for no greater crime than making his fiancée pregnant. His sister, a novice nun, appeals for mercy but is offered his life only at the price of her own chastity. The play signals the notorious difficulty involved in forming an adequate conception of justice and mercy, and in striking an appropriate balance between their distinct and apparently sometimes competing claims.

The words 'justice' and 'mercy' bear a multiplicity of senses in *Measure for Measure*. Minimally, however, we may interpret justice as concerned with the application of rules, paradigmatically properly enacted laws. On this bare conception, justice is a matter of treating like cases alike, where the criterion of likeness is picked out by the legal rule itself, which is to be strictly applied in accordance with its literal terms. Justice, as the strict application of a legal rule, is not influenced by the law-applier's independent grasp of the underlying values that the rule itself was fashioned to advance, let alone by the bearing of any extraneous considerations that may arise, whether they be moral in nature or considerations of self-interest or expediency. On a comparably minimalist construal, mercy is exhibited by any lenient deviation from the strict and impartial application of a legal rule; that is, by any deviation that ameliorates or removes some hardship that someone was liable to suffer through the rule's strict application. Lenient deviations from legal rules, broadly understood, do not only arise with regard to the punishment of criminals; they also bear on the application of any legal rule whose strict application would result in the imposition of some kind of burden on another. Understood in this minimalist fashion, justice and mercy are not obviously values—genuine sources of practical reasons—in all circumstances, but perhaps at best proto-values.[8] This is because it is far from obvious that there is always a genuine reason, let alone a moral reason, either to apply a law strictly according to its terms or else to exercise leniency in its application.

Against this background, we can interpret two of the main protagonists of *Measure for Measure*—Angelo and the Duke—as personifying radically contrasting attitudes to the question of strictness and leniency in the application of the law. Although their positions occupy opposite ends of the spectrum, both embody a defective grasp of the genuine values in play. Insofar as Nuttall and others interpret the play as oscillating

---

[6] Raysor, *Coleridge's Shakespearean Criticism*, 113–15.

[7] Kermode, *Shakespeare's Language*, 164.

[8] According to H.L.A. Hart, however, the impartial application of the law 'equally' according to its terms is a requirement of justice, Hart, *The Concept of Law*, 160.

between the two extremes of a strict legalism and an uncritical leniency, they offer us an unduly restricted range of options.[9] The real message of the play is that the question of when to apply the law strictly and when to exercise leniency is often highly complex, and that a half-way satisfactory response to it transcends both the rigour of the 'precise' Angelo and the laxity of the self-indulgent Duke.

As *Measure for Measure* opens, Duke Vincentio is preparing to leave the city that he has ruled for more than 19 years, a period in which Vienna has become a centre of depravity, vice, and criminality. It is not that he wanted the city to suffer this fate, nor even that he simply does not care about its citizens; rather the Duke has a personal inability to enforce the law and administer justice. As he later explains:

> We have strict statutes and most biting laws
> The needful bits and curbs to headstrong jades,
> Which for this fourteen years we have let slip;
> Even like an o'er-grown lion in a cave
> That goes not out to prey. Now, as fond fathers,
> Having bound up the threatening twigs of birch,
> Only to stick it in their children's sight
> For terror, not to use, in time the rod
> Becomes more mock'd than fear'd: so our decrees,
> Dead to infliction, to themselves are dead,
> And Liberty plucks Justice by the nose,
> The baby beats the nurse, and quite athwart
> Goes all decorum. (I, iii, 19–31)

Quite simply, he is the cause of the city's troubles. There were indeed laws, but finding them too harsh, the Duke has granted mercy to almost all, the end result being a legal system that has become something of a joke. A central theme of the play, then, is the rightful conduct of government through the application of law: the considerations that properly bear on whether law should be strictly applied (justice, in the minimalist sense) or whether leniency should be shown (mercy, in the minimalist sense). Indeed, given the need for legal rules in protecting us against anarchy and disorder, a special concern is with how properly to integrate leniency within a scheme of government: how to distinguish between 'devilish mercy' (III, i, 64) or mercy that proves itself a 'bawd' (III, i, 147), on the one hand, and 'lawful mercy' which is 'nothing kin to foul redemption' (II, iv, 113), on the other. Another way of putting the distinction in question: how to separate out leniency that manifests the arbitrary will of the ruler from that which is properly regulated by authentic values, including the values of justice and mercy in some non-minimalist sense. So, for example, considered as a genuine value, mercy is not realized, or given its proper weight, in every act of official leniency. Rulers can be deeply mistaken as to the demands of both justice and mercy, and they can also be mistaken about how those demands are to be integrated in reaching a judgement as to what they should do, all things considered.

---

[9] Nuttall, *Shakespeare the Thinker*, 266–7.

Sadly, while the Duke acknowledges that it is his own inability to administer justice that has led to trouble in Vienna, his prevailing attitude is not sorrow at the pitiful condition of his subjects, but rather a slightly piqued concern that his 'mercy' has not been appreciated, and that the law, and by implication he himself, has become an object of ridicule. There is a strong element of self-indulgence in his description of himself as a lion that will not hunt, a doting father who spares the rod and spoils the child, and yet the images are perversions of the natural order. Ending, as he does, on a half-line, the word 'decorum' is given heavy emphasis. Its Renaissance definition is complex. For the Duke what is paramount is the loss of the dignity accorded to his office: there is something unseemly about this nose-plucking state of affairs that he feels reflects badly upon himself. But a further meaning lurks behind this one that has nothing to do with outward show; it is concerned instead with making judgements proper to the circumstances and requirements of a given case.[10] It is primarily this second meaning of decorum that should matter to the Duke, but repeatedly in the play he concerns himself with appearances over substantive matters. He likes the look of mercy, finds it becoming to a ruler, but has failed to exercise it with due judgement. His is the kind of arbitrary leniency, manifesting the brute power of rulers, which has traditionally given mercy a bad name.

Something of this sense is present in the imprisoned Claudio's likening of the law to 'unscour'd armour, hung by th' wall' (I, ii, 1.156). The Duke thinks only of the law as a sharp weapon, that he refuses to use to 'strike and gall' (I, iii, 36) his people. But Claudio's image of rusty armour is a reminder that the law also protects, and that displays of mercy towards those guilty of crimes can result either in further harm to their victims, or more widespread harm in the ensuing spirit of lawlessness.[11] The consequences of his acts to unknown others are never accorded their proper significance by the Duke; instead, he is overly concerned with immediate action, and the way in which he is perceived by the wrongdoer and his subjects generally. Incapable of restoring law and order to Vienna, he has temporarily handed power to his deputy, Lord Angelo, in the expectation that Angelo will administer the law with enough severity to clean up the mess. He is not, however, being brought in as some kind of executioner. The Duke admittedly gives him less than five lines of instruction while taking 18 lines to say that he really does not have time to talk, but it is clear that Angelo has been granted the power to be merciful where he sees fit:

> Mortality and mercy in Vienna
> Live in thy tongue, and heart. (I, i, 44–5)

> …Your scope is as mine own,
> So to enforce or qualify the laws
> As to your soul seems good. (I, i, 64–6)

---

[10] *Antony and Cleopatra* has instances of both: I, i, 67, and V, ii, 19.

[11] According to Aquinas, the reproof of others' wrongdoing can be based either on the harm the wrongdoer does to himself or the harm caused to others, including upsetting the balance of the common good. The first sort of reproof is an act of charity; the second, which can take a coercive form, is a matter of justice, understood as a specific value among others to which the law should be attentive (the full set of these values can be understood as legal, general, or universal justice). *ST* II-II, q.33, a.1. Omitting punishment in a case of the second sort, out of fear of upsetting the offender or public opinion, is a mortal sin. *ST* II-II, q.33, a.2, ad.3; a.6.

It is not, however, clear to Angelo. As soon as the Duke has been waved off (ostensibly to Poland, but in reality only around the corner in order that he might secretly monitor proceedings), both Angelo and the deputy Escalus confess that neither of them is sure of their new role, and in spite of the scope of the power given to him, Angelo's understanding of justice turns out to be a narrow legalism. For him, justice is a matter of consistency with a given rule, where the rule in question is embodied in the positive legal order. More disturbingly, he appears to regard the law as exhausting the genuine reasons that bear on him in his capacity as a public official.

We might have anticipated this. Confronted with the Duke's plan to surrender power, Angelo's reservations are couched in terms that portray himself as a stamped coin:

> Let there be some more test made of my metal,
> Before so noble and so great a figure
> Be stamp'd upon it (I, i, 47–9)

It is an extension of the Duke's earlier metaphor, 'What figure of us, think you, [Angelo] will bear?' (I, i, 16). Our 'angel', it emerges, is not a heavenly being, but rather the 16th-century English coin of the same name; and just as the coin is blank until stamped, Angelo lacks an appreciation of the requirements of public morality independent of the law. He operates exclusively within the structure imposed by a system of extraneously posited legal rules, with no basis on which to justify deviations from their strict application. He is 'the voice of the recorded law' (III, iv, 61) whatever that turns out to be, and under the newly resurrected law code of Vienna, it turns out to be a truly terrifying voice. The pendulum has swung from the capricious leniency of the Duke to the rigid law enforcement of Angelo. His narrow, formalistic construal of justice, which he takes to exhaust the whole of public morality, is as defective as the Duke's universal pardon.

First, Angelo's 'precise' adherence to the rules prevents him from seriously entertaining the critical question as to whether a given law represents a generally adequate attempt to advance the public good. So, for example, the severity of the repressive sexual laws in Vienna is never a cause for concern on the part of Angelo.[12] That the law lays down the death penalty for sex outside marriage is conclusive for him. It is left to the fools, as so often in Shakespeare, to remind the higher powers of the limitations of human nature, and to point out the futility of rules that deny those limitations. Thus, the bawd Pompey Bum, informed by Escalus of the reinstated law against pre-marital sex, inquires, 'Does your worship mean to geld and splay all the youth of the city?' (II, i, 227). Similarly, the rake Lucio comments that while Vienna may have given itself over to sexual freedom, 'it is impossible to extirp it quite,/ . . . till eating and drinking be put down' (III, ii, 98–9).[13]

---

[12] It is noteworthy that Shakespeare himself would have stood condemned under such a law had it applied to his time.

[13] Now, as Finnis has rightly pointed out: 'Aristotle and Aquinas insisted that, though it is a principle of natural law that crimes should be punished, there is no natural measure of punishment; the degree and kind of punishment is in fact a traditional stock-example of what is left to pure positive law: *NE* 1134b22; *ST* I-II, q.95, a.2c.)', in *CEJF* III.10, 159; see also *CEJF* III.12, 178–9. But, of course, the fact that natural reason does

The truth of these observations is clear, but there is no room for such truths in Angelo's Vienna. The fact remains that Claudio must die. Claudio's explanation for the plight in which he and Juliet find themselves is less clear-cut than Angelo's condemnation of it. They are very willingly betrothed, and merely prevented by lack of funds from seeking the church's formal approval of their union; but Angelo's concern is with exactly the 'outward order' (I, ii, 138) they lack. It is not entirely clear how extreme a form of legalism he embraces. At one point he seems to assume that legal wrongs exhaust all wrongs, with the implicit suggestion that it is the very fact of their being illegal that *makes* those forms of conduct morally wrongful: 'Why, every fault's condemn'd ere it be done' (II, ii, 38). On the other hand, it is significant that Angelo does offer a justification for imposing the death penalty for sexual relations outside marriage. But the very nature of that justification partly serves to underline his legalism, for it turns on a strained analogy between bringing about the birth of an illegitimate child and taking a life through murder:

> It were as good
> To pardon him that hath from nature stolen
> A man already made, as to remit
> Their saucy sweetness that do coin heaven's image
> In stamps that are forbid. 'Tis all as easy
> Falsely to take away a life true made,
> As to put mettle in restrainèd means
> To make a false one. (II, iv, 42–9)

Never far from his 'stamping' metaphors, Angelo's argument is that illegitimate birth is a form of forgery; forgery is a form of theft; and theft of a life is murder, murder clearly being a crime. The argument is an *ad hominem* one: if you believe that murder is wrong, then in consistency you are committed to believing that fornication is also wrong. There is a question, perhaps, whether Angelo would have regarded murder as wrong if it were not a crime according to law. But even if we do not foist on him the extreme legalist view that action being illegal is both necessary and sufficient for anything being a moral wrong, it remains the case that his moral outlook is unduly uncritical of the content of existing law. The law is, for him, fundamentally something to be applied according to its terms, not to be assessed against an independent moral touchstone.

Second, Angelo's attitude to the law prevents him from taking seriously the possibility that, even if the laws in question are in principle legitimate and effective means of furthering the public good, their application in certain unforeseen or unusual circumstances, both generally and the particular case, may yield an excessively harsh result, thereby providing a compelling reason for leniency in their application. This possibility is flagged by other characters, most notably the other judge, Escalus, whose presence in the play provides a counterpoint to the actions and beliefs of Angelo. Dealing with the

not yield a uniquely correct verdict about the appropriate measure of punishment for any given crime, which along with other rational considerations creates the need for a legal-institutional stipulation, is perfectly consistent with natural reason setting important constraints on the acceptable range of stipulations, as well as on the forms of activity that are properly subject to criminal sanction.

legal disputes of the comic sub-plot, Escalus proceeds with patience and good humour. First, he shows himself sensitive to the point that, having been dormant for so many years—nine or 15 years, the very indeterminacy of the period of desuetude only serving to underline the point—suddenly to apply these draconian laws constitutes a failure to give due notice to those whose interests are liable to be adversely affected by them. Therefore, he is lenient to Pompey on the grounds that the latter has had insufficient notice of the new strict regime of enforcement. Next time, and it is clear from the tenor of Pompey's asides to the audience that there will be a next time, 'in plain dealing' (II, i, 246), he shall be whipped; but for now he has been given due warning. The scene ends with Escalus' observation that, 'Mercy is not itself, that oft looks so;/Pardon is still the nurse of second woe' (II, i, 280–1). He is, unlike the Duke, sensitive to the reper-cussions of the noble pardon; and he can see the force in Angelo's assertion that the criminal who is punished for one crime, 'Lives not to act another' (II, ii, 105), but Pompey has been given the benefit of the doubt, this time. Escalus has no wish, however, to imitate the Duke's incontinent leniency, and he does not hesitate to punish the repeat offender Mistress Overdone.

Escalus is also helpful in illustrating the need to distinguish between different levels of severity in the violation of laws. Here, in particular, it is arguable that Claudio, in view of the pre-contract, has committed a violation that is much less culpable than the sort anticipated by the law, even if we assume that the death penalty is a deserved punishment in the general run of cases. With this second case, we are in the domain of Aristotelian *epieikeia* or equity: the idea that unanticipated circumstances may arise in which one must deviate from the strict application of a law that is otherwise generally acceptable in order to avoid an unjust result. A law demanding the return of a weapon to its owner can be set aside when the latter has become dangerously insane, as can a law requiring the closure of the city gates at a specified hour when doing so would leave those defending the city at the mercy of invaders. In Aquinas' lucid rendering:

> [B]ecause human acts about which laws are made exist as particular happenings, infinitely variable, there is no possibility of laying down a rule of law that would cover every case. Legislators rather take into account what is ordinarily the case and formulate a law accordingly. Yet observing this law in some situations runs counter to the rightness of justice and the public good intended by all law ... Thus in these and similar cases to follow the word of law would be an evil; a good to follow what the meaning of justice and the public good demand, letting the letter of the law be set aside. Epieikeia—we call it equity—is addressed to this end and so clearly is a virtue (*ST* II-II, q.120, a.1).

Or, in the familiar Latin maxim, *summum ius summa iniuria*, which supplies us with the proper context for understanding Escalus' observation concerning Angelo that 'my brother-justice have I/found so severe that he hath forced me to tell him he is indeed Justice' (III, ii, 240–2). Notice that equity, so understood, does not have an inherent link to leniency: the situation-specific considerations overlooked by the law may be such as to justify augmenting, rather than mitigating, the legally stipulated punishment. However, the proper exercise of equity in criminal adjudication will systematically tend towards leniency because of the constraining influence of the principle of fair notice discussed above, this time in the guise of another maxim, *nulla poena sine lege.*[14]

A third major defect in Angelo's approach to the law is that he is blind to the possibility of mercy in a more specific sense. This is the sense according to which there is reason to temper, out of charitable concern for the wrongdoer, a punishment that is actually deserved by the latter as a matter of retributive justice.[15] Retributive justice here bears the meaning of a specific moral standard, among others, to which the criminal law should be attentive. So, even if we confine ourselves to the situation in which the punishment laid down by law is not only generally the deserved punishment for a wrong, but also the deserved punishment in this particular case, there may be additional, leniency-justifying considerations that may be taken into account, these considerations giving the official a reason to punish the wrongdoer less severely than retributive desert alone would allow. For example, although an offender's subsequent repentance does not alter the gravity of his original wrongdoing, and therefore the punishment he deserves for it, it may be a reason to punish him less severely than a focus exclusively on desert would permit. Mercy is grounded in a proper concern for the offender's interests. Although there may be a duty to show such mercy in certain circumstances, the offender does not have a right to it, hence mercy does not fall within the boundary of justice, but is instead one legally relevant value among others.[16] The words of Escalus once again force a comparison with Angelo as he claims that, 'If my brother wrought by my pity, it should not be/so with him' (III, ii, 204–5).[17] Claudio would not be condemned to die if Angelo felt the pity that Escalus feels, and such pity motivates his advice:

> Let us be keen, and rather cut a little,
> Than fall, and bruise to death. Alas, this gentleman,
> Whom I would save, had a most noble father. (II, i, 5–7)

But Angelo allows no autonomous role to considerations of mercy or pity. Instead, insofar as pity is a legitimate consideration, it is subsumed under his master-value of strictly applying the law according to its terms. When Claudio's sister, Isabella, begs that he show some pity, Angelo responds: 'I show it most of all when I show justice;/For then I pity those I do not know' (II, ii, 101–2). In its own way, this is a fair point, and one that the Duke would have done well to consider, but it cannot be the whole story. Angelo claims that his would be 'the very cipher of a function' (II, ii, 39–41) were he to register Claudio's wrongdoing and, in deference to Isabella's plea for mercy, refrain from punishing him. But, ironically, it is the very extreme nature of his legalism that turns him into such a cipher: 'It is the law, not I, condemn your brother' (II, ii, 80),

---

[14] For a discussion of the interplay between equity and rule of law considerations, including *nulla poena sine lege*, see Tasioulas, 'The Paradox of Equity'.

[15] For one account of mercy in this sense, see Tasioulas, 'Mercy' and Tasioulas, 'Punishment and Repentance'.

[16] To the extent that it is one legally relevant value among others, mercy forms part of justice in an expansive sense, see Tasioulas, 'Where is the Love?'

[17] Pity is here to be understood as *misericordia*, or what is often translated as 'mercy', which consists in 'compassion for the misery of another'. *ST* II-II, q.30, a.1, ad.2.

since he renounces the independent judgement that a judge must exercise in deciding whether or not strictly to apply the law.

Angelo's general insensitivity as a judge to any reasons beyond those encoded in the law, his lack of a capacity for emotionally and intellectually registering their importance, is underlined by the descriptions and imagery used by others in relation to him. They portray him as cold, hard, inhuman, lacking in fellow-feeling: 'begot between two stockfishes', his urine 'congealed ice' (III, ii, 106–7). With typical perspicacity, the rake Lucio sees him for what he is: a 'motion' (III, ii, 108), a mere puppet. So, in Angelo, it is arguable that a lack of *sensibility*, especially fellow-feeling, is bound up with an inability to see the *sense*—the good reasons or normative significance—of a range of considerations that can justify lenient deviations from the strict application of the rule of law. In particular, his inhumanity (lack of capacity for fellow-feeling) explains his inability to grasp the idea that mercy may justify tempering the law's application. To the extent that sensibility creeps into Angelo's world, it is not feelings of humanity that are attentive to the needs and suffering of others, but rather lustful urges that are essentially self-centred, treating Isabella as an object of their gratification.

Isabella is by nature a character who desires restraint, a novice nun whose first words in the play seek confirmation that the rules in the convent will be strict enough for her. Nevertheless, discovering that her brother has been sentenced to death for making his fiancée pregnant, Isabella goes to Angelo to plead for his life. As life or death entreaties go, however, hers is strangely reluctant: a chiasmic play on the difference between what she wants to do and what she must do, in which the repetition and rhetoric serve only to diminish the force of her apparent desire. She leads with a firm declaration that fornication is a crime that must be punished by the 'blow of justice', an unfortunately evocative term given the precarious state of her brother's neck:

> There is a vice that most I do abhor,
> And most desire should meet the blow of justice;
> For which I would not plead, but that I must,
> For which I must not plead, but that I am
> At war 'twixt will and will not. (II, ii, 29–33)

She seems very ready to concede that in strict justice—not just in terms of the law, but of independent moral desert—the death penalty is a justified punishment for Claudio. A further three lines of explanation take her to the end of her suit, and a refusal by Angelo to pardon her brother. At least, Isabella takes it as a refusal. In fact, it is a question in which Angelo asks whether we can condemn the sin and not the sinner, but Isabella is so ready to give up that her response condemns her brother to death before any appeal is concluded: 'O just but severe law!/I had a brother, then: heaven keep your honour' (II, ii, 42–3).

It is only the presence of Lucio, directing from the sidelines, that prevents her leaving, but in response to Lucio's urgings to pluck at Angelo's sleeve, and beg him for her brother's life, she enquires instead into Angelo's use of the auxiliary 'will':

> Ang. I will not do't.
> Isab. But can you if you would?
> Ang. Look what I will not, that I cannot do. (II, ii, 51–3)

It is all too cold for Lucio's taste: he wants her to play the supplicant, weep and beg for mercy. But Isabella wants to engage in a rational argument. She wants mercy for her brother, but she expects it to be the result of a reasoned decision on the part of the judge, not a knee-jerk response to the sight of a weeping woman. However, for Angelo the law is what it is, and his will has nothing to do with it. The very nature of her question, however, shows that this is not the case for Isabella. She respects the law and she regards her brother as guilty of wrongdoing, but she hesitantly arrives at the understanding that we do not have to accept the contrast between the mindsets of Angelo and the Duke as exhaustive of the moral possibilities. We are not saddled with a stark choice between the strict enforcement of the laws laid down, on the one hand, or else lenient deviations motivated by whim on the other. The capacity to reason enables us to stand back, both from the existing law and from any given array of personal inclinations we might have, to ask whether acting on the law or the inclination makes sense in this particular context. It enables us to assess them in the light of genuine values, including justice and mercy. In so doing, it holds out the prospect that the question of whether strictly to apply the law or else to exercise leniency is a matter for rational assessment, hence justifiable in light of objective reasons, and not simply hostage to one's subjective commitments.[18] This fits with Isabella's seemingly consistent commitment to rational persuasion. Her question to Angelo, 'Who is it that hath died for this offence?/There's many have committed it' (II, ii, 88–9) is very much to the point, and of all the characters in *Measure for Measure* she asks the most probing questions about punishment and desert.

However, Isabella does not stop there. She explores the notion that in arriving at rational assessments regarding matters of value, emotion need not be a hindrance, indeed it may even be an indispensable aid to the process. Her earlier chiasmus as she awkwardly begged for her brother's life on the grounds of strict justice is now employed to evoke empathy: 'If he had been as you, and you as he' (II, ii, 64) she claims, there would have been mercy shown. The point here is not so much that emotions are subject to rational assessment, i.e. that we can have reasons for or against a particular emotional response. Rather, the idea is that reason and emotion, feeling and thought, have to work harmoniously together if we are to register the import of certain values. Sense (good sense, reason) and sensibility (capacity for an emotional response) do not necessarily stand in an antagonistic relationship; they may be cooperative partners in determining the content of justice and mercy and how to integrate their demands in justifiable official action. On this diagnosis, Angelo's inability to register the import of a whole range of considerations is bound up with his cold character, devoid of empathy or fellow-feeling, while the Duke's similar inability is due to the fact that his feelings, although by no means entirely lacking in concern for others, are not sufficiently

---

[18] The point is particularly worth emphasizing regarding mercy, which is often unfairly tarred with the accusation of being an expression of subjective whim. In the context of this discussion of the reason-governed character of mercy, we should note the distinction Aquinas draws between two kinds of pain over another's misfortune (mercy). One is a movement of the sense appetite, an emotion or feeling unregulated by reason, hence not a virtue. This can fly in the face of reason's counsel. The other is a movement of the intellective appetite and, as such, 'can be regulated by right reason and, thus regulated, can in turn regulate the movements of the lower appetite' (*ST* II-II, q.30, a.3). When thus regulated mercy is a virtue.

disciplined by the critical perspective of reason. By contrast, the ideal implicit in some of Isabella's pleas involves access to an enhanced moral understanding of a situation through the integrated workings of reason and feeling, sense and sensibility:

> ...Go to your bosom,
> Knock there, and ask your heart what it doth know
> That's like my brother's fault. If it confess
> A natural guiltiness, such as is his,
> Let it not sound a thought upon your tongue
> Against my brother's life. (II, ii, 137–42)[19]

What is more, Isabella apparently recognizes that there is a place for mercy in appropriate cases as a counterpoint to retributive justice. Not indiscriminate leniency, but rather a suspension or tempering of the deserved punishment on the basis of a due regard for the interests of the wrongdoer. Mercy so understood falls beyond the scope of justice; even if there is an obligation to bestow it, it is not something to which the offender has a moral right. Thus, she calls for Claudio's imminent execution to be halted on the grounds that, 'He's not prepar'd for death. Even for our kitchens/We kill the fowl of season' (II, ii, 85–6). As she proceeds, Isabella also sets her sights higher, invoking the mercy of heaven itself:

> Why, all the souls that were, were forfeit once,
> And He that might the vantage best have took
> Found out the remedy. How would you be
> If He, which is the top of judgement, should
> But judge you as you are? O, think on that,
> And mercy then will breathe within your lips,
> Like man new made. (II, ii, 74–8)

This is her 'Portia' moment, but pretty as it is, it does not quite sustain the Christ-like mercy of its opening. The movement is downwards, away from heaven towards a much more expedient, 'judge not that you be not judged' argument. It is no more effective in eliciting mercy from Angelo than it was in getting Shylock to change his mind. Shylock's response to the argument that the 'quality of mercy is not strained', is: 'My deeds upon my head! I crave the law' (*The Merchant of Venice*, IV, i, 203), and Angelo's response is similar: this is nothing to do with him; it is the law that condemns Claudio. As such, his sins, his interests, his inclinations are all immaterial.

In the end, Isabella fails to convince Angelo, but it remains an extraordinary scene in that it lays before us an array of arguments in favour of mercy, to which Angelo's answers are certainly limited. He is the hedgehog to Isabella's fox, tight and defensive as she approaches him from all angles. He knows only that the law is the law, and Isabella's appeals make no difference. It is only desire for her that makes Angelo finally say that he will stay the execution. Being Angelo, of course, it does not occur to him

---

[19] As Aquinas points out, there are two ways in which we can come to see another's misfortune as our own: if we bear some special relationship to them, e.g. friendship, or if we regard their misfortune as one to which we also might have been prey, hence: 'those who regard themselves so fortunate and powerful as to imagine that no evil can befall them: such have no pity' (*ST* II-II, q.30, a.2).

that he could simply declare his interest in Isabella; nor is straightforward blackmail to his taste. Instead, he confronts her with a legal dilemma, the logic of which manifests his typically truncated view of the relevant considerations: if leniency to Claudio is justified, then Isabella should have no qualms about submitting to Angelo. If she does not submit to him, then in consistency she is committed to believing that Claudio should be punished. But Isabella will not be fooled by his sleight of hand. Nor will she be tricked into using the word 'mercy' to describe the offer of Claudio's life for her chastity, nor consider herself 'unmerciful' in refusing the bargain. She has spent too long considering what mercy is and what it might do to think that any act that releases someone from punishment, no matter its cost or motivation, can be denominated 'mercy':

> Ignomy in ransom and free pardon
> Are of two houses: lawful mercy
> Is nothing kin to foul redemption. (II, iv, 111–13)

Too often critics fail to see the distinction and label Isabella as unmerciful towards her brother for refusing to trade her body for his life.[20] Of course, Angelo has no intention of releasing Claudio and secretly calls for his execution regardless, but this is sometimes overlooked in a general stampede to condemn Isabella. Partly, this stems from critical sympathy with Angelo's self-serving argument that if Claudio has committed no wrong, then it would not be wrong for Isabella to do likewise. But Isabella does not believe that Claudio is innocent, and none of her arguments ever proceed from this standpoint. Instead, she believes there are reasons of mercy for remitting something of a punishment that could be inflicted as deserved according to retributive justice or, at least, law. In the end, the problem is not so much that she fails to accede to the demand to surrender her body in order to save Claudio's life; after all, arguably the upshot of doing so, at least in her judgement, is eternal damnation. Instead, the point is more that she dismisses the possibility of giving in to Angelo to save Claudio out of hand, with great vehemence, and even with a rhyming couplet: 'Then, Isabel live chaste, and brother, die:/More than our brother is our chastity' (II, iv, 183–4). But Shakespeare has anticipated our concern that Isabella is not compassionate enough, and ensures that if we are heading in that direction then we are going to find ourselves keeping company with Angelo:

> . . . Be that you are,
> That is, a woman; if you be more, you're none.
> If you be one—as you are well express'd
> By all external warrants—show it now,
> By putting on the destin'd livery. (II, iv, 133–7)

He wants her weak and compliant, preferably on her knees as Lucio had earlier urged her to be, but Isabella will not succumb, not to him, and not to any kind of demand for a dumb-show petition for 'mercy'. She will not be beaten, but nor can she win. The law cannot help her because Angelo is the law in Vienna, and at any rate, as he chillingly

---

[20] See Bloom, Shakespeare, 374, on Isabella's 'plain nastiness'.

says, slipping insidiously into the intimate pronoun, 'Who will believe thee, Isabel?' (II, iv, 153).

The ensuing interview with her brother in his prison cell is not Isabella's finest hour. Claudio, one of the cast of 'half-contemptible young men' who regularly appear in Shakespeare's comedies,[21] does not give a much better account of himself, but, of course, he has a sentence of death hanging over him. As for Isabella, she has the unenviable task of telling her brother that she could save his life but will not do so. And yet, strange as it may sound, accusations of coldness here against Isabella are misplaced. There is vulnerability in her need somehow to get him to say that he does not want her to surrender her chastity for him; and there is deep emotion in her prevaricating, 'O, I do fear thee, Claudio' (III, i, 74), for what can she fear in him, unless it is her own knowledge that her love for her brother might weaken her resolve? She is not cold, but she is pitiless in her overwrought state as she accuses him of cowardice, dishonesty, and even incest (in some twisted logic whereby Claudio would be given life by her). No doubt Portia would have handled it better, but Portia, unlike Isabella, always holds the cards. When speeches about mercy fail to get her what she wants, she reveals great facility as an interpreter of contracts. We may not have seen it coming, but Portia is always in control, and no pound of flesh need be surrendered. Isabella does not have this kind of power, nor does she have any desire to be cleverer than the law. She is powerless and vulnerable, and no more able to surrender her flesh than Antonio.

The Duke, however, has been watching everything, and he has a plan. As a man with a prevailing interest in appearances, and a habit of playing to his audience, it is not at all surprising that he should turn out to have a taste for the theatre, and what he proposes is to save the day by means of a well-known comedy plot. It emerges that Angelo had been betrothed to a certain Mariana, but had abandoned her when her dowry was lost. The Duke therefore proposes the traditional 'bed-trick': Isabella will pretend to give in to Angelo's blackmail; Mariana will be substituted in the bed in Isabella's place; Claudio will be saved; and Mariana will gain a husband through consummation. There are, of course, flaws in the plan, not least of which is the fact that Mariana will be doing what Isabella had claimed would mean the death of her soul; and Angelo will then be guilty of a wrong that she believes is rightly punished by law (and for which Claudio has been sentenced to death). *This* is the real paradox in Isabella's attitude, rather than the dilemma with which Angelo confronts her: it is perfectly consistent to say that sexual relations outside marriage are wrong, but that mercy should be shown to some of those who engage in them; it is quite another thing to affirm their wrongfulness and then engage in a plot aimed at bringing about such wrongdoing on the part of others. This suggests a narcissistic concern with her *own* chastity rather than with the morality of the situation. Still, these moral blemishes do not preclude the possibility that Isabella is the main conduit of the positive moral message of the play; in fact, they serve to highlight the theme that judgements of strictness and leniency, justice and mercy, fall to be made by fallible and flawed human beings, and that their shared fallible and

---

[21] Nuttall, *Shakespeare the Thinker*, 256.

flawed nature is an indispensable part of the background in understanding and acting upon these considerations.

The bed-trick works, of course (no one in a comedy is ever capable of telling one woman from another in the dark) and the Duke is able to save Claudio from execution by substituting the head of a conveniently dead lookalike (though he holds this particular piece of information in reserve for now). He then gets to satisfy his longing for the dramatic by revealing himself at the critical moment: a far-from-*Deus ex machina*. Angelo's confession is instant and he demands the death penalty for his own crime. The severity that he applied to others he has no hesitation in applying to himself, and there is no thought on his part of evading the law. In its own limited way it is an admirable response. But while he speaks of his shame, there is no mention of remorse. It may be implied in his desire for death, but he certainly does not want to talk about his actions, or have them scrutinized, or consider what other people might want from him. He simply wants to die now, immediately. His final words in the play are addressed to Escalus:

> I am sorry that such sorrow I procure,
> And so deep sticks it in my penitent heart
> That I crave death more willingly than mercy. (V, i, 472–4)

Insofar as he can muster an emotional response, it is merely a mirroring of what he encounters in others: sorrow at causing their sorrow. The burden of their mercy is more than he can bear, and execution would be so much simpler. Angelo is Angelo to the end, cleaving to the words with which he originally dismissed Escalus' plea for mercy on behalf of Claudio: 'When I that censure him do so offend,/Let mine own judgment pattern out my death,/And nothing come in partial' (II, i, 29–31).

As for the Duke, much as he has enjoyed playing the severe judge, he is now itching to display some leniency, and a suitably unworthy recipient is going to have to be found. Enter Barnardine: a convicted felon, inmate of death row, 'careless, reckless, and fearless of what's past, present, or to come' (IV, ii, 141–2). In other words, an ideal candidate for the kind of pardon that the Duke had been guilty of issuing at the play's opening, and which he is intent on issuing at the play's close. The unreformed and unrepentant Barnardine is to be set loose on the streets of Vienna. We shudder for 'those we do not know' in Angelo's earlier words, for this is the 'bawd' mercy that Isabella had condemned. That it should be a self-aggrandizing whim and not some manifestation of charity on the Duke's part is made clear by the sentencing of Lucio at the same time. The wittily acerbic Lucio is guilty of most of the play's one-liners, and the Duke has been the persistent butt of his jokes. Of all the 'crimes' in the play, this is the only one of which the Duke is the victim. But in fact, it is the only wrong that he is unwilling to cancel out, and Lucio is punished by marriage to the punk, Kate Keep-down. Ironically, the only case in which the Duke refuses to show mercy belongs to the only type of case regarding which that stern critic of legal mercy, Immanuel Kant, judged it permissible for a ruler to be merciful, i.e. crimes against the ruler himself.[22]

---

[22] 'Of all the rights of a sovereign, the *right to grant clemency* to a criminal (*ius aggratiandi*), either by lessening or entirely remitting punishment, is the slipperiest one for him to exercise; for it must be exercised

Like Angelo, the Duke has learned nothing about justice and mercy. Our last hope is Isabella.

It is not clear what the Duke wants of Isabella in the final scene. He has said that Angelo will be executed as just retribution for the execution of Claudio; but, of course, the Duke is aware that Claudio is not dead, and indeed he will imminently produce him like a rabbit from a hat. Ostensibly, he could be providing her with the opportunity to show great mercy to Angelo, forgiving him even for the death of her brother; but in fact it is more likely that he wants to deflect her from this path. He claims that Claudio would turn in his non-existent grave, were Isabella to beg for Angelo's life, and even resorts to a spot of ghostly ventriloquism:

> The very mercy of the law cries out
> Most audible, even from his proper tongue:
> 'An Angelo for Claudio; death for death.
> Haste still pays haste, and leisure answers leisure;
> Like doth quit like, and Measure still for Measure.' (V, i, 405–9)

That the seemingly straightforward law of the play's title should re-emerge in the mouth of a man pretending to be the ghost of a man he knows is not dead, demanding the death of a man who did not kill him, no doubt amused Shakespeare. Justice is not easy and mercy is harder still. It is, however, lost on the Duke, who seems intent on arrogating all acts of mercy to himself, and is therefore simply goading Isabella. But, to her credit, Isabella will not be goaded. She does not share the Duke's tendency towards emotional indulgence, nor does it matter to her how she is perceived, which is why it is unfair of the critics to latch on to the beginning of her petition for Angelo as the vanity of a woman taken with her own sexual power: 'I partly think/A due sincerity govern'd his deeds/Till he did look on me' (V, i, 443–5). This is not the self-referential attitude of the Duke, rather it is a re-assertion of the old Isabella, the one who wants rational consideration of the merits of the case, and surely the hitherto blameless life of the defendant merits such consideration. Indeed, as pleas go, it is a logical one. She ignores the Duke's emotional manipulation, and insists, as she has done throughout, that Claudio merely had justice. As for Angelo, given that he was in bed with a different woman entirely, he did not in fact commit the crime he intended to commit against Isabella, and his thoughts cannot be treated in the same way as actions, not even by a Duke with an obsessive interest in what his subjects think of him:

> . . . My brother had but justice,
> In that he did the thing for which he died:
> For Angelo,
> His act did not o'ertake his bad intent,
> And must be buried but as an intent,

in such a way as to show the splendor of his majesty although he is thereby doing injustice in the highest degree. With regard to crimes of *subjects* against one another it is absolutely not for him to exercise it; for here failure to punish (*impunitas criminis*) is the greatest wrong against his subjects. He can make use of it, therefore, only in case of a wrong done *to himself* (*crimen laesae maiestatis*). But he cannot make use of it even then if his failure to punish could endanger the people's security. This right is the only one that deserves to be called the right of majesty', Kant, *The Metaphysics of Morals*, 145[337].

> That perish'd by the way. Thoughts are no subjects;
> Intents, but merely thoughts. (V, i, 442–52)

Of course, her plea fails to take Mariana into account, and the fact that Angelo deserves whatever 'justice' Claudio had, given that they have committed the same act in the eyes of the law. But properly so: Isabella is not being asked to judge the case, she is speaking as one of the victims, and as such she can only comment on the wrongs done to her. In the end, it may be taken primarily as a plea for fairness and equity, rather than mercy proper (although, insofar as her plea for leniency is responsive to Angelo's repentance and to his past 'sincerity', it may also fall into the latter category). She also, for the first time in the play, gets to her knees in order to beg for a life, the life of the man whom she believes has killed her brother, and who had plotted to rape her; prompted by compassion, perhaps for him, or perhaps for Mariana. Lucio, with his stage directions, could not accomplish this; nor could Angelo with his threats. Empathy and reason combine in this, her final speech.

But the Duke is unimpressed: 'Your suit's unprofitable. Stand up, I say' (V, i, 452). He does not want serious considerations of justice and mercy to intrude on the theatrics of his final scene. He has Claudio to bring back from the dead, prisoners to release, and multiple weddings to arrange. What he does not want is Isabella stealing his thunder or denying him the opportunity to indulge in a final orgy of his own brand of 'mercy'. She is, therefore, effectively silenced. We hear no more from Isabella, not even when her brother is revealed to be alive, not even when the Duke throws two marriage proposals in her direction. In attempting to understand justice, and in her attempt to be responsive to both equity and mercy, Isabella has transcended the limited viewpoints of both Angelo and the Duke; but in doing so it is as though Angelo's words come true: 'If you be more, you're none' (II, iv, 135). Isabella is still a presence on stage but she is a ghost of her former self, and as the Duke leads off the traditional line of couples it is not her hand but her 'willing ear' (V, i, 535) he requests. The talking from now on is going to be done by him. Of course, this has always been the Duke's play, right from the moment that he decides to disguise himself and manipulate events from behind the scenes, and he has decided that it is a comedy. The serious questions that the play raises about the relationship of mercy to justice are going to be swept aside. Isabella has been silenced, Angelo has failed, and the Duke will fail again. Earthly law is in the hands of,

> … man, proud man,
> Dressed in a little brief authority,
> Most ignorant of what he's most assured,
> His glassy essence, like an angry ape
> Plays such fantastic tricks before high heaven
> As makes the angels weep, who, with our spleens,
> Would all themselves laugh mortal. (II, ii, 120–6)

Angels might weep for Vienna, but we, being ourselves 'desperately mortal' (IV, ii, 143) are invited to laugh as the characters exit: a procession of human striving and failing, two by two.

Bibliography

Aquinas (2006a), *Charity* (vol.34 2a2ae. 23–33 *Summa Theologiae*) ed. R.J. Batten O.P. (Cambridge: Cambridge University Press).

Aquinas (2006b), *Virtues of Justice in the Human Community* (vol.41 2a2ae. 101–22 *Summa Theologiae*) ed. T.C. O'Brien (Cambridge: Cambridge University Press).

Bloom, Harold (1999), *Shakespeare: The Invention of the Human* (London: Fourth Estate).

Finnis, John (2011a), 'Hart's Philosophy of Punishment', in John Finnis, *Human Rights and the Common Good. Collected Essays: Volume III* (Oxford: Oxford University Press), Ch.10.

Finnis, John (2011b), *Natural Law and Natural Rights* (Oxford: Oxford University Press).

Finnis, John (2011c), 'Retribution: Punishment's Formative Aim', in John Finnis, *Human Rights and the Common Good. Collected Essays: Volume III* (Oxford: Oxford University Press), Ch.12.

Hart, H.L.A. (2012), *The Concept of Law* 3rd edn. (Oxford: Oxford University Press).

Kant, Immanuel (1991), *The Metaphysics of Morals*, trans. M. Gregor (Cambridge: Cambridge University Press).

Kermode, Frank (2000), *Shakespeare's Language* (London: Penguin).

Nuttall, A.D. (2007), *Shakespeare the Thinker* (New Haven, CT: Yale University Press).

Parker, M.D.H. (1955), *The Slave of Life: A Study of Shakespeare and the Idea of Justice* (London: Chatto & Windus).

Raysor, T.M. (1930), *Coleridge's Shakespearean Criticism* (London: Constable & Co).

Shakespeare, William (1965), *Measure for Measure*, ed. J.W. Lever (London: Methuen).

Shakespeare, William (2003), *Antony and Cleopatra*, ed. John Wilders (London: Methuen).

Shakespeare, William (2010), *The Merchant of Venice*, ed. John Drakakis (London: Methuen).

Tasioulas, John (1996), 'The Paradox of Equity', *CLJ* 55, 456–69.

Tasioulas, John (2003), 'Mercy', *Proceedings of the Aristotelian Society* 103, 101–32.

Tasioulas, John (2006), 'Punishment and Repentance', *Philosophy* 81, 279–322.

Tasioulas, John (2011), 'Where is the Love? The Topography of Mercy', in R. Cruft et al. (eds), *Crime, Punishment, and Responsibility: The Jurisprudence of Antony Duff* (Oxford: Oxford University Press), 37–53.

15

The Basis for Being a Subject of Rights: the Natural Law Position

Patrick Lee

What is the basis for full moral worth or being a subject of rights? What property or nature must an entity possess in order to be a subject of rights? It seems that there is a distinction between those beings it is permissible to use as mere means, on the one hand, and other beings we have a duty to respect, and even to treat as we would have others treat ourselves, on the other. The question is: by what criterion do we draw the line between those two sorts of beings? What is the basis in reality for drawing the line between subjects of basic rights, and beings that are not subjects of rights?

Various criteria have been proposed. One popular criterion among philosophical circles these days is a developed capacity—in the sense of a proximate or immediately exercisable capacity, or a disposition—for rational acts, such as self-consciousness and self-conscious desires.[1] Here I shall defend the criterion for having basic rights that has been explained and defended in various places by John Finnis, namely, being an individual substance with a rational nature (which is the traditional definition of "person"[2]). I will draw on Finnis's guidance at many points in the argument.

There are two main parts to this position. First, the basis for full moral worth is being a certain kind of substance, as opposed to possessing an accidental attribute or attributes. Second, the specific type of substance that merits full moral worth is a *rational* substance, or, more clearly, a substance with a rational nature. It is helpful to distinguish these two parts of the criterion for full moral worth. The rational support for the one part is not necessarily the same as that for the other.

I will advance two arguments that primarily provide support for the first part of this criterion—namely, that the basis for being a subject of rights is the kind of substance an entity is. Then I will present a defense of the position that the specific kind of substance that has full moral worth is a *rational* being. Finally, I will briefly explain how this position provides a coherent account of how every human being has an equal fundamental dignity.

---

[1] See, for example: Tooley, "Abortion: Why a Liberal View is Correct." Peter Singer and David Boonin hold that an individual must actually have a desire for continued life as a subject of experiences to be someone with full moral worth. However, they mean a disposition to have a desire, or a dispositional desire—such that when one wakes in the morning one may remember one has a desire for X. Since such a disposition is acquired some time after one has been alive, it also is a development of a capacity that is previously possessed. See Singer, *Practical Ethics*, Chs 4–6; Boonin, *A Defense of Abortion*, Chs 2–3.

[2] For a discussion of the term: Thomas Aquinas, *Summa Theologiae*, I, q.29, a.1.

I. A Type of Substantial Entity

The first argument appeals to a thought-experiment. It is not a strict demonstration, but a dialectical argument. It is meant to show that the position that the basis for being a subject of rights is the type of substance one is, is more coherent, and provides a better account for commonly accepted moral convictions than its alternatives. Let us suppose I have something seriously wrong with my brain, and unless I have brain surgery I will die very soon. So, let us suppose that next week I will be admitted to a hospital, where I will undergo major brain surgery. But it is also virtually certain that one of the side effects of this surgery is that I will suffer complete amnesia—even to the point of losing all my linguistic abilities, abilities to walk, to eat with a fork, and so on. Now of course I wish I could avoid these side effects. I do not want to lose all my memories, personality traits, and so forth. After the surgery I will not remember my wife, my children, any of my friends, or my deeply held beliefs. In a way, I will be starting all over. In fact, after the surgery, it will also take some time, say, several months, for me even to regain consciousness—I will gradually regain consciousness—but not the same content that I had before—and from there I will have to gradually acquire knowledge, human relationships, and so on.[3]

Now, during those few months in which I completely lack consciousness and during the later months in which I am gradually acquiring new conscious memories and skills, I still exist. If someone told me now that, although I will not remember who I am, I will suffer excruciating pain after the surgery, I would be very afraid. It seems that the person after the surgery, the entity who at that time refers to himself as "I," will be identical to the person writing this essay right now.

So, the first point this thought-experiment suggests is this: what makes me me—the person that I am—is not my consciousness as such. Rather, it is me both before and after the surgery—and I would say that that is because what I am is a rational, animal organism, and it is the same rational animal organism before and after the surgery even though there is no continuity of consciousness and there is a long period of time in which the substantial entity that I am completely lacks consciousness.[4]

But the second, and crucial, point for our purposes is this. Just as it is wrong to kill me now, so it would be wrong to kill me when I am unconscious, and it would be wrong to kill me during the time that I am gradually acquiring rational consciousness. What makes it wrong to kill me now is not that one would be killing something that is presently conscious or even presently able to be conscious. Rather it seems that it is sufficient for me to have a right life that I am identical to the being that eventually will have self-awareness and other rational capacities. It seems that any entity that is constituted in such a way that she has an active disposition to develop herself to the stage of having rational consciousness must be a subject of basic rights. Why will it be wrong to kill me after my surgery? Is it because I once *was* conscious? But by

---

[3] This is similar to Francis Beckwith's thought experiment about "Uncle Jed": Beckwith, *Defending Life, A Moral and Legal Case Against Abortion Choice*, Ch. 6.

[4] For more discussion of this position: *CEJF*.II.2; Lee and George, *Body-Self Dualism in Contemporary Ethics and Politics*, Ch. 1. Also see Williams, "The Self and the Future," 161–80.

hypothesis I am not going to regain any of *that* consciousness. Why should that consciousness or self-consciousness matter? I think it would be wrong to kill me immediately after the surgery. And I think the best explanation of why it would be wrong to kill me then is that in that situation I am an entity that has a nature orienting me toward reasoning and shaping my life by deliberate choice. I have the internal resources and active disposition to develop myself to the stage at which I would have actual rationality and deliberate choice.

The hypothetical scenario I have imagined is, of course, in relevant respects similar to the position of human embryos and fetuses. Human embryos and fetuses are human beings—animal organisms with the internal resources and active disposition to develop themselves to the point where they will be actually rational and shape their lives by deliberate choices. Thus, just as it would be wrong to kill me after my surgery, while I am still absolutely unconscious but slowly developing to the point where I will be self-conscious, so it is wrong to kill human embryos or fetuses, for they are human beings, animal organisms actively developing themselves to the stage where they will shape their own lives by rationality and deliberate choice. To express the point somewhat differently: these considerations suggest that what makes you and me intrinsically valuable as a subject of rights is not attributes that we might have in addition to being the things that we are; rather, what makes you and me intrinsically valuable as subjects of rights is the fundamental kind of being that we are. And so, you and I are intrinsically valuable from the moment we come to be. We do not come to be at one time and only at a later time become intrinsically valuable as subjects of rights.

A second argument for the position that the criterion for full moral worth must be a kind of substance is as follows. We treat beings with basic rights in a radically different way than we treat beings we think do not have rights. Most people believe it is permissible to use, experiment on, dismember, and even kill, for our own purposes, beings that do not have rights, even though we think we should not cause unnecessary pain to them when doing so. By contrast, we believe, that at least in general, we should not intentionally kill beings with rights, and even that we should treat them as we would have them treat us.[5]

Such a radical difference in the way we *treat* different classes of beings must surely be based on some radical difference *in reality* between those classes of beings. Now, there *is* a radical difference between substances with a rational nature, on the one hand, and other types of entities, for example, cells or human tissue, on the other.[6] In particular, considering the beginning of human life, there is a radical difference in kind between a sperm and an ovum on the one hand, and an embryo, from the zygote stage onward, on the other. The former are sex cells, parts of larger organisms (the paternal and maternal organisms respectively); the latter is a human being at her early stage of development, and is the same substantial entity that will later be born, crawl, walk,

---

[5] I hold we should *never* intentionally kill entities that possess basic rights, but that need not be discussed here.

[6] It is worth noting that natural kinds are classified by their basic natural capacities, not their immediately exercisable ones: kittens for example are classified as carnivores, precisely because they are constituted (have a nature) to develop themselves to the point where their mode of life will importantly include eating flesh.

talk, and eventually reason and shape her own life. But once the human being comes to be, there is only a difference in degree between her and the subsequent stages of that same human being. There is no radical difference between a human being at one stage of her development, and that same human being at another stage of development.[7]

Hence those who propose an accidental attribute, such as an immediately exercisable capacity (or nearly immediately exercisable capacity) for self-consciousness, as the basis for being a subject of rights, are basing a radical difference in the way we treat different beings on a mere quantitative difference, or a mere difference in degree, among those beings treated differently. Moreover, the selection of the degree of difference that will count as morally significant is arbitrary—the selection of *this* degree of difference rather than *that* degree is an arbitrary decision. Such arbitrary line-drawing regarding the question of which beings have basic rights and which do not is unjust.

True, in some areas we cannot avoid making an arbitrary (or somewhat arbitrary) selection of when to treat different people differently—for example, in determining when to count someone as intoxicated, or at what age to allow someone to drive an automobile. But in those cases there is no morally relevant radical difference one could select. Here, on the contrary, regarding basic rights (as opposed to, say, specific rights to perform specific actions) there *is* a nearby and morally relevant radical difference. Thus, proponents of the position that the basis for being a subject of rights is an accidental attribute are ignoring that radical difference and are picking out a mere quantitative difference as the basis for radically different types of treatment. It is, on the contrary, more reasonable to base the right to life on the *substantial nature* of the entity, rather than an accidental attribute, such as an immediately exercisable capacity for self-consciousness, or self-conscious desires (whether dispositional or fully actual).[8]

To avoid this conclusion, one might hold that the basis for having rights is not an immediately exercisable capacity, but the fact that one has actually performed a self-conscious desire. Then, one might say that before an entity performs an act of self-conscious desire it does not have rights, but after it has performed that act then it does have rights. And that would be an either/or matter. The problem with this position, however, is that it is unclear why something that was true of an individual in the past, and may no longer be true of her, could be a basis for her now having basic rights. Why would the fact that I had self-conscious desires in the past ground my having rights now, such as a right to life? If for example I am now in a coma, I do not now have any self-conscious desires. Why would past desires give me a right to life now?

---

[7] Note that the argument is not just that there is no radical difference between any two *adjacent* stages of development of a human being. Rather, the difference between a human being at one stage of development and that same human being at *any* other stage of development is only one of degree. Hence the objection that this argument commits the sorites fallacy, as is sometimes claimed, is mistaken. See, for example: Sandel, *The Case Against Perfection*, 118. A more detailed reply to Sandel's objection will be found in Lee and George, *Body-Self Dualism in Contemporary Ethics and Politics*.

[8] For further discussion of this issue, see Lee, "Substantial Identity, Rational Nature, and the Right to Life," 23–42.

Or one might hold—as Peter Singer does in his book *Practical Ethics*—that even if I am in a coma I still have the desire to continue to live; namely, a dispositional, as opposed to an actual, desire.[9] However, a dispositional desire is really a disposition to have an actual desire. It is the effect of an act, a determination of the basic capacity. That is, it is a type of development of the basic capacity, and so the difference between having such a disposition to desire and not yet having one, or not yet quite having one, is still a mere difference in degree. Why select a disposition for a certain type of act, rather than a nature orienting one to such an act? In the development of a living being, as it approaches its first actualization of a capacity, that capacity is more and more disposed to be actualized, and so there is a sense in which there *is* a disposition to act already in a capacity before it acts, though of a different sort than the disposition to act after it has acted. Now, the selection of a disposition rather than a capacity, and the selection of this type of disposition rather than of another type of disposition, is an arbitrary selection.

I conclude that the more reasonable position is that the basis for being a subject of rights is being a certain kind of substance. From this, it follows that you and I are subjects of rights from the time that we come to be, and we remain intrinsically valuable as subjects of rights until we die.

II. Rational Beings

So far, I have concentrated on the first part of what I believe is the criterion of having full moral worth or being a subject of rights; namely, being a certain type of substance. Now I move to the second part of the criterion. The particular type of substance that qualifies as having basic rights is a rational substance, that is, an individual substance with a rational nature. Let me note, however, that even if one just held the first part of the criterion, one would have made considerable progress. For, even if we remained divided about what specific type of substance an individual must be to have basic rights, it would still follow that human embryos and fetuses, and the elderly demented and unconscious have basic rights. Suppose one said that those who have basic rights are sentient beings, or even all living beings. Then it would still follow that, since it is the kind of substance that is the basis for having rights, that substance will have rights from the moment it (he or she) comes to be, and continue to have basic rights for as long as it lives. However, it is important, I think, to see that not all animals, and not even all mammals, have basic rights. For, in my judgment, the move toward animal rights is, in practice, not actually extending full rights to animals but diluting the concept of basic rights.

So, I now move to considerations that support the position that the specific type of substance that is a subject of rights is a rational substance; that is, a substance with a rational nature. In these considerations we must go back to the first principles of morality—that is, the first principles of the natural law.

We do not first establish some general moral norm and then deduce from it that we ought to promote and respect the well-being of others, and determine, by further

---

[9] Singer, *Practical Ethics*, 76–81.

argument, which others we ought to respect. Rather, the practical knowledge that we ought to promote the well-being of others, and which others, should be implicit in the first principles of practical reason itself; that is, in the natural law.

We begin to deliberate about what to do when we find ourselves in situations in which we understand there are different actions we could perform, and we understand something distinctively appealing or beneficial in each performance, but we cannot do both. I could do A or I could do B. Action A has some benefit in it (either in the action itself, or as bringing about some benefit distinct from the action) and action B offers a different benefit (for example, going to the gym would contribute to my health and perhaps friendships; going to the library would enable me to learn). The good recognized as offered by each course of action is a reason for doing it, a reason for action.

Of course, in many cases the benefit or good that is offered by the action is a merely instrumental good—for example, one earns money, not for its own sake but for what it can buy. But not all goods can be merely instrumental. Hence there must be some ultimate reasons for one's choices, some goods which one recognizes as reasons for choosing, which are not mere means to some further good. These are *basic* goods; they are sufficient to motivate one to act in order to realize or participate in them.

Such ultimate reasons for choice are not arbitrarily selected. These goods are not just what we happen to desire, different objects for different people. The goods we recognize as worth pursuing are those conditions or activities that are genuinely fulfilling or perfective of me and of others like me (or at least parts or fragments of such fulfillments). We are moved to act and deliberate about doing so when we apprehend that there are conditions or activities that are *really fulfilling* or *perfective* (of me and of others like me).

Such basic goods include human life and health, speculative knowledge or understanding, aesthetic experience, harmony with other people, harmony among the different aspects of the self, and other actualizations of our basic potentialities. The objects we apprehend as being fulfilling and worth pursuing are not individual or particularized objects. I do not apprehend merely that *my* life or knowledge is intrinsically good and to be pursued. I apprehend that life and knowledge, whether instantiated in me or in others, are good and worth pursuing. For example, seeing an infant drowning in a shallow pool of water, I understand, without an inference, that a good worth preserving is in danger and so I reach out to save the child. But the question remains: I apprehend that life is a good to be pursued, but what sort of life—the life of any organism, the life of any sentient being, or the life of rational beings? I will argue that the basic goods worthy of pursuit are *intelligible goods*, and so the basic goods of rational beings.

I understand that life, health, knowledge, and so on, are goods worthy of pursuit. At the same time I apprehend that I have a *responsibility* toward these goods as opportunities.[10] This is not yet "responsibility" in the full moral sense—which presupposes

---

[10] Speaking of these basic goods, Joseph Boyle says: "The options supported by judgments of value make a kind of demand on the acting person, not necessarily the unconditional obligation of morality, but surely something more than the urgency of desire." Boyle, "Reasons for Action: Evaluative Cognitions That Underlie Motivations," 195. The demand he refers to there is what I am calling a responsibility that is not necessarily yet moral.

that I see some options for choice as reasonable and others as not fully reasonable—but it is an apprehension that it would be worthwhile to pursue some of these goods and that I ought to take account of these goods when I act. Moreover, in understanding there are goods worth pursuing I also apprehend myself as an agent and as someone whose being and fulfillment are worthwhile.

Now, I also apprehend that the person sitting in the desk next to me, for example, is similarly situated toward these same basic goods: the possibilities I view are possibilities she views, and the basic responsibility I apprehend she, evidently, apprehends. And so I understand that the goods worthy of pursuit are the fulfillments of those who are presented (or can be presented) with the same type of view, and who see (or can see) the same type of responsibility. And as I apprehend that I am a person persisting through time, and am worthwhile, I see that *in just the same way* the human being sitting in the desk next to me also is a person persisting through time and is worthwhile. John Finnis richly explains this point as follows:

> For: reflection on the continuity of one's identity and life—through sleep, through traumatic unconsciousness, through the unrememberable eventfulness of one's infant life, through one's life in the womb and, as it may be, one's future life in senility and dementia (Shakespeare's "second childishness")—makes evident that what is valuable for oneself is valuable and significant in a qualitatively similar way for any being with the same capacities as oneself.[11]

And by "capacities" here he means *radical* capacities, that is, having a constitution or nature orienting one to active development to the stage where one does perform such actions—as opposed to an immediately exercisable capacity.

As *my* life, health, knowledge, and so on *matter*,—are worth pursuing—in the same way, the life, health, truth, and so on, of others who are similarly related to such goods are worth pursuing, and they themselves are worthwhile. Being an object of animal urges, or sheer desires, does not ground or justify the choice-worthiness of their objects. However, *being a fulfillment that one's practical reason can apprehend as a reason for action*, does. Thus, the responsibility toward goods to be pursued extends to the goods, including the being and fulfillment, of all those who can—either now, or potentially—understand these goods as worth pursuing.

The claim is not that one first apprehends one's own individual good, and then infers that fairness enjoins recognizing such goods in others. Rather, the point is to uncover the extension of the first practical principles themselves—to make explicit what is known when one apprehends that life, knowledge, etc., are goods worthy of pursuit for myself and others like me. Implicit in the first principles of practical reason is the truth that what is to be pursued, promoted, protected, is the well-being of *rational* beings— beings with a rational nature.

This analysis also provides further support for the point that it is *substantial entities* with a rational nature who are bearers of basic rights. The beings I care for—myself and all others similarly situated toward these intelligible goods—are agents, beings who persist through time; in other words, in Aristotelian language, substances. And I care

---

[11] *CEJF* III.Introduction, 5.

about—and ought to care about—what happens to me and to beings like me, not only when they are actually conscious, but also during those periods of their lives—which can be considerable—when they are unable to respond to commands, to painful stimuli and the like. So, the things that I care about are particular kinds of substantial entities, and these substantial entities exist before their basic natural capacities for self-conscious acts and deliberate choice have developed to the stage where these capacities are immediately exercisable. And these substantial entities are valuable during those periods when, because of injury or illness, their capacities for rationality are not immediately exercisable. So, to say that it is rational beings who are worthwhile and whose being and fulfillment I should respect as I respect my own, is to take the word "rational" as denoting a type of substance, not as an ability conceived of as an accidental attribute, which can come to be at some time after the rational individual herself comes to be, and can cease to be before this individual ceases to be. Hence the basis for distinguishing between those beings I should treat always as ends and never as mere means and those I can use as mere means is not an accidental attribute but a distinct kind of substance. I should care about my self for my own sake and for others who are like me for their own sake. And the relevant likeness (to me) is being a substance with a rational nature.

Every human being is an animal with the basic natural capacity to reason and make deliberate choices, even though something may prevent the actualization of that natural capacity. This is true of unborn human beings and of infants, and it also is true of a human being with severe dementia, or in a coma, or in a so-called persistent vegetative state. They possess the basic natural capacity to reason and make deliberate choices, but they also may suffer from some impairment that prevents the actualization of that capacity.

III. Equal Fundamental Rights

This view supports the position developed above, that all human beings have equal fundamental rights. The basis for this is that such rights are due to every individual with a rational nature. Being a certain kind of thing, that is, having a specific type of substantial nature, is an either/or matter—a thing either is or is not an individual with a rational nature. But the accidental attributes that could be proposed as criteria for full moral worth come in varying and continuous degrees: there is an infinite number of degrees of the relevant developed abilities or dispositions, such as for self-consciousness or intelligence. So, if persons were valuable as subjects of rights only because of such accidental qualities, and not in virtue of being a particular type of substance, fundamental rights would also be possessed by human beings in varying degrees. The proposition that all human beings have equal fundamental rights would have to be classified as a mere superstition. Rather, although human beings differ immensely with respect to talents and accomplishments, that is, in the degrees of *development* of their basic natural capacities, they all are equal as being individuals with a rational nature (persons).

Recently, Jeff McMahan has posed two objections to this position. First, he argues that not all human beings have the radical capacity for rationality (he refers to this as an internal directedness toward having a rational nature—but by rational nature he means the proximate capacity for rational actions). And, second, he argues that internal directedness toward rationality comes in degrees, and so this position—he contends—does not ground *equal* fundamental rights, since it would seem to follow that if rights are based on properties that vary in degree the rights themselves will vary in degree also.[12]

McMahan claims that not *all* human beings have an internal directedness toward rationality.[13] He supposes that the position that all individuals have a rational nature involves the claim that, "the inherent tendency toward rationality is present in the human genome, which the radically impaired share with the rest of us." He then points out that in some cases of radically impaired humans the genes necessary for the proper growth of the brain are present but something prevents their activation or blocks their action. McMahan concedes that such individuals do have an intrinsic potential, or an internal directedness to rationality. But, he continues, in other cases of radically impaired humans, "the defective growth of the brain results not from the blocked action of normal genes but from defects in the genes themselves."[14] In such cases, McMahan contends, the individuals are plainly human beings and yet they lack any internal directedness toward rationality. Thus, according to McMahan, an internal directedness toward rationality will not ground equal fundamental rights for all human beings—but, at best, only for some.

Let me note, first, that human nature, or internal directedness toward the mature stage of a rational animal, is not located solely in the genes. Rather, the genetic-epigenetic state of the cells of a conceptus or embryo is a material cause, and having the right sort of genetic-epigenetic constitution is a necessary condition, and an indication that what is present is a rational animal. But the main problem with this objection is that it overlooks the point that, *rational animal* is a definition of a natural kind. That is, *rational animal* expresses the essential, substantial nature that you and I possess, the nature without which you or I do not exist. Thus, if an individual *does* lack internal directedness toward rationality—as opposed to having a blocked potentiality for that—then this individual is *not* a human being. There are types of entities—for example, complete hydatidiform moles[15]—that have a human genome but whose cells lack the epigenetic state providing them with an orientation or active disposition to develop a brain (each of the cells has the human DNA but the genes are not modified in the way required for the cascaded, internally directed growth to the mature stage of a human being). Now, what is valuable as a subject of rights is a rational being (in humans, a rational animal). So, if an entity does not have an internal directedness toward rational acts—which, if it is a mammal, requires either that it have a brain suitable to be the substrate of conceptual thought, or the capacity to develop such a

---

[12] This is a significant admission on McMahan's part. His position does not seem to escape the grave difficulty raised by this point.

[13] McMahan, "Challenges to Human Equality," 88 ff.

[14] McMahan, "Challenges to Human Equality," 88 ff.

[15] Complete hydatidiform moles are generated when two spermatozoa penetrate an oocyte and the genetic material from the oocyte is ejected but the cells begin to replicate and produce some differentiated but not globally organized growth.

brain—then it does not have a rational nature. If it is not a rational animal then it is not a whole human being.[16]

It is important to note that if a human conceptus has the potential to develop a brain suitable for being the substrate for *any* awareness, then the potential for having *rational* awareness—which could consist in a simple awareness of oneself as an agent, as an I—cannot practically be excluded. It also is important to note that it seems possible for an organism to have a disposition or dynamic orientation toward developing a brain suitable to be the substrate of conceptual thought, but also have a genetic defect that will cause an illness that will prevent the actualization of that disposition. So, it is much more difficult than McMahan seems to assume to conclude of a given cognitively impaired individual that she does not engage in rational acts, and lacks any internal directedness to do so.

McMahan's second objection to the position that having a rational nature is the ground for having basic rights is that there are degrees of internal directedness toward rationality, and so the position that bases full moral worth on having a radical capacity for rationality cannot—any more than the alternative position—defend equal fundamental rights. McMahan argues as follows:

> In a paradigmatic case of internal directedness or intrinsic potential, all that is needed from an external source for the realization of the potential is nutrition, hydration, shelter, and so on. But there is then a spectrum of possible cases in which in each succeeding case just a little more is needed from the outside for an individual to develop a rational nature. There is no threshold that marks a sharp separation between cases of intrinsic potential and extrinsic potential.[17]

However, the distinction between an intrinsic potential and an extrinsic potential does not consist in how many external factors are needed. Rather, the distinction is that between the capacity of a thing to *produce* an effect that is in structure or form proportionate to itself (an intrinsic potential), and the capacity of a thing to be changed by something else, where the end product is not proportionate to the thing with that passive capacity (an extrinsic potential). Thus, the coming to be of a new human organism—which is a substantial entity—is the coming to be of a new entity with a distinct intrinsic potential to develop itself toward its mature stage, where it will have the immediately exercisable capacities for rational thought and deliberate choices. Such a coming to be does indeed mark a sharp discontinuity. The human organism cannot come to be gradually; rather, it must come to be all at once.

McMahan's argument implicitly supposes that a human organism comes to be gradually—but that could be so only if the human organism were a process instead of a substance. A process is spread out in time, so that it has temporal parts as well as spatial parts; examples are a song or a baseball game. And thus a process does not exist as a whole all at once, but it exists as a whole only in a duration. By contrast, a substance

---

[16] Thus, complete hydatidiform moles, parthenotes, and teratomas are human growths but are not whole human beings. For more on this issue: Lee, "Distinguishing Embryos from Non-embryos"; Lee and Grisez, "Total Brain Death: A Reply to Alan Shewmon," 275–84.

[17] McMahan, "Challenges to Human Equality," 92.

exists as a whole at each moment that it exists. And, since that is so, the substance cannot exist only partially—at each moment it either exists as a whole or it does not exist at all, there is no middle ground. The substance cannot, therefore, come to be gradually, but must come to be all at once—otherwise there would be moments where it was partially and not wholly present. Organisms, including human organisms, are substances. Some of the evidence that an organism—including human organisms—is a substance, not a process, is as follows.

While we can explain some processes by referring to other processes that occurred earlier, in many central explanations processes are explained by reference to something that persists. This is because processes are extended in time and often composed of smaller processes or events, and what one needs to explain about such sets or series of processes is precisely their regular and ordered sequence. But what ultimately explains such order and regularity in sequences of processes extended in time is an *agent* that persists through time.

For example, we must affirm the existence of animals—including ourselves—as agents, and as agents that persist through long stretches of time, in order to account for the complex processes of growing, perceiving, reacting to stimuli, crawling, walking, running, and so on. The actions initiated and sustained by animals—including complex actions such as chasing prey, eating meals, and mating—are complex actions which take time. To suppose that organisms are processes instead of substances is to make it very difficult to account for or make room for these kinds of basic explanations. Moreover, from the internal, first-person perspective, I seem to be directly aware that it is the same agent who first deliberates about which option to perform, then chooses to do one rather than another, and finally carries out what I have chosen.[18]

Thus, McMahan's supposed spectrum of cases where an extrinsic potential gradually morphs into an intrinsic potential—so that there would be no sharp line between things which lack a rational nature and things which have a rational nature—is logically inconsistent with the fact that rational animal organisms are substances. The human organism, the rational animal, must come to be all at once, not gradually. Many changes *precede* this substantial coming to be, but these are changes that dispose, more and more, the materials out of which the substance will come to be, to that substantial change. The bringing together of the spermatozoon and the oocyte, and the penetration of the oocyte by the spermatozoon, is a gradual process that results in the coming to be of a new organism. But the organism itself—with a constitution providing her a disposition to actively develop herself to the stage where she can reason and make deliberate choices, does not exist until that process—the bringing together and the joining of the spermatozoon and the oocyte—is completed. Prior to the completion of this process it is not correct to say that the new organism partially exists. And when it does come into existence, it comes into existence as a whole organism—though at an immature stage. So, there is no continuum stretching between an extrinsic potentiality and an intrinsic potentiality—at least not of the sort that is fundamental in the nature of an organism.

---

[18] For a more detailed development of this point: *CEJF* II.2.

McMahan additionally objects that it is hard to believe that such a small change—one on the level of genes—could have such a profound significance—namely, the difference between whether a human being, with full moral worth, exists or not.[19] But the small genetic changes themselves are not directly the ground for that profound significance. Rather, an accumulation of small changes gives rise to, or at least allows the coming to be of, a new substance; and this coming to be marks a radical discontinuity. There is nothing at all surprising in the fact that a substantial change may be *caused by* a small change in the composition or arrangement of smaller components. It is true that just a small change in a sequence of processes or groups of entities cannot itself be of profound significance. But a small change can *cause* or *allow* the coming to be of something else that is significantly different. For example, a certain degree of heat is required to effect many significant chemical changes, such as explosions; water arises from hydrogen and oxygen, where just a little less heat would not enable that substantial change.[20] And so here the joining of the human spermatozoon and the human oocyte—the completion of which on one level is a small incremental movement (namely, the penetration of the oocyte by the spermatozoon)—gives rise to the coming to be of a new substance, a new human organism (which is a sharp discontinuity).

An individual's having a rational nature means that she is inherently, that is, in virtue of what she is, oriented to conceptual thought and deliberate choice, and to shaping her own life, constituting by her free choices how good or bad a person she will be. Having a nature orienting one to shaping his or her own life has no degrees; either a being has such a nature or not.

So, there is a fundamental respect in which all rational beings, all persons, are equal, namely, each has a nature orienting her to shaping her life morally well or morally badly. Other factors in an individual that may facilitate her shaping her life well, or make it more difficult to shape her life well, do not make a difference with respect to whether she has fundamental dignity and fundamental rights. Consider a human person who will have an IQ of 160 when mature to one with a much lower IQ: the high IQ person is not on that basis a better person. Moreover, even those who later *are*, in one sense, better persons—that is, are *morally* better persons—and therefore later *do* deserve better treatment in some contexts, do not on that account have more *fundamental* personal dignity than the morally less good or morally bad (who also could change their ways by free choice).

It also is true that not all *persons* have the same nature, even though they are the same with respect to being persons. Non-human rational animals, if there are any (whether extra-terrestrial or not), angels, and God, are (in the sense I am using the term) rational beings, persons. These different natures are unequal in various ways, but those important differences are not connected to whether one has fundamental rights. Such fundamental rights are based on a respect in which all persons are equal

---

[19] *CEJF* II.2, 91. McMahan's own position—that the central wrong of killing consists in the frustration of a being's interest in continuing to live—does not escape this fundamental difficulty.

[20] I am supposing that the formation of water is a substantial change, in the Aristotelian sense, that is, the generation of a new substance. If that is not so, then it is still not impossible, which is all that is needed for the point.

(including humans, angels, and even God—God will not just use us for his own purposes). There is a radical difference between non-rational beings and all rational beings, and that difference constitutes a non-arbitrary line. Above that line, although they may be unequal in various ways, their inequalities are irrelevant to the possession of equal fundamental rights.

Having basic rights—moral immunity from being killed or enslaved, the right to be treated as others would have themselves be treated—follows upon being an individual with a rational nature. It does not follow on a property that varies in degrees (such as a certain degree of development of the basic capacity for rationality), nor on factors in one's constitution that will aid or impede the more complete development of one's rational nature.

Other rights are based on the varying degree of ability to reason (scholarships, for example), on moral goodness (rewards and punishments), or on acquired skills (for example, the right to play in the Masters golf tournament). But having basic rights to begin with is based on being a certain type of substance or subject. Rights that are based on varying properties may themselves vary in degree. So, if there are equal basic rights—as opposed to rights that are merely conveniently treated *as if* equal—then what they are based on must also be equal. And it seems that the only morally relevant respect in which all human beings are equal is in the kind of substance—person—they are, not in any accidental attribute or attributes.

It is a merit of this position that we can say truthfully what was asserted in the Declaration of Independence, and reaffirmed by Lincoln at Gettysburg, that, All men are created equal, and endowed by their Creator with certain unalienable rights.

Bibliography

Aquinas, Thomas, *Summa Theologiae.* 5 vols. (Madrid: Biblioteca Autores Cristianos, 196).

Beckwith, Francis, *Defending Life, A Moral and Legal Case Against Abortion Choice* (Cambridge: Cambridge University Press, 2007).

Boonin, David, *A Defense of Abortion* (Cambridge: Cambridge University Press, 2002).

Boyle, Joseph, "Reasons for Action: Evaluative Cognitions That Underlie Motivations," *American Journal of Jurisprudence* 46 (2001).

Lee, Patrick, "Substantial Identity, Rational Nature, and the Right to Life," in Christopher Tollefsen (ed.), *Bioethics with Liberty and Justice: Themes in the Work of Joseph M. Boyle.* (New York: Springer, 2011), 23–42.

Lee, Patrick, "Distinguishing Embryos from Non-embryos," in Antoine Suarez and Joachim Juarte (eds), *Is This Cell a Human Being?* (New York: Springer, 2011).

Lee, Patrick, and Robert P. George, *Body-Self Dualism in Contemporary Ethics and Politics* (New York: Cambridge University Press, 2008).

Lee, Patrick, and Germain Grisez, "Total Brain Death, A Reply to Alan Shewmon," *Bioethics* 26, 5 (2012), 275–84.

McMahan, Jeff, "Challenges to Human Equality," *The Journal of Ethics* 12 (2008), 81–104.

Sandel, Michael, *The Case Against Perfection* (Cambridge, MA: Belknap Press of Harvard University, 2007), 118.

Singer, Peter, *Practical Ethics*, 3rd edition (New York: Cambridge University Press, 2011).

Tooley, Michael, "Abortion: Why a Liberal View is Correct," in *Abortion: Three Perspectives* (New York: Oxford University Press, 2009).

Williams, Bernard, "The Self and the Future," *The Philosophical Review* 79 (1970), 161–80, reprinted in *Problems of the Self* (Cambridge: Cambridge University Press, 1976).

16

Constitutional and Other Persons

Gerard V. Bradley

I

In *Roe v. Wade*[1] the Supreme Court affirmed three propositions about the status of unborn children as human persons.

The first proposition was that the unborn are *not* constitutional persons. The Court asserted that the word "'person' as used in the Fourteenth Amendment, does not include the unborn" [156]. This conclusion was important because, as the Court plainly stated, the case for abortion liberty would otherwise "collapse[], for the fetus' right to life would then be guaranteed specifically by the Amendment" [156–7]. The Court concluded, more specifically, that *if* the unborn were recognized as constitutional persons, only abortions to save a pregnant woman's life could be consistent with equal respect for the life of the unborn.[2]

Writing for the *Roe* Court, Justice Blackmun treated the constitutional-person question as one about past legal usage, as an inquiry about a technical term whose meaning in *Roe* depended upon how it was understood in the 19th century. He considered just two kinds of historical evidence to be relevant.[3] By far the more critical to his reasoning were the 20 or so uses of the term "person" in the Constitution (such as that no "person shall be elected President more than twice"). Blackmun concluded that none of these usages indicated, "with any assurance, that it has any possible pre-natal application."[4] "All this, together with our observation that throughout the major portion of the 19th century prevailing legal abortion practices were far freer than they are today,"[5] Blackmun added, "persuades us that

---

[1] 410 U.S. 113 (1973). Page references in brackets in the text are to this volume.

[2] See 410 U.S. at 157, n. 54, where the Court said that "if the fetus is a person who is not to be deprived of life without due process of law, and if the mother's condition [namely, a life-threatening pregnancy], is the sole determinant, does not the Texas exemption appear to be out of line with the Amendment's command?" The Court worries in the same footnote, too, that, if the unborn are Fourteenth Amendment "person[s]," even Texas' restrictive law might not be restrictive enough. The Court asked, for example, whether any penalty for a criminal abortion less than the penalty for murder could be constitutionally justified. This worry is not so well grounded as the one expressed in the text, which simply identifies the effect of applying with equal force the laws governing acts which cause death of persons, born and unborn.

[3] The Court did not explore the Congressional drafting or the state ratifications of the Fourteenth Amendment, with a view to discerning what "person" was understood to mean in the provision precisely at issue in *Roe v. Wade*. One such exploration appears in Part IV, *infra*.

[4] None of the usages considered by the *Roe* Court conveyed the full extension to all instances of a kind or to every member of a class, as the Fourteenth Amendment does in declaring that "no state" shall deprive "any" person of Due Process or "deny" to "any person" Equal Protection of the laws.

[5] The Court described the wave of increasingly restrictive abortion statutes which began just before, and was in full swing when, the Fourteenth Amendment was drafted, debated, and ratified. The Court recognized that these reforms owed in significant part to lawmakers' realization that persons began at

the word 'person' as used in the Fourteenth Amendment does not include the unborn" [158].[6]

This first proposition affirmed by the *Roe* Court had no connection to the subject matter of the second and third. These latter two affirmations had to do with whether the unborn really are persons. The common concern of these two propositions is the question: when do persons truly begin? Do they really begin at conception, or at any other time before live birth?

"Texas urges," Blackmun wrote in *Roe*, that apart from the Fourteenth Amendment, "life begins at conception and is present throughout pregnancy" [159]. Texas further argued that "[o]nly when the life of the pregnant mother herself is at stake, balanced against the life she carries within her, should the interest of the embryo or fetus not prevail" [150]. On this view, the state has a "compelling interest"—indeed, a duty—to "protect[] that life from and after conception." The sources of this "duty" no doubt included Texas' constitutional obligation to accord all persons within its borders the "equal protection of the laws."

The *Roe* Court neither affirmed nor denied the state's proffered answer to the question about when persons begin. The Court instead declared its incompetence in the matter: "We need not resolve the difficult question of when life begins. When those trained in the respective disciplines of medicine, philosophy, and theology are unable to arrive at any consensus, the judiciary, at this point in the development of man's knowledge, is not in a position to speculate as to the answer."[7] This is the second proposition about unborn persons affirmed by the *Roe* Court: persons—or, in the Court's phrase, "life, as we recognize it" [161]—*may* truly begin at conception, or at some later time before birth. But it is not for the judiciary to say that they do, or that they do not.

The third proposition affirmed in *Roe* had to with whether *legislators* are similarly incompetent to authoritatively judge when persons begin. *Roe* implicitly determined that they are *not* so incompetent. The evidence that *Roe* affirmed Proposition Three is not limited to the Court's silence; that is, to the fact—and it is a fact—that nowhere in *Roe* does the Court *say* that legislators may not judge when persons truly begin. The Court also reviewed various areas of law where legislators predicated valuable rights of the unborn child [161–2]. The Court questioned none of these legal regimes. The majority concluded from this review only that the "unborn have never been recognized in the law as persons *in the whole sense*"; that is, in every respect, or to the extent that

---

conception. But the majority's analysis of whether the unborn might be among those "persons" who were guaranteed "equal protection of the laws" (including those against homicide) did not consider the possible significance of this coincidence.

[6] This conclusion, Justice Blackmun wrote, "is in accord with the results reached in those few cases where the issue has been squarely presented" [158].

[7] The Court's metaphysical diffidence in a case which announced such a novel, controversial constitutional right is striking. But the Court's affirmation of Proposition One, along with ambient notions of judicial supremacy in constitutional interpretation, supported the Justices' apparent belief that they could resolve the abortion issue by categorically separating the subject matters of Proposition One and of Propositions Two and Three. They maintained throughout *Roe* the position that the truth about when persons begin—whatever it might be—had no bearing on whether the unborn are Fourteenth Amendment persons.

adults (for example) are so recognized [162; my emphasis]. The Court did not expressly reject the predicate of Texas' contention that it bore a "duty" to ban abortion because persons begin at conception. The Court instead sidestepped the predicate while denying the conclusion: "Logically," the state's asserted interest in protecting the unborn "need not stand or fall on acceptance of the belief that life begins at conception or at some other point prior to live birth" [15]. And a woman's interest in abortion generally outweighed that state interest, whatever exactly it might be.

The stated reasons for the abortion liberty supply further evidence of *Roe's* affirmation of Proposition Three. The Court stated that legislators may affirm what they wish about the unborn, so long as they do not, "by adopting one theory [of when] life [begins], override the rights of the pregnant woman that are at stake" [162]. Those "rights" were rooted neither in a judicial conclusion about when persons begin (Proposition Two), nor in the denial of legislative competence in the matter (Proposition Three). The ground of the abortion liberty articulated in *Roe v. Wade* was, instead and unquestionably, the "detriment that the state would impose upon the pregnant woman by denying her" the abortion option. The Court listed seven such "detriments": "medically diagnosable harm" even in early pregnancy; "psychological harm"; "additional offspring" may herald a "distressful future"; "mental and physical health may be taxed by child care"; "the stigma of unwed motherhood"; the "distress for all concerned, associated with the unwanted child"; and "the problem of bringing a child into a family already unable, psychologically and otherwise, to care for it" [153].[8]

Proposition Three was confirmed and more explicitly asserted by the Supreme Court in the 1989 *Webster* decision.[9] Missouri's legislators declared that the "life of each human being begins at conception." They defined "unborn children" to include "all ... offspring of human beings from the moment of conception until birth at every stage of biological development." They mandated that "the laws of this state shall be interpreted and construed to acknowledge on behalf of the unborn child at every stage of development, all the rights, privileges, and immunities available to other persons, citizens, and residents of the state,"[10]subject only to federal constitutional limitations (chiefly, those found in *Roe* and its progeny).

The Supreme Court in *Webster* upheld all these provisions. The Court interpreted its prior cases to mean that "only that a state could not justify an abortion regulation *otherwise* invalid under *Roe v. Wade* on the ground that it embodied the state's view" of when people begin (emphasis added).[11]

State v. Holcomb[12] illustrates the sweep of the legislative competence expressed in Proposition Three. *Holcomb* was a prosecution for first degree murder. The Missouri appellate court upheld the defendant's conviction for killing his own unborn child,

---

[8] "All these are factors the woman and her responsible physician necessarily will consider in consultation" [153].

[9] *Webster v. Reproductive Health Services*, 492 U.S. 490 (1989).

[10] 492 U.S. at 504.

[11] 492 U.S, at 505. When the Court affirmed the basic holding in *Roe* in 1992 (*Planned Parenthood v. Casey*) the Court said that "the State has legitimate interests from the outset of pregnancy in protecting ... the life of the fetus," so long (again) as the pregnant woman's rights were respected, 505 U.S. at 846.

[12] 956 S.W. 2d 286 (Mo. App. W. D. 1997).

where the victim was expressly declared to be, simply, a "person" for purposes of the state murder law. The *Holcomb* court observed that "[i]t is basic doctrine of *Roe v. Wade*, and it is understood by persons on all sides of the abortion controversy, that *Roe* limited to the mother the legal right to consent to the destruction of her unborn child."[13] For the rest of the world, "destruction of the unborn child" was criminal homicide.

The combined effect of these *Roe* propositions is paradoxical, at least. Propositions One and Two mean that even if the unborn really are human persons (who would, obviously, benefit greatly from legal protection against being killed), they are still *not* "persons" whose lives are protected by the Constitution. Proposition Three means that legislators may (in fact, have) recognize the unborn as real persons with the same right not to be killed as everyone else, save that *Roe* means that what would be unjustified homicide by anyone requires no articulated justification at all by the unborn person's mother.

II

This trio of propositions affirmed by the *Roe* Court was no casual grouping. Each one played an essential role in the majority opinion.

Proposition One was essential to the Court's holding. Even Roe's attorneys "conceded as much on reargument" [157]. The hypothesized "collapse" of the appellant's case owed to the effect of extending equal protection of the laws governing justified use of deadly force to the "person" *in utero*.[14] The *Roe* Court correctly saw that the constitutional-person question was gatekeeper of these laws. Proposition One had no point or significance in *Roe* save to block the bringing of abortion under the ordinary laws about killing. In other words: *Roe's* statement that "the word 'person' as used in the Fourteenth Amendment does not include the unborn" is transparent for, and has no meaning apart from, the proposition that the decision to kill the unborn was exempted from the operation of the criminal law's homicide proscriptions, including its provisions about justified use of deadly force.

Proposition Two was essential to *Roe's* legitimacy. The *Roe* majority opinion begins with an argument, not about abortion or about the personhood of the unborn, but about the Court's peculiar competence to resolve this "sensitive and emotional" question, one plagued by "vigorous opposing views," and to end a debate marred by "the deep and seemingly absolute convictions that the subject inspires." The Court's warrant (so to speak) lay precisely in its capacity "to resolve the issue by constitutional

---

[13] 956 S.W. 2d 286 (Mo. App. W. D. 1997), at 292.

[14] The *Roe* Court curiously attributed this assimilative prospect to the Due Process Clause. But there was no question in *Roe* (and there is none about abortion generally) of *state* deprivation of life. The question is rather about private violence, and the suspension of ordinary protection of the law in the case of the pregnant woman seeking an abortion. It is also hard to see which "process" might be "due" so as to justify a hypothetical state-imposed abortion. In any event, the *Roe* majority's concerns about restricting abortion to life-threatening cases (among other concerns), make it clear that an *equal* right to be protected by the criminal laws was on the Justices' minds.

measurement, free of emotion and predilection" [116]. Such was the *Roe* Court's self-described "task."

This special competence depended upon the Justices' detachment from the "philosophic" issues raised by abortion; that is, upon Proposition Two. It (the detachment) allowed and equipped them to resolve the divisive abortion question in a uniquely credible and authoritative way. That way was free of emotion, partisanship, and of either side's "absolute[ness]." That way was a third way, a distinct path between the warring sides' moral arguments.[15] As the *Casey* Justices said when they affirmed the central holding of *Roe* in 1992: "Men and women of good conscience can disagree about the profound moral and spiritual implications of terminating a pregnancy." The *Casey* plurality added: "Our obligation is to define the liberty of all, not to mandate our own moral code."[16]

Proposition Three is not strictly entailed by Proposition Two. The *Roe* Court *could* have consistently held that it was incompetent to judge when people begin, and that legislators are too. But some alternatives to Proposition Three were incompatible with Two. The *Roe* Court might have said, for example, that in truth *nobody* comes to be before birth. But that would have voided the second proposition, and thus sabotaged the Court's credibility. The Court might have said that there is no true answer to the question of when persons begin, that it is all a matter of opinion. This, too, would have voided the second proposition, and thus undermined the Court's legitimacy. Saying that there is no true answer to a philosophical question is itself a philosophical assertion.

The Justices might have avoided an open clash with Proposition Two by saying that the truth of the matter about whether persons begin before they are born—assuming for argument sake (the Court could have said) that there *is* such a truth—is entirely beyond the government's competence to ascertain.[17] One problem with this possibility

---

[15] That the *Roe* Justices did not personally believe that persons begin at conception suggests that Proposition Two was an all the more deliberate choice. Lewis Powell's biographer, University of Virginia law professor John Jeffries, clerked for Powell during the *Roe* term. Jeffries reports "the surprising lack of antiabortion sentiment inside the Court. White and Rehnquist voted to uphold [Texas'] laws, but chiefly for the reason that abortion was not covered by the Constitution, not on the ground that it was intrinsically wrong. The Court's only Catholic, William Brennan, supported freedom of choice. So did Powell's closest friend on the Court, Potter Stewart." Jeffries, *Justice Lewis Powell: A Biography*, 350. Jeffries adds that Powell would not have changed his mind even if he had been confronted by an articulate defender of the right-to-life. "Powell was not personally religious nor otherwise much given to abstraction. The idea that a fertilized embryo was a fully recognized life would always seem to him unacceptably remote from ordinary experience. That this belief was closely associated with the Catholic Church only made it easier for him to dismiss. No argument would have persuaded Powell that the disturbing realities of unwanted pregnancy and back-alley abortion should be subordinated to religious dogma," Jeffries, *Justice Lewis Powell: A Biography*, 350.

[16] *Planned Parenthood v. Casey*, 505 U.S. 833, 850 (1992).

[17] This is roughly how the Religion Clauses handle questions of doctrine, worship, and church organization. The First Amendment effectively holds that the truth (or falsity) of positions about such revealed matters must not be a predicate of government action. See *Oregon v. Smith*, 494 U.S. 872, 877–8 (1990). Several members of the *Roe* Court held a view about abortion that seems to intersect their views about religion. The *Roe* opinion rooted abortion liberty in the pregnant woman's concrete experiences and interests, in the "distressful life" which a state would impose upon a woman by denying her the choice to abort. See 410 U.S. at 153. Against this impressive *fact* stood—as several Justices repeatedly said in internal correspondence—an abstraction, a speculative possibility, "potential" or inchoate life. The Justices (to varying degrees) regarded those who believed that persons began at conception as moved by religious belief or by moral beliefs which were neither facts nor consensus "values," and thus in some sense ethereal, and perhaps unreal. The normative calculus

is that it would have flown in the face of centuries of contrary legal practice (all the ways in which the unborn *were* treated as persons, if not in the "whole sense"). To clothe its declaration with the desired legal force, moreover, the Court would have had to have the Constitution say that when people begin is a question which no public authority in America is authorized to answer. This would have been a real challenge.[18]

The strategy adopted by the *Roe* Court to resolve the contentious debate about abortion is clear enough. It is effectively conveyed by Propositions One, Two, and Three. Most simply put, the Court thought that Proposition One blocked any constitutional requirement of equal protection for the unborn. The Court also thought that its holding in *Roe* blocked any legal requirement of equal protection. Proposition Two establishes the Court's warrant for putting into practice Proposition One. Proposition Three protects Proposition Two, and conforms to other practical and logical requirements of *Roe's* establishment of abortion rights.

The *Roe* Court believed, in other words, that *if* the unborn were not constitutional persons *then* ordinary criminal law principles prohibiting the use of lethal force, unless in justified defense of self or others, were inapplicable to a woman's abortion decision (and its implementation by herself or her agents). This belief was mistaken. Proposition Three opened a second path to that destination, another route by which homicide law and its justification principles would supervene upon a pregnant woman's deliberations, namely, constitutional challenges by men convicted under one of the 38 or so "feticide" laws enacted since 1973.

III

Matthew Bullock and Lisa Hargrave were having a baby. Hargrave was 22 to 23 weeks pregnant on New Year's Eve 2002, when she and Bullock consumed some alcohol and cocaine at a party. After returning to their apartment, Hargrave did some more cocaine. Bullock asked her to stop for the baby's sake. When Hargrave ignored his request, they argued and—according to Bullock's later statement to the police—he blacked out. Next thing he knew he was on top of Hargrave, strangling her. Because he feared that Hargrave would call the police on him, Bullock bound and gagged her. After she struggled to break free Bullock returned and strangled her to death. Their unborn child died, too, as a result.[19] Just after Christmas 2006 the Pennsylvania Supreme Court

---

appropriate to these circumstances was also expressed by Brennan, privately to Douglas: "moral predilections must not be allowed to influence legal distinctions... the law deals in reality not obscurity—the known rather than the unknown. The law does not deal in speculation." See Garrow, *Liberty and Sexuality*, 537. These words were almost verbatim taken from a 1969 law review article justifying abortion rights by retired Justice Tom Clark. Clark's treatment of the matter is, unfortunately, deeply confused and, at times, stupid. See Clark, "Religion, Morality, and Abortion."

[18] Indeed, it would have required a reading of the Fourteenth Amendment which—as we shall see in Part IV—is wholly at odds with its history and logic. A deeper and truly catastrophic flaw in this possibility apparently did not occur to the *Roe* Court. The Justices there seem to have assumed that the Constitution declares—holds, settles, says authoritatively—that every human being who is born is straightaway a "person." The Court evidently further assumed that the Constitution's agnosticism about when people begin was limited to putative persons *in utero*. But the Constitution contains no such stipulation. See text accompanying notes 45–6.

[19] These facts are taken from *Commonwealth v. Bullock*, 913 A. 2d 207 (2006).

affirmed Bullock's multiple convictions, including one for Voluntary Manslaughter of his (and Hargrave's) unborn child.[20]

Barry Holcomb was convicted in Missouri state court of strangling his girlfriend Laura Vaughan to death. Her unborn child perished with her. For the child's death Holcomb was convicted of first-degree murder, just as he was for killing Vaughan. Holcomb knew that Laura was pregnant, and prior to the murders he had threatened to kill both of them. Under Missouri law, the location of a homicide victim *in utero* made absolutely no difference to Holcomb's criminal liability. Holcomb received consecutive life sentences, without possibility of parole.[21]

Airman First Class Scott Boie was charged with intentionally killing his unborn child. This crime was punishable just the same as it would have been if his victim had been 50 years old, or five. Boie had married his girlfriend shortly after learning that she carried their child. But he was never happy about the pregnancy. Before long, he asked her to have an abortion. When his wife refused his request, Boie bought some Misoprostol, a known abortifacient commonly used in lawful chemical abortions. He ground the drug into a powder and secretly put some of it into his wife's food and drink on four different occasions. She soon miscarried. After admitting what he had done during a secretly recorded conversation with his wife, Boie pleaded guilty under the federal Unborn Victims of Violence Act to the lesser offense of attempting to kill his child. Boie was dishonorably discharged, and sentenced to nearly ten years in prison.[22]

Erica Basoria was pregnant with twins by Gerardo Flores. By the time she discovered it and concluded that she wanted an abortion, it was too late: her doctor said that neither he nor any other local doctor could safely perform the abortion. Basoria testified at Flores' trial for capital murder that she then asked him to terminate her pregnancy by stepping on her abdomen. He did so, but only after—as the appellate court recounted Basoria's testimony—repeatedly asking him to. Basoria supplemented Flores' efforts with some of her own. The court which affirmed Flores' convictions wrote: "[b]y the last week of her pregnancy, she was striking herself every day" [434]. Basoria subsequently delivered stillborn twins. Flores was sentenced to life in prison.[23]

Criminal laws protecting the life of unborn children govern deadly transactions even where the child survives unscathed. Jaclyn Kurr stabbed her boyfriend, Antonio Pena, to death. She was convicted after trial, notwithstanding her contention that she killed Pena after he "punched her two times in the stomach and [after she] warned Pena not to hit her because she was carrying his babies." Evidence at trial indicated that Kurr had indeed recently become pregnant. The trial court nonetheless denied her request that the jury be instructed about *justification*.[24] Her proposed instruction was the standard

---

[20] Bullock's conviction for third-degree murder of Hargrave was not at issue on appeal.

[21] These facts are taken from *State v. Holcomb*, 956 S.W. 2d 286 (Mo. App. W. D. 1997).

[22] These facts are taken from *United States v. Boie*, 2011 WL 5986774 (A.F. Ct. Crim. App. 2011).

[23] These facts are taken from *Flores v. State*, 245 S.W. 3d 432 (Ct. Crim. App. 2008).

[24] *Justification* "involves conduct which would otherwise be criminal, but which under the circumstances is socially acceptable and which deserves neither criminal liability nor even censure," (LaFave, *Criminal Law*, 471, quoting Paul Robinson). "Thus burning a field in order to create a firebreak preventing a raging fire from reaching nearby homes," conduct which would otherwise be criminal mischief, is justified (LaFave, *Criminal Law*, 471). Using lethal force against and even killing—both ordinarily serious crimes— are justified when done in self-defense or in defense of another. *Justification* is very different from *excuse*.

one, commonly used in every American jurisdiction. It is precisely what the *Roe* Court presupposed when it said that, if the unborn counted as persons, abortion laws would have to be very restrictive. Kurr asked that the jurors be told that her use of lethal force against Pena was justified if she had a reasonable fear that he was going to kill, or cause serious bodily harm, to her or to unborn baby.[25]

Kurr's conviction was overturned on appeal. The higher court held that Michigan's unborn children's protection act law established that deadly force could be justified in defense of an unborn child of any age. "Indeed, she may under the appropriate circumstances use deadly force to protect her fetus even if she does not fear for her own life." This holding undoubtedly extends to third parties, too. A friend (or stranger) who happened upon Pena assaulting Kurr could justifiably harm or kill Pena, based upon a reasonable fear that he was going to kill Kurr, or her baby *in utero*.[26]

Thirty-eight states as well as the national government have enacted laws specifically against fetal homicide, or *feticide*: the unjustified killing of an unborn child. These laws identify the unborn child as a distinct victim; the legal harm of killing the child is not part or derivative of any injury to the mother. The tiny victim's description in these laws ranges from "child *in utero*" to "human being" to "person." Harm to the woman carrying the child is not an element of these offenses. These laws include an *explicit* immunity for women seeking to terminate their own pregnancies, because these laws would otherwise naturally extend to abortions.

The federal Unborn Victims of Violence Act (UVVA)[27] of 2004 is typical of these feticide laws. In pertinent part it says that "whoever" "causes the death of, or bodily injury to," a "child who is *in utero*" is guilty of an offense distinct from any accompanying offense against the women carrying the child. This separate offense is subject to the same punishment as would be the identical misconduct if it were committed against the "unborn child's mother"—which would be the same punishment as if the offense were committed against anyone else. A "child *in utero*" is, according to the federal law, a "member of the species homo sapiens, at any stage of development, who is carried in the womb." Nothing in the federal act authorizes prosecution of a "any woman with respect to her own unborn child," or of anyone conducting a "lawful abortion."[28] This express reservation stops the UVVA from limiting abortions to those

---

Excuse pertains to situations where the misconduct is criminal and morally reprehensible, but where holding a particular person criminally responsible for the misconduct is judged to be inappropriate. Criminal acts are excused, not on the basis of the net value of any act, but due to characteristics of the actor, usually some sort of extraordinary stress or diminished capacity. Paul Robinson explains that "'justified' conduct is correct behavior that is encouraged or at least tolerated . . . An excuse represents a legal conclusion that the conduct is wrong, undesirable" but that punishment is inappropriate. "Excuses do not destroy blame" (LaFave, *Criminal Law*, 473). They do, however, reduce or eliminate culpability.

[25] These facts are taken from a copy of the slip opinion in *Michigan v. Kurr* (Mi. Ct. App. 2002), a copy of which is in the author's possession.

[26] To the obvious challenge that its reasoning would justify anti-abortion protestors using force to interrupt abortions, the *Kurr* court simply cited *Roe* for the proposition that such imminent harm to another's life was "lawful."

[27] 18 U.S.C. 1841 (2004).

[28] So Erica Basoria could not have been prosecuted as an accomplice to murder under the UVVA, even if she had consented to Gerardo Flores' stomping upon her stomach. (In fact, Flores' conviction implied that the jurors rejected Basoria's testimony about asking Flores to assault her.) The *Flores* court said that, "[o]nly

justified by a threat to a woman's life or of serious bodily harm, which is where its plain meaning in light of justification principles would go.[29] In sum: the unborn child has the *same* legal right not to be killed as does everyone else in the jurisdiction, save the case where the child's mother procures a lawful abortion.

There have been many prosecutions under these laws. The most famous of these was surely that of Scott Peterson for killing his wife Laci and their unborn son Conner on or about Christmas Eve, 2002.[30] (Peterson is currently on death row in San Quentin Prison.) Every one of these convictions challenged on appeal has been affirmed. Every one of those appeals raised constitutional objections based on *Roe*. Each of the convicted defendants who pursued these appeals maintained that treating the unborn as homicide victims is to treat them as persons, and that treating the unborn as persons violated *Roe*. All the appellate courts have correctly rejected this claim. They have rightly cited what we have called Proposition Three, or the *Webster* case, or both. They have said, provisionally at least, that legislators are free to predicate the same right not to be killed of persons born and unborn, so long as they do not "otherwise" violate *Roe*.[31]

These courts have failed wretchedly, however, to deal with the deeper Equal Protection challenge which Messrs. Holcomb, Boie, Bullock, and Flores have made to their convictions. This is the challenge which we identified at the end of Part II, the challenge which depends upon the incapacity of Proposition One to wall-off the abortion decision from ordinary justification principles by denying that the unborn are "constitutional persons." In fact, these feticide laws make no mention whatsoever of "constitutional persons."

Barry Holcomb stated the challenge plainly. The court which affirmed his conviction said that "Holcomb argues that all intentional and unjustified killings of pre-born children must be treated the same."[32] The challenge is this: how can the law hold that a father is *never* justified in killing his unborn child, while the identical act performed by the child's mother—producing the same harm, for the same reasons, executing the

---

if the acts were consensual could appellant [Flores] argue that the statute treated him and Ms. Basoria unequally by allowing the State to prosecute [him] but not Ms. Basoria for the same acts," 245 S.W. 2d at 437.

[29] This federal exemption goes further than *Roe* requires. In 1997 the Supreme Court of South Carolina affirmed Cornelia Whitner's conviction for injuring her own unborn child. She ingested crack cocaine during the third trimester of her pregnancy, so extensively that her child was subsequently born with cocaine in his system. Whitner was sentenced to eight years in prison for criminal child neglect. Whitner claimed that her right of privacy—as affirmed in *Roe v. Wade* and other cases—required reversal. She argued that the unborn child was not a rights-bearing entity, and that the "state" had no interest of its own in the unborn child over and against the pregnant woman's wishes. She said that the law accorded "legal rights to the unborn only where the mother's or the parents' interests in the potentiality of life . . . are sought to be vindicated." The *Whitner* court said that a criminal prosecution vindicates precisely the public's interest in a distinct "person's" life and health. "[I]f, as Whitner suggests we should, we read [a parallel] case only as a vindication of the mother's interest in the life of her unborn child, there would be no basis for prosecuting a mother who kills her viable fetus by stabbing it, by shooting it, or by other such means, yet a third party could be prosecuted for the very same acts." See *Whitner v. State* 492 S.E. 2d 777 (1997).

[30] Section 1 of the federal UVVA says that it may be cited as "Laci and Conner's Law."

[31] I say "provisionally" because this affirmation is undercut by these courts' treatment of the "deeper Equal Protection challenge," which I next consider in the text.

[32] 956 S.W. at 292.

same choice by the same behavior—is *always* justified? Or, rather, that the same act by the mother is entirely exempt from the norms of justification?[33]

After all, Conner Peterson's demise is just the same *harm*, whether it is perpetrated by his father or by his mother. The chosen *object* of the vast majority of abortions is the same as the objective of the feticide defendant—that the unborn child no longer exist, for the further object of avoiding the burdens of being a parent.

Roe listed seven types of "distress" as reasons for abortions. Only one of the seven had to do with carrying a child in the womb: "medically diagnosable harm" during pregnancy. The other reasons had to do with anticipated burdens of raising a child; call this "post-natal distress." These burdens of child-rearing included (in *Roe's* words) the prospect that "[m]aternity, or additional offspring, may force upon the woman a distressful life and future." In addition, "[p]sychological harm may be imminent. Mental and physical health may be taxed by child care. There is also the distress, for all concerned, associated with the unwanted child, and there is the problem of bringing a child into a family already unable, psychologically and otherwise, to care for it" [153].

Only one of these post-natal "distresses" is distinctive to women. But that one—"the stigma of unwed motherhood"—has evaporated since 1973. The remaining "distresses" are real enough. But they are not distinctively maternal. None would morally justify any mother or father in harming a child once born. The law is also settled and unequivocal: *Roe's* list of parental "distresses" could never justify anyone killing anyone else.

Sometimes, the behavior by which a choice to terminate a child in the womb is carried out is the same as an abortion (as with Airman Boie's administration of Misoprostol, or Gerardo Flores' invited stomping). To this skein of identity—same choice, same intention, same act, same harm, and occasionally the same behavior—is added the same *norms* of justification. Holcomb and the others are not arguing for fetal personhood; quite the contrary, they maintain that *Roe* necessarily reduces the unborn's status to that of some non-personal human entity. They do not seek to overturn Proposition One. Each appellant nonetheless argues on behalf of an indubitable "constitutional person," namely, himself. Each argues that *once* the legislature has decided to treat the unborn as homicide victims (under authority of what we have called Proposition Three), the law may not hold *him* responsible while completely exempting *her* for doing exactly the same thing. *This* discrimination (they say) violates the Fourteenth Amendment's guarantee of Equal Protection of the law.

So far stated, their argument is sound. It is no rebuttal of it to simply cite *Roe v. Wade*. Besides the fact that *Roe held* nothing about the challenge they pose, the Court there made clear its opinion that elective abortions could *not* be morally justified.

The challenge is therefore grave. It has not been met.

Among the attempted rebuttals is one commentator's suggestion that the "personhood of the fetus [be] determined entirely by the mother's subjective intent." This

---

[33] *Roe v. Wade* listed several reasons why women should enjoy an abortion liberty. But no particular woman has to prove that any such reason obtains in her case. So it is not the case that the abortion liberty amounts to a finely calibrated, woman-specific *application* of justification principles. The abortion liberty represents the abandonment of justification principles altogether.

argument is that when the mother chooses abortion, the fetus is not a legal person, but when the father destroys the fetus, the victim is a person. This commentator charitably says: "though a legal fiction, the regime is nevertheless workable."[34] "The regime" is a desperate flight from reality. Whether any specific being is a human person has nothing to do with the desires or needs of someone seeking to destroy it.

> *The notion that when Paul killed little Bill at 4 pm Thursday last it was murder because Bill was a person but that when Julie killed little Bill at 4 pm Thursday last it was fine because Bill was not a person, makes no legal or moral sense.*

The *Bullock* court responded to the challenge by saying that "the mother is not similarly situated to everyone else, as she alone is carrying the unborn child."[35] This is true in an important but limited sense: the presence of a child within the mother's body gives rise to possibilities of justified use of force that arise for no one else. Only the pregnant woman may face an imminent threat of death or serious bodily harm due to the pregnancy itself. Ordinary principles of justification would thus permit her to terminate her pregnancy, and thus to knowingly end the unborn child's life, if she reasonably feared her own death or her own serious bodily injury.[36]

There is no point in denying the "uniqueness" of a mother's relationship with her child. Nor is there profit in denying a father's distinctive bond with his daughter or son, or the special quality of any man's love for a woman. The relevant point is that, when it comes to violence, all such relationships are subject to the common governance of the same legal norms. That is what equal justice under law means. Criminal law is the great equalizer. Homicide statutes deal strictly in anonymous "persons." If one "person intentionally and without lawful justification causes the death of another person," it is murder. Full stop. It matters not that the victim was a bad son or husband, or that he was the greatest. It makes no difference that the murderer was prince of the city or the lowest of the low. Relationships, roles, one's character, and personal identity are irrelevant to killing and to justification. The criminal law cares only about acts and results and objective harms. It is built upon an unwavering conviction that everyone's life counts the same. The law of justification is not ignorant of pregnancy's pains and trials, just as it is not ignorant of the burdens people face more generally as parents, as workers, as friends, as enemies, as neighbors, as strangers. It is simply that the criminal law of justified killing puts all this aside.

> *The notion that Paul may be guilty of murdering his son little Bill but that Julie cannot be guilty because she is little Bill's mother makes no legal or moral sense.*

---

[34] Curran, "Abandonment and Reconciliation," *Duke L.J.* 1135.

[35] 913 A. 2d at 216.

[36] One version of the pregnancy-is-unique justification for abortion-on-demand holds that "[e]ven if the fetus [is] a person, a woman is justified in killing it because of what it does to her when it imposes a wrongful pregnancy, whatever might be her personal reasons for doing so," Ramsey, "Restructuring the Debate Over Fetal Homicide Laws," *Ohio St. L. J.*, 760. *Roe v. Wade* imposes no prerequisite of a "wrongful pregnancy," however, much less one "imposed" by the fetus. The abortion liberty there articulated extends even to pregnancies greeted with joy by a mother who later changes her mind, for any reason or none, and has an abortion.

Several courts have relied upon the legal requirement that a pregnant woman must *consent* to an abortion to distinguish the feticide situation. It is true that consent makes a difference to how the law evaluates bodily intrusions. It is also true that almost any assault upon an unborn child will involve an assault upon the pregnant woman as well. That latter intrusion is a crime. It is punishable (in all our cases) along with the crime against the unborn child. There may also be civil liability for depriving a woman of the relationship with her child. It is nonetheless a bedrock principle of our criminal law that, while the permissibility of certain touches and intimacies and physical contact depends upon consent, no one can consent to one's own murder, much less to the murder of someone else.

> *The notion that it was OK for Paul to murder little Bill because Julie, Bill's mom and Paul's wife, consented to it makes no legal or moral sense.*

Some courts affirming feticide convictions—those in *Bullock* and *Boie*, for example— have replied to Holcomb's argument in another manner which defies succinct summary. The *Bullock* court asserted—contrary to the plain terms of the Pennsylvania feticide law—that "the statutory language does not purport to define the concept of personhood or establish when life as a human being begins and ends."[37] The *Bullock* court added (here relying upon language from an earlier feticide appeal) that "whether an embryo is a human being [is] irrelevant to criminal liability under the statute."[38] Quoting from a different feticide case, *Bullock* said that "[t]he statute only requires proof that, whatever the entity within the mother's womb is called, it had life and, because of the acts of the defendant, it no longer does."[39] The Armed Forces appellate court in Boie's case adopted all this language, and concluded that the issue was whether the "embryo" "had the properties of life and whether [Boie] attempted to end that life by poisoning" his wife's food.[40]

Justice Baer concurred in the *Bullock* result. He wrote separately to "emphasize certain matters implicit" in the Court's decision. Judge Baer "emphasized" that, although the conviction was in all respects indistinguishable from that of killing the deceased mother, it "should not, and cannot, be interpreted as an attempt in any way to define, generally, a fetus as a life-in-being or as endorsing the notion that the interruption of the reproductive process is the killing of human life."[41]

The misfortunes of this position are legion. For one thing, it is a frank abandonment of *Roe's* Propositions Two and Three (albeit due to dismay upon recognizing the collapse of Proposition One as a fence between the abortion liberty and ordinary justification principles). Another problem is the frank rejection of the plain meaning of these statutes. These laws plainly recognize the unborn child as a rights-bearing human being, distinct from its mother and equal in value to everyone else (with the *Roe*-mandated exception for the pregnant woman). Pennsylvania's lawmakers "called" the manslaughter victim in *Bullock* an "unborn child," which they defined as a member

---

[37] 913 A. 2d at 212.
[38] 913 A. 2d at 213, quoting the Minnesota Supreme Court in *State v. Merrill*, 450 N.W. 2d 318, 324 (1990).
[39] 913 A. 2d at 213, quoting *People v. Ford*, 581 N.E. 2d 1189, 1201 (Ill. App. 3d 1991).
[40] 2011 WL 5986774.   [41] 913 A. 2d at 219.

of the "species homo sapiens"—that is (according to any standard dictionary): one of humankind, a human being. In Holcomb's case, the murdered unborn child was simply a "person."

The "victim" in these judicial imaginings seems to be either an internal organ of the mother or her interest in some foreign biological "entity" within her. Upon what reasonable basis these courts nonetheless affirm "manslaughter" and "murder" convictions is unstated, much less has any of these courts explained how those who slay indeterminate "entities" may end up on Death Row, adjacent to those who have slaughtered real folks.

> *These courts' utterances make no legal or moral sense. If Paul kills a sub-personal human entity which we could call "little Bill," and he receives a life sentence for doing so, on what grounds is Julie immunized from all criminal liability when she performs the identical act?*

Re-describing the unborn child as a hapless, anonymous "entity" may lessen the burden of justification for extinguishing it, on the view that pre-personal "bill" is less intrinsically valuable than little Bill. But that devaluation does nothing to close the gap between Paul and Julie.[42]

The last stand against the Holcomb challenge was given expression by Justice Baer, concurring in *Bullock*. His stance is, however, implicit in all these cases and amounts to a tacit confession that Holcomb's challenge is unanswerable without putting the scope of *Roe's* abortion liberty into play. Baer wrote: "*Roe* and its progeny remain the law in this nation and any attempt based upon the legislature's choice of language... to undermine its constitutional imperative, is unavailing."[43]

This is not nonsense. It is instead the declaration of a settled determination to retain the abortion liberty established by *Roe* as a brute judicial stipulation impervious to moral criticism and, even, to the constitutional requirements that no state deny to any person the Equal Protection of the laws.

IV

We saw in Parts I and II that the *Roe* Court's conclusion about constitutional persons— our Proposition One—was instrumentally necessary to keep homicide and justification principles away from abortion. In Part III we saw that the instrument is broken.

---

[42] The *Roe* Court and these feticide courts may countenance a scarcely stated view that no pregnant woman should suffer unwillingly for a "theory" (of when life begins), especially for someone else's (a legislator's?) "theory." This is evidently to suppose that the harm involved in abortion is conceptual, that someone's intellectual scheme has been assaulted. See also note 17. This way of thinking about thinking (if you will) is wrong, and dangerous. A "theory" of life is what one believes to be the case—really, on the ground, in the flesh—about people, just as a "theory" about torture or health care or unjustified killing is what one believes to be someone else's moral due, and what counts as an injustice against him or her. If no one should suffer for a "theory" of when persons begin, why should they bear any sacrifice for a "theory" of *justice*, which is an "entity" even more mysterious and ethereal than any baby in the womb. Besides, there is no good reason to arraign only those who would protect unborn persons as speculators and "theorists," for *any* account ("theory") about when persons begin is inseparable from an account ("theory") of why we consider *any* putative person to be a rights-bearing individual.

[43] 913 A. 2d at 220.

Proposition One is a broken instrument. Justice Baer and the other feticide courts evidently recognize that the abortion liberty is now dangerously exposed. They recognize that it is incompatible with laws equally protecting the lives of unborn human individuals against the whole world minus one (the mother). They see too that *Roe* opened the door to these laws, and that it offers no grounds for rebutting these laws' equal protection implications. Though these jurists so far offer no aid to imprisoned men who—according to these judges—did not kill the "persons" they were convicted of killing, they are ready to meet the danger at hand. They are prepared to defend abortion *and* to completely abandon *Roe's* Proposition Two. They have decided to "resolve the difficult question of when life begins."[44] They are prepared to say that life begins at birth.

As an unadorned piece of judicial philosophizing this declaration will not do the job it is meant to do. Idle judicial theorizing lacks coercive authority. Even occasional authoritative judicial sorties (such as affirming a feticide conviction) will not cabin legislators possessed of the belief that persons begin at conception. They must somehow be disabled from acting upon that belief. The only way effectively to do that is to declare that the *Constitution* establishes that people begin at birth.[45]

The flaw in this strategy is that the claim that the Constitution stipulates that persons do not begin before birth is so demonstrably false, that it is transparent for the judicial philosophizing it is meant to dress up.

Let me explain.

Justice Blackmun wrote in *Roe* that the "Constitution does not define 'person' in so many words" [157]. Indeed, it does not. He then sought to extract a definition—or at least an answer to the question about the unborn—by scanning the Constitution for references to "persons." Blackmun found many such references. All of them predicated certain duties or advantages or eligibilities or penalties of "persons." Blackmun's inquiry yielded such information as that slaves are "persons" (in the Fugitive Slave Clause and in the infamous three-fifths apportionment compromise), and that only older "persons" could hold political offices (various age qualifications for President and members of Congress). But these stipulations have no tendency to "define"—specify, explain—who or what a "person" is, any more than a law saying that "no person may obtain a driver's license before attaining eighteen years of age" establishes that the term "person" does not include pedestrians, or children.

One reason why Justice Blackmun might have chosen this gross methodology is that he thought the downside risk was very shallow. The *Roe* majority seems to have

---

[44] In saying that these judges "have decided to 'resolve the difficult question of when life begins,'" I do not mean to imply that they believe otherwise. Many may truly believe that persons begin at birth. It is apparent, however, that all of them believe that abortion liberty entails that the law hold that persons begin at birth (or possibly at viability, if a particular defender of abortion liberty is willing to cede regulation of that small number of elective abortions done in the last trimester).

[45] Such a declaration against fetal personhood would not solve all the problems of legal and moral incoherence surrounding feticide. But settling once and for all that the unborn are to be treated legally as pre-personal "entities"—or as "potential" life—does reduce the threat which today's unborn victims of violent acts pose to the abortion-liberty regime. Disconcerted judges (among others) may even see settling the matter once and for all as a long-term solution to the question about how to coherently and cogently justify abortion rights.

presumed that the Fourteenth Amendment extended to *everyone*, once he or she was born. The first words of the Fourteenth Amendment say: "All persons born or naturalized in the United States...are citizens" thereof. If read inattentively this provision could seem to be a declaration that everyone born of woman is, for that reason alone, a "person." But that is not what those words say or imply.

The opening words of the Fourteenth Amendment could just as naturally be read to mean that birth is an event in the course of a "person's" life, as it would be if persons begin at, say, conception. This opening language could also naturally be read to mean that human individuals (biologically speaking) come to be at some point prior to the emergence of genuinely "personal" existence. In this view, the elevation of a sub-personal human organism to genuinely "personal" status would be established by the appearance or acquisition of certain active capacities or experiences, such as self-consciousness. Retired Justice Tom Clark wrote (in his article anticipating *Roe*) that the fetus' inability to "interact with other human beings" meant that it lacked "life."[46]

On this view, one's body comes to be before one comes to be. The organism precedes the person. On this view, "persons" is a qualitative term. Then the Constitution's "all persons born" language could naturally be read to mean that even infants (and adults) who lack the distinctive active capacities or experiences of "persons" are not constitutional persons. These unfortunates would therefore lack—on *Roe's* account—any right not to be killed.

Moreover: it is *only* in the Due Process and Equal Protection Clauses that the term "person" appears in its full extension: no state shall "deprive *any* person of life, liberty, or property without due process of law; nor deny to *any* person within its jurisdiction the equal protection of the laws" [emphasis added]. In every other instance examined by Blackmun "person" is accompanied by an adjectival predicate. "Person" is everywhere else qualified by some attribute, status, or achievement, such as being "free" (not enslaved) or as "holding an office," being convicted of a crime, or having arrived at a certain age. Even the opening words of the Fourteenth Amendment parcel "persons" present into "citizen" and non-citizen categories. None of this implies, however, that persons begin at birth.

The truth is that the Constitution *nowhere* tells us when persons begin. The Constitution *nowhere* tells us who or what counts as a "person." We need (for lack of a better term right now) a "theory" of life to identify *any* "constitutional person." If detectable "distress" is to trump any "theory" of life, then no one's right-to-life is very secure. We shall all then reside in a Hobbesian state of nature, in which only the presumptuous would buy green bananas.

Roe's methodology is deficient in another important respect. None of the opinions in *Roe v. Wade* considered the voluminous record of Congressional debate of the Fourteenth Amendment itself. None of the opinions considered the surviving records—also voluminous—of the state legislative ratifications of the Amendment. None made reference to any federal judicial decision indicating, shortly after ratification, what the common understanding of "person" was.

---

[46] 2 *Loyola L. Rev.* at 5.

In fact, these records confirm the meaning of "person" evident on the face of the constitutional language: *every*—that is "any," without exception—member of a natural kind or class, namely, "person" is constitutionally entitled to Due Process of Law and to the Equal Protection of the laws. The evidence that Fourteenth Amendment "persons" are everyone who is truly a person is overwhelming. "Person" here (as elsewhere) in the Constitution references a natural kind.[47]

A. Congress proposes

Ohio Representative John Bingham sponsored the Fourteenth Amendment in the House of Representatives. During the debate over what is now Section One he said that its coverage was "universal." It applied, Bingham declared, to "any human being." Congressman Bingham's counterpart in the Senate, Senator Jacob Howard, emphasized that the amendment applied to every member of the human family: Howard stated that "[i]t establishes equality before the law, and it gives to the humblest, the poorest, the most despised of the race the same rights and the same protection before the law as it gives to the most powerful, the most wealthy, or the most haughty." Howard told the Senate that Section One abolished "all class legislation... and [did] away with the injustice of subjecting one caste of persons to a code not applicable to others." The predominant tenor was precisely to explain "section one" *in toto* in two terms: *everybody* (without qualification) and *impartial* (and cognates: non-arbitrary, equal, non-discriminatory).

Pennsylvania Congressman Thaddeus Stevens said in 1866 during his House campaign that Section One meant that "the same laws must and shall apply to every mortal, American, Irishman, African, German or Turk."[48]

B. The states ratify[49]

On 31 January 1867, Pennsylvania Representative Kinney said: "[the amendments] urge that we come back to those ideas of government enunciated in the immortal Declaration of Independence..." Later in the debate, Representative Allen said that Section One embodied the premise of the Declaration. State Senator Browne recited the language of the Declaration in his explanation and defense of the amendment, as did Representative Mann on the House side. The common message was that "all men are created equal." Representative Day urged ratification to insure that, "...the rights to life, liberty and property; in short, the inalienable rights enunciated in the Declaration of Independence, not...be accepted as 'glittering generalities' but as original, self-

---

[47] Available space requires that this presentation of evidence be limited to a very brief survey. I am certain, however, that the evidence presented in text speaks for the vast bulk of all the surviving evidence.

[48] "The Pending Canvas!" Speech of Thaddeus Stevens, Delivered at Bedford, PA on Tuesday Evening, 4 September 1866, 11.

[49] Here I follow closely the research findings of constitutional historian James Bond. I have relied in particular upon his "The Original Understanding of the Fourteenth Amendment in Illinois, Ohio, and Pennsylvania." See generally Bond, *No Easy Walk to Freedom*.

evident truths, fundamental in their character and essential elements in the ground-work of our Republican system of government."

These proponents believed that everyone had natural rights, and they repeatedly emphasized their belief that Section One protected these fundamental rights. Senator Bingham spoke of the "birthright of every human being," Representative Ewing, of "the common right of humanity." Senator Lowry declared that "every child of God shall stand upon equality before the law, and shall have and enjoy equal and exact justice." Toward the end of the debate in the Senate, Senator Browne implored his colleagues to recognize that respect for "the rights of man is fundamental to the national existence."

Typical of the relevant phrases as reported in newspapers covering the Congressional debate and state ratifications were "all men"[50]; "all persons"[51]; "all men as equals before the law of God and man."[52] Indiana Governor Oliver Morton addressed a large crowd on 18 July 1866, and declared that Section One "intended to throw the equal personal and proprietary protection of the law around every person who may be within the jurisdiction of the state."[53] Two weeks later the *New York Times* said: "The equal protection of the laws is guaranteed to all, without any exception."[54]

C. Judicial decision

In one important judicial investigation of who counted as a "person," a federal judge in Nebraska considered its extension to Native Americans:

> The most natural, and therefore most reasonable, way is to attach the same meaning to words and phrases when found in a statute that is attached to them when and where found in general use. If we do so in this instance, then the question cannot be open to serious doubt. Webster describes a *person* as "a living soul; a self-conscious being; a moral agent; especially a living human being; a man, woman, or child; an individual of the human race." This is comprehensive enough, it would seem, to include even an Indian . . . On the whole, it seems to me quite evident that the comprehensive language used in this section is intended to apply to all mankind—as well the relators [that is, the "Indian" party] as the more favored white race.[55]

D. The logic and structure of section one

The only way to make sense of Section One of the Fourteenth Amendment is to understand that the word "person" is an exhaustive reference to a natural kind. The most prominent historian of the Amendment's adoption writes that "the only effect of the amendment was to prevent the states from discriminating arbitrarily between different classes of citizens. As long as a state treated its citizens equally, distinguishing between them only when there was a basis in reason for doing so, the state would

---

[50] Quoted in Thomas, "Newspapers and the Fourteenth Amendment," 27, n. 91.
[51] Thomas, "Newspapers and the Fourteenth Amendment," 28.
[52] *NYT*, 30 June 1867.
[53] Thomas, "Newspapers and the Fourteenth Amendment," n. 97.
[54] *NYT*, 31 July 1866 (quoted in Thomas, "Newspapers and the Fourteenth Amendment," n. 101).
[55] 25 *F. Cases* 695 (D. Neb. 1879).

remain immune from federal intervention pursuant to the Fourteenth Amendment."[56] Though there many other references to "citizens" in like statements, many expressions of the basic aim establish that it was laws "equal, impartial to all."[57] But all these aspirations would be defeated, if it were possible for those exercising public authority to "define" some human individuals as non-persons, or to stipulate that some human individuals be treated as "persons" for some purposes but not for others, so as to evade the often inconvenient moral demands of equality.

* * *

The constitutional text, its purpose, and the history of its ratification all show that the "word 'person' as used in the Fourteenth Amendment" is transparent for the truth of the matter. This does not by itself establish that the unborn (or, for that matter, any other specifiable group, such as Armenian-Americans, southpaws, or dwarves) *are* Fourteenth Amendment persons.[58] It establishes that they are constitutional persons if it is the case that they really are persons.

According to *Roe v. Wade*, legislators but not judges are competent to resolve the philosophical question about persons. The evidence marshaled in this Part shows that this is to say that legislators but not judges are competent to determine the matter of constitutional persons; that is, they are competent to ascertain the scope of that class protected by the Equal Protection and Due Process Clauses. Any legislator who conscientiously believes that persons begin at conception is, so far considered and by dint of a sworn duty to uphold the Constitution, *obliged* to equally protect the unborn from harm. This is not at all—again, so far considered—a matter of "reversing" *Roe* or of usurping the role of the judiciary. It is rather a case of legislators making the most sense they can of the Constitution, once *Roe's* reasoning has manifestly imploded.

Against this duty, Judge Baer and others similarly disposed might throw up their own declaration that the unborn possess only "potential" life, and that the Constitution itself establishes this in-between status for the child *in utero*. The evidence marshaled here shows, however, that such a declaration could only be issued by someone culpably ignorant of or indifferent to the truth about the Constitution. Indeed, such a declaration would be transparent for Baer-like judicial willfulness: any legislative attempt to "undermine [*Roe's*] constitutional imperative, is unavailing."

Just so.

---

[56] Nelson, *The Fourteenth Amendment*, 115.

[57] Nelson, *The Fourteenth Amendment*, 117.

[58] The question of constitutional coverage today is not dependent upon what the ratifiers of the Fourteenth Amendment more precisely thought—or would think today—about the status of, say, Native Americans, Chinese contract workers, mentally or physically defective children, or the unborn. (Just as it is the case, for example, that the meaning of "religion" in the First Amendment today does not depend upon what the Founders thought or might think of Christian Science, Catholicism, Islam, or Native-American spirituality.) The Constitution makers (in 1791 or 1868) meant to establish and did establish an open-ended *class* or *kind* of beneficiaries. They did not mean to establish nor did they establish a closed aggregate list of exemplars or members. As a matter of fact, there is substantial evidence among the records of state legislatures which ratified the Fourteenth Amendment that they understood the word "person" to include the unborn. See Witherspoon, "Reexamining *Roe*."

V. Conclusion

When the Supreme Court reaffirmed in 1992 what it called the "central holding" of *Roe v. Wade* the Justices adhered to very little of Justice Blackmun's reasoning. The decisive "joint opinion" of Kennedy, O'Connor, and Souter instead took refuge in two facts. The first was the fact that *Roe* established in 1973 a very wide abortion liberty. The second fact affirmed in *Planned Parenthood v. Casey* was this: "[F]or two decades of economic and social developments people have organized intimate relationships and made choices that define their views of themselves and their places in society, in reliance on the availability of abortion in the event that contraception should fail." The joint opinion writers added that "[t]he ability of women to participate equally in the economic and social life of the Nation has been facilitated by their ability to control their reproductive lives."[59]

The question about unborn constitutional persons is suppressed.[60]

Evidently, the *Roe* initiative has gotten too big to fail.

Casey's alleged necessity for abortion rights is really beside the point. For those who believe that people begin at live birth, *Casey* supplies much more than they need to affirm *Roe's* "constitutional imperative." For those who believe that people begin at conception, the million and more persons sacrificed annually is way too high a price to pay for "backup contraception," a price which they know no one would endorse if it were payable in more visible persons like you and me.

For those who are unsure or who have not yet thought about it, justice requires, not unreflective acquiescence in *Casey's* claim about structural justice (or injustice, depending on whether the unborn are really persons). Justice requires that those undecided figure out the truth about the unborn, and then join one or the other side accordingly.

Bibliography

Bond, James, "The Original Understanding of the Fourteenth Amendment in Illinois, Ohio, and Pennsylvania," 18 *Akron L. Rev.* 435 (1984–85).

Bond, James, *No Easy Walk to Freedom: Reconstruction and Ratification of the Fourteenth Amendment* (Westport, CT and London, UK: Praeger, 1997).

Clark, Tom, "Religion, Morality, and Abortion: A Constitutional Appraisal," 2 *Loy. L. Rev.* 1 (1969).

Curran, Douglas, "Abandonment and Reconciliation: Addressing the Political and Common Law Objections to Fetal Homicide Laws," 58 *Duke L.J.* 1107 (2009).

Garrow, David, *Liberty and Sexuality: The Right to Privacy and the Making of Roe v. Wade*, (Berkley, CA and London, 1994).

Jeffries, John, *Justice Lewis Powell: A Biography* (New York, 1994, 2001).

LaFave, W., *Criminal Law*, 5th ed. (St Paul, MN, 2010).

---

[59] 505 U.S. at 836. President Obama expressed the same thought in his 23 January 2012 remarks upon the 39th anniversary of *Roe*: "As we remember this historic anniversary, we must also continue our efforts to ensure that our daughters have the same rights, freedoms, and opportunities as our sons to fulfill their dreams."

[60] President Obama did not mention the unborn, either.

Nelson, W., *The Fourteenth Amendment: From Political Principle to Judicial Doctrine* (Cambridge, MA and London, UK, 1988).

Ramsey, C., "Restructuring the Debate Over Fetal Homicide Laws", 67 *Ohio St. L. J.* 721 (2006).

Thomas, George, "Newspapers and the Fourteenth Amendment: What Did the American Public Know About Section 1?", 27, n. 91 (2009), available at: <http://ssrn.abstract=1392961>.

Witherspoon, J., "Reexamining *Roe*: Nineteenth-Century Abortion Statutes and the Fourteenth Amendment," 17 *St. Mary's L. J.* 29 (1985).

17

Bioethics after Finnis

(Most Rev.) Anthony Fisher OP

Twentieth-century bioethics was a big disappointment.[1] Unparalleled advances in medicine occurred at a time of decline in academic ethics and often in professional practice. Despite articulation in oaths, textbooks, and courses, 'medico-morals' proved no obstacle to shameful experiments conducted not just by Nazi or Stalinist doctors but also by researchers in the 'free world' where human rights were paid more lip-service.[2] Attitudes in medicine and medical research, to the unborn, handicapped, mentally ill, black, poor, and elderly were uneven at best. Medicine became in many ways a service for a fee or a tool of ideologies without reference to its internal goals and without a coherent ethic.

The reinvention of medico-morals as 'bioethics' from the 1970s onwards also proved no barrier, as medicalized killing, especially by abortion, later by embryo experimentation, achieved astonishing proportions. Bioethics now offered health professionals and the general public two main models for decision-making: a *buffet bioethic* where autonomous agents choose according to taste from a range of principles so as to get the permissions they want; and a *ledger bioethic* that purports to balance various debits and credits, again usually in favour of prior preferences.[3] The weaknesses of both have been well exposed by other commentators on the history and foundations of bioethics.[4] Important among those criticisms are: first, such approaches situate the pursuit of health and healthcare within a severely impoverished conception of the human good and practical reason. Second, such *thin* conceptions of the good are matched by a failure to attend to the kind(s) of character appropriate to healthcare and research. Third, an equally thin conception of profession, community, and the common good leaves bioethics with little to say about the place of traditions of practice or about social responsibility for provision. Fourth, liberal and utilitarian ethics are ultimately

---

[1] On its history and deficiencies see: Eckenwiler and Cohn, *The Ethics of Bioethics*; Jecker et al., *Bioethics*; Jonsen, *A Short History of Medical Ethics*; Rothman, *Strangers at the Bedside*.

[2] Lafleur et al., *Dark Medicine*; Reverby, *Examining Tuskegee*; Presidential Commission for the Study of Bioethical Issues, *Ethically Impossible*.

[3] E.g. the works of Peter Singer, Michael Tooley, and John Harris, the textbook by Beauchamp and Childress, *Principles of Biomedical Ethics* (seven editions so far) and articles by admirers of principlism in Gillon, *Principles of Health Care Ethics*.

[4] Finnis's critiques include: *FoE*, 80–108; *NDMR*, 177–274; 'Incoherence and Consequentialism (or Proportionalism)—A Rejoinder' (with J. Boyle and G. Grisez) (1990f); *MA*; 'Theology and the Four Principles of Bioethics: a Roman Catholic View' (with A. Fisher) (1993d). Other critics include: Clouser and Gert, 'Morality *vs.* Principlism', 251–66; DuBose, Hamel and O'Connell, *A Matter of Principles?*; Fisher, 'Rethinking Principlism'; Grisez, 'Against Consequentialism' (1978); Irving, 'The Bioethics Mess'; Jamieson, *Singer and his Critics*; Maclean, *The Elimination of Morality*; MacIntyre, *Whose Justice?*; Oderberg and Laing, *Human Lives*; Pellegrino et al., *Biotechnology and the Human Good*.

incompatible with and can offer no reasoned basis for the Hippocratic tradition carried forward in the post-war codes of the international and local medical associations.[5] And finally, though providing rhetorical justifications for the preferences of the medical and research establishments, much contemporary bioethics fails to offer ordinary practitioners or patients any clear direction. If bioethics is to support more than medibusiness and the bioethics industry itself, it must follow the best of recent moral philosophy into the richly textured terrain of human goods, norms, and commitments, natural and supernatural virtues, narratives, communities, and traditions; it must also have a sound understanding of the science, history, and craft of healthcare.

Some of these concerns are addressed directly in the moral philosophy elaborated by John Finnis, most fully in *Natural Law and Natural Rights*[6] but also in many articles on moral and legal theory, some written in collaboration with Germain Grisez, Joseph Boyle, William E. May, Robert George, or others. Recently Finnis featured in the Nobel Peace Prize acceptance speech by Aung San Suu Kyi who noted gratefully that it was Finnis who nominated her for the prize in view of her heroic and peaceable stance in Burma. This example of Finnis's politics and influence, like his defense of anti-nuclear bomb and anti-abortion protestors in court, is a performative utterance of this theory. This 'new natural law theory' draws upon the classical tradition of natural law, the underlying philosophy and specific conclusions of Catholic moral theology, and the thinking of some modern writers about practical reason;[7] there is also some overlap with the new virtue ethics and communitarianism. While Finnis has not written a bioethics textbook or elaborated a full bioethic, he has explored a number of particular bioethical questions in more than 20 articles on contraception,[8] the beginning of life,[9] the reproductive technologies,[10] abortion,[11] euthanasia and the withdrawal of care,[12] the end of life,[13] and nuclear deterrence.[14] These articles show that his conclusions are broadly compatible with the classical ('Hippocratic') tradition and might offer

---

[5] E.g. World Medical Association, *International Code of Medical Ethics* (1949); *Oath at the Time of Being Admitted as a Member of the Medical Profession* ('Declaration of Geneva') (1948); *Ethical Principles for Medical Research Involving Human Subjects* ('Declaration of Helsinki') (1964).

[6] *NLNR*; *FoE*; Introduction to Finnis, *Natural Law* (1991e).

[7] Finnis responds to the claim that he has betrayed the natural law tradition in favour of Humean and Kantian assumptions in: *CEJF* IV.5; *CEJF* I.1; *CEJF* I (Introduction); *NLNR*, 432–42.

[8] Finnis on contraception: 'Personal Integrity, Sexual Morality and Responsible Parenthood' (1985e); '"Every Marital Act Ought to Be Open to New Life": Toward a Clearer Understanding' (with G. Grisez, J.M. Boyle and W.E. May) (1988e); *CEJF* V.23.

[9] Finnis on the beginning of life: 'The Legal Status of the Unborn Baby' (1993b); *CEJF* II.15; *CEJF* II.16.

[10] Finnis on the reproductive technologies: 'IVF and the Catholic Tradition' (1984d); 'Debate over the Interpretation of *Dignitas personae*'s Teaching on Embryo Adoption' (2009k); *CEJF* II.17.

[11] Finnis on abortion: *CEJF* IV.22; *CEJF* I.16; 'Abortion, Natural Law and Public Reason' (2000c); *CEJF* III.19. Likewise: Grisez, *Abortion: the Myths, the Realities, the Arguments*; Lee, *Abortion and Unborn Human Life*.

[12] Finnis on euthanasia and withdrawal of care: *CEJF* III.15; *CEJF* III.19; 'The Value of Human Life and The Right to Death' (1993e); 'Living Will Legislation' (1994h); *CEJF* III.14; *CEJF* III.15; *CEJF* III.16. Likewise: Grisez and Boyle, *Life and Death with Liberty and Justice*; Gormally, *Euthanasia, Clinical Practice and the Law*; Keown, *Euthanasia Examined*; Keown, *Euthanasia, Ethics and Public Policy*; Paterson, *Assisted Suicide and Euthanasia*; Jackson and Keown, *Debating Euthanasia*; and Keown, *The Law and Ethics of Medicine*.

[13] Finnis on the end of life: *CEJF* II.18. Likewise: Tollefsen, *Biomedical Research and Beyond*; Gormally, *The Dependent Elderly*.

[14] Finnis on nuclear deterrence: *CEJF* III.13; *Nuclear Deterrence, Morality and Realism* (1987g).

contemporary bioethics the foundations it so sorely needs. In this essay I will try to construct and comment on a *Bioethic after Finnis*.

I. The Goods of Life and Health

A. The basic goods

Practical thinking is the activity of deliberating towards and making choices. All intelligible acts are chosen and performed for a *purpose*: we hope to achieve something, to bring about some state of affairs, through or in our action.[15] Such reasoning and choice has several important aspects.

(1) A rational act is one performed with one or more particular ends or benefits that are the object of the agent's willing. Some will be merely instrumental, a means to some more ultimate end. When we press the question of why a person chose or did something—e.g. why she went to the pharmacy and bought medicine—we shall come eventually to the real reason why anyone would be interested in doing such a thing—e.g. 'I bought the medicine hoping it would make me well'. So buying medicines is to be explained by the good of *health* to which this action is ultimately directed.

(2) All intelligible human activity is aimed at *participating* in some such ultimate good(s) by realizing, protecting, or promoting that good(s) in some way.[16] These *basic goods* are self-evidently choice-worthy and irreducible to other goods or ends.

(3) We do not choose our basic goods. They are intrinsic to all human persons, corresponding to the inherent complexity of human nature, and fulfilling aspects of it. So *flourishing* ('happiness') is more than a series of pleasurable experiences or fulfilled preferences: it is the ideal of realizing, as richly as possible, *the range* of human goods within the confines of one's nature, circumstances, and proper commitments.

(4) Though we do not invent our basic goods, we do choose actions which either promote or subvert participation in them and may adopt personal hierarchies among them. No particular choice will exhaust once and for all the good(s) we pursue.

(5) True flourishing is the ideal of realizing the basic goods not just in oneself but, as far as possible *in all persons*, living together in harmony—'the integral human fulfillment of persons in community'. 'As intelligible, the basic goods have no proper names attached to them.'[17]

B. Life

What are these basic goods? The most direct way to uncover them is to ask concerning the range of human actions: 'Why do that?' Persisting with such questions eventually

---

[15] Finnis on the human act: *CEJF* II.8; 'Natural Law and the *Is-Ought* Question' (1981e); 'The Basic Principles of Natural Law' (with G. Grisez) (1982a); 'Practical Reasoning, Human Goods and the End of Man' (1984); *CEJF* I.10; *NDMR*, 275–93; *Aquinas*; *CEJF* II.14.

[16] Following Finnis I use the term 'participate' in this way, without intending to imply a Platonic account of the good.

[17] Grisez et al., 'Practical Principles' (1987f), 114.

yields a small number of *for-the-sake-ofs* such as life, health, truth, beauty, creativity, leisure, friendship, marriage, integrity, and religion.

Life is such a basic good.[18] Here life signifies organic or bodily existence, its preservation, prolongation, and transmission. It is the opposite of death, decay, and sterility. It must be distinguished from: life as some mysterious ghostly property (*élan vital*, etc.); liveliness or vivacity (a temperamental or emotional quality); life-as-lived in its various dimensions (such as business life, social life, etc.); life-as-lived in its totality of objects (flourishing or 'the good life'); and life as the existence of various institutions, systems, or inanimate things. Such metaphorical uses of 'life' depend for their significance upon a prior organic understanding.

Organisms such as human beings are said to have a natural (or species-typical) *lifespan*, 'the life-span of most of us in the absence of specific mortal diseases and fatal accidents'.[19] There does seem to come a time in life, even if not always sharply defined, beyond which most people would not feel robbed or cheated were they soon to die, and death would not be judged or grieved as premature; at this stage a person might be said to have had 'a fair innings'. Then a prudent person might prepare self and others for death, and no longer apply as much effort to postponing death. Just where this stage is will be partly a matter of traditional expectations (e.g. the 'threescore years and ten or fourscore for those who are strong' of Psalm 90) and partly a matter of present-day statistical averages; and it will be part-biological, part-environmental.

C. Health

Finnis and his colleagues group life and health together as one good, just as others might group marriage with other friendships. For the purposes of elaborating a bioethic it can be useful to distinguish these two goods more clearly. While many actions in healthcare are explicable in terms of the pursuit of both life and health, some prolong participation in life with little or no increased participation in health (e.g. resuscitation, artificially feeding the persistently unresponsive) and vice versa (e.g. palliative care); indeed, some prolong life at the expense of health (e.g. pre-emptive breast removal) and some serve health and comfort at the risk of shortening life (e.g. high doses of opiates given to relieve the pain of those with already reduced respiration).

As rational animals, human beings have various systems and capacities, both organic and psychological, which can function well or ill, individually or in relation to each other. Health is *normal psychosomatic functioning of the whole organism*. This definition has a number of aspects:

(1) Health is 'normal' functioning both in the statistical sense ('normality' or 'species typical function') and in the teleological sense ('normativity', what is reasonably to be expected of a member of that species; sound, well-integrated, successful functioning, etc.). In human beings this will include certain biological prerequisites for 'animal' activities, such as nutrition, sentience, motility, and fertility, and certain

---

[18] Finnis on the good of life: *NDMR*, 300–9; *Aquinas*, 140–3.
[19] Kass, *Toward a More Natural Science: Biology and Human Affairs*, 301.

psycho-biological prerequisites for specifically 'human' activities, such as the capacities for human emotions, rationality, learning, and language.

(2) Healthy function is commonly a range rather than a point, with two unhealthy extremes (e.g. obese or malnourished) or with a rough threshold below which one is unhealthy and/or disabled (e.g. legally blind).

(3) The World Health Organization definition of health—as 'a state of complete physical, mental, and social well-being'[20]—is too broad. Much of what contributes to well-being is not health or medicine; nor are all evils experienced by human beings illnesses or for want of healthcare.[21] Adopting such an all-encompassing conception of health, sickness, and healthcare can lead to inappropriate analysis of situations, inappropriate 'solutions', and the misdirection of efforts and resources.

(4) On the face of it health might seem to be relative to people's own temperaments, cultures, plans, and preferences. Dyslexia is no problem in an illiterate culture; restricted mobility may matter less to someone not inclined to move much. Yet this only shows the relativity of the impacts of health and sickness; it does not deny the objective reality of ill-health.

D. Life and health as basic goods

Finnis's articulation of the basic goods—including life and health in bioethics—is the least controversial part of his moral theory and has met the most immediate support amongst most philosophers and theologians. Suffice it to say, participation in life and health makes intelligible (whether or not moral in the circumstances) an enormous range of personal activities from getting up in the morning, washing and breakfasting, looking both ways before crossing the street, going to work, rearing children, cooking, and exercising, through to sending of birthday, get-well, and condolence cards, demonstrating outside nuclear bases or abortion clinics, paying health insurance and resuscitating people. It likewise explains a range of social institutions and activities such as: grocers, pharmacies, disaster relief operations, road safety laws, criminal courts, vaccination programmes, cars with sirens, medical and nursing schools, hospitals, secretaries of state for health and their departments, health insurers, and so on.

Some or all of these things might be explained instrumentally. Life, we might say, is only 'worth living' because of what it enables. I want to go on living so I can care for my children, play tennis, write my *magnum opus*; without these things I might not want to carry on. When we talk of 'a good life' (or a bad one), we refer to those experiences, relationships, and achievements that constitute a biography and for which being alive and healthy are merely means to an end.[22] But the instrumental uses to which life and health are put do not exhaustively explain their value. Life and health are also enjoyed 'for their own sake'. That is why people are not generally expected to give further

---

[20] From the *Constitution of the World Health Organization* (1946).
[21] Cf. Kilner, *Who Lives? Who Dies?*, 160.
[22] An example of such reasoning in law was in *Airedale NHS Trust v. Anthony Bland by his guardian ad litem The Official Solicitor* [1993] AC 789 which Finnis examined in *CEJF* II.19. See also: Fisher, 'On Not Starving the Unconscious'.

reasons for promoting life, avoiding death and so on: these are sufficient reasons *in themselves*. So, too, people can say meaningfully 'it's good to be alive' and 'she's the picture of health' without having to explain what the person is doing with that life or health. This sense that life is *intrinsically* valuable is also behind our talk of the sanctity or inviolability of life, the right to life, and so forth.[23]

Finnis et al. have argued convincingly that the alternative thesis—that life and health are merely instrumental goods—presupposes a tendentious and ultimately indefensible dualism. In particular, it seems to require not merely a distinction but a separation between person and life. A related problem with instrumentalist views of human life is a depreciation of our animality and corporeality. To treat the animal, organic, bodily aspect of my life as somehow distinct from 'the real me'—my 'self' or, as Richard Rorty calls it, my 'mind-stuff'—as merely something I *have, own* or *use*, is to adopt an anthropology both dualist and denatured. Human beings are rational *animals*, living organisms, not angels or spirits; their life is bodily life; they experience their physical and mental lives as dynamically unified, psychosomatic actors.[24] Nonetheless, many people outside the Abrahamic religions and some within them remain dissatisfied with the claim that mortal bodily life is a fundamental good, always worthy of being promoted and protected.

Of course, Finnis recognizes that to say that life is an end *in itself* is not to say that we desire it *by itself*. People want not merely to live but to live well, to flourish consciously pursuing their own life plans and participating in the range of basic goods. People living in a persistently unresponsive state or in late dementia may enjoy only a very reduced participation in the goods of life and health and participate in other goods not as agents but only as the beneficiaries of others' friendship, knowledge, caring work, etc. Nonetheless, they *are* still living human beings: their life is their very reality as persons and as such remains a good, even if not consciously enjoyed by them and not attractive to others; their death is a loss, even if welcomed by some. This explains why we still care for them, including the provision of artificial nutrition and hydration: such care ensures they continue to participate in such goods as they can; it maintains bonds of interpersonal communion with them; it expresses our benevolence and respect for them as living, if profoundly handicapped, members of our human family. It also explains why we do not kill them or hurry their deaths or bury them alive, take organs from them or experiment upon them, sexually abuse them, throw them on the dump,

---

[23] Some examples of legal authorities for this notion: *Blackstone's Commentaries* (1765) I, 130 and VI, 189; *Bland's Case per* Bingham MR, Hoffmann LJ and Lord Goff; *Auckland AHA v. A-G* [1993] 1 NZLR 235, 244; *McKay v. Essex AHA* [1982] 2 All ER 771, 781–2. That the sanctity of life principle applies as clearly to medical situations as elsewhere has also been insisted upon by the courts: *R v. Adams* [1957] Crim LR 365; *Re J* [1992] 4 All ER 614; *R v. Arthur* 12 BMLR 1 (1981); *R v. Cox* 12 BMLR 38 (1992). The House of Lords Select Committee on Medical Ethics, *Report* (1994), vol. 1, §238 concluded: 'Society's prohibition of intentional killing...is the cornerstone of law and of social relationships. It protects each one of us impartially, embodying the belief that all are equal. We do not wish that protection to be diminished.'

[24] *CEJF* II.5; *CEJF* I.2, 53–4; *NDMR*, 307–9; Grisez and Boyle, *Life and Death with Liberty and Justice*, 377–80; Lee and George, *Body-Self Dualism in Contemporary Ethics and Politics*; Boyle, 'The American Debate about Artificial Nutrition and Hydration', 28–46; Haldane, 'Rational and Other Animals', 120–9; May, 'Feeding and Hydrating the Permanently Unconscious and Other Vulnerable Persons' 203; Midgley, *Beast and Man*.

or otherwise subject them to harm or indignity.[25] Those who say we should not feed (artificially or at all) those who are persistently unresponsive or otherwise at a very low ebb have trouble explaining these taboos or else themselves abandon them.

To say that life and health are basic goods is not to say that the prolongation and transmission of life, and the maintenance and improvement of health, are reasonably to be pursued by everybody, all the time, whatever the circumstances or costs to self and others, and by whatever means; nor does it mean that life and health are the only or the most important values. The pursuit of goods such as life and health makes some human choices intelligible, but not necessarily reasonable 'all things considered'. While there will always be good reasons to do things which promote participation in life and health, there may well concurrently be good reasons *not* to do so—such as one's other goals or responsibilities or the burdens of such care.

E. Priorities among the basic goods

The basic goods are called 'good' in irreducibly different senses, and none can meaningfully be said to be objectively 'more good' than another. But life and health do have a certain *natural* priority over other basic goods, just as some would say integrity and religion have a certain *supernatural* or *metaphysical* priority.[26] Reasons include:

(1) Life and health are structural requirements of human choice, for the obvious reason that one cannot choose without being alive, being well enough mentally to be able to exercise free rational choice and being physically and mentally healthy enough to act upon our decisions.

(2) Choices are made in the context of commitments, plans, and strategies: without some security that we will live over a certain stretch of time and be healthy enough to see through our purposes we cannot plan, commit, or choose.

(3) All other goods serve participation in life and health. By acting to ensure one's survival and pursuing good diet, hygiene, and healthcare, for example, life and health serve each other. Participating in the good of play by exercise and rest; in the good of truth by education in health, disease, substances, and lifestyle; in the good of friendship by assisting in healthcare or turning to others for assistance—in all these health and life are served. Mental health likewise requires the pursuit of all the other goods.

(4) Life and health are goods that qualify the pursuit of all the others: thus one can have life-giving, lively, or healthy work, play, worship, relationships, life plans. So, while life and health are not supergoods transcending all others, they are attained through the pursuit of all the goods and in turn unite, order, and qualify participation in other goods.

---

[25] *CEJF* III.16, 192–3 makes an important observation about the systematic and sinister confusion of the emotionally repugnant aspects of long-term coma (extrinsic indignities suffered, or 'undignified' aspects of dependence) with lack of intrinsic or essential human dignity in, for example, talk of 'vegetables' and 'vegetative states'. See also *NDMR*; *CEJF* II.19; Fisher, 'Artificial Nutrition: Why Do Unresponsive Patients Matter?'

[26] One could develop other examples of natural priorities among basic goods: e.g. *CEJF* I.3, 80, note; Grisez et al., 'Practical Principles' (1987f), 138–9.

Thus life and health have some natural or logical priority over other basic goods and any rational life plan must make prudent provision for those things necessary for life and health. Hence infant mortality and life-expectancy are the most commonly used indices of social development, need satisfaction and deprivation; and, next after these, indices of morbidity and morbidity prevention such as vaccination rates.

F. Healthcare

Another important way in which life and health are properly given priority is as the objects of *life plans* or *vocations*.[27] Commitment to a life plan gives an identity or narrative unity without which our choices would be incoherent and contradictory.[28] Healthcare is one such life plan. Some people commit themselves to the study, profession, and practice of healthcare and so ultimately to the pursuit of life and health. This consumes a great deal of their time and energy, gives them particular skills, expertise, and recognition, and structures their other choices. While there are various roles possible in healthcare, all genuine healthcare seeks the prolongation of life, the promotion of health, the prevention of disease, and/or care and symptom relief in the meantime.

Not everything doctors and nurses do contributes to these ends: some of what they do is useless; some actually harmful; some serves other goals such as consoling relatives, providing consumer wants, maximizing provider income, avoiding litigation, achieving social objectives such as eugenics, and so on. Such activities are not true healthcare: their justification, if any, lies elsewhere. Nor is professional healthcare the only way to pursue the goods of life and health: also important are nutrition, exercise, housing, access to clean water, sanitation, and informal healthcare provided at home. But more complex forms of care require considerable training and resourcing of doctors and nurses.

This kind of selectivity, concentration, or commitment to a healthcare vocation need not mean arbitrarily limiting appreciation and respect for other basic goods, let alone acting directly against them. Some people might count life and health lower among their personal priorities, taking considerable (though not arbitrary) risks in developing mountaineering skills or focusing their attention on academic philosophy, without thereby 'saying' that life and health do not matter to them or at all. Likewise, others will focus on curing the sick, possibly at some cost to the attention they might otherwise have given to sport or philosophy. By 'professing' to do this they undertake to pursue those ends within a tradition of practice. Here Finnis's account might usefully be enriched by the ideas of Alasdair MacIntyre on tradition as contexts for practical reasoning and action.[29]

---

[27] On the idea of a coherent plan of life see *NLNR*, 103–5 and on the hazards of this idea 452–3.

[28] See *NLNR*, 104 on how life plans require 'direction and control of impulses, and the undertaking of specific projects...the redirection of inclinations, the reformation of habits, the abandonment of old and adoption of new projects, as circumstances require, and, overall, the harmonization of all one's deep commitments'.

[29] MacIntyre, *After Virtue*.

G. Healthcare virtues

Finnis et al. have been criticized for their underdeveloped moral psychology—some call it 'anthropology' or even 'metaphysics'—and for the priority they give to principle over virtue in articulating their ethics.[30] I think that complaint is to some extent justified, reflecting a certain suspicion of emotions and passions in their writings. Any moral pedagogy and professional formation focused on principle without work on forming character in virtue will be insufficient. Nonetheless, there is plenty of room here for the idea of *virtues* in the sense of cultivated character traits or sensibilities that structure and integrate passions, reason, and will in pursuit of the good. The self-constitutive or reflexive aspects of choice—inclining us to make like choices in the future—is in fact a strong theme in Finnis's theory.[31] Principle does have a logical priority to virtue: without it we could not criticize any community's model of 'the virtuous man' or 'the good life' or know which excellences we ought to cultivate in ourselves and our children and professionals. But good habits clearly develop in tandem with morally right thinking and choosing. Writers such as Edmund Pellegrino have taken up this lacuna in practical reasoning.[32]

Virtues traditionally regarded as constitutive of good character in health professionals and patients include:

- *respectfulness* and *fellow-feeling*, which ensure an inclination always to treat one's patients and carers as one's moral equals and to seek their good, especially their life and health;
- *practical wisdom*, which enables quick, morally reasonable treatment decisions;
- *courage* and *patience*, including both stretching oneself and coming to terms with finitude;
- *temperance*, including taking responsibility for health and moderating healthcare expectations;
- *justice* which considers the demands of the common good and prioritizes allocations according to need;
- *mercy* or active compassion in the face of 'crying need';
- *fidelity* to those with whom one has a special relationship of care;
- *truthfulness* and *confidentiality* towards patients.

---

[30] Finnis responds to this criticism in *NLNR*, 421–2.

[31] E.g. *CEJF* III.16, 191: 'Whichever proposal is adopted or recommended, the choice (or recommendation) is one which will impact on the character of the chooser (or recommender) and of every potential chooser, on the character of healthcare professionals, on the relationship of trust between healthcare professionals and their clients, on the attitude of everyone to his or her own body and bodily life, on the whole substance of solidarity between the strong and the weak at all stages of life.'

[32] Pellegrino and Thomasma, *Virtues in Medical Practice*; Pellegrino and Thomasma, *The Christian Virtues in Medical Practice*. Likewise the works of writers such as Robert Adams, Raimond Gaita, Leon Kass, Mary Midgley, Nancy Sherman, Charles Taylor and Paul Waddell.

II. From Goods and Virtues to Bioethics

A. Some principles

The ancient aphorism that 'good is to be pursued and done and evil avoided' is the preeminent norm of practical reason, akin to the principle of non-contradiction in speculative reasoning.[33] This principle requires all human action be undertaken for some benefit and that pointless or arbitrary choices be shunned. Because basic goods are self-evidently choice-worthy, they provide the intentional premises of practical reasoning. These most basic principles, such as 'preserve life' and 'promote health', are determinations of the goods themselves and, like the goods, both underived and self-evident.[34]

A choice is always between at least two possibilities, each with its own attraction but rivals for that choice. It may be between something morally good and something wicked (though attractive and intelligible), in which case the choice is clear (if possibly difficult). But it may instead be between competing good or mixed alternatives: how then is one to decide?

Finnis et al. explain that we ought to choose 'only those possibilities whose willing is compatible with a will toward integral human fulfillment'.[35] They unpack ('specify') this foundational norm in a series of intermediate principles ('modes of responsibility'), such as those requiring impartiality and fairness, respect for the freedom and conscience of others, detachment, fidelity and purity of heart, and excluding violence, vengefulness, and prejudice.[36] From the most basic principles and these modes of responsibility, specific moral laws may be deduced, explained, critiqued, and/or qualified. These include positive or *orientation* norms, such as 'respect the dignity of others as your equal', 'follow the Golden Rule', 'help those in need', 'foster the common good in your communities', and 'redistribute surplus wealth'; and negative or *limit* precepts, such as 'do not murder', 'never directly harm the innocent', 'abandon none committed to your care', and 'do not lie'. Such moral laws make up the bulk of common morality.

Bioethics considers the goals and practices internal to medicine and applies the precepts of common morality to the dilemmas that arise in life, death, and healthcare. Thus the Hippocratic oath included orientation norms such as 'I will always act for the benefit of the sick', 'I will deal justly and honestly with my patients', and 'I will respect professional confidences', and limit precepts such as 'I will do no harm', 'I will never prescribe a poison', 'I will never assist in an abortion', and 'I will never abuse a patient sexually'.[37] Likewise the modern codes of medical and nursing practice have

---

[33] This section owes much to Grisez et al., 'Practical Principles' (1987f), 119–29. See also St. Thomas Aquinas, *ST*, I–II, 94, 2.

[34] *NLNR*, 68–9 lists several (self-evident) rationality norms. Grisez et al., 'Practical Principles' (1987f), 106–13 offer an analysis of *per se nota* and defend the notion of self-evidence.

[35] Grisez et al., 'Practical Principles' (1987f), 128.

[36] The derivation of some of these 'intermediate principles', 'basic requirements of practical reasonableness' or 'modes of responsibility' is treated, if only briefly, in *NDMR*, 284–7; and *CEJF* V.22.

[37] On the goals internal to medicine as understood in the Hippocratic and Judeo-Christian traditions: Kass, *Toward a More Natural Science*; Ashley et al., *Health Care Ethics*; Tollefsen, *Bioethical Research and Beyond*.

sought to specify the ways that common morality applies to the particular realm of healthcare.

Sometimes we may be tempted to abandon reason and follow preference or prejudice at the expense of others: this is increasingly common in Western societies with respect to the unborn, disabled, and elderly. Or reason and feelings may collude in rationalization, as occurs in the buffet and ledger bioethics described above. Hence the importance of precepts against arbitrary preference amongst persons (the 'Golden Rule' to treat others as you would have them treat you; 'act only on principles that can be applied universally'; 'never treat a person as a means only, but always as an end in themselves') and against arbitrary preference amongst goods (the 'Pauline Principle' that evil may not be done that good may follow; 'the end does not justify the means').[38] Without commitment to such principles inviolable human rights are doomed, as are any serious professional codes of ethics.

Of course any choice seeking participation in some basic good will come at the 'opportunity cost' of not promoting some others; it may even have the unintended side effect of reducing or damaging someone's participation in some good(s). But this is quite different morally from intending to destroy, damage, or impede someone's participation in a basic good.[39] Directly to attack someone's participation in a basic good is intrinsically wrong, as a good in and of itself only ever provides a reason to act for it; if done in the hope of securing some supposed 'greater good' it amounts to an incoherent attempt at commensurating diverse goods and evils, arbitrarily playing favorites among the goods or persons or both.[40]

B. Personal responsibility for health and healthcare

Responsibility for health and healthcare begins with the individual concerned and his/her family. People should seek and act upon reliable information about health and hygiene, diet, rest, exercise, substances, and disease prevention, seeking to avoid illness and injury as far as reasonable. They have a duty, and should be given the room, to challenge contemporary practices which threaten their health (e.g. work patterns, fashions, sexual mores) and to practice moderation. When necessary they should seek the assistance of health professionals; but even then they ought not to abdicate responsibility for their own health and healthcare, assuming the role of 'victims' and passive recipients of technology and attention. In all, people should develop a style of life suited to their true flourishing as human beings.

The emphasis on personal responsibility for health, true as far as it goes, is accompanied in much Anglo-American bioethics, including that of the new natural law

[38] See Rom 3:8. The derivation of the limit precepts against arbitrary preference amongst persons and arbitrary preference amongst goods is treated in *NLNR*, 105–10, 419–23; *NDMR*, 263–7, 285–94; *CEJF* II.1; *CEJF* I.15; and *Aquinas*, 170–6. Similar points are made in Christian moral theology (e.g. Grisez, *Christian Moral Principles*, Chs 7 and 8) and in Kantian ethics (e.g. Donagan, *The Theory of Morality*).

[39] *NLNR*, 118–24; Fisher, 'Killing and Letting Die: What's the Difference?'; Gormally, *Euthanasia, Clinical Practice and the Law*.

[40] Similarly incoherent and deceptive is the notion of balancing or trading-off efficiency and principle, for efficiency is a judgment regarding the means to an end, and this end (with the means proposed) must first be judged good or not in principle. See *CEJF* I.15.

writers, by a diminished role for the state in healthcare. Suspicion of state involvement is one of the factors that has underpinned the long resistance to universal healthcare in the United States and leaves these theories undeveloped with respect to social provision of healthcare and its complexities such as the allocation of healthcare resources.

With respect to personal responsibility for healthcare, Finnis's approach means no orientation norm can be *absolute* in the sense of being exhaustively fulfillable or over-riding all other orientation norms: for example, we cannot help all the needy, in every way and all the time. But some limit precepts are absolute or exceptionless since they are fulfillable and cannot be breached without acting directly against the good: e.g. we can and should avoid ever murdering anyone.[41]

The duty to promote one's own or other people's health, as with all other orientation precepts, is not absolute. We do what we can and what we must. When, therefore, would it be appropriate to forgo medical treatment? I have already implicitly identified two situations where treatment should not be applied:

(1) Where the treatment proposed does not in fact contribute to participation in life or health (e.g. ineffective or at most marginal tests or therapies, substance abuse, and most contraception, sterilization, abortion, IVF, and 'sex change' surgery).

(2) Where the healthcare proposed does indeed contribute to participation in life or health but only in ways that are morally unreasonable (e.g. killing patients to obtain organs, using stem cells taken from human embryos, other ethically dubious therapies, or research).

Treatments may reasonably be forgone:

(3) Where it is judged by the patient (or other appropriate decision-maker where the patient is incompetent) to be disproportionately burdensome in terms of the pain, physical side effects, indignity, disruption, confinement, risk, or cost to that individual or others.

(4) Where a patient reasonably judges that a particular proposed treatment would be inconsistent with his/her responsibilities. While harmonizing one's healthcare choices with other elements of one's life plan will not justify neglecting life and health entirely, it may be appropriate to forgo certain healthcare opportunities for the sake of rival personal goals or the needs of others. Thus a man might reasonably decide to receive simpler treatments at home, rather than leaving and bankrupting his family to receive a more expensive and experimental therapy.

Here Finnis's theory critiques over-treatment as much as under-treatment, physicalist obsession with maximizing lifespan as much as the quality-of-lifist rejection of the lifespan we are given.

C. Duties of health professionals

If the primary responsibility for healthcare lies with the individual (and his/her family), health professionals often act as agents or delegates of the individual. This delegation is, arguably, the source of the principle of informed consent so strongly advocated in

---

[41] Finnis on absolutes: 'Absolute Moral Norms: Their Ground, Force and Permanence' (1988f); *CEJF* I.12; *MA*.

contemporary healthcare. However, health professionals are not 'hired guns' offering their services to all comers for a fee. Independently of the demands of patients, colleagues, managers, and insurers they must make a judgment about what is medically appropriate and ethically permissible in each case. As moral agents, health professionals are bound, like anyone else, by the precepts of practical reason and shaped, like anyone else, by the virtues; as professionals and practitioners of a particular craft, they are bound to the ends and ethic internal to their vocation and recognized in its tradition; as persons licensed and often resourced by the community, they have certain social responsibilities also.

III. Some Unethical Healthcare Decisions

A. Directly homicidal healthcare decisions

There are many opportunities deliberately to save life or to kill people in medicine, whether by action or by calculated course of omission. Finnis's approach shows why direct attacks upon innocent lives are always gravely immoral, whether as an end or a means to another end. Such lethal attacks include: murder, surgical abortion, abortifacient drug use, human embryo destruction, most uses of reproductive technologies, search-and-destroy genetic tests, infanticide, suicide, assisting in suicide, active euthanasia (voluntary or not) and euthanasia by neglect of basic care (e.g. denying feeding to handicapped babies, or 'PVS' patients judged unworthy of life or better off dead).

Of course, the choice to kill a patient might be motivated by more than simple malice, such as the desire to respond to patient or a family request, to free women from the burden of bearing and raising or else giving up for adoption an unwanted child, to relieve those suffering from irremediable pain, to release family and carers from the burden of caring well for a long-term patient, to 'clear the beds' for other patients, to recover life-saving organs for another patient, or to reduce the burden on healthcare resources, and so on. At least until the growing acceptance of abortion (from the 1970s), the norm of common morality against killing the innocent was reflected in medical law, codes of professional ethics, and healthcare practice: killing, it was generally agreed, was among the ways in which health professionals may not deal with their patients.[42] As the Hippocratic Oath promises: 'I will not give anyone a lethal drug, even if asked, nor advise such a plan; similarly I will give no woman an abortifacient.'

One tactic to avoid compromising the prohibition on medical killing while allowing abortion has been to deny the individuality, humanity, or personhood of the unborn child. Finnis argues that the integrated organic functioning of the human being begins at conception and that, while immaturity and inexperience preclude the embryo from demonstrating many distinctively human behaviours (such as conscious thought), it is already the kind of being to which such behaviours are proper. A being only develops to the stage of *demonstrating* such behaviours because it already has the *inherent capacity* for them. A man may not (yet) speak Norwegian but he has the capacity to speak it

---

[42] *CEJF* II.20; Finnis and Fisher, 'Theology and the Four Principles' (1993d). Also: Emanuel, *The Ends of Human Life*; Kass, *Toward a More Natural Science*; Ramsey, *The Patient as Person*.

because he is human. Finnis criticizes the unargued-for materialism underlying many accounts of the human person in bioethical debates, as if human beings are no more than sophisticated wiring and plumbing, and the equally untenable dualism referred to above, as if some 'real self' popped in and out of the human body at different stages of development or sickness.[43]

Such obfuscations aside, to choose to kill the innocent is generally recognized to be a choice against the good of life and against the victim, even if it serves some good ulterior purpose. It also involves a willingness to impede instances of other goods that depend upon life, such as health and friendship. Such killing fails to satisfy the Golden Rule and the duty to care for others and contravenes limit precepts such as the Pauline Principle and those against murder and lying. Its reflexive effect is, of course, to make the health professionals concerned into killers, and this will have a corrupting effect not only on their character and future practice but on their profession and community if these are complicit in the killing.

Finnis gives the example of the 'politicized and manipulative' vocabulary used not only to cloak the real meaning of abortion but also of the reproductive technologies. All production of embryos by natural means, IVF, or cloning is *reproductive*; all uses of embryos as sources of tissues or cell-lines to benefit some other human being are *non-therapeutic*. So the distinction, common in rhetoric and regulation, between reproductive and therapeutic cloning (or other embryo manufacture) is plain deceptive—and lethally so. Finnis defends his claim that this violates the World Medical Association's *Declaration of Helsinki on Research on Human Subjects* against the objections that embryos can split into twins, are too small, lack self-direction, etc. Like much of the obfuscation in warfare, so now in the research lab early human lives may be relabelled as 'pre-embryos' or 'research materials' and their killing as 'therapeutic' or 'research', but what is contemplated is, in fact, direct homicide.[44]

B. Importance of intention

Not all decisions by health professionals that foreseeably result in death intend such harm. Utilitarians commonly elide responsibility for all foreseeable consequences of one's actions, whether these are intended or not; the civil law, however, more often than not takes intention into account and the natural law account of Finnis insists on the crucial relevance of the agent's intention, end or purpose.[45] Sometimes, as noted above, there will be good grounds for withholding or withdrawing treatments; sometimes there will be insufficient resources to save or heal everyone. But if shortening the life or harming the health of a patient is no part of the reason for such chosen conduct, there is no reckless disregard and there is a good enough reason to tolerate the foreseen risks or side effects, the health professional is not to be held responsible for a death that ensues. To say that a heart surgeon, who did all in his power but failed to save a patient dying of heart disease, 'killed the patient' and should be held responsible for that is to misunderstand the human act and moral responsibility.

---

[43] *CEJF* II.15; *CEJF* II.16; 'The Other F-word' <http://www.thepublicdiscourse.com/2010/10/1849>.
[44] *CEJF* II.17.   [45] *CEJF* I.14; *CEJF* V.22.

Of course, sometimes health professionals neglect to provide an appropriate treatment or give a medically inappropriate one precisely because they think death would be in their patient's best interests or that of others. In that case, the choice is directly homicidal and thus immoral. With forensic precision Finnis identifies potentially lethal obfuscations in some philosophical accounts of life, death, intending, and acting, such as those of Peter Singer and John Harris, and in some recent legal decisions, such as most famously in *Bland's Case*.[46] By their own admission the Law Lords' reliance on the distinction between acting and omitting in that case, rather than focusing on intention (including intentional neglect to provide due care), has left the law in this area 'almost irrational' and 'morally and intellectually misshapen'. Nowhere do they explain how their decision can be reconciled with the long legal tradition not only on homicide-by-neglect but also on the added responsibility the law imposes upon agents to provide for the needs of their own dependent children, parents, or patients. It is long established law that to neglect to fulfill that duty can be murder, manslaughter, assault, or negligence.[47]

Much of Finnis's work, like that of Elizabeth Anscombe before him, has depended upon a view of the meaning and significance of intention in the human act (and its cognates 'unintended side effect', 'double effect', 'direct', and 'indirect').[48] This has helped to clarify how giving high doses of pain-relieving agents or removing overly burdensome treatments, even at a risk of shortening life, need not be euthanasia; why a surgical procedure or drug commonly used to make people permanently or temporarily sterile may rightly be used for another purpose even if it has a sterilizing side effect; when vaccines grown on cell-lines taken from aborted fetuses may ethically be used; what incremental improvements might be made in imperfect laws or bills without being morally complicit in the bad laws; and so on.[49] Here Finnis's conclusions align with the classical moral tradition while his analysis of the human act helps explain apparent exceptions or inconsistencies in that tradition. However this same action theory can lead to some very unsettling conclusions, e.g. regarding the permissibility of craniotomy in difficult labours.[50] This has led some to doubt the whole edifice upon which the new natural law theory is built; in my own case it has left me thinking that, like Churchill's description of democracy, Finnis's is the worst action theory except for all the others.

C. Directly harmful healthcare decisions

Just as the healthcare relationship involves many opportunities to save life, so it occasions many acts of curing or care; there are likewise many ways and means to

---

[46] *CEJF* II.17; *CEJF* III.15; *CEJF* II.20.

[47] *R v. Bubb* (1850) 4 Cox CC 455; *R v. Gibbins & Proctor* (1918) 13 Cr App Rep 134; *R v. Instan* [1893] 1 QB 450; *R v. Marriott* (1838) 8 C & P 425; *R v. Nicholls* (1874) 13 Cox CC 75; *R v. Stone & Dobinson* [1977] QB 354; [1977] 2 All ER 341; *R v. Unnamed 44 year old man, The Times*, 8 March 1994; *Bland's Case* per Lord Keith at 362.

[48] Finnis on intention: *CEJF* II.8; *CEJF* II.9; *CEJF* II.10; *CEJF* II.12; *CEJF* II.13.

[49] E.g. *CEJF* IV.22; Finnis, 'Restricting Legalised Abortion is not Intrinsically Unjust' (2005f); Finnis, 'A Vote Decisive for ... a More Restrictive Law' (2005g).

[50] *CEJF* II.3.

harm people, whether by action or omission of appropriate care. Finnis's theory shows why non-lethal attacks upon psychosomatic integrity are unethical, such as torture, maiming (including destroying a healthy bodily function), permanent or temporary sterilization, much 'sex change' surgery, various kinds of 'brain washing', and substance abuse. To choose to harm the innocent is to choose to destroy or impede instances of the good of health, which is wrong even if it serves some good ulterior motive such as freeing a person from unwanted fertility or gender, prosecuting the security interests of the state or achieving temporary euphoria. Furthermore, such acts often involve a willingness directly to compromise participation in other basic goods, such as life or friendship. Directly harming or deliberately neglecting people, like directly killing them, breaches the limit precepts against harming and pragmatism and fails to satisfy orientation norms such as the Golden Rule and the duty to care. Such interventions are not *healthcare* at all.

The choice to harm a patient might be driven by a desire to respond to a patient request, to minimize their suffering, to harvest live organs for a life-saving transplant, to obtain important research data, to keep a voice high by castration or to maximize a beggar's chances by amputation. Despite the recent tendency to treat health professionals as mere for-fee service providers, and the growing tolerance of procedures such as sterilization and sexual reassignment surgery, medical law and ethics still generally uphold the norm against harming the innocent: no health professional may deliberately harm or neglect a patient. As the Hippocratic Oath promises: 'I will prescribe only regimens that are good for my patients and do no harm'.

Much that goes on in the area of reproductive technology amounts either to directly *lethal* activity (e.g. disposing of embryos judged unfit for implantation, 'selective reduction' when too many embryos have implanted, search-and-destroy genetic testing and abortion, and so on) or to directly *harmful* activity (e.g. freeze-thawing embryos which damages many of them). One interesting harm that Finnis analyses is the manufacture ('production') of human beings in laboratories rather than the procreation ('reproduction') of them in the marital bed. Finnis argues that aiming to supply people with babies by manufacturing embryos *in vitro* and selectively implanting them treats the embryos as sub-personal 'products'. To treat people in this way, as valuable only for the uses others have for them, rather like slaves, is a moral harm to them—even if they are harmed *in the very process of coming into being*, even if their life is good in itself and even if those who ultimately care for them genuinely love them.[51]

D. Some other healthcare norms

Using the same kinds of practical reasoning about the ends and ethic internal to healthcare it is possible to reason to the range of bioethical precepts which have been articulated in the great medical oaths and codes of practice.[52] These include orientation

---

[51] *CEJF* II.17, 298–301; Finnis, 'IVF and the Catholic Tradition' (1984d).
[52] On the axiomatic values in the history of Western medicine see, for example, *CEJF* III.16,191 and the writings of Leon Kass, Edmund Pellegrino, Gilbert Meilaender, and Christopher Tollefsen.

norms requiring reverence for the person, doctor-patient trust, responsiveness to needs, activity aimed at saving, curing and caring, and special care for the most disadvantaged; and limit precepts forbidding assaults, non-consensual interference, manipulation, exploitation, neglect, lying, breaches of confidentiality, and unjust discrimination in healthcare.[53] Thus the World Health Organization's *Declaration of Geneva*, a modern version of the Hippocratic Oath, requires physicians to consecrate their life to the service of humanity; to make 'the health of my patient' their first consideration; to prevent 'considerations of religion, nationality, race, party politics, or social standing coming between my duty and my patient'; to 'maintain utmost respect for human life from its beginning'; and not to use their medical knowledge 'contrary to the laws of humanity'. A similar ethic properly applies to nurses.

E. Prejudiced healthcare decisions

Feelings can sometimes motivate unreasonable choices in healthcare, as elsewhere in life, and reason may also play accomplice to prejudice. Thus some people have been denied the care appropriate to them on the basis that they were too young or small, too poor or powerless, insufficient social contributors, 'old and useless', or 'better off dead'. The Golden Rule exposes such judgments as unjust. Of course choices between persons are sometimes required: healthcare, for instance, is given to the sick (and first to those most urgently in need of attention) rather than to everyone equally; there is scope for reasonable preference for one's self, family, friends, and community. But when all reasonable allowance is made for that, this principle remains 'a pungent critique of selfishness, special pleading, double standards, hypocrisy, indifference to the good of others whom one could easily help ("passing by on the other side"), and all the other manifold forms of egoistic and group bias'.[54] There is more to be done to address the biases this ethic unveils, e.g. against those with poor mental health.

IV. Conclusion

As a young student of law and bioethics I was graced to encounter some early writings by John Finnis on abortion.[55] That led me to his then just-published *magnum opus* on natural law which in turn opened up for me a whole new vista on moral argument. Finnis has long continued to teach me by his writings and his influence has been profound on many who have read him. He has genuinely advanced legal and moral theory, offering both a much sounder grounding than generally secured in our age.

Sometimes the bioethical positions of believers are brushed aside as relevant only to members of that confession[56] and those of the Hippocratic tradition as outmoded. But Finnis's bioethic demonstrates the logical soundness and enduring practical significance

---

[53] Some of these are explored more fully in Fisher and Gormally, *Healthcare Allocation*, which follows a similar approach to Finnis's.

[54] *NLNR*, 107.

[55] Finnis, 'Abortion and Legal Rationality' (1970c(i)); *CEJF* III.18.

[56] Finnis responds in several essays collected in Part One of *CEJF* V.

of the conclusions of those traditions, while giving them much-needed underpinnings in a rich conception of the human good and practical reason. In the process he shows bioethics a way out of the morass of being little more than self-justification for some medical researchers or practitioners, titillation for a public eager for exciting dilemmas, and fuel for the endless expansion of the bioethics industry. Whatever the limitations of this theory, it will, I think, be his enduring legacy in bioethics more than his normative conclusions. Finnis's approach shows people how to respond well to real-life difficulties and provides a 'pre-evangelization' platform for that evangelization our healthcare culture, and the wider societal 'culture of death', so desperately need.[57]

Bibliography

Aquinas, Thomas, *Summa Theologica* I–II, 94, 2.

Ashley, Benedict M., J. deBlois, and K.D. O'Rourke, *Health Care Ethics: A Catholic Theological Analysis* (5th edn, Georgetown: Georgetown University Press, 2007).

Beauchamp, T.L. and J.F. Childress, *Principles of Biomedical Ethics* (7th edn, Oxford: Oxford University Press, 2012).

Boyle, Joseph, 'The American Debate about Artificial Nutrition and Hydration' in L. Gormally (ed.), *The Dependent Elderly* (Cambridge: Cambridge University Press, 1992), 28–46.

Clouser, K.D. and B. Gert, 'Morality *vs.* Principlism' in Gillon, R., (ed.) *Principles of Health Care Ethics* (London: John Wiley & Sons, 1993), 251–66.

Constitution of the World Health Organization (1946), *British Medical Journal* 2 (4570): 302–3, 7 August 1948.

Donagan, Alan, *The Theory of Morality* (Chicago, IL: University of Chicago Press, 1977).

DuBose, E., R. Hamel and L. O'Connell (eds), *A Matter of Principles? Ferment in U.S. Bioethics* (Virginia: Trinity Press International, 1994).

Eckenwiler, L.A. and F.G. Cohn (eds), *The Ethics of Bioethics* (Baltimore, MD: The Johns Hopkins University Press, 2007).

Emanuel, E.J., 'The Ends of Human Life: Medical Ethics in a Liberal Polity (Cambridge, MA: Harvard University Press, 1991).

Finnis, John, *Natural Law and Natural Rights* (Oxford: Oxford University Press, 1980; 2nd edn, 2011).

Finnis, John, 'Natural Law and the "Is"–"Ought" Question: An Invitation to Professor Veatch' (1982) 26 *Catholic Lawyer*, 266.

Finnis, John, *Fundamentals of Ethics* (Washington, DC: Georgetown University, 1983).

Finnis, John, 'IVF and the Catholic Tradition' (1984) 246 *The Month*, 55.

Finnis, John, 'Practical Reasoning, Human Goods and the End of Man' (1984) 58 *Proceedings of the American Catholic Philosophical Association*, 23; also in (1985) 66 *New Blackfriars*, 438.

Finnis, John, 'Personal Integrity, Sexual Morality and Responsible Parenthood', *Anthropos* [now *Anthropotes*], 1 (1985).

Finnis, John, *Moral Absolutes: Tradition, Revision and Truth* (Washington, DC: Catholic University of America Press, 1991).

Finnis, John, 'The Legal Status of the Unborn Baby' (1992) 43 *Catholic Medical Quarterly*, 5.

Finnis, John, 'The Value of Human Life and The Right to Death' (1993) 17 *Sthn Illinois ULJ*, 559.

Finnis, John, 'Living Will Legislation', in L. Gormally (ed.), *Euthanasia, Clinical Practice and the Law* (1994), 167.

Finnis, John, 'Euthanasia and Justice' (1995) *CEJF* III.14.

---

[57] On the corrupting effects of the culture of death even within Catholic theology, see *CEJF* V.22.

Finnis, John, *Aquinas: Moral, Political, and Legal Theory* (Oxford: Oxford University Press, 1998).

Finnis, John, 'Understanding Dignitas Personae on Embryo Adoption', (2009) 9(3) *The National Catholic Bioethics Quarterly*, 461.

Finnis, John, *The Collected Essays of John Finnis, Volume I: Reason in Action* (Oxford: Oxford University Press, 2011).

Finnis, John, *The Collected Essays of John Finnis, Volume II: Intention and Identity* (Oxford: Oxford University Press, 2011).

Finnis, John, *The Collected Essays of John Finnis, Volume III: Human Rights and Common Good* (Oxford: Oxford University Press, 2011).

Finnis, John, *The Collected Essays of John Finnis, Volume IV: Philosophy of Law* (Oxford: Oxford University Press, 2011).

Finnis, John, *The Collected Essays of John Finnis, Volume V: Religion and Public Reason* (Oxford: Oxford University Press, 2011).

Finnis, John, 'Discourse, Truth, and Friendship' *CEJF* I.2 (Oxford: Oxford University Press, 2011).

Finnis, John, 'Scepticism's Self-Refutation' *CEJF* I.3 (Oxford: Oxford University Press, 2011).

Finnis, John, 'Action's Most Ultimate End' *CEJF* I.10 (Oxford: Oxford University Press, 2011).

Finnis, John, 'Intention in Direct Discrimination' *CEJF* II.14 (Oxford: Oxford University Press, 2011).

Finnis, John, 'When Most People Begin' *CEJF* II.14 (Oxford: Oxford University Press, 2011).

Finnis, John, 'Organic Unity, Brain Life, and Our Beginning' *CEJF* II.15 (Oxford: Oxford University Press, 2011).

Finnis, John, 'Persons and Their Associations' *CEJF* II.5 (Oxford: Oxford University Press, 2011).

Finnis, John, 'On Producing Human Embryos' *CEJF* II.17 (Oxford: Oxford University Press, 2011).

Finnis, John, 'Brain Death and Peter Singer' *CEJF* II.18 (Oxford: Oxford University Press, 2011).

Finnis, John, 'Intentionally Killing the "Permanently Unconscious"' *CEJF* II.19 (Oxford: Oxford University Press, 2011).

Finnis, John, 'Economics, Justice, and the Value of Life' *CEJF* III.15 (Oxford: Oxford University Press, 2011).

Finnis, John, 'Euthanasia and the Law' *CEJF* III.16 (Oxford: Oxford University Press, 2011).

Finnis, John, 'Justice for Mother and Child' *CEJF* III.19 (Oxford: Oxford University Press, 2011).

Finnis, John with Joseph Boyle and Germain Grisez, 'Incoherence and Consequentialism (or Proportionalism—A Rejoinder' (1990f) 64 *American Catholic Philosophical Quarterly*, 271.

Finnis, John with Joseph Boyle and Germain Grisez, *Nuclear Deterrence, Morality and Realism* (Oxford: Clarendon Press, 1987).

Finnis, John with Anthony Fisher, O.P., 'Theology and the Four Principles: A Roman Catholic View I', in *Principles of Health Care Ethics*, ed. Raanan Gillon (Chichester, England: John Wiley, 1994), 31.

Finnis, John and Germain Grisez, 'The Basic Principles of Natural Law: A Reply to Ralph McInerny' (1982) 26 *American Journal of Jurisprudence*, 21.

Finnis, John, with Germain Grisez, Joseph Boyle, and William E. May, '"Every Marital Act Ought to Be Open to New Life": Toward a Clearer Understanding', (1988) 52 *Thomist*, 365.

Fisher, Anthony, 'Killing and Letting Die: What's the Difference?' (1993) 21 *Signum*, 16

Fisher, Anthony, 'On Not Starving the Unconscious' (1993) 74 *New Blackfriars*, 130.

Fisher, Anthony, 'Rethinking Principlism: Is Bioethics an American plot?' (2010) 21(2) *Bioethics Outlook*, 1.

Fisher, Anthony, 'Artificial Nutrition: Why Do Unresponsive Patients Matter?' in *Catholic Bioethics for a New Millennium* (Cambridge: Cambridge University Press, 2011), Ch. 8.

Fisher, Anthony and Luke Gormally, *Healthcare Allocation: An Ethical Framework for Public Policy* (St Augustine Pr Inc, 2001).

Gillon, R., (ed.), *Principles of Health Care Ethics* (Chichester: John Wiley & Sons, 1993).

Gormally, L. (ed.), *The Dependent Elderly* (Cambridge: Cambridge University Press, 1992).

Gormally, Luke (ed.), *Euthanasia, Clinical Practice and the Law* (Linacre Centre for Health Care Ethics, 1994).

Grisez, Germain, *Abortion: the Myths, the Realities, the Arguments* (New York and Cleveland: Corpus Books, 1970).

Grisez, Germain, 'Against Consequentialism' (1978) 23 *AJ Juris*, 449.

Grisez, Germain, *Christian Moral Principles* (Chicago, IL: Franciscan Herald Press, 1983).

Grisez, Germain and J. Boyle, *Life and Death with Liberty and Justice* (Notre Dame: University of Notre Dame Press, 1979).

Grisez, Germain, John Finnis and Joseph Boyle '"Direct" and "Indirect": A Reply to Critics of Our Action Theory' (2001) 65(1) *Thomist* 1.

Haldane, John, 'Rational and Other Animals', in *Reasonable Faith* (New York: Routlege, 2010), 120–9.

Irving, Dianne, 'The Bioethics Mess' (2001) 19(5) *Crisis*, 16.

Jackson, E., and J. Keown, *Debating Euthanasia* (Oxford: Hart Publishing, 2012).

Jamieson, D., (ed.), *Singer and his Critics* (Chichester: Wiley-Blackwell, 1999).

Jecker, N.A., A. Jonsen, and R. Pearlman, *Bioethics: An Introduction to the History, Methods and Practice* (2nd edn, Burlington: Jones & Bartlett Learning, 2007).

Jonsen, Albert, *A Short History of Medical Ethics* (New York: Oxford University Press, 2008).

Kass, Leon, *Toward a More Natural Science: Biology and Human Affairs* (Simon and Schuster, 1985), 301.

Keown, John (ed.), *Euthanasia Examined* (Cambridge: Cambridge University Press, 1995).

Keown, John, *Euthanasia, Ethics and Public Policy* (Cambridge: Cambridge University Press, 2002).

Keown, John, *The Law and Ethics of Medicine: Essays on the Inviolability of Human Life* (Oxford: Oxford University Press, 2012).

Kilner, J.F., *Who Lives? Who Dies? Ethical Criteria in Patient Selection* (New Haven, CT: Yale University Press, 1990), 160.

Lafleur, W.R., G. Böhme and S. Shimazono (eds), *Dark Medicine: Rationalizing Unethical Medical Research* (Bloomington: Indiana University Press, 2008).

Lee, Patrick, *Abortion and Unborn Human Life* (2nd edn, Washington, DC: Catholic University of America, 2010).

Lee, Patrick and Robert George, *Body-Self Dualism in Contemporary Ethics and Politics* (New York: Cambridge University Press, 2009).

MacIntyre, Alasdair, *Whose Justice? Which Rationality?* (Notre Dame: University of Notre Dame Press, 1988).

MacIntyre, Alasdair, *After Virtue* (3rd edn, Notre Dame: University of Notre Dame Press, 2007).

Maclean, A., *The Elimination of Morality: Reflections on Utilitarianism and Bioethics* (London: Routledge, 1993).

May, William E., 'Feeding and Hydrating the Permanently Unconscious and Other Vulnerable Persons' (1987) 3 *Issues L Med*, 203.

Midgley, M., *Beast and Man: The Roots of Human Nature* (Rev edn, London: Routledge 1995).

Oderberg, D., and J. Laing (eds), *Human Lives: Critical Essays on Consequentialist Bioethics* (London: Macmillan, 1997).

Paterson, C., *Assisted Suicide and Euthanasia: A Natural Law Ethics Approach* (London: Ashgate, 2008).

Pellegrino, E., and D.C. Thomasma, *Virtues in Medical Practice* (Oxford: Oxford University Press, 1993).

Pellegrino, E., and D.C. Thomasma, *The Christian Virtues in Medical Practice* (Washington, DC: Georgetown University Press, 1996).

Pellegrino, E., et al., *Biotechnology and the Human Good* (Washington, DC: Georgetown University Press, 2009).

Presidential Commission for the Study of Bioethical Issues, *Ethically Impossible: STD Research in Guatemala 1946 to 1953* (Washington, DC: 2011).

Ramsey, Paul, *The Patient as Person* (New Haven, CT; London: Yale University Press, 1970).

Reverby, S., *Examining Tuskegee: The Infamous Syphilis Study and Its Legacy* (Chapel Hill: University of North Carolina Press, 2009).

Reverby, S., *Examining Tuskegee: The Infamous Syphilis Study and Its Legacy* (Chapel Hill: University of North Carolina Press, 2009).

Rothman, D., *Strangers at the Bedside: A History of How Law and Bioethics Transformed Medical Decision Making* (New York: Basic Books, 1991).

Tollefsen, C., *Biomedical Research and Beyond: Expanding the Ethics of Inquiry* (New York: Routledge, 2008).

World Medical Association, *International Code of Medical Ethics* (London: World Medical Association, 1949).

World Medical Association, *Oath at the Time of Being Admitted as a Member of the Medical Profession* ('Declaration of Geneva') (World Medical Association, 1948).

World Medical Association, *Ethical Principles for Medical Research Involving Human Subjects* ('Declaration of Helsinki') (World Medical Association, 1964).

18

A New Father for the Law and Ethics of Medicine

John Keown

I. Introduction

John Finnis is internationally recognized as an eminent scholar of legal philosophy and of constitutional law. He should also be recognized, this essay will contend, as a leading authority on the law and ethics of medicine.

In the UK, Glanville Williams has been described as the 'grandfather' of the discipline—largely because he wrote one of its earliest and most influential books, *The Sanctity of Life and the Criminal Law*[1]—and Ian Kennedy as one of its 'fathers'. Although their work has stimulated valuable debate, it has been shown to be philosophically flawed.[2] Williams noted that for lawyers to engage with other disciplines such as ethics involved 'risky trespasses outside the lawyer's proper sphere'.[3] Much of his and Kennedy's writing proves the point. This essay will suggest that the prolific contribution of John Finnis to the discipline over the last 40 years provides, because of its combination of legal expertise and philosophical rigour, a far sounder intellectual foundation for the discipline than that offered by Williams or Kennedy.

As the previous essay helpfully explained, Finnis's work is informed by a coherent and clearly articulated natural law framework of ethical principles, in particular the principle of the 'sanctity' or 'inviolability' of life (IOL), or what he understandably prefers to call 'the ethics of equality in right to life'.[4] This is important, not least because the natural law tradition has historically shaped English medical law. This remains the case even though the law has, by extensively permitting abortion and research on human embryos *in vitro*, increasingly reflected the sort of utilitarian thinking advocated by Glanville Williams. Anyone who has read Finnis's work will be well equipped to spot misunderstandings of key concepts of the IOL framework—intention, 'double effect', and 'proportionate' and 'disproportionate' treatments—which permeate the work of Williams and Kennedy.

As we shall see, Finnis has produced a discrete and substantial body of work in relation to the law and ethics of medicine, a body of work which calls for a volume in its

---

[1] Williams, *The Sanctity of Life and the Criminal Law*.
[2] Keown, *The Law and Ethics of Medicine*, Chs 2 and 3 respectively. In particular, Williams and Kennedy misunderstand the natural law tradition, which has informed English medical law, and fail to articulate anything approaching a coherent alternative.
[3] Williams, *The Sanctity of Life and the Criminal Law*, 11. Some leading medical lawyers, like Peter Skegg and Margaret Brazier, have, with considerable distinction, focussed on medical law. Many other medical lawyers have, however, followed Williams and Kennedy in making risky trespasses into ethics.
[4] *CEJF* II.18, 312.

own right. Not only do the prolific quantity and unparalleled quality of his scholarly output mark him out as one of the world's leading authorities in the field, it is not easy to think of other scholars who bring to the discipline such a powerful combination of legal and philosophical expertise. Much of Finnis's work addresses, like that of Williams and Kennedy, controversial issues at the beginning and end of life.

II. The Beginning of Life

One of Finnis's best-known essays is 'The Rights and Wrongs of Abortion' (1973), his classic response to J.J. Thomson's ingenious paper 'A Defense of Abortion', a response in which he trenchantly questions her analogy between terminating an unwanted pregnancy and disconnecting an unwanted violinist.[5] This paper is reproduced in his *Collected Essays*, as are five others on the beginning of life. 'Justice for Mother and Child' (1993) (written by invitation in the vernacular of the 'four principles' approach to bioethics) argues that the intentional killing of human persons, as an end or as a means, offends the principles of justice and non-maleficence, and that the only reasonable judgment is that the unborn are human persons.[6] In '"Public Reason" and Moral Debate' Finnis asks why Rawls draws the boundary of justice, fairness, and reciprocity at birth.[7] How could it be rational to think that the child just before birth has no rights while the child just after birth has the rights of a citizen free and equal to other citizens? Why should the child a week before birth be subject to destruction at someone else's 'balancing of values'?[8] Finnis observes: 'The public reason of the United States, as manifested in the loquacious judgments of its Supreme Court, has after a quarter of a century uttered not a sentence that even appears intended to offer a rational response to that question.'[9]

The papers reprinted in the *Collected Essays* consider the status of the unborn child not only *in vivo* but also *in vitro*. For example, 'Justice for Mother and Child' maintains that any experimentation or observation which is likely to endanger the embryo is maleficent, unjust, or both, unless the procedures are intended to benefit that embryo.[10] Ethical concerns about *in vitro* fertilization (IVF) are pursued in 'CS Lewis and Test-Tube Babies' (1984)[11] which notes that the IVF child comes into existence 'not as *a gift supervening on an act expressive of marital unity*, and so not in the manner of a new partner in the common life so vividly expressed by that act, but rather in the manner of a product of a making...'[12] The 'great evils of destructive experimentation, observation, and selection' are signs of the same moral flaw: viewing human children as products.[13] And children they are: since the culmination of the process of fertilization, each human embryo possesses a genetic constitution and organic integration.[14] This theme is taken up in 'When Most People Begin' (1993)[15] which, rejecting the arguments of Tooley, Donceel, and Ford that personhood does not begin at conception, concludes that 'reason can find no event or principle or criterion by which to judge that

---

⁵ *CEJF* III.18.   ⁶ *CEJF* III.19, 307.   ⁷ *CEJF* I.16, 267–8.
⁸ *CEJF* I.16, 268.   ⁹ *CEJF* I.16, 268.   ¹⁰ *CEJF* III.19, 313.
¹¹ *CEJF* III.17.   ¹² *CEJF* III.17, 276.   ¹³ *CEJF* III.17, 279.
¹⁴ *CEJF* III.17, 279.   ¹⁵ *CEJF* II.16.

the typical adult or newborn child or full-term or mid-term unborn child is anything other than one and the same individual human being—human person—as the one-cell, 46-chromosome zygote the emergence of which was the beginning of the personal history of that same child and adult'.[16] His paper 'Organic Unity, Brain Life, and Our Beginning' (1988) replies to Michael Lockwood's argument that human beings begin with the capacity for consciousness and end when it ends, and that we are not human organisms but are 'ensconced in' a human organism during a phase of that organism's life.[17] Finnis identifies the dualism in Lockwood's position, which renders inexplicable the unity in complexity of which we are aware in each of our conscious acts. 'On Producing Human Embryos' (2000)[18] addresses human cloning. It notes the 'politicized and manipulative' description of cloning as 'therapeutic'[19] as distinct from 'reproductive' when in reality *all* human cloning reproduces a human being and none of it intends therapy for that human being. It adds that even human cloning in order to produce a live birth would remain open to objection: 'The radical separation of IVF from the act of marital union is only more radical and dramatic in generation by cloning which neither incarnates that union, as procreation does, nor even reproduces both father and mother, as sexual generation even in vitro does, but instead replicates a single person...'[20] Finnis has written much more which merits mention on the beginning of life, on both abortion and IVF. First, abortion.

A. Abortion

In 1986 the Catholic Bishops' Joint Committee on Bioethical Issues published a paper on the ethical and legal aspects of the 'morning after' pill (MAP).[21] This paper, like several others published by that committee, was drafted by Finnis. Besides containing a nuanced analysis of the ethical aspects of the MAP, it considered whether its administration or supply constituted a criminal offence. Section 58 of the Offences against the Person Act 1861 prohibits the use of means with intent to procure 'miscarriage'. Did an intent to prevent the implantation of any embryo which had been conceived after intercourse amount to an intent to procure 'miscarriage'? The paper noted that until recently it had been universally accepted that section 58 operated from fertilization. Glanville Williams, no less, had stated as much in *The Sanctity of Life*: 'The foetus is a human life to be protected by the criminal law from the moment when the ovum is fertilized.'[22] However, in May 1983 the Attorney-General informed Parliament in answer to a written question that 'miscarriage' should be interpreted as it was ordinarily understood in 1861, and that it was clear that the ordinary use of the word related to interference after implantation. There were, Finnis's paper commented, strong grounds for doubting the Attorney's opinion. Indeed, before the Attorney-General announced his decision, Finnis had supplied him with a detailed analysis of the medico-legal usage

---

[16] *CEJF* II.16, 291.   [17] *CEJF* II.15, 280.
[18] *CEJF* II.17.   [19] *CEJF* II.17, 294.
[20] *CEJF* II.17, 299–300. See also 1998a, an amended version of which appears as *CEJF* I.16.
[21] Catholic Bishops' Joint Committee on Bioethical Issues, 'The Morning After Pill'.
[22] Williams, *The Sanctity of Life and the Criminal Law*, 141.

of 'miscarriage' in the 19th century, showing that it was used to refer to the interruption of pregnancy from fertilization, not implantation.[23] How the Attorney could have told Parliament otherwise remains a mystery.

One possibility is that he had been influenced by Glanville Williams. The second edition of his *Textbook of Criminal Law*, published in 1983, declared:

> Formerly it was thought that the vital point of time was fertilization, the fusion of spermatozoon and ovum, but it is now realised (though the point has not come before the courts) that this position is not maintainable, and that conception for legal purposes must be dated at earliest from implantation.[24]

Williams neither adverted to his earlier statement of the law nor gave any legally relevant reason for departing from it. Finnis, in a letter to *The Times* in April 1983, before the Attorney-General announced his decision, recalled that statement.[25] Williams promptly replied: 'I was stating the general opinion as to the law; but my concern was to criticise it'.[26] Williams had indeed criticized the law: as President of the Abortion Law Reform Association he had campaigned for its relaxation. But his statement in *The Sanctity of Life* of what the general opinion as to the law *was* could hardly have been clearer. Williams' letter appeared to be an attempt to cover his tracks. Perhaps in the mind and office of the Attorney-General he succeeded.

Finnis's other contributions to the literature on abortion law include his pioneering analysis in 1970, at a time when the legal regulation of abortion was the subject of intense debate, not least in the US, of three schemes of regulation. The three schemes it considered were: the prohibition of all abortion except where the life of the woman is threatened; the permission of abortion under wider medical or quasi-medical conditions; and the permission of abortion (save by those unqualified to perform it).[27] The goal of the first scheme was to suppress abortion in all but a few cases and to witness society's commitment to the value and inviolability of life.[28] In considering whether the scheme was effective in suppressing abortion, he noted that the answer had to be 'very circumspect'. The figures for illegal abortion were 'everywhere very unreliable' and he questioned the bases of the high estimates by abortion advocates in both the US and the UK.[29] Moreover, it could hardly be doubted that transition from the first to the second and third schemes was liable to be accompanied by marked increases in the total (as it has since been in both the UK and US). Finnis concluded that the first scheme was effective in suppressing, if not eliminating, abortion.[30] He observed:

[23] The analysis was later published as Keown, '"Miscarriage"'. See also Keown, *The Law and Ethics of Medicine*, Ch. 6.

[24] Williams, *Textbook of Criminal Law*, 294. For criticism of the restricted interpretation of 'miscarriage' advanced by both Glanville Williams and Ian Kennedy see Keown, *The Law and Ethics of Medicine*, 157–60.

[25] Finnis, 'Letters'.   [26] Williams, 'Letters'.

[27] Finnis, 'Abortion and Legal Rationality' (1970c(i)), 432.

[28] Finnis, 'Abortion and Legal Rationality' (1970c(i)), 436.

[29] Finnis, 'Abortion and Legal Rationality' (1970c(i)), 437. Williams cited estimates of 42,000–250,000 cases per year, lamenting that their proponents did not state the way they arrived at their conclusion. He arrived at an estimate of 52,000, without stating the way he arrived at his. *The Sanctity of Life*, 192–3.

[30] Finnis, 'Abortion and Legal Rationality' (1970c(i)), 439. In another paper he noted that the number of maternal deaths in the UK from illegal abortion was low and had been falling even before the enactment of the Abortion Act 1967, Finnis, 'The Abortion Act' (1971b).

It is, of course, a main aim of the criminal law to eliminate undesired conduct. But the criminal law is not futile if it succeeds in doing little more than manifesting society's continuing commitment to its preferred values. Examples of such laws are many—laws against speeding, against perjury, against domestic murder, against prostitution, once upon a time against duelling, and now against certain forms of racial discrimination.[31]

In a paper in 1989 Finnis criticized the (in)famous 'Historians' Brief',[32] an *amicus curiae* brief submitted to the US Supreme Court in *Webster v. Reproductive Health Services*.[33] Signed by no fewer than 281 historians, the brief urged the Court that abortion was not an offence at common law and that the statutory restriction of the law by the wave of 19th-century anti-abortion legislation did not have as even one of its aims the protection of the unborn child. Finnis showed these claims to be bogus. Nor were they of merely academic interest. In *Roe*, Justice Blackmun had paved the way to fashioning a constitutional right to abortion by concluding that historically the law had treated abortion leniently, and even by doubting that abortion was an offence at common law. Moreover, Ronald Dworkin rested his key argument that the unborn are not constitutional persons on the brief's claims that the anti-abortion legislation was adopted not to protect them but to protect the health of the mother and the privileges of the medical profession.[34]

Also noteworthy is Finnis's paper in 1992 on 'The Legal Status of the Unborn Baby',[35] essential reading for lawyers who blithely assert that the unborn child has 'no legal status'.[36] The full and equal protection of the state's laws against homicide should, he argued, be accepted as extending to the unborn: there should be no special law prohibiting abortion.[37]

B. *In vitro* fertilization

Finnis has also made a signal contribution to reflection about the law and ethics of the new reproductive technologies. In addition to the papers noted above which address IVF, in the 1980s he drafted three important documents published by the Catholic Bishops' Joint Committee on Bioethical Issues: the Committee's submission in 1983 to the Committee on Human Fertilisation and Embryology, chaired by Dame Mary Warnock[38]; its response in 1984 to the report of the Committee[39]; and its response

---

[31] Finnis, 'Abortion and Legal Rationality' (1970c(i)), 436.

[32] Finnis, '"Shameless Acts" in Colorado' (1994d). For further criticism of the brief see Keown, *The Law and Ethics of Medicine*, Ch. 5. For a rebuttal by Finnis of a comparable argument doubting the Catholic Church's historical condemnation of abortion see Finnis, 'IVF and the Catholic Tradition' (1984d).

[33] 492 U.S. 490 (1989).

[34] Finnis, '"Shameless Acts" in Colorado' (1994d), 12.

[35] Finnis, 'Legal Status of the Unborn' (1993b).

[36] See also his critique of jurisprudential attempts to support that assertion in *CEJF* II.1, 21–35.

[37] Finnis, 'Legal Status of the Unborn', 8. See also, on abortion and public reason, Finnis, 'Abortion, Natural Law and Public Reason' (2000c), and on the justice of voting to restrict laws permitting abortion, Finnis, 'Restricting Legalised Abortion' (2005f) and Finnis, 'A Vote Decisive for...' (2005g).

[38] Finnis, 'In Vitro Fertilisation: Morality and Public Policy' (1983e).

[39] Finnis, 'Response to the Warnock Report' (1984c).

in 1987 to the Department of Health and Social Security's Consultation Paper on Legislation on Human Infertility Services and Embryo Research.[40] Moreover, in 1984 he wrote an unpublished paper analysing the question whether it was a criminal offence to create an embryo *in vitro* and deliberately not to transfer it to the womb.[41] This was one of the earliest papers on the legal status of the human embryo *in vitro* and, it appears, the only one to contend that the *in vitro* embryo enjoyed the protection of the criminal law. The paper considered possible liability for child abandonment or exposure, contrary to section 27 of the Offences against the Person Act 1861, and for homicide. As for the crime of homicide, it noted that *Archbold* stated (at 20–59) that 'If a grown-up person chooses to undertake the charge of a human creature helpless from infancy..., he is bound to execute that charge without gross neglect...'[42] The applicability of the law of assault, and therefore presumably of homicide, to even pre-viable embryos was, noted Finnis, clearly affirmed by Glanville Williams in 1978 when he wrote in his *Textbook of Criminal Law*: 'If an aborted fetus is alive it is a person, no matter how short the period of gestation, and using it for an experiment would in law be at least an assault upon it. If doctors wish to perform these experiments legally they must seek statutory authority'.[43] Williams was treating the criterion of legal protection as extra-uterine live existence, not age, viability, or appearance, and this appeared to be in line with the whole course of the common law. Finnis also considered possible liability for the common law crime of abortion, which has never been abolished. He concluded that if, as was far from certain, the common law crime required proof of 'quickening', it was only because of problems of proof and that where, as in the IVF situation, there was no comparable problem of proving the existence of a live human being, there was no reason why the protection of the common law should not be extended in the way suggested by Williams.[44] The common law was concerned not so much with the distinction between early and late fetal life, but with the distinction between being inside and outside the womb: 'What was inside was invisible, and especially so before the first tangible stirrings; and what might affect it was treated as not securely knowable. What was outside was a human being *in rerum natura* or "in being", and was and is protected by the criminal law'.[45] The principle that the common law develops even to extend the criminal law squarely covered the novel circumstances of IVF embryos.

In the House of Lords debate on the Warnock Report, Lord Denning, the former Law Lord, took a similar view:

> I would suggest that the only logical point at which the law could start is that the child, the human being, starts at the moment of conception and fertilisation. From that point onwards there is a gradual development in its environment. So I would hold— and I hope the judges would hold—that from that moment there is a living, human being which is entitled to protection just as much as the law protects a child.[46]

---

[40] Finnis, 'On Human Infertility Services' (1987j).

[41] Finnis, 'Memorandum'. The paper, though unpublished, is discussed in Keown, *The Law and Ethics of Medicine*, 198–201.

[42] Finnis, 'Memorandum', 6.   [43] Williams (1978), 263, n. 8.

[44] Finnis, 'Memorandum', 9.   [45] Finnis, 'Memorandum', 11.

[46] *Hansard*, H.L. (1983–84), vol. 456, col. 541, at 542.

Lord Denning's hopes were to be dashed. The Human Fertilisation and Embryology Act 1990 adopted the Warnock Committee's recommendation that the law should allow the embryo to be frozen, donated, discarded, or subjected to destructive research, thereby in essence treating the embryonic human not as a person but as a chattel. The courts have, moreover, resiled from the opportunity to hold that the *in vitro* embryo enjoys a right to life under Article 2 of the European Convention of Human Rights. In ruling to the contrary, they have failed to produce a reasoned rebuttal of the ethical and legal arguments advanced by Finnis and Denning. Indeed, they have scarcely even confronted them, just like those (very few) medical lawyers who have addressed the legal status of the *in vitro* embryo.[47] Glanville Williams, for example, in his brief consideration of whether the scientist who discards an *in vitro* embryo commits murder, simply asserted: 'The sensible solution is to say that the embryo has not reached a sufficient stage of development to be a "reasonable creature" within the law of homicide.'[48] How does this 'solution' square with his earlier statement that a living aborted fetus is a person, no matter how short the period of gestation?

III. The End of Life

An appropriate bridge between Finnis's writing on the beginning and on the end of life is a paper he wrote anonymously about the important trial in 1981 of a consultant pediatrician, Dr Leonard Arthur, for the murder of a disabled newborn baby by 'sedation and starvation'.

John Pearson was born with Down's syndrome and was 'rejected' by his parents. Dr Arthur told the nurses that the baby's parents did not wish him to survive and wrote on the notes that he was to receive 'nursing care only'. In other words, the baby was to be kept comfortable but not fed. Moreover, Arthur prescribed regular doses of an analgesic in order (as he later admitted to the police) to stop the baby seeking sustenance. John Pearson died three days later. Arthur stood trial at Leicester Crown Court for his murder.

Evidence tendered by the defence pathologist indicated that the baby had defects of the heart, lung, and brain. The prosecution, to avoid the difficulty of proving that it was Arthur's conduct, not the baby's poor health, that had been the cause of death, amended the indictment to attempted murder. Arthur, who did not give evidence, was acquitted. One reason was undoubtedly the summing-up of the trial judge, Mr Justice Farquharson, which favoured the defence. Finnis anonymously penned a meticulous and withering analysis of his direction to the jury.[49]

Finnis exposed the confused and contradictory nature of the summing-up, not least the judge's notion of a 'holding operation'. According to the judge, a 'holding operation' was revocable and involved the 'setting up' of conditions, conditions that were set up 'in the hope that' the child, who was not dying, would die as a result of infection

---

[47] See Keown, *The Law and Ethics of Medicine*, Ch. 8. For Finnis on the ethics of adopting frozen embryos see 'Embryo Adoption' (2009k).

[48] Williams, *Textbook of Criminal Law* (2nd edn), 290, n. 6.

[49] Anonymous, *Regina v. Arthur* (1981).

or similar, for 'the object is to allow the child to die'. Those who embarked on a 'holding operation' knew it was a regime which would 'inevitably lead to death' unless the parents revoked it in time. The drugs used were not intended to hasten death but solely to reduce any suffering. A 'holding operation' was, said the judge, 'neutral', a case of 'allowing nature to take its course'.

Finnis identified major problems with the judge's notion. First, a regime could not be 'neutral' when it was set up in the hope that the child would die and when it was known that death would be the inevitable outcome. Moreover, it was impossible to reconcile 'allowing nature to take its course' with the deliberate 'setting up' of conditions in which it was hoped the child would die and because of which he would die. Second, the judge contradicted himself. He stated that, as a matter of law, a 'holding operation' could not amount to attempted murder because it was revocable, but he also said that the fact that an action was revocable did not mean that it could not be an attempt.

Furthermore, the judge explained that attempted murder required clear evidence of intent to cause death combined with an act which was immediately connected with the crime, an act not merely preparatory to the commission of the offence but proximate to it. But a 'holding operation' as defined by the judge satisfied these requirements. The intent was clear: it involved the deliberate setting up of conditions in the hope that the child would die, in the belief that he would not otherwise die, and in the knowledge that the regime would inevitably lead to death unless revoked. Nor was the conduct merely preparatory. Not only had the regime of non-feeding and drugging begun: there was no further decision to be made. Once initiated, it was not a preparatory stage, it was the only stage. A child who was starved and drugged was bound to deteriorate. A 'holding operation' was not, despite the implication of the word 'holding', a plateau: it was a steady descent toward death even if (for a time) reversible.

In any event, asked Finnis, was baby Pearson's regime, on the facts, a 'holding operation' at all? Was there any evidence of revocability? Was there any evidence that Dr Arthur and the others involved had any expectation of saving the baby? If so, why did the nurses and the junior doctor in charge think not? Why were only incomplete medical records kept? Why did no one contact the mother after she had left the hospital to ask if she had changed her mind? Why did Arthur evidently not see the baby again after he first prescribed the regime? Though such questions were repeatedly pressed by the prosecution to show that there was in fact no expectation of any reversal, the judge in his summing-up made it clear that he took seriously the claim that nothing irrevocable had been set in train when Dr Arthur initiated the regime.

Nor, added Finnis, did the judge make enough of a crucial fact about baby Pearson, namely, that Dr Arthur presumed he was dealing with a healthy Down's baby. The evidence tendered at trial by the defence pathologist, that the baby had medical complications, was irrelevant to Arthur's intent. Arthur did not think he was confronted with a dying baby, or a baby who needed 'extraordinary' treatment. As far as Arthur knew, the baby needed nothing more extraordinary than milk.

Finnis identified other flaws in the summing-up. For example, throughout the trial prominence was given to the fact that the baby had been 'rejected' by his parents, yet the judge failed to instruct the jury that the law did not confer on parents the power of life and death over their children. The judge also revealed ignorance about and prejudice against children with Down's syndrome. He stated, erroneously, that Down's children had little chance of adoption. He described their 'lolling tongues' and 'oriental appearance' and said that a 'mongol' was faced with 'the most appalling handicap'. The judge also displayed an exaggerated deference to medical witnesses who testified for the defence. To cite but one instance, he quoted with no sign of disapproval the statement by one of the doctors that 'Many respected members of the profession regard the not giving of food as allowing nature to take its course. This area is so sensitive that doctors regard that as a matter between them, their consciences and their patients.'

Finnis's critique showed that a central aspect of the summing-up—the direction that while it is murder intentionally and actively to kill any baby, it is not illegal for a doctor intentionally to kill a baby by planned omission, at least a Down's baby who has been rejected by his parents—was flawed. This direction was not only bad law—cases such as *R v. Gibbins and Proctor* established that those having the care of a child are under a duty to feed it—it was bad ethics. There is obviously no ethical difference between intentionally killing a baby by drugs and intentionally killing a baby by starvation (and Arthur, of course, did both). Finnis would later target the same distinction between killing by deliberate act and by planned omission in the landmark case of *Airedale NHS Trust v. Bland*.[50]

Bland, one of the most important cases in English law, concerned the lawfulness of withdrawing tube-feeding from Tony Bland, a patient in a 'persistent vegetative state' (PVS). The Law Lords held that withdrawal would be lawful because it was an omission to provide medical treatment which was no longer in the best interests of the patient. It was no longer in his best interests because it was futile, and it was futile because, at least in the opinion of a 'responsible body of medical opinion', life in PVS was not a benefit. Finnis produced probably the first, and certainly the most penetrating, analysis of the case.[51]

He pointed out that what was novel and gravely significant was that in the view of a majority, at least, of the Law Lords, discontinuing tube-feeding may be lawful even when decided upon precisely with the intention of killing the patient. A number of their Lordships recognized that this left the law, as Lord Mustill put it, in a 'morally and intellectually misshapen' state, prohibiting the intentional ending of life by an act but permitting the intentional ending of life by planned omission. Finnis wrote that while cases such as *Gibbins and Proctor* did not address the argument successfully raised in *Bland*—that one who has undertaken a duty of care may yet have no duty to exercise that care so as to sustain life—the proper application or extension of their rule to meet that argument was surely this: 'those who have a duty to care for someone may never exercise it in a manner intended to bring about that person's death'.[52]

He also called attention to the disturbing implications of the case for other mentally compromised patients. The Law Lords endorsed the criterion of responsible medical opinion, the '*Bolam* test', to determine which patients' lives were of no benefit. But what qualified *doctors* to decide such questions of justice and human worth for the whole community? Moreover, the judges seemed to concur with the dualistic

---

[50] [1993] A.C. 789.   [51] *CEJF* II.19.   [52] *CEJF* II.19, 317.

understanding of the patient's life implicit in the medical opinion to which they deferred, as if patients comprised a non-bodily person and a non-personal body. (Brown P, for example, commented that Tony Bland's 'spirit' had left him and all that remained was a 'shell'.) But each of us, maintained Finnis, has a human life, not a vegetable life, plus an animal life plus a personal life. Further, another judge (Hoffmann LJ) denied that the case had eugenical implications, but the same judge described Tony Bland's life as an indignity, a 'humiliation'. Not only did this, commented Finnis, confuse undignified circumstances with inherent dignity, but epithets of indignity and humiliation could easily be applied to various classes of severely handicapped people: 'Many are those who might be rescued from undignified conditions by benevolent termination of their life.'[53]

Again, the Law Lords ruled that it was the duty of physicians to discontinue life-sustaining measures when, in line with a responsible body of medical opinion, they considered 'invasive' measures no longer to be in their patient's best interests. But what counted as 'invasive' measures? The Law Lords referred to 'medical treatment *or* care' as the appropriate description for the life-sustaining measures whose removal the law authorized (and required). Would this not include ordinary feeding?[54] And why was tube-feeding regarded as a 'medical treatment'? Finnis observed that the judgments all seemed to embrace a fallacious inference: that if tube-feeding is part of medical treatment it is therefore *not* part of non-medical (home or nursing) care which decent families and communities provide for their dependent members. To stop providing food and basic hygiene to patients who are not imminently dying and to whom such provision involves no significant burden seems either to intend to bring about their death or to cease caring for them which, in an affluent society, amounts to a denial of their personhood by breaking off solidarity with them.[55]

Tony Bland, though in a state of permanent unconsciousness, was neither dying nor dead, at least according to the standard definition of death as the cessation of integrated organic functioning. Some philosophers reject that definition and would regard as 'dead' anyone who, like Bland, had permanently lost higher brain function. In 'Brain Death and Peter Singer'[56] Finnis underscored the importance of distinguishing between the definition of death in conceptual, factual, and operational terms. While defending the conceptual definition of death as the cessation of integrated organic functioning, he doubted that this criterion is factually established by death of the brain. This is but one of several issues which merit much more attention from medical lawyers than they have received. And, while Finnis's contribution to the question of when patients are dead is important, his contribution to the ongoing debate about the ethics of making them dead is even more so.

In his three celebrated exchanges with John Harris,[57] Finnis maintained, against Harris, that euthanasia is concerned with the intentional and not merely foreseen shortening of life, whether by act or by omission; explained why intention is of moral

---

[53] *CEJF* II.19, 321. For an essay criticizing the thinking of those US Supreme Court Justices in the case of *Cruzan v. Missouri Dept. of Health* 497 US 26 (1990) who denied that the life of the PVS patient in that case was a benefit see Finnis, 'Reflections on *Cruzan*' (1993e).

[54] *CEJF* II.19, 315.   [55] *CEJF* II.19, 319–20.   [56] *CEJF* II.18.   [57] *CEJF* III.14.

significance; and gave an account of the wrongness of intentionally killing any human being, even the very young, the very ill, or the very old.[58] He criticized Harris' attempt to link being a 'person' with having an ability to value one's life. To attach key importance to a human being's presently exercisable mental ability rather than to the radical capacity inherent in their nature which grounds that ability is vague, arbitrary, dualistic, and discriminatory.[59] Finnis also took issue with Harris' concept (borrowed from Dworkin) of 'critical interests', interests that if satisfied make one's life genuinely better. Finnis noted that this notion cuts both ways for, if it is the case that those asking for euthanasia are tragically misinterpreting the value and meaning of their lives, how can it be, as Harris claimed, a denial of respect for those persons to prevent them acting on that misinterpretation?[60] Finnis also questioned Harris' apparent reinterpretation of 'critical interests' so as to equate a person's intrinsic interests with that person's subjective opinion about what it means for his or her life to go well. Not only does such a subjectivizing of Dworkin's concept abandon the very notion of objective, critical interests but, if nothing else about human existence is of objective importance, why should the individual's opinion be so?[61] The Finnis-Harris debate classically illustrates key philosophical disagreements in the euthanasia debate. It also illustrates one important area of agreement: neither thinks that euthanasia can rationally be confined to the voluntary variety.

Finnis returned to the link between the voluntary and the non-voluntary varieties in his euthanasia debate with Ronald Dworkin. Although euthanasia campaigners invoked individual autonomy and privacy, Finnis maintained, their proposals required that candidates satisfy a certain degree of illness or suffering. What was being proposed was not a private act, but an act in which assistance was sought by another, sharing an intent to end the patient's life. It was no more private an act than an agreement to sell oneself into slavery.[62] The bottom line was clear: when should we allow some people to sit in judgment on the life of another so as to authorize themselves or others to carry out that person's request for death? And, if such judgments about the worthlessness of a person's life were decisive, why not permit them when the request for death cannot, or has not, been made?[63] Moreover, even supposing there was a right to choose to be killed, there was even more evidently a right to choose not to be killed. Which legal framework would take those rights most seriously? That was a largely empirical question and one which Dworkin had wholly failed to answer plausibly.[64] Finnis cited the widespread breach of guidelines in the Netherlands, not least the regular practice of non-voluntary euthanasia and the common failure of doctors to report cases to the authorities. This evidence had influenced two expert committees, the New York State Task Force on Life and the Law and the House of Lords Select Committee on Medical Ethics, unanimously to reject the arguments for decriminalization, including those adduced by Dworkin, to which they carefully replied.[65]

---

[58] *CEJF* III.14, 211–23. See also *CEJF* III.15 on the importance of maintaining solidarity with the dependent elderly.

[59] *CEJF* III.14, 224–8.   [60] *CEJF* III.14, 229–30.   [61] *CEJF* III.14, 230.

[62] *CEJF* III.16, 258.   [63] *CEJF* III.16, 259.   [64] *CEJF* III.16, 262.   [65] *CEJF* III.16, 263.

Mention of the House of Lords Select Committee leads us to another dimension of Finnis's contribution to the law and ethics of medicine. He has been influential not only in the academic but also in the political sphere. In the wake of *Bland*, the House of Lords established the Select Committee on Medical Ethics, chaired by Lord Walton (and including Lord Mustill). A central concern of the Committee was whether to recommend the decriminalization of active euthanasia and physician-assisted suicide. The Linacre Centre for Health Care Ethics in London (now the Anscombe Bioethics Centre in Oxford), on whose Board of Governors Finnis has served for many years, filed a substantial submission with the Select Committee. The submission was jointly drafted by the Centre's then Director, Luke Gormally, and by Finnis.[66] The Select Committee also received submissions and heard testimony (including from Ronald Dworkin) in favour of decriminalization. The Committee's unanimous rejection of that case may well have owed much to the Linacre Centre submission. Not only did one member of the Committee comment that it was the best submission the Committee had received, but the Committee's Report reflected several of the key points made in the submission. Endorsing 'double effect', the Committee distinguished between intending to kill and merely foreseeing the hastening of death as a side effect of palliative treatment. It rejected the argument that 'double effect' was a cloak for widespread euthanasia and amounted to medical hypocrisy.[67] The Committee was not persuaded that arguments like those adduced by Dworkin were sufficient reason to weaken the prohibition on intentional killing: 'That prohibition is the cornerstone of law and of social relationships. It protects each one of us impartially, embodying the belief that all are equal.'[68]

Unfortunately, the Committee fudged the issue which had led to its establishment: the propriety of withdrawing tube-feeding from patients in PVS. Members were divided on the issue, though they agreed that the question need not and should not arise in practice, since in a case like that of Tony Bland, antibiotics could have been withheld on the ground that recovery from the complications of infection 'could add nothing to his wellbeing as a person'.[69] The law remained, therefore, in the same 'morally and intellectually misshapen' state identified by Lord Mustill in that case. Until, it seems, the Mental Capacity Act 2005.

That Act established a comprehensive framework for the treatment and care of mentally incapacitated adults. Finnis was an adviser on the Bill to the Catholic Bishops of England and Wales, and as adviser to the responsible Bishop participated in deliberations on the Bill, both in public statements and private discussions with the responsible Ministers and their officials. In the light of concerns expressed by the Bishops and

---

[66] The submission was later published: Gormally, *Euthanasia, Clinical Practice and the Law*, Book Two, Ch. 1. Chapter 2 is a valuable analysis by Finnis of the law and ethics of 'living wills' or 'advance directives': Finnis, '"Living Will" Legislation' (1994h). He would later assist another Select Committee, the House of Lords Select Committee which considered Lord Joffe's Assisted Dying for the Terminally Ill Bill, not least by drawing to its attention the 'eye-opening' statement by leading Dutch defenders of euthanasia that it is now the duty of patients to make it clear, while competent, if they do *not* want to be euthanized should they became incompetent. See Keown, *The Law and Ethics of Medicine*, 243.

[67] House of Lords Report, *Report of the Select Committee on Medical Ethics*, para. 243.

[68] House of Lords Report, *Report of the Select Committee on Medical Ethics*, para. 237.

[69] House of Lords Report, *Report of the Select Committee on Medical Ethics*, para. 257.

others about the danger of giving legislative endorsement to the intentional killing of patients by planned omission of treatment or tube-feeding, the government inserted a provision in the Act. Section 4(5) of the Act provides that 'Where the determination [of what is in the person's best interests] relates to life-sustaining treatment [the person making the determination] must not, in considering whether the treatment is in the best interests of the person concerned, be motivated by a desire to bring about his death.' In his subsequent legal and ethical analysis of the Act,[70] Finnis wrote:

> What we have in s.4(5), with its talk of not being motivated by a desire to bring about death, is not as satisfactory as what we had urged and continued to the end to urge: an exclusion of any *purpose* of bringing about death. But it is not as bad as it may look. The phrase 'motivated by a desire' has been used in the courts, by judges, as equivalent to the phrase 'influenced by a desire', which is found in the Insolvency Act 1986, s.239 (5). These judgments show that the courts treat the motivating desire not just as a matter of primary motives and ultimate ends but as including also all purposes which affect the decision-maker's deliberations and shape or enter into its conclusions—that is, all the kinds of purpose which are referred to when one says that in carrying out one's decision one has an intent to … or a purpose of …[71]

Whether s.4(5) is interpreted by the courts to prohibit attempts to hasten death by planned omission remains to be seen. Even if it is, Finnis identified another problem: s.4(5) does not apply to advance refusals of treatment made by the patient. It therefore appears that even an advance refusal which is patently suicidal—such as one made by a euthanasia campaigner to undermine the law—is binding on doctors. The government's opinion that such a refusal would be evidence of mental incapacity to make an advance direction was, Finnis aptly observed, self-deception, and its opposition to amendments which would have invalidated advance decisions manifesting a suicidal purpose have left the Act open to this obvious abuse of the right to refuse treatment, an abuse which would, moreover, confront morally upright doctors with difficult questions of moral cooperation in suicide.[72]

A further problem he identified is the Act's loose definition of 'best interests'. Section 4(6) speaks of the relevance of a person's 'past and present wishes and feelings'; his 'beliefs and values'; and 'other factors' he would be likely to consider. Section 4(7) directs the person making the determination to take into account the views of certain others as to what is the person's best interests, if it is practical and appropriate to consult them. This appearance of 'unrooted subjectivity', Finnis observed, remains a 'deep weakness' in the Act's treatment of best interests.[73]

Clearly, much will depend on how the courts interpret 'best interests' and s.4(5). It is to be hoped that they will be guided by Finnis's reflections. On more than one occasion, Finnis has had a more direct input into judicial deliberation, for he has helped draft more than one brief filed with the courts in cases involving end of life questions.

---

[70] Finnis, 'The Mental Capacity Act' (2009j).
[71] Finnis, 'The Mental Capacity Act' (2009j), 101–2, footnotes omitted.
[72] Finnis, 'The Mental Capacity Act' (2009j), 104–5.
[73] Finnis, 'The Mental Capacity Act' (2009j), 100.

In the *Dianne Pretty* case, the claimant, who had motor neurone disease, asked the Director of Public Prosecutions (DPP) for a guarantee that he would not prosecute her husband under the Suicide Act 1961 for the crime of assisting suicide, should her husband assist her to commit suicide. The DPP refused. She sought judicial review of his refusal. The House of Lords held that the DPP had no power to guarantee that he would not prosecute her husband. As Lord Bingham noted, the power to dispense with and suspend laws and the execution of laws without the consent of Parliament was denied to the Crown and its servants by the Bill of Rights 1689.[74] The Law Lords rejected her contention that she enjoyed a right, under the European Convention of Human Rights, to be assisted in suicide. She appealed to the European Court of Human Rights.

The Court held that the UK's blanket ban on assisting suicide did not violate the Convention. The Court's judgment on the applicant's claim under Article 8 was, however, both cryptic and controversial. Pretty argued that the Article protected the right to self-determination, which included the right to choose when and how to die. The Court agreed that personal autonomy was an important principle in interpreting the Article: the very essence of the Convention was respect for human dignity and freedom.[75] It also stated that the blanket ban on assisting suicide imposed by the Suicide Act 1961 prevented her from exercising her choice to avoid what she considered an undignified and distressing end to her life, and that the Court was 'not prepared to exclude' that this constituted an interference with her right to respect for private life, guaranteed by Article 8(1).[76] The blanket ban was, however, saved by Article 8(2), as being imposed by law with the legitimate aim of safeguarding life and thereby protecting the rights of others. Clear risks of abuse did exist, and it was primarily for states to assess the risk and the likely incidence of abuse if the general prohibition were relaxed.[77] Neither the blanket ban nor the DPP's refusal to give an advance undertaking were disproportionate.[78]

A brief filed with the Court by the Catholic Bishops' Conference of England and Wales, which Finnis drafted with Eleanor Sharpston QC, questioned the relevance of autonomy to Article 8. The brief submitted:

> ...Article 8 does not encompass a right to self-determination as such. Rather, Article 8 relates to the right to private and family life in respect of the manner in which a person conducts his life. Where rights under Article 8 are engaged, it is to protect the physical, moral and/or psychological integrity of the individual...Such rights may—indeed, sometimes do—include rights over the individual's own body. However, the alleged right claimed by Mrs Pretty would ineluctably and necessarily extinguish the very benefit on which it was purportedly based, namely respect for her private *life*. The ending of a life is not a private matter, but is a legitimate concern of public authorities whose duty is to protect the lives of citizens within their jurisdiction.[79]

---

[74] *R (Pretty) v. Director of Public Prosecutions* [2001] UKHL 61 at [39].
[75] *Pretty v. United Kingdom* (2002) 35 EHRR 1 at [65].
[76] *Pretty v. United Kingdom*, at [67].
[77] *Pretty v. United Kingdom*, at [74].
[78] *Pretty v. United Kingdom*, at [76]–[77].
[79] Catholic Bishops, Intervention of the Catholic Bishops' Conference of England and Wales, para. 33.

Like the Law Lords, the brief concluded that Pretty's rights under Article 8 were not engaged at all.

The Law Lords in *Pretty* affirmed the blanket ban on assisting suicide. However, in the later case of *Purdy*, they would undermine that ban, employing reasoning about privacy no less questionable than that of the European Court in *Pretty*. Finnis has produced the leading critique of their Lordships' reasoning.[80]

In *Purdy* the claimant, who had multiple sclerosis, contemplated asking her husband to assist her to travel to Switzerland to commit suicide, or to Belgium for euthanasia. She asked the DPP to inform her of the criteria he applied in deciding whether to prosecute cases of assisting suicide, in particular in the kind of circumstances she contemplated. He refused. She sought judicial review of his refusal, arguing that, in the absence of an 'offence-specific' policy by the DPP concerning the exercise of his discretion, the prohibition on assisting suicide was not 'in accordance with law' as required by Article 8(2) of the European Convention. The Divisional Court and Court of Appeal dismissed her claim. Remarkably, the Law Lords allowed her appeal.

The Law Lords' ruling (a 'swansong' because it was their last ruling before they metamorphosed into the Supreme Court of the United Kingdom) was, observed Finnis, 'astonishing'. They were wrong to think that the decision to commit suicide engaged the Article 8 right to privacy:

> That same right to privacy is engaged in countless offenses, serious and minor: whatever one does in one's home or in one's correspondence to advance some criminal purpose, from mass murder to evasion of licence fees, engages the right. Is one entitled, whenever one's privacy right is thus engaged, to the assistance of the courts in determining, in advance, how likely it is that the prosecuting authorities will judge a prosecution contrary to the public interest?[81]

Moreover, while Purdy was not, like Pretty, seeking a guarantee of non-prosecution, she was, as the Court of Appeal had observed, seeking 'the nearest thing possible to a guarantee' that her husband would not be prosecuted.[82] Further, added Finnis, it had apparently been entirely overlooked that she would herself be committing a crime by inciting her husband to furnish assistance.[83] Finally, the information she sought from the DPP was information sought, and granted, precisely for the purpose of committing a crime. 'This alone', he commented, 'would make the Lords' swansong eerie'.[84] Why, he asked, should the DPP's duty to give guidance to prosecutors be converted into a duty to give guidance to prospective offenders about their chances? What received scant attention in the judgments was the public interest in maintaining a clear and exceptionless prohibition. That prohibition had been upheld by the European Court in *Pretty*, along with a prosecutorial discretion which would accommodate many factors, while creating no legitimate expectation of immunity, thereby leaving in place the deterrent effect so important for many. For good measure, that overriding public

---

[80] Finnis, 'The Lords' Eerie Swansong' (2009i).
[81] Finnis, 'The Lords' Eerie Swansong' (2009i), 2.
[82] Finnis, 'The Lords' Eerie Swansong' (2009i), 3.
[83] Finnis, 'The Lords' Eerie Swansong' (2009i), 4.
[84] Finnis, 'The Lords' Eerie Swansong' (2009i).

interest had been reaffirmed, while the Law Lords were writing their judgments, by the clear rejection by the House of Lords of a legislative attempt to exempt from the prohibition the sort of assistance in travel that Purdy was contemplating.[85]

An even more eerie aspect to the swansong was its implication that, if Purdy's right to privacy entitled her to know when it was safe for her chosen assistant to help her to travel to Switzerland, the same right entitled her to know when it would be safe for her assistant to hand her a lethal dose at home.[86] Finnis's analysis was prophetic: the guidance for prosecutors subsequently issued by the DPP draws no distinction between the two forms of assistance.[87] As Finnis concluded: 'It is hard to imagine a more unfitting end to their great jurisdiction.'[88]

IV. Conclusion

This overview of John Finnis's contribution to the law and ethics of medicine indicates that it easily qualifies him as one of the most eminent international authorities in the discipline. Indeed few, if any, scholars have made a contribution which is as prolific or which combines such legal and philosophical expertise. His contribution ranges across some of the most complex and controversial questions, from cloning to brain death. Involving no risky trespasses, it exhibits a command not only of medical law, criminal law, constitutional law and legal history, but of legal, moral, and political philosophy. It also demonstrates an assured grasp of theology and biological science. Moreover, although his contribution has mainly taken the form of scholarly papers (many, but not all, of which have been touched on in this essay) it has also taken other forms, whether public debate with other scholars, court briefs, and advice on legislative drafting.[89] Nor has he shied away from the media.[90]

The fact that many of those working in the law and ethics of medicine, in the UK and beyond, have yet seriously to engage with much of his scholarship is more a reflection on the state of the discipline than on his contribution to it.

---

[85] Finnis, 'The Lords' Eerie Swansong' (2009i), 5.

[86] Finnis, 'The Lords' Eerie Swansong' (2009i), 6–7.

[87] Crown Prosecution Service, *Policy for Prosecutors in Respect of Cases of Encouraging or Assisting Suicide*.

[88] Finnis, 'The Lords' Eerie Swansong' (2009i), 7. Another significant brief which Finnis helped draft, with Eleanor Sharpston QC and Angela Patrick, was filed by the Catholic Bishops Conference of England and Wales, intervening on appeal in the case of *The General Medical Council v. Leslie Burke* [2004] EWHC 1879 (Munby J). The brief, which contained a clear and cogent ethical and legal analysis of patient autonomy, challenged the exaggerated importance attached to autonomy by Munby J, who asserted, for example, that it was for the patient to determine what was in his own 'best interests' and that the 'sanctity of life' must take second place to autonomy. Catholic Bishops' Brief (2009), at para. 16. Reversing his decision, the Court of Appeal stated that, although much in his judgment was uncontroversial, 'we counsel strongly against selective use of Munby J's judgment in future cases' [2005] EWCA Civ 1003 at [24].

[89] And a balanced, educational book for schoolchildren on the issue of abortion: Finnis and Flynn, *What Do You Know About Abortion?*

[90] He has, for example, debated embryo research with Mary Warnock on BBC's *Newsnight* and with Jonathan Glover in *The Channel 4 Debate*; discussed euthanasia with a leading Dutch euthanasiast on the same channel's *After Dark*, and written on eugenic abortion in *The Sunday Telegraph*: Finnis, 'Abortion for Cleft Palate' (2003l).

Bibliography

Anonymous (1981), *A verdict on the Judge's summing-up in the trial of Dr. Leonard Arthur, November 1981* (Leamington Spa: LIFE).

Catholic Bishops' Joint Committee on Bioethical Issues (1986), 'The Morning After Pill. Some Practical and Moral Questions about Post-Coital "Contraception"' Briefing 16: 33–9; 254–5.

Catholic Bishops (2002), Intervention of the Catholic Bishops' Conference of England and Wales Pursuant to Article 36§2 of the Convention in *Dianne Pretty v. United Kingdom*. <http://www.catholic-ew.org.uk/CBCEW-Media-Library/Archive-Media-Assets/Files/Department-of-Christian-Responsibility-and-Citizenship-files/Briefing-Papers/Diane-Pretty-Bishops-Conference-intervention-pursuant-to-Article-36.2/(language)/eng-GB>.

Catholic Bishops (2005), Intervention of the Catholic Bishops' Conference of England and Wales on appeal in *The General Medical Council v. Leslie Burke*. <http://www.catholic-ew.org.uk/CBCEW-Media-Library/Archive-Media-Assets/Files/Healthcare/CBCEW-submission-Lesley-Burke-case-May-2005-pdf/(language)/eng-GB>.

Crown Prosecution Service (2010), *Policy for Prosecutors in Respect of Cases of Encouraging or Assisting Suicide* (London: Crown Prosecution Service).

Finnis, J.M. (1970), 'Abortion and Legal Rationality', *Adelaide L Rev* 3: 431.

Finnis, J.M. (1971), 'The Abortion Act 1967: What Has Changed?', *Crim LR*: 3.

Finnis, J.M. (1983), 'Letters', *The Times* (5th April).

Finnis, J.M. (1983), 'In Vitro Fertilisation: Morality and Public Policy', Evidence submitted by the Catholic Bishops' Joint Committee on Bio-ethical Issues to the Committee of Inquiry into Human Fertilisation and Embryology.

Finnis, J.M. (1984), 'Response to the Warnock Report', submission to Secretary of State for Social Services by the Catholic Bishops' Joint Committee on Bio-ethical Issues.

Finnis, J.M., (1984), 'IVF and the Catholic Tradition', *The Month* 246: 55.

Finnis, J.M. (1984), 'Memorandum Re Possibility of Criminal Proceedings in Respect of Human Embryos Conceived in vitro and Deliberately Not Transferred to the Womb'. Unpublished.

Finnis, J.M. (1987), 'On Human Infertility Services and Embryo Research', response by the Catholic Bishops' Joint Committee on Bio-ethical Issues to the Department of Health and Social Security.

Finnis, J.M. (1993), 'The Legal Status of the Unborn Baby', *Catholic Medical Quarterly* 43: 5.

Finnis, J.M. (1993), 'The "Value of Human Life" and "The Right to Death": Some Reflections on *Cruzan* and Ronald Dworkin', *Southern Illinois University LJ* 17: 559.

Finnis, J.M. (1994), '"Shameless Acts" in Colorado: Abuse of Scholarship in Constitutional Cases', *Academic Questions* 7/4: 10.

Finnis, J.M. (1994), '"Living Will" Legislation', in Gormally, L. (ed.), *Euthanasia, Clinical Practice and the Law* (London: The Linacre Centre), 167.

Finnis, J.M. (2000), 'Abortion, Natural Law and Public Reason', in George, R.P. and Wolfe, C. (eds.) *Natural Law and Public Reason* (Washington DC: Georgetown University Press), 71.

Finnis, J.M. (2005), 'Restricting Legalised Abortion is not Intrinsically Unjust', in Watt, H. (ed.), *Cooperation, Complicity & Conscience* (London: Linacre Centre), 209.

Finnis, J.M. (2005), 'A Vote Decisive for . . . a More Restrictive Law', in Watt, H. (ed.), *Cooperation, Complicity & Conscience* (London: Linacre Centre), 269.

Finnis, J.M. (2009), 'The Lords' Eerie Swansong: A Note on *R (Purdy) v Director of Public Prosecutions*', Oxford Legal Studies Research Paper 31. <http://papers.ssrn.com/sol3/papers.cfm?abstract_id=1477281>.

Finnis, J.M. (2009), 'The Mental Capacity Act 2005: Some Ethical and Legal Issues', in Watt H. (ed.), *Incapacity & Care: Controversies in Healthcare and Research* (London: The Linacre Centre), 95.

Finnis, J.M. (2009), 'Debate over the Interpretation of *Dignitas personae*'s Teaching on Embryo Adoption', *National Catholic Bioethics Q* 9: 475.

Finnis, J.M. (2011), '"Public Reason" and Moral Debate', in Finnis, J.M., *Reason in Action: Collected Essays Volume I* (Oxford: Oxford University Press), Ch. 16.

Finnis, J.M. (2011), 'The Priority of Persons', in Finnis J.M., *Intention & Identity: Collected Essays Volume II* (Oxford: Oxford University Press), Ch. 1.

Finnis, J.M. (2011), 'Organic Unity, Brain Life, and Our Beginning', in Finnis, J.M., *Intention & Identity: Collected Essays Volume II* (Oxford: Oxford University Press), Ch. 15.

Finnis, J.M. (2011), 'When Most People Begin', in Finnis, J.M., *Intention & Identity: Collected Essays Volume II* (Oxford: Oxford University Press), Ch. 16.

Finnis, J.M. (2011), 'On Producing Human Embryos', in Finnis, J.M., *Intention & Identity: Collected Essays Volume II* (Oxford: Oxford University Press), Ch. 17.

Finnis, J.M. (2011), 'Brain Death and Peter Singer', in Finnis, J.M., *Intention & Identity: Collected Essays Volume II* (Oxford: Oxford University Press), Ch. 18.

Finnis, J.M. (2011), 'Intentionally Killing the "Permanently Unconcious"', in Finnis, J.M., *Intention & Identity: Collected Essays Volume II* (Oxford: Oxford University Press), Ch. 19.

Finnis, J.M. (2011), 'Euthanasia and Justice', in Finnis, J.M., *Human Rights & Common Good: Collected Essays Volume III* (Oxford: Oxford University Press), Ch. 14.

Finnis, J.M. (2011), 'Economics, Justice and the Value of Life', in Finnis, J.M., *Human Rights & Common Good: Collected Essays Volume III* (Oxford: Oxford University Press), Ch. 15.

Finnis, J.M. (2011), 'Euthanasia and the Law', in Finnis, J.M., *Human Rights & Common Good: Collected Essays Volume III* (Oxford: Oxford University Press), Ch. 16.

Finnis, J.M. (2011), 'C.S. Lewis and Test-Tube Babies', in Finnis, J.M., *Human Rights & Common Good: Collected Essays Volume III* (Oxford: Oxford University Press), Ch. 17.

Finnis, J.M. (2011), 'The Rights and Wrongs of Abortion', in Finnis, J.M., *Human Rights & Common Good: Collected Essays Volume III* (Oxford: Oxford University Press), Ch. 18.

Finnis, J.M. (2011), 'Justice for Mother and Child', in Finnis, J.M., *Human Rights & Common Good: Collected Essays Volume III* (Oxford: Oxford University Press), Ch. 19.

Finnis, J.M. and Flynn, C.W.A. (1980), *What Do You Know About Abortion?* (revised edn) (Oxford: Oxford Schools Publications).

Gormally, L. (ed.) (1994), *Euthanasia, Clinical Practice and the Law* (London: The Linacre Centre for Health Care Ethics).

House of Lords (1993–94), *Report of the Select Committee on Medical Ethics* (Paper 21—I).

Keown, I.J. (1984), '"Miscarriage": A Medico-Legal Analysis', *Crim LR*: 604.

Keown, I.J. (2012), *The Law and Ethics of Medicine: Essays on the Inviolability of Human Life* (Oxford: Oxford University Press).

Williams, G. (1958), *The Sanctity of Life and the Criminal Law* (London: Faber and Faber).

Williams, G. (1978), *Textbook of Criminal Law* (London: Stevens and Sons)

Williams, G. (1983), 'Letters', *The Times* (13th April).

Williams, G. (1983), *Textbook of Criminal Law* (2nd edn) (London: Stevens and Sons).

PHILOSOPHY OF LAW

19

Value, Practice, and Idea

N.E. Simmonds

In an early essay, Finnis identified a problem that lies at the heart of jurisprudence. After pointing out that jurisprudential inquiry into the nature of law is widely assumed to be the theoretical investigation of a social phenomenon, he explained that 'the relations between law and the activities of making, maintaining, applying, evading, etc., the law are, in the context of those activities, generally understood as relations between reason for action and action'. Yet 'the relation between the categories, "reason for acting" and "social phenomenon", seems quite obscure, and the "theorists" of law have not offered explicit accounts of it'.[1]

In the years following that essay, many legal theorists were to concentrate their efforts upon the relationship between law and practical reason, thereby revealing only one of a number of respects in which Finnis's work has been profoundly influential for modern jurisprudence, even though the influence has been insufficiently acknowledged. In spite of these efforts, however, the nexus between social phenomena, such as practices and institutions, and the domain of reasons and values, remains poorly understood. Although some progress can be made by close attention to the role of conventions, plans, and decisions in practical reason, the most fundamental problems are less amenable to a quick fix. The issues are large, casting a long shadow over the surrounding moral and intellectual landscape.

I. Practice and Value

One part of the problem springs from a tendency radically to separate the realm of practice from that of reason and value without acknowledging the extent to which values must be found within our forms of association if they are to be more than empty illusions. Our ethical life is reflective and self-critical in a way that creates the permanent possibility of discrepancy between our practice and the ideals that the practice seems to suggest and embody. The customary way in which things are done will always be potentially open to criticism and consequent revision. But this critical openness can easily be misunderstood. For, as Finnis points out, while the set of moral opinions held by a group of persons is 'never determinative', it is nevertheless true that 'one cannot reach a critical morality without working through the morality in which de facto one was brought up'.[2]

The process of becoming a moral agent is one in which we learn to detach ourselves from our private and individual situation, and view affairs from a perspective that is

---

[1] *CEJF* I.6, 105.   [2] *CEJF* IV.11, 270.

capable of being shared between persons. We acquire an understanding of this view-point, and explore its resources, through dialogue with others, and through our never-fully-completed grasp of a moral and evaluative language, together with our knowledge of the patterns of life of which that language is a part. It is this shared domain, with its refined distinctions and slowly acquired forms of perception, that gives both structure and content to even our most private and personal reflections. The image of the philosopher escaping from the cave is a vivid expression of the need for independent critical reflection, but it should not be taken as suggesting the possibility of an ethical knowledge that is wholly independent of our associating together, and of the customs that structure our daily interactions with our fellows. Values must be inhabited before they are reflectively understood.[3]

We must each decide for ourselves what is to be done, and, in making that decision, we must not slavishly and uncritically follow what others do, but must exercise judgement. From these undoubted truths we can all too easily conclude that what others think and do can have no bearing upon what 'ideally' ought to be done. Our ways of associating together, and our established practices, are then seen as merely the accidental upshot of the vicissitudes of history and the dispositions of power. Values are thought of as expressions of an unmediated subjectivity, or as located in a realm quite remote from the shared world of practice. Within this outlook, the domain of practices and institutions is stripped of intrinsic value and is seen as an appropriate object of moral critique but not a potential source of moral knowledge. The idea that reason might be itself articulated within those practices seems puzzling and mystificatory.

In our desire to maintain a critical and reflective posture towards the social world around us, we loosen our attachment to familiar ways of life and turn our faces towards more remote ideals. But there are dangers in this shift of orientation. As Oakeshott points out, when detached from an established pattern of conduct, 'every moral ideal is potentially an obsession . . . (I)n our eagerness to realize justice we come to forget charity, and a passion for righteousness has made many a man hard and merciless.' Since 'Every admirable ideal has its opposite' which is 'no less admirable', the orientation towards detached ideals, by 'directing our attention always to abstract extremes, none of which is wholly desirable' makes us 'see double', transforming our moral life into a series of dilemmas.[4] This can foster the idea that moral life has been fragmented beyond the possibility of repair.[5] More commonly, it encourages a kind of disengaged pluralism that, in the guise of the 'analysis' of value concepts, seeks to strip our moral and political ideas of the suggestiveness and fertility that is so manifest in the history of our discourse, thereby foreclosing important dialogic resources and leaving in their place only the vortex of radically ungrounded choice.[6]

Whether morality is thought to find its truest expression in that which is entirely personal and inward (the light of individual conscience), or in highly abstract

---

[3] 'How but in custom and in ceremony/Are innocence and beauty born?' (W.B. Yeats, 'A Prayer for my Daughter').

[4] Oakeshott, 'The Tower of Babel' (1962), 68–9.   [5] MacIntyre, *After Virtue*.

[6] Simmonds, *Law as a Moral Idea*, 176–82.

principles against which practice must be judged (the principle of utility; the categorical imperative), it comes to be denuded of real content. While abstract principles may provide the colourful banners of various tribes within the university and beyond (Kantians versus consequentialists, and so forth) the *application* of such principles to particular circumstances is unavoidably problematic, so that no outward practice can be viewed as a clear and unambiguous expression of the morality that is reflectively espoused. The person's relationship to events and to other persons comes to be subordinated to principles which particular situations instantiate only imperfectly and ambiguously. Ultimately, for the scrupulous moral agent, the messy complexities of reality foster an unwillingness to endorse as fully 'moral' anything that possesses a concrete existence in the public realm beyond the privacy of his or her imaginings: an empty simulacrum of ethical life proves to be the final destination of the turn to inwardness and abstraction. It is in this context that Hegel writes of 'the beautiful soul' that is 'entangled in the contradiction between its pure self and the necessity of that self to externalise itself and change itself into an actual existence'.[7]

By contrast with this, the tradition of political thought that stems most evidently from Aristotle directs its gaze outwards, towards established habits of conduct and ways of life. The institutions of human society (institutions such as law, government, property, the market, and the family) are considered in relation to the idea of excellence in human life. It is an error to interpret Aristotle as attempting to derive our knowledge of the good from a metaphysics of nature.[8] Aristotle does not seek an Archimedean viewpoint, outside of ethics, from which our knowledge of the ethical realm can be derived. A knowledge of the good, however imperfect, is an integral part of our nature as that nature is realised in the institutions of a human community. Such knowledge can be deepened, not by the discovery of metaphysical foundations, but by a form of reflection that enables us to see how the various elements of our ethical life are articulated (no doubt imperfectly) within the familiar ways of arranging our life together, and our conceptions of what is to be done or not to be done.

It is a mistake to assume that we must *first* arrive at some general conception of the good life and *then* address the question of how far a life of that sort is fostered and inculcated by the institutions in question. Rather, we can come to understand our own nature (our only partially realised potential for excellence) by reflecting upon the expression of that nature in the characteristic institutions of human society. Of course, as Finnis rightly emphasises throughout his work, there is no question here of arriving at an understanding of the good by deduction from the observable facts of what is typically done. Rather, an inchoate understanding of the good is already engaged in the enterprise from the start, and is brought to full and self-conscious flowering by the task

---

[7] Hegel, *Phenomenology of Spirit*, 406. In a recent essay John Gardner has pointed to Hart's ambivalence about the nature of morality, suggesting that Hart had doubts about the status, as truly moral, of even admittedly sound principles of justice. It seems to me that we can see in these doubts the retreat of morality into an ineffable subjectivity, a retreat that mirrors positivism's supposedly 'demystified' picture of the public realm. See Gardner, 'Hart on Legality, Justice and Morality'; Simmonds, 'Reply: The Nature and Virtue of Law', 278–9.

[8] Those aspects of Aristotle's thought that often create a contrary impression are best construed as seeking to *locate* ethics and politics *within* Aristotle's account of nature, not as seeking to *derive* ethics and politics *from* the account of nature.

of reflection. As Finnis reminds us, 'the disciplined acquisition of accurate knowledge about human affairs' can enable us to move from unreflective practical prejudices to sound judgements concerning 'what is good and practically reasonable', thereby bringing about 'a modification of the judgments of importance and significance with which one first approached the data as a theorist'.[9]

II. Law as Idea

If one part of our problem springs from a failure to see the articulation of values within practice, another part springs from complexities that are concealed within the correct observation that law is a social phenomenon. The existence of law in a community involves the existence of certain established patterns of behaviour, along with a complex structure of distinctive ideas, understandings, and expectations. There is, of course, a straightforward sense in which the existence of such an assemblage of ideas and practices is a social phenomenon. Yet it is easy to be misled. The concept of 'law' is not best thought of as a simple label that applies to a distinctive type of social institution, for it is also an orienting idea that plays a vital role within the very institution to which it applies. Understanding that orienting idea is essential, even if what we seek is a wholly detached and descriptive account of a type of social phenomenon.

It is not by accident that legal positivist theories tend to downplay, or even deny, the role played by the concept of 'law' within the practices composing a legal order. Hart regards the basic rule of recognition as forming an outer bounding limit on the framework of legal thought, and allows no room within his theory for juridical questions concerning the status as law of the system of which the rule of recognition forms a part.[10] Raz adopts much the same position rather more explicitly, arguing that questions concerning the nature of law are no more likely to arise in court than questions of astrophysics or biology. According to him, the judges' duty is a duty to decide in accordance with the rules of the system under which they sit, 'and it matters not at all whether these rules are legal ones'.[11]

In fact, and quite contrary to such theories, many of the ideas and understandings that constitute the existence of a legal order themselves make reference to the notion of 'law'. Legislators do not issue orders or prescriptions, even orders or prescriptions of a general and standing kind. Rather, they claim to enact 'laws', and they take the status of their enactments as law to be fundamental to any claim that the enactments have upon the citizens' conduct. This is one reason why the legislature's prescriptions will normally be applied to the citizen only in accordance with juristic doctrines that it is the judge's duty to understand and safeguard. For the judiciary is charged with the task of deciding in what way the decrees of the legislature have law-making effect; and, while powerful persons may decide for themselves what dictats they will issue, the effect of legislative decisions in changing the law is determined in accordance with

---

[9] *NLNR*, 17.   [10] Simmonds, *Law as a Moral Idea*, 119–36.
[11] Raz, *Between Authority and Interpretation*, 81–5. I have criticised Raz's view elsewhere: Simmonds, 'Reflexivity and the Idea of Law', 11–12.

principles that transcend the momentary will of particular individuals or groups, reflecting the nature of law as such. In many jurisdictions the content of these principles will be unsettled and in dispute, with the various interpretative approaches embodying somewhat different conceptions of the nature of law.

Similarly, judges do not decide cases by reference to the standards that they think most just, or wise, or reasonable; nor by reference to standards that they and their colleagues accept for reasons of self-interest, or even for general moral and political reasons (as in MacCormick's idea of 'underpinning reasons'[12]). The standards applied by judges are applied because they are the requirements of the law. Judges decide cases by reference to the law, and it is the status of the relevant rules and principles as law that is thought to give them their justificatory force and to render them the appropriate basis for decisions that can control and direct the state's coercive force against individuals. The judge's fundamental duty is not one of applying a basic rule of recognition; nor should it be thought of as simply a duty to apply the rules of the system under which the judge was appointed: the judge's fundamental duty is a duty of fidelity to law.[13] The question of law's nature is therefore implicitly addressed by all intelligent and responsible judges, even if they do not think of the question in precisely those terms.

Within a legal order, therefore, the status of a rule as 'law' is thought to give the rule a special claim upon the conduct of individuals, and a special justificatory force. The source and basis of this special claim and justificatory force may seem to be obscure; but the nature of law is itself obscure. For example, the law is created by men and women: but it also governs its own creation, so that acts can create law only when legally authorised so to do. Within ordinary doctrinal arguments, this feature can give rise to a good deal of confusion,[14] but in a general reflection upon the nature of law it suggests problems of circularity or infinite regress that can be resolved only by careful philosophical thought. Furthermore, law depends upon the authority of statutes and precedents but also somehow goes beyond the available authorities, so that lawyers may possess an equally sound knowledge of the statutes and precedents and nevertheless disagree about the law's content. Many legal rules are thought of as having been created by the judges, and expressly formulated rules are frequently modified by judges in the course of adjudication. Yet this continuous judicial modification of the rules is assumed somehow to be compatible with the judge's duty to apply pre-existing law. The ordinary forms of legal discourse suggest that, although the law depends upon authoritative texts, it cannot be straightforwardly identified with the contents of those texts. The law is always, as Philip Allott astutely observes, 'somewhere else and something else'.[15]

In this way we find ourselves asking what 'law' must be, that these various understandings can reflect its character. Indeed, the law seems to exhibit a range of

---

[12] MacCormick, *Legal Reasoning and Legal Theory*, 139–40. For criticism see Simmonds, *Law as a Moral Idea*, 131–3.

[13] Simmonds, *Law as a Moral Idea*, 119–43.

[14] As, for example, when public lawyers misguidedly argue that Parliament *must* derive its law-making power from the common law, there being no other possible source from which the power could be derived.

[15] Allott, *The Health of Nations*, 43.

characteristics that are hard to imagine being coherently combined in one institution. Little wonder that some have concluded that traditional conceptions of law embody a mysterious incarnation of the ideal within the real,[16] or the suggestion of a 'brooding omnipresence in the sky': we are urged to rid ourselves of these illusions by a focus upon the voice of power, or by purely predictive frameworks of thought that strip from the law any internal connection to practical reason.[17]

Jurisprudential inquiry into the nature of law resembles the search for a focal point that will draw our various understandings together into a coherent picture. One tradition seeks to locate that focal point in something relatively mundane and devoid of intrinsic moral value, such as commands backed by organised force, or a basic rule accepted, perhaps for wholly non-moral reasons, by officials. Another, older, approach sees the institutions of law as, in a sense, pointing beyond themselves to ideals and aspirations that are only partially realised in the concrete facts of actually existing legal orders. And, to some extent sharing this latter outlook, but taking it to a quite different conclusion, there are those who view the framework of legal thought as a dangerous source of illusions, to be eradicated by a wholesale revision of legal ideas.

III. Expression and Reflection

The attempt to assemble our various understandings of law into a coherent picture of law's nature is, of course, not an isolated and self-standing enterprise. We want our understanding of law to fit coherently with other settled understandings concerning the nature of morality, the character of political and ethical communities, and even the bases of human knowledge.

It is at this point that the abstract and one-sided understanding of the relationship between practice and value (discussed earlier) comes to be a problem. For we are inclined to think of our practices as attempts to realise or implement values that were conceived independently of the practice. Whereas, in the instances most relevant to jurisprudence, this is not so. Here, the relation between the practice and the values embodied in the practice must be conceived as comparable to that between aesthetic values and the works of art that realise those values.[18]

The point can be developed by reference to a variety of traditions of philosophical thought,[19] but here I will draw upon the essay by Oakeshott from which I quoted earlier.[20] Here Oakeshott discusses what he calls 'the denial of the poetic character of all human activity', a denial which is manifested in the assumption that 'moral activity' consists in 'the translation of an idea of what ought to be into a practical reality'. This 'prosaic tradition of thought' even extends itself into the understanding of poetry,

---

[16] Ross, *Towards a Realistic Jurisprudence*, 11, 20.

[17] 'The common law is not a brooding omnipresence in the sky, but the articulate voice of some sovereign or quasi sovereign that can be identified.' Justice Oliver Wendell Holmes in *Southern Pacific Company v. Jensen*, 244 U.S. 205, 222 (1917).

[18] See Collingwood, *The Principles of Art*.

[19] Elsewhere I have discussed the issue as it appears in the work of Gadamer: Simmonds, *Law as a Moral Idea*, 145–50.

[20] Oakeshott, 'The Tower of Babel' (1962), 68–9. Oakeshott published another, quite different, essay under the same name in his book *On History and Other Essays*.

which is thought of as beginning with an idea that is then given expression in words. But, Oakeshott tells us, 'A poem is not the translation into words of a state of mind':

> Nothing exists in advance of the poem itself, except perhaps the poetic passion. And what is true of poetry is true also, I think, of all human moral activity. Moral ideals are not, in the first place, the products of reflective thought, the verbal expressions of unrealized ideas, which are then translated (with varying degrees of accuracy) into human behaviour; they are the products of human behaviour, of human practical activity, to which reflective thought gives subsequent, partial and abstract expression in words. What is good, or right, or what is considered to be reasonable behaviour may exist in advance of the situation, but only in the generalized form of the possibilities of behaviour determined by art and not by nature.[21]

The 'prosaic tradition of thought', as Oakeshott describes it, has been a persistent problem within contemporary jurisprudence. For it obstructs and obscures the very possibility upon which the jurisprudential inquiry into the nature of law depends: that is, the possibility that reflection upon a body of human practices can reveal to us values that could be understood in no other way, while the practices in question cannot adequately be understood except by reference to the relevant values (towards which they are oriented). Once that thought is allowed to evaporate, we are inevitably led to conclude that, in being an inquiry into actual institutions rather than abstract values, jurisprudence cannot be other than a morally disengaged and purely descriptive enterprise. At the same time, values are no longer thought of as publicly expressed in the fabric of our form of association, but retreat inward to a purely private realm, accessible only as a matter of 'intuition'. A supposedly descriptive enterprise of theorising law (an enterprise persistently and understandably wracked by doubts about its own status, coherence, and value) is then contrasted with a 'normative' enterprise of seeking reflective equilibrium within our moral intuitions (while carefully overlooking the extent to which those intuitions are bound up with established practices). Since it is far from clear why we would need a general theoretical 'description' of law, it is not surprising that the enterprise proves to be almost exclusively one of attempting to dispel the appearance that value is in some way intrinsic to law. To some of those attempts we can now turn.

IV. Concession and Avoidance: Law's Claims

There are various aspects of law that are most strongly suggestive of a close and necessary connection between law and morality. We speak of the law as conferring rights and imposing duties, and this way of speaking seems to be integral to our notion of law: a regime that imposed coercive demands and punished people without any pretence to be enforcing their duties, or protecting their rights, would not be a legal order. But philosophers of law have frequently wondered whether it is possible to regard law as imposing duties and conferring rights without assuming that the law is

---

[21] Oakeshott, *Rationalism in Politics*, 72–3.

morally binding or morally valuable. When we ascribe to the law a power to create rights and duties, do we not assume that moral value is intrinsic to law's nature?

Similarly, law seems to have an unusually close association with the value of justice. We are all required to act justly, but the requirement seems more stringent and different in character when applied to judges, law-makers, and legal systems. A judge who decides cases without regard to justice fails in his duty as a judge, and not simply in respect of the general duty, incumbent upon everyone, to act with justice. Were we to encounter a constitution and code of law that does not even pretend to pursue justice, but only to serve the interests of the rulers, we might well wonder whether it should properly be thought of as a system of law at all. In much the same way, when we encounter a clearly wicked exploitative system that does not seem to be informed by any good faith conception of justice, we may feel that it should perhaps be regarded not as law but as a purely coercive apparatus dressed in misleading juridical trappings.

The uncertainty of our reaction to such instances is normally taken as reflecting the indefinite nature of our semantic intuitions regarding the concept of 'law', and the consequent need to offer a clarified theoretical account of that concept. But our uncertain reactions could equally be viewed as embodying insight into the moral complexities of the situations considered. For even wicked systems of governance, motivated by purely selfish aims, will find it in their interest to enact and enforce provisions that to some extent comply with the requirements of justice. There are likely, for example, to be laws prohibiting violence by citizen against citizen, because the regime will wish to maintain its monopoly on the use of force, the better to implement its policies without obstruction. And even a purely exploitative regime may wish to maintain the efficiency and productivity of the market by enforcing contracts and providing remedies for tortious injury, for a thriving economy may be a precondition of the regime's ability to extract lucrative taxes. Wicked regimes are therefore likely to enforce as law many provisions that they will share with just legal systems. Finally, the adherence to rules which is a necessary feature of law may be thought to possess intrinsic moral value, for it realises (to a degree) a form of freedom that distinguishes the free man from the slave.[22]

The approach of Hart's legal positivism to such resemblances between law and morality was a tough-minded one. According to Hart, the language of legal rights and duties expressed rule-based demands but not moral requirements, while the close association between law and justice was partly to be explained by reference to conceptual connections between formal justice and rule-following. Features of law (such as its characteristic form or content) that might be thought to be of intrinsic moral value were said not to embody any necessary connection with morality, because 'compatible with great iniquity'.[23]

These arguments are certainly not without merit and they still have their defenders. But the consensus has tended to move against Hart in certain key respects. It is difficult to see how legal rights and duties could intelligibly be invoked as justifications in the adjudicative context if they are not, in some sense, moral concepts. How, for example,

---

[22] See Simmonds, *Law as a Moral Idea*, 99–111; also Simmonds, 'The Nature of Law', 618–21.
[23] See discussion in Simmonds, *Central Issues in Jurisprudence*, 258–9.

could a judge invoke a rule as a justification for his decision, while openly acknowledging that his only reasons for accepting the rule are reasons of self-interest? If law is intelligibly to be offered as a justification for the imposition of a sanction, must that not be on the assumption that the law serves some moral value?

Mindful of such problems, Hart's positivist heirs have in recent years adopted a more moderate line. They have silently conceded that there is some merit in the criticisms of Hart that were put forward by legal positivism's opponents. But, by offering what they see as a subtle, nuanced, qualified version of positivism, they have tried to show that the positivist can make such concessions while nevertheless retaining legal positivism's core insights. Considerable uncertainty regarding the nature and identity of those core insights has followed in the wake of these manoeuvres, leading to the situation referred to by Finnis when he says that the question of what is to be understood by 'legal positivism', and whether any truth is conveyed by it, is 'a gloomy jungle into which it is best never to stray'.[24]

One strategy that is employed involves the ascription to law of certain 'claims'. Thus, it is conceded that the law speaks in a fundamentally moral language of rights and duties. But this is said to show, not that 'law' is an intrinsically moral concept, but that it is part of law's nature to *claim* to be morally valuable or morally binding. A system of rules that did not, in this way, claim to possess moral value could not be a system of law. But it does not follow that a system which (while making the relevant claim) fails to possess any such value is not law, or is law only in an extended or 'non-focal' sense.

How do we know what 'claims' to ascribe to the law? We are told that the law's 'claims' are identifiable by reference to the presuppositions of the speech-acts of the law's officials: 'If it turns out—as it does—that it is in the nature of law to have institutions which can purport to grant rights to people, it is in the nature of law to claim entitlement to confer rights on people.'[25]

At this point we need to remember that, according to Raz, the concept of 'law' plays no necessary part within the practices composing a legal order: questions concerning the nature of law are no more likely to arise in court than questions of astrophysics or biology; and the judges' duty is not one of fidelity to law, but a duty to decide in accordance with the rules of the system under which they sit, 'and it matters not at all whether these rules are legal ones'.[26] These views play an important part in sustaining the plausibility of the ascription to law of certain 'claims'. For they help to obscure the fact that it is, for the most part, in the very act of *judging the system of rules to be law* (or, in the case of law-makers, presenting their enactments as law) that the officials attribute to the rules their moral properties. In other words, rather than the law making 'claims' through its officials, the position is that the concept of law (the concept that orients and informs the practices that compose the legal order) is the concept of a system of rules possessing a moral value that is sufficient to give rise to rights and duties.[27] If we are to understand the practices composing a legal order, even for purely

---

[24] *CEJF* IV.1, 44.   [25] Raz, *Between Authority and Interpretation*, 2.

[26] Raz, *Between Authority and Interpretation*, 81–5.

[27] Cf. Finnis's observation that law is rightly conceived of as 'by its nature morally valuable', together with his clarification of that observation: *CEJF* IV.1, 27–8.

descriptive purposes, we need to understand that concept of law. It is an integral part of our ethical life and form of political association.

In some contexts it may be helpful and appropriate to speak of law's 'claims'. This is so, for example, when we wish to emphasise that the mere fact that a certain language is typically employed within a practice does not in itself show that the language is always justified or appropriate. Sometimes, indeed, practices may not be the practices that they claim to be, but are best understood as fraudulent simulacra of what they claim to be. At times, important practical issues may be raised by the decision to describe the law as making 'claims' rather than (as in my alternative proposal) thinking of the concept of 'law' as the concept of an intrinsically valuable body of rules.

Suppose, for example, that we are reflecting upon a regime that makes no attempt to serve the demands of justice, even though it dresses its decrees and decisions in the language of legal rights and duties. If we think of certain 'claims' as being essential to the nature of law, we will have no difficulty in treating such a system of prescriptions as a fully fledged instance of 'law'; for, in employing the relevant language, it clearly makes the relevant claim (to be morally valuable, binding, or just). If, however, we think of it as part of the nature of law that the law's prescriptions should at least *aim* to serve justice and the common good (even if they fall short of achieving that aim) our perception of the regime will be quite different. We will not see it as a core instance of a legal system, albeit one that happens not to pursue the justice that it claims to pursue. Rather, we will be more likely to say that, in presenting as 'law' a system of rules that is not intended to serve justice (or any other moral aim), the officials are guilty of a falsehood. Even if we judge that, for some purposes, it might be misleading to insist that the system in question is *not really* law, we may nevertheless conclude that, for other purposes, it is equally confusing to insist that it *is* law. We may conclude that it should be regarded as law only in a corrupted, watered-down or 'non-focal' sense.

Ever since Hart's criticisms of Radbruch, many positivists have insisted that no practical issue can turn upon the question of whether or not the decrees of such a regime are 'law'. If moral decisions always consisted in a direct comparison between sets of particular facts and categorically binding moral principles they might be right. But, of course, our moral life is not like that. We settle upon certain principles, dispositions, or habits of conduct as appropriate to certain types of situation. We are always prepared to question the guidance thereby offered if we consider that there is some reason for doing so. Yet our perception of a situation as a normal one of its type (or, as a highly unusual example) is likely to have an important bearing upon our ultimate decision. Since law is a pervasive aspect of our lives, we inevitably form certain general attitudes governing our responses to the law's prescriptions (such attitudes might in principle range from uncritical compliance, through a reflective presumption of compliance grounded in civility, to antinomian scepticism and rejection). It is for this reason that the perception of a regime as a core instance of legality, or as a marginal and corrupt abuse of the very idea of legality, can make a significant difference to our individual decisions and to overall outcomes. The decision to think of law in terms of moral 'claims' rather than moral 'aims' is, therefore, not only intellectually misleading but may also have damaging practical consequences.

V. Concession and Avoidance: Law's Aims

Some positivists have pursued the strategy of concession and avoidance further. Shapiro, for example, has proposed that it is an 'essential truth about law'[28] that law has a moral aim. He calls this his 'Moral Aim Thesis'.[29] A moral aim can be ascribed to the law primarily on the basis of the law's moral vocabulary. As Shapiro puts it:

> By describing legal demands as 'obligating', not merely 'obliging', and power as based on 'right', not merely 'might', elites present their practice as something other than a criminal enterprise or self-interested pursuit of pleasure, profit, or glory. They depict it, in other words, as an activity that is supposed to solve moral problems and should be obeyed for that reason.[30]

This may seem to be a significant concession to the opponents of positivism. But it is not so, in Shapiro's view. For 'what makes the law *the law* is the fact that it has a moral aim, not that it satisfies that aim'.[31]

Such an acknowledgement that law must, as part of its essential nature, *have* a moral aim, but need not *achieve* that aim, may seem to be an insightful move for the positivist. For it accommodates the associations between law and morality that are suggested by the law's vocabulary (and by the close conceptual connections between law and justice) and relied upon by the critics of positivism. At the same time, in pointing out the difference between having an aim and achieving the aim, it renders the thesis compatible with the possibility of grossly unjust, yet fully legal, rules and systems of governance.

However, few theorists seem to doubt the possibility of unjust law. What they are more likely to question is the possibility of laws that are not even *intended* to serve justice, but serve only the selfish interests of the law-makers. Even when the doubt focuses upon the grossly unjust content of the laws, rather than upon the motivation that lies behind them, the underlying idea may be that a content so grossly at odds with justice can only be explained by a lack of any good faith concern for justice on the part of the law-maker. In instances of this type, we might think, it does not help to point out that it is the moral *aim* that is essential to the nature of law, and not the achievement of that aim: for it is precisely the genuine existence of the aim that is called into question.

Most surprisingly, however, Shapiro appears to reject any distinction between regimes that have a moral aim that they fail to achieve, and regimes that employ the moral vocabulary of law but nevertheless lack any genuine moral aim. Rejecting any such distinction, he argues that unjust regimes are to be thought of as 'broken clocks' that simply fail to do what clocks ought to do, rather than as 'decorative clocks' that are designed to produce the appearance of being a clock without actually having time-keeping as an aim.[32] We are told that, even in 'a legal system staffed by officials who merely pretend to pursue noble aims, but are solely after their own material gain... It would nevertheless be true that the aim of legal activity in that system is moral in

---

[28] Shapiro, *Legality* (Cambridge, MA: Harvard University Press, 2011), 216.
[29] Shapiro, *Legality*, 213 *et seq.*   [30] Shapiro, *Legality*, 217.
[31] Shapiro, *Legality*, 214.   [32] Shapiro, *Legality*, 391.

nature (much as the aim of assertion is to convey true information even though the asserter is lying).'[33]

It is important to notice that Shapiro is not simply saying that law *generally* serves moral aims, although it can also be employed to serve wicked aims. If he was to make such a point, as part of an argument concerning the *concept* of law, it would strongly suggest a reliance upon Finnis's notion of 'focal meaning', and this is an approach that Shapiro dismisses as guilty of an elementary confusion between different senses of the word 'ideal'.[34] This is why Shapiro is careful to say that, even in an evil exploitative system, 'the aim of legal activity *in that system* is moral in nature' (italics added).

But how can this be? The main thesis of Shapiro's work is that laws are plans, embodied in constitutions and posited rules. How can such a thesis be combined with the claim that, even where the rules enacted by the powers-that-be are intended only to serve selfish aims, nevertheless the law can be said to have a moral aim?

To eliminate the contradiction we have to construe Shapiro's 'Moral Aim Thesis', not as ascribing to the law-makers any intention to serve any moral aim, nor as suggesting that the law actually advances this or that valuable state of affairs. Rather, the Moral Aim Thesis must be read simply as pointing out the special normative requirements to which law is subject.

Thus, when Shapiro tells us that 'It is simply an essential truth about law that it is supposed to solve moral problems',[35] the supposition that he has in mind must be a normative requirement, rather than a factual assumption ('supposed' is ambiguous). This makes Shapiro's analogy with a lying assertion clear: when one makes a lying assertion one subjects oneself to a special range of normative requirements that do not apply to storytelling or the recitation of poetry. Clearly there is no other sense in which even a lying assertion can be said to have truth as its aim.

What this shows us, however, is that Shapiro's argument is broken-backed. For his Moral Aim Thesis can be reconciled with the existence of wholly exploitative legal systems only if the 'moral aim' in question is construed as a matter of moral prescriptions applying to the law, rather than moral goals that the laws are actually serving to advance. But (as we saw above) the Moral Aim is ascribed to law in the first place on the basis that it is presupposed by the law's moral vocabulary. And this ascription requires that the Moral Aim be construed quite differently.

In fact, Shapiro relies upon the ambiguity of the word 'supposed'. Those who describe their governance in legal terms of rights and duties are said 'to depict it . . . as an activity that is supposed to solve moral problems and should be obeyed for that reason'.[36] In this context, 'supposed' must be read as referring to an assumption that law actually advances or is intended to advance some morally valuable state of affairs, for the law's exposure to special normative requirements cannot in itself (and apart from the assumption that it is going some way towards satisfying those requirements) supply us with a reason for obeying it. But, when Shapiro needs to persuade us that the Moral Aim is an essential feature of law that is present even in wicked systems (thereby

---

[33] Shapiro, *Legality*, 216.
[34] Shapiro, *Legality*, 390–2. For criticism, see Simmonds, 'The Logic of Planning and the Aim of the Law'.
[35] Shapiro, *Legality*, 216.   [36] Shapiro, *Legality*, 217.

reducing decorative clocks to broken clocks that simply fail to achieve their aim) he relies upon a different sense of 'supposed': only in that sense can it be said that, even in a system where the law-makers wholly eschew moral aims, 'It is simply an essential truth about law that it is supposed to solve moral problems.'[37]

VI. Law and the Common Good

In the opening chapter of *Natural Law and Natural Rights*[38] Finnis explores the character of general descriptive theories of the nature of law. Beginning from the observation that a social scientific understanding of human practices must understand the point of the practices as conceived by the participants, he notes that this poses a problem for a general theory of law, since such conceptions will vary greatly from person to person and from one community to another. When we move from the description of particular contexts (e.g. in historical description) to a general theory (such as a general theory of the nature of law) we must therefore determine the most appropriate viewpoint from which the theory is to be constructed. How is an appropriate viewpoint to be selected in a non-arbitrary way? In answer, Finnis points out the intellectual benefits that have come from careful attention to the relationship between law and practical reason, in the work of both Hart and Raz. But, he argues, the 'internal point of view', as described by Hart, provides only an unstable intellectual vantage point: it is itself acknowledged by Hart and Raz to be an amalgam of different views, some of which would be considered to be marginal or parasitic even by those who hold the attitudes in question. Having decided to construct our theory of law from the viewpoint of practical reason, there is no stable position within practical reason that we can justifiably choose other than the viewpoint of the fully practically reasonable agent.

The bulk of Finnis's book aims to explain, clarify, and give substance to the viewpoint of the fully practically reasonable agent, and to reveal the way in which law is a response to the problems set by practical reason. The opening words of *Natural Law and Natural Rights* inform us that 'There are human goods that can be secured only through the institutions of human law, and requirements of practical reasonableness that only those institutions can satisfy.'[39] Finnis's view seems to be that, even if our ultimate goal is a general descriptive theory of the nature of law, we must begin by understanding the range of 'human goods' and appreciating the way in which some of these goods can be realised only through the law. Only when we have grasped how law is the necessary solution to a problem set by practical reason can we really understand law's nature.

Finnis's argument offers us an attractive way of overcoming some of the more impoverishing features of contemporary jurisprudence, without abandoning some of its corresponding insights. For example, one frustrating feature of much modern jurisprudence has been its apparent disconnection from any broad philosophical reflection upon the human condition. This is combined with the most extreme uncertainty about the general nature of the enterprise that jurisprudential inquiry represents.

---

[37] Shapiro, *Legality*, 216.   [38] *NLNR*.   [39] *NLNR*, 3.

Neither accusation could be levelled at *Natural Law and Natural Rights*. For, in that volume, we are presented with a sweeping and persuasive theory that takes us from the most fundamental questions of reason and human flourishing right through to wise and insightful reflections upon the major features of law, of justice, and of authority in human communities. This wide and integrated vision is one of the striking features of the book, rendering it unlike almost all of the other texts making up the staple diet of contemporary jurisprudence.

Although wide-ranging, *Natural Law and Natural Rights* is a very carefully structured book. At the apex of the structure, almost precisely in the centre, we find Chapter Six, which concerns 'Community, Communities, and Common Good'. All of the preceding chapters work up to this, and almost all of the following chapters work out its implications. Indispensable foundations for the idea of the common good are established by earlier discussions of practical reasonableness and friendship: for the peculiar nature of a civil community can be understood only in the light of its capacity to foster the independent agency of citizens, and to express the mixture of concern and respect that is the essence of civic friendship. The chapter on community and the common good explores 'the network of overlapping relationships in which and for which all individual lives are to be lived', thereby providing 'an indispensable foundation for all the subsequent explorations of justice, rights, authority, law and obligation'.[40] Furthermore, the chapter offers the core of Finnis's attempt to resolve a key philosophical problem, concerning the unity of practical reason: thus the chapter undertakes 'a fuller analysis of the proper relationship between one's own well-being and the well-being of others'.[41]

It is the notion of the common good that provides, for Finnis, the link between descriptive and normative jurisprudence. In his opening chapter, Finnis argues that the general phenomenon of law is to be understood by reference to those 'focal instances' where law serves the common good. Consequently, the primarily normative and evaluative analyses of later chapters (chapters which explain the way in which law can contribute to the realisation of the common good) also have an important bearing upon the descriptive project. As he explains in the early essay from which this essay began, the role of law in human affairs is to be understood 'by reference to the role it has for those who engage in it out of... civil or communal friendship'.[42]

This breadth and vision, however, comes at a certain price. For, while Finnis's discussions of the rule of law[43] are remarkably insightful, they are developed as aspects of the broader notion of 'the common good'. The principal object seems to be to reveal how full human flourishing within a just community requires the rule of law: governance by law is, as it were, the only possible solution to a problem set by practical reason. But the rule of law also has great value and importance even within the context of wicked and exploitative regimes that make no attempt to serve the common good.

---

[40] *NLNR*, 135.

[41] *NLNR*, 134. At the same time, Finnis notes, the chapter 'does not complete that analysis, even in outline' for the issue finally demands 'the venture of speculative reason' undertaken in his final chapter (p. 135).

[42] *CEJF* I.6, 123.   [43] *NLNR*, 270–6.

Although such regimes will generally lack any self-interested reason for maintaining the rule of law, they may nevertheless sometimes find themselves constrained by practices of observing the rule of law that they have inherited from their predecessors.[44] Where this is so, their observance will significantly constrain the regime's coercive power and will confer upon individual citizens at least a *degree* of what I call 'freedom as independence': a value that centrally contributes to the distinction between slaves and free men; and that, within the context of a human community, can be realised in no other way than under the rule of law.

Hart, no doubt, might point out that compliance with the rule of law is compatible with great iniquity. But this is not a reason for doubting the status of the rule of law as a moral value. For forms of government, as for people, there can be distinct virtues. Sometimes the requirements of different virtues conflict: thus, the demands of kindness may sometimes conflict with the requirements of scrupulous honesty. Occasionally, it may even be the case that the most scrupulous honesty goes hand in hand with great unkindness. But none of this shows that honesty is not a moral virtue, or that its moral claims are contingent upon consequence and circumstance.

Admittedly, there may come a point at which the wickedness of a regime is so great that it is hard to attach any real moral importance (even of a non-conclusive kind that is liable to be outweighed by conflicting considerations) to the regime's adherence to the rule of law. But, if that is so, it is perhaps also the point where the entire framework of legal thought (with its vocabulary of rights and duties, responsibility and justice) has been emptied of all real significance and can serve only to mislead. Finnis tells us that 'it is not conducive to clear thought, or to any good practical purpose' to deny legal validity to grossly unjust enactments that have been 'recently affirmed as legally valid and obligatory' by the highest courts.[45] In general, we can accept this. But, when the observation is considered in the context of grossly evil regimes, I am not sure that it does not represent an error that Finnis has elsewhere been anxious to point out and avoid. For everything that 'clear thought' requires in such contexts can be adequately captured by talk of what is 'accepted by the courts as law', while the reflective citizen is able to reserve judgement on the actual status as law of what has been so accepted.

VII. Concluding Observations

Legal positivists have often presented their theories as attempts to 'demystify' the law,[46] to rid our legal thinking of residual ideas of 'transcendence',[47] or the 'incarnation' of the ideal within the real.[48] These proclamations gesture towards metaphysical commitments which are assumed rather than explored or explained. In this essay I have tried to suggest that a principal motivation for legal positivism is the desire to maintain a moral metaphysic wherein abstractly conceived values or principles confront neutrally described facts. This distorts our understanding of law, which is at its core a body

---

[44] For this possibility, see Simmonds, *Law as a Moral Idea*, 61.   [45] *NLNR*, 357.
[46] The latest example, following Bentham and Hart, is Shapiro. See Shapiro, *Legality*, 388–9.
[47] Kelsen, *Introduction to the Problems of Legal Theory*, 21.
[48] Ross, *Towards a Realistic Jurisprudence*, 11, 20.

of practices oriented towards the idea of the rule of law, and therefore towards a central value of political association. But it also distorts our understanding of values, which can only with great impoverishment be understood in abstraction from the practices and forms of association that partially embody them. If we are to arrive at an adequate understanding of morality and politics, we must recover a more adequate sense of the complex relations between practice and value. To that end, we could do worse than focus our energy on the philosophy of law; and, in the search for a better philosophy of law, the writings of John Finnis provide an invaluable stimulus and guide.

Bibliography

Allott, Philip, *The Health of Nations: Society and Law Beyond the State* (Cambridge: Cambridge University Press, 2002).

Collingwood, R.G., *The Principles of Art* (Oxford: Clarendon Press, 1938).

Finnis, John, *Natural Law and Natural Rights* (Oxford: Oxford University Press, 1980).

Finnis, John, 'Reason, Authority and Friendship', in *Reason in Action: Collected Essays, Volume 1* (Oxford: Oxford University Press, 2011).

Finnis, John, 'Hart as a Political Philosopher', in *Philosophy of Law: Collected Essays, Volume IV* (Oxford: Oxford University Press, 2011).

Finnis, John, *Reason in Action: Collected Essays, Volume 1* (Oxford: Oxford University Press, 2011).

Finnis, John, *Philosophy of Law: Collected Essays, Volume IV* (Oxford: Oxford University Press, 2011).

Gardner, John, 'Hart on Legality, Justice and Morality' (2010) 1(2) *Jurisprudence* 253.

Hegel, G.W.F., *Phenomenology of Spirit*, translated by A.V. Miller (Oxford: Oxford University Press, 1977).

Kelsen, Hans, *Introduction to the Problems of Legal Theory* (1934), translated by B.L. Paulson and S.L. Paulson (Oxford: Clarendon Press, 1992).

MacCormick, Neil, *Legal Reasoning and Legal Theory*, revised edition (Oxford: Clarendon Press, 1994).

MacIntyre, Alasdair, *After Virtue* (London: Duckworth, 1981).

Oakeshott, Michael, 'The Tower of Babel', in *Rationalism in Politics* (London and New York: Methuen, 1962).

Oakeshott, Michael, 'The Tower of Babel', in *On History and Other Essays* (Oxford: Blackwell, 1983).

Raz, Joseph, *Between Authority and Interpretation* (Oxford: Oxford University Press, 2009).

Ross, Alf, *Towards a Realistic Jurisprudence* (Copenhagen: E. Munksgaard, 1946).

Shapiro, Scott, *Legality* (Cambridge, MA: Harvard University Press, 2011).

Simmonds, Nigel, *Law as a Moral Idea* (Oxford: Oxford University Press, 2007).

Simmonds, Nigel, *Central Issues in Jurisprudence*, third edition (London: Sweet and Maxwell, 2008).

Simmonds, Nigel, 'Reflexivity and the Idea of Law' (2010) 1 *Jurisprudence* 1.

Simmonds, Nigel, 'Reply: The Nature and Virtue of Law' (2010) 1(2) *Jurisprudence* 277.

Simmonds, Nigel, 'The Nature of Law: Three Problems With One Solution' (2011) 12 *German Law Journal* 601.

Simmonds, Nigel, 'The Logic of Planning and the Aim of the Law' (2012) 62 *University of Toronto Law Journal* 255.

20

The Irony of Law

Timothy Endicott

Jurisprudence, like philosophy in general, is generative. Good work solves problems, yet the common stock of problems worth addressing does not decrease as a result. It tends to increase. This essay studies the generativity of a piece of good work: John Finnis's elaboration of the 'central cases' method for the construction of concepts in social theory. The exposition of the method, in Chapter 1 of *Natural Law and Natural Rights*, was a landmark in analytical jurisprudence. The issues I will address illustrate the fruitfulness of the method both for resolving problems, and for generating new ones.

I will start with a puzzle for that method (which will turn, in fact, into a putative paradox). Finnis says that central cases of the concepts of social theory (such as the concept of law) fully instantiate values that are instantiated in more-or-less watered-down ways in peripheral cases. Yet the instances of some such concepts (such as the concepts of slavery, of tyranny, and of murder) do not instantiate any value.[1] I will propose that the best solution to this puzzle (while compatible with his work) is actually simpler than Finnis suggests: the central cases of such concepts focally instantiate certain *ills*. Some of the concepts essential to social theory are to be understood in relation to central cases that have no value. The central case of a concept essential to social theory may excel in some good *or* in some ill, or in neither, or in both.

What about law? In seeking an articulate grasp of the concept of law, we should not start from a preconception that its central cases are good. Finnis does not start from a preconception; his work in *Natural Law and Natural Rights* and elsewhere involves a sustained and convincing argument that the central cases of a legal system, and central cases of particular laws, instantiate certain goods—'the things which ... make it important from a *practical* viewpoint to have law'.[2] But I will argue that law is an evaluatively complex practice. The central cases of a legal system, or of a law, do indeed involve goods that Finnis ascribes to them; the central cases also involve certain ills. That is the irony of law. It secures essential goods for a community, *and also* (and, in fact, by the same token) it incurs certain ills that are necessarily involved in its specific techniques for securing those goods.

The irony is not just a theoretical tension; it works itself into a tension over a legal system's regulation of the validity of its own particular legal norms. I seek to explain that tension in Section IV of the essay.

---

[1] Nick Barber makes this point in *The Constitutional State*, 14.
[2] *NLNR*, 16.

I. The Central Cases Method

Finnis ascribes the central cases method to Aristotle and also to Weber, Hart, and Raz,[3] and counts it as an advance, in the work of Hart and Raz, over the attempts of John Austin and Hans Kelsen to construct a theory of law by identifying one thing common in all instances of law.[4] The method is an important device for the formation of theoretical concepts, because it corresponds to a principle of analogy in human concept formation in general.[5] Finnis illustrates the method with Aristotle's explanation of the 'homonymous' nature of the concept of friendship. 'Homonymy' simply means using the same word for one thing and another; the homonymy becomes interesting in the case of friendship, because of the significant differences among things that are called by the same name. The sense of the term 'friend', and the intension of the concept of a friend, are to be understood by identifying the features of the central case[6]; the term refers to less central cases, too (and the extension of the concept includes cases of friendship that are not central), insofar as their similarities to central cases justify calling someone a 'friend', or calling a relationship a 'friendship'.

This understanding of concepts such as the concept of a friend, and of the meaning of words such as 'friend', raises two questions: what makes something a central case? And what are the limits of homonymy? That is, given that something is not a central case, how similar to a central case must it be, in order for it to count as a peripheral case (rather than not a case at all)?

There can be no abstract answer to either question (any more than there can be a theory of the extension of concepts in general). In the case of any particular concept, each question may be answered differently from different points of view that might (more or less reasonably, or unreasonably) be taken toward the subject matter. 'The idea of central cases and focal meanings is itself an analogical idea',[7] as Finnis says. The subject matter may permit various criteria of centrality, for different purposes, in different contexts, and corresponding to different points of view. Consider the concept of a human being. A person can from one point of view become less human as his actions become radically unreasonable, or irrational (he becomes 'inhuman', as people say), but from another point of view (or, we might say, in another sense), he remains simply—and unambiguously—a central case of a human being.

Finnis used the method of central cases to explain the old saying that an unjust law is not a law.[8] The saying bears a superficial air of paradox—as if there can be an instance of a concept that is not an instance of the concept. But there certainly are (for example) arguments that are not arguments at all.[9] And counterfeit $20 bills are not $20 bills, and so on. The lack of paradox is explained by Finnis's method.

---

[3] See *NLNR*, 9–10, 20.   [4] See *NLNR*, 5–6, 9–10, 13, 20.
[5] See Endicott, 'How to Speak the Truth'.
[6] Note that by speaking of 'the central case', I do not at all mean to suggest that there is a single such case, or a single way of securing the goods (or the ills) at stake. Finnis's convincing account of incommensurabilities among goods (*NLNR*, 112–23, 422–3) yields the view that, in the case of a practice as complex as a legal system, there is no way of maximizing the attainment of the goods at stake, so that if there are two different legal systems with very different arrangements, it may be that both are central cases, and that neither is more central than the other.
[7] *NLNR*, 430.   [8] *NLNR*, 363–6.   [9] See *NLNR*, 438.

The method is based on a crucial insight: there is an inherent connection between what counts as a friend, and what counts as a *good* friend. Your grasp of the concept of a friend depends on your having some grasp of what counts as a good friend. Consider the ways in which a friendship may be deficient; those very features, if exacerbated, may tend to result in its not being a friendship at all. And yet, there are bad friends (and there is bad medicine, and there are bad arguments). The central cases method of conceptual analysis needs to leave room for bad instances of a concept that are, nevertheless, instances. And the method allows that room, insofar as the limits of homonymy extend beyond central cases, so that a bad friend can still be understood *as* a friend (and so on). The intelligibility of bad friends or bad medicine or bad arguments involves both a grasp of the good involved in the central case, and a grasp of the similarities that make sense of saying *both* that the bad friend (for example) is a friend, and that he or she is no friend.

It may seem that the grasp of the concepts of social theory generally depends on a grasp of the goods that are instantiated by the central cases, plus a capacity to extend the concept by analogy. And concerning law, Finnis says quite explicitly that the right point of view for a theorist is the point of view in which instituting law and obeying it 'are recognised as at least presumptive requirements of practical reasonableness itself'.[10]

But the central cases of some concepts are no good for anything. How do we explain the intelligibility of those concepts?

II. The Paradox of Evil

Natural Law and Natural Rights suggests that central instances of the concepts of social theory are good things.

> Descriptive social theory...cannot in its descriptions do without the concepts found appropriate by men of *practical* reasonableness to *describe to themselves* what they think worth doing and achieving...[11]

But theorists and people of practical reasonableness also need to describe to themselves the things that are worth refraining from and preventing. Finnis emphasizes this point: a sound theory must 'differentiate the really important from that which is unimportant or is important only by its opposition to or unreasonable exploitation of the really important'.[12]

If central cases of social practices (such as law) are those which focally instantiate the potential *value* of those practices, what about practices that have no value? Finnis insists that social practices are best understood from the point of view of the practically reasonable person, who sees value in, for example, law.[13] The practically reasonable person sees no value in murder or slavery. Does this mean that vicious practices are unintelligible? Or that they are to be understood from the point of view of a practically

---

[10] *NLNR*, 15.   [11] *NLNR*, 16.   [12] *NLNR*, 18.   [13] *NLNR*, 14–15.

unreasonable person who falsely sees value in them? Finnis addresses these questions in his 2011 'Postscript' to *Natural Law and Natural Rights*:

> What then is to be said of widespread and well-rooted practices which oppose important human goods? Are there central cases of prostitution? Slavery? Concentration camps? Extermination camps? Tyrannies? Burglaries? From the viewpoint of those who choose such acts or ways of life or institutions or ideologies, *efficacy and sustainability* in service of their individual purposes, whatever the cost to the victims, is doubtless a primary criterion of centrality. From the viewpoint of practical reasonableness, such acts and practices earn a place in social *theory* only by their opposition (harm, threat) to and/or parasitism on those goods and requirements of practical reasonableness that they harm and flout, or imitate with unreasonable deviations and restrictions.[14]

Finnis never actually *answers* his question of whether there are central cases of prostitution, tyrannies, and so on. It is a matter of the intelligibility of evil, and it creates a seeming paradox. The right viewpoint for social theory is the viewpoint of the practically reasonable person, and that person sees no rational point in evil. Tyranny does not involve a good that is focally instantiated in its central cases. And then a practice such as tyranny seems to be incomprehensible, unintelligible. The *concept* of tyranny, therefore, seems to be no concept at all, since concepts are by their nature capable of being grasped.

A. Specific quality

This paradox—that vicious practices seem to be inconceivable—can, in fact, readily be dissolved: the central case of tyranny excels in a specific and quite intelligible sort of ill. Let's call that ill its 'specific quality'. It would be tempting to call it the 'specific excellence' of tyranny,[15] since the central case excels in that ill just as the central case of friendship excels in a good. But let us use 'quality', to avoid calling the abuse of a community for the arbitrary pleasure of an autocrat an 'excellence'. This quality of tyranny is specific because it defines the practice (as mutualized concern for the good of another person[16] is the specific quality of friendship).

The idea of *opposition* to goods—which Finnis mentions—is all that social theory needs for the explanation of such practices. Why does Finnis talk of efficacy, sustainability, and parasitism? The reference to efficacy and sustainability might seem to point to a way of avoiding the paradox, because those technical virtues have a rational point, which can be comprehended in light of (for instance) the *good* ruler's concern for the efficacy and sustainability of a just legal system (or the good doctor's concern for the efficacy and sustainability of a hospital). It might seem that we can analogize from apt concern for the efficacy and sustainability of good institutions, to the concern of a tyrant for an efficacious and sustainable tyranny.

---

[14] *NLNR*, 430.
[15] As Socrates said, the specific excellence or virtue (*arête*) of a human being is justice (Plato, *Republic*, Book I, 335c).
[16] For a fuller explanation, see *NLNR*, 141–4.

It is true that the central cases of a tyranny are efficacious and sustainable. But these technical virtues—precisely because they are rather generally central to intentional practices and institutions—do not help us to grasp what is specific to, for example, tyranny. We could say the same, of course, of the role of efficacy and sustainability in hospitals or in law. The central cases of hospitals and of legal systems are efficacious and sustainable, but these technical virtues do not explain the specific quality of those good institutions, and they cannot do so for unjust institutions, either. We cannot make sense of the concepts in question, without answering the question, 'why make *this* (a tyranny, a legal system, a hospital) efficacious and sustainable?' The paradox of evil seems to remain unaffected, if we cannot find a rational point in pursuing a vicious purpose in an efficacious and sustainable way.

Finnis's reference to parasitism on good pursuits may suggest a way of avoiding the paradox, because a good pursuit *does* have a rational point. The suggestion is that we can understand vicious pursuits as peripheral instances of good pursuits, intelligible in light of the good purposes of the central case of the good pursuit (although involving the pursuit of those purposes in a deviant or misconceived way). Finnis says that:

> Slavery is parasitical on wage labour and on property in things. Concentration camps are deviant forms of reasonable prisons, detention centres, holding centres, and quarantine arrangements.[17]

It is certainly true that many vicious practices involve the unreasonable pursuit of some intelligible good—and are therefore deviant instances, as one might say, of reasonable practices. But this fact gives us no help with certain other practices which are of great concern to social theory, which are in no way parasitic on reasonable practices, and which are evils unmitigated by any analogy to reasonable pursuits. Murder is the obvious example (along with its varieties such as assassination and terrorist atrocities and genocide). The central case of a murder is an action taken—successfully—for the purpose of securing a certain sort of ill: the death of the victim. The specific quality of murder is the intentional accomplishment of death.

It might be tempting to see all murders as deviant or non-central cases of other categories of action that are reasonable in their central cases (retribution, or self-expression, or wage labour, etc.). But it would be a mistake to try to explain the concept on that basis, *even if* all murders are instances of some such action. Even if a particular murder is, for example, a way of earning money, we can conceive of it *as murder* not because it is a degenerate means to the intelligibly good end of making money (that is merely accidental to the concept of murder), but only as the successful pursuit of a specific ill. Particular murders have a unifying feature that gives murder its specific intelligibility (which, of course, is what makes the concept of murder a *concept*), and its usefulness in social theory.

The central cases of murder are central because of the focal way in which they display the specific viciousness of pursuing the death of the victim. The central cases are those that aim most purposefully and reflectively (and, of course, successfully) at

---

[17] *NLNR*, 430.

the evil (the murders that are called 'first degree' in some jurisdictions). The peripheral cases reflect more-or-less watered down versions of that vicious pursuit. A premeditated killing-for-hire is a central case; merely half-hearted murders, murders committed with muddled or conflicting intentions, felony murder, and any killing in which the killer had diminished responsibility, are more or less peripheral instances, if they are instances at all. Wink murder (in the children's game in which a player dies when the murderer winks at him or her) is a murder that is not a murder. It is not a murder because it does not involve the specific ill that characterizes the central case.

We can say similar things of any political or social concept whose instances are necessarily unjust. Tyranny is such a concept: an important category for social theory, which is not a deviant instance of the pursuit of reasonable governance. Tyrannies may involve various practices, such as kangaroo courts, which are deviant forms of reasonable techniques of governance. The state may be called a 'Republic' and the tyrant may be called 'President', and then the state and the tyrant are watered-down instances of a republic and of a president. But in itself—in its essence—tyranny is intelligible not in light of the watered-down instantiation of any good, but as the practice of a specific form of *bad* governance. We can say the same of all the concepts by which we conceive of social practices that are intrinsically unreasonable, such as abuse of power, bias, corruption, racism, and so on: what makes something an instance of such a practice is not that it is a deviant instance of a practice whose core cases are good, but that it is a specifically bad practice. More generally, and most abstractly, instances of the concepts of injustice, of evil, and of wrongfulness in general (all useful concepts for social theory) are not deviant cases of categories whose central cases are reasonable.

We can also say the same of practices such as prostitution and slavery, which Finnis portrays as intelligible by relation to certain goods (explaining their wrongness in terms of the deviation from reasonable pursuit of those goods). There are central and peripheral cases of prostitution and slavery; their central cases do indeed bear relations of analogy to other, good relationships. But the central cases are central by virtue of their focal instantiation of the evil that they involve. Serfdom and temporary indentured servitude are forms of slavery, in a sense, but they are only peripheral cases of slavery, because they involve *watered-down forms of the evil* of slavery. They can also be understood as peripheral forms of employment. But slavery itself is not best understood as a degraded form of employment; its central cases excel in the treatment of a human being as a thing to be owned, as chattels are owned. The treatment of a person as property is the specific quality of slavery. The specific quality that renders a human practice intelligible may be good or bad.[18]

In the discussion of the central cases method in his book *Aquinas*, Finnis addresses 'those institutions, such as slavery, which seem to be, not deviant versions of something else, but flourishing examples of vicious attitudes and practices'. He says that:

---

[18] Do murderers necessarily view the death of the victim as a good? Or can they act rationally in pursuit of something they understand to be evil? I will not enter into this underlying question of whether action is intelligible as rational only on the hypothesis that it aims at something that the actor believes (possibly wrongly) to be good. It is enough for present purposes to say that murder is intelligible as aimed at something that is bad.

What may seem the central case of slavery—say slavery in the early Roman empire or the *ante bellum* South—is an intelligible system stabilized by law which, however inadequately, mitigates the most radical consequences of the idea of treating one human being as the mere property and tool of another. The 'purest' cases of slavery are arrangements such as the forced-labour camps of wartime Nazi Germany, where the labourers are used up hugger-mugger like, or even as, mere material. Systems such as the Roman or the *ante bellum* American pay their own tribute to virtue in their self-interpretation... These systems are deviant versions of proper institutions such as penal detention, wage service, and inheritance.[19]

The suggestion is that the intelligibility of slavery is to be found in analogies to good practices, and it is left unclear how the 'purest' cases are intelligible—or whether they are at all. Perhaps Finnis means to suggest that Roman and American slavery are intelligible only in virtue of their techniques for mitigating the ill that slavery involves, so that the 'purest' cases are not central cases of the concept, but are merely irrational practices.

Slavery in which the owner uses up his property is a particularly evil form of slavery, but it is not a more central case *of slavery* than a case in which the owner carefully protects and nurtures his property, if the protection and nurture are for the sake of preserving the owner's property. Ownership of a car is not more specifically *ownership* if the owner destroys the car. Likewise, the specific quality of slavery is the treatment of a person as property, not destruction of the person. And then the American and Roman forms of slavery really are central cases insofar as they treated persons fully as property. But they departed from the central case—they did not fully instantiate the specific quality of slavery—if they included protections for the slave, in virtue of his or her humanity, against the full implications of status as a chattel.

It is unquestionably important to see the connections between various institutions of slavery and reasonable property and commerce (and the resulting potential for rationalizations of the practice of slavery). But the specific quality of slavery—the thing that gives intelligibility to the concept—is an ill. Social theory, I think, would be falling short of its aspiration to explain, if we were to seek to portray vicious practices generally as parasitic on good ones.

This conclusion does not contradict Finnis's account of vicious practices. On the contrary, it points out that his account of vicious practices could be simpler: all it really needs is his idea that such practices 'earn a place in social *theory* only by their opposition (harm, threat)'[20] to goods. And to be clearer, the account should recognize that the ills of such opposition supply the specific qualities of the concepts by which we conceive of such practices. As Finnis says, a theorist must 'differentiate the really important from that which is unimportant or important only by its opposition to or unreasonable exploitation of the really important'.[21] But we should say that opposition

---

[19] *Aquinas*, 49–50. [20] *NLNR*, 430.

[21] *NLNR*, 18. Does Finnis need a theory of ills, and of practical unreasonableness, that is distinct from the theory of goods and of practical reasonableness offered in *NLNR*? That conclusion is not supported by the point I have made. Social theory certainly needs the equipment to account for injustice and wrongdoing, and to account for straightforward *malice*, and not merely for unreasonable pursuit of goods. But for all I have said here, the idea of opposition to the basic goods that Finnis lists, and the explanation of

to goods plays a focal and pre-eminent role in the explanation of vicious practices. The rest—efficacy, sustainability, parasitism on reasonable pursuits—is incidental to the intelligibility of intrinsically vicious practices (it may be involved in the intelligibility of various connections between practices that are and are not vicious). The specific qualities of vicious practices are ills, and their central cases exemplify those ills in paradigmatic ways.

And still, the paradox can be dissolved. The paradox, remember, was that practices are intelligible in light of the goods pursued in their central cases, so that some vicious practices seem to be unintelligible. The dissolution is this: the central case of a *purpose* is not a *good* purpose, but is simply something that can intelligibly be gone after. A theory of purposes (which would be a crucial element in any complete social theory) does need to account for good purposes, and for the principles by which they may be pursued. But it need not account for purposes as generally good; it needs to be prepared to account for purposive behaviour aimed merely *against* a good. Such behaviour is not a watering-down of good behaviour; it is opposed to the good. This does not render concepts such as murder or tyranny or evil or injustice unintelligible. Those concepts are all too intelligible to any human being, even though their central cases are, from the point of view of practical reasonableness, deeply pointless. Each of us can understand, from the internal perspective, the pursuit of ends that are, from a truer perspective, not to be pursued.

B. Action, practice

There is further reason to question the general notion that social concepts are to be understood by reference to goods. Even within the practical domain, concepts whose instances are not necessarily vicious may admit of practically unreasonable instances that are central cases. Think, most abstractly, of the concept of action. Accept for the sake of argument the account of the proper purposes of action in Finnis's ethics.[22] The proper purposes of action do not give criteria of centrality for the application of the concept. An action does not become less truly an *action* as it departs from the reasonable pursuit of goods. Murder is, you might well say, a degenerate form *of action*. But its degeneracy is accidental to its character as an action; that is, a murder is not a less good example of an action, in virtue of being a vicious action.

It is still true that even with the concept of action, there are central cases and peripheral cases, and they are so in relation to the specific quality of action. Intentional actions, we might say, are central cases (such as voting for your chosen candidate in an election). There are borderline cases of intentional action, and they are still actions, but not paradigmatic cases (such as voting with your eyes closed, or after misreading the candidates' names). And then there are really peripheral cases of action, such as the instinctive jerk of a hand on touching something hot. But accept that the reasonably

---

unreasonableness implicit in his theory of practical reasonableness, are enough. Murder, for example, is intelligible in terms of the good of life (but only as *opposed* to that good, and not as, in its essence, parasitic on any good).

[22] As explained in Chapters III to VI of *NLNR*.

principled pursuit of goods is what makes action worthwhile, and you should still conclude that the resulting unbounded array of good purposes do not provide a criterion of centrality for the concept of an action. An action does not become less centrally an action, insofar as it becomes unreasonable.[23]

It is the *specific* quality of a category that provides criteria of centrality. Actions are good or bad as they meet or fail to meet the requirements of justice and other virtues; they are more or less truly *actions* not in respect of *those* qualities, but only in respect of the specific quality of action, which is to give effect to the actor's purposes. And unreasonable purposes (and preferences, hopes, and longings, etc.) are purposes (and preferences, etc.) *simpliciter*.

Likewise, a practice—a general form of action—does not become less truly a practice as it becomes unreasonable. A policy is not necessarily less truly a policy if it is foolish. We can say similar things about directives and orders and arrangements and institutions and customs, and you see how close we are coming to the practice of law. Are its central cases, as Finnis argues, necessarily good? I will argue that they are necessarily good *and* necessarily bad; law in its nature is evaluatively complex. We can use democracy as an example to demonstrate the possibility and the significance of such an evaluative complexity.

C. Evaluatively complex practices—the example of democracy

The specific quality of democracy is the quality of rule of a community by the people. That quality is complex—it is typically good (it is often extraordinarily good, and necessary) for a community to be ruled by the people. And yet it should be painfully obvious that rule by the people also involves ills. This obvious truth is obscured by much of the history of a worldwide and still ongoing struggle for responsible government, over long bloody centuries in which no alternative to democracy has proven useful. Winston Churchill was undoubtedly right to say, in Great Britain's fairly democratic Parliament, that 'democracy is the worst form of Government except all those other forms that have been tried from time to time'.[24] It is a history in which the value of democracy has been so exigent, that its advocates and defenders have found rhetorical purposes in concealing its ills.

We could find or imagine more or less central cases of democracies, and more or less peripheral cases, as they display the specific quality of rule by the people more or less. That complex specific quality is a good (insofar as control over government by the governed does a great deal to support responsible government, and prevents certain abuses). It is also bad (insofar as control by the people inclines government to actions the justice of which is distorted by the preferences of the people, and distorted by the

---

[23] And yet, we might say that there is a general good in action, in a sense. Even though there are unreasonable actions, the practically reasonable person necessarily takes action (whereas one particularly striking and radical way of being unreasonable would be to abnegate action altogether). I think that this aspect of the good of action does not contradict the conclusions I have drawn, because it does not mean that actions are *prima facie* good, or that an action is a less truly an action if it is unreasonable.

[24] HC Deb., 11 November 1947, vol. 444, cc207: <http://hansard.millbanksystems.com/commons/1947/nov/11/parliament-bill#column_207>.

processes by which they rule).[25] The good of democracy involves distribution of power, away from the few who might abuse the power that oligarchy or monarchy would give them. The many are 'like the greater quantity of water which is less easily corrupted than a little'.[26] But people are not incorruptible just in virtue of being many. The dangers of corruption in monarchy and oligarchy are simply worse.

In its need for practical techniques for rule by the people, democracy involves an inherent, standing tension between participation and representation, with dangers such as mob rule on one side, and the collapse into some form of oligarchy on the other side. The central case, of course, involves a mean between those two, and yet the tension remains a feature of the central case, because although real human communities can have better or worse techniques for reconciling the values of representation and participation, each involves dangers, and there is no perfect reconciliation. Every democracy involves elements of mob rule, and elements of oligarchy.

And degradation of political deliberation by populism and political correctness, and corruption of political practice by media interests and by campaign finance (or whatever other techniques the particular democracy may afford for trafficking in influence over the electorate or influence over the representatives), are inherent to democracy. So is the tendency toward short-termism that arises from the essential temporal aspect of democracy. Without periodic measures of control by the people in elections or otherwise, the goods of democracy would be lost; with periodic measures of control, officials accountable to the people work to an artificial rhythm that does not support good policy formation.

Democracy is evaluatively complex. Central cases are good in some respects; they are also bad in some respects (even if all the other forms of government are worse), in virtue of being central cases. Law, like democracy, is an evaluatively complex concept. It is different from the related but more abstract concepts mentioned above (customs, practices, etc.), because law is specifically systematic and specifically authoritative, and it has a specific, complex set of social functions. Unlike practices in general, there is something intrinsically valuable about it. But the complexity in its specific quality involves an ironic mixture of good and ill; ironic because it involves the practically reasonable person in inflicting certain ills on a community, and in sustaining them.[27]

---

[25] I think that you can agree with this even if you see additional, extraordinary goods in democracy that I have not mentioned. And if you think of democracy as a pure form of equalization of political power among persons (with all abuses accidental and not a part of democracy in itself as form of governance), reflect that there is no form of democracy that treats every person affected by the decisions of the polity as an equal member in the polity. No democratic state, for example, gives a vote to all the outsiders who might be affected justly or unjustly by the state's decisions; if it tried to do so, the state would deform its democracy by losing hold of the principle of subsidiarity, which can be a reason for citizens and not others to have political power in the state. So democracy, like oligarchy or aristocracy, subjects persons who have no say in the polity's decisions (if only outsiders and visitors) to the exercise of political power by other persons; its virtue is that it gives political power in some form to members of the polity.

[26] Aristotle, *Politics*, Book III.xv.

[27] Cf. Barber, *The Constitutional State*, 14: 'Our ethically informed test of importance can pick out bad features of a practice as well as the good.'

III. The Irony of Law

The systematicity of law and its authoritative nature, and its functions, secure the rule of law. The specific functions reflect the aspects of the life of a community that the law must regulate, if the community is to have the rule of law.[28] The systematic and authoritative aspects of law secure regulation in the distinctively transparent, stable, prospective, and reflexive fashion that distinguishes the rule of law from military rule, and from gangsterism, and from other forms of arbitrary rule. This systematic and reflexive form of rule of the life of a political community is valuable.[29] The central instances of the concept of a legal system are valuable in ways that may be (and are, in modern states) simply essential to justice and good governance.

The specific quality of law is the attainment of the rule of law. The rule of law carries with it ills that correspond to its virtues. It has the inevitable concomitant that its generality, and its corresponding institutionalized techniques, will stand in the way of justice in some situations. The system could not secure its essential purposes if it were left to every official and every person to decide what is permissible. The system would have to do that, in order to leave every person free to act justly; but if it did so, the system would subject us all to arbitrary rule (in fact, it would no longer be a system at all).

The ills of law are various. Those arising from the generality of law are the most salient in their essential role in the central case of law, but there are many others. The processes that prevent arbitrary government involve ills, because there is no way to tailor the processes to the benefits that need to be secured. In adjudication in particular, the provision of fair hearings necessarily offers facilities to the malicious for evading justice, for forcing the community into prevarication and irresolution and multiplication of pointless proceedings, and merely for spending the other side's money. Legal systems typically involve *professions*—and you might say that the central case of a legal system involves professions, because its sophistication will mean that many in the community will need representation and advice (and all will need access to both). The legal profession involves ills. It is not an accident that every sophisticated legal system involves failures and abuses by lawyers, or that the cost of good representation is high in every system; these ills result from the very conditions that make the legal profession a potentially great profession, and lawyering a potentially great vocation—such as the good willingness of judges in open courts to listen to arguments of counsel, and to hold the highest powers in the state accountable to the strength of those arguments.

Consider one typical function of law in modern societies, to illustrate the ills of central cases of the concept of a legal system: taxation. It is essential to the rule of law that state revenue should be collected in a way that is ordered prospectively by legislation, and enforced by officials whose institutions are framed to prevent corruption, with adjudication of disputes by tribunals that, while independent of the legislature and the executive, have no power of their own to depart from the legislation. It is also essential to the common good and therefore (in Finnis's theory of law) to the central case

---

[28] See Raz, 'On the Functions of Law'.

[29] *NLNR* is a sustained argument in favour of this proposition.

of law, that the substance of the revenue legislation should promote the common good, reflecting a sound assessment of the economy of the country, wise estimates of the effect on the economy of the revenue law, and a sound sense of social justice. Therefore, in the central case of a legal system, the substance of the tax law is substantively just and effective for its purpose, *and also* is laid down by a responsible law-maker and enforced with integrity, with disputes resolved by independent tribunals.

The resulting ills include the subjection of each taxpayer to the say-so of the legislature (and, in the *best* case, to the ills of democracy, discussed above). Assume the best as to the wisdom and justice of the legislature; still, because of the very nature of law, each taxpayer will be subjected to a general rule that will not be able to respond sensitively to relevant considerations such as the individual's capacity to contribute. Responding to all those considerations would take endlessly individuated decisions; that would be unfeasible, and if it could be arranged, it would diminish or abolish the protections against arbitrariness that are secured through the rule of law. So the central case of a legal system involves certain ills, which are bound to be incurred if the system attains the goods that characterize the central case. In this respect the law of taxation is only an illustration: for another, think of all the motor vehicles around the world sitting at red traffic lights where there is no traffic going through the intersection. The ill is obvious, even though there is good reason for them to sit there, and there was good reason for their communities to implement the regulation that involves the corresponding loss.

These ills are inherently in tension with the good of the rule of law. In the central case of a legal system, the tax law will promote the common good, *and* the tax rates will be general rules chosen by the say-so of a human institution and enforced and applied by other institutions. The positing of rules for the coordination of a community by authorities is, as Finnis has shown, central to the concept of law. That means, for example, that courts do not have unbounded jurisdiction to overrule unjust decisions of other institutions (and if they did, we would have arbitrary rule by judges). A proclivity to bias,[30] and a huge complex potential for human error, and the ills of generality, are therefore ills inherent to the central case of a legal system.

The specific quality of law is the pursuit of the common good in a form that involves intrinsic ills. Legal ordering involves tendencies toward waste and stupidity and even injustice: an alienation from sympathy and generosity in community relations[31]; a conservatism in dealing with new challenges and opportunities for the community; a systematically clumsy and bureaucratic resistance to equity.

None of these ills can count as a reason against having a legal system. None is unmanageable, and they can be managed better or worse. A good system will institutionalize techniques (and will devise new techniques ad hoc) for managing them well:

---

[30] Discussed in Endicott, 'Morality and the Making of Law'.

[31] Cf. Joseph Raz's sobering caveat about the rule of law: 'It is . . . not an ideal free from blemish. It brings in its wake the problems of denial of effective access to the courts, and of alienation from the law. To some extent there is no escape from these blemishes. We have to be chastened by an awareness of their existence, do our best to minimize them, and be modest in our pride in the rule of law', Raz, *Ethics in the Public Domain*, 362. That is true, in Raz's view, even when the rule of law is essential (as it is, he says, in 'modern industrialized societies', 356).

progressive income taxes, equitable jurisdictions in courts, case management in litigation, legal aid, professional disciplinary processes, these techniques and very many more can be used to reduce or to counteract the law's own inherent ills. Yet we cannot expect any legal system ever to escape them, because they accompany the goods that justify creating and sustaining legal systems. They are features of the central case of a legal system, and the specific quality of law includes ills as well as goods.[32]

At the centre of the irony of law is the fact that it is for the common good that acts of making and applying law should be effective whether they promote the common good or not. Whatever you think law is for, you have no reason to deny this irony. The ideal of promotion of the common good,[33] the ideal of independence of the arbitrary will of others,[34] the ideal of restraint of state coercion in accordance with the principles of a community of equals[35]; view any of these as the purpose of the law, and, ironically, that purpose can only be pursued in a system that gives effect to decisions whether they accomplish the purpose or not, and whose techniques for pursuing the purpose will themselves generate ills. The irony of law reflects the poignant irony on the face of the old slogan, 'a government of laws, and not of men'.[36] A government of laws *is*, of course, a government of people, constrained in ways that are so extraordinarily valuable that the practice is worth sustaining in spite of the many evident and inevitable ills of a government of people, and in spite of the ills involved in restraining the people who govern from doing justice as they see fit.

IV. The Irony Illustrated: the Law Regulates its Own Authenticity

Is it possible to differentiate between a 'law' that is *not* a law, and a bad law? This question of the limits of homonymy is to be answered in light of the specific quality of law. And here there is a tension, because it is a feature of the central case of a law that the appropriate legal authority happens to have made it. Take the example of a bad scheme of taxation. Imagine that it inflicts unjust burdens on some taxpayers, or (since every revenue scheme is part of the state's whole approach to economic governance) that the taxes are kept low as part of a structural failure in the pursuit of social justice. You might say that this law is like a friend who betrays you: you can say, quite truly, that he is an unfaithful friend, or alternatively you can say, quite truly, that he is no friend. As the title of Chapter XII of *Natural Law and Natural Rights* presupposes ('Unjust Laws'), and as its whole argument explains, on Finnis's view of the central case method, a peripheral case *is* a case.[37] The unjust law is a law. And in a sense, it is also

---

[32] Leslie Green points out that Hart expressed a similar view in his debate with Lon Fuller: 'law's nature as an institutionalized system of norms makes it endemically liable to become alienated from its subjects . . . For Hart, the fallibility of law is *internally* connected with law's nature and is not merely a result of some kind of external pollution', Green, 'Positivism and the Inseparability of Law and Morals', 1057.

[33] *NLNR*, 276.

[34] Pettit, *Republicanism*; Simmonds, *Law as a Moral Idea*.

[35] See Dworkin, *Law's Empire*.

[36] *Marbury v. Madison*, 5 U.S. 1 Cranch 137, 163 (1803), John Marshall; Constitution of the Commonwealth of Massachusetts, 1779, Article 30. The Americans were almost quoting Aristotle, who said that 'it is preferable that the law should govern than any one of the citizens' (Aristotle, *Politics*, Book III.1287a).

[37] See in particular *NLNR*, 363–6.

not a law. And there is no contradiction in these assertions, because of the 'supple subordination of words to a shifting focus of interest', and their resulting 'systematic multi-significance'.[38] The seemingly contradictory statements are possible because similarities to and differences from the central cases allow you to extend the limits of homonymy to cover the faithless friend, or the bad law, or not. There are different viewpoints from which you might accurately describe the situation in one way or another.

Should we simply say the same of the bad tax? And can a judge take the viewpoint from which the situation is well described by saying that the 'tax' is no tax at all (or the 'law' is no law)? Finnis says:

> Law that is defective in rationality is law only in a watered-down sense... This proposition is not offered as immediately applicable in a court of law (or other intra-systemic context); nor does it entail that a court or a citizen ought not to comply with such a law...[39]

It is true that such a proposition (the defective law 'is law only in a watered-down sense') is not typically or generally applicable in a court of law (and indeed, this is part of the irony of law). But it can be so.

In *Centre for PIL v. Union of India* (3 March 2011[40]), the Supreme Court of India quashed a recommendation for the appointment of a Central Vigilance Commissioner. The Commissioner heads the federal anti-corruption commission. Indian law provides for the Commissioner to be appointed on the recommendation of a High Power Committee ('HPC'—the Prime Minister, the Home Minister, and the Leader of the Opposition). The recommended candidate, Mr Thomas, had been a minister in the Kerala state government. After a change of government, he became one of eight defendants in a prosecution alleging corruption in government contracts. Thomas had not been found guilty; the prosecution had been stayed for many years. But the Supreme Court held that the law 'required due weightage to be given' to the charges against him. On the ground that the HPC had not duly considered the implications of the charges for its decision, the Supreme Court declared that 'the recommendation made by the HPC on 3rd September, 2010 is non-est in law'.[41] 'Non est' is Latin for 'it does not exist'.[42]

The HPC did undoubtedly recommend Thomas. It seems a mere contradiction to say that a recommendation is not a recommendation. Was the Court's decision irrational, or perhaps a localized rebellion *against* the law? Or was it simply a sensible application of the central cases method? These questions concern an aspect of legal

---

[38] *NLNR*, 364, nn. 13 and 10.   [39] *NLNR*, 294.
[40] Writ Petition (C) No. 348 of 2010.
[41] *Centre for PIL v. Union of India*, para. 33.
[42] The phrase 'non est' has a history in Indian law; the Supreme Court has applied it:

   —hypothetically, to a provision of the Constitution if it were repealed (*Raja Suriya Pal Singh v. State of Uttar Pradesh* 27/05/1952),
   —to legislation that has been held to be a nullity on the ground that it is contrary to the Constitution (*Behram Khurshed Pesikaka v. State of Bombay* 19/02/1954),
   —generally to invalid legal instruments (*Nagubai Ammal v. B.Shama Rao* 26/04/1956).

reasoning that is very important and yet quite delicate to describe, and provocative and dangerous in practice.

A recommendation of an anti-corruption commissioner is a purposive action, and we might say that the central case of such a recommendation is a case in which the proper purposes of the action are pursued successfully, through an appropriate process, by the proper agency. The central case of such a particular legally effective decision has a dual aspect: it is the proposal *made by the authorised committee*, and it is also a proposal that furthers the anti-corruption purposes of the office to which the appointment is to be made. Moreover, the central case involves *success* in the pursuit of the purposes of the appointment, so it also exemplifies *wisdom* in judgments as to the character and gifts of potential candidates, and in assessment of the implications of a person's past both for their character and the likely effect of their appointment, and also in assessment of the institutional and cultural and political context in which the appointment is being made, and of the ways in which others will react to the candidate's appointment in a particular political environment.[43]

There are many ways in which a recommendation might depart from the central case: the simplest example is the pseudo-recommendation that might be falsely recorded in a document titled 'Recommendation of the HPC' and drawn up as a spoof, or a forgery. Or think of a 'recommendation' from the HPC in which the wrong candidate was named through a clerical error. Or suppose that the Prime Minister purported to announce the 'recommendation' of the HPC without consulting the other members of the HPC. Or imagine a corrupt recommendation, or a recommendation based on partiality toward or against a candidate's race or class, or a recommendation made with inadequate information about the candidates, or after a careless glance at the information, or without sound judgment as to the character of the candidate, or as to the political symbolism and impact of an appointment, or a recommendation of a less well-qualified person when a better-qualified person is available, and so on.

Which of these departures from the central case justifies the conclusion that a purported 'recommendation' is not a genuine recommendation? It might seem that the genuine ones are those decided by the authorized body in the prescribed manner and form. Yet suppose that the members of the HPC were to act jointly on a bribe: then it seems that the HPC would not *genuinely* be exercising its duty to recommend at all. In that case, far from exercising the authority that had been given to them, they would be deciding to go after the bribe *instead*, through a corruption of their authority. Their 'recommendation' would a mere sham, rather than a genuine recommendation as to who ought to be Commissioner. If that is right, then you might say that the reason the corrupt recommendation is not a genuine recommendation is that the decision-makers

---

[43] It is worth re-emphasizing (see note 6) that the idea of a 'central case' does not imply that there is in any context a single ideal recommendation; on Finnis's approach, there may be multiple incommensurable respects in which different candidates may be preferable, so that there may be no rational ground for concluding that one potential candidate is preferable to another. And the judgment will involve predictions as to the future, and will require the prioritizing of particular policy goals, and while it is possible for these predictions and priorities to be unreasonable, it is also possible that different decision-makers might adopt different predictions and priorities without one set being less reasonable than another.

were not acting on the considerations that ought to guide a recommendation. And then it seems attractive to say more generally that if they do not act on the relevant considerations, they are not really carrying that duty out, either. But then if they do not give the true weight to those considerations, it seems that they are not carrying out their duty, either. And so it is possible to traverse (in a way that courts throughout the common law world have traversed, in various ways and to various extents, in judicial review of executive action) from a seemingly irreproachable doctrine that a public authority must make a genuine exercise of its power, toward a doctrine that the courts must quash a decision of another public authority if a different decision would have been better.[44]

Not every purported recommendation is a *genuine* recommendation (think of the spoof and the forgery). *Some* departures from the central case obviously mean that the so-called 'recommendation' is not really a recommendation. But if we were to say that any 'recommendation' that departs in any way from the central case is not really a recommendation, we would obliterate the distinction between good and bad recommendations. It is essential to be able to distinguish between a bad recommendation, and a purported 'recommendation' that does not count as a recommendation at all. We ought to hold onto the distinction between a *bad* recommendation and a *non*-recommendation, because it is useful for critical reflection and, therefore, significant for good governance in India. It offers a tool for a significant differentiation in assessment of the HPC's actions: there is a difference, which a good critic needs to discern, between the HPC doing its job badly, and the HPC not doing its job at all.

Yet it may be tempting to say that there is no such distinction, because the HPC's job was to make a *good* recommendation. And of course, that *was* their job! We seem to be landing in another paradox: nothing can count as a recommendation unless it is a good one.

The central cases method certainly does not support that kind of paradoxical thinking; in fact, it dissolves the confusion: far from claiming that anything that departs from the ideal recommendation is *not* a recommendation, the method allows that it may well be a recommendation—that it may truly be called 'a recommendation' or 'no recommendation' from different viewpoints—and that it is intelligible as a recommendation by analogy to the central cases of a recommendation. The dissolution of the confusion lies in the potential to understand a particular bad recommendation as a recommendation that *departs* from the central case; you may say that such a recommendation would reflect a failure by the HPC to carry out its duty, but you can still differentiate it (in the way that I suggested is important) from a failure to make a recommendation at all.

Given the potential for homonymy by reference to the central case of a recommendation (that is, for calling an action 'a recommendation' in virtue of its similarities to the central case), what are the limits of homonymy? When a court says 'non est', it asserts (or, more precisely, it presupposes) a legal power. Different conclusions as to the limits of homonymy allocate power differently. Imagine a very limited rule governing

---

[44] For discussion of the 'genuine exercise' doctrine, and of some ways in which English judges have performed this traverse, see Endicott, *Administrative Law*, 269–70.

the extent of the 'non est' doctrine, giving the court a role only in an unimportant range of circumstances (such as to give a declaration that a so-called 'appointment' was a nullity where a purported candidate had forged a document purporting to record a recommendation of the HPC), and no power to decide that a recommendation 'non est' if the HPC presents it as its recommendation. Or imagine a second rule, that a recommendation 'non est' if it is not made on due consideration of the relevant information (which is, roughly, the rule on which the Indian Supreme Court acted). Or we might imagine a third rule, that a recommendation 'non est' if the candidate is not the best candidate for the job. These rules would allocate power over the anti-corruption commission (between the HPC and the Court) in different ways; the third rule would give the Court a form of general veto over recommendations. The first would leave the HPC free both to make good recommendations informed by the right familiarity with the real considerations at stake, and also to abuse their power.

There would be nothing illogical, or necessarily contrary to the rule of law, in a regime with any of these rules. The gains that each rule offers India (in potential for prevention of bad appointments to the Vigilance Commission) need to be reconciled with the losses (in potential for ill-informed interference with good appointments, and in the judicialization of this aspect of the country's politics, with a concomitant dilution of the political responsibility of the members of the HPC).

If the Supreme Court of India invented the second rule (let us assume that the Court has constitutional power to do such a thing), was it right to do so? This is a question of good legal policy which could not possibly be answered without a full understanding of the law and politics of India (and, in particular, the law and politics of the complex movement against corruption). The question is not simply whether a recommendation made on irrelevant grounds *is* a recommendation; the question is whether there is a potential for the judicial power to improve things, in a way that is worth pursuing in light of the potential losses. But we can certainly say that the judges have taken on a remarkable power: they are prepared to nullify any HPC decision, if it is made on the basis of judgments of relevance with which they disagree.

The Thomas case illustrates the irony of law: the central case of a recommendation (that is, a good recommendation) has two independent features that are potentially in tension: it is *the HPC's* recommendation, and it is also *good in its substance*. We can say similar things of the central cases of contracts, and wills, and statutes—they are the acts of the persons or institutions authorized to make them, and they are also good for their purposes. We can say of a particular legal measure such as a recommendation, as we can say of a whole legal system, that it counts as an instance *not* simply insofar as its substance promotes the common good, but also insofar as it has an authoritative feature (the mere *fact* that it was made by the authorized person or institution) that is potentially at odds with the substantive good of the measure.

So here is an illustration of the irony of law, in respect of individual legal measures: the law must regulate the authenticity of its own instruments (contracts, wills, statutes, recommendations, etc.), and in this self-regulation, the aspects of the central cases are in tension. The central case of a contract is a good agreement, and is the agreement that happens to have been made by the parties. The central case of a will makes a good disposition of property, and also represents the say-so of the testator. The central case of a recommendation of an anti-corruption commissioner is the recommendation of a good candidate, and it is the choice of the HPC. If it were up to judges to decide whether a contract is a good agreement, or a will makes a good disposition, or a statute is advisable, or a recommended candidate is a good candidate, then the law would lose the value of the central case, in an attempt to secure the value of the central case.

The central cases method offers techniques for understanding legal decision-making, and for the critique of legal decision-making, and not only for construction of theoretical concepts. What it does not do, of course, is to provide a technique for identifying the limits of homonymy—that is, for drawing the crucial distinction between departures from the central case that do and do not have the consequence that a purported instance of some legal category is no longer to be counted as an instance at all. And those limits depend quite radically on particularities. The language and the concepts of the law do not tell the courts what those limits are; where to draw them is a question of craftsmanship in the law's self-regulation.

As a result, there can be no general 'non est' doctrine in any legal system. It might be quite wrong for judges to assume power to nullify a will on the ground that it was made without attention to the relevant circumstances, and yet quite right for them to assume a power to nullify a recommendation to an anti-corruption commission that was made without attention to the relevant circumstances. It is even hard to generalize about what powers a court ought to have to review the decisions of other public authorities. But perhaps one very general principle for legal control of the authenticity of legal decisions ought to be that it should not generally be the role of a court to replace other people's decisions (to make a contract or will, to enact a statute, to take an administrative decision, to entrench a constitution, etc.) with better decisions.

The need for law to regulate its own authenticity is also shown, conversely, by patently invalid measures that the law treats as valid. Consider a decision that is *not* a decision—e.g., a decision made by a judge who is sitting without being lawfully qualified to consider the matter. In *Coppard v. Customs and Excise Commissioners* [2003] QB 1428 (Court of Appeal), the losing party appealed a decision after finding out that the judge had not been authorized to sit in the Queen's Bench Division, though he believed that he was authorized. Lord Justice Sedley, for the Court of Appeal, said that the case raised the question, 'when is a judge not a judge?' (para. 2). He concluded that someone who was certainly not a lawfully qualified judge, was a judge:

> There is uncontested evidence that but for an oversight in the Lord Chancellor's Department he would have been formally authorised under section 9. He was well qualified to sit. This is therefore not a case of usurpation, nor of lack of the requisite competence or qualification. On established principles of law, Judge Seymour was a judge-in-fact of the High Court and his judgment therefore a judgment of the High Court. (para. 24)

The Court of Appeal had suggested in an earlier case that the decision of a judge who knew he had no jurisdiction would be 'a decision that never was' (*Fawdry & Co v. Murfitt* [2003] QB 104 Ward LJ para. 61), and that view was upheld in *Coppard*. But Lord Justice Sedley said that the judge in *Coppard* was 'a judge-in-fact of the High Court and his judgment therefore a judgment of the High Court'.

It is an aspect of the irony of law, that a recommendation made by the authorized committee may be no recommendation, and a 'judgment' may count as a judicial decision even if made by a judge who was not a judge.

V. Conclusion

Progress in philosophy does not tend to diminish the common stock of problems that are worth addressing. That is true in particular of the progress that John Finnis made through his method in *Natural Law and Natural Rights*. The book gave the best explanation of the necessity—for elucidating the concept of law—of accounting for the goods served by central cases of legal systems, and of legal rules. And it generates new problems.

I have argued that the central cases of the concepts of social theory may be central because of ways in which they instantiate goods, or ills, or even (in the case of abstract categorical concepts such as action) neither. And in particular, analytical jurisprudence (unlike the law itself) needs to account for what is good *and* bad about law. Ironically, the two go together.

This irony is such a focal aspect of the nature of law, that it is not overemphasizing it to call it *the* irony of law. But it is not a paradox, or even a peculiarity of law. It is related to the irony of democracy (captured in Churchill's truth that it is the worst form of government except for the others). The irony of law shares in the more general irony of authority: that acting in obedience to an authority may be justified by the authority's capacity to serve some purpose, *whether the authority is doing so or not*. It is analogous to the irony of parenting (which involves, from the child's point of view, tensions between the wisdom and the danger of doing what the parent says and, from the parent's point of view, tensions between the need to guide the child and the need to let the child develop her autonomy).

Even human friendship involves a related form of irony. In its central case, friendship involves, ironically, *not* a concern for the central case of a friend, but a personalized, mutualized concern for *that actual person*—warts and all.

Bibliography

Aristotle (1996), *The Politics and the Constitution of Athens*, 2nd ed. (Cambridge: Cambridge University Press).

Barber, Nick (2010), *The Constitutional State* (Oxford: OUP).

Dworkin, Ronald (1986), *Law's Empire* (Cambridge, MA: Harvard University Press).

Endicott, Timothy (2001), 'How to Speak the Truth', *American Journal of Jurisprudence* 46, 229–48.

Endicott, Timothy (2010), 'Morality and the Making of Law', *Jurisprudence* 1, 267–75.

Endicott, Timothy (2011), *Administrative Law*, 2nd ed. (Oxford: OUP).

Green, Leslie (2008) 'Positivism and the Inseparability of Law and Morals', *NYULR* 83, 1035–58.

Pettit, Philip (1997), *Republicanism: A Theory of Freedom and Government* (Oxford: Clarendon Press).

Raz, Joseph (1971), 'On the Functions of Law', in A.W.B. Simpson (ed.), *Oxford Essays in Jurisprudence: Second Series* (Oxford: OUP), 278–304.

Raz, Joseph (1994), *Ethics in the Public Domain* (Oxford: OUP).

Simmonds, Nigel (2007), *Law as a Moral Idea* (Oxford: OUP).

21

Ideas of Easy Virtue

Timothy Macklem

The normal justification of authority, according to Joseph Raz, is to be found in the capacity of authority to enable those who follow its directives to do better than they would do were they to exercise their own judgment, where the alternatives of heeding the authority's direction and reasoning for oneself are evaluated according to the same standard. In other words, authority, when properly exercised and properly attended to, can help us to comply more fully with reasons that otherwise apply to us. When an authority functions in this way it is justified; otherwise it is not. For those who understand the justification of authority in terms of the constitution of authority, Raz's account looks for the justification of authority in the wrong place, and so offers, even when fully satisfied and hence at its most robust, an account of justified authority that is narrow, insubstantial, and at odds with the everyday experience of law and the workings of a legal system. For yet others, however, of whom John Finnis is the most notable, Raz's account and those of his constitutional critics, despite their differences, are in fact united by a common, yet utterly profound misapprehension of law, and as a consequence miscarry for the same basic reason; namely, that they both fundamentally misunderstand the very essence of the relationship between law and its justification. Justification, according to Finnis, is not some kind of exercise that one performs upon law, whether successfully or unsuccessfully, or whether in the setting of the constitution or of the application of legal authority; rather it is an all-but-essential aspect of the very fabric of law itself, so as to make it ultimately impossible to comprehend law, in any substantial sense, other than in terms of what might justify its existence and place in our lives. One could say, put rather briefly, that law is intricately constituted by its own justification, in the sense that justification is the life force of law, in all its richness, complexity, and perhaps even mystery. Without justification there would certainly still be law, as Finnis is quick to make clear (so distancing himself from views such as those of Dworkin), and that fact matters greatly to the good that law can do, but a law that fails to discover the justification that law exists to live up to is law that miscarries in terms of its very reason for being, and so is law in name only, an artefact stripped of its life purpose.

Finnis's claim is set out persuasively, with admirable clarity and succinctness, in the justifiably famous opening chapter of his *Natural Law and Natural Rights*.[1] He relies upon Aristotle, albeit tempered by Max Weber, for the basic thought. In attempting to contemplate an object or practice, such as the social institution of the law, one is bound

---

[1] The claim is renewed in the Postscript to the second edition, at 426–36, and in the Introduction to *CEJF* IV.

to isolate the practice from its conceptual neighbours, first, by attending to its point, and second, by distinguishing central cases of the practice from those that are peripheral. Indeed, it might be said (though Finnis himself does not put it this way), it is this that makes something such as a practice an *object* of our reflection: we look to it (the object) with a purpose in mind. Given that we have many reasons to contemplate a practice such as the law, and so may have as many purposes possibly in mind, a person who wishes to describe the practice without endorsing any purpose in particular (a person such as a legal theorist) is able to establish a stable picture of the practice only by identifying central cases of the purposes we might possibly have in mind and, through them and by extension, central cases of the practice itself. According to Finnis, this is to be done by identifying, not the most common, but the most reasonable cases of self-interpretation on the part of those who are engaged in the practice. In doing so, one identifies the point of the practice. In the setting of the law, he suggests, the central point of view is that of practical reasonableness, and the most reasonable case of that point of view is the view that is in fact practically reasonable, and that is as a consequence free (or at least as free as we can make it) of contingency, misunderstanding, and myth. It follows that we can only understand law by understanding what would make law practically reasonable, that is, what would make it both good and effective as a design for living. In short, justification is an intrinsic aspect of our understanding of law.

One prominent feature of this way of thinking of the law is to give new life to the old proposition that an unjust law is not a law. Finnis offers a delicate reinterpretation of this idea: as he sees it, an unjust law is recognizable as law but barely so, like a paring knife that cannot pare, or a friend who is constitutively prepared to betray one's friendship. Set out like that, Finnis's position clearly courts without quite falling into an equivocation as to the meaning of law, because it embraces the apparent paradox of laws that are not laws, or (to pursue my own illustrations) paring knives that are not paring knives and friends who are not friends, while distancing itself from the possibility that such laws are laws in one sense but not in another, and so on for paring knives and for friends. Yet striking though the proposition is on its face, it is rather less clear what might be interesting about it, even in its reinterpreted form. After all, both Finnis and those, such as Raz, whom he seeks to take issue with on this point agree that a person is justified in not attending to such a law. How much does it matter then, and for what purposes, whether what a person rightly rejects the claims of in such a setting remains fully law or only formally so, whether legal obligation in that setting is non-existent or entirely hollow? Is there anything more at stake here than the rationality of regret?

It seems to me that the interest and significance of Finnis's position become a good deal clearer when viewed from the opposite perspective. If an object or a practice is indeed tied to a point or purpose (presumably a human purpose that other creatures might have access to, since purposes must find their origins and direction in the mind of some agent, and Finnis clearly has human agency in view), closely enough to make that purpose all but an essential element of the identity of the object or practice in question (although not quite essential, given that Finnis makes clear that something of the object will survive even in the face of complete failure to fulfil this purpose), then the connection between non-basic goods (objects or practices) and what they are good for is not only necessary, as he alleges, but also unified, stable, and closed.[2] Law exists to serve practical reasonableness and no other, as paring knives exist for paring, and friendship exists for whatever the point of friendship is taken to be. It is not open to human beings to invent or, to put it from the opposite perspective, objects and practices are not open to acceptance of, not susceptible to finding themselves the bearers of, fresh points, fresh purposes, new values and disvalues, or unfamiliar admixtures of various values, disvalues, or values and disvalues wrapped up together. This is not to say that such inventions and attributions do not take place. Rather, it is to say that, on the logic of Finnis's account, when they take place they must be peripheral rather than central cases of the practice, or they must be once peripheral but now central cases that have come to displace some formerly central case of the practice, or that their intervention in the practice must be sufficiently alien and of sufficiently long standing as to have given rise over time to new objects and practices, which have thereby become descendants of and neighbours to the objects and practices in which those new points were first deployed. Unity, relative stability, and closure are central to the concept of point as Finnis deploys it.

Are these several variations in fact exhaustive of the ways that practices and values interact in our lives? Is it not possible to believe that the relationship between practices and values is multiple, fluid, transitory, and open-ended? If so, it would be misleading or conclusory to speak of a central case, or a point (singular), other than from a sociological perspective perhaps, a perspective that Finnis specifically sets aside, precisely because it would bind practices to perceptions of their point and correspondingly detach them from their true potential for value (or lack thereof). Is it not further possible that the point of certain practices may be, or at least may include, a bad one, so that the relationship of certain practices to practical reasonableness is just to that extent negative? In particular, might law not have or, more precisely, be capable of having many points, including bad ones; might it not even be the case that law is on the whole more of a bad thing than a good thing, more the enemy of practical reasonableness than its friend? To return to the general perspective once more, could the significance of description in the project of human understanding be thought to lie in anything other than the fact of its evaluative promiscuity? Are descriptions not, at their core, ideas of easy virtue, placeholders for the various values and disvalues with which their objects may be from time to time infused, in the course of manifold engagements with those objects by agents from different backgrounds with different purposes in mind? Is it not their relative distance from evaluation that makes them valuable in themselves, as descriptions, what makes them something more, in other words, than mere placeholders, makes them vital resources in the realization of value by agents through the exercise of their reason, imagination, and will?

Begin with what is helpful and true in what Finnis has to say. Underlying the broad claim that Finnis is seeking to make about the relationship between social practices and

---

[2] When Finnis maintains that a practice cannot be understood apart from its point, he cannot be taken to be maintaining that the practice cannot be understood apart from its value, or he would be assuming his conclusion.

what is said by him to be their point, or in particular, between the phenomenon of law and the pursuit of practical reasonableness in circumstances of moral and human diversity, is an entirely sound observation, and indeed a worthy reminder of an Aristotelian insight, as to the basic elements of the rational quest both for value and for the understanding needed to attain it, and the role that social practices, and our comprehension of them, may have to play in that quest and in its success or failure, whether the latter be in whole or in part. Our encounters with the world, and the various concepts that we call upon to organize, direct, and reflect upon those encounters, are all undertaken with some species of evaluation in mind. Our interest in the features of the world, including its purely moral features, our very capacity to identify them as features, is always and only ever with what ought to be in mind (or, more precisely, with our perception of what ought to be); in that sense every ought is an is, all values are facts, and all facts are evaluatively inspired. It is simply not possible to comprehend the world rationally apart from a sense of the value or disvalue that comprehension might be thought to yield, directly or indirectly. Where neither value nor disvalue is at stake, actually or potentially, one can identify features of the world only by extension and with an accompanying attitude of something close to bafflement: what, one might ask, could one possibly make of such a feature, and why, assuming that one could possibly make something of it, would one have any interest in it? Comprehension is nothing more nor less than comprehension of the possibility of value and its place in our lives: just as our eyes register light waves, and our ears register sound waves, our cognitive faculties register value (and disvalue), sometimes entirely by dint of their own internal operations, and sometimes, perhaps more often, by their interaction with what our external, sensory perceptions have registered, separately or in combination, that is, with what we have seen, heard, smelled, touched, or tasted.[3]

So, for example, when we come across an unfamiliar object we seek to grasp, and are bound so to seek, just what the object might be good for, as it is often put colloquially, or more precisely, since the thought that the object might be good *for* something focuses on instrumental value, potentially to the exclusion of intrinsic value, just what to make of the object in question in terms of its value or disvalue. Adept as we normally are in navigating our particular circumstances, and conventional and controlled as most of those circumstances are in relatively stable cultures, the experience of seeking to grasp the value of an object or practice is somewhat unusual in the course of adult life in one's native culture, all the more so the older, and more practised, and more settled one becomes there. Yet, as we have all had occasion to observe, the experience is entirely familiar to children, and by the same token, as familiar an aspect of adult engagements with children. Objects the value of which is entirely obvious to an adult are often turned over uncomprehendingly in a child's hand, then perhaps put in the mouth to taste and feel, then dropped, as apparently meaningless, or in a more dramatic response, firmly rejected, apparently on the basis that they either are or might soon become a source of disvalue in the child's present scheme of activity. While less common, a similar incomprehension invades adult life as and when one

---

[3] This is to assume that comprehension is sound when in fact, of course, it is often not so. I will return to the issue of misperceptions of value below.

strays into a culture, or some aspect of a culture, the objects and practices of which are foreign to one's experience in some way: according to many narratives of voyages of exploration, aboriginal peoples have frequently been baffled by certain aspects of their engagement with the objects and practices of non-aboriginal peoples, and vice versa; according to stereotype, and not always falsely so, the old are often baffled by the ways of the young, and vice versa; artists are often baffled by the views and practices of scientists, non-technophiles are often baffled by technophiles, and so on.

In all these settings people find themselves baffled just because the value that is latent in certain objects or practices, objects and practices that are in the salient respect alien to the people in question, is quite literally imperceptible to them, thereby rendering the objects or practices themselves incomprehensible. Those objects and practices, and the values that underpin them, are such that they can only be grasped by those among us who are cognoscenti, of the appropriate kind and in the appropriate degree. This does not, it should be emphasized, make such objects and practices in any sense unusual as objects or practices. On the contrary, the value or disvalue of any object or practice is only ever intelligible to those who are cognoscenti. Comprehension is always and only ever comprehension of the possibility of value or disvalue, so that in any setting where one is, for whatever reason, not in a position to be cognizant of the possibility of value or disvalue, one is consequently in no position to comprehend the object or practice in question, be the object or practice valuable in itself, or be it partially constitutive of a value; be it a vehicle for the realization of value, or be it a component of such a vehicle. The experience of incomprehension is unfamiliar in adult life only because and to the extent that we normally operate in domains in which we are cognizant of most of the objects and practices that we are liable to encounter and of at least some of the values and disvalues that they are capable of giving rise to. Yet that normalcy is for the most part the product of learning and habituation: the intellectual passage from childhood to adulthood, from a relatively limited, visceral, native response to the presence or possibility of value and disvalue, to a much more sophisticated, reflective, wide-ranging, and contemplative grasp of the range and depth of what the world has and might have to offer, is in large part a transition to the position of a cognoscente.

All this simply goes to confirm much of the moral instinct and conceptual insight that Finnis is seeking to vindicate in the opening chapter of *Natural Law and Natural Rights*. Broadly speaking, and so setting aside for the moment the admittedly vital nuances of what has just been said, there is no essential divide between description and evaluation, no fundamental separation between law and morals, as long, of course, as one remembers to speak, or at least to think, of the latter in the plural. Yet that last rider is crucial, for its presence breaks the connection between the evaluative underpinning of description and the identification that Finnis is seeking to make, of description with evaluative purpose. It is that fact, that the realm of what ought to be, the realm of evaluation and of morals, is multi-faceted, and fundamentally so, that makes description (as a qualitative rather than a quantitative exercise) possible and indeed necessary, and so distinguishes the project of description from its indispensable companion, the project of evaluation. It is the further fact that the objects and practices that description captures are typically susceptible to the ongoing direction of imagination and will, be it human or otherwise, a direction that makes them the bearers of different values and disvalues in different hands and at different times (and also susceptible to misdirection), that makes it highly unusual to be able to bind description to evaluation with regard to any given object or practice. That is all the more so when the object or practice in question is, like law, multi-faceted and complex, even when evaluation is understood compendiously, as it is in Finnis's rendering of law.

Consider some everyday cases. A saw, so it would seem, is a tool that was originally designed, however long ago, as a way of cutting wood. It is, of course, far from being the only way of cutting wood (axes and adzes are older and in some ways superior means of performing many of the same tasks that a saw is called upon to perform), so something of its original purpose is shared with other tools. What is more, wood is not the only material that a saw can cut (there are hacksaws for metal and there are water-cooled saws for stone and concrete), which is to say that a saw has acquired purposes other than the one for which it was originally designed. More strikingly, and perhaps more surprisingly, a saw is also, at least in its form as a handsaw, a musical instrument. In serving this purpose it is not in any sense reconfigured; on the contrary, it is simply repurposed, and that only temporarily, for something of the significance of a musical saw lies in the fact that its musicality is compatible with its original and more familiar purpose of cutting wood. When people seek to make music, yet lack either conventional instruments or the skill to draw music from them, they often explore the percussive and melodic possibilities of what surrounds them. If the exploration is successful, and if the lack that inspired it is a common one, then the consequent musical exploitation of the everyday may become conventional, as in the case of a saw, a washboard, or a steel drum. Each of these musical instruments is a straightforward instance of finding a new purpose for an article that was designed with an entirely different purpose in mind.

If one moves from the setting of an artefact to that of a social practice a similar pattern emerges. Marriage, whatever its antediluvian origins, by the 19th century came to acquire in English law the purpose of voluntarily uniting a man and a woman for life, to the exclusion of all others.[4] That was, one might have been tempted to say, its point. Yet each and every aspect of that familiar purpose (or point, to speak that way for the moment) even as enshrined in English law, has subsequently come under pressure, most interestingly, in ways that qualify but do not displace the original purpose as embodied in law. Marriage today may be arranged, and so be something less than fully voluntary; it may, in many though not all of the jurisdictions that have inherited English law, unite members of the same sex; it need not last for life (though for the time being it must be intended to do so); it need not be to the exclusion of all others (polygamy aside, in many jurisdictions descending from English law adultery is not recognized as a ground for divorce unless it amounts, on separate considerations, to the ground of marriage breakdown). In short, the ongoing development and extension of the possible purposes of marriage, and of the many values and disvalues that the institution of marriage can consequently give rise to, is almost as straightforward a case as that of the ongoing development and extension of the purposes and possibilities

---

[4] *Hyde v. Hyde and Woodmansee* (1866) L.R. 1 P. & D. 130.

of a handsaw, once again amounting to the development of, in this case, a social practice, along lines that invest that practice with new purposes, without thereby turning it into a different practice (other than *pro tanto*). In fact, quite to the contrary.

What is most noticeable about such developments of purpose, and most controversial in the case of the currently broadening palette of the possible purposes of marriage, is that each new purpose depends for a significant portion of its meaning and value on the continuity of the contemporary, multi-purposed practice with its more narrowly purposed forebears, and indeed, on the compatibility of the contemporary practice with the purpose or purposes that those forebears expressed and facilitated and that the contemporary practice continues to express and facilitate. As with the musical saw, something of the significance of same sex marriage lies in the fact of its compatibility with marriage's older and more familiar purpose of uniting heterosexual couples for life. Indeed it is precisely that fact, of concomitance and compatibility, that makes the investment of marriage with new purposes as controversial as it is. In respecting the social practice that they elect to engage in for its traditional and most familiar purpose, husbands and wives today are bound to respect the other (valuable) purposes for which that practice may also be engaged in now, for the simple reason that those other purposes are every bit as at home in the practice as is the one that they have chosen to embrace, and for that reason must to some extent necessarily be engaged with by any and all of those who engage with the practice, albeit that they do so for other reasons, with other purposes in mind. Were that not the case, and were concepts actually tied to particular purposes (or points) in the way that Finnis contends they are, nobody would or could be arguing, in either one direction or the other, about the proper purposes of marriage, for such a thought could not be the basis for an argument that anyone could rationally pursue. Marriage between members of the same sex would be logically impossible rather than, as in fact all participants in the current argument of necessity take it to be, morally desirable or undesirable.

Underpinning these observations is a more profound point that can be brought out by a final example. In certain settings evaluative promiscuity runs rather deeper than the previous two instances would suggest, to the extent that openness of purpose becomes partially constitutive of the practice itself (or less commonly, of an artefact). To put it more precisely, in the setting of certain social practices, and of our concepts of them, the development of new purposes is not simply a possibility, something that may happen to the practices in question, given the energy of human beings, the richness of human imagination, and the plasticity of the practices, but rather constitutes a significant, perhaps definitive aspect of the practices as we know and pursue them. Consider, as a relatively familiar case in this regard, the theatre, by which I mean the set of interrelated practices of writing, performing, and participating in drama, whether as an author, actor, or member of a theatrical audience, in the last instance whether it be in a physical theatre, before a screen, or as the reader of a script. What can possibly count as drama is frequently the question, and the challenge, that animates not only particular dramas but the broader social practice of the theatre of which they are a part, certain presently prevailing conceptions of which it is the purpose of those particular dramas to develop, extend, and on occasion even confound, by advancing a dramatic agenda that self-avowedly presents itself as having no less a degree of theatrical value, and no more remote a connection to the realm of theatrical practice, than the prevailing conceptions that their agenda challenges. We engage in theatre, in part at least, just to discover what theatre might be capable of.

Each of these examples can certainly be reconciled with the terms of Finnis's account, simply by identifying one of the many possible purposes to which the practice in question might be put as central to the practice, and thus as the point of the practice. Yet the crucial question is, of course, just how is one able to do this and, even granted the ability, at what price? Finnis would, it seems to me at least, almost certainly take the purpose of a handsaw to be that of cutting wood; the purpose of marriage to be the union of a man and a woman for life, to the exclusion of all others; and the purpose of theatre (I am on more speculative ground here) perhaps to be the oral presentation of imagined experience, by one or more actors in a public setting, in a manner that is both entertaining and instructive to its audience. But just what is it that might be thought to make these or any other purpose *central* in the sense that Finnis has in mind, the sense in which it becomes possible to describe a particular purpose as the *point* of an object or practice and by that means to identify whatever value may be yielded by the realization of that purpose with the very meaning of the object or practice in question? Finnis rightly discounts the possibility that such centrality is to be discovered by an empirical canvas of the purposes that people actually have in mind when engaging in the practice, so as to discover the purpose for which the practice is in fact most commonly engaged in, for that would simply be to identify the value of a practice with the most common perception of that value, and thereby render the meaning of the practice vulnerable to whatever is the most common misperception of its value.

Finnis suggests instead that centrality is to be discovered by identifying the most reasonable cases of self-interpretation on the part of those who are engaged in the practice. Yet it is clear that this suggestion requires a degree of refinement if it is to be at all plausible, given that a great many, perhaps most, practices are characterized by, or at least are susceptible to, a wide range of competing cases of self-interpretation on the part of those who are engaged in them, not all of which can be discounted as unreasonable. Might one seek to identify the central case of such self-interpretations by weighing the various reasonable purposes for which they are undertaken against one another, so as to determine which of them is the most reasonable? Finnis clearly does not think so, for that kind of approach would be dependent for its success upon the commensurability of value, something that Finnis not only rightly denies but that the essence of his account of law is dependent on the denial of. Might one identify the central case of a practice with the original or foundational purpose for which the practice was first engaged in? Surely not, for that would be to return to the empirical canvas, and so once again would be to identify the value of a practice with a perception of that value, in this case a historical rather than a contemporary perception. It is true, of course, that certain longstanding practices have come to be closely associated with their originating purpose, in a way that has made them relatively resistant to attributions of any different purpose, but that fact in itself tells us only of the strength of cultural convention in certain settings, of the limitations of human imagination and will in the face of such conventions, and of the brute character of certain practices. It does not yield any general insight about the relationship of purposes to practices, let alone an insight that would explain what criterion makes a purpose central.

Might one say then, as Finnis actually does with respect to the social practice of law, that the central point of view is that of practical reasonableness? On its face that would seem simultaneously in part to assume one's conclusion (that the point of a practice must be practically reasonable rather than practically unreasonable), and in part to beg the question, which after all is just which aspect of practical reasonableness, as manifested in the various purposes for which people engage in the practice, is to be regarded as central to the practice, in a manner and to an extent that makes it sensible to regard that aspect of practical reasonableness as the very point of the practice. Reference to practical reasonableness will not help us to distinguish cutting wood and making music, or traditional marriage and same sex marriage, all of which are practically reasonable as purposes and yet only one of which can be regarded as central in each case if the practice in question is to have a point (singular). And even if it did help us in those particular cases (as Finnis would have it) it could not be expected to do so more broadly, for the question of centrality of purpose arises because and to the extent that a practice can be engaged in for more than one practically reasonable purpose.

Yet underlying these several difficulties, it seems to me, is a much more fundamental question, namely, how might a point of *any* kind, be it central or otherwise, come to be connected to a practice? Granted that the meaning of a practice is intrinsically connected to its value and disvalue, what basis is there for believing that the same is also true of point? On the face of it, purposes proceed from people, or more precisely, from agents,[5] and practices have a point, therefore, just to the extent that they are invested with a sense of purpose by those who engage in them. This is certainly what Finnis assumes. If that is the case, however, then it would be a mistake to attribute point to a practice other than as one aspect of the record of a particular engagement with the practice by an agent with a certain purpose in mind, a purpose that to the extent of the engagement had become the point of the practice or, at least, of a particular instance of it. To think otherwise would be to connect value and its perception (which necessarily underpins and informs purposes) in precisely the way that Finnis is at pains to reject, as he does in rejecting the identification of point with the most common cases of self-understanding on the part of participants in the practice. If that much is true, then it would further seem that it is a mistake to allow oneself to think that there is, other than in certain highly specialized cases, a special bond between a social practice and any value in particular, a bond that could be captured by the idea of a central case and its associated point, other than the aptitude of the practice for the realization of the value in question, in the setting of a particular project that is pursued by an agent or agents with a particular purpose in mind, just the sort of connection the rational basis of which is discoverable through the application of the normal justification thesis (where authority is at stake) and the other bases of which are to be found in the exercise

---

[5] I am here bracketing the possibility of passive practices.

of imagination and will, in the manner certain elements of which I have sought to trace elsewhere.[6]

It is important to be rather careful here, however, lest one run purpose and point together in a way that may be encouraged by certain terms of Finnis's account yet is not required by them. There must be a significant conceptual distance between purpose and point, or it would not make sense to think of them separately, other than as something approaching synonyms. What is more, the significance of the distinction aside, there would be no need for those who engage in a practice with a certain purpose in mind to invest the practice with a corresponding sense of point, the sense that roots, however transiently and contingently, the purpose that they have in mind, or at least certain crucial aspects of it, in the practice. It seems to me that the explanation of these phenomena is along the following lines. The distinction between purpose and point is real and important, but its significance is to be discovered in the equivocal character of point, lying as it does between the realms of purpose and of value, while partaking opportunistically of both. It is the investment of practice with purpose that gives practice its alleged point, and in return (here reversing the direction of influence), it is the identification of point with the meaning and value of practice that allegedly imbues a purpose (which drives the attribution of point) with some portion of what has been independently recognized as the meaning and value of the practice. This process of identification and attribution lends practices, in the form of what is taken, from time to time and agent to agent, to be their point, an appearance of singularity of point, call it centrality, that they in fact derive from the capacity of purpose, in the hands of certain agents on certain occasions, to be singular and focused.[7] The appearance of singularity obscures the multiple possibilities for meaning and value that exist for virtually all practices, while simultaneously imbuing purposes with value, or purporting to do so, thereby diminishing or even concealing the role played by perception in the identification of purpose, and correspondingly diminishing the consequent prospects for error that are embodied in any purpose that proceeds from an agent capable of error, and that are accordingly and consequently translated into point. In short, the attribution of point is a way of colonizing a practice and its value, so as to align the practice with the purpose that the agent has in mind, and in doing so to invest the agent's purpose with some portion of the value that the practice is capable of giving rise to.

Yet it is also important not to overstate this qualification. The idea of point may occupy a place, equivocally and opportunistically, between the realms of purpose and of value, but it does so because its role is to associate purpose (in the case of law, human purpose) with the value or values, real or perceived, that animate purpose. That being the case, it exists as a byproduct of purpose, a companion in the same endeavour, and for that reason is subject to all the possibilities and all the frailties that purpose is subject to. Objects and practices that are engaged in with a purpose or purposes in

---

[6] *Law and Life in Common* (forthcoming March 2015).

[7] Purposes can of course be multiple and shifting, and often are, and so can be much like the value of a practice in that respect; what I am emphasizing here is that they can also be fastened upon, and that it is when they are fastened upon in the course of engagement with a practice that it becomes possible to speak of the point of the practice in terms of them.

mind may be successfully invested with a wide range of points, as wide in fact as the range of purposes that inspire those points, for good and for ill. They may correctly be said to have many points, and not all of those are good ones.

If this much is true then the difficulty in the story that Finnis sets out to tell about the point of law as a social practice, and more generally, about the relationship between the meaning of social practices and their value, stems from his dual commitment to the idea of a central case and its identification as the point of a practice. That idea is but a metaphor, which only has purchase in terms of a purpose, and indeed and more precisely, in terms of certain kinds of purposes. It is in terms of purposes of those kinds that a point may be rightly regarded as central. Yet the identification of such a purpose necessarily takes place against the background of the variety of values that are to be discovered in a practice, the variety of purposes for which the practice may be engaged in that are discernible through the exercise of reason and imagination, the capacity to fasten upon one purpose rather than another through the exercise of reason and will, and the vulnerability of the whole enterprise to rational error on the part of agents, however that error may be engendered. To extend the metaphor of the central case any further than this, in the way that Finnis seeks to do, is to suppress the roles of imagination and of will in the identification of purpose, as well as to suppress the governing role of reason in supervising, however imperfectly, the exercise of those capacities.

What does this imply for the project of description, be it of the practice of law or of anything else? What criteria should a person call upon in order to describe a social practice correctly? Clearly descriptions are necessary, not only to reflection upon engagement with practice, but also to engagement itself, where that engagement is self-conscious. Yet if a practice lacks a central case, how can a theorist ever establish a stable picture of the practice, in order to meet the challenge that Finnis sets himself, that of describing a practice, and so determining its point, without endorsing any purpose in particular? The short answer is that a theorist can only do so with a particular purpose in mind, a purpose that the theorist must be prepared to account for in such a way as to warrant the presence and absence of the features that the description so favoured by the theorist includes and excludes. It is simply not possible to arrive at a description neutrally, in a way that does not have evaluative implications, foreclosing certain prospects for value and fostering others. Nor is it possible to arrive at a description neutrally in a different sense, namely, in a way that shields the purposes that inform the description from evaluative contention, whether by calling those purposes central or otherwise. In short, convention aside, there is no such thing as a central, stable, correct description. Rather there are many possible such descriptions, of which many are in turn central to one purpose or another, so that a standard description can only be established by convention, and even then will always remain both tied to the context in which the convention exists and vulnerable to the wide range of challenges that can be offered to conventions. Yet it is also important to recognize that there is nothing in any of this to be particularly dismayed by. On the contrary, it is precisely these features that lend descriptions their value.

The underlying point of descriptions is to identify an object or practice without thereby identifying it with any value in particular.[8] The consequent and converse point of much of descriptive practice is to speak of an object or practice in such a way as to trade on the open and uncommitted features of description while simultaneously offering a particular rendering of the object or practice the effect of which is to close and commit its description in such a way as to serve better a certain evaluative purpose. Descriptions, as a project, exist at least in part in recognition of this evaluative permissiveness. That being the case, they can be couched in a host of different ways, with as many different implications for the values to be realized from what is described. Certain forms of couching will by their nature make certain evaluative pursuits more central to a description than will others. When those forms of couching claim such centrality for themselves they enter the realm of persuasive definition. Other forms of couching trade upon their evaluative plasticity, and of course between those two poles there is a rich continuum of actual and possible descriptions, each with its own evaluative potential.

In analytic philosophy, the conventional approach has been to be as minimal as possible about the elements of description so as to be as catholic as possible about the potential for value and disvalue of engagement in the social practice as so described. It is in that spirit that one might propose philosophically that law, for example, is constituted by the union of primary and secondary rules, or must claim authority for what it requires, or must seek to create a life in common. Doing so minimizes the degree to which one's philosophical conclusions are assumed as part of one's premises for analysis and discussion. Yet such an approach is nothing more than a familiar tradition in philosophy, one that makes certain insights possible at the expense of others. What is important to recognize as a more general matter is that even when descriptions are tightly tied to a particular evaluative point the distance between the two is not a fiction, for the simple reason that while descriptions exist to aid evaluations they are neither evaluations themselves nor constituents of evaluation.[9]

What then of paradigmatic descriptions? How are they to be understood? The answer follows reasonably straightforwardly from what has already been said. Descriptions become paradigmatic for a certain community when the sharing of those descriptions, and of the concepts that they embody, yields or is believed to yield a value or access to values that would be inaccessible or at least less accessible in the absence of that shared access. Paradigmatic descriptions enjoy no greater status than this, no greater bond to the social practices that they seek to capture, no greater immunity from the possibility of repurposing, or from losing their status as paradigmatic.

---

[8] This is to put the claim idiomatically. Lest I contradict myself in doing so I should perhaps say, more precisely, that one of the chief (that is, both characteristic and successful) functions of descriptions is to identify an object or practice without thereby identifying it with any value in particular. Of course the promiscuity (or catholicity) runs in more than one direction: descriptions also identify values without thereby identifying them with their instantiation in any particular object or practice, in all its complexity, admixture, and potential for disvalue.

[9] The account offered here is in accord with what is proposed by Julie Dickson in *Evaluation and Legal Theory*, other than in the account's denial of any special status to the species of evaluation that she describes as meta-theoretical. That species of evaluation is distinctive in all the ways that she describes, but it is not, in my view, in any other sense an evaluation of a special kind, with an evaluative status that differs from the status of other evaluations.

Where does this leave the idea that an unjust law is not a law, even in the delicately nuanced form that Finnis presents that idea? In what circumstances might moral error be thought to threaten description? It is tempting to think never, that evaluative failures depend on conceptual success, and so have no capacity to threaten description. A knife that cuts well or badly is a good or bad knife only because it is indisputably a knife, that is, because it has already succeeded in falling under that description. Other articles that cut well (such as scissors) or badly (such as chopsticks) do not for that reason become or cease to be knives; it is only when *knives* cut well or badly that they either live up to or fail to live up to their descriptive status as knives. If that were the end of the matter, and if the enabling of practical reasonableness were the point of law, the failure of law to be practically reasonable would be something that one could identify only in and through the identification of a certain social practice as law, and thus as burdened with the project of practical reasonableness in terms of which it had been found to have failed. If that were true, then an unjust law would necessarily be a law, albeit a deviant instance of law, given its failure of point. In recent writing Finnis himself has offered a view along these lines, although in doing so he does not explore in any detail the idea of deviance, and so does not explain the sense in which an unjust law is both fully a law (so as to be in a position to be adjudged to have failed as a law) and yet barely a law (because of its profound evaluative failings).[10] Yet it seems to me that the thought that connects evaluative failures to conceptual success is rather too neat, rather too quick. In most settings evaluative failures do not in fact trade on conceptual descriptions, and so do not in any sense depend on the success of those descriptions. In certain settings, however, evaluative judgments do indeed trade on conceptual descriptions, with the result that evaluative failure may threaten those descriptions, just as evaluative success may confirm them. That is the case when evaluative success in a particular respect is taken to be a necessary albeit not a sufficient condition of falling under the description.

When a knife is dull one normally notices that fact alone, the fact of a failure to realize a particular value, and so reaches for another knife or a pair of scissors with which to perform the task at hand without thereby reflecting or needing to reflect upon the impact of dullness on the knife's description as a knife. Suppose, however, that the blade of a spreading knife snaps just as one is in the course of using it, leaving one with but a stub of the blade. It seems to me that once again one would normally continue to treat the article as a spreading knife, perhaps to be thrown away as unfit for further use, perhaps as a candidate for repair by fastening a new handle to the shortened blade (indeed I have undertaken such a repair and still have the knife in my drawer), so addressing the specific inability of the knife to spread effectively without reflecting on its status as a knife, or more precisely, taking its continued status as a knife for granted. But suppose that one is on an airplane, or at a picnic, and is presented with a plastic knife with which to cut rather than to spread one's food. As most of us have discovered to our frustration, cutting is a task that is often difficult to perform satisfactorily with a plastic knife, and it seems to me that when confronted with the failure of a plastic knife to cut satisfactorily one's reaction to the inadequacy of the article for its appointed task

---

[10] *CEJF* IV, 7.

might well be to question its status as a knife, despite its physical profile and suggested use. The question is why and in what circumstances that should be so, or more precisely, why that reaction should be regarded as a sound one.

The answer, it seems to me, is that because descriptions of articles and social practices are typically couched in such a way as to encompass and accommodate the aptitude of those articles and practices for the realization of a wide range of values, and because the relationship of descriptions to the values that are capable of being realized through the articles or practices to which those descriptions refer is both malleable (in all the ways set out above) and evolving, descriptions are typically not in any way threatened by the failure of a given article or practice to realize a value in particular. On the contrary, descriptions are threatened by failures of value only as and when those failures are either comprehensive or critical in character. Failures of value are *comprehensive* in character when it is impossible to imagine a value that might be realized through the article or practice in its failed state, or more precisely, when it is impossible to imagine the realization of a value that could fall anywhere within a description of the article or practice either as it stands or as it might be amended (it is possible that the broken knife is now just junk but it is also possible that it could become a pick or a scraper of some kind). Failures of value are *critical* in character in all those settings in which achievement of some value in particular through the article or practice is a condition precedent of recognizing the article or practice as falling under the description in question. That might possibly be true of the failure of what is presented as a knife to cut one's airplane meal satisfactorily, not because cutting is central to knives but because what is presented to one as a knife on one's airplane tray is a knife for that purpose alone (I am here bracketing its alternative function of spreading butter on one's airplane roll), so that a failure to satisfy that purpose is also failure to satisfy its definition as a knife.

All this is but to say that failures of value and of definition are cross-cutting and cannot be mapped onto one another. Their connection is a contingent one, so that it would be a mistake to suggest either that an unjust law is never a law or that an unjust law never fails to be a law by reason of its injustice, as much of a mistake, and for connected reasons, as it would be to suggest that there is a central case of law and that it is to be looked for in the purpose for which law is most reasonably engaged in. This is a conclusion, needless to say, that on its face is at odds with the terms of Finnis's account yet, paradoxically, it is not entirely clear how far Finnis himself is in fact committed to rejecting the conclusion by embracing anything like a mistake of either kind, for he is deeply equivocal about the extent to which he is committed to the idea that laws are laws without regard to the question of their justice and, to the opposite effect, that unjust laws fail to be law by reason of their injustice. In particular, as he has subsequently emphasized in the Postscript to its second edition, the opening chapter of *Natural Law and Natural Rights*, pungent as it may be, is not strictly necessary to the extremely illuminating account that follows of the various contributions that law is capable of making to the pursuit of practical reasonableness in circumstances of human frailty, moral abstraction, and value pluralism.

Herbert Hart was famously criticized by Joseph Raz for advancing what Raz called a practice theory of norms, that is, for believing that norms are constituted by practices.

One could make a like observation, albeit to the opposite effect, about the work of John Finnis, Hart's pupil, for Finnis advances what might be called a norm-based theory of practices, that is to say, he believes that practices are inherently constituted by morally valid norms, thus making any practices not so constituted deviant by definition. The implications of this position run very much deeper than the question of whether unjust laws are or are not laws, for Finnis thinks of the social practice of law in this way just because he thinks of any and all social practices in this way. That is a real shame, for just as Hart was led by his practice theory of norms to neglect the significance of morality in any account of law, so Finnis is led by his norm-based theory of practice to neglect the like significance of social practice, however normatively soundly, or unsoundly, or soundly and unsoundly, the social practice in question may be inspired and directed. It is true that this neglect is only partial, which is why Finnis is free to suggest that the first chapter of *Natural Law and Natural Rights* is not strictly necessary to what follows. Yet the neglect is also central, for it runs like a thread through the book, in particular in Finnis's reluctance to follow through on the logic of the book's rich central observations on the value that law, as a social practice, is capable of bringing to the project of practical reasonableness. The significance of social practice is something that Finnis is comprehensively committed to capturing in regard to particular laws, at least when speaking positively of the ways in which the moral project of a good life, collectively and individually, can be furthered by law, but is equally set against acknowledging with regard to the broad social practice of law itself.

As I have said, that is a real shame, because it amounts to a failure to recognize the full significance of instantiation in human endeavour, a failure to recognize the full implications, for good and for ill, in artefacts and otherwise, of the surviving cultural record of a distinctive and telling series of interplays among the human faculties of reason, imagination, and will, interplays that have yielded, in a way that is fundamental to our political and social orders, the legacy not only of particular laws but of the very idea of law itself. It is a shame, finally, because *Natural Law and Natural Rights* does so much to transcend the pseudo-conflict between those who think of law as a natural phenomenon and those who think of it as a human artefact, so much to show that the connections between law and morality, or put more broadly, between law and other forms of reasoning about value and how to realize it in one's life, individually and collectively, are central to the idea of law.

Bibliography

Dickson, Julie, *Evaluation and Legal Theory* (Oxford: Hart Publishing, 2001).
Finnis, John, *Natural Law and Natural Rights*, second edition (Oxford: OUP, 2011).
Finnis, John, *Philosophy of Law: Collected Essays of John Finnis, Volume IV* (Oxford: OUP, 2011).
Macklem, Timothy, *Law and Life in Common* (in manuscript).

22

Law and Its Theory: a Question of Priorities

Julie Dickson

I. Introduction

Throughout his distinguished career, John Finnis has contributed to philosophical thinking about law in myriad ways. One area of his work which has particularly engaged me is his contribution to jurisprudential methodology. In many of his important works developing his general theory of law, Finnis combines arguments regarding the nature of law with analyses and insights concerning the nature of the theory of law, considering questions such as: What are the criteria of success of theories of law? How should legal philosophers approach and execute the task of trying to understand law's nature? And what role do evaluative judgements play in characterising law accurately and adequately?

In this essay, I return to the task of exploring certain aspects of Finnis's views on law and its theory.[1] However, I do so here from a particular and novel angle: by means of an analysis of several senses of 'explanatory priority' which feature in the views of several contemporary legal theorists, including Finnis, as they seek to explain the nature of law, and to justify their particular methodological approach to that task. In a certain sense, then, the title of this essay is slightly misleading, for I will claim that it is not a question of priorities, but many questions regarding several senses of explanatory priority which we must identify, differentiate, and explore if we are better to understand law and its theory.

The essay is structured as follows. In Section II, I outline a certain important and challenging duality in law's nature, and discuss those aspects of Finnis's views which attempt to do justice to it. Section III lays out and begins to analyse several different senses of explanatory priority which play important roles in various legal theorists' understanding of law and of jurisprudential methodology. Section IV then discusses Finnis's position in respect of these priorities, and critically analyses the consequences of his views as regards his attempts to do justice to various aspects of law's nature.

---

[1] I have discussed aspects of Finnis's views on jurisprudential methodology in previous work, notably Dickson, *Evaluation and Legal Theory*, especially Chs 2–4; Dickson, 'Methodology in Jurisprudence', 117–56; Dickson, 'Is Bad Law Still Law? Is Bad Law Really Law?'; Dickson, 'Legal Positivism: Contemporary Debates'.

II. Law's Dualities and Finnisian Natural Law

A leading legal philosopher has recently expressed the view that:

> General theories of law struggle to do justice to the multiple dualities of the law.
> The law combines power and morality, stability and change, systemic or doctrinal
> coherence and equitable sensitivity to individual cases, among others...
>   ... [A]re the concepts commonly used in legal theory adequate to the task of explaining
> these dualities and the attendant conflicts or tensions in our understanding of the law?[2]

In this essay I intend to explore some of the challenges generated by law's dualistic
character. I will do so, however, by focussing on a different duality, namely that of law
as both a *social* and a *normative* phenomenon. As with many terms featuring in legal
philosophical discourse, much ink has been spilled exploring what is meant by law as
a social and as a normative phenomenon respectively. I will focus only on certain
questions and issues arising from law's social and normative nature, in large part those
which play an important role in John Finnis's views on the nature of law and the nature
of the theory of law.

In speaking of law's social nature in the present context, then, I have in mind two
main points:

(1) Law is a social artefact which exists in virtue of the fact that human beings and the
    social institutions they create—such as legal officials, legislatures, and courts—have
    decreed or decided or recognised or practised or enforced a given set of norms.
(2) The existence and content of valid legal norms is ultimately to be determined by
    reference to social facts, in particular, by reference to law's social sources, and not
    by reference to the merits of the legal norms in question.

These theses, especially the second, are controversial and contested in some quarters, and
may be regarded by some as being the province of one particular approach to understanding law, namely legal positivism.[3] Several important legal philosophers have expressed
doubts regarding carving up the jurisprudential field in terms of 'teams' of legal positivists,
natural lawyers, and others.[4] But whatever the merits of dispensing with such classifications, as we shall see below, John Finnis, a legal theorist primarily associated with the
natural law rather than legal positivist tradition, claims in his general theory of law both to
recognise, and to do justice to, those aspects of law's social nature referred to above.

What of the other aspect of the duality of law referred to above, namely law as a
normative phenomenon? This aspect of law's nature, and what is required in order to do
justice to it potentially involves many different questions and issues: how we should
interpret legal ought statements of the form 'according to law, X ought to ϕ'; whether
such statements can be reduced to combinations of social facts or to statements about
other people's beliefs; whether 'ought' means the same thing in legal and moral contexts,

---

[2] Raz, *Between Authority and Interpretation*, 1.
[3] Indeed, in rendering them here, I draw upon my attempt to characterise the core of legal positivist
thinking in Dickson, 'Legal Positivism: Contemporary Debates', Section IA.
[4] See e.g. MacCormick, *Institutions of Law, an Essay in Legal Theory*, 278; Raz, 'The Argument from
Justice, or How not to Reply to Legal Positivism', 35.

and what it does mean in each of those contexts; what grounds the validity of legal norms; how to understand law's claim to be morally binding and to generate genuine reasons for action; what would vindicate law's claim to be morally binding and to generate genuine reasons for action; what am I to do, given the presence of law; which value or values ought law to realise, and under what conditions does it succeed in so doing, etc.

For present purposes, I will focus only on certain of these issues. Law claims to state that which we have genuine reason to do, and to pre-empt and exclude other reasons for action we may have.[5] In order to understand the nature of law, therefore, it is important to understand the character of those claims; the conditions, if any, under which they are justified; and thus address the question of what we ought to do, given the presence of law. Moreover, given that law is a system of conduct-guidance which attempts to get individuals, and the societies in which they live, to act in particular ways, it is also important to consider whether, and in what sense, there is any overall point or value to law which might contribute to its justification conditions. In attempting to do justice to law's normative character, then, it is important for legal theorists to address the following questions: (1) Under what conditions are law's claims to generate genuine reasons for action justified? (2) Does law have an overall normative point or value?

As has been mentioned above, John Finnis apparently seeks to capture both the social and the normative aspects of law's nature in developing his general theory of law. Finnis makes seemingly powerful claims in his work that his theory does adequate justice to law's social nature, and to law as a man-made and posited phenomenon:

> ...human law is artefact and artifice, and not a conclusion from moral premises[6]
>
> ...why deny that the facts which are referred to as 'human positing'—custom, legislation, judgments—can all be identified by lawyerly historical methods, without 'moral argument'?[7]

Indeed, it is Finnis's view that natural law theorising, from Aquinas onwards, attempts to recognise and explain the posited character of human law within the natural law approach. In a sense, then, Finnis does not regard legal positivism as a rival position to the form of natural law thinking he espouses, rather he regards it as redundant, for he believes that natural law theory can and should do adequate justice to law's positivity, as well as identifying and explaining law's ability to generate genuine reasons for action, and its moral point or value.[8]

In espousing this view, Finnis takes himself to have disabused the jurisprudential community of several falsehoods which he believes have featured in the views of legal philosophers such as Hans Kelsen, such as that natural law theory has no specifically legal notion of validity, or that it gives no important role to positive law, seeing it as a mere copy of pre-existing natural law.[9] This apparent attempt to do justice to law's

---

[5] In this I follow the views developed by Joseph Raz in Raz, *Practical Reason and Norms*, and Raz, *The Morality of Freedom*, especially Chs 2–4, and by John Finnis in *NLNR*, 233–7, 255, 308–14, 345, 352.

[6] Finnis (1996c), 205.

[7] Finnis (1996c), 205.

[8] See Finnis (1996c), 195–205; Finnis (2003b), *passim*, but especially 115–16 and 122; Finnis (2007c), Introduction.

[9] *NLNR*, 26–9.

social and posited nature, and to a specifically legal notion of validity, has also led some to claim that Finnisian natural law reconciles or at least lessens pointless mutual opposition between legal positivist and natural law scholars,[10] though Finnis himself sometimes adopts a less than reconciliationist position on this issue.[11]

Turning to the other aspect of law's nature under consideration here, i.e. law as a normative phenomenon, Finnis attempts throughout his general theory of law to address questions regarding the conditions under which law's claims to generate genuine reasons for action are justified, and whether law has an overall normative point or value.[12] Indeed, not only does he address these questions, but it would not be an exaggeration to say his view of law is largely characterised by the distinctive answers which he gives to them: that law's overall normative point is reasonably to resolve coordination problems for the sake of societal common good, thus allowing citizens successfully to pursue basic goods or values in their lives,[13] and that law generates genuine reasons for action and ought to be obeyed largely when and for the reason that it achieves that normative point.[14]

All this, therefore, seems to indicate Finnis's desire to do justice to both law's social and its normative character. On closer inspection, however, doubts begin to emerge regarding the sense in which, and the extent to which, this is really the case. But before attempting to explore and expose Finnis's particular commitments in this regard, I will outline more generally four different senses of explanatory priority which seem to be at work in contemporary jurisprudence. In my view, paying greater attention to the character of and differences between these senses of explanatory priority will assist our understanding of the importance of various of law's features in constituting its nature, and of the relative merits of different methodological approaches within jurisprudence.[15] For present purposes, outlining the following four senses of explanatory priority will also provide a useful classificatory schema facilitating better understanding and critical analysis of Finnis's distinctive position.

III. Four Senses of Explanatory Priority

A. Explanatory priority #1: priority as order of explanation *or* does it matter where you start?

The first sense of explanatory priority to be explored here has to do with whether (and, if so, why) it matters where we start in our theoretical investigations into law's character. Is there a particular property or sub-set of properties of law which it is either necessary or explanatorily superior to *start* with, in order for a general theory of

---

[10] See e.g. MacCormick, 'Natural Law and the Separation of Law and Morals', especially 106–10, 120, 122.

[11] Claiming, for example, that: 'Positivism is not only incoherent. It is also redundant', Finnis (2002a), 23.

[12] These issues are discussed at more points in Finnis's work than could possibly be referenced here. However, the declaration of intent contained in the opening sentences of *NLNR* makes the point well enough: 'There are human goods that can be secured only through the institutions of human law, and requirements of practical reasonableness that only those institutions can satisfy. It is the object of this book to identify those goods, and those requirements of practical reasonableness, and thus to show how and on what conditions such institutions are justified...' *NLNR*, 3.

[13] *NLNR, passim*, but see especially Chs VI, IX, X.

[14] *NLNR*, especially Chs XI, XII.

[15] This is a topic which I intend to explore further in future work on jurisprudential methodology.

law to be successful? If the answer is yes, then those properties of law will have explanatory priority over other properties it may possess, in the particular sense that it will be (depending on the version of the thesis espoused) either necessary, or explanatorily superior, to begin one's investigation into law's nature by investigating those properties. To put things in terms of the particular duality of law discussed here, does it matter whether we start by investigating matters to do with law's social facticity and institutional character, or whether we instead begin with questions such as whether law has an overall normative point or value and whether and under what conditions its directives ought to be followed?

Now, even if it were to be established that this sense of explanatory priority properly features in legal philosophical investigation, further questions would emerge as to which properties of law the priority attached to, and for what reasons. The aims and focus of the current discussion preclude full consideration of these matters here. For present purposes, however, some examples may help illustrate further both the character of, and some possible reasons for, such priority.

The first example is drawn from some of my own work on jurisprudential methodology. In *Evaluation and Legal Theory* I argue that legal theorists can identify, understand, and explain important and significant features of law without yet taking a stance on whether and under what conditions those features of law are morally valuable and/ or morally justified.[16] My contention is that although legal theorists must engage in a kind of evaluation—in the book I refer to it as 'indirect evaluation'—in order to identify and explain law's important and significant features; such a task does not entail, and need not be supported by, 'directly evaluative judgements' regarding law's moral value or moral justification conditions.[17] In the closing chapter of the book I then make a further claim: that certain questions in jurisprudence, questions that have to do with the particular sort of social institution that law is, and the particular procedures and means via which it operates, must be answered prior to asking and attempting to answer questions such as whether and under what conditions legal norms ought to be obeyed and which values legal systems ought to live up to.[18] The reason for this, I claim, is that the first set of questions must be adequately answered so that we can formulate the second set with the requisite degree of precision and accuracy, and so that we have the relevant information to try to answer them:

> If we are to be capable of answering directly evaluative questions such as whether and under what conditions legal norms ought to be obeyed, then we need to know quite a bit about how those norms, and the social institution which issues them, operate. Otherwise, how are we to know *what* exactly we are asking the question, 'ought we to obey it?' of?[19]

In a similar vein, in 'Legal Positivism: 5 ½ Myths', John Gardner claims that questions characteristically asked and answered by legal positivists regarding the character and

---

[16] Dickson, *Evaluation and Legal Theory*, *passim*.
[17] Dickson, *Evaluation and Legal Theory*, especially Ch. 3.
[18] Dickson, *Evaluation and Legal Theory*, Ch. 7, especially 134–7.
[19] Dickson, *Evaluation and Legal Theory*, 135.

conditions of legal validity are, in his words, 'logically prior' to what might be thought of as characteristic questions of the natural lawyer, such as which distinctive ideals law ought to realise, and whether its norms are morally binding.[20] Again, for Gardner, the reason for this seems to be that it is only once we ask and answer certain questions about the nature of legal validity that we have a sufficiently clear view regarding exactly what we are asking questions concerning ideals and justification conditions *of*:

> For [legal positivism's thesis regarding the conditions of legal validity] tries to answer a logically prior question. What is this field of human endeavour, to which the natural lawyer's proposed criteria of success and failure apply? What makes something a candidate for being accounted a success or failure in these terms? What is this *lex*, such that it ought to be *ius*?[21]

It should be noted that this is a position from which Gardner has explicitly resiled in later work,[22] and I will return to his more recent position in Section III(C). For present purposes, however, the examples above should begin to flesh out what I have in mind by explanatory priority in the 'order of explanation' or 'does it matter where you start?' sense.

B. Explanatory priority #2: priority as explanatory dependence

Explanatory priority in the second sense I have in mind has to do with whether a certain feature of law, or subset of features of law, explains certain other, or all other, features of law, such that those other features of law depend on the character of the first feature or set of features. An illustration of this can also be found in a discussion of jurisprudential methodology by John Gardner, in which he addresses in passing the issue of the relation in Ronald Dworkin's work between determining the existence and content of law on the one hand, and law's overall moral point or objective on the other.[23] Gardner claims that, for Dworkin:

> ...the point or objective of law, as realized in the central case, explains all the other defining features of law, including all those that obtain in the limit cases where the point or objective is not realized. How law is depends entirely on how it ought to be. Law is comprehensively tailored to its purpose.[24]

In making these points, Gardner has in mind Dworkin's well-known claim that in order to know which propositions of law are true and what they require of us, we must engage in an exercise of 'constructive interpretation' which aims to assign a general justifying point or value to legal practice as a whole, and then to interpret that practice in its best light in terms of the point or value in question.[25] For Dworkin, at least the Dworkin of *Law's Empire*, the point or value of legal practice is properly to constrain

---

[20] Gardner, 'Legal Positivism: 5 ½ Myths', 226–7.
[21] Gardner, 'Legal Positivism: 5 ½ Myths', 226–7.
[22] Gardner, 'Nearly Natural Law', 16, and especially n. 27.
[23] Gardner, 'Nearly Natural Law', 14–16.
[24] Gardner, 'Nearly Natural Law', 14–15.
[25] Dworkin, *Law's Empire*, *passim*, but see especially 46–53, 90–6, 225–38, 254–8, 410.

and thus render justified the use of governmental collective force. Which propositions of law are true and what they require of us is thus to be determined by ascertaining the normative point or value underpinning law—the justification of state collective force—and then determining which legal propositions flow from that point so assigned, and hence which legal duties are justifiably imposed on citizens in light of that normative point. This being so, in Dworkin's general theory of law in *Law's Empire*, certain features of law—namely the existence and identification of legal rights and duties—are determined by another feature of law, namely its normative point or value. The existence and identification of legal rights and duties thus depend on, and are explained by, law's normative point, and the latter can be said to have explanatory priority over the former in this second sense.

It is important to note the ways in which this form of explanatory priority differs from explanatory priority #1 ('EP #1') discussed in Section III(A). First of all, although on first consideration it may seem as though any features of law which could be established to have priority over other features of law in this second sense would *also* have priority in the 'order of explanation' sense (i.e. that legal theorists should start by investigating those properties of law which explain certain other of its properties), I am not convinced that this is necessarily so. Suppose that it is indeed the case that some subset of law's properties, subset A, explains another such set, subset B, such that subset B is explanatorily dependent on subset A. It could nonetheless be the case, for example, that a legal theorist could have a significant theoretical interest in, and a well-developed intuitive awareness of, the properties of law forming subset B, thus facilitating her beginning by doing some explanatory theoretical work as to their character, before moving on to investigate the character of subset A upon which subset B depends, and the precise relation of dependence between them. Second, this second form of explanatory priority ('EP #2') is in a sense 'stronger' than EP #1. In the first sense of priority, two different subsets of law's features could illuminate relatively independent aspects of law's nature such that subset A does not explain or in some sense determine subset B nor vice versa. Rather, all that is claimed regarding priority #1 is that, for some reason, it is necessary or explanatorily more adequate to start with either subset A or subset B respectively and to explain them in a certain order. The claim made regarding priority #2, however, is not about order of explanation but about explanatory *dependence*, that subset A of law's features *explains* and/or in some sense *determines* subset B such that the latter are explanatorily dependent on the former.

C. Explanatory priority #3: identificatory priority

A third sense of explanatory priority featuring in some legal theorists' accounts of law involves the claim that certain of law's properties are more important than others to the task of *identifying* law as a distinctive entity. An illustration of such a claim may be found in a recent article by Leslie Green entitled, 'Law as a Means'.[26] Green discusses whether law is, in a certain sense, best understood in terms of being a specific social

---

[26] Green, 'Law as a Means', 169–88.

means to various ends, or in terms of any end or ends it may serve. As the argument proceeds, Green makes various moves to try to render more plausible the thesis that:

> ...law's means are more important in *identifying* law as a social institution than are law's ends...what makes law special are the means by which it serves those ends. Moreover, law's ends, even if they are proper ideals for law, are not distinctive: there are no ends universal among or unique to all legal systems, no ends that unify and explain all features of its means.[27]

It is important to note that in this passage Green is not claiming that, in understanding law *tout court*, law's means are more important than any ends it may have. Rather, the more particular point he is making is that certain features of law—in his view, the means by which it operates—are more specific to it, and hence will better help us to *identify* law and pick it out as something distinctive, than will other of its features, namely its ends. On this view, law's end or ends could still be something vitally important about it, and could be important to understand as part of law's nature. Indeed, law's end or ends could even be *more* important in understanding law, and/or more important in understanding law's nature, than its specific social means. It could be the case, for instance, that those properties which allow us to pick out and identify something as law may not be amongst the most important things about it, *tout court*, and/or that its more interesting properties are not particularly useful in identifying it as the thing that it is. Moreover, law's specific social means might not be particularly interesting in terms of our current legal theoretical or wider intellectual interests, and its ends might be much more interesting in this regard.[28] The claim that is made for this kind of explanatory priority is distinctively that in respect of *one* vitally important task of legal philosophy, that of *identifying* law as law, some of its properties—in Green's view its means—are more important to focus on than others.

At this stage in the inquiry, questions may arise as to whether, and, if so, in what sense, this third sense of explanatory priority differs from EP #1: priority as order of explanation. For it might be supposed that a general theory of law should *begin* by identifying that which counts as law, and that hence any properties of law having explanatory priority in sense #3—that of better enabling us to pick out and identify law as law—would also have explanatory priority in sense #1—priority in terms of order of explanation. This supposition might be further bolstered by the fact that when discussing reasons for EP #1 in Section III(A), the examples I gave, from my own work, and from some of John Gardner's, each seemed to contend that the reason for beginning by investigating certain of law's properties was that it was in some sense necessary to identify exactly what law is and how it operates before we can ask morally evaluative questions about those ideals to which it should aspire or conditions under which we ought to follow its directives.

For all this, however, I believe that there are good reasons to distinguish EP #1 from EP #3. First of all, the examples I gave in Section III(A) were just that, some examples of

---

[27] Green, 'Law as a Means', 173 (my emphasis).
[28] For discussion of the phenomenon of jurisprudential topics coming into and going out of intellectual fashion, see Dickson, 'The Central Questions of Legal Philosophy'.

claims by particular legal theorists that there are certain reasons why it is explanatorily necessary or beneficial to start with certain features of law and not others in our jurisprudential investigations. However, a fuller account of EP #1 would need to investigate, inter alia: (i) whether and why particular theorists' views in this regard are correct,[29] and (ii) whether there may be several different reasons justifying beginning by investigating certain properties of law and not others in our theories. That we need to identify exactly that which we wish to go on to morally evaluate may be one such reason, but there could well be other reasons as well. This tack, however, might lead some to the view that although EP #1 and EP #3 do not mark out identical categories, nonetheless EP #3 would always be *one reason for* EP #1 such that any properties of law possessing EP #3 would also possess EP #1. Even this interpretation, however, would be a mistake in my view, for it obscures another possible methodological stance which certain theorists appear to adopt, namely that it *does not* matter where you start, but that nonetheless, certain properties of law have explanatory priority for the task of identifying law and picking it out as distinctive.

This may be John Gardner's more recent view of the way in which legal theorists ought to approach the task of understanding law. In his 2007 article, 'Nearly Natural Law', Gardner alters his position from that discussed in Section III(A). He attempts to refute Dworkin's view (discussed in Section III(B)) that law's overall normative point explains and determines all the other features of law, by claiming that:

> ...a moment's thought shows that one already needs at least some other relatively independent criteria to identify the thing in question, such that one can begin to discuss *its* (that very thing's) point or objective.[30]

This seems at first glance to repeat Gardner's claim discussed in Section III(A) that legal theorists should *start* with criteria for identifying law which are independent of any normative point or value which it may have. Appearances are deceptive, however, for Gardner goes on to claim that:

> Our conclusion should not be that these other criteria have explanatory priority over the study of law's point or objective. Our conclusion should be that study of the nature of law, or indeed of the nature of anything, is like the mid-ocean reconstruction of Neurath's boat. As each aspect of the nature of law is elucidated, other aspects need to be held constant in the background to orientate the investigation; one can in principle begin one's investigations with any aspect of the nature of law so long as one does not attempt to open up everything else at the same time...[31]

Gardner thus seems to espouse the methodological stance that: (a) it *does not* matter where you start in investigating various aspects of law's nature, but that (b) one important explanatory task of jurisprudence is to pick out and identify what counts

---

[29] In future work on this topic I hope to have an opportunity to reflect further on my own views in this regard, as well as those of others.

[30] Gardner, 'Nearly Natural Law', 15.

[31] Gardner, 'Nearly Natural Law', 15–16. A footnote internal to this quote explicitly states that: 'I erred in suggesting otherwise at the end of '"Legal Positivism: 5 ½ Myths", *American Journal of Jurisprudence* 46 (2001) 199, 226.'

as law, and certain features of law are more important than others to this particular explanatory task. If my interpretation is correct, then this position demonstrates another sense in which there is distinctive space for explanatory priority #3 to occupy.

D. Explanatory priority #4: priority as relative importance for law's nature

The final sense of explanatory priority to be considered here holds that certain of law's features have priority over others in terms of their relative importance for law's nature, or, to put it another way, in terms of their relative importance as regards what makes law into what it is. The best illustration of this sense of explanatory priority comes from the work of Finnis himself. Finnis's position in this regard will be subject to critical analysis in Section IV; in the present section I merely present aspects of it in order to exemplify the kind of explanatory priority which I have in mind.

As was discussed in Section II, Finnis presents himself as a legal theorist who realises the need to do justice to both the social and the normative aspects of law. He claims that his particular brand of natural law theory can adequately account for law's positivity, and for legal systems' possessing intra-systemic tests for legal valid-ity, while remaining faithful to the need to explain law's overall normative point of reasonably resolving coordination problems for the common good, and hence gen-erating moral reasons for action. However, an interesting position emerges when we consider Finnis's view of how we should understand instances of legal systems which meet the relevant social facts criteria for accounting them as law (for example, they consist of norms of a practised system emanating from the social institutions of that system and meeting its intra-systemic tests for legal validity), but which fail in terms of fulfilling law's normative point or value (i.e. those norms, and the system of which they are a part, do not coordinate for the common good, or perhaps even coordinate in order to produce morally bad outcomes).

According to Finnis, although there is a certain sense in which such systems, and the norms which constitute them, can still be accounted as law,[32] he is keen to point out that they are also to be regarded—depending on the force of his turn of phrase—as not really law,[33] less than fully law,[34] law only in a secondary, watered down, non-central or distorted sense,[35] or, simply, not law.[36] The social fact properties of law hence seem, to Finnis, less central to law's nature, less central to its being law, than its ability successfully to realise its overall normative point or value.

That this is Finnis's considered view is further revealed by a remark he makes in 'Law and What I Truly Should Decide' in response to a challenge by Joseph Raz as to why law should be regarded as not really or fully law when it is bad, whereas novels or paintings or people still remain novels or paintings or people even when they are bad.[37] Finnis's response to Raz is that: '... like argument, medicines, and contracts, law *has a*

---

[32] *NLNR*, Ch. XII.4; Finnis (2007c).   [33] *NLNR*, 277–8.
[34] *NLNR*, 279.   [35] Finnis (2007c), Section 4.
[36] Finnis (2003b), 114. The discussion in the remainder of this section, and in Section IV(D), draws on Section IIB of Dickson, 'Legal Positivism: Contemporary Debates'.
[37] Finnis (2003b), 114–5, and especially n. 9.

focused and normative point to which everything else about it is properly to be regarded as subordinate.[38] Those features of law which go to its social nature—such as norms meeting intra-systemic tests of legal validity, and which are recognised and enforced by legal officials—are thus regarded by Finnis as subordinate qualities of law, and law that exhibits those qualities, but that does not instantiate law's overall normative point or value, is seen as a watered down or secondary kind of law (when it is seen as law at all). Law's 'focused and normative point', i.e. its moral task of reasonably resolving coordination problems for the common good, is hence what is regarded as most important to its being law. This being so, although Finnis often claims that natural law thinking is interested both in law's social facticity, and in its normative point and propensity to generate reasons for action, he appears to regard the latter qualities, and the explanation of them, as having explanatory priority in this fourth sense.

IV. Finnisian Priorities

A. Does it matter where you start? Finnis and explanatory priority #1

Some of Finnis's clearest statements regarding his stance on EP #1 are to be found in his article, 'Law and What I Truly Should Decide'.[39] Finnis argues that it *does* matter where we start in our legal philosophical investigations, and that the starting point should be to ask and try to answer the question of why we should favour introducing, having, maintaining, and complying with law.[40] In claiming that we should begin by inquiring into why we should have law, and under what conditions we ought to comply with it (and in claiming that the answers to those questions involve moral deliberation), Finnis places himself squarely on the 'normative' side of the social/normative duality of law as regards which of law's qualities we must tackle first in terms of the order of explanation of them that we adopt. One reason he gives for this is that, 'The primary reality of the law is rather in its claim, as itself a moral requirement, on my deliberating about what to decide',[41] and that this 'reality' of law is primary:

> . . . because the rational force of this claim is fully intelligible even before one knows anything much about the content of the law and certainly before one has been taught anything about law in general or 'the concept of law'.[42]

Finnis seems to be saying, then, that one reason why we need to begin our legal philosophical investigations with a consideration of aspects of law's normative character, is that law's *claim* to have a moral point or value and to supply us with moral reasons for action is the first thing that strikes us about law when we consider its presence in our social world, and is intelligible with a priority and immediacy over any other of law's properties. Finnis also claims in 'Law and What I Truly Should Decide', as he does elsewhere, that natural law theory can and does adequately account for the social reality and actually posited character of law,[43] but stresses time and again that those social properties of law can be accounted for within a theory of law that, '. . . has

---

[38] Finnis (2003b), 114, n. 9 (my emphasis). [39] Finnis (2003b), 107–29.
[40] Finnis (2003b), 107. [41] Finnis (2003b), 112.
[42] Finnis (2003b), 113. [43] Finnis (2003b), 116, 122.

been worked out from the *starting point* of the one hundred percent normative question, what should I decide to do . . . '[44] and which does not make the 'philosophical mistake'[45] of assuming that, in developing theories of law, ' . . . you can answer the question What is it? Before you tackle the question Why choose to have it, create it, maintain it, and comply with it?'[46]

Several points can be raised here as regards Finnis's stance on EP #1. First of all, is Finnis correct that the first thing that strikes us about law, and which is intelligible before any other of its properties, is its moral claim over us and over our processes of deliberation? One might think, for example, that some if not many of those who frequently come into contact with the law are likely to hold views to the effect that it, and its officials and executive agencies, are *not* justified as regards their claims and actions, and hence do not operate in the domain of changing and shaping our moral reasons for action at all.[47] Even if such views are correct, of course, that does not mean that law is not *making* a moral *claim* on us, even if such a claim turns out—either sometimes, or always—to be false. My point is, however, that for those holding views (views which may have arisen from longstanding experience) to the effect that law does not operate such as to shape and change moral reasons for action, the first thing that strikes them about law, and that they find intelligible about it, is highly unlikely to be law's moral claim on our deliberative processes. Rather, I would suggest, the first thing that strikes them about law is likely to be its characteristic use of force, and its perceived tendency to a kind of 'blunt instrument over-inclusiveness'. By this I mean that persons holding such views might attribute to the law, or at least to certain of its executive agencies—the police for example—attitudes such as that persons of a certain age demographic, and/or ethnicity, and/or hailing from a certain residential area have tendencies toward criminal activity of a certain kind, and are to be treated accordingly. The veracity or otherwise of these speculated-upon perceptions is not my concern here. Rather, my claim is that for those holding such views—and we know that such persons and views exist[48]—the first thing that hits one about law is highly unlikely to be its moral claim over their deliberative processes. It may rather be the case that one *already* has to think of law as actually being, or having the potential to be, moral in character, and capable of generating moral reasons for action, in order for what *Finnis* regards as its 'primary reality' to be something which initially occurs to you about law. Many people do not see law this way, and, arguably, and at least to some extent, with good reason.

Moreover, even if we do grant, *arguendo* that, at least for some, or for some in some situations, law is initially perceived as making a moral claim upon what we ought to do, why should we think that this therefore means that the first matters we ought to

---

[44] Finnis (2003b), 115 (my emphasis).
[45] Finnis (2003b), 129.   [46] Finnis (2003b), 129.
[47] Considerable empirical data supporting this point emerges from the ongoing project attempting to understand the causes and consequences of the riots in England in August 2011, 'Reading the Riots, Investigating England's Summer of Disorder', a collaboration between the *Guardian* newspaper and the London School of Economics, supported by the Joseph Rowntree Foundation and the Open Society Foundations and available online at: <http://www.guardian.co.uk/uk/series/reading-the-riots>.
[48] See 'Reading the Riots', especially the section entitled, 'Riots Were "a Sort of Revenge" Against the Police', available at <http://www.guardian.co.uk/uk/2011/dec/05/riots-revenge-against-police>.

investigate about law lie in its normative rather than its social character? For example, suppose that I accept that one of the first and initially important things to strike me about law is its claim to play a certain role in determining, morally, what I ought to do. It would not necessarily follow that I would conclude that the first thing(s) I should investigate about it are its moral point or purpose and whether and when it creates genuine reasons for action. Rather, given my understanding of the seriousness of the claim which law purports to make upon me—that it claims to operate in the domain of the moral, and to exclude and replace some of 'my own' reasons for action which I would otherwise act upon[49]—I might first of all think it sensible to establish matters such as: Where does this law come from? What is the exact character and structure of the claims which it makes upon me? What, precisely, does it demand of me? By whose purported authority is it a law? What will the consequences be if I do not obey it? All of these questions—which I may well view as having investigatory priority once I understand the nature of law's claim over me—can only be answered by delving into aspects of law's *social* character, such as the social sources whence it hails, and the practical reality of its means and modes of enforcement. Additionally, even if Finnis were to claim in response that I would seek answers to the above sorts of questions *in order* ultimately to know whether and when I ought to obey law, and to understand any moral purpose it may have, this does not change the point that I might well attempt to get there by first of all considering aspects of law's social character such as those mentioned above. Indeed, this point—that one reason why it is important to pick out and adequately explain certain 'social' features of law is that an understanding of them may, later down the line, facilitate the asking and answering of morally evaluative questions such as which values a legal system ought to live up to, and under what conditions are legal systems justified—was one which I made myself in *Evaluation and Legal Theory*.[50]

B. Finnis and explanatory priority #2

In Section III(B), I discussed EP #2, namely the idea of priority *qua* explanatory *dependence*: that subset A of law's properties explains and/or in some sense determines subset B such that the latter are explanatorily dependent on the former. Does some such relation of explanatory dependence hold in Finnis's theory as between law's normative and social properties? This is a difficult question to answer and one which may well repay further consideration. For now we can note that Finnis does appear to envisage some significant relations between, for example, law's positivity, and its overall moral point or value. Law's overall point or value—that of reasonably resolving coordination problems for the common good and so enabling us, in common, to pursue things of value in our lives—gives to posited law its point or purpose. According to Finnis, the reason why we have positive law is that certain features of it are particularly apt as regards resolving the coordination problems to which any society seeking in common to pursue the basic goods is necessarily subject. Moreover, this also

---

[49] Here, once again I follow the views of Finnis and Raz on this topic; see n. 5.
[50] Dickson, *Evaluation and Legal Theory*, Ch. 7.

reveals another kind of connection between law's positivity and its overall point or value: certain social features of law—including its positivity, its ability to pick out and promulgate those solutions the community has agreed upon (via its legal and political procedures) for now, its enforcement mechanisms, and abilities to stop 'free riding'— are necessary in order that law can fulfil its central moral task of reasonably resolving coordination problems for the common good. So law's overall normative point or purpose infuses posited law with its rationale; and law's positivity and other aspects of its social character enable law to function well as the resolver of coordination problems and so enable it to realise its overall normative point or value.[51]

As I mentioned above, the exact character of these connections would repay further consideration. However, it is already clear that whatever Finnis envisages in this regard, it is not the 'strong' sort of explanatory dependence discussed in Section III(B), such as features in Dworkin's view that law's overall point or value explains and determines all the other features of law, such as which propositions of law are true. Rather it seems that, for Finnis, law's positivity enables it to perform certain tasks which contribute to the successful attainment of law's overall point or value, and law's overall point or value infuses positive law's existence with a rationale, but that neither explains all aspects of, nor determines all features of, the other.

C. Some considerations concerning explanatory priority #3

As we have seen from the discussion in Section IV(A), Finnis regards the investigation and understanding of certain properties of law—namely its overall normative point or value, and its ability to generate reasons for action—as having explanatory priority in the sense that in developing our theories of law we should start by thinking about and trying to understand those normative aspects of law, rather than some of its social properties. Does this mean, however, that Finnis *also* regards law's normative point or value as having explanatory priority in the sense that it is more important than are other properties of law to the task of picking out and *identifying* law as a distinctive entity?

Interestingly, if this were to be Finnis's position then he would be espousing close to the diametrically opposite view to that held by Leslie Green in 'Law as a Means'.[52] As was discussed in Section III(C), in that paper, Green argues that the social means by which law operates are more specific to it, and hence will better help us to identify law and pick it out as something distinctive, than will other of its properties, namely any ends it may have. In my view, however, Finnis does not have a definitive position on this issue. Nonetheless, a few remarks can be made here which may begin to shed some light on the topic.

One point which is interesting to note in this regard is that it is possible to hold the view that law, in virtue of its nature, has an overall moral point or value, while rejecting the thesis that this aspect of law is more important than are other of its properties as

---

[51] These points arise throughout Finnis's work, but see e.g. Finnis (2003b); Finnis (2007c), especially Section 1; *NLNR*, *passim*, but especially Chs IX and X.

[52] Green, 'Law as a Means'.

regards picking out law and identifying law as a distinctive entity. For example, in 'About Morality and the Nature of Law',[53] Joseph Raz argues that law, by its nature, has a specific moral task to perform, namely:

> ... to secure a situation whereby moral goals which, given the current social situation in the country whose law it is, would be unlikely to be achieved without it, and whose achievement by the law is not counter-productive, are realised.[54]

However, Raz does not claim that this task is *unique* to law:

> I doubt that there are important tasks that are unique to the law, in the sense that they cannot at all be achieved any other way.[55]

On this view, then, as law is not unique in its moral task, focussing on that task may not be particularly helpful in picking out law as a distinctive entity.

Finnis, however, may well hold a different view on this issue which could affect his stance on EP #3. Finnis claims at certain points in his work that *only* law is capable of performing the task of reasonably resolving coordination problems for the common good.[56] If he is correct that *only* law can perform this task successfully, then this task, or at least its successful achievement, *will* be unique to law. If this were so, then, were we able to identify successful instances of the reasonable resolution of coordination problems for the common good of those living together in a political society, then, according to Finnis, we may, via this route, be able to identify that which—for him— counts as law.[57]

D. Finnis and explanatory priority #4: what makes law into what it is?

As was discussed in Section III(D), for Finnis, instances of legal systems which meet the relevant social facts criteria for accounting them as law (for example, they consist of norms of a practised system emanating from the social institutions of that system and meeting its intra-systemic tests for legal validity), but which fail in terms of fulfilling law's normative point or value (those norms and the system of which they are a part do not coordinate for the common good), are not really law,[58] less than fully law,[59] law only in a secondary, watered down, non-central or distorted sense,[60] or, simply, not law.[61] The social fact properties of law hence seem less central to law's nature, less central to its being law, for Finnis, than are its ability successfully to realise its overall normative point or value.

---

[53] Raz, 'About Morality and the Nature of Law'.
[54] Raz, 'About Morality and the Nature of Law', 12 (emphasis in original).
[55] Raz, 'About Morality and the Nature of Law', 11.
[56] *NLNR*, 3, and Chs IX and X, especially 232, 266–70; Finnis (1984b), 119–21, 133–7.
[57] Space precludes further investigation here of those aspects of Finnis's position which would be necessary to ascertain precisely his views on these issues, and of whether Finnis or Raz has the better argument regarding the uniqueness to law of any moral task it may have. See also Section IV(D) for further discussion of that which counts as law for Finnis.
[58] *NLNR*, 277–8.   [59] *NLNR*, 279.
[60] Finnis (2007c), Section 4.   [61] Finnis (2003b), 114.

As was also mentioned in Section III(D), Finnis's views on this matter are underlined further by a response he gives in an exchange with Joseph Raz, noted in 'Law and What I Truly Should Decide':

> On the occasion of the Lecture, Joseph Raz asked why law should be thought to be like argument, medicine or contracts, rather than like novels or paintings, or people, that still novels or paintings, or people, even if they are bad. One answer is that, like argument, medicines, and contracts, law has a focused and normative point to which everything else about it is properly to be regarded as subordinate. Novels and paintings, on the other hand, can have incompatible points, e.g. to entertain or arouse (like kitsch or porn) or to tell a truth with artistry. People exist in the natural order as living substances even if they are not functioning adequately or at all in the orders of logic and thought, deliberation, and/or exercises of skill.[62]

However, this promotion of law's normative point or value, and concomitant demotion of its social fact properties as regards what makes law into what it is, is extremely problematic, both in itself, and specifically as regards Finnis's claim that his brand of natural law theory can adequately account for and do justice to law's social nature and to its positivity.

Finnis's stance is problematic per se for the following reasons. Legal systems are institutionalised normative systems in which interrelated norms are created, modified, applied, and enforced by social institutions such as legislatures, courts, and tribunals, the police and other executive agencies. In any jurisdiction governed by law, some such institutions exist and they and the norms they generate and apply have a deep and pervasive impact on the social reality of those living in the society in question. People fall under the jurisdiction of the legislature, courts, and other legal institutions, are subject to their norms, stand liable to have them forcefully applied to them in case of non-compliance, and know and view as important these characteristics of law. More-over, these features of law, and their impact on the lives of those living under it, persist irrespective of whether law successfully realises any moral point or value which it may have. Law and people are hence not so disanalogous as Finnis claims in the quotation above: although the social reality of law is very different in character from the biological reality of people, both persist even when those entities fail to live up to those standards which they ought to, and both are properties of considerable importance in demar-cating those entities' character and making them into what they are. In the case of law, the importance of those social properties stems from the fact that law's social and institutional character plays a deep and pervasive role in people's lives irrespective of its moral justification, and from the fact that those living under law regard those social features of law as important and significant.[63] Law's social facticity—the fact that it is 'out there' in and has a profound effect upon the social reality of people's lives irrespective of whether it fulfils any normative point it may have—is hence something extremely significant about law which it is important to foreground and adequately explain in accounts of its nature. It is not something to be regarded as subordinate to

---

[62] Finnis (2003b), 114, n. 9.
[63] For further discussion of this point, see Dickson, *Evaluation and Legal Theory*, 59–60, 120–1, 139–43.

other of law's properties and hence of significantly reduced importance as regards making law into what it is.

In addition to being problematic per se, Finnis's demotion of law's social and posited character also casts serious doubt on his claim that his brand of natural law theorising can adequately account for and do adequate justice to the social aspects of law. As is argued above, the social and posited character of law is extremely important as regards people's self-understanding in terms of law, and in terms of the deep and pervasive impact on people's lives which these properties of law have. In claiming that such properties are of significantly less importance to law's nature than its normative point or value, Finnis fails to do adequate justice to these aspects of law or their effects on those living under law. Finnis's claim that his natural law theory sufficiently explains both law's normative and its social properties thus rings hollow.

V. Conclusion

This essay has sought to discuss an important duality of law—that law is both a social and a normative phenomenon—and has examined John Finnis's general theory of law in terms of its ability adequately to account for and explain this duality. In the course of the discussion, I have explored four different senses of explanatory priority which feature in contemporary jurisprudential methodology. In my view, differentiating between and properly understanding these senses of explanatory priority will help us better to understand the character of jurisprudential claims and what grounds them. Finnis's distinctive brand of natural law theory has been critically examined in light of these priorities in order that we may probe further his particular commitments as regards his view of the nature of law, and of the nature of the theory of law. Despite Finnis's claims that his general account of law does adequate justice to both law's normative and its social character, I have argued that this is not in fact the case, and that aspects of his stance unacceptably demote law's social properties in terms of their importance for the nature of law, and for our understanding of the nature of law. Notwithstanding this conclusion, however, I hope that it is apparent that I regard John Finnis's views on law and its theory as a rich and rewarding source of jurisprudential debate.

Bibliography

Dickson, J. (2001), *Evaluation and Legal Theory* (Oxford: Hart Publishing).

Dickson, J. (2003), 'The Central Questions of Legal Philosophy' in M. Freeman (ed.), 56 *Current Legal Problems*, 63–92.

Dickson, J. (2004), 'Methodology in Jurisprudence: a Critical Survey', 10 (3) *Legal Theory*, 117–56.

Dickson, J. (2009), 'Is Bad Law Still Law? Is Bad Law Really Law?' in M. Del Mar and Z. Bankowski (eds), *Law as Institutional Normative Order* (Farnham, Surrey: Ashgate), 161–86.

Dickson, J. (2012), 'Legal Positivism: Contemporary Debates' in A. Marmor (ed.), *The Routledge Companion to Philosophy of Law* (New York: Routledge), 48–64.

Dworkin, R. (1986), *Law's Empire* (London: Fontana Press).

Gardner, J. (2001), 'Legal Positivism: 5 ½ Myths', 46 *American Journal of Jurisprudence*, 199–227.

Gardner, J. (2007), 'Nearly Natural Law', 52 *American Journal of Jurisprudence*, 1–32.

Green, L. (2010), 'Law as a Means' in P. Cane (ed.), *The Hart-Fuller Debate in the Twenty-First Century* (Oxford: Hart Publishing), 169–88.

MacCormick, N. (1992), 'Natural Law and the Separation of Law and Morals' in R.P. George (ed.), *Natural Law Theory: Contemporary Essays* (Oxford: Clarendon Press), 105–33.

MacCormick, N. (2007), *Institutions of Law, an Essay in Legal Theory* (Oxford: OUP).

Raz, J. (1986), *The Morality of Freedom* (Oxford: Clarendon Press).

Raz, J. (1990), *Practical Reason and Norms* (2nd edn, Princeton, NJ: Princeton University Press).

Raz, J. (2003), 'About Morality and the Nature of Law', 48 *American Journal of Jurisprudence*, 1–15.

Raz, J. (2007), 'The Argument from Justice, or How not to Reply to Legal Positivism', in G. Pavlakos (ed.), *Law, Rights and Discourse: The Legal Philosophy of Robert Alexy* (Oxford: Hart Publishing), 17–36.

Raz, J. (2009), *Between Authority and Interpretation* (Oxford: OUP).

'Reading the Riots, Investigating England's Summer of Disorder', a collaboration between the *Guardian* newspaper and the London School of Economics, supported by the Joseph Rowntree Foundation and the Open Society Foundations, available online at: <http://www.guardian.co.uk/uk/series/reading-the-riots>.

23

Finnis on Legal and Moral Obligation

Maris Köpcke Tinturé

'The law...tries to isolate..."legal thought"...from the rest of practical reasoning' (318),[1] says John Finnis. Legal thought 'systematically restricts' the 'feedback' of moral considerations on legal requirements (312). In 'strictly legal thought', the strength of one's moral reasons for conforming to law 'never becomes a topic of consideration' (317). 'In contemplation of law', legal obligation is 'invariant in force' (317) and has a 'black-and-white quality' (312): '[t]here are, legally speaking, no degrees of legal obligation, just as there are no degrees of legal validity' (309). The 'methodological counterpart' of this, according to Finnis, is the 'legal postulate' that there are no gaps and no conflicts in the law (269, 311). The law 'presents itself as a seamless web',[2] and as such claims to occupy the same space in our deliberations as morality.[3] But it does not claim to be morally obligatory, Finnis argues: it only claims to be legally obligatory.[4] A reasonable person, however, will presume, defeasibly, that the law creates a generic moral obligation of variable force and extent.[5]

The purpose of this essay is to unpack and evaluate this intriguing set of propositions. They bring together some of the central themes in Finnis's legal philosophy and, I will argue, they are best understood in light of those wider themes. These propositions appear at a crucial juncture in *Natural Law and Natural Rights* (*NLNR*): they are primarily developed in the two core sections (XI.3 and XI.4) of Chapter XI on Obligation, by far the longest and one of the most difficult chapters in the book. They encapsulate Finnis's position on the moral need for positive law—that is, on the *moral* need for legal thought to *isolate* itself from moral thought. They provide the essential link between Finnis's portrayal of positive law (in Chapter X) and his conclusions about the moral obligations that positive laws may generate (in Chapter XII).

Part of what makes these propositions complex, and worth unpacking in some detail, is that they are not fully explained in the pages in which they are formally stated. For the argument of Chapter XI has a peculiar structure, a structure which reflects a key methodological insight that in some ways runs through the entire body of Finnis's work. The explanation of obligation in Chapter XI proceeds along a series of 'levels of explanation'. It starts with an account of facts about people's behaviour and attitudes relating to obligations, and gradually moves towards a critical consideration of the practical reasoning (actual or potential) of the persons involved. That shift of

---

[1] Bracketed page and chapter references in the main text are to *NLNR*.
[2] *CEJF* IV.2, 50; *CEJF* IV.3, 71.
[3] Finnis, 'Jurisprudence: Some Main Questions', lecture 6.
[4] Finnis, 'Jurisprudence: Some Main Questions', lecture 6; Introduction to *CEJF* IV, 6, n. 13.
[5] *NLNR*, 318–9, 359–61, 362, 473–4; *CEJF* IV.2, 46ff.

emphasis from a third-person report of what *other people* speak of and treat as reasons for action, to a *first-person* engagement with such reasons *qua* (good) reasons, unfolds along a number of stages, such that each stage builds upon the previous one and yet transcends it—a bit like opening a Russian doll, layer after layer. The propositions reproduced at the start, which appear relatively early on in the chapter, only gain their proper significance when interpreted in the context of the further layers of analysis that Finnis digs through in the latter half of the chapter, and in related texts.

The methodological insight reflected by the structure of Chapter XI can be summed up as a gradual move *from fact to reason*. In a recent essay on Hart, Finnis evokes this methodology with a memorable analogy suggested to him by his mentor. Hart once remarked to Finnis, self-referentially, that what started his interest in philosophy, as a boy, was the breakfast cereal packet. As Finnis explains the remark: 'from the 1890ies [. . .], packets of Quaker oats have depicted a substantial Quaker man holding a Quaker oats packet depicting a substantial Quaker man holding a packet of Quaker oats . . .'[6]

Finnis shows in that essay that Hart's legal philosophy made progress by 'prioritiz-ing. . . the internal attitude or attitudes to law' (230) and 'our inner lives of thought, judgment, and decision' (231). Finnis aims to capitalize on that progress and that method of building up an account of law. But unlike Hart's, Finnis's account of law is built up, self-consciously, by following a long chain of moral argument, a chain reflected in the structure of Part II of *NLNR*, in the structure of *Aquinas* (1998), and again in the very sequence of the five volumes of *Collected Essays* (2011). The chain of thought begins at basic, pre-moral experiences and insights about what is good and bad in human life, and stretches all the way through the importance of groups and communities to the need for justice, and to law's ability to help secure it (and finally considers ultimate questions about the point of doing good and being just). Characteristically, the first sentence of Volume I of *Collected Essays* discusses the act of deliberation—the act closest and most immediate to the reader. And Volume IV, on legal philosophy, opens with the reflections of a seven-year-old (you or me, some decades ago) faced with a first exposure to an everyday injustice. In Chapter XI of *NLNR* and elsewhere, Finnis's methodology moves—as did once the eyes of the young Hart at breakfast—from what is most immediate, easily observable, to what is less apparent but richer in meaning and can shed new light on the reality we apprehend.

Our most immediate object of analysis is the text of Chapter XI of *NLNR* and related passages, such as the endnotes to it and the Postscript's remarks about it. Therefore, the next section summarizes Finnis's argument, retaining the original order of exposition so as to chart the sequence of explanatory levels that make up the discussion of legal obligation. In Section II I try to reconstruct the key idea of the law's isolation from moral reasoning, and in Section III I consider whether and why the law's isolation (thus understood) is morally needed. The final section raises some doubts about Finnis's view that it follows from this argument that the law does *not* claim to be morally obligatory.

---

[6] *CEJF* IV.10, 231.

I. Chapter XI of *Natural Law and Natural Rights*: An Explorer's Report

After some introductory clarifications on the jargon of 'obligation' in Section XI.1, Section XI.2 discusses promissory obligation, 'that form of obligation with which the word has a particular affinity' (298). A promissory obligation is seemingly created by the very act of signalling one's intention to assume that obligation. Finnis considers a first level of explanation of this phenomenon, focused on the language and attitudes which make up the practice of promising, and then a second level of explanation, focused on the significance, in a person's practical reasoning, of the adverse consequences that follow a promise's breach. He finds that neither of these two kinds of account can satisfactorily explain why promises bind or even why they are judged to bind, particularly promises the breach of which is likely to go undetected. The binding force of promises can only be made sense of by a 'third-level' explanation that concentrates on the moral need, for the common good, of the practice of promising. Finnis develops this 'third-level' explanation at some length (303–8). He portrays the moral need for the practice of promising in terms of its enhancement of individual autonomy, its ability to sustain fairness amongst persons who share the benefits of shouldering comparable burdens, its role in shaping human identity and relationships and, generally, its capacity to durably solve coordination problems for the benefit of all. The point of this practice would be defeated, says Finnis, if one's expression of an intention to be bound were not a necessary (albeit not a sufficient) condition for one's being so bound (308).

This analysis along three levels is then applied to legal obligation. Section XI.3 begins by observing that legal obligation, unlike promissory obligation, is 'invariant' in force (though not in content): as a matter of law there is no room for defendants to plead that their legal obligation was diminished or outweighed by competing non-legal obligations (311), and only exceptionally, through designated institutions, does the legal system permit the 'feedback' of non-legal 'value' or 'policy' considerations on legal requirements (312). This 'invariant' or 'black and white' quality of legal obligation, he says, 'is part of the data, which an explanation of law must take into account and explain (and not explain away)' (312). But, as he goes on to show, it is not adequately explained by either a 'first-level' analysis focused on 'social pressures', or by a 'second-level' analysis which looks only to coercion or similar unwelcome social pressure (313–4). Section XI.4 therefore offers a 'third-level' analysis of legal obligation.

In so doing, Finnis distinguishes two senses of 'legal obligation': 'legal obligation in the legal sense' (or 'in the intra-systemic sense', or 'in contemplation of law'), and 'legal obligation in the moral sense'. The first sense of 'legal obligation' is the lawyers' sense: it is the sense routinely used by legal professionals or laypeople in pointing out that some kind of conduct is required by law. The second, moral, sense expresses the speaker's view that what is legally obligatory in the first sense is truly, all-things-considered, i.e. *morally* required of the subject(s) in question. (In other writings Finnis refers to this second sense as simply the 'moral obligation to obey the law'.)[7]

Legal obligation in the moral sense, says Finnis, is 'relatively weighty' (319) but 'variable in force' (318). He represents it with the following simplified schema of practical reasoning, which is the 'good citizen's' reasoning schema:

A. We need, for the sake of the common good, to be law-abiding;
B. But where ϕ is stipulated by law as obligatory, the *only* way to be law-abiding is to do ϕ;
C. Therefore, we need [it is obligatory for us] to do ϕ where ϕ has been legally stipulated to be obligatory (316).

The obligation, expressed in the conclusion C, gains its force from the first, moral, premise A, in conjunction with the second, predominantly factual, premise B. But the strength of premise A 'will vary according to the subject-matter of the law and the circumstances of a possible violation' (318). (I discuss this further in Section III.) Unlike legal obligation in the moral sense, legal obligation in the *legal* sense is 'invariant' and 'black-and-white'. The law, says Finnis, 'anticipates' the good citizen's schema of reasoning and seeks to give it 'an unquestioned or dogmatic status' (318). 'Whence'—he asks—this unquestioned status, this 'legally invariant force of legal obligation'? He answers: 'from step B, taken together with an interpretation of step A as an undiscussed postulate, isolated by legal thought from the general flow of practical reasoning' (316–7). So, on this analysis, the fundamental difference between legal obligation in the legal sense and in the moral sense is that, in the case of the legal sense, step A (and, by implication, steps B and C) is 'isolated' from moral reasoning—isolated, that is, 'from those general values and principles' which can 'give[] it as a premiss a moral force' (317, 318), a force that would be 'variable'. The legal sense of legal obligation, Finnis adds, is the primary concern of 'specifically legal science' (319) and perhaps also of 'positivists', who rightly insist on tracing the 'sources' of legal rules in 'past acts and facts' (320).

At this point Finnis announces that the rest of the chapter will 'consolidate the analysis of both these senses of "legal obligation"...by considering two long-standing controversies', one about the legal sense and one about the moral sense, and then 'using that discussion to clarify the precise role of the legislator's..."will" in the creation and explanation of obligation' (320–1). He does not say it explicitly, but in so proceeding the rest of the chapter adds new 'levels of explanation' to the three he has nominally envisaged thus far.

The controversy about legal obligation in the legal sense that he selects for consideration (Section XI.5) concerns whether the obligation generated by contracts should be understood, legally, as an obligation to perform what was undertaken, or as a disjunctive obligation to *either* perform *or* pay compensatory damages. Finnis observes that this second reading, defended by Holmes, is not continuous with actual legal rules and

---

[7] The distinction between the first and second senses also echoes the distinction between 'detached' and 'committed' statements of legal obligation (Raz, *Practical Reason*, 171–7; *NLNR*, 320 with 234ff); I will not explore these parallels here.

would serve the common good rather poorly (besides effectively dissolving the notion of obligation). Notice that a disjunctive understanding of legal obligation is not the same as a 'second-level' explanation that reduces obligation to the coercive threat of sanction (or other unwelcome social pressure): even if it is unlikely that the sanction will be exacted, the disjunctive *obligation* (to either perform or undergo the sanction) still holds good. The disjunctive understanding and its rejection add a further refinement, indeed a further 'level', to a 'third-level' type of explanation: they stress that what follows from steps A and B is precisely C, the positive direction to ϕ, rather than an alternative direction to *either ϕ or* pay damages.

The controversy about legal obligation in the moral sense (Section XI.6) has a structure similar to the controversy about the legal sense. It concerns whether, and if so when, the obligation imposed by positive laws should be understood, morally, as an obligation to perform the stipulated act, or instead as a disjunctive obligation to *either* perform the act *or* submit to the legal penalty. According to Finnis, medieval and early-modern Spanish jurists who endorsed a version of a 'purely penal law theory' held, in essence, that positive laws impose a disjunctive moral obligation whenever the law-maker so intended.[8] The reason why this controversy matters is not that it exposes the flaws of a disjunctive understanding of legal obligation. They have already been exposed in XI.5. The reason it matters, as Section XI.7 begins to make plain, is that it exposes the flaws of an understanding of legal obligation as being purely the *effect of the law-giver's will*. And this mistaken understanding repays discussion because it builds unsoundly on a sound consideration that is worth dwelling on: namely, that the law-giver's will—his or its sheer decision—is an important aspect of legal obligation, in both the moral and the legal sense. Indeed, legal obligation (in the standard case)[9] arises upon the law-giver's expression of will. This is part of the very meaning of the above syllogism, in steps B and C: to say that the law 'stipulates' ϕ is (in the standard case) to say that someone (person or body) with legal authority has declared that ϕ ought to be done.

Defining the precise *role* of the law-giver's will yields a new level of explanation of legal obligation (in both senses). This level of explanation has crucial but not fully expressed parallels to the initial discussion of the promisor's will. As Finnis puts it, legal obligation arises upon, but is not created precisely and simply by, the law-maker's expression of will. Contrary to what the 'purely penal law theory' suggests, the law-giver cannot choose to impose or withhold obligation from a stipulation. A law-making stipulation of ϕ is a sheer fact which, to give rise to an obligation, must be inserted—as a minor, factual premise—into 'a normative framework *which is not of the law-giver's making*' (335).[10] The law-maker's deliberate stipulation is a necessary but not a sufficient condition for the obligation to arise.

---

[8] More or less crude ways were proposed to ascertain the law-maker's 'will' to that effect, including the law's verbal formulation, the stipulation of a sanction, or subtler pointers such as tradition, the sanction's severity, or the importance of the subject matter (325–30).

[9] This simplifies the important truth (recently stressed by Finnis: Introduction to *CEJF* IV, 5–6; *NLNR*, 472) that in a legal *system* there is typically no one-to-one correspondence between the legal meaning of a discrete law-making act and the propositional content of a complete legal rule.

[10] Finnis explains this through analogy with delegated legislation (*NLNR*, 332–4).

And yet, this minor premise can be further unpacked. There is a sense in which the sheer stipulation, although it is only a factual precondition of the obligation, can *itself* be taken to reflect and express the *full* syllogism. This unravelling of the law-giver's act of will is done in Section XI.8: yet another layer of obligation is peeled off. Finnis argues that the law-giver's stipulation (in the central case) expresses the law-giver's *imperium* (341). One's *imperium*, as Aquinas explained, is the last stage in the process leading to a free and deliberate human act: it involves the rational representation to oneself, before (and in) acting, of the value of one's objective and the appropriateness of one's chosen action as a means to it.[11] What motivates me to act by carrying out my choice is not merely the fact that I chose so to act, but my understanding of the *point*, the (prospective) benefit, of that action. And understanding the point of my action means understanding the means-ends relationship that renders that precise action worth undertaking (and in some cases also necessary and/or obligatory). My *imperium* is my representation-to-myself of that means-ends relationship: it is my 'formulated resolve to act' (342). The *imperium* of a reasonable law-giver, therefore, is his representation-to-himself of the value of the common good and the appropriateness of (stipulating) φ as a means to it. In other words, the propositional content of the law-giver's *imperium* is the full syllogism A–C. This is why the 'good citizen' can reasonably treat the law-giver's expressed *imperium* 'as if it were his own *imperium*' (341), and why it makes sense to say that the law-giver 'anticipates' the 'good citizen's' reasoning (318) in making the stipulation. Roughly speaking: the stipulation *is* premise B, but it *expresses* premises A–C.

In an ultimate level of explanation, Section XI.9 (in conjunction with Chapter XIII) explores the foundation of moral obligation itself, showing it to be relatable, albeit not reducible, to a sheer 'exercise of divine will'. I will not discuss this here.

The journey of thought that unfolds in Chapter XI, from fact to reason, starts by observing that in some social practices certain acts of will are taken to have obligatory force, and explains that obligatory force (and at the same time the practice of making such predications of obligation) in terms of the reasons for the relevant practice, summarized in a practical syllogism. Legal obligation in the legal sense, it is argued, is the conclusion of that practical syllogism when the syllogism is 'isolated' by legal thought from unrestricted moral reasoning. The conclusion of the syllogism rests on the important factual premise of somebody's deliberate act of stipulation: a sheer fact, yet itself (in the central case) a response to reasons for the practice. For, as Finnis says in an endnote, 'the genuine "logic of the will" ... is the logic of practical reasoning (349)'.[12]

II. Law's Isolation: What Is It?

An important step in this journey of thought is somewhat undeveloped: the idea of an *isolated* syllogism. That legal obligation in the legal sense is 'invariant', 'black-and-white' and relatively 'isolated' (317, 318, 320), 'sealed off' (355) or 'detached' (319) from moral reasoning is the distinctive feature or set of features of legal obligation

---

[11] *NLNR*, 338ff; *Aquinas*, 68 and 71 with 63, 256–7.
[12] And in the Postscript: 'will is one's *responsiveness* to reasons for action (...)' (*NLNR*, 475).

which Finnis highlights at the start of Section XI.3 as something in need of explanation (and not to be explained away). Section XI.4 does indeed repeatedly refer to such isolation: we are told that, inasmuch as the syllogism is 'artificially isolated' (320) from moral thought, step A is treated as a 'framework principle or postulate' (317) whose 'basis and force... never becomes a topic for consideration' (317); but that it can always be 'relocated' (318) or 'integrated' (320) in the flow of moral reasoning and thereby given 'moral force' (318). However, beyond these metaphoric formulations, relatively little is said in Section XI.4 to make clear just what this isolation or 'insulation' (344, 354) consists in, how it is effected, and what reality or set of realities it refers to. And, from Section XI.5 (320) onwards, the idea of the law's isolation is never nominally returned to. For everything Finnis discusses from that point on is a clarification of the practical syllogism as such (namely, of its conclusion C and of the 'stipulation' in step B). But the practical syllogism is the *common* basis of explanation of the legal and moral sense of legal obligation. The idea of isolation is a feature of the legal sense only: it is precisely what *distinguishes* the legal sense of legal obligation from the moral one.

In fact, as Finnis suggests in the Postscript (473), the idea of the law's isolation is touched on in a range of different passages in the book, including Chapter XII (355–6) and (albeit not nominally) Chapter X on Law. Building on these passages, and Chapter XI as a whole, this section and the next will try to reconstruct and state Finnis's position on what he himself calls '[the] concern' of Chapter XI: namely, 'to explain the practical reasons for a working postulate of legal thought, and the consequences of the postulate in legal reasoning' (344).

The present section argues that the idea of the law's isolation from moral reasoning is best understood as a combination of four different elements, which I will call: positivity, determinacy, ease of identification, and conclusiveness.

(a) *Positivity:* A starting point to understand Finnis's position on this matter, which is the classical position, is the insight that law is positive. By this I simply mean that legal requirements are determined by the legal meaning of human law-making *acts* (usually deliberate),[13] *rather than* by appeal to moral considerations which are not part of the legal meaning of law-making acts. Law-making acts are the 'acts of stipulation' referred to in step B of the practical syllogism. Law is, in an important sense, the result of human acts of will. This idea runs through the entire book, and is expounded in particular in Chapter X on Law.[14] As Finnis puts it in XII.3,

> The enterprise of exercising authority through law proceeds by positing a system of rules which derive their authority not from the intrinsic appropriateness of their content but from the fact of stipulation in accordance with rules of stipulation (355).

'Not from the *intrinsic* appropriateness of their content' does not rule out the possibility that judgments of appropriateness, including moral appropriateness, are legally

---

[13] Finnis speaks of 'past acts' (*NLNR*, 269, 268) or 'past acts or facts' (320), which include, prominently, 'acts of deliberate or at least datable creation or amendment' (320). At the end of Chapter X he generically refers to the 'act of "positing" law' (290).

[14] Especially at 268–9 (on the law's 'special technique' of treating 'past acts' as giving reasons to act in the present), and again at 320 (where Finnis also speaks of 'sources'); see further *CEJF* IV.12, 296–7.

relevant to establishing what the law requires *in so far as posited rules make these judgments legally relevant*. Indeed, criteria of legal validity set out by the corresponding 'rules of stipulation' (power-conferring rules) may, and usually will, refer not only to questions of 'form and originating fact' but also to questions of 'content',[15] and either kind of question, but especially the latter, may (though it need not) involve moral judgment. It will involve moral judgment where, for example, a law stipulates that 'unfair' agreements are unenforceable, or that 'arbitrary' administrative decisions are void (and no legal definition of these terms is given).[16] When criteria of validity thus include moral tests, it may well be that 'what would otherwise be an indubitable legal obligation is in truth not (*legally*) obligatory because it is unjust' (356–7). But in so far as criteria of validity do not include moral tests, or the right kind of tests, or in so far as a doctrine of finality takes hold (e.g. *res judicata*), there remains, on Finnis's account, a standing possibility that what is legally required is not morally sound.[17]

The affirmation of law's positivity, thus understood, is an all-or-nothing position. It does not, as such, take a stance on how many and which moral tests of validity a legal system can afford to be 'permeated by' (356). The more the moral tests of validity, the less the law is 'isolated' from morality. This issue falls under the next two headings.

(b) *Determinacy*: Finnis argues that the law 'presents itself' as a 'seamless web',[18] that is, as a wholly determinate set of rules. It is a 'working postulate' of legal thought, he says, that there are 'no gaps' (269) in the law and 'no overlapping and conflicting legal duties' (311). (The latter is the 'methodological counterpart' of the 'invariability in the formal force of every legal obligation' (311).) Gaps and unresolved normative conflicts cause the law to be *pro tanto* underdetermined. A prominent source of gaps in the law is the use of vague legal language, and very especially the use of (legally undefined) moral terms and concepts.[19] This is because moral requirements in many ways radically underdetermine what ought to be done in numerous concrete situations, as Finnis elaborately shows in the central chapters of *NLNR*. If a law stipulates that 'unfair' agreements are invalid, only the validity of clearly fair and of clearly unfair contracts is legally determinate: in so far as a contract's fairness is (morally) indeterminate, so is its legal validity. Strictly construed, the postulate 'no gaps' would entail, amongst other things, 'no moral criteria'. Although, as Finnis notes, the postulate is fictitious (269), it is worth asking what truth there is to it so that it could be plausible to attribute to law this self-presentation.

Complete determinacy of law (absence of gaps) at any particular point in time is not conceivable, even barring human error. For it would rule out the distribution of decision-making authority on which every legal system relies by empowering officials and private legal agents to change legal positions within a pre-existing legal framework. Determinacy through time—what we might call diachronic determinacy—is more

---

[15] *CEJF* I.1, 19.

[16] For the contrary view, Raz, *Authority of Law*, 75; Gardner, 'Justification under Authority', 23, 71–2; I cannot discuss here why I think this contrary view is misguided.

[17] For: 'It is not conducive to clear thought ... to smudge the positivity of law by denying the legal obligatoriness *in the legal or intra-systemic sense* of [the relevant unjust] rule' (*NLNR*, 357).

[18] *CEJF* IV.2, 50; *CEJF* IV.3, 71.   [19] Endicott, 'Raz on Gaps', 107–8.

easily conceivable. A mature legal system does, in principle, have the ability to settle, through a stipulated procedure, any question in need of settlement which has not been settled already.[20] The broad jurisdiction of a legal system's courts, coupled with the legal doctrine of precedent, do indeed suggest that legal systems strive towards complete diachronic determinacy, and (for that same reason) not towards complete synchronic determinacy. And yet, as Finnis's discussion rightly suggests, legal systems typically strive to be *synchronically determinate to a degree*. Familiar symptoms of this ambition include the 'casuistical refinement of legal rules', the 'legal effort for exhaustiveness and coherence of stipulation' (311) and the pervasiveness of 'analogical reasoning'. The extent of the law's determinacy varies greatly between different areas and levels of legal regulation. But overall, from a primarily descriptive standpoint, it is probably true to say that an organization could not de facto succeed in coercively regulating many forms of conduct across a wide territory and population unless it provided sufficiently precise directions on a sufficiently wide range of matters. So, if only for the sake of efficacy (we will consider other reasons in Section III), a working legal system needs to (amongst other things) 'systematically restrict' the 'feedback' on legal reasoning of open-ended moral standards: it needs to make sure that step A is not too often 'relocated' in unrestricted moral reasoning and its moral force assessed. One way that legal systems carry through this 'restriction' is by empowering specific institutions, such as supreme courts, to conduct a moral assessment of legal requirements, an assessment from which other elements of the system are debarred (e.g., a supreme court empowered to overrule its own previous decision on grounds of moral error).

(c) *Ease of identification*: Even moral questions that have determinate answers may be ill-suited to serve as tests for the validity of law. This is because moral questions, even to the extent that they are rationally determined, are controversial as a matter of fact. People of different cultural backgrounds, natural abilities, or ideological outlooks do in fact strongly disagree about what is reasonable or fair. In order for a legal system to be efficacious, however, a critical mass of the population must be able broadly to converge on identifying what counts as a legal requirement (identifying, that is, either directly or with the aid of professionals). Hence, also for this reason, legal systems must (for the sake of efficacy) 'restrict' the occasions and the respects in which identifying legal requirements turns on moral (and otherwise controversial) judgment. This is particularly manifest in the bulk of routine transactions and ordinary dealings, as well as in situations where certainty is so paramount that adherence to certain procedural steps (forms, stamps, signatures, etc.) may be taken *legally* to override a breach of other legal rules: as with, for example, property registry entries, notarial deeds, or *res judicata*. Finnis implicitly raises the point about ease of identification when discussing the law's role in settling disputes in large human communities.[21]

---

[20] A legal gap exists in so far as the law fails definitely to settle (including settlement via a closure rule) a question in need for definite settlement, a need typically established by pointing to a relevant similarity to a justiciable question already definitely settled; this is compatible with the discussion in Raz, *Authority of Law*, 70–7.

[21] E.g. *CEJF* IV.3, 71; *CEJF* IV.12, 296–7; *CEJF* IV.10, 244; *CEJF* IV.13, 302, 314; *NLNR*, 269, 279.

(d) *Conclusiveness*: Assume that the content of your legal obligation has been determined, with or without moral tests, perhaps only after the supreme court has pronounced. It is now fruitless to plead that your legal obligation, thus determined, is '*outweighed* and *diminished* or *deferred* or in some other way *modified* by other considerations, however "reasonable"' (311). The law is conclusive: it will not take into account any considerations that have not themselves been anticipated or catered for by the system's provisions, either directly by being built into general rules as exceptions, exemptions, excuses, justifications, etc., or indirectly by a conferral of discretion on the relevant officials ('*de minimis*' rule, sentencing bands, pardon, etc.). In a sense, conclusiveness is linked to determinacy: given the law's 'postulate' that it has settled or can now settle all questions in need for settlement, the law cannot consistently accept that its final settlement is validly defeated by other considerations. Typically, the law is at its most determinate and conclusive in legally final decisions. A main difference between determinacy and conclusiveness, and hence a reason for discussing these issues separately, is that the content of the 'postulate' of determinacy is not generally true as a matter of fact, but conclusiveness is. The law *will not* accept a pleading like the above.

Finnis does not say that legal obligation in the legal sense is conclusive. He says that it is 'invariant in force': that all legal obligations in the legal sense are 'of the same strength'.[22] I prefer to speak of conclusiveness (or non-defeasibility) rather than of invariance, because the term 'invariance' has an ambiguity. The penalties for legal wrongs vary greatly: some are rather mild, some are very harsh. This might reasonably be taken to mean that, in contemplation of law, there are degrees of wrongfulness: all penalized kinds of conduct are wrongful in contemplation of law, but some are more seriously wrongful than others. Important debates on the proportionality of penalties focus on this issue. It is probably implausible, and at any rate unnecessary, to hold that all legal obligations are of the same strength in *this* sense, in the sense of moral seriousness. When Finnis points out that the law does not legally authorize subjects to second-guess their obligations once legally determined, he means that legal requirements are always *non-defeasible* in contemplation of law. They can be non-defeasible (in contemplation of law) even if they vary in moral seriousness (in contemplation of law). Step A is 'undiscussed', 'unquestioned' (318): it is not for the subject to discuss, to question, the suitability of ϕ as a means to the common good. In contemplation of law, what you ought to do, all things considered, is precisely ϕ: whether by a wide or a narrow margin, the balance of reasons is tilted in favour of you ϕing. As Finnis sometimes puts it (following Raz), the law purports to provide protected reasons[23]: that is, reasons that reflect what the subject ought to do, and that are not amenable to being outweighed or defeated by a range of other ('excluded') reasons that would otherwise bear on what he ought to do.

Finnis also calls legal obligation 'black-and-white' and 'all-or-nothing', synonymously with 'invariant'. 'Black-and-white' and 'all-or-nothing', I think, express the

---

[22] He synonymously speaks of 'formal invariance' (*NLNR*, 313), 'all-or-nothing deontic force' (314), and '*equal* obligation in law of *each* obligation-imposing law' (318).

[23] *NLNR*, 319 with IX.2 (233ff) and endnote 255.

conjunction of conclusiveness with determinacy. In so far as the law is determinate, it gives a *definite* answer (279) to the two main questions it is in the business of answering: namely, whether a given kind of conduct is obligatory (prohibited) or not, and whether a given kind of conduct amounts to an exercise of legal powers (and so is legally valid) or not.[24] This is why the 'black-and-white' quality of legal obligation is comparable to that of legal validity (309, 312). There are only two possible answers to either question. The law is determinate in so far as it definitely answers *either* one thing *or* the other; it is underdetermined in so far as it gives both answers, or neither, or no clear answer. Conclusiveness, by contrast, speaks to the *quality* of the two options that the law is to definitely choose between. The law is to definitely choose whether a kind of conduct is non-defeasibly obligatory, or not obligatory at all. It is to definitively choose whether a kind of act is legally (fully) valid, or not valid at all. The choice is one between two extremes: either 'all' (non-defeasibly obligatory, valid) or 'nothing' (not at all obligatory, not at all valid)—either 'black' or 'white', not either 'dark grey' or 'light grey'. The law is to definitively settle a choice (determinacy) between two extremes (conclusiveness).

We can now link together all the elements that constitute the law's 'isolation'—the isolation of the syllogism from the 'general flow of practical reasoning', the isolation of 'strictly legal thought' from moral thought. There is a sense in which the isolation, as Finnis describes it, is absolute: 'invariant', 'no degrees', 'black-and-white', 'all-or-nothing'. And there is a sense in which the isolation, as he describes it, is a matter of degree: 'systematically restricts', 'tries to isolate', 'wherever it reasonably can' (320), 'permeated by' (356). Each of these senses corresponds to two aspects of the isolation, as I have portrayed it. It is absolute in the first and fourth respects: all law is positive, and all law is conclusive in its claimed obligatory force. But it is a matter of degree in the second and third respects: the law 'restricts' but does not eliminate the 'feedback' of moral considerations in determining the content of legal requirements. The less restriction, the less determinacy and ease of identification. The four aspects build on one another. That law is positive is a prerequisite of it being sufficiently determinate and easy to identify to serve as a common standard. And legal requirements must be (made) determinate before they can be conclusive.

III. Law's Isolation: What Is It For?

So far I have looked at the law's isolation primarily as a fact. I have sought to single out this peculiarity of legal obligation in the legal sense. In an efficacious legal system, law is positive, conclusive, and relatively determinate and easy to identify. But we will learn more about the law's isolation if we consider it not merely as a fact but as a response to reasons—as Finnis recommends that we do. It is time to ask about the 'practical reasons' for this feature of legal thought: to ask, that is, about the *moral* reasons for the law's *isolation* from morality.

---

[24] This corresponds to Hart's sound (and widely accepted) individuation of legal norms into duty-imposing and power-conferring (Hart, *The Concept of Law*, especially Ch. 3).

Finnis's answer corresponds to what he calls the moral sense of legal obligation. But, as he himself notes in the Postscript (473), this sense is insufficiently explained at the place where it explicitly 'comes into view' (Section XI.4, 318–9; and, one could add, Chapter XII.3), and should be understood in connection with the discussion of fairness in the section on promissory obligation (XI.2) and in some other writings[25] (including the Postscript at 473–4). We have a *presumptive* generic moral obligation to obey the law, Finnis argues. The presumption can be defeated if the law is unjust in any of the ways identified in Chapter XII.2 (352–4), but there is a reason why there is a presumption in the first place. The reason, which is packed into steps A and B (interpreted in the full moral sense), has to do with the moral need for the techniques and structures of a legal system. The common good of human communities, says Finnis, especially because it is open-ended and can take many different forms, calls for public, general, and stable mechanisms for the coordination of manifold kinds of human conduct. The characteristic techniques and procedures of legal systems are uniquely suited to furnish this needed coordination, primarily by publicly settling on concrete requirements that respond to, but are often more specific than, moral standards; and, secondarily, by securing compliance with those requirements. Only *law* can do this settling and enforcement in a way that is fair, reliable, and predictable across a wide range of subject matters and periods in time.

The very elements that make up the law's isolation are central to the law's ability to thus coordinate. Settling on concrete courses of conduct characteristically calls for a process of *determinatio*: that is, for rendering open-ended moral standards more 'determinate', by drawing lines where morality does not draw any. A coordination problem, in the sense relevant here, arises where attaining a morally needed goal requires a collective course of conduct (which may involve any combination of action, abstention, tolerance, etc.), and there are in principle two or more available and appropriate—but mutually exclusive—routes which, if collectively followed, would bring about the goal. The existence of *more than one* available and appropriate route is sometimes the result of indifference between the options (should we drive on the left or right?), and sometimes the result of incommensurability (should we ban firearms?). Either way, such bifurcations are constantly encountered by law-makers designing a detailed and workable plan for a community to live together. In selecting *one* route to the exclusion of others, at *each* juncture, reasonable law-makers *determine*—give concrete shape to—what justice requires of individuals on specific occasions. And in being publicly marked, the chosen route becomes salient[26] and so capable of being convergently followed, and *pro tanto* morally obligatory. Because morality, as such, is too underdetermined and controversial to provide the concrete guidance, public salience, and predictability we need, something other than morality ought to be the 'source' of our common standards: law ought to be positive, relatively determinate, and conclusive in its force, and legal validity ought predominantly to turn on easily identifiable factors that many different people can broadly converge on.

---

[25] He quotes from *CEJF* IV.3, 70–2.
[26] E.g. *CEJF* IV.2, 59, 60, 63–4; *CEJF* IV.3, 67, 70; *CEJF* IV.5, 150; *CEJF* IV.10, 256.

The benefit of treating decision-making *acts* as 'sources' of law lies not merely in the fact that they bring into our dealings a degree of determinacy and ease of identification that morality, as such, lacks. More can be said about the *kind of act* to which legal systems typically attribute law-making force, and the reasons for this. Finnis's discussion at the end of Chapter XI gets us into the right zone. He portrays a law-making act as being *itself* (in the central case) a response to the reasons for having law, a response made up of an interplay between 'reason' and 'will' (properly so called): the reasonable law-maker, having chosen ('willed') one of the various appropriate patterns of conduct, stipulates it as legally obligatory on the strength of his understanding that doing so (going ahead with that underdetermined choice) is a suitable means to the common good and that the chosen pattern of conduct, because chosen and legally stipulated, is (as from now) morally obligatory. What kind of act is this stipulating? It is not just any voluntary act. It is not just any expression of an intention. It is an act that expresses the acting person's, the law-giver's, intention to do something (and that does it) *by the very expression of that intention*. More concretely, it is an act whereby the acting person expresses his intention to bring about a change in normative positions (and that does so) *by the very expression of that intention in a designated form*. The nature of exercises of legal powers is an intricate and fascinating topic. Suffice it to note here what Finnis points out when discussing promises (XI.2, 308), and when characterising the main features of a legal order (X.3, 269). There is good reason for attributing law-making significance to this kind of act, and not to other kinds of expressions of intention or voluntary acts. This attribution yields a technique that enables individuals and groups knowingly to shape, now, the framework of their own and/or other people's future relationships, in a way that does not excessively cramp human communication or sacrifice certainty to spontaneity.

Each of these benefits of the law's isolation comes with some inevitable drawbacks. Or perhaps they are not so much drawbacks as part of the 'package deal' of being governed by a relatively predictable framework of general rules and stable institutions.[27] Over- and under-inclusiveness are unavoidable consequences of the existence of sufficiently determinate general rules, which draw lines beyond the point where right reason calls for a distinction. '[E]xquisite refinement and narrowness of draftsmanship' (311) can reduce but can never fully eliminate this vice. The stipulated form for valid exercises of legal powers promotes ease of identification and certainty, but may also belie the subject's actual intentions or yield a nullity for mere defect of form. Positivity entails that what has been decided is decisive, whether or not I would have voted for it, and whether or not anyone should have voted for it. And a conclusive decision may well be mistaken on the facts or on the law, and yet become legally final as the opportunities for appeal or collateral challenge elapse.

None of these drawbacks necessarily amounts to an injustice of a kind that could outweigh, from the point of view of the common good, the benefits of the rule of law. There is, so to speak, a *range* of drawbacks which it would be unjust *not* to tolerate and go along with. For—as Finnis insists—they correspond, directly or indirectly, to

---

[27] For a discussion of such 'drawbacks', see Köpcke Tinturé, 'Law Does Things Differently'.

benefits for other community members (and myself), who in turn on other occasions shoulder comparable burdens which directly or indirectly benefit me. It is only fair for me (barring serious injustice) to take the benefits of community life along with its burdens, burdens more or less closely linked to the law's isolation like paying my share of tax, complying with formalities that enhance certainty, or acquiescing in a misguided resolution that puts an end to a wearying dispute. This rationale of fairness amongst persons, combined with the acknowledgement that legal technique brings inevitable rigidities and imperfections, yields the essential truth behind step B: the law is entitled to be treated, presumptively, as a 'seamless web', as a *system* of rules 'which cannot be weighed or played off one against the other' (317) and so are generically morally binding. Because not every drawback will exceed the tolerable range, it makes sense to start one's assessment with a *presumption* that what is experienced as an inconvenience or burden is in fact a practically inevitable symptom of the law's morally needed isolation. In short: both the benefits *and* the inevitable drawbacks of the law's isolation warrant the presumption that what is obligatory in law is also morally obligatory.

However, where the drawbacks or errors *do* exceed the tolerable range, the presumption is defeated and the law's moral binding force is qualified in force and extent. Moderate under-inclusiveness may be not unjust, but, for example, disproportionate discrimination is, and so is a judicial mistake that effects a serious setback to critical human interests. Legal obligation in the *moral* sense (the 'moral obligation to obey the law') is 'variable', i.e. defeasible in force: there is a standing possibility that steps A and B lose some or all of their purchase in the face of some kind of injustice that overrides the very good reasons for having a system of positive law.

IV. Does the Law Claim to be Morally Obligatory?

Finnis explains legal obligation in the legal sense by appeal to the same practical syllogism that expresses the moral obligation to obey the law, and argues that in the legal sense the syllogism is 'isolated' from moral reasoning. I have discussed what this isolation amounts to in practice, and why it is a good thing. I am now interested in a further interpretation of this reality. The idea that the law treats premises A and B as 'unquestioned' suggests that the law treats them as being always satisfied, fulfilled. Presumably, this is why legal obligation in the legal sense is of 'invariant' (conclusive, non-defeasible) force, and why legal obligation in the moral sense—which allows one to second-guess the premises—is of 'variable' (defeasible) force. It makes sense, in my view, to say that the law presents itself as being non-defeasibly (conclusively) morally obligatory. After all, the law can hardly intelligibly present itself as being unjust, that is, as placing unreasonable burdens or otherwise exhibiting flaws of the kind that could defeat or override the law's moral obligatory force. The thought that the law presents itself as being non-defeasibly morally obligatory reminds one of the idea, popular with some writers, that the law *claims* to be (non-defeasibly) morally obligatory.[28]

---

[28] E.g. Raz, *Ethics in the Public Domain*, 215–6; Raz, *Authority of Law*, 158–9; Simmonds, *Law as a Moral Idea*, 138–40; Gardner, 'How Law Claims'; Endicott, 'Interpretation, Jurisdiction', 17; see further Alexy, *Begriff und Geltung des Rechts*, 65ff.

Perhaps surprisingly, in recent works Finnis has categorically denied the proposition that the law claims to be morally obligatory.[29] The law, he says, contextually and implicitly claims to be legally obligatory, and to be reasonable. But it does not claim to be morally obligatory. The reason why some may find Finnis's position surprising is that several passages of *NLNR*, although they do not explicitly take up this issue, appear to commit him to the very proposition he denies. For a start, unlike other authors, Finnis has no significant quarrel with the idea that 'the law' makes a 'claim'. The 'claim', he rightly says, is 'contextual and implicit'; as Simmonds and Soper put it, attributing a claim to law is not the description of a fact but a way of making sense, theoretically, of our settled understandings about law and its morally intelligible purpose.[30] Finnis speaks in this same spirit of the law 'present[ing] itself' as seamless. He also intriguingly refers to the legislator's 'expressed *imperium*, the promulgated "intention of the legislator"' (341). Whatever is meant by such 'expression', it is clearly not a literal, verbal expression in the wording of the promulgated stipulation, for what is thus 'expressed' is the legislator's *imperium*, that is, the full *moral* A–C syllogism which in turn 'anticipates...the "good citizen's" schema of practical reasoning' (318). This is not what we literally read in most legal texts.

And indeed, the idea that 'the law' implicitly makes a moral claim, expresses a moral syllogism—or at least its moral conclusion—seems quite naturally to follow from Finnis's characterization of legal obligation in the *legal* sense in terms of a *moral* syllogism, a syllogism that, moreover, in its extended version uses the very same notation ('if p, q, r, then $XO\phi$') to represent the moral obligation and the legal sign that 'signifies' the legal obligation (315–6). The only difference in notation is that the formula appears in *quotation marks* when it refers to the legal sign (316)—suggesting that the expressed legal obligation is truly a *claimed* moral obligation, not a different species of practical necessity. Finnis repeats that the law's version of the syllogism would be 'empty' (316, 317, 355) were the corresponding piece of moral reasoning not available. I agree: what could be the non-moral sense of 'need...for...the common good' (316)? Finnis insists that there is such thing as 'normativity (and thus obligation) which is *legal* (and so far forth not moral)',[31] but I am not able to find in Chapter XI, to which he points, a positive characterization of legal normativity (obligation) as a distinct entity, not reducible or explicable by reference to (a claimed) moral obligation. The weight of the argument in that text is carried by the idea of isolation. But I have explained at some length what this idea plausibly refers to, and I have not needed to appeal to 'legal normativity'. Finnis says that the law claims to 'occupy the same space in practical reasoning...as morality'.[32] But what else, other than a *moral* syllogism, could be 'offer[ed]' (317) to the 'good citizen' for adoption as 'his own' (341)? In the last analysis, what else, other than morality, can occupy the space of morality—can be as 'decisive for choice'[33] as morality?

---

[29] Finnis, 'Jurisprudence: Some Main Questions', lecture 6; Introduction to *CEJF* IV, 6, n. 13.
[30] Simmonds, *Law as a Moral Idea*, 138–40; Soper, 'Law's Normative Claims', 215–8, 229–31.
[31] Introduction to *CEJF* IV, 6, n. 13.
[32] Finnis, 'Jurisprudence: Some Main Questions', lecture 6.
[33] Finnis, 'Jurisprudence: Some Main Questions', lecture 6.

An argument Finnis has given for his denial that the law makes a moral claim is that 'legal thought' has 'moments of isolation' such as '*res judicata*': a potentially mistaken final decision is to be applied by other elements in the legal system as though it were correct (although possibly everyone involved knows that it is not). But this argument is not convincing. Perhaps the decision is truly unjust, but the law cannot plausibly admit to this. We are left with an 'incorrectness' of a kind that is an inevitable downside of systemic, large-scale coordination. But as we have seen, and Finnis himself stresses, there is a moral reason for such 'isolation' of legal thought, indeed a reason so strong that it warrants a presumption *in favour* of the law's generic moral binding force. The law's isolation from morality is morally required, and so does not stand in the way of a moral claim: if anything, it warrants the claim. The law can plausibly claim that an incorrect (but not unjust) *res judicata* decision is morally needed, and thus morally binding.

The real ground behind Finnis's position must, I think, be found in a distinction that perhaps becomes clearest in *Aquinas* (163–4) and the Introduction to *Collected Essays*, Vol. IV (6–7, 8).[34] On Finnis's view, the strength of the law's moral binding force is reduced or extinguished not only where a legal rule *as such* is unjust, but also where a legal rule—even a just rule—conflicts with a particular subject's moral responsibilities arising in particular circumstances. All affirmative moral obligations, says Aquinas, are subject to the second kind of override: they hold '*semper sed non ad semper*' (always but not on every occasion).[35] They necessarily become subject to exceptions—defeasible— as they are brought to bear on particular circumstances. Finnis regards the obligation to obey the law as an affirmative moral obligation, and so as subject to exceptions and overrides down to a degree of specificity that cannot possibly be anticipated or otherwise catered for by even the most careful law-maker and the most conscientious law-applier. Therefore, he appears to conclude, were the law to make a *moral* claim, it would either have to be a claim to be non-defeasibly binding—which cannot be true, and so cannot plausibly be attributed to law; or it would have to be a claim to be defeasibly binding—which sits uneasily with the law's refusal to accept non-legally-recognized moral overrides (conclusiveness). Hence, Finnis reasons, the law cannot intelligibly be said to make a moral claim.

Pace Finnis, I do not think it is implausible to attribute to law the claim that it is non-defeasibly morally binding, binding *semper et ad semper*. For what is true of general moral norms—namely, that they 'leave it to one's moral judgment to discern the times, places, and other circumstances of their directiveness'[36]—is *not* true of the moral obligation to obey the law in contemplation of law. The law's effort is precisely to take over that very specification (*determinatio*) of general moral norms, offering its stipulations as authoritative determinations of the times, places, and other circumstances of the moral norms' directiveness. Any mature legal system has a range of mechanisms to carry out a wide-ranging specification of moral duties, both *ex ante* by incorporating the specification into general rules (explicitly or contextually), and via mitigating policies of diverse kinds at the stages of application and enforcement.[37]

---

[34] It is foreshadowed in *CEJF* IV.17.   [35] *Aquinas*, 164.

[36] *Aquinas*, 164.   [37] One might add 'equity' and 'desuetude' (*CEJF* IV.17, 372).

Moreover, as Finnis points out, there is a sense in which a legal system claims to be gapless (Section II(b)): and this means that it claims to have taken into account all relevant considerations, to have settled all questions in need for settlement, and therefore, plausibly, to have built in all relevant moral overrides—not just some. It may be unlikely, in practice, for a legal system to cater for all relevant overrides; but then it is unlikely for a legal system to be wholly gapless, or wholly reasonable, and yet we meaningfully speak of the law claiming as much.

We attribute a claim to law as part of our effort to render law morally intelligible. '[T]o refer to what "the law" claims', says Soper, 'is to refer to what any sensible individual ... in the position of a representative of the legal system ... ought to recognize as the implicit claim that accompanies such official action'.[38] My sense is that we cannot render the law morally intelligible unless we understand it to claim (contextually and implicitly) vis-à-vis the convict that he failed to do what he had a moral obligation to do *in the particular circumstances*—which include the circumstance that the potentially imperfect (but not unjust) moral specification he disobeyed was part of a legal system that in some respects needs to be overbroad, blunt, or otherwise 'isolated' from morality in order to fulfil a morally urgent task that is the responsibility of all.

Bibliography

Alexy, Robert (1992) *Begriff und Geltung des Rechts* (München: Karl Alber) (translated into English as *The Argument From Injustice: A Reply to Legal Positivism* (Oxford: OUP, 2003)).

Endicott, Timothy (2003) 'Raz on Gaps—The Surprising Part', in L. Meyer, S. Paulson and T. Pogge (eds), *Rights, Culture and the Law: Themes from the Legal and Political Philosophy of Joseph Raz* (Oxford: OUP), 99.

Endicott, Timothy (2007) 'Interpretation, Jurisdiction, and the Authority of Law', *American Philosophical Association Newsletter on Law and Philosophy* 6, 14.

Finnis, John (2008) 'Jurisprudence: Some Main Questions', lecture 6 at the Faculty of Law, University of Oxford, 13 May 2008 (transcript on file with the author).

Gardner, John (2008) 'How Law Claims, What Law Claims', in M. Klatt (ed.), *Institutionalized Reason: The Jurisprudence of Robert Alexy* (2012) (Oxford: OUP).

Gardner, John (2010) 'Justification under Authority', *Canadian Journal of Law and Jurisprudence* 23 no. 1, 71.

Hart, H.L.A. (1994) *The Concept of Law* (2nd edn, Oxford: OUP, 1994).

Köpcke Tinturé, Maris (2010) 'Law Does Things Differently', *American Journal of Jurisprudence* 55, 201.

Raz, Joseph (1975) *Practical Reason and Norms* (London: Hutchinson).

Raz, Joseph (1979) *The Authority of Law* (Oxford: OUP).

Raz, Joseph (1995) *Ethics in the Public Domain: Essays in the Morality of Law and Politics* (rev. edn, 1995) (Oxford: OUP).

Simmonds, Nigel (2007) *Law as a Moral Idea* (Oxford: OUP).

Soper, Phillip (1996) 'Law's Normative Claims', in R. George (ed.), *The Autonomy of Law* (Oxford: OUP).

---

[38] Soper, 'Law's Normative Claims', 218.

24

Constitutional Principle in the Laws of the Commonwealth

*Richard Ekins**

I

Reflecting on the residual constitutional links between the United Kingdom and Australia, John Finnis, then Rhodes Reader in the Laws of the British Commonwealth and the United States in the University of Oxford, stressed 'that the constitution (small "c") includes not only the law that judges can declare and enforce on the motion of litigants, but also the conventions that responsible ministers and legislatures (all those persons whom I will call "authorities") acknowledge as authoritative and binding'.[1] This positive law and these conventions are in turn framed and supported—animated—by constitutional principles, which are 'not merely a matter of general normative propositions' but rather are 'those elements of the common good which the law [and practice] of our constitution articulates and promotes'.[2] This essay considers a fraction of Finnis's study of constitutional principle, attending to some of the ways in which the constitution informs how the political community acts over time for the common good, as well as to why the unity and identity of that community is itself a matter of constitutional principle.

II

From 1968–1976, Finnis wrote essays on constitutional law in the *Annual Survey of Commonwealth Law*.[3] The essays outlined and considered recent developments in the constitutional practice of the members of the British Commonwealth, surveying legislative and judicial action, as well as political change more generally. Of particular note is Finnis's attention to the judicial response to the revolutions or *coups d'état* in Pakistan, Uganda, Rhodesia, Cyprus, and Ghana. This analysis informed his 1971 paper, 'Revolutions and Continuity of Law'.[4] The target of that paper—the first of his two notable contributions to the series *Oxford Essays in Jurisprudence*[5]—was Kelsen's theory of discontinuity, viz. that every breach of an original historical constitution forms a new constitution and hence a new legal system. This theory distorted the attempts by judges to reason about their duty in the wake of revolutionary change,

* I thank the Marsden Fund of the Royal Society of New Zealand and to the Federalist Society for their support. I am grateful also to Nicholas Aroney, Grant Huscroft, Paul Rishworth, Philip Sales, Grégoire Webber, Paul Yowell, and especially John Finnis for helpful comments. The usual disclaimer applies.

[1] 1983a, 91–2.   [2] *CEJF* III.9, 134.
[3] 1968b; 1969a; 1970d; 1971c; 1972e; 1973f; 1974a; 1975; 1976a.
[4] *CEJF* IV.21.   [5] The other is *CEJF* II.1.

suggesting that the courts had either to stand by the pre-revolutionary constitution under which they were appointed or to adopt in full the revolutionary constitution. Not so, Finnis argued in his *Annual Survey* essays: the courts need not make any such stark choice and the fact of past appointment, at the time by lawful power, warranted the continued discharge of judicial duty.

Kelsen's theory of discontinuity proved unable to explain either how coups occur within a continuous legal system or how lawful devolution is possible. The attempt by some scholars to argue that the coup does not fracture the original constitution failed, for the coup is defined by unlawful departure from rules of succession. Yet this is the only change the coup need involve and all other legal rules may remain valid and continue in force until such time as repealed or amended. Likewise, the legal rules in force prior to independence continue after independence and the ground for their validity remains that they were enacted by the exercise of lawful authority, notwith-standing that the legislative body in question, say the Imperial Parliament, no longer has authority to change the law of the newly independent system. In this way, past rules of recognition remain relevant to legal reasoning. Finnis argued that this present relevance of past action is consistent with the law and logic of repeal, in which repealed lawmaking acts may retain, in various ways, legal significance. These reflections culminated in his insight into the general principle of continuity: 'A law once validly brought into being, in accordance with criteria of validity *then in force*, remains valid until *either* it expires according to its own terms or terms implied at its creation, *or* it is repealed in accordance with conditions of repeal in force *at the time of its repeal*.'[6]

The principle is a central entailment of the very idea of positive law, for:

> ... the general principle presupposes, expresses, and realizes (or secures) the most general and basic *function* of 'the law'—namely, to relate the past to the present, by providing a present guide to actions which take place and have effect in the future (when this present will be in the past).[7]

This passage foreshadowed Finnis's later articulation of the nature and point of positive law. The reason to take past acts to settle the present in this way is to make possible a stable, fair form of social life, in which persons (and communities) have the capacity by acting now to settle what will be done in the future, and thus to plan their (and our) lives over time. The principle's central implication is that 'the continuity and identity of a legal system is a function of the continuity and identity of the society in whose ordered existence in time the legal system participates'.[8] Indeed, the general principle is a disposition of the political community, especially of the officials who represent the community, a disposition that follows from the reasonableness of ordering public life in this way. One sees the disposition, and its limits, in Lord Mansfield's judgment in *Campbell v. Hall*,[9] maintaining (inter alia) that the laws in force in some conquered or ceded territory continue in force, save for laws contrary to fundamental principle (say, authorising torture or outlawing Christianity). Here, the Crown recognises the

---

[6] *CEJF* IV.21, 63.   [7] *CEJF* IV.21, 65.   [8] *CEJF* IV.21, 69.
[9] (1774) 1 Cowp 204; see further 2003k, [878].

continuity of law, tempered by assertion of its own capacity to rule and refusal to maintain certain unjust laws, even in the absence of explicit repeal.

The continuity of law turns on the continuity of the political community: after unconstitutional change, valid legal rules need not, per the general principle, derive from the new rule of recognition. Still, the general principle does not entail legal pluralism. The continuing relevance of past rules of recognition, such that what the Queen in Imperial Parliament *enacted* settles the law for Australia, does not mean that the legal system includes multiple, unranked rules of recognition. Equivocation about the location of lawmaking authority is reckless. The past rules of recognition, and the present rules of identification that point to them, are not derived from, but may very well be subordinate to, the new rule of legislative competence.[10]

The general principle's centrality to how a reasonable community constitutes itself over time bears on how EU law stands within the UK. The repeal of the European Communities Act 1972 would plainly be a significant act. Would its repeal merely terminate the continuing lawmaking competence of the organs of the EU, such that, per the general principle, the body of EU law at the time of repeal would continue in force until later repealed by particular Acts of the Westminster Parliament? No, the repeal would terminate the continuing validity of past propositions of EU law within the UK, such that Acts disapplied by reference to s. 2(4) of the 1972 Act would again direct how one should act. The reason for this conclusion—the discontinuity of EU law—is that at no time have the criteria for legal validity in the EU been accepted on their own terms by the political community of the UK. Rather, that community, by way of a particular rule valid by reference to its criteria (in relevant part: what the Queen in Parliament enacts is law), made provision for the content of another legal system to have effect within its own legal system.[11]

The rules of European law were not made in accordance with criteria of validity in force in the UK at the time of making. They do not continue beyond the demise of the rule that gives them legal force in the UK (absent a savings clause). This confirms the obvious, but neglected, point that the UK continues to conceive of itself as a distinct political community, apart from the EU. The relationship between them is not analogous to a state in a federation that has a constitutional right of secession (or a dominion within the imperial constitution that may lawfully devolve, on adoption of the Statute of Westminster perhaps). For the state (or dominion) forms part of a larger political community and shared criteria for lawmaking (at the federal, imperial level) prevail throughout the entire community. By contrast, the UK (like other member states) remains a distinct political community which makes provision for the rules of the EU to have (some) effect within its territory, the scope and nature of which effect is to be settled by the constitutional order of the UK, notwithstanding the EU's insistence on the supremacy of its law over contrary national law.

---

[10] *CEJF* IV.21, 58–9.
[11] The proposition made out in this paragraph has been affirmed in the European Union Act 2011, s. 18.

III

The central reality of lawful devolution is not unconstitutional rupture but the recognition of (the emergence of) a distinct political community, which has its own common good and its own capacity to act to secure that good by way of reasoned self-government. For this reason, the typical provisions of an Independence Act announce that from some appointed date Her Majesty's Government in the United Kingdom shall cease to be responsible for the territory in question and subsequent Acts of the Parliament of the United Kingdom shall not extend to the territory as part of its law.[12] The termination of legislative responsibility for former colonies has not always been so clear. For the UK Parliament long retained responsibilities under the constitutions of some independent communities that formerly were but parts of the imperial whole. The question of how these responsibilities should be exercised illuminates the central-ity of constitutional conventions and principles, in addition to positive law, in the constitution and turns, again, on judgments about the nature—the character, even—of the communities in question.

The Statute of Westminster 1931 made provision for the lawful devolution of (in effect) sovereignty to the Dominions, empowering the Parliament of each Dominion to enact laws repugnant to imperial statute and with extra-territorial effect. However, s. 7 provided that nothing in the Act was to apply to the repeal or amendment of the British North America Acts 1867 to 1930 (the BNA Acts), which were central to the consti-tution of Canada. That is, any such repeal or amendment would continue to require legislative action on the part of the Parliament of the United Kingdom. In 1980 and 1981, the question arose whose request was necessary and sufficient to legitimate amendment of the Acts by the UK Parliament. The Canadian Government argued forcefully that it spoke for the independent state of Canada and that the UK authorities should therefore not look behind any federal request for amendment of the Acts; whatever role the provinces might play in relation to amendment was of no concern to the UK. The Foreign Affairs Committee of the House of Commons undertook to inquire into the role of the UK Parliament in relation to the Acts and especially to determine whether the UK Parliament was indeed bound by convention or principle to act automatically on any request from the Canadian Government. Finnis served as advisor to the Committee and its three reports bear his unmistakable mark.

The question before the Committee was not one of strict legality, for the UK Parliament's power to amend the Acts (with legal effect in Canada) was never in dispute; neither of course was the truth that Canada is, and was then, an independent state. Rather, the question was how the UK Parliament should exercise its competence to amend the BNA Acts. The Committee's first report set out a very thorough study of the precedents, which consisted in past requests for amendment and the responses on the part of the UK authorities, both before and after the enactment of the Statute of Westminster.[13] The report identified the central principles that should inform the UK Parliament's constitutional responsibility. First amongst these was the federal principle:

---

[12] 2003k, [719].   [13] 1981a.

Canada is a federally structured community. The UK Parliament's responsibility was to act in response to the wishes of the Canadian people, expressed in a way consistent with its federal nature. Thus, when a proposed amendment had some bearing on the scope of provincial powers and responsibilities, the concurrence or otherwise of the provinces was relevant to how the UK Parliament should receive a federal request for amendment. The precedents to this effect were grounded in sound principle.

The UK Parliament was not strictly the guardian of the provinces *qua* provinces. Instead, it had to respond to a request from Canada as a federally constituted people. While it was not for the UK Parliament to judge the merits of any proposed amendment, it had a duty to consider the constitutionality of the process of request, for it had been invited to continue to exercise, and in the Statute of Westminster had reluctantly agreed to continue to accept, this very responsibility. This was responsibility within the Canadian constitutional order, per the principles and precedents of that order, within which the federal nature of Canada was central. Hence, it would be wrong to subvert this responsibility by acquiescing in a claim that the federal government spoke for Canada in relation to foreign states, including the UK: the UK Parliament was not acting as a foreign state in exercising its power to amend the constitution of Canada. Still, this residual responsibility, and the importance of the federal nature of Canada, did not entail any duty to investigate whether the provinces consented. It was reasonable for the UK Parliament to presume consensus until such time as provincial opposition was made known by way of the proper channels. Further, the responsibility of the UK Parliament to respond to a proper request from the Canadian people did not entail any requirement of provincial unanimity. It would be unreasonable to insist on unanimity, for this would frustrate the principle of constitutional self-determination, viz. that the community should have the capacity to constitute its governing arrangements. And the constitutional actors in the Canadian federation at no relevant time proceeded on the basis that even fundamental constitutional self-determination was conditional on unanimity—rather, they took substantial consensus to be sufficient.

The Committee's careful report elicited a sharp, argumentative response from the Canadian Government to which the Committee replied in turn and in kind.[14] The Supreme Court of Canada's subsequent decision on the constitutionality of the proposed federal request closely (albeit silently) followed the path set out by the Committee's reports, in particular their fundamental distinction between law and convention *within* the category of *constitutional requirements*, and their solution to the unanimity question.[15] The sound grasp of the principles and conventions governing the exercise of the UK Parliament's residual responsibility—a grasp not manifested by the posture of the UK and Canadian governments in 1981—helped avoid the surrender to an unconstitutional federal request for change notwithstanding considerable provincial opposition.[16] In this way, the UK Parliament did its duty in evaluating the constitutionality of the process that culminated in its enactment of the Canada Act 1982 (UK). Confronted by the Supreme Court's judgment on the

---

[14] 1981c.
[15] *Reference re Amendment of the Constitution of Canada* (1981) 125 DLR (3d) 1.
[16] 1981d.

convention-based requirement of substantial consensus, and the strong possibility that the UK Parliament would decline to act in defiance of that requirement, the Canadian federal and provincial governments negotiated until they attained the required degree of consensus (short of unanimity).

The principles relevant to Canada extended also to Australia. Writing in 1983, three years before the Australia Act 1986 (UK), Finnis argued that the UK Parliament's residual responsibilities in the Australian constitution (which is much more than the Constitution of the Commonwealth of Australia[17]) turned on the federal structure of that constitution, such that these responsibilities could not rightly be undermined by appeal to the Federal Parliament's external affairs power (an appeal similar in kind to the Canadian Government's). For in this context the UK Parliament was not an external power, but one which acted or could act within the Australian order, given the invitation to do so, and acceptance of such. The rationale for the principle that governed the exercise of this residual responsibility was the significance of preserving federal structure, not for its own sake but because this remained the way the community was ordered, which should not be lightly overthrown, certainly not by way of a formal schema that denies the continuity of the legal orders and the consequences of such principled continuity for the constitutional order. Hence the UK Parliament should (and did) understand its constitutional position in this way. Again, as in Canada, Finnis's close engagement with the legal and political history illuminated the relevant practice, which grounded his articulation of relevant principles going to the federal nature of the polity and the constitutionality of processes of constitutional change. Thus, in relation to both Dominions, the UK Parliament's residual responsibility was to assist the exercise of collective self-government consistent with the federal form.

The resolution of these questions, and the reasoning of the UK Parliament's cross-party select committee, confirms that the constitution is more than its positive law. It was rational for the Canadian people to repose trust in the UK Parliament, which exercised that authority consistent with the principles that focus on the constitution-ality of process (rather than the merits of amendment), to which the nature of the Canadian political community and the good of its self-rule were relevant. The reality, vitality, and constitutionality of this kind of political responsibility are often overlooked.

IV

The theory of responsible government was and is central to the imperial constitution. The separation of powers for which that constitution made provision, and which framed responsible government, was in issue in the *Bancoult (No. 2)* litigation,[18] where leading English judges entertained a challenge to the vires of an Order in Council reinstating restrictions on entry and residence in the British Indian Ocean Territory

---

[17] 1983a, 92.

[18] See especially: *R (Bancoult) v. Secretary of State for Foreign and Commonwealth Affairs (No. 2)* [2007] EWCA Civ 498, [2008] QB 365; and *R (Bancoult) v. Secretary of State for Foreign and Commonwealth Affairs (No. 2)* [2008] UKHL 61, [2009] 1 AC 453.

(BIOT). These restrictions, made other than by Order in Council, had been struck down four years earlier in *Bancoult (No. 1)*[19]; they had been imposed with a view to the building and maintaining of an important US military base, with the agreement of the UK Government. The application challenged the making and content of the Order on a range of public law grounds: ultra vires, irrationality, and breach of legitimate expectation.

The Foreign Secretary argued that the Colonial Laws Validity Act 1865 (CLVA) settled the validity of colonial laws, including Orders in Council, and left the court with no jurisdiction or right to impeach such laws on the grounds of their repugnance to the English public law of judicial review. The Court of Appeal, like the Divisional Court, disagreed. For, Sedley LJ reasoned, the CLVA concerned the *priority* of otherwise valid law—colonial law, imperial statute, and the common law of England—not the *power* to enact law.[20] The modern judicial power to review the exercise of the royal prerogative was not recognised in the nineteenth century, which means that the kind of challenge mounted to the legislative act in this case could not have been in the minds of the drafters or legislators in 1865.[21] Therefore, he concluded 'the 1865 Act had neither the purpose nor the effect of barring all such challenges'.[22]

In a working paper later relied on in part in argument before the House of Lords,[23] Finnis refuted the Court of Appeal's account of the origin, point, and legal effect of the CLVA.[24] In settled colonies, the Crown had no capacity to legislate while a representative legislature existed (and even otherwise it had only constituent power, viz. to establish a legislature and other authorities). In ceded/conquered colonies, per *Campbell v. Hall*, the Crown had prerogative power to legislate but not to legislate contrary to fundamental principles.[25] For some settled colonies, the imperial statute instituting legislative power imposed a qualification along the lines that 'no such law should be repugnant to law of England'.[26] The Law Officers in their Opinions of 1862, 1863, and 1864, which led to the enactment of the CLVA, advised that this invalidated laws in violation of fundamental principle, but that there was no clear way to discern the fundamental from the non-fundamental. These references to 'fundamental principle' were imported to settled colonies from the regime for conquered/ceded colonies and Orders in Council for their governance.[27]

The legislative aim, Finnis inferred, was to abolish the whole repugnancy doctrine, which had become standard in settled colonies (where the Crown rarely legislates), but had its origin in relation to ceded/conquered colonies (where the Crown routinely legislates), which itself had been made the standard for other imperial territories.[28] Therefore, Parliament would have reasoned, one should address ceded/conquered colonies and other imperial territories by making provision for *some* Crown legislating to come within the new freedom from invalidation by way of repugnance—viz. the most public, responsible kind of prerogative legislative act, which is an Order in

---

[19] *R (Bancoult) v. Secretary of State for Foreign and Commonwealth Affairs (No. 1)* [2001] QB 1067.
[20] *Bancoult (No. 2)* (CA) [22].   [21] *Bancoult (No. 2)* (CA) [23–4].
[22] *Bancoult (No. 2)* (CA) [25].   [23] [2009] 1 AC 453, 465 and 470.
[24] 2008e.   [25] 2008e, [2].   [26] 2008e, [3].
[27] 2008e, [4].   [28] 2008e, [6].

Council rather than letters patent or other acts. The Court of Appeal's judgment that the CLVA concerns priority not powers was unsound. Boothby J, the wayward Adelaide judge, would often declare local legislation void on the grounds that the legislature had no *power* to enact laws repugnant to English law.[29] The CLVA aimed (i) to eliminate a doctrine qualifying the power of makers of colonial law by reference to fundamental principles of the common law, principles and doctrine which had pervaded the entire imperial constitution, and (ii) to reaffirm the supremacy of imperial statute.[30] It follows that the Act's 'reference to voidness (and thus to validity), especially as distinguished from and coupled with reference to inoperacy, must be taken to deal with both power and priority, at once'.[31]

On the merits, the CLVA aside, the Court of Appeal had held that the Crown's power to legislate for BIOT was limited to the peace, order and good government of *that* territory, such that its exercise for the defence interests of the United Kingdom was unlawful. This holding turned on a serious misreading of the authorities on 'peace, order and good government'. More significant still, argued Finnis, its account of the relationship between the UK and its territories was unsound. The court's narrow focus on the interests of BIOT echoed the Lords' ruling in *Quark*[32] that royal instructions communicated to a colonial governor by the Foreign and Commonwealth Secretary are not acts of the UK Government and cannot be given in the interests of the UK. That decision, Finnis explained, was flatly unconstitutional.[33] The UK Government is responsible for its dependent territories. Hence the standard terms of an Independence Act provide that from some appointed date Her Majesty's Government in the United Kingdom will no longer be responsible for the territory. This responsibility is grounded, Finnis argued, on the legal reality/principle that he had articulated in *Halsbury*: the UK and its dependent territories form one realm having one undivided Crown.[34] And '[t]he legal doctrine that there is one undivided realm corresponds to the moral and political reality that the common good of each part is dependent on the common good of the whole'.[35]

The House of Lords had held in *Quark* that when Her Majesty gives instructions through a Secretary of State to a governor she is (and only is) Queen of the particular territory and the Secretary is merely her mouthpiece. However, the term 'through a Secretary of State' refers to the theory of responsible government, pursuant to which the Queen acts only on the advice of a responsible minister. In relation to royal instructions to colonial officers, this would and should have always been understood to mean they are subject to instructions (in proper form) of the UK Government which is responsible for them. The giving of instructions 'through a Secretary of State' is 'an act of Her Majesty in right not only of her dependent territory..., but also, indeed primarily, in right of the UK, which forms one undivided realm with all its dependent territories'.[36] Finnis concluded that Orders in Council legislating for BIOT were exercises of the UK Government's responsibility for the common good of the UK

---

[29] 2008e, [9].   [30] 2008e, [11].   [31] 2008e, [11].

[32] *R (Quark Fishing Ltd) v. Secretary of State for Foreign and Commonwealth Affairs* [2005] UKHL 57, [2006] 1 AC 529.

[33] 2008e, [16–19].   [34] 2003k, [716].   [35] 2008e, [20].   [36] 2008e, [19].

and all its dependencies. It was profoundly unconstitutional to deny the legality of those acts, the CLVA aside, on the grounds that it was improper to act for the defence of the undivided realm.

V

Finnis's argument was accepted in part in the House of Lords. Lord Hoffmann cited with approval the key passage in *Halsbury*[37] and went on to say, rather quietly,[38] that having read Finnis's paper he conceded that his decision in *Quark* was unsound. Indeed, it was common ground, if not quite explicitly, in *Bancoult (No. 2)* that *Quark* was wrongly decided and that the Crown in Council rightly acts for the undivided realm. However, confusion about the relationship between imperial and local good (and imperial and colonial law) continues to pervade the judicial and scholarly discussion.

Lord Mance, with whom Lord Bingham agreed, accepted that in legislating for BIOT the Crown in Council may act for the interests of the UK and its other territories. However, he denied that this power to legislate extended to 'depopulating the whole of a habitable territory in the interests of the United Kingdom or its allies' for it 'is a power intended to enable the proper governance of the territory, at least among other things for the people inhabiting it'.[39] That is, the power is limited by reference to local rather than imperial good. Likewise, Elliott and Perreau-Saussine argued that even if *Quark* was wrongly decided, still 'it does not follow that the Crown acting in relation to BIOT in right of the United Kingdom can do so for the purpose of advancing the latter's interests exclusively'.[40] The court should intervene, they contended, if the Crown fails to balance these interests appropriately: in relation to BIOT 'the Crown [was] guilty of a fundamental category error', for to act for the peace, order and good government of a territory is to act for the good of the territory's population.[41] These assertions repeat the failing of *Quark* and ignore the central principle of the imperial constitution—that the UK and its dependencies form one undivided realm, such that action for the good of the undivided realm is not to be contrasted with, and held to be limited by, the good of the territory in question.

The judicial confusion about the relationship between territory and undivided realm also informed the majority's reading of the CLVA. Lord Bingham and Lord Mance followed Lord Hoffmann, who *rejected* the Court of Appeal's argument that the CLVA concerns the priority of otherwise valid colonial laws, on the grounds that Finnis had 'persuasively argued' that the repugnancy doctrine was always understood to limit the *powers* of colonial lawmakers.[42] However, Lord Hoffmann continued:

> ... the Act was intended to deal with the validity of colonial laws ... from the perspective of their forming part of the local system of laws administered by the local courts. ... But these proceedings are concerned with the validity of the Order, not simply as part of the

---

[37] *Bancoult (No. 2)* (HL), [47].
[38] *Bancoult (No. 2)* (HL), [48].   [39] *Bancoult (No. 2)* (HL), [157].
[40] Elliott and Perreau-Saussine, 'Pyrrhic Public Law: Bancoult and the Sources, Status and Content of Common Law Limitations on Prerogative Power' [2009] *Public Law* 697, 709.
[41] Elliott and Perreau-Saussine, 'Pyrrhic Public Law', 710.
[42] *Bancoult (No. 2)* (HL), [39].

local law of BIOT but, as Professor Finnis says, as imperial legislation made by Her Majesty in Council in the interests of the undivided realm of the United Kingdom and its non-self-governing territories.... The fact is that Parliament in 1865 would simply not have contemplated the possibility of an Order in Council legislating for a colony as open to challenge in an English court on principles of judicial review. It was concerned with the law applicable by colonial courts not English courts.[43]

Lord Hoffmann concluded that 'from the point of view of the jurisdiction of the courts of the United Kingdom to review the exercise of prerogative powers by Her Majesty in Council, the Constitution Order is not a colonial law'.[44] This argument misstates the nature of the Crown's legislative act, introducing a gloss on the statute that is entirely unsupported by logic or principle and which frustrates the scheme of the Act.

Section 1 of the CLVA provides that 'The term "colonial law" shall include laws made for any colony either by such legislature as aforesaid or by Her Majesty in Council'. The CLVA is an imperial statute, which settles the validity of colonial law throughout the imperial legal system, which includes the English courts. In legislating for the colony—that is, in changing the law in the territory in question—the Crown acts for the undivided realm. However, that the Crown (or Imperial Parliament legislating for a territory) acts for the whole does not entail that the laws it makes for the part are colonial laws only from the perspective of the colonial courts. They are just colonial laws (not imperial legislation), the validity of which is upheld by the CLVA. Finnis did *not* say that the Order was imperial legislation. It was a colonial law, which per the theory of responsible government and the separation of powers in the imperial constitution, was properly made in the interests of the realm at large. The majority take for granted that a finding of invalidity in the English courts undermines validity in the BIOT. Their reading thus shatters the Act's separation of powers, making provision for the English courts to entertain challenges to colonial law, on the very ground that they are repugnant to the law of England!

Parliament plainly contemplated that colonial laws would be challenged in the English courts—this was the very situation in *Campbell v. Hall*, from which follows the repugnancy doctrine and the CLVA itself. In this way, an Act to settle the validity of colonial law—as the title and preamble, not to mention the main operative provisions, make very clear was its point—is interpreted by the *Bancoult (No. 2)* majority to be an entirely different rule of jurisdictional priority, requiring challenges to colonial laws to be litigated in England rather than in the colonies. Lord Rodger and Lord Carswell rightly denied this arbitrary reading.[45] However, they went wrong in taking the CLVA to rule out challenge on the grounds of fundamental principle but not to exclude the ordinary grounds of judicial review: legality, rationality, and natural justice.[46] They thus remain open to an application to quash an Order in Council (or an Act of a representative legislature) on the grounds that it is irrational (unreasonable) or in breach of natural justice. Their position, like the majority's, reintroduces repugnancy, and justiciable constraints of fundamental principle, which the CLVA forbids.

---

[43] *Bancoult (No. 2)* (HL), [40].
[44] *Bancoult (No. 2)* (HL), [41].
[45] *Bancoult (No. 2)* (HL), [97].
[46] *Bancoult (No. 2)* (HL), [104–5].

The missteps in *Bancoult (No. 2)* are not of mere historical interest.[47] The judicial willingness to sidestep the CLVA and to entertain judicial review of prerogative legislation has implications for the devolved legislatures of the UK. This is confirmed by the Supreme Court's holding in *Axa* that the Scottish Parliament is in principle amenable to review on common law grounds.[48] True, almost all the members of the court held that irrationality (unreasonableness) review was not available,[49] yet the prospect of review for breach of fundamental rights or the rule of law was held open.[50] The court's reasoning was simplicity itself: the Scottish Parliament is a statutory body and does not enjoy sovereignty, therefore is subject to the rule of law, which entails judicial review.[51] However, the Scotland Act 1998 very clearly institutes a representative, responsible legislature with full lawmaking power, subject to carefully specified limits: compatibility with the European Convention on Human Rights (ECHR) (itself justiciable) and subject matter reserved for Westminster alone. For the courts to insert into this scheme a further power of judicial review is at best unwise and at worst usurpation. The judicial confidence that the rule of law demands that every public power—including elected, responsible legislatures—be subject to judicial review, above and beyond the grounds of review clearly chosen by Parliament, is unwarranted. It fails to grasp the inaptness of approaching *legislating* as if it were ordinary administrative action or to heed the lessons of the imperial constitution. The fleeting reference to *Bancoult (No. 2)* in *Axa* served mainly to bolster the judicial confidence that there was no impediment to asserting review,[52] confidence that Finnis's critique should unsettle.

VI

The confusion in *Quark* and *Bancoult (No. 2)* about the political community for whom lawmakers act has its counterpart in *Belmarsh*,[53] where the House of Lords failed to perceive the constitutional significance of nationality and alienage. The received wisdom has it that in *Belmarsh* the court quashed (or at least denounced) an unlawful, discriminatory scheme for the indefinite detention of foreigners suspected of terrorism. Finnis argues instead that the judgment was an exercise in lawless judging, displaying neglect both of controlling constitutional principle and of plain statutory duty. His critique elucidates the significance for our constitutional arrangements of membership of the political community.

Finnis traces in some detail the history of the distinction between alien (foreigner) and national (citizen) in English law. Aliens within the realm enjoy the equal protection of

---

[47] They remain of direct practical importance in relation to the rule of British Overseas Territories. In *Misick v. Secretary of State for Foreign and Commonwealth Affairs* [2010] EWCA Civ 1549 and [2009] EWHC 1039 (Admin), the English courts considered, but dismissed, an application for judicial review challenging the legality of the Turks and Caicos Islands Constitution (Interim Amendment) Order 2009.

[48] *Axa General Insurance Limited v. The Lord Advocate* [2011] UKSC 46 at [47], per Lord Hope and [139], per Lord Reed.

[49] The exception is Lord Mance at [97].

[50] *Axa*, [51], per Lord Hope and [149] and [153], per Lord Reed.

[51] *Axa*, [46], per Lord Hope and [149–53], per Lord Reed.

[52] *Axa*, [141], per Lord Reed, although cf. [146].

[53] *A v. Secretary of State for the Home Department* [2004] UKHL 56, [2005] 2 AC 68.

law. This equality, he explains, is grounded on the maxim of reciprocity, articulated in *Calvin's Case*, that 'presence within the realm entitles foreigners to the protection of subjects and entails the obligation of subjects'.[54] Whether the Crown had prerogative to expel (friendly, non-enemy) aliens has not always been clear.[55] However, high judicial authority in the early 20th century affirmed the state's power to refuse to permit aliens to enter the realm and to expel them at its pleasure. And Parliament 'has [since] vigorously asserted, and ever more carefully regulated, our state's (nation's, political community's) capacity lawfully and rightfully to exclude'.[56] Thus, legislation has made repeated provision for exclusion of aliens and for their deportation. Two legal-constitutional principles may be discerned. First, apart from employment conditions imposed on entry and liability to the Crown's authority to expel them, aliens within the realm have equal rights and obligations to nationals. Second, the citizen can now never be excluded from the realm.

The principle that underlies the executive's authority to expel aliens is that 'the political community, while it cannot shift to other communities the risks presented by one of its own nationals, need not unconditionally accept the *risk presented by aliens*'.[57] This means that 'risks to the public good which must be accepted when arising from the presence of a national need not be accepted from the presence of an alien and may be obviated by the alien's exclusion or expulsion'.[58] The principle supports the power to expel and an adjunct to that power, the power to detain the alien pending removal or even pending decision about removal. That power is affirmed in Art. 5(1)(f) of the ECHR, which specifies that 'the lawful ... detention of a person ... against whom action is being taken with a view to deportation' does not infringe the right to liberty and security of person.

The atrophy of this power, by reason of the neglect of relevant principle, is evident in the House of Lords' declaration in *Belmarsh* that s. 23 of the Anti-Terrorism, Crime and Security Act 2001 (ACSA) was incompatible with Arts 5 and 14 of the ECHR. Where an alien had been certified to be a security risk under s. 21 of ACSA, s. 22 made it possible to make a deportation order '(1) ... despite the fact that (whether temporarily or indefinitely) the action cannot result in his removal because of—(a) a point of law[59] which wholly or partly relates to an international agreement, or (b) a practical consideration'. Section 23 (astonishingly, never set out in the judgment) provided:

(1) A suspected international terrorist may be detained under a provision specified in subsection (2) despite the fact that his removal or departure from the United Kingdom is prevented (whether temporarily or indefinitely) by—
    (a) a point of law ... or
    (b) a practical consideration.

---

[54] *CEJF* III.9, 134; essay 9 is 2007a, less sections V and VI of the published original. I refer to those sections, and hence to 2007a rather than III.9, at various points below.

[55] *CEJF* III.9, 135–6.   [56] *CEJF* III.9, 137.   [57] *CEJF* III.9, 139.

[58] *CEJF* III.9, 140; the original text was all in italics.

[59] The point of law in question is that one may not deport a person to a country where they may be tortured.

The two provisions specified in (2) are both to be found in the Immigration Act 1971: the second is 'paragraph 2 of Schedule 3 to that Act (detention pending deportation)'.

Finnis argued that s. 23 should have been read in light of the relevant judicial authorities, which stress that legality turns on a continuing purpose of removal. The relevant statutory language, 'detention pending deportation', made this restriction plain. Finnis continued: 'If s.23(1) lifted temporal restrictions (removal "within a reasonable period"), s.23(2) plainly implied that detention would nonetheless be or become unlawful if the purpose of removing the alien were absent or abandoned, or reduced to mere idle wish.'[60]

This interpretation was obvious. It was also required by s. 3 of the Human Rights Act 1998 (HRA),[61] which the courts have often invoked to justify interpretations that are considerably less obvious. Finnis concluded that *Belmarsh* is to this extent *per incuriam*.[62] The judicial assumption that s. 3 of the HRA was irrelevant to the interpretation of s. 23 seems—but we are left with speculation since the relevance of s. 3 was never addressed—to have turned on the fact that a Derogation Order was made on the day the bill (which became the ACSA) was introduced to Parliament. However, the text of the Order (again, never quoted in the judgment) made out, Finnis argued, only a conditional intention that if s. 23, read per s. 3 of the HRA, is not compatible with Art. 5(1)(f) then it is nonetheless to take effect, as an emergency derogation under Art. 15 of the ECHR.

Their Lordships declared s. 23 incompatible with Arts 5 and 14, reasoning that it was irrational to limit a regime of indefinite detention for suspected terrorists to foreigners when nationals were equally capable of terrorism and that such limitation was discriminatory. Finnis's central objection to these declarations is that they wholly ignore the constitutional principle—nationality-differentiated risk-acceptability—that explains the regime, on which principle Parliament seems (or at least should be understood) to have acted. When that principle is in clear view, the detention of aliens pending deportation is not an arbitrary limitation to some subset of 'suspected terrorists', nor is it unjustified discrimination (if one is tempted to think justified discrimination an empty category, recall that even routine liability to deportation without detention 'discriminates' on nationality: aliens may be deported, nationals may not). Ironically, in neglecting controlling principle, the court failed to extend to detainees the protection that for continued detention to be lawful the executive need maintain an ongoing purpose of removal.

The principle of nationality-differentiated risk-acceptability grounds the liability of aliens to expulsion and the immunity of nationals from expulsion. This disjuncture, together with rules limiting statelessness, affirms that the human community is and should be structured into distinct political communities, in which arrangement persons may live well.[63] The continuity of legal order turns on the unity over time of the

---

[60] 2007a, 430. Finnis said 'If' here because he also made, as a distinct argument, the point that what is a reasonable period depends on such factors as the security risk and the obstacles to removal.

[61] The section provides that as far as possible the courts must read other legislation consistently with the ECHR.

[62] 2007a, 431.   [63] *CEJF* III.9, 146.

political community itself and that unity presupposes the willingness of members to act jointly, to conceive of each other as members of a continuing group, with and for whom they should share and sacrifice. This self-conception involves and reproduces general-ised trust that overcomes competing calls on one's loyalty, surrender to which imperils the project of stable, ordered public life.[64] The distinction between members and non-members, nationals and aliens, is indispensable to this group unity. For the citizens of some political community are disposed to, and have good reason to, accept the risks that arise from other citizens and yet not from aliens. The maxim of reciprocity, which warrants equal treatment while aliens are amongst us, also grounds action to maintain the unity and stability of the political community over time.

VII

In the first paragraph of his 'Nationality, Alienage and Constitutional Principle', Finnis says: 'the presumption that statutes do not overturn [constitutional] rights and principles qualifies the ordinary subordination of common law to parliamentary authority'.[65] Better I think to say that the presumption is consistent with the centrality of constitutional principle in the deliberation of the legislature (and executive). Indeed, Finnis's later discussion makes clear that the reciprocity of legislative and judicial reasoning is premised on the legislature's capacity to act for reasons. The legislature has the first, immense, responsibility for securing the common good by deliberating about and choosing what should be done. No scholar has done more than Finnis to refute the reductive account of legislating that has such a hold in legal-scholarly discourse, evident in Lord Hope's casual assertion in *Axa* that the courts safeguard minority rights while the legislature acts for the country at large.[66]

The jurisprudence that grounds Lord Hope's separation of powers (and responsi-bilities) is the object of Finnis's 1985 Maccabaean lecture.[67] The lecture's title[68] posed the question whether Britain should entrench the ECHR in domestic law, authorising judicial review of legislation. However, the main point of the lecture was not to answer this contingent question, but rather to expose the confusions and utilitarian presuppos-itions of modern rights adjudication and to outline the unity of the common good, which consists in, and is not to be contrasted with, (specified) rights. Finnis denied 'that courts are the uniquely appropriate forum for practical judgment about those rights and principles which comprise the bulk of manifestos like the European Convention'.[69] The responsibility of every legislature, he maintained, is 'to hold in view... goods and evils, opportunities, and perils, and to *choose commitments*, backed by legal compul-sion'.[70] The distinct responsibility of the courts is to 'ensure that their decisions are consistent with (i.e. "fit") the derivative, *institutional* rights and principles created by the public commitments already made by the relatively determinate sources which can

---

[64] *CEJF* III.9, 147–9.   [65] *CEJF* III.9, 133.   [66] *Axa*, [49].   [67] *CEJF* III.1.
[68] 'A Bill of Rights for Britain? The Moral of Contemporary Jurisprudence'; the lecture was reprinted, as essay 1, under the title 'Human Rights and Their Enforcement'.
[69] *CEJF* III.1, 41–2.   [70] *CEJF* III.1, 41.

be the subject of legal *learning*.[71] The specification of rights, and hence the justice of legislation, is not one that can be mastered by legal learning.

Finnis did not strictly conclude that Britain should not introduce a justiciable bill of rights. He denied that there was 'a grand balance sheet' on which to calculate the merits of such change.[72] The phrase echoes his earlier disavowal of the argument that the courts would make worse decisions than Parliament. It is true, Finnis said, that Anglo-American courts 'have a record disfigured with unjust or malign and ill-reasoned decisions . . . But legislatures, too, fail in justice, or promote injustice'.[73] More importantly, 'it is absurd to seek an "overall balance" sheet, identifying possible worlds with and without judicial review of legislation as better and worse states of affairs all things considered'.[74]

I agree that the separation of powers is contingent. However, general principles frame the choice. For example, when the authorities are (very) corrupt and intent on (grave) injustice, it may be reasonable for the military to overthrow the constitution and to rule. Yet the military is very obviously not an institution capable of ruling well. There are good reasons to limit the military to the defence of the realm, notwithstanding that in extremis it (like others capable of action) should act otherwise. Finnis's discussion concluded with just such a general case:

> . . . adopting a bill of rights, in any form now practicable, means accepting a time-bound text which downgrades some human rights by its flawed craftsmanship and its failure to envisage more recent challenges to justice—flaws magnified by the European Court's interpretative methods. It also means accepting into our country's institutional play of practical reasoning and choice a new, or greatly expanded element of make-believe, and new or ampler grounds for alienation from the rule of law.[75]

This is a powerful argument, when taken together with his analysis of the special responsibility of each institution, that the legislature is in general better placed than the judiciary to choose well. Thus, one need not draw up an incoherent balance sheet to conclude, as I argue Finnis in effect did in 1985 in relation to the ECHR, that *ceteris paribus* instituting judicial review in this form is unwise (not choiceworthy).

Finnis did not rely on an argument from democratic principle.[76] The objection that judicial review is undemocratic fails, he argued, because 'the majority' is an elusive, unstable object and because, 'in a North Atlantic type of political order, the free citizen's power over judicial appointments is not less than his influence on legislation'.[77] An example of the latter proposition: '[t]he campaign to secure that all new federal judges will oppose the *Roe v. Wade* "right to an abortion" seems to be going smoothly'.[78] The example has been overtaken by events, for the campaign has faltered—in part because of a general problem in the equivalence Finnis here draws between judicial appointment and legislation. The true equivalence is between judicial *decision* and legislation and over the former the free citizen has very little power, much less than over legislation. Why? Judges enjoy secure tenure and their deliberation proceeds by way of, or at least is articulated in, legal learning,

---

[71] *CEJF* III.1, 42.   [72] *CEJF* III.1, 44.   [73] *CEJF* III.1, 21.   [74] *CEJF* III.1, 21.
[75] *CEJF* III.1, 44.   [76] *CEJF* III.1, 21–2.   [77] *CEJF* III.1, 22.   [78] *CEJF* III.1, 23.

whereas legislators contest elections over time and legislative deliberation is open (and transparent) to the public, with legislators willing to argue directly about the merits of legislation.

Citizens should have a share in self-government and their peaceful joint exercise of power itself forms part of the common good. This line of thought is perhaps presupposed in Finnis's argument that there is 'a special humiliation'[79] or a 'special insult added to the injury done' when the judiciary invalidates just legislation, which 'is the inauthenticity of the appearances which the courts in these cases kept up—the appearance of doing what courts characteristically do when doing justice according to law'.[80] The point is somewhat obscure in this formulation. The exercise of judicial review may tell a lie: viz. that the invalidation of some legislative act is entailed, dictated, by the community's own commitments, when in truth it follows from an open judicial choice. The principal reason why the insult stings, however, is that the judicial act (and the prospect of further such action, unmoored from the community's past commitments, save the introduction of judicial review itself) undercuts the efforts of a free people to govern itself.

In many ways, for many ends, our judges should speak and act for us, but *not* in reviewing the choices we make about open questions, when our self-constitution is engaged. The special virtue of judicial deliberation and action is its continuity with positive law, with past commitments of the political community. For citizens to exercise self-government, they must have some capacity to act jointly to choose for reasons. Framing a constitution by convention and public ratification is such a mode of action but so too is ordinary legislating. And importantly, the exercise of constituent power cannot reasonably rule out extensive room for subsequent legislative choice. Otherwise the community arbitrarily curtails its subsequent reasoning, adopting commitments more specific than warranted by reason. If the first principle of constitutional order is that those with capacity should exercise authority,[81] the second is that the location of authority should be settled by authority.[82] In that second type of act, one should aim to institute a body capable of holding in view that which is relevant and choosing reasonably, in a way that enables self-government.

VIII

Finnis's study of the constitutional law and practice of the members of the British Commonwealth makes clear the central significance of the unity and identity of the political community itself, for whose common good authority is instituted and exercised. The elements of the common good that constitutional principles articulate frame the deliberation and action of legal and political authorities and thus inform law and convention. Positive law is central to, but does not exhaust, the constitution, and the importance of the rule of law does not entail judicial supremacy in the separation of

---

[79] *CEJF* III.1, 41.   [80] *CEJF* III.1, 43.   [81] *NLNR*, 246.   [82] *NLNR*, 249–50.

powers. Thus, Finnis's reflections on the continuity of law, the residual responsibilities of institutions in former parts of an imperial whole, the theory of responsible government in the imperial polity, the distinction between nationals and aliens, and the separation of judicial and legislative power illuminate the ways in which a constitution orders the life over time of a free people.

25

Intention and the Allocation of Risk

*Neil M. Gorsuch**

Others have, and will for years to come, write and speak about, learn from and debate John Finnis's contributions to ethics, philosophy, even Shakespearean scholarship and theology. But as a workaday judge, my daily bread does not consist of such high cuisine. It is instead made up of a comparatively pedestrian—if wholesome and filling—stew of statutes and precedents, regulations and rules. Yet, from time to time Finnis has been kind enough to dine with those of us who subsist on such doctrinal fare—and here, too, he has applied his remarkable talents in important and enduring ways. He is, after all, not just a philosopher but a fine lawyer and a member of the Bar (Gray's Inn). And it is on an aspect of his scholarship in the legal arena that I have been asked to comment.

But before I get to that, I seek (and in any event assume) a point of personal privilege. This to offer a brief recollection of John Finnis not as philosopher or even as lawyer but in the role I know him best—as teacher. Many years ago, I was lucky enough to study under his supervision. It was a time when legal giants roamed among Oxford's spires. John Finnis, Ronald Dworkin, and Joseph Raz were all there, busy with their seminal works, their lectures and seminars open to any curious graduate student, their debates the stuff of student coffee house legend. As a graduate student at the same college where Finnis has spent almost a half century, I was fortunate to have him assigned as my dissertation supervisor. And as busy as he was with his research and scholarship, while a leading figure in his field on an international stage, there was never any question about the degree of his devotion to his students. He took on many (and many thankless) tasks in aid of student life, serving variously as the college's dean of graduates, director of undergraduate studies, and vice-master, even reportedly assuming for a time the position (dreaded by many students) of estates bursar, the keeper of the college finances.[1] Not every great scholar is also such a devoted teacher, taking to heart his role as leader in the daily life of a collegiate community.

Finnis's concern for his students manifested itself in many other and more personal ways. Like the red ink he poured so carefully—and generously—over the papers we produced. Or the gentle but exacting cross-examinations we endured while sweating next to (but never raked over) the coal fire in his paneled college room. To those lucky enough to have experienced all this, we recall well how the good professor (really,

* Many thanks to Gerry Bradley, Holly Cody, Daniel Furman, Sean Jackowitz, John Keown, Daniel Klerman, Chris Mammen, Jason Murray, Bob Nagel, Eugene Volokh, Phil Weiser, and Steve Yelderman for their helpful comments. Despite such generous assistance, I alone am responsible for any remaining errors and the views expressed here. This essay was originally delivered as a talk at Notre Dame Law School in September 2011.

[1] *University College Record* (2010), 15(3): 19–27.

Doctor to many of us, before the Americanism crept in) patiently and generously read draft after draft we produced, always encouraging our efforts but also always testing, always questioning, and never tolerating a weak argument or an implicit or untested premise—let alone the syntactical sin of a misplaced modifier or split infinitive. I have encountered few such patient, kind, and truly generous teachers in my life.

And I am hardly alone in this assessment. On his (semi-)retirement from Oxford in 2010, University College published a number of recollections from Finnis's former students. A couple are evocative of my experience and emblematic of the sort of teacher Finnis was and is. Nicola Lacey, now a fellow at All Souls, recalled the time she began as one of Finnis's students. Finnis asked her what law courses she intended to study. She replied that she would surely take the popular courses on Jurisprudence and Criminal Justice but that just as surely she intended to avoid the dry stuff of Restitution. Finnis looked at her with intense seriousness and thought for a moment. Then, perhaps peeking out over his glasses—as he does when he wishes to emphasize a really important point—he replied, "But, Mrs. Lacey, Restitution is good for the soul." Needless to say, she took Restitution. Philip Gawith, who later went on to serve as CEO of the Maitland communications agency, recalled a time when his tutorial partner triumphantly concluded that a certain argument was "circular." To which Finnis responded—accompanied, we might imagine, by his characteristically gentle sigh— "and what is a circle but a collection of points equidistant from the center?" As Gawith observed, Finnis had certain quiet and dry ways of letting us know that what we considered to be a good argument was not quite so good.[2] I am just happy to know that, while Finnis may now have largely retired from Oxford, students at a university in my own country (Notre Dame) will continue to have the chance to get to know him not just as a philosopher whose works they encounter in print but as a kind and careful teacher to be enjoyed in person.

And with that point of personal privilege exercised, let me turn to comment on an aspect of Finnis's legal scholarship. Space constraints will allow me to share just one example. But it will, I think, easily suffice to illustrate his enduring importance to the law.

In crime and tort, legal liability has often and long depended on a showing that the defendant *intended* to do a legal wrong. When it comes to inchoate offenses such as attempt and conspiracy, the presence of an unlawful intent is frequently what separates criminality itself from legally innocuous behavior.[3] The same holds true when it comes

---

[2] *University College Record* (2010), 15(3): 19–27. For these and other recollections, I am indebted to Dr Robin Darwall-Smith, the University College archivist who directed the college's published tribute to Finnis, for allowing me to retell here some of the stories he took the time and effort to compile and record.

[3] See, e.g. *Braxton v. US*, 500 US 344, 351 n. * (1991); *US v. Bailey*, 444 US 394, 404–5 (1980); *Direct Sales Co. v. US*, 319 US 703, 711 (1943); Model Penal Code §2.02, Comment 2, §5.01, Comment 2; LaFave, *Substantive Criminal Law*, § 5.2(b) and n. 9, §11.3; Bishop, *New Commentaries on the Criminal Law Upon a New System of Legal Exposition*, §729.4. To be sure, the drafters of the Model Penal Code have suggested extending attempt liability to those who believe their conduct would cause (not intend to cause) an unlawful result. Model Penal Code §5.01(1)(b). As the Code's commentators admit, however, they have advocated an exception to the common law's usual requirement of intent and their proposal has not been adopted in most American jurisdictions. Model Penal Code §5.01 comment 2; LaFave, *Substantive Criminal Law*, §11.3 (a) n. 28.

to accessory liability.[4] The law of homicide, as well, "often distinguishes either in setting the 'degree' of the crime or in imposing punishment" between intended and unintended killings.[5] And many of our most serious torts (say, battery and assault) are denominated *intentional* torts. Of course, what *qualifies* as "intentional" and thus sufficient to render the defendant liable in the civil context is broader than in the criminal context—embracing knowing as well as truly purposeful wrongs in American law. And perhaps this is so for good reason, given that in tort only money, not individual liberty, is at stake.[6] But it remains a fact that the nature of liability (punitive damages, for example) is generally more expansive and serious for what tort law deems an *intentional* wrong than for wrongs involving only lesser *mens rea*.[7]

In comparatively recent years some have argued for tearing down this traditional legal edifice. These theorists have suggested that the presence or absence of an intent to perform a legal wrong should be neither here nor there when it comes to assigning legal liability; that the common law's traditional reference to intention should be scrapped or revised; that a better way forward exists. In the space I have, let me outline just two of the challenges to our received tradition and then highlight some of the defects associated with those efforts, defects that Finnis's scholarship has helped illuminate.

The bolder of the two challenges is perhaps most emblematically identified with the prolific Judge Richard Posner. In Judge Posner's view, legal liability in tort should turn on a comparison of social costs and benefits. Whether a legal wrong is done intention-ally is more or less beside the point. Intentional torts merit stiffer penalties than those done recklessly or negligently only if and to the extent economic efficiency requires that outcome.[8] To explain why this is so, Judge Posner asks us to consider the case of *Bird v. Holbrook*[9]—a chestnut that many of us encountered in law school and that, as it happens, involved an actual bird and, perhaps even better still, a bed of tulips.

So let us begin with the facts of that case. In *Bird*, the defendant owned a walled garden where, as the court put it, he "grew valuable flower-roots, and particularly tulips, of the choicest and most expensive description."[10] To protect the garden, the defendant-owner set up a hidden spring gun, a shotgun rigged to fire when any trespasser stumbled over a contact wire.[11] The plaintiff, a William Bird, was a young man of 19 who saw a neighbor's female servant in distress. She was in distress because a wandering pea-hen apparently belonging to her employer had escaped and "alighted in the defendant's garden."[12] So young Will Bird, a well raised young man it would seem, volunteered to collect the bird. He clambered to the top of the defendant's garden wall

---

[4] See, e.g. Model Penal Code §2.02, Comment 2, §2.06, Comment 6(c); *US v. Peoni*, 100 F 2d 401, 402–3 (2d Cir. 1938) (Hand, J).

[5] *Bailey*, 444 US at 405.

[6] *Restatement (Second) of Torts* (1965), §8A.

[7] See, e.g. Keeton et al., *Prosser and Keeton on the Law of Torts*, §8.

[8] Posner, *Economic Analysis of Law*, 260–5.

[9] (1828) 4 Bing 628, 130 ER 911. Judge Posner used the case as the focus of one of his earliest articles on law and economics, and he continues to use it as the focus of his discussion of intentional torts in his textbook. Posner, "Killing or Wounding to Protect a Property Interest," 209; Posner, *Economic Analysis of Law*, 260–5.

[10] 4 Bing at 631, 130 ER at 912.   [11] 4 Bing at 632, 130 ER at 912.

[12] 4 Bing at 632, 130 ER at 913.

and called out two or three times to see if anyone was around. Receiving no reply, he jumped into the garden. Once in the garden he saw that the pea-hen had taken shelter near a summer house and so he went to collect it.[13] Seeking to pluck the bird, not pick the flowers, he was nonetheless rewarded for his troubles with a spray of swan shot from the defendant's hidden spring gun.[14]

When his case for damages eventually made it to court, the English bench found the garden owner liable.[15] The court did so on the basis that it is unacceptable (at least without notice, it said) for anyone to maim others *intentionally* simply for picking tulips.[16] The *intentional* harming of another's person is a grave thing and generally impermissible at law, even for the protection of property. Neither, the court pointed out, was the defendant really even seeking to defend his tulips. By leaving a hidden spring gun lying around, the owner demonstrated that he was just as happy to injure someone who had *already* picked his flowers as he was someone *about* to pick them. And no doubt in the owner's view punishing the completed picker was a useful deterrent, a way to dissuade other future would-be pickers from even trying. But this was a serious wrong because, as counsel for Mr Bird put it, the sanction of law is required "to give effect to punishment, and pain [intentionally] inflicted for a supposed offence, at the discretion of an individual, without the intervention of a judicial sentence, is a mere act of revenge."[17]

Now back to Judge Posner. For his part, Judge Posner encourages us to analyze *Bird*, and tort law generally, in a radically different way. In his view, the case can be and is perhaps better understood *not* as involving an intentional wrongdoing but as involving an effort to achieve the optimal social balance between two perfectly "legitimate activities, raising tulips and keeping peahens."[18] Spring guns, Judge Posner suggests, may well be an efficient, perhaps even the most efficient, way of protecting tulips in a time and place where police protection is not readily available; conversely, spring guns may be inefficient in times and places where other means of protection are more accessible and accidental shootings more likely.[19] The real trick, Judge Posner argues, and what he says judges already may be doing subconsciously, is "design[ing] a rule of liability [in tort] that maximize[s] the (joint) value of both activities, net of any protective or other costs (including personal injuries)."[20] Neither does Judge Posner confine his critique to the realm of civil liability. In criminal law, too, he argues that intent has significance only as a *proxy* for other variables in an economic cost-benefit analysis.[21] So it is that, under his approach, the fact that a defendant may have *intended* to kill or maim others is itself really "neither here nor there."[22]

---

[13] 4 Bing at 633, 130 ER at 913.
[14] 4 Bing at 633, 130 ER at 913.   [15] 4 Bing at 633, 130 ER at 913.
[16] 4 Bing at 640–6, 130 ER at 916–18.   [17] 4 Bing at 636; 130 ER at 914.
[18] Posner, "Killing or Wounding to Protect a Property Interest," 209.
[19] Posner, "Killing or Wounding to Protect a Property Interest," 214–16.
[20] Posner, "Killing or Wounding to Protect a Property Interest," 210.
[21] Posner, *Economic Analysis of Law*, 295.
[22] Posner, *Economic Analysis of Law*, 206.

To those who might object that liability for intentionally killing or maiming another human being should not turn on a balancing of economic costs and benefits, Judge Posner offers this reply:

> It is surely not correct to say that society never permits the sacrifice of human lives on behalf of substantial economic values. Automobile driving is an example of the many deadly activities that cannot be justified as saving more lives than they take. Nor can the motoring example be distinguished from the spring-gun case on the ground that one who sets a spring-gun intends to kill or wound. In both cases, a risk of death is created that could be avoided by substituting other methods of achieving one's ends (walking instead of driving); in both cases the actor normally hopes the risk will not materialize. One can argue that driving is more valuable and spring guns more dangerous; but intentionality is neither here nor there.[23]

A second, perhaps more modest, challenge to our received legal tradition, though one headed in much the same direction, might be identified with Glanville Williams and his theory of "oblique intention." While Williams did not insist that intention (however defined at law) is entirely irrelevant to the assignment of legal liability, he argued for collapsing intent with foresight or knowledge and treating the two the same when it comes to determining culpability in the criminal law, much as American law typically does in tort.[24]

To make his point, Williams once offered this example—a colorful and complex one in its own right. Suppose a spy is discovered to be ferrying a top secret and highly sensitive device to a hostile state by way of an international flight. Detected in air, the spy fears he will be prevented from completing his mission, so he seizes a hostage and demands that the flight steward prepare a parachute so that he can escape with the device intact. The steward (apparently steeped in national security matters himself) recognizes that the consequences will be dire if the secret device falls into the hands of the enemy, so he discreetly cuts the parachute's ripcord. In a rush, the spy fails to check the parachute, leaps from the plane, and the device (along with the spy) is destroyed upon hitting the ground. Applying his oblique theory of intention, Williams had this to say:

> It seems clear that, as a matter of law, the steward must still be credited with an intention to kill the criminal. He foresees the certainty of the criminal's death if the events happen as he sees they may, even though he does not desire that death.[25]

Of course, the steward's killing might be legally justified on other grounds, say perhaps because of the affirmative defense involving the defense of others. But Williams used his hypothetical to make a different point. He used it to argue that whether the steward intended the spy's death or merely knew it would happen should not matter when assessing his legal liability or access to any affirmative defense. In Williams's view there

---

[23] Posner, *Economic Analysis of Law*, 206.
[24] Williams, "Oblique Intention"; Williams, *Textbook of Criminal Law*, 84–7; Williams, *The Mental Element in Crime*, 52–3.
[25] Williams, *The Mental Element in Crime*, 51–3.

is no point in distinguishing between at least intended and foreseen homicides because all that does is "involve the law in fine distinctions, and make it unduly lenient."[26]

With Judge Posner's and Glanville Williams's views now (albeit very briefly) sketched, we might begin to ask some analytical and normative questions about their project, questions that Finnis's scholarship has suggested and illuminated. Once scattered across various journals and years, Finnis's efforts in this area have been recently and happily married together, and can be found published as essays 10 and 11 in Volume II, and essay 16 in Volume IV of Oxford University Press's recent collection of Finnis's work.

Let us begin with the analytical. Judge Posner rests his argument in large measure on the notion that intended harms (however defined) and purely negligent harms are much the same because both involve the imposition of a risk of harm on someone else. In particular, the automobile driver and the spring gun operator, he says, are essentially indistinguishable. Both take actions that create some risk of harm, even though both *hope* that harm will not materialize. Whether any harm is intended is beside the point, neither here nor there, because the risk of the unhoped-for harm is just an inherent cost associated with performing two generally beneficial activities, driving and tulip growing.

But we might well question whether this line of analysis conflates two different things, hoping and intending. After all, as Finnis asks, cannot one "*intend* to achieve a certain result without *desiring* it to come about"?[27] Cannot one "choose and intend to do what is utterly repugnant to one's dominant feelings"?[28] Consider the spring gun owner. We can all agree with Judge Posner that he may well *hope* everyone stays away from the trap he sets. But if he thinks that many will be deterred and only a few will come, then does not he really *intend* to shoot those few?[29] Is it not the whole point of a spring gun deterrent that the owner *intends* to injure or kill those who ignore or test it, however repugnant that result may be to the owner's *hopes*? In this way, does not the spring gun owner *intend* to maim or kill even if he may *hope* not to have to do so? And, having observed this much, can we really say the negligent driver is in the same position as the spring gun owner? After all, the negligent driver neither hopes *nor intends* to hurt anyone when he takes to the road. He may hurt someone by accident, but killing or maiming is simply not part of his plan or intent—as either a means *or* as an end.[30] Any injury he might cause would be grounds for serious regret, not the fulfillment of any intention he harbors. In this way, the cases of the spring gun owner and driver come to us in very different postures analytically—not at all indistinguishable as Judge Posner's analysis would have us posit.

A similar analytical question attends Williams's effort to equate intent and knowledge or foresight. We might approach that question by asking whether it is really fair to say that Williams's steward is guilty of an *intentional* killing. To be sure, the steward *knew* the spy would die; but did he *intend* that death? Or might there be, as Finnis suggests, a strong argument that Williams's steward "did not intend to kill the spy, though he foresaw and accepted that his own choice would certainly bring about

---

[26] Williams, "Oblique Intention," 425.   [27] *CEJF* II.10, 174 (emphasis added).
[28] *CEJF* II.10, 175.   [29] *CEJF* IV.16, 342.   [30] *CEJF* IV.16, 345.

[the spy's] death"?[31] Indeed, might it be a fairer view of the facts that the spy's "free-fall and death are side effects of the steward's plan to destroy the...device" that might do harm to his country?[32] After all, and for all we know from Williams's hypothetical, if the steward could have destroyed the device without killing anyone he gladly would have done so.

And this leads us to the real analytical question confronting Williams's project: Is he right that *no* meaningful distinction exists between intent and foresight that the criminal law might recognize, at least sometimes? In answering this question, it is hard to do better than Finnis once did with this illustration:

> Those who wear shoes don't *intend* to wear them out [even though they may foresee that as an inevitable consequence]. Those who fly the Atlantic foreseeing certain jetlag [likewise] don't do so with the *intention* to get jetlag; those who drink too heavily rarely *intend* the hangover they know is certain. Those who habitually stutter foresee with certainty that their speech will create annoyance or anxiety, but do not *intend* those side effects. Indeed, we might well call [Williams's] extended notion of [oblique] intent the Pseudo-Masochist Theory of Intention—for it holds that those who *foresee* that their actions will have painful effects on themselves *intend* those effects.[33]

Plainly, a meaningful analytical distinction *does* exist between intending and foreseeing a consequence. Recognizing exactly this, the Model Penal Code acknowledges that a line can and sometimes should be drawn in American criminal law "between a [person] who wills that a particular act or result take place and another who is merely willing that it should take place."[34] So, too, the US Supreme Court, which has emphasized that, at least in the criminal law, the idea that "knowledge is sufficient to show intent is emphatically *not* the modern view."[35] Tellingly, even Williams himself ultimately conceded that in certain areas of law—treason, for example—society *should* require proof of intention rather than knowledge before imposing liability. Yet, Williams notably failed to explain *why* this should be so or *how* it might be reconciled with his claim elsewhere that the intent-knowledge distinction lacks force.[36] His ambiguity and equivocation seem the product of a largely unexplored (if ultimately correct) intuition that, at least sometimes, intent *does* matter.

Not only does Finnis help us see that the traditional intent-knowledge distinction in law bears analytical power overlooked by its critics. He also helps expose the undergirding normative reasons for the law's traditional cognizance of intention. He reminds us, for example, that some of the law's harshest punishments are often (and have long been) reserved for intentional wrongs precisely because to *intend* something is to endorse it as a matter of *free will*—and freely choosing something *matters*.[37] Our intentional choices reflect and shape our character—who we are and who we wish to be—in a way that unintended or accidental consequences cannot. Our intentional choices define us. They last, remain as part of one's will, one's orientation toward the

---

[31] *CEJF* II.10, 185.   [32] *CEJF* II.10, 185.   [33] *CEJF* II.10, 183 (emphases added).

[34] Model Penal Code §2.02, Comment 2, n. 6 (quoting National Commission on Reform of the Federal Criminal Laws, *Working Papers* 1: 124).

[35] *Giles v. California*, 554 US 353, 368 (2008).

[36] Williams, "Oblique Intention," 435–8.   [37] *CEJF* II.10, 194.

world. They differ qualitatively from consequences that happen accidentally, unintentionally: after all, even a dog knows the difference between being tripped over and being kicked.[38] Even to the dog, it is not simply the result that matters so much as, sometimes at least, the intention behind it. Intending to do a legal wrong to another person is something special because, as Finnis puts it,

> [t]o intend something is to choose it, either for its own sake or as a means; and to choose is to adopt a proposal (a proposal generated by and in one's own deliberation). Once adopted, the proposal, together with the reasoning which in one's deliberation made that proposal intelligently attractive, *remains*, persists, in one's will, one's disposition to act.[39]

This is a view, of course, that has long and deeply resonated through American and British jurisprudence, and indeed the Western tradition. It is precisely why the law treats the spring gun owner who maims or kills intentionally so differently from the negligent driver whose conduct yields the same result. As Roscoe Pound once put it, our "substantive criminal law is," at least at minimum, "based upon a theory of punishing the vicious will. It postulates a free agent confronted with a choice between doing right and doing wrong."[40] At bedrock, and whatever else it may require of citizens, our law rests on what Justice Jackson called the "belief in freedom of the human will and [the] consequent ability and duty of the normal individual to choose between good and evil."[41] Finnis reminds us of the normative power lurking behind familiar precepts and proclamations like these.

But there are still other normative justifications for the special emphasis the law places on intentional conduct. One has to do with human equality. When someone *intends* to harm another person, Finnis encourages us to remember, "[t]he reality and fulfillment of those others is radically subjected to one's own reality and fulfilment, or to the reality and fulfilment of some other group of persons. In *intending* harm, one precisely makes their loss one's gain, or the gain of some others; one to that extent uses them up, treats them as material, as a resource."[42] People, no less than material, become means to another's end. To analyze *Bird v. Holbrook* as the challengers to extant law would have us, we ask merely whether superior collective social consequences are produced by ruling for the plaintiff or defendant. On this account, there is nothing particularly *special* about the individual. Like any other input or good, it gives way whenever some competing and ostensibly more important collective social good is at stake. But it is exactly to prevent all this that the law has traditionally held, in both crime and tort, that one generally ought not *choose* or *intend* to harm another person, and that failing to observe this rule is a particularly grave wrong. This traditional rule "expresses and preserves each individual person's . . . *dignity* . . . as an equal."[43] It recognizes that "to choose harm is the paradigmatic wrong; the exemplary instance of denial of right."[44] It stands as a bulwark against those who would allow the human individual

---

[38] Holmes, *The Common Law*, 3.   [39] *CEJF* IV.16, 347.
[40] Pound, "Introduction," xxxvi–vii.
[41] *Morissette v. US*, 342 US 246, 250 (1952).
[42] *CEJF* IV.16, 347–8; Kant, *Groundwork for the Metaphysics of Morals*, 46–8.
[43] *CEJF* IV.16, 349.   [44] *CEJF* IV.16, 349–50.

to become nothing more than another commodity to be used up in aid of another's (or others') ends.[45]

Assigning legal liability based on intent can serve still other virtues. While Williams said that requiring a showing of intent rather than knowledge leads to unduly fine distinctions and too much leniency in criminal matters, law-makers and courts have frequently found these distinctions necessary to avoid results they perceive as unjust. So, for example, when it comes to attempt and conspiracy crimes, a showing of intent is often required to establish criminal liability, even though a lesser *mens rea* may suffice to establish liability for the same completed offense.[46] And even when criminal liability attaches to the primary criminal offenders on a lesser *mens rea* showing, proof of intent is typically required to hold liable those only tangentially involved with the illegal enterprise as accessories.[47] While of course legislators are free to vary these rules and sometimes have, these rules largely persist and are no doubt what the Supreme Court has called a product of "an intense individualism . . . root[ed] in American soil" willing to attach criminal sanction for actions just indirectly (or not at all) responsible for harm befalling others *only* if a *choice to do wrong* is present.[48] In this way, attention to the defendant's intent can help address and prevent what Learned Hand once called a "drag net" effect of sweeping up "all those who have been associated in any degree whatever with the main offenders."[49] The intent requirement in attempt, accessory, and conspiracy law ensures that there is no criminal prosecution, for example, when a utility provides telephone service to a customer "knowing it is used for bookmaking" or "[a]n employee puts through a shipment in the course of his employment though he knows the shipment is illegal."[50] In this way, American law seeks to allow the liberty of normal commerce and communication between individuals without forcing them always to be on guard against Williams's "oblique" intentions.

In response to all this, one might imagine Judge Posner or Williams replying that all the doctrine of intent does could be done just as easily through a system that looks purely to social consequences. Or arguing that intent doctrine does, in some sense, serve to maximize collective social welfare because of the very features that distinguish it. But replies like these would, of course, only serve to demonstrate that the fine gradations of *mens rea* traditionally recognized in the common law are *not* beside the point (neither here nor there) as both Judge Posner and Williams have suggested (albeit in their own different ways). In this respect, an argument along these lines would be nearly self-defeating. Neither would responses like these answer the objection that the common law's frequent focus on intent has meaning *for the reasons* the law has traditionally given (free will, equality, liberty)—reasons that seem to be justifiable on bases independent of any underlying social welfare calculus. Nor would they address the objection that the common law's stated reasons for focusing on intent are its true and accurate reasons—that the law possesses an integrity and deep logic to it. And they would do little to confront the argument that the law's prohibition of intentional

---

[45] *CEJF* IV.16, 349–50.   [46] See n. 3.   [47] See n. 4.
[48] *Morissette*, 342 US at 251–2.
[49] *US v. Falcone*, 109 F 2d 579, 581 (2d Cir. 1940) (Hand, J).
[50] Model Penal Code §2.06, Comment 6(c).

wrongs should sometimes trump even (and perhaps especially) when a utilitarian calculus suggests a different result.

To be sure, much more could be said about Finnis's contribution to the question of intention in crime and tort. There is a great deal more complexity and subtlety both to his arguments and to those of his antagonists than I can stitch out in these few pages. And many more difficulties to explore. Like the incommensurability problems Finnis argues can sometimes attend consequentialist explanations of the law. Or the complexities involved in trying to distinguish intended means and ends from unintended side effects. Or the question when exactly the law should and should not take special cognizance of intent and distinguish intended consequences from those merely known or foreseen. After all, while Finnis reminds us that the law *may* take cognizance of an analytically and normatively meaningful distinction between intended and unintended conduct, he hardly suggests that the law always *must* do so or that other bases for legal liability should not exist—two positions that would themselves be plainly mistaken.

But while these questions are more appropriately material for other discussions, and certainly more than I might manage to address in these few pages, let me offer one example of how the intent-foresight distinction might play a critical role in the debate over one issue of contemporary interest: the law of assisted suicide and euthanasia. As I explained in my book on that subject, Anglo-American assisted suicide law has long depended on the intent-knowledge divide. As with many other accessory offenses, liability here traditionally falls upon those who *intend* to kill another human being but not on those who *foreseeably* cause death but intend no such thing.[51] In this way, assisted suicide laws have generally sought to ensure that only actors most closely associated with the enterprise are subject to liability; others more loosely affiliated are not swept into the drag net. Unsurprisingly, both Judge Posner and Glanville Williams have sought to level the law's traditional distinction in this arena (too), all in aid of an effort to undermine and undo altogether laws prohibiting assisted suicide and euthanasia.

Their work in the assisted suicide context, however, merely revives and echoes the analytical and normative difficulties and questions we have identified. Using his theory of oblique intention as a starting point, Williams argued that the case for legalizing assisted suicide follows ineluctably from the fact that law already permits a physician to prescribe a lethal dose of palliative drugs to a patient in order to relieve pain, even if he knows that doing so may (even will) cause the patient's death. In Williams's view, the doctor who performs the same act intending to end the patient's life is in essentially the same position. But here again, one might ask whether Williams conflates two analytically different things. Cannot the law draw a rational distinction (as, in fact, it long has) between the act of a caring physician who administers morphine to ease his patient's grave pain, foreseeing death without any intent to kill, and the act of a Dr Kevorkian who injects his patients with potassium chloride in order (intending) to see them

---

[51] Gorsuch, *The Future of Assisted Suicide and Euthanasia*, Ch. 4.

dead?[52] In *Vacco v. Quill*, the Supreme Court expressly recognized and endorsed the historical pedigree and analytical validity of laws that have long made just this distinction between foreseen and intended deaths in the assisted suicide context; are we really sure it was wrong to do so?[53]

And if we do pull down the law's traditional dependence on intention in this arena, we might ask, what would be the upshot for our commitment to human equality? Judge Posner contends that assisted suicide should be legalized because (in his view) the balance of social utility appears to justify it. But his utilitarian argument for legalization leaves him forced to concede that some human lives are worth greater legal protection than others because of their comparative instrumental value; on his account, some lives should never be taken, but others can (and perhaps should) be.[54] Yet, if human lives bear only instrumental value, how do we decide which lives have sufficient utility to warrant the law's protection and which do not? And if some human lives lack sufficient instrumental utility to merit protection against being intentionally taken, what are we saying about our commitment to human equality?[55] Might existing law do more to protect equality than the would-be authors of its demise might wish to admit?[56]

Other large questions follow, too. If we throw over existing law and permit some persons' lives to be taken intentionally, how are we supposed to go about the business of sorting out which lives may be so taken? Whose life may be taken and who decides? Does it even matter whether we have the consent of those to be killed, at least if we can confidently conclude their lives really lack (what someone deems to be) sufficient instrumental value? Peter Singer's work advocating infanticide reveals just how far the logical progression ignited by this line of inquiry may take us.[57]

But let me leave that preview there, with those dangling questions asked but unanswered. The permutations and even just some very tentative answers took me a long book to spell out. For our purposes here it is enough to note that Finnis has done much to remind us that the law's use of intention as a basis for liability is not always and wholly beside the point; that the law's focus on intent can, at least sometimes, be both analytically and normatively justified; and that all this can make a significant difference in the analysis of many legal questions across many fields and in many different ways. Finnis's work has helped explain and defend the thicket of the common law's traditional *mens rea* rules, reminding us of the intellectual pedigree of those rules and of the reasons why the law has often and for so long taken care with what sometimes seem complex and unduly fine distinctions. No doubt the debate will continue, with rejoinders made, new lessons learned, and echoes heard in the assisted suicide and many other debates for years to come. But no one seeking

---

[52] Gorsuch, *The Future of Assisted Suicide and Euthanasia*, Chs 4, 9 (discussing Williams's theory, among others).

[53] 521 US 793, 802 (1997) (distinguishing assisted suicide from acceptable medical practice on exactly these grounds, explaining that "[t]he law has long used actors' intent or purposes to distinguish between two acts that may have the same result").

[54] Gorsuch, *Future of Assisted Suicide and Euthanasia*, 160 (discussing Posner, *Aging and Old Age*, 241).

[55] Gorsuch, *Future of Assisted Suicide and Euthanasia*, Chs 7–9.

[56] Walton Report, para. 237 ("Th[e] prohibition of intentional killing ... is the cornerstone of law and of social relationships. It protects each one of us impartially, embodying the belief that all are equal.").

[57] Gorsuch, *The Future of Assisted Suicide and Euthanasia*, Ch. 9 (discussing Singer, *Practical Ethics*).

to raze or reimagine the law's protective *mens rea* forest in favor of some (surely well-intentioned) alternative vision will be able to do so without first confronting Finnis's defense. And that, though but a very small part of Finnis's body of work, represents a significant achievement indeed.

Bibliography

Bishop, Joel Prentiss (1892), *New Commentaries on the Criminal Law Upon a New System of Legal Exposition* (8th edn, Chicago, IL: T.H. Flood & Co.).

Finnis, John (1990), "Allocating Risks and Suffering: Some Hidden Traps," in John Finnis, *Collected Essays, Volume IV: Philosophy of Law* (Oxford: OUP), 337.

Finnis, John (1991), "Intention and Side Effects," in John Finnis, *Collected Essays, Volume II: Intention and Identity* (Oxford: OUP), 173.

Gorsuch, Neil M. (2006), *The Future of Assisted Suicide and Euthanasia* (Princeton, NJ: Princeton University Press).

Holmes, Oliver Wendell (1881), *The Common Law* (Boston, MA: Little, Brown & Co.).

Kant, Immanuel ([1785] 2002), *Groundwork for the Metaphysics of Morals* (trans. Allen W. Wood) (New Haven, CT: Yale University Press).

Keeton, W. Page, et al. (1984), *Prosser and Keeton on the Law of Torts* (5th edn, St. Paul, MN: West Publishing Co.).

LaFave, Wayne R. (2003), *Substantive Criminal Law* (2nd edn, St. Paul, MN: West Publishing Co.).

National Commission on Reform of the Federal Criminal Laws (1970), *Working Papers* (Washington, DC: US Government Printing Office).

Posner, Richard A. (1971), "Killing or Wounding to Protect a Property Interest," *J Law & Econ* 14: 201.

Posner, Richard A. (1995), *Aging and Old Age* (Chicago, IL: University of Chicago Press).

Posner, Richard A. (2011), *Economic Analysis of Law* (8th edn, New York, NY: Aspen Publishers).

Pound, Roscoe (1927), "Introduction," in Francis Bowes Sayre, *A Selection of Cases on Criminal Law* (Rochester, NY: Lawyers Co-Operative Publishing Co), xxix.

Report of the House of Lords Select Committee on Medical Ethics (Walton Report) (HL Paper 21–I of 1993–94).

Singer, Peter (1993), *Practical Ethics* (Cambridge: CUP).

Williams, Glanville (1965), *The Mental Element in Crime* (Jerusalem: Magnes Press).

Williams, Glanville (1983), *Textbook of Criminal Law* (2nd edn, London: Stevens).

Williams, Glanville (1987), "Oblique Intention," *Cambridge L J* 46: 417.

PHILOSOPHY, RELIGION, AND PUBLIC REASONS

26

The Right to Religious Liberty
and the Coercion of Belief

A Note on *Dignitatis humanae*

Thomas Pink

I. Liberty of Religion

What is the meaning of Vatican II's declaration *Dignitatis humanae*?[1] The declaration is commonly understood to teach a right not to be coerced in matters of religion that is uniform in relation to all kinds of authority, being grounded in the dignity of the human person. In particular, liberty of religious belief is taken to be inviolable; and the further right to freedom from coercion in the public practice of religion is subject only to the just limits of public order.

But it is not clear that this is an accurate reading of the declaration. True: in *Dignitatis humanae* the Church opposes and forbids religious coercion by the state or other civic institutions—including forms of religious coercion that once she actually called for and required. But in Catholic doctrine the true bearer of an authority to coerce, or to forbid coercion, in matters of revealed religion has historically been the Church, not the state. And Vatican II's declaration on religious freedom, as was clear by design, does not address the coercive authority of the Church. So *Dignitatis humanae* in no way denies the doctrine of the right and authority to pressure religious belief as well as public practice on which the Church's past policies, once very coercive indeed, were historically based. Policy may have changed through the Vatican II declaration, but the underlying doctrine of coercive authority has not.

II. The Coercive Authority of the Church: Trent and Canon Law

The problem of religious liberty is nowadays seen as a problem about limits to state authority. For today it is the state that is seen as having the ultimate right and authority to coerce—to authorize the use of force, and to give directions backed up by threats of punishment. And so for Church teaching about religious liberty people look to encyclicals about the state from the 19th-century papacy, from *Mirari vos* onwards, as well as to Vatican II's *Dignitatis humanae*.

In fact it was the Church that was traditionally seen as having the authority to direct religious belief and practice, and to enforce its directives by threats of punishment.

---

[1] *Dignitatis humanae*, declaration of the Second Vatican Council on religious freedom, in Tanner and Alberigo, *Decrees of the Ecumenical Councils*, volume 2, 1001–11.

And the basis of the Church's legislative authority was baptism, the sacrament that unites all Christians. For according to traditional teaching, it is the baptized that have, under the divine law of the New Covenant, an obligation of fidelity to the Church, to enforce which the Church has an authority to direct and to punish. So past fundamental teaching about religious liberty and coercion is to be found in two other places: in past conciliar teaching about baptism, and in the canonical tradition of the Church.

One figure who triggered conciliar teaching on this subject was Erasmus. In the preface to his *Paraphrases on Matthew*[2] he had proposed that those baptized as children be asked on growing up publicly to reaffirm their baptismal commitment to Catholic fidelity in belief and practice; and that they not be subjected to any coercion back into fidelity save exclusion from the sacraments if they were unwilling to provide the reaffirmation. This Erasmian challenge to the use of temporal penalties to pressure the baptized into fidelity had already been criticized by theologians in Spain and France well before Trent.[3] Trent specifically cites Erasmus's proposal, and in canon 14 of the decree on baptism imposes an anathema upon it:

> If anyone says that when they grow up (*cum adoleverint*), those baptized as little children should be asked whether they wish to affirm what their godparents promised in their name when they were baptized; and that, when they reply that they have no such wish, they should be left to their own decision and not, in the meantime, be coerced by any penalty into the Christian life (*suo esse arbitrio relinquendos nec alia interim poena ad christianam vitam cogendos*), except that they be barred from the reception of the eucharist and the other sacraments, until they have a change of heart: let him be anathema.[4]

This canon was understood as *de fide* support for the right and authority punitively to enforce baptismal obligations to fidelity. And that right was clearly understood by theologians and canonists from long before Trent as a right to coerce not only public practice, but also belief—a fundamental baptismal obligation being to faith. The central Catholic doctrine of the metaphysical freedom of the individual in respect of religious belief and action set barriers to religious coercion, but these were not absolute and uniform. The unbaptized had no obligation of fidelity to the Church, and so could never rightly be coerced into Catholic belief or practice. But the baptized did have such obligations; and so, once properly instructed, they could be threatened with punishments to coerce them into the faith, should their unbelief ever be expressed.[5]

---

[2] Erasmus, *In evangelium Matthei paraphrasis*.

[3] See Homza, 'Erasmus as Hero, or Heretic?'

[4] *Council of Trent*, Decree on baptism, canon 14, in Tanner and Alberigo, *Decrees of the Ecumenical Councils*, volume 2, 686.

[5] For a frequently cited canonical text, see the fourth council of Toledo of 633, forbidding coercion into the faith of the unbaptized; but requiring that, where necessary, the act of faith be coerced in the baptized (Friedberg, *Corpus iuris canonici*, volume 1, 161–2). See also Aquinas, *Summa theologiae* 2a2ae, q. 10, a. 8, *Utrum infideles compellendi sint ad fidem?*; Bellarmine *De laicis* in his *De controversiis christianae fidei, adversus huius temporis haereticos*; and Suarez *De fide*, in volume 12 of his *Opera omnia*. For later discussion of Trent's canon 14, see Billuart, *Summa sancti Thomae, tractatus de fide*, dissertation 5, article 2, *utrum infideles cogendi ad fidem?*; Perrone, *Praelectiones theologicae*, volume 7, *tractatus de baptismo*, 103–11; Hurter, *Theologiae dogmaticae compendium*, volume 3, tract 9 §§315–16 at 281–2.

Trent's teaching is a dogmatic canon. And the Church still teaches her possession of a coercive jurisdiction over the baptized, and in respect of belief as well as external practice. The present 1983 Code of Canon Law for the Latin Church states as canon 1311:

> The Church has the innate and proper right to coerce (*coercere*) offending members of the Christian faithful (*christifideles*) with punitive sanctions (*poenalibus sanctionibus*).

And the Christian faithful (*christifideles*) are defined within the Code in canon 204 §1, and in a way fully continuous with tradition, as the baptized:

> The Christian faithful are those who, inasmuch as they have been incorporated in Christ through baptism, have been constituted as the people of God.

So the 1983 Code of Canon Law, the 'code of Vatican II', undoubtedly maintains the traditional teaching that the Church possesses a coercive jurisdiction over the baptized.[6] Moreover the penalties applied are not restricted to the spiritual. For example, expiatory penalties (penalties that serve both to deter and to repair harm done) can include those that are temporal, removing some earthly good, as canon 1312 §2 affirms:

> The law can establish other expiatory penalties which deprive a member of the Christian faithful of some spiritual or temporal good and which are consistent with the supernatural purpose of the Church.

Along with apostasy and schism, heresy, which is defined in canon 751 as: 'the obstinate denial or obstinate doubt after the reception of baptism of some truth which is to be believed by divine and Catholic faith' is still punishable under canon law by the medicinal penalty, oriented towards cure of the offender, of excommunication. But it is also, in the case of those baptized who are Catholic clerics, punishable by expiatory penalties beyond exclusion from the sacraments, such as restriction of movement and loss of office and privilege (see canons 1364 and 1336). One can be punished by being forbidden to travel or by the loss of one's job. Granted, this is far from the more drastic penalties that we are familiar with in the pre-modern Church. But to be threatened with, say, the loss of one's job is not a trivial matter either. And the issue is not about this or that past form of coercion and its morality, many cases of which may indeed have been grossly immoral, but the very legitimacy of the coercive direction of anyone, including any of the baptized, in religious belief and practice.

---

[6] Canon 11 of the 1983 code decrees that, by contrast to the 1917 code, 'merely ecclesiastical laws' are now imposed by the Church only on Catholics. But this limitation is very importantly not cited in canon 1311's statement of the general coercive authority of the Church, which is still held to extend over *christifideles* without further qualification. Moreover 'merely ecclesiastical laws' are creations of human ecclesial legislation, such as the obligation to Friday penance, that can be humanly and canonically revised. They are not obligations under divine law, such as the basic obligation to fidelity applying to the baptized under the law of the New Covenant, which the Church's very authority to legislate presupposes and which the Church cannot revise. So canon 11 does not restrict the Church's authority to coerce—an authority which remains over the baptized in general as canon 1311 states. And this is a reading I share with the very thorough University of Navarre Commentary on the 1983 Code: my thanks to Fr Paul Hayward for the reference.

If these penalties are deliberately being imposed for, amongst other purposes, that of directing and influencing people either into remaining religiously faithful in the first place, or, through the disliked effects of actual imposition, into returning to fidelity, then it might look as though we have a coercive structure, however mild compared to any in the past, that in the case of some of the baptized is being applied to pressure religious belief and practice.

Could the penalties be too mild to engage any prohibition on religious coercion such as to be found *Dignitatis humanae*? That is not plausible. If governments threatened loss of employment as the penalty for expressing certain religious beliefs, and did so as part of a general policy of deliberately discouraging people from holding them, then surely this would be quite enough to violate *Dignitatis humanae*'s teaching.

It might be suggested that the Church's insistence on orthodoxy is merely a form of membership or employment condition, to protect the integrity of the institution, and is not actually intended as part of a coercive structure to deter offenders or to reform them. On this view, the canon law on heresy is not aimed at coercively influencing what beliefs certain people hold and express. It is no more so coercively intended than any other simple membership or job qualification. But this fails to take into account the penal language. The code specifically addresses infidelity or heresy not as a simple failure to meet conditions on membership or employment, but as a wrong or crime—a *delictum*—deserving punishment—*poena*. And the loss of communion or office or privilege that follows is described in explicitly punitive terms. And for the Church to threaten a clearly unwelcome outcome such as job loss specifically as a punishment for wrongdoing, is precisely to act like any authority seeking coercively to regulate and influence what people believe and do and to pressure them away from whatever is being classed as wrong. By attaching real costs to heresy, and describing those costs as punishment for what is presented as a crime, the Church is conveying the very same coercive message that states do when they attach similarly penal costs to actions classed by them criminal—namely that what has been penalized really is wrong, and so is not to be done. The Church is doing exactly what she describes herself in canon 1311 as having the right to do, namely to give coercive direction to the baptized—in this case to use the threat of punishment to influence what the baptized believe, directing them away from the crime of heresy.

If the Church treats heresy and apostasy as punishable wrongs, and punishable by outcomes materially unwelcome to the offender, then it seems she is morally committed to what follows from this—the licitness in at least some cases and under some circumstances of using some form of penal coercion, beyond mere exclusion from the sacraments, as a means to holding people to their baptismal obligations. Which is precisely what Trent claims to be legitimate. At issue behind Trent's condemnation of Erasmus is the seriousness with which the Church means what she says in the formulations of her own canon law.

III. Religious Coercion and the Authority of the State

Dignitatis humanae is often presented as if in opposing religious coercion by the state, it involved some change in Church teaching about the authority of the state, and in this a departure from 19th-century papal teaching. But this is not obviously true. Gregory XVI's *Mirari vos*, Pius IX's *Quanta cura*, and Leo XIII's *Immortale dei* do all make claims about the state and its religious duties. Some of these duties are to profess the true religion, which is the Catholic faith. Thus *Immortale dei* says

> So, too, it is a crime for the state to act as if there were no God, or not to have a care for religion, as something beyond its scope, or as of no practical benefit; or out of the many forms of religion to adopt whatever one it likes; for states are bound absolutely to worship God in that way which he has shown to be his will.[7]

This teaching about the state's duty to profess the true religion clearly concerns a duty of reason under natural law:

> As a consequence, the state, constituted as it is, is clearly bound to fulfil the many and weighty duties linking it to God, by the public profession of religion. Nature and reason, which command every individual devoutly to worship God in holiness, because we are under his authority, and because having come from him we must return to him, bind also the civil community by the same law.[8]

Now *Dignitatis humanae* does not explicitly teach this natural law duty on the state to profess the true religion. But nor does the declaration explicitly deny this teaching either. There is then left open the possibility of at least a 'soft' or non-coercive Catholic religious establishment. Vatican II's declaration directly opposes not establishment, but the state's involvement in religious coercion. So is this opposition to religious coercion by the state really what some assert it to be—a change in doctrine that is social, about the nature of the state? I shall suggest that it marks not any doctrinal change, but rather a change in the Church's policy—in the use of her own authority.

Certainly the 19th-century papacy did teach a duty on the state to coerce on behalf of the Catholic faith. Thus in *Quanta cura*, those people are condemned who assert

> that it is the best condition of civil society, in which no duty is recognized, as attached to the civil power, of coercing by enacted penalties, offenders against the Catholic religion, except in so far as public peace may require.[9]

So Pius IX certainly talked of the state as having an *officium coercendi* or duty to coerce on behalf of the Catholic faith in matters of religion. But where, according to papal teaching, does this duty come from? Does the state have an authority of its own to direct and coerce the religious belief and practice of its subjects, an authority it should exercise on behalf of the true faith? Or does the authority to direct and coerce religion belong to the Church, so that the duty on the state is imposed on it by the Church, and is a duty to help the Church in the exercise of her authority?

Quanta cura does not actually answer this crucial question. That was left to Leo XIII, who explained which coercive power, Church or state, has the authority to direct and legislate for the practice of religion. His doctrine is clear. That authority very clearly

---

[7] Leo XIII, *Immortale dei*, §6.
[8] Leo XIII, *Immortale dei*, §6.
[9] Pius IX, *Quanta cura*, §3.

attaches to the Church, not to the state. For it is the role of the Church, not the state, to direct humans to supernatural ends, and—as the modern Code still proclaims—to authorize coercion for those same ends. In *Immortale dei* he expressly claims:

> In truth Jesus Christ gave his Apostles free authority in matters sacred, together with a true power to legislate and what follows therefrom, the twofold power to judge and to punish... Hence, it is the Church, and not the State, that is to be man's guide to heaven: and it is to the same Church that God has assigned the charge of seeing to, and legislating for, what concerns religion.[10]

And

> The Almighty, therefore, has given the charge of the human race to two powers, the ecclesiastical and the civil, the one being set over divine, the other over human, things... While one of the two powers has for its immediate and chief object care of the goods of this mortal life, the other provides for goods that are heavenly and everlasting. Whatever, therefore, in things human is in any way of a sacred character, whatever belongs either of its own nature or by reason of the end to which it is referred, to the salvation of souls or to the worship of God, is subject to the power and judgment of the Church.[11]

Nor was Leo XIII's teaching novel. We find it also three centuries before in papally approved teaching coming out of the Roman College. So when *Dignitatis humanae* says

> Furthermore, those private and public acts of religion by which people relate themselves to God from the sincerity of their hearts, of their nature transcend the earthly and temporal levels of reality. So the state, whose peculiar purpose it is to provide for the temporal common good, should certainly recognise and promote the religious life of its citizens. With equal certainty it exceeds the limits of its authority if it takes upon itself to direct or prevent religious activity.[12]

we shall easily find texts of approved Roman theology from the counter-reformation that, regarding the state, say much the same. Thus Suarez, in a papally commissioned text of 1613, the *Defensio fidei catholicae*, asserts against James I of England limits to his or any state's authority in matters of religion:

> Punishment of crimes only belongs to civil magistrates in so far as those crimes are contrary to political ends, public peace and human justice; but coercion with respect to those deeds which are opposed to religion and to the salvation of the soul, is essentially a function of spiritual power [the power of the Church], so that the authority to make use of temporal penalties for the purposes of such correction must have been allotted in particular to this spiritual power.[13]

The ends natural to this life that were the particular competence of the state simply did not justify coercion on behalf of any revealed religion. So we had a natural right not to

---

[10] Leo XIII, *Immortale dei*, §11.
[11] Leo XIII, *Immortale dei*, §§13–14.
[12] *Dignitatis humanae*, §3, in Tanner and Alberigo, *Decrees of the Ecumenical Councils*, volume 2, 1004.
[13] Suarez, *Defensio fidei catholicae*, Bk 3, Ch. 23, §19, in *Opera omnia*, volume 24, 320–1.

be so coerced on the state's authority. Vatican II's statement above of the state's lack of authority in matters of religion is not novel at all.

How then was the state ever involved in religious coercion? For everyone knows that Catholic states were once very heavily involved. Heresy could be a crime under state law. And Catholic states were still being encouraged into the 19th century, as a matter of duty, to protect their subjects from error by restricting non-Catholic practice and proselytization in the public sphere. If all this religious coercion was under the authority of the Church, then its basis must lie in what founds that authority—the sacrament of baptism and the moral obligations on the baptized that baptism brings. Traditionally understood, these may include a duty, when so directed, to aid the Church in her rightful use of force, whether to enforce baptismal obligations on the baptized themselves, or to resist and ward off threats to the Church's mission from without, such as by protecting the baptized from exposure to non-Catholic religious practice or proselytization. And that is how the state came into the picture: through such obligations on the baptized so to assist the Church. For if the state is Christian, its rulers as baptized can in particular be under an obligation to assist the Church in coercion for religious ends, should such assistance be requested. But the authority behind such religious coercion is, as Leo XIII insisted, that of the Church, not that of the state. This is a coercive authority that exists independently of that of the state, that serves supernatural ends quite distinct from those proper to the state, and that would still exist whether or not the state existed.

To take one example, from what is as much a general Council of the Church as Vatican II: Lateran IV clearly committed itself to the existence of an obligation on baptized rulers to assist the Church in the exercise of her coercive jurisdiction, should that assistance be requested. That Council conveyed the teaching in the most direct way possible: by making the provision of such assistance a condition of rulers' continued communion with the Church.[14] Baptized rulers unwilling to follow Church instructions to remove heresy could be excommunicated, the Council decreed—a penalty that was imposed by a pope after the Reformation on one otherwise faithful Habsburg ruler who dared to tolerate Protestant belief and practice among his subjects.[15]

IV. Religious Liberty as a Political Liberty

Dignitatis humanae nowhere addresses the coercive authority of the Church. This was by intent, as was made plain by the conciliar commission for the declaration. For it was objected to the declaration by worried canonists among the Council fathers that there were examples of religious coercion exercised by the apostles over the baptized that could be drawn from the New Testament itself.[16] In reply the Commission noted:

---

[14] See Fourth Lateran Council, Constitution *De haereticis* in Tanner and Alberigo, *Decrees of the Ecumenical Councils*, volume 1, 234.

[15] See Wilson, *Europe's Tragedy: A History of the Thirty Years' War*, 68.

[16] One such traditionally alleged example being, for example, the deaths of Ananias and Saphira, often seen as an apostolic penalty imposed by St. Peter on errant baptized.

Examples and statements brought against the text taken from the New Testament (and also many from the Old Testament) either concern the internal life of the religious community of Israel, in which Jesus and the Apostles lived, or the intra-ecclesial life of the early Christian community. And the declaration does not treat of this life.[17]

And again, in reply to the suggestion that the Declaration affirm as compatible with religious liberty that the Church use sanctions to impose her doctrine and discipline on those subject to her, the Commission replied that proposal was not admitted since the Declaration was not to treat of the question of freedom within the Church herself.[18]

The declaration plainly declares at the outset that its purpose is to address the rights of individuals and groups in civil society, and, in particular, in relation to the state. The declaration is entitled: *On the right of persons and communities to social and civil liberty in religious matters.* And the declaration further announces in the first paragraph that since its concerns are with civil liberty, nothing in the declaration affects traditional teaching concerning people's obligations to the Church, including those of the baptized:

> Indeed, since people's demand for religious liberty in carrying out their duty to worship God concerns freedom from compulsion in civil society, it leaves intact the traditional catholic teaching on the moral obligation of individuals and societies towards the true religion and the one Church of Christ.[19]

This passage is often taken to be, at best, a sop to nostalgia for some form of Catholic state establishment. But the significance of this passage is more fundamental. The declaration was intended to bypass the coercive authority of the Church. And what else is included in the 'traditional teaching' that the declaration is supposed to preserve? Clearly included are the moral obligations to the Church of the baptized. These obligations base and constitute the Church's coercive jurisdiction, and as traditionally understood include obligations on the baptized to aid the Church in exercising her authority. One effect of the clause is, exactly as required, to ring-fence what was supposed to be ring-fenced—the coercive authority of the Church.

The part of the declaration entitled 'The general principle of religious freedom' that states and argues for this principle then relies primarily on appeal to natural reason— not on appeal to revelation, on which an account of the coercive authority under the New Covenant of the Church would have very importantly to depend. For the Council admits that the right not to be coerced with which it is concerned—a right not to be coerced by the state—is not dealt with in revelation:

> ...revelation does not expressly affirm the right of immunity from external coercion in religious affairs.[20]

---

[17] *Acta Synodalia Sacrosancti Concilii Oecumenici Vaticani II*, volume 4, part 6, 763.
[18] *Acta Synodalia Sacrosancti Concilii Oecumenici Vaticani II*, volume 4, part 6, 770.
[19] *Dignitatis humanae* §1, in Tanner and Alberigo, *Decrees of the Ecumenical Councils*, volume 2, 1002.
[20] *Dignitatis humanae,* §9, in Tanner and Alberigo, *Decrees of the Ecumenical Councils*, volume 2, 1006.

It is only in a final section entitled 'Religious freedom in the light of revelation' that the Council does make some appeal to revelation, and to the history and past teaching and official conduct of the Church. But this is certainly not to enunciate a comprehensive doctrine about the authority of the Church. The appeal is being made only at the end of the declaration, and only to support and reinforce a case that has already been made for what is a civil liberty—and a case that has already been made from reason. The case is certainly not built on any overall account of the history, conduct and past teaching on coercion generally of the Church. Rather two points alone are emphasized. First, emphasis is placed on what is a clearly revealed doctrine—the metaphysical freedom of the act of faith:

> And first and foremost religious freedom in the social order is fully congruent (*congrua*) with the freedom of the act of christian faith.[21]

Second, the conduct of the Church in relation to those already baptized is not explicitly discussed. Rather, having announced as one of the chief Catholic doctrines that no one must be forced to embrace the Catholic faith against their will, the declaration then emphasizes the fact that from the apostles on, the Church never, at least officially, relied on coercion to evangelize the *unbaptized*. The declaration's account of Church history in relation to the non-coercion of faith is entirely centred on the Church's constant opposition to any coercion of the non-baptized:

> The apostles, taught by Christ's word and example, followed the same course. From the very beginning of the Church the followers of Christ strove to convert people to the confession of Christ as Lord, not by any coercive measures or by devices unworthy of the Gospel, but chiefly by the power of God's message.[22]

There is, it is true, the following rather more general statement about past Church teaching on coercion:

> Although at times in the life of the people of God, as it has pursued its pilgrimage through the vicissitudes of human history, there have been ways of acting less than in conformity to the spirit of the gospel, indeed contrary to it, nevertheless it has always remained the teaching of the Church that no one's faith is to be coerced.[23]

But this statement occurs at the end of a general account of evangelization of non-Christians, and is plausibly to be understood as referring to the communication of faith in the context of such evangelization. For read as an account of Church teaching regarding coercion of the faith of the baptized, and given her own continuing imposition of penal sanctions on the baptized for the crimes of heresy and apostasy, this statement about 'what has always remained the teaching of the Church' would be a plain falsehood. There is certainly no more detailed account given of the Church's past teaching on and policy in relation to coercion generally, and especially with respect to coercion of those already baptized. Such an account would be deeply relevant

---

[21] *Dignitatis humanae*, §9, in Tanner and Alberigo, *Decrees of the Ecumenical Councils*, volume 2, 1006.
[22] *Dignitatis humanae*, §11, in Tanner and Alberigo, *Decrees of the Ecumenical Councils*, volume 2, 1008.
[23] *Dignitatis humanae*, §12, in Tanner and Alberigo, *Decrees of the Ecumenical Councils*, volume 2, 1009.

to—indeed a compulsory feature of—any serious account of the jurisdiction specifically of the Church.

Dignitatis humanae supports its account of Church history by references, in footnote 8, to the pre-1917 *Corpus iuris canonici*. This canonical material is cited by the declaration to support the claim that the Church historically forbad coercion into the faith. The material from the *Corpus* cited is very exact. It specifically condemns the use of coercion to evangelize the unbaptized, such as the coercive baptism of Jews and Moslems. Indeed, one canonical authority referenced is that much-cited traditional canonical plank for the coercion of the faith in heretics, the fourth Council of Toledo, which having condemned coercion into baptism, then, in the very same passage referred to by *Dignitatis humanae*, and in the same terms and with the same force, demands coercive measures to retain within the faith those who, having been baptized, then attempt to leave.[24] The declaration is clearly not telling some story about how Church teaching has always opposed the coercion of religious belief as such—a story that would anyway be utterly false. The non-coercive story told is very clearly restricted to the case of the unbaptized.

Why then in the second section on revelation did the Council concentrate just on two specific points—the metaphysical freedom of the act of faith and the Church's teaching and conduct concerning the evangelization of the unbaptized? The answer is that though such a selective treatment both of revelation and of the past is dangerously misleading for any general account of the jurisdiction of the Church—and obviously so since the history of non-coercion given precisely addresses only the conduct of the Church towards the belief of those *not yet within her jurisdiction*—it is deeply relevant to what was the Council's true and immediate concern, which is the coercive authority (or rather lack of it) in matters of religion of the state and other civil institutions.

Why might the policy of the Church towards those not yet baptized be peculiarly relevant to an argument concerned with a specifically civil liberty of religion? After all, it might be thought, states may well be able licitly to do lots of things not open to, or not the business of the Church. Why should limits to what the Church can rightly do, and in one specific case, be relevant to determining limitations on state action? In fact the answer is fairly obvious. According to perfectly traditional teaching, the metaphysical freedom of the act of faith leaves the unbaptized believer standing in relevantly the same normative relation to the Church as all people, baptized or unbaptized, stand in relation to the state. So if revealed teaching rules out coercion into the faith of the unbaptized by the Church, that supports the case initially made at the level of reason against religious coercion by the state.

Why is the relation of the metaphysically free believer to Church or to state in these two cases in relevant respects normatively the same? Because in both cases the bearer of authority is dealing with a being in possession of metaphysical freedom who is not yet bound by a religious obligation to that authority. Why cannot the Church coerce the unbaptized into Christianity? Because, the traditional answer would go, although the metaphysically free believer has a moral obligation to God to believe the true divine

---

[24] See again Friedberg, *Corpus iuris canonici*, volume 1, 161–2.

revelation, being unbaptized he has as yet no such obligation to the Church. Therefore given the person's metaphysical freedom and the lack of any such obligation binding him specifically to the Church, the Church simply has no authority to coerce him into Catholic fidelity. But something similar would hold of the state, and whether or not the person is baptized. He is metaphysically free, has an obligation to God in respect of the true religion—but whether baptized or not has no specifically religious obligations to the state. Since no one has any religious obligations to the state, so the state has no specifically religious authority, and so no authority of its own to coerce or direct anyone in any way in religious matters. The parallel between limits to the coercive powers of the Church and those of the state is in this particular case clear. The incompleteness of the declaration's account of Church teaching and history is not a problem; or, at least, it is not a problem as part of an argument that is primarily based on natural reason, and that specifically concerns the coercive jurisdiction not of the Church herself but of the state and other like civil institutions.

V. The Scope of *Dignitatis Humanae's* Teaching

So *Dignitatis humanae* in no way impugns religious coercion as such. Its subject matter is state and civil coercion under natural law; and it teaches the moral wrongness of the state's involvement in religious coercion. And that wrongness plainly follows given, first, the state's lack of any authority of its own for such coercion—hardly a new idea, but Counter-reformation and Leonine teaching; and given, second, the Church's present and evident refusal to license such coercion by states on her authority. But is this refusal relevant? Was the Church not just wrong in the past to license state involvement in religious coercion, and even demand that Christian states coerce on her behalf and on her authority? Opinions will differ on what is a very complex question. But this is a question concerning the coercive authority of the Church herself, and not one that *Dignitatis humanae* actually addresses. All the declaration states is that, as things stand, and given rights against the state attaching to human nature, state coercion of religion cannot be justified.

Dignitatis humanae in no way denies that the Church's past policy, particularly towards those subject to her jurisdiction, the baptized, was highly coercive; nor does the declaration in any way disavow or contradict the Church teaching that consistently endorsed such coercion, when carried out under her authority. The declaration even cites, we have seen, and without condemnation, canonical authority supportive of such coercion. The whole declaration sidesteps very carefully the issue of the Church's own coercive authority, and the legitimacy of past religious coercion applied under that authority.

The Church's present policy regarding state coercion on her behalf is abundantly clear, and is not likely to change soon. But the complete Catholic doctrine on the issue goes beyond this. It depends on the moral obligations of the baptized, including baptized state officials, towards the Church; and it depends on the nature of those obligations not just under present conditions, but also under conditions such as those that held in the past, when state populations were overwhelmingly made up of the baptized, and Church policy was very different. Beyond expressly undertaking to preserve traditional teaching about such obligations—and the *Corpus iuris canonici* and cases such as Lateran IV suggest something about the possible content of this teaching—the declaration does not itself tell us what these obligations could involve. The declaration in effect guarantees traditional teaching about the authority of the Church to direct and coerce, without itself telling us what that teaching is.

VI. How to Model the Right to Religious Liberty

Catholic teaching on religious liberty is distinctive in two ways. First, it bases a normative freedom, a right not to be coerced, on a metaphysical freedom—on people's power of control over belief and action. This appeal to metaphysical freedom is unlike much modern secular liberalism, and itself deserves discussion. Second, the teaching involves a model of religious liberty that is jurisdiction-centred rather than purely person-centred.

On the person-centred view the right not to be religiously coerced is uniform in relation to all kinds of authority, being set directly, without any intervening juridical considerations, by the character and dignity of the human person. On a jurisdiction-centred view, the right of a person not to be coerced in matters of religion still involves recognition of their dignity—but the recognition due is variable, and depends on what kind of juridical authority is behind the coercion, and also on whether the person falls under that authority's jurisdiction. So the state can lack an authority to coerce religion that the Church possesses. This difference is explained by something else besides human nature itself—by the different ends served by the two forms of authority. It is the temporal ends served by the state, and the fact that religion transcends those ends, that limits state authority over religion. The limit is not uniformly fixed, for all authorities, by human nature alone—as *Dignitatis humanae* makes clear:

> So the state, *whose peculiar purpose it is to provide for the temporal common good*, should certainly recognise and promote the religious life of its citizens. With equal certainty it exceeds the limits of its authority if it takes upon itself to direct or prevent religious activity.[25]

The historical Catholic view is jurisdiction-centred. And *Dignitatis humanae* seems designed to respect this. This is plain from the careful structure of the declaration and its very effective ring-fencing of the coercive authority of the Church. The appearance of a person-centred account arises from the declaration's failure explicitly to address the Church herself as a coercive authority—a conception of the Church that in fact some supporters of the declaration, such as John Courtney Murray, anyway did not fully share[26]—so that the declaration can easily be read as concerned with religious coercion in general. But the declaration's talk of the incapacity of 'human' authorities to direct and coerce religion clearly does not include the Church. 'Human' in this context does not mean 'staffed by humans' but rather serving ends natural to humanity, as opposed to the supernatural ends served by the Church. This is plain when we read:

---

[25] See again *Dignitatis humanae*, §3.
[26] See Pink, 'Conscience and Coercion'; and Pink, 'The Interpretation of *Dignitatis humanae*'.

For the practice of religion, of its very nature, consists principally in internal acts that are voluntary and free, in which one relates oneself to God directly; and these acts can neither be commanded nor forbidden by any merely human power.[27]

It cannot be denied that as an authority the Church precisely commands and requires of the baptized that they maintain and remain true to their baptismal faith. Canonically, the Church still claims a right to direct and coerce the beliefs of the baptized.[28]

The traditional teaching of the Church is that our right to religious liberty is juridically conditioned, and is not a simple and direct function of our metaphysical status. In particular, the liberty of the baptized is limited and conditioned by baptismally generated obligations to the Church. Since *Dignitatis humanae* can be interpreted—indeed itself *demands* that it be interpreted—so as to respect and leave intact traditional teaching concerning these obligations, then everything in it has to be read with the appropriate qualification. Whenever the right to liberty is grounded by the declaration on considerations X and Y, it must be left open that X or Y might not strictly be enough—that also necessary must be an absence of the kind of normative or juridical relation that a baptized person has to the Church. What would follow for the baptized given the presence of that relation must remain up to the traditional teaching to determine.

So when we read

But people are only able to meet this obligation [to truth] in ways that accord with their own nature, if they enjoy both psychological freedom and freedom from external coercion. Thus the right to religious freedom is based on human nature itself, not on any merely personal attitude of mind.[29]

this affirmation certainly establishes that coercively to pressure people in the exercise of their metaphysical freedom and their rationality is, considered in itself, something very undesirable—indeed that given our rational and free nature, such coercion is an injury and wrong done to the person coerced unless, of course, the coercion has some special and weighty justification. The text of the declaration also states, very clearly, that when the coercion is applied on political or civic authority, and when moreover it occurs to pressure someone's religious belief, such justification is always lacking. The metaphysical freedom of the believer does in that case give him an absolute right not to be coerced, a right he enjoys given the state's lack of any authority to coerce him. That the coercion would be equally wrong when the person is baptized and the authority behind the coercion is the Church cannot be assumed to follow; and certainly, given the declaration's self-proclaimed subject matter and the self-imposed restrictions on its interpretation, it is not expressly claimed by the declaration itself to follow.

Is not any attempt to coerce belief objectionable just as a direct assault on human rationality? Not obviously. Legal coercion is not just a brute force, like a kick or a shove. The legislator's threat of punishment is intended to influence, but not to replace, the

---

[27] *Dignitatis humanae*, §3, in Tanner and Alberigo, *Decrees of the Ecumenical Councils*, volume 2, 1003.
[28] See the 1983 Code: canon 750 directs us to believe certain truths, and subsequent canons characterize heresy as involving the punishable doubt or denial of such truths.
[29] *Dignitatis humanae*, §2, in Tanner and Alberigo, *Decrees of the Ecumenical Councils*, volume 2, 1003.

exercise of our rationality, and to influence, in particular, what we believe, and in ways already modelled in Suarez's counter-reformation account of the coercion of belief. For Suarez, the coercion of belief does not involve the Hobbesean or Lockean caricature of it as pointless inquisitional cruelty: a blank command, accompanied by threats, to believe something without reason, such as that two plus two equals five. The function of canonical penalties is indeed intended to motivate compliance through exploiting dislike of the penalties; but dislike of the threatened penalties is supposed to work by engaging the attention of those threatened, and motivating and directing them seriously to consider a case that is being argued, on the basis of reasoning or credible testimony, and which they had wilfully and culpably been ignoring. In relation to belief the function of coercion is not to replace argument and evidence, but to reinforce them.[30]

The laws imposed by modern states arguably work rather similarly in relation to the various kinds of non-religious action which those states justly coerce and direct. The function of penal coercion in the criminal law is often to use the threat of a penalty to engage attention and help communicate a message that there are anyway prior grounds to believe—that the action threatened by punishment really would be seriously wrong.[31] The function of sanction-backed criminal law is in part to drive home an argument and change what people—not non-rational animals but beings equipped with reason—actually believe. No matter how terrible and unwarranted the means adopted by the 16th-century Church's agents, their conception of the use of law to coerce the baptized into meeting their obligations was not so very different. The canonical punishments for heresy and the like threatened by the counter-reformation Church, or by the modern Church, are similar in intended function to the criminal penalties threatened by today's liberal state: to communicate testimony or witness to the truth given by representatives of the coercing authority—witness or testimony that should anyway be enough to support and warrant assent; and by impelling attention to the message and its grounds, to pressure those subject to the authority into believing it.

So when *Dignitatis humanae* says in its first introductory paragraph that 'truth imposes itself solely by the force of its own truth' this cannot sensibly be understood to rule out the use of coercive penalties to communicate truth and to persuade. The modern liberal state makes such use of penalties the whole time. Of course coming to believe a claim, whether through uncoerced enquiry or after being subject to coercive pressure, is indeed always to come to see the claim as true. Coercive pressure cannot bypass this essential feature of belief. One cannot come to believe a claim just as a strategy for avoiding a punishment, but without *ipso facto* coming to see that claim as true. So coercive pressure to be effective in communicating belief must operate exactly as Suarez envisaged. It must affect how the truth appears, and do so by leading people to attend to genuine grounds for the belief by way of evidence or testimony. And

---

[30] See Suarez's illuminating general discussion of the coercion of belief in *De fide*, disputation 18, section 4, §§7–8 in volume 12 of his *Opera omnia*, 450–1.

[31] For a modern theory of the expressive function of punishment see Feinberg, *Doing and Deserving*. The idea that *liberal* punishment cannot seek to address and change people's thoughts and beliefs—to direct and form their conscience as well as their external actions—is naive both about liberalism and about punishment.

certainly in so far as the truth does then actually 'impose itself' on one's belief, one will indeed come to believe the truth just because it is the truth—just by the force of its own truth, because that is how the truth now appears.

VII. Conclusion

The issue is not the overall morality of the Church's past coercive policies, such as her past choice of sanctions and her choice of targets. Much imprudence and outright cruelty was involved, scarcely justified by the supernatural ends the coercion was supposed to serve. The issue is the Church's very authority and right to coerce religious belief and practice. Is her possession of such an authority a matter of Catholic faith? It seems in fact to be so.

The modern Catholic debate about religious liberty has been conducted as a debate about the state and its competence and authority in matters of religion. The focus has been on this: apparent, and considerable, variation over time in the levels of state coercion of religion that the Church has been willing to endorse. To the end of the Counter-reformation, the Church often required the state to aid in the coercive reconversion to Catholic fidelity of baptized Protestants—a coercion that, even before Vatican II, she eventually came to forbid. Then, during the 19th century, and to the 1960s, she might encourage the restriction, in Catholic countries at least, of non-Catholic practice in the public sphere. And now, subject to just public order, she forbids the state to coerce religiously at all; and concordats with Catholic countries have been rewritten to reflect this.

The debate about the significance of such apparent variation in permitted state coercion is proving interminable. Indeed, the debate seems impossible to resolve when limited to the history of teaching specifically on the state. And now we see why. For all along the real coercive authority in religion was the Church, not the state.

So until the debate moves from what is, where religion is concerned, the secondary issue of the authority and competence of the state, and addresses what is fundamental, the authority of the Church over those subject to her, the controversy about religious liberty cannot be resolved. We particularly need what is currently lacking—a theology of the Church that properly acknowledges what seems *de fide*, her own divinely given authority to coerce belief as well as practice, and which explains the doctrinal basis of and limits to the Church's power of coercion. This will centrally involve an appropriate theology of baptism and, in particular, of the obligations to the Church incurred through baptism. For Erasmus's anti-coercive heresy was about baptism, not about the state. So it is baptism and its juridical and moral significance that will be key to settling the debate about religious liberty.

Bibliography

Acta Synodalia Sacrosancti Concilii Oecumenici Vaticani II (1970) (6 volumes) (Vatican City).
Aquinas, Thomas (c.1265–73), *Summa theologiae*.
Bellarmine, Robert (1599), *De controversiis christianae fidei, adversus huius temporis haereticos* (Ingolstadt).

Billuart, Charles-René (1746–51), *Summa sancti Thomae* (Liège).

Codex iuris canonici (1983) (Vatican City).

Erasmus, Desiderius (1522), *In evangelium Matthei paraphrasis* (Basel).

Feinberg, Joel (1970), *Doing and Deserving: Essays in the Theory of Responsibility* (Princeton, NJ: Princeton University Press).

Friedberg, Emil (ed.) (1881) *Corpus iuris canonici* (2 volumes) (Leipzig).

Homza, Lu Ann (1997), 'Erasmus as Hero, or Heretic? Spanish Humanism and the Valladolid Assembly of 1527', *Renaissance Quarterly* 50: 78–118.

Hurter, Hugo von (1908), *Theologiae dogmaticae compendium* (Innsbruck).

Leo XIII (1885), *Immortale dei* (Rome).

Perrone, Giovanni (1845), *Praelectiones theologicae* (Milan).

Pink, Thomas (2012), 'Conscience and Coercion', *First Things* 225: 45–51.

Pink, Thomas (forthcoming 2013) 'The Interpretation of *Dignitatis humanae*', *Nova et Vetera*.

Pius IX (1864), *Quanta cura* (Rome).

Suarez, Francisco (1856–70), *Opera omnia* (Paris).

Tanner, Norman and Alberigo, Giuseppe (eds) (1990), *Decrees of the Ecumenical Councils*, 2 volumes (Georgetown).

Wilson, Peter (2009), *Europe's Tragedy: A History of the Thirty Years' War* (London: Allen Lane).

27

Natural Law and the Transcendent Source of Human Fulfillment

Germain Grisez

John Finnis points out that, although the basic aspects of human well-being are really and unquestionably good, further practical questions arise, including ones "about the possibility of a deeper explanation of obligation" and "the point of living according to the requirements of practical reasonableness."[1] I shall not deal in this essay with what Finnis has written about those questions. Instead, I will first summarize the view Finnis and I share about the emergence of the moral *ought* and explain its inherent normative force. Second, I will sketch out my own view of what that *ought* gains in normative force from what one can know by philosophical reflection about the Creator and about the ultimate end for which human beings should act. Third, I will sketch out my view of what the moral *ought* can gain in normative force—for people who live by the light of faith in the Lord Jesus Christ—by theological reflection on the Kingdom of God.

I. The Moral *Ought:* Its Emergence and Inherent Force

Moral norms are often confused with positive laws or with informal sociocultural norms—rules that depend on the choices of societies' law-makers or opinion leaders. Young children, unable to understand the reasons behind any of the norms they are taught, inevitably consider all of them binding inasmuch as adults enforce conformity. Some passages of the Old Testament (Hebrew Bible) are easily misunderstood as implying that moral obligations depend on God's will and might well be different. Both those who entirely reject many of the moral norms included in those sacred writings and people who violate those norms while regarding them as binding are likely to conveniently regard them as arbitrary rules.

Finnis, Joseph Boyle, and I explained that moral norms are truths underlying sound moral judgments and are one kind of practical truth. We argued that there are self-evident practical truths, which take the form: X is a basic human good to be promoted and protected. These self-evident practical principles direct human beings toward various intelligible aspects of the well-being and flourishing of individual persons and of communities. The basic human goods are: life, including health and bodily integrity; skillful work and play; knowledge and esthetic experience; harmony among a person's own judgments, choices, feelings, and behavior; harmony with other human

---

[1] *CEJF* V, 26–9, 31–3, 56–79, 135–8, 179–88, 193–202, 370–1; *FoE*, 136–53; *Aquinas*, 294–334; *NLNR* 371–413, 424–5, 477–9.

beings; harmony with the transcendent source of meaning and value, which we call *God*; and marriage, including parenthood.[2]

While the first principle of practical reasoning—*Good is to be done and pursued, and evil is to be avoided*—demands one to be reasonable enough to avoid pointless behavior, the first principle of morality makes a stronger demand: to be entirely reasonable. "*Right reason* is nothing but *unfettered reason*, working throughout deliberation and receiving full attention."[3] When one's feelings incline one to make a choice on grounds one knows to be less than fully reasonable, the directiveness of practical knowledge becomes moral normativity: *is-to-be* becomes *ought-to-be*. "The ought-to-be which calls for morally right choice represents the full directiveness of practical knowledge, while the is-to-be which commends the morally wrong choice represents a fragment of that directiveness operating in isolation from the whole."[4]

We proposed a rather complex formulation of the first principle of morality.[5] I now think that the self-evident truth underlying intermediate moral principles is simpler. In its contest with feelings, reason of course rules in favor of itself: *When one's feelings incline one to choose what reasons indicate is not to be chosen or not to choose what reasons indicate is to be chosen, one ought to choose in accord with reasons.*

Being self-evident, that principle cannot be demonstrated. But it can be explained. Since *every* option for choice has the support of some feelings (without such support nothing becomes an option for choice[6]), choosing in accord with reasons involves subordinating one's feelings, not disregarding them. Moreover, since all the principles of practical reasoning together direct actions toward the fulfillment of every aspect of a human being as a whole person, no part of oneself would be neglected if one consistently chose in accord with reasons, whereas some part of oneself is neglected or ill-treated whenever one chooses in accord with insubordinate feelings.

In our works, Finnis, Boyle, and I call intermediate moral principles *requirements of practical reasonableness* or *modes of responsibility*.[7] Like the first principle of morality, these intermediate principles do not refer to specific kinds of acts. So, philosophers sometimes mistakenly regard one or another of them as the first principle of morality.

Perhaps the most widely recognized intermediate moral principle is fairness: In the absence of a *reason* for treating different people differently, one ought not treat them differently according to one's special feelings toward them.[8] Another intermediate moral principle forbids taking revenge and otherwise intentionally harming others: One ought not implement feelings of anger and hatred by choosing to harm another (reason always forbids intentionally violating anyone's good). Again, desire, fear, and lethargy unintegrated with reason ought to give way to reasons: someone dieting for

---

[2] Grisez et al., "Practical Principles, Moral Truth, and Ultimate Ends" (1987f), 102–20.

[3] Grisez et al., "Practical Principles, Moral Truth, and Ultimate Ends" (1987f), 121.

[4] Grisez et al., "Practical Principles, Moral Truth, and Ultimate Ends" (1987f), 125.

[5] Grisez et al., "Practical Principles, Moral Truth, and Ultimate Ends" (1987f), 127–9.

[6] Grisez et al., "Practical Principles, Moral Truth, and Ultimate Ends" (1987f), 122–5.

[7] Grisez et al., "Practical Principles, Moral Truth, and Ultimate Ends" (1987f), 127–8. Russell Shaw and I introduced the expression *modes of responsibility* in Grisez and Shaw, *Beyond the New Morality*, 108, where they also were called *guidelines for love*.

[8] Of course, one sometimes does have a reason for treating different people differently according to one's special feelings for them.

health's sake ought not gorge on rich foods; someone fearing cancer ought not avoid a checkup that might find it; and someone who has undertaken a difficult job ought not delay setting to work. Then too: One ought not follow feelings that incline one to destroy, damage, or impede an instance of a basic good so as to attain a purportedly greater good or prevent a purportedly greater evil (the alleged reasons for doing so are always rationalizations).[9]

Even without any sophisticated philosophical or theological reflection, mature and thoughtful people notice that a person's free choices and the actions that carry them out not only have or fail to have their intended effects but also affect the agent himself or herself. "You will know them by their fruits" (Mt 7:16) is a common-sense saying. People who regularly make morally good choices are morally good people, and people who make morally bad choices are morally bad people. Morally good people have an integrity that morally bad people lack. That integrity, although likely to be more or less misconceived due to morally defective sociocultural structures, is recognized and valued by those who strive to be good.

Quite often, one cannot act for a good without cooperating with another or others. Those cooperating ought, of course, to be fair to one another. Whatever good all the cooperating parties intend is their common good, and the parties, in fairness, should intend not only benefit to themselves but to the others. If some parties fail to carry out their fair part in the cooperation, they deprive the others of their fair share of benefit. Thus the moral *ought* of fairness in cooperating constitutes a moral bond between the parties. What each party ought to do is a moral obligation and duty, and corresponding to that moral obligation and duty is the other parties' right to their fair share of benefits.[10]

St. Thomas Aquinas thought that the first morally significant act of unbaptized children is either to direct themselves to God as their true, ultimate end or to sinfully fail to do that.[11] However, the Second Vatican Council teaches that people can faultlessly lack explicit knowledge of God who nevertheless strive—with the help of divine grace, which, however, they need not be aware of—to live upright lives, and so can be saved.[12] As St. Paul observed, people naturally understand moral requirements and can apply them to their own actions (see Rom 2:12–16).

Aquinas also held that, in making choices and acting, one must intend as one's ultimate end something that one expects will so completely satisfy that it will leave one nothing else to desire, and that one therefore cannot intend two different ultimate ends at the same time.[13] In this matter, both his premise and his conclusion seem unsound.

Anything that is not a person tends toward a fulfillment fixed by its nature and environment. But although the basic human goods are unchanging, the ways of realizing them are not fixed. Rather, we human beings develop new ways of being fulfilled. Therefore, we never need to be satisfied with the fulfillment we already have,

---

[9] See Finnis, et al. "The Futility of Consequentialist Arguments," Ch. 9, *NDMR*, 238–72.

[10] While not everything one ought and ought not to do is an obligation of the sort explained here, there is a general moral obligation of a different sort, which will be explained in the next part of this essay.

[11] See *ST* 1–2 q. 89 a. 6 c. and ad 3.   [12] *Lumen gentium*, 16.

[13] See *ST* 1–2 q. 1 a. 5 c.

and we can intend something as our ultimate end without supposing that it ever will be realized in a way that will leave nothing more to be desired. In fact, not all those making morally significant choices, and perhaps very few of those doing so, suppose that anything they can hope to realize in and by their actions and can intend as an ultimate end promises such complete satisfaction that its attainment would leave nothing to be desired.[14]

Aquinas himself holds that infidels—that is, people who sinfully refuse to accept the gift of faith—need not sin in everything they do, because their unbelief does not completely destroy the good of human nature. So, infidels can do good deeds that they do not order to the end of their unbelief but intend for some natural good.[15] According to Aquinas, one always must be acting for *some* ultimate end.[16] So, infidels must intend as an ultimate end distinct from that of their unbelief either the natural good they intend in their good acts or some other good ulterior to it. *Pace* Aquinas, such infidels must, therefore, have at least two ultimate ends at the same time.

Many people simultaneously pursue for their own sakes—and therefore for no other ultimate end—two or more different goods, such as their marriage and family, their career, their favorite form of recreation, and their eventual life after death in heaven. Even those who engage in religious activities and avoid mortal sins for the sake of the last of these may find it impossible to see how pursuing the first three can contribute anything to the last and how pursuing the last can contribute anything to the first three. With loose life plans, such people juggle diverse interests rather than coordinate them, much less subordinate them to some single ultimate end.

From the preceding points it follows that some people know and live in accord with a good deal of moral truth, even if not all of it, without knowing God and/or without acting for a single ultimate end. For such people, the moral *ought* not only has the inherent appeal of its reasonableness and of the acting person's own integrity but the essentially related appeal of the specific human goods that moral norms promote and safeguard.

Fairness toward others and abstaining from intentionally harming them make for harmony among people, not just the unstable harmony that is sometimes brought about by manipulation and/or domination, but the more stable harmony of transparency and mutuality. While doing evil to achieve good is likely to seem promising in the short run, it often proves disastrous in the long run. Subordinating desires and fears and lethargic feelings to reason promotes and protects real goods likely to be damaged if insubordinate feelings have their way.

The benefits of morally good choices and actions generally are so real and so obvious that most moral norms bearing on one's own good may seem to be plain good sense. Of course, habitual conformity to some moral norms, especially those subordinating sexual feelings, yields less obvious intelligible goods—for example, the ability to say no that is essential for a fully meaningful yes, friendships in which unsatisfied erotic

---

[14] See Ryan, "Must the Acting Person Have a Single Ultimate End?"
[15] See *ST* 2–2 q. 10 a. 4 c. and ad 2; cf. q. 23 a. 7 ad 1; *Sent*, II d. 41 q. 1 a. 2; *De malo* q. 2 a. 5 ad 7.
[16] See *ST* 1–2 q. 1 a. 4.

attraction is fully integrated with mutual good will, and the wonder of intimacy first experienced by a couple who have made an unbreakable commitment to each other.

Nevertheless, immoral people often seem to win out and prosper while virtue seems to be its own punishment. Many large organizations proclaim ethical ideals that they do not practice. When people who lead upright private lives assume the responsibilities of office in a government, a business, a university, or a church, they generally seem to think that to protect and promote the organization's interests it is necessary to do evil—especially but not only to lie and to cooperate with evildoers.

II. How the Creator and the Ultimate End Enhance the Normative Force of the Moral *Ought*

The existence of anything we experience or can imagine is contingent upon the fulfillment of conditions outside the thing.[17] The fact that each contingent thing exists is not included in what the thing is. Finding oneself in a universe of things that do not exist of themselves and seeking to account for the existence of these contingent things, one reasonably posits an ultimate cause that depends on nothing else. I will call that ultimate cause *the Creator*. The Creator exists of itself: what it is includes that it is. But nothing can lack anything included in what it is. So, the Creator of contingent things cannot lack existence. It *necessarily* is.

Reflecting on this argument makes it clear that the Creator is utterly mysterious. The argument shows that the Creator's existence is included in what it is. By contrast, the existence of creatures neither is included in nor flows from what they are or from any characteristic they have. It follows that whatever the Creator is cannot be what any creature is. And whatever any creature is, the Creator is not. Thus, whenever one uses a word in the same sense it is used to say something true about a creature, what one says about the creature must be denied of the Creator.

Thus, the Creator is not a body, matter, or energy; is not spatial or temporal; does not evolve or change in any way. But the Creator's changelessness does not imply fixity or rigidity, for those also are intelligible characteristics of creatures. If the Creator is not a body, neither is it a mind or conscious subject—using *mind* and *conscious subject* in the same sense we use them about ourselves. By experiencing ourselves and one another, we learn what it is to know, to choose, to be a person. But using words with the same sense they have when we talk about ourselves, we must say: the Creator does not know, does not choose, is not a person. Indeed, using words in the same sense they have when we talk about creatures, we must say that the Creator is not a substance and has no nature.

Can we even say the Creator causes? Not in any of the senses in which we say a creature causes. However, while we cannot know what the Creator is, we can know something about it by considering how creatures are related to it. To adapt a saying of

---

[17] The treatment of God here is adapted from Grisez, "Natural Law, God, Religion, and Human Fulfillment," 11–14. The argument is articulated more fully and defended against philosophical objections in Grisez, *Beyond the New Theism*, 19–272.

Aquinas: We cannot grasp what the Creator is, but what it is not, and how other things are related to it.[18]

The question about contingent realities that initiates the argument leading to the existence of the Creator poses a problem unlike any other: Why do such things exist? That why leads to a unique because; it leads to the Creator as the source of the being of everything else.

Various sorts of things within our experience are called "causes" in diverse senses. For instance, the fact that these words are on a printed page is caused in diverse ways by the author's choice of them, the typesetter's work, and the physical-chemical properties of paper and ink. Though accounting in diverse ways for the fact that the words are on the page, all those causes are called "causes" because they answer why questions. So, when we ask, "Why do contingent things exist?" whatever answers that why question also is said to be their cause, using *cause* in a unique sense.

Where did that unique sense of *cause* come from? It developed in the argument and emerged from it, along with a unique sense of *is*, when one concluded that there is a cause of contingent things. That instance of fresh meaning emerging is like other instances that occurred when people asked other why questions and answered them by discovering other sorts of causes.

In sum, our knowledge about the relationship of created things to the Creator enables us to say, with a sense that is definite but unique, that the Creator causes. So, without understanding what the Creator is, we know that the Creator has what it takes to account for the actual being of the universe.

Something of what we know about human knowing and willing also can be attributed by analogy to the Creator. Since creatures need not be, they need not have been created. So, the Creator need not have created anything. Its creating, therefore, must have been free. On this basis, it is reasonable in thinking about the Creator to use the model of human agency through deliberation and free choice.[19] Of course, such predications must be not only based on the relationships that authorize them but limited to what those relationships authorize.

When we consider other things and ourselves as creatures of an intelligent and free Creator, we naturally attribute to him the order we find in the world around us and in ourselves. Included in that order is the directiveness of the principles of practical reason. Just as the truth that a universe of contingent things exists is obvious but points to the Creator, so the truth that our human goods are to be realized is evident but points to the directive intelligence of the Creator, who is in and of himself completely real and so not like us, who must *act* to realize (*real*-ize) ourselves.

This account of the transcendent source of the prescriptivity of practical principles is unlike a moral argument for God's existence that regards conscience as consciousness of divine commands. Some versions of that view claim that God could make anything morally obligatory by commanding us to do it. More plausible is the idea that human goods can be known theoretically, and that divine commands, which presuppose that

---

[18] "Non enim de Deo capere possumus quid est, sed quid non est, et qualiter alia se habeant ad ipsum" Aquinas, *ScG* I c. 30.
[19] See Grisez, *Beyond the New Theism*, 255, 268–72.

theoretical knowledge, supply the *ought*. But even that notion fails to recognize the truth of self-evident practical principles.

As I explained in the first part of this essay, moral normativity arises from the prescriptivity of the principles of practical reason, when that prescriptivity is confronted by feelings that incline one to behavior inconsistent with what reasons prescribe. Consequently, the rational cogency of any moral guidance we receive from others presupposes our own insight into basic human goods, just as everything we learn from others about the natural world presupposes our own experience and basic understanding of that world. Thus, the commands of others—even commandments taken to be God's—can make a *moral* claim on us only by appealing to the full directiveness of the principles of practical reason.

When we understand that directiveness as guidance provided by our Creator, our sense of its dependability deepens, and with that the normative force of the moral *ought* which it generates increases, and general moral obligation emerges. This emergence can be explained.

Children who follow their parents' guidance cooperate with their parents. Similarly, if one thinks that the Creator has provided the principles of practical reason to guide us to our fulfillment, one will suppose that one is cooperating with the Creator when one follows the direction of practical reason in promoting and protecting basic human goods. By the same token, following emotions against reasons will be failing to cooperate with the Creator and disobeying his guidance.

Like parents interested in their children, the Creator obviously is interested both in the realization of the goods toward which he directs human beings, by providing them with the principles of practical reason, and in the moral integrity of human agents. So, disobeying the Creator's guidance deprives him of what he wished to realize in and through the cooperation. Therefore, whenever one is aware of a moral *ought*, one is aware not only of practical reason's moral demand but of moral obligation, of being bound to obey the Creator.

Still, one first knows the prescriptivity of practical reason's principles; only then does one become aware both of the moral norms to which that prescriptivity gives rise and of its transcendent source. And only with that twofold awareness can one become aware of moral obligation, of being bound by the source of practical reason's prescriptivity to follow it integrally rather than to follow feelings at odds with the Creator's integral guidance.

There are two ways in which people in cooperative relationships can fulfill their responsibilities to one another.

In one way, they can treat each other fairly, each intending that the other receive his or her fair share in the common good they intend to realize by cooperating. For example, if I buy a new car and sell my old one to a teenage girl who responds to my ad, she and I cooperate for the common good of a mutually beneficial exchange. I fulfill my responsibility by being honest and asking a fair price—not, for instance, taking advantage of her inexperience or urgent need to make a deal—thus willing that she obtain her fair share of the common good.

In another way, the parties in a cooperative relationship can treat each other lovingly, each intending to benefit the other for his or her own sake, and thus intending that the other receive, not only his or her fair share of the common good they intend by cooperating, but that and more, as a contribution to his or her overall good. For example, two men who are true friends go golfing together. Each not only wills the other to receive his fair share of the common good of the morning's golfing but, loving the other, wills the other's overall good for his own sake, and so wills the share of the common good of that morning's golfing as a contribution to his friend's overall good. As a result, each will strive to make the morning's play beneficial and enjoyable for the other, and along the way they will chat about their families, their work, and so on.

Aware that they are created, people should acknowledge that they owe their very being and everything they have to the Creator. So, they should be grateful to him. Harmony with this transcendent source of meaning and value is one of the basic human goods. As children grateful to their parents love them for their own sakes, people grateful to the Creator can and should will the Creator's overall good for his own sake. If they do, they will fulfill their moral obligations as their contribution to that overall good. In this way, they will seek not only the harmony of submission to the Creator but the harmony of what can only be thought of as friendship.

If one is aware of cooperating with the Creator and fulfilling obligations to him, one also is aware that different people's capacities to act for their own and others' benefits differ and that different people can be benefited in different ways. So, it is reasonable to assume that the Creator intends the particular benefits to which the principles of practical reason direct each individual, given his or her unique set of capacities and opportunities.

Since the principles of practical reason direct all present and future created persons to all the particular benefits available to them according to their particular gifts and opportunities, the Creator is interested in the realization of all those goods. To will the Creator's overall good for his own sake, therefore, is to will all of those goods. One can do that only by intending all of the benefits to oneself and anyone else that one rightly chooses to bring about as contributions to that ulterior end—namely, all of those goods for the Creator's own sake—which thus will be the single ultimate end of every morally good act one does.

Someone intending that ultimate end regards the Creator and all created persons together as, potentially, a single, universal community. Insofar as created persons and particular communities reject moral obligation, they set themselves outside that community. Still, inasmuch as the principles of practical reason direct action to the realization of the goods of such people, the Creator remains interested in them, and the goods that will truly fulfill them continue to pertain to the common good that is the ultimate end. As the all-inclusive common good of a potentially universal community, that ultimate end can be called *integral communal fulfillment*.[20]

---

[20] Integral *human* fulfillment (IHF) was mentioned in many of my earlier works. I regarded it as an ideal that rectifies the will. In Grisez et al., "Practical Principles, Moral Truth, and Ultimate Ends" (1987f), 131, we define IHF thus: "The ideal of integral human fulfillment is that of the realization, so far as possible, of all the basic goods in all persons, living together in complete harmony." I now propose that human persons and groups can and should take integral *communal* fulfillment (ICF) as their ultimate end. IHF and ICF differ in several ways. (1) In IHF, "all persons" referred to all human beings, past, present, and future; in ICF, the potential community includes the Creator and all present and future created persons.

In sum, when we take into account that we are creatures and that the Creator directs us by the principles of practical reason to our own fulfillment and that of others, the moral *ought* becomes moral obligation. And if we will for the Creator's own sake the satisfaction of his interest in the goods to which he directs created persons, we will intend integral communal fulfillment as our ultimate end and contribute to its realization by gratefully fulfilling our moral obligations.

Even if some philosopher without faith in divine revelation not only concluded that the universe is created—something I do not think has ever happened—but worked out the entire view sketched out above, living according to that view would not be easy. Many people and groups seem to ignore moral norms, making life difficult for those who conform to them. Moreover, even the finest life ends with death, and eventually the entire world will pass away. That transience makes one wonder whether anything one does or fails to do finally matters.

III. How the Kingdom of God Further Enhances and Transforms the Moral *Ought*

"I must preach the good news of the kingdom of God," Jesus says, "for I was sent for this purpose" (Lk 4:43; cf. Mk 1:38). He proclaims the kingdom's *imminent* coming: "Now after John [the Baptist] was arrested, Jesus came into Galilee, preaching the gospel of God, and saying, 'The time is fulfilled, and the kingdom of God is at hand; repent, and believe in the gospel'" (Mk 1:15; cf. Mt 4:12–17).

People understood Jesus' proclamation of the kingdom's coming in light of the psalms they prayed and the Scripture readings they heard in their synagogues.[21] The only true God had created the universe, and it manifests his kingly wisdom and power. In choosing Israel, freeing her from Egypt, and making a covenant with her, God acted as her king. Sinful Israel is dominated by pagans, but when the time is right, God will rescue her, restore the broken world, and raise the dead. Even the pagans will recognize God as their Lord. Perfectly manifesting his righteousness, the renewed creation will be God's everlasting kingdom.[22] He will bring about *shalom*—completeness, wholeness, health, peace, welfare, safety, soundness, tranquility, prosperity, perfectness, fullness, rest, harmony.[23] Divine sovereignty on earth will be exercised by the Son of Man, who may be the Davidic messiah.[24]

---

(2) By wishing for (not intending) IHF, morally good will was specified by it; by intending ICF, morally good will is specified by it. (3) Ideally, the fruit of morally good will would be IHF; the actual fruit of taking ICF as their ultimate end by all the persons who do so is whatever well-being and flourishing their actions bring about in their community and in each of them. (4) With their wills specified by wishing for IHF, morally good persons settled for the happiness they had in benefiting themselves and others as they lived their good lives; with their wills specified by intending ICF, morally good persons hope for the realization of the Creator's purpose in creating, friendship with him, and the happiness of increasing well-being and flourishing in themselves and other created persons.

[21] See Fitzmyer, *The Gospel According to Luke I–IX*, 557 and 154–9.
[22] Wright, *The New Testament and the People of God*, 147–338.
[23] See Strong's *Concordance*, 7965.
[24] See Dan 7:13–14; Viviano, *The Kingdom of God in History*, 17.

It could be prophesied of Jesus: "The Lord God will give to him the throne of his father David... and of his kingdom there will be no end" (Lk 1:32–33). Anticipating Jesus' birth, some faithful Jews expected God to scatter the proud, put down the mighty from their thrones, exalt the lowly, fill the hungry with good things (see Lk 1:51–53), save God's people from their enemies, free them to serve him without fear, remove them from death's shadow, and guide them to *shalom* (see Lk 1:71, 73–75, 79).

Thus, when Jesus proclaimed that the time was fulfilled and the kingdom of God was at hand, and established his credibility by "healing every disease and every infirmity among the people" (Mt 4:23), many of the common people understood his message, believed him, and were electrified by the prospect of the kingdom's imminent coming.

The kingdom was incipient in Jesus' healing of illnesses and casting out of demons— "If it is by the Spirit of God that I cast out demons, then the kingdom of God has come upon you" (Mt 12:28; cf. Lk 11:20)—for in these healings and exorcisms the complete conquest of evil had begun. Jesus himself made the kingdom present—"The kingdom of God is in the midst of you" (Lk 17:21)—for in Jesus' perfect obedience the Father's will was already being done on earth.[25]

Nevertheless, the definitive kingdom remained, and still remains, an object of hope for the future: "According to his promise we wait for new heavens and a new earth in which righteousness dwells" (2 Pt 3:13). Jesus taught his disciples to pray: "Thy kingdom come, Thy will be done, *on earth* as it is in heaven" (Mt 6:10). That prayer implies that the kingdom will not be a spiritual realm apart from this world.[26] It also implies that the kingdom is not yet fully realized.[27] The kingdom will fully come only when the glorious Son of Man—Jesus risen from the dead—comes again, the dead are raised,[28] and the whole world renewed.[29] Then it will be true to say: "The kingdom of the world has become the kingdom of our Lord and of his Christ, and he shall reign for ever and ever" (Rev 11:15). The new Jerusalem will come down out of heaven from God, and he will dwell in the midst of his people in an entirely renovated world (see Rev 21:1–5).

Jesus teaches his disciples to seek first the Father's kingdom and his righteousness and assures them that all the goods about which people in general are anxious will be theirs as well (see Mt 6:33; Lk 12:31). The kingdom is so precious that one reasonably gives everything one has to possess it (see Mt 13:44–45). Entering the kingdom will be difficult for the wealthy (see Mt 19:23). It will be far easier for the poor: "Blessed are you poor, for yours is the kingdom of God" (Lk 6:20). Childlike humility also is necessary (see Mt 18:1–4). The moral commandments given the Israelites are still in full effect, and meeting the socially accepted standard of rectitude will be insufficient to enter the kingdom (see Mt 5:19–48, 19:16–22, 22:37–40). Doing the Father's will, not mere lip service, is necessary (see Mt 7:21). The Son of Man, identified with the King, will discern which people are fit to enter the kingdom prepared *from the foundation of the*

---

[25] Meier, *A Marginal Jew*, 398–506, especially 450–4.
[26] Viviano, *The Kingdom of God in History*, 19, explains that Jesus did not say "My kingship is not *of* this world" but "My kingship is not *from* this world" (Jn 18:36).
[27] See Meier, *A Marginal Jew*, 289–302.
[28] Meier, *A Marginal Jew*, 309–17.
[29] See O'Callaghan, *Christ Our Hope*, 39–73.

world on the basis of their serving or failing to serve the needy, with whom the King/Son of Man identifies himself (see Mt 25:31–46).

When asked whether only few will be saved, Jesus earnestly replies: "Strive to enter by the narrow door; for many, I tell you, will seek to enter and will not be able" (Lk 13.24).[30] And Jesus makes it clear that failing to enter the kingdom will mean unending misery. The King/Son of man will say to those who do not serve the needy: "Depart from me, you cursed, into the eternal fire prepared for the devil and his angels" (Mt 25:41). It is better to give up whatever one must to enter the kingdom than "be thrown into hell, where their worm does not die and the fire is not quenched" (Mk 9:47–48; cf. Is. 66:24). "And the smoke of their torment goes up for ever and ever" (Rev 14:11). St. Paul teaches that anyone who commits certain sorts of sins will not "inherit the kingdom of God" (1 Cor 6:10, Gal 5:21) and, having disobeyed the gospel, "shall suffer the punishment of eternal destruction and exclusion from the presence of the Lord" (2 Thess 1:9).

While the vivid expressions used in that teaching are symbolical language,[31] the common Christian tradition maintained the realism of scriptural teaching about hell more firmly than it did the realism of scriptural teaching about the kingdom. Taking for granted the received understanding of the kingdom, Jesus did not need to describe it in detail. Still, he mentions people reclining "at table in the kingdom of God" (Lk 13:29), says "Blessed is he who shall eat bread in the kingdom of God" (Lk 14:15), and tells his apostles that he has arranged a kingdom "for you that you may eat and drink at my table in my kingdom" (Lk 22:29–30). Jesus thus leads his disciples to expect the good things of human life in the kingdom.

After Jesus' resurrection, the kingdom of God was the topic of his conversation with his disciples (see Acts 1:3). They were still expecting him to "restore the kingdom to Israel" (Acts 1:6). After the Holy Spirit came, Philip's message—and thus the infant Church's initial creed—is summarized by saying that he "preached good news about the kingdom of God and the name of Jesus Christ" (Acts 8:20). Paul's great work of evangelization could likewise be summarized as "preaching the kingdom of God and teaching about the Lord Jesus Christ" (Acts 28:31; cf. 14:22, 17:7, 19:8, 20:25, 28:23).

While the kingdom preached by the infant Church retained all the down-to-earth realism of Israel's hoped for kingdom, Jesus introduced an entirely new requirement for entry and a new conception of the sublimity of membership in the kingdom. Jesus is the Word who was with the Father in the beginning—the Word through whom all created things came to be—and he became man to enable those who welcomed him to become children of God (see Jn 1:1–3, 12–14). Entry into the kingdom requires that one be born again by the water of baptism and the Holy Spirit (see Jn 3:5), and thus share in the Word's divine nature (see 2 Pt 1:4), as the Word shares in our human nature.

St. Paul likewise explains that the Spirit makes those who are in Christ share in Jesus' sonship. By adoption (see Rom 8:15, 23), they become "children of God, and if

---

[30] Fitzmyer, *The Gospel According to Luke I–IX*, 1025, comments: "many... will not be able. So Jesus answers indirectly the question put to him. Many may crowd before the narrow door, but not all of them will succeed in passing through it."

[31] See John Paul II, General Audience, 7.

children, then heirs, heirs of God and fellow heirs with Christ" (Rom 8:16–17; cf. Gal 4:4–7). They are therefore entitled to enjoy not only human *shalom* but the *shalom* that properly belongs to the divine persons—the "peace of God, which passes all understanding" (Phil 4:7). At the same time, Paul makes it clear that those who are in Christ will enjoy that more-than-human fulfillment while also sharing in Jesus' resurrection life (see Rom 8:11, 23).

To reach fulfillment *as children of God*, Christians must be united with Jesus. He teaches: "He who eats my flesh and drinks my blood abides in me and I in him" (Jn 6:56). Philip asks Jesus to show them the Father, and Jesus tells him that, having seen him, they have already seen the Father (see Jn 14:8–9). Jesus then explains that he and the Father are in each other (see Jn 14:10–11), and that after his death they will again see him, and "in that day you will know that I am in the Father, and you in me and I in you" (Jn 14:20). Again, Jesus prays for all his disciples "that they may all be one; even as thou, Father, art in me, and I in thee, that they may be one in us" (Jn 17:21). Paul similarly teaches that the hope of Christians depends on their oneness with Jesus. All of them are baptized by the Spirit into the one body of Christ (see 1 Cor 12:13). And, since the Eucharist is a participation in the blood and body of Christ, "we who are many are one body, for we all partake of the one bread" (1 Cor 10:17). Those who "belong to Christ" will be raised to glory with him (see 1 Cor 15:18, 23).

The disciple who keeps Jesus' commandments loves him and will be loved by the Father, and Jesus promises: "I will love him and will manifest myself to him" (Jn 14:21). What form will Jesus' self-manifestation ultimately take? "We are God's children now; it does not yet appear what we shall be, but we know that when he appears we shall be like him, for we shall see him as he is" (1 Jn 3:2). "Blessed are the pure in heart, for they shall see God" (Mt 5:8). Paul similarly speaks of the perfect knowledge to which Christians can look forward: "When I was a child, I spoke like a child, I thought like a child, I reasoned like a child; when I became a man, I gave up childish ways. For now we see in a mirror dimly, but then face to face. Now I know in part; then I shall understand fully, even as I have been fully understood" (1 Cor 13:11–12). In the new Jerusalem, the blessed will worship God and the Lamb, and "they shall see his face" (Rev 22:4). From a present immature and childlike relationship with God, the blessed, having died in Christ, will advance to such intimacy with him that they will know God on the basis of mutuality—"we shall be like him" and "understand fully, even as I have been fully understood"—and thus share fully in the *shalom* of God.

As Jesus himself lived a full human life while also sharing fully in the *shalom* of God, those who die in him will share fully in the *shalom* of God while also sharing fully in the human *shalom* of the definitive kingdom. During the first two centuries, Christian writers retained the New Testament's realistic understanding of the definitive kingdom. Unfortunately, however, Church Fathers formed by the mold of Greco-Roman classicism—beginning with Origen (*c.*185–254) and culminating with St. Augustine (354–430)—reduced human sharing in the *shalom* of God to human intellectual contemplation of God, an activity essentially like, though far more perfect than, Christian mystics enjoy briefly in this world. Those same Fathers reduced the human *shalom* of the definitive kingdom to one or more of the following: the individual's interior and spiritual perfection, Jesus himself, the earthly Christian empire, the Church in this world and in heaven, the group of those seeing God.[32]

The resurrection of the blessed will be a renewal of their own bodies so that they will be like Jesus' body, and imperishable as his is.[33] That resurrection will be part of the transformation of the entire created universe (see Rom 8:19–24). God's plan is to gather up all things in Christ, "things in heaven and things on earth" (Eph 1:10; cf. Col 1:20). Moreover, the good deeds of those who die in the Lord accompany them (see Rev 14:13). Good human works will survive (see 1 Cor 3:12–14). So, after stressing the realism of resurrection, Paul exhorts: "Be steadfast, immovable, always abounding in the work of the Lord, knowing that in the Lord your labor is not in vain" (1 Cor 15:58).[34] In a remarkable passage, the Second Vatican Council goes considerably further:

> After we have promoted on earth, in the Spirit of the Lord and in accord with his command, the goods of human dignity, familial communion, and freedom—that is to say, all the good fruits of our nature and effort—then we shall find them once more, but cleansed of all dirt, lit up, and transformed, when Christ gives back to the Father an eternal and universal kingdom: "a kingdom of truth and life, a kingdom of holiness and grace, a kingdom of justice, love, and peace." On this earth the kingdom is present in mystery even now; with the Lord's coming, however, it will be consummated.[35]

The Council apparently takes for granted that the good deeds of the blessed will accompany them. It asserts that all the good *results* both of their good works and of natural human functioning will somehow be salvaged, freed of any residue of sin, glorified, and worked into the entirely renovated heavens and earth. Nothing, it seems, will be excluded but evil.

Think what that means. Jesus advises: "Lay up for yourselves treasures in heaven" (Mt 6:20). But the Council's understanding of a kingdom rich in human goods goes far beyond what most Christians have previously imagined they could lay up for themselves by taking up their crosses and following him. And if all these human goods are to be found again in the kingdom, they, like the vastly improved bodies of the blessed, plainly will not be there as trophies in a heavenly museum.

Human life will go on in the kingdom. One will find again every good relationship begun, without any of its defects and obstacles, ready to be taken up and joyously carried on, forever becoming better and deeper. Those one knows when one arrives in the kingdom will introduce one to others, and they to still others. One will find again every good interest and skill, again freed of defects, ready to be taken up and pursued. One can remember the very best days, the very best moments in one's life, and hope to find again whatever it was that made them so good, not so as to recapture them, but so as to live a life that will be at every moment as good as those best moments, and growing ever better.

[32] See Viviano, *The Kingdom of God in History*, 30–56.

[33] Wright, *Surprised by Hope*, 154–56, explains why 1 Cor 15:44 should not be translated "It is sown a physical body, it is raised a spiritual body."

[34] Some recent non-Catholic authors cite this text to make precisely this point; see Wright, *Surprised by Hope*, 192–205; Alcorn, *Heaven*, 133–9.

[35] See *Gaudium et spes*, 39; the internal quotation is from *Roman Missal*, Preface of the Feast of Christ the King.

With that hope, the normative force of the moral *ought* increases tremendously. One is less tempted to do evil to achieve and/or protect human goods. Moreover, one is motivated not only to avoid sin, but to do good in dealing with others. One is freed to make worthwhile efforts that may well fail, knowing that anything good begun well will somehow be stored up in the kingdom, so that failure in the present age will not be lasting loss. Indeed, one is freed from living for what the present age's future might bring. For nothing one does—nothing hard one must do and no suffering one must undergo—is merely for the present age's future. Rather, all of it is for the far more important future of the age to come. And in that age, the real meaning and value of everything one did, in the Spirit of the Lord and in accord with his command, to promote and protect human goods in the present age will be gloriously manifest.

Bibliography

Alcorn, Randy (2004), *Heaven* (Carol Stream, IL: Tyndale House).

Aquinas, Thomas, *Quaestiones de malo*.

Aquinas, Thomas, *Scriptum super Sententiis*.

Aquinas, Thomas, *Summa contra gentiles*.

Aquinas, Thomas, *Summa theologiae*.

Finnis, John (1980), *Natural Law and Natural Rights*, 2nd ed. 2011 (Oxford: Oxford University Press).

Finnis John (1983), *Fundamentals of Ethics* (Washington, DC: Georgetown University Press).

Finnis, John (1998), *Aquinas: Moral, Political, and Legal Theory* (Oxford: Oxford University Press).

Finnis, John (2011), *Collected Essays of John Finnis*, vol. 5, *Religion and Public Reasons* (Oxford: Oxford University Press).

Finnis, John, with Joseph Boyle and Germain Grisez (1987), *Nuclear Deterrence, Morality and Realism* (Oxford: Oxford University Press).

Fitzmyer, Joseph A. (1981), *The Gospel According to Luke I–IX* (New York: Doubleday).

Grisez, Germain (1975), *Beyond the New Theism: A Philosophy of Religion* (Notre Dame, IN: University of Notre Dame Press); reprinted with a new preface: *God: A Philosophical Preface to Faith* (South Bend, IN: St. Augustine's Press, 2005).

Grisez, Germain (2001), "Natural Law, God, Religion, and Human Fulfillment," *AJJ* 46: 3–36.

Grisez, Germain, with Joseph Boyle and John Finnis (1987), "Practical Principles, Moral Truth, and Ultimate Ends," *AJJ* 32: 99–151.

Grisez, Germain, with Russell Shaw (1974), *Beyond the New Morality: The Responsibilities of Freedom* (Notre Dame, IN: University of Notre Dame Press).

John Paul II (1999), General Audience, 2–3, *L'Osservatore Romano* (English), Aug. 4, 1999, 7.

Meier, John P. (1994), *A Marginal Jew: Rethinking the Historical Jesus*, vol. 2, *Mentor, Message, and Miracles* (New York: Doubleday).

O'Callaghan, Paul (2011), "*Parousia*," in *Christ Our Hope: An Introduction to Eschatology* (Washington, DC: The Catholic University of America Press).

Ryan, Peter F. (2001), "Must the Acting Person Have a Single Ultimate End?" *Gregorianum* 82: 325–56.

Vatican Council II (1964), *Lumen gentium* (*Constitutio Dogmatica de Ecclesia*), *AAS* 57: 5–71.

Vatican Council II (1965), *Gaudium et spes* (*Constitutio Pastoralis de Ecclesia in Mundo Huius Temporis*), *AAS* 58: 1025–120.

Viviano, Benedict T. (1988), *The Kingdom of God in History* (Wilmington, NC: Michael Glazier).

Wright, N.T. (1992), *The New Testament and the People of God* (Minneapolis, MN: Fortress Press).

Wright, N.T. (2008), *Surprised by Hope: Rethinking Heaven, the Resurrection, and the Mission of the Church* (New York: Harper Collins).

REFLECTIONS AND RESPONSES

28

Reflections and Responses

John Finnis

The 27 foregoing essays were generously contributed by their authors in the spirit, I believe, of the Oxford graduate seminars that for many of us have been unsurpassed forms of intellectual work and life—for me the seminars, above all, with Joseph Raz (often also with Ronald Dworkin) and Timothy Endicott. Here everyone meets, as equals in the discussion of a single text or, before long, of a single pair of 'texts', the second responsive to the first, and each then the matter for searching questions and a free flow of probings and suggestions, with no final pronouncement or attempted consensus. The participants, from anywhere in the world, carry away, each one, their own individual reflections and judgments. My essay here is 27 little essays, each to be taken as setting up the *second of a pair of texts* for the reader's own probings, reflections and judgments or suspensions of judgment. It was by no means the least part of the contributors' generosity—for all of which I am very grateful—that they gave me the last word within the confines of the book. In every case there is much of substance that I have not mentioned.

The following reflections and responses refer fairly frequently to my own writings. The five volumes of my *Collected Essays*, in particular, are sprawling and scattered in their treatment of the issues; the index to them (to be found, for all of them, in each volume) is much enhanced in the paperback edition; to compensate for the original edition's weakness on subjects/topics I have here been rather free with these inter-textual cross-references. They keep up, for a little longer, my part in a discussion in which, when all is said and done, others will have the last say.

I. Reasons, Goods, and Principles

1.

Joseph Raz is interested in knowing what it is about knowledge that makes it of value. This is, he cautions, a question that 'has nothing to do with' whether knowledge *is* of value—*is* a value, an intelligible good. Rather, he is asking what explains that it is. (But he questions whether certain kinds of knowledge have any value at all: knowing how many cats there were in 720 A.D., for example.) He mentions the thought that 'an answer to the question what makes A good could only refer to some other good, B, and state that A is good because it is B' [p. 18]. As he points out, this holds only if A is a derivative good, not basic. So that is not how he takes his question's key phrase—'*makes it* a value'.[1] As he

---

[1] But before we leave behind this strategy of explaining what makes knowledge a good, we should notice some of the ways in which knowledge is valuable not merely instrumentally (as when one knows where to find the cheapest coffee, or what kind of explanation the History examiners expect to find in candidates'

says, it is possible that basic, irreducible goods can be explained, for although such explanations 'will be circular in that they will explain evaluative concepts using evaluative concepts', the fact is that 'the fundamental concepts all thought relies on cannot be explained in a non-circular way, but some wide circles have explanatory power'[p. 18].[2]

That is certainly how *NLNR* tackled his question. It did not 'invoke self-evidence to rebut scepticism'[3]; or claim that self-evidence is 'a source of knowledge'; or follow Descartes and suppose (as Raz counsels) that adequately understanding basic goods is a matter of 'contemplating a clear and distinct idea'; or appeal to any 'sense of certainty, or feelings of self-evidence'[4] [p. 20]. The proper response to scepticism about a basic human good is, I think, to invite sceptics both (a) to articulate any reason they may have in mind for doubting that this (say, knowledge) is intrinsically good (a distinct, irreducible element of human flourishing), and (b) to attend closely to the relevant field of human possibility, and to instances of the states of affairs in which this good is realized, and of the states of affairs in which it is possible but *not* realized (but rather ignored, impeded, destroyed . . .). Whether or not Raz's requests for explanation intimate some scepticism about knowledge's intrinsic value, I think an explanation of the kind he seeks can indeed be supplied.

Knowledge is a state of affairs instantiated, centrally, when someone has grasped and correctly followed the reasons for judging a true proposition true, or a false proposition false. It is (so far forth) a leaving behind of ignorance and muddle, an avoiding of error, misinformation, and delusion. Indifference to its value makes one all too likely to remain the dupe of falsehood and illusion, to be myth-ridden, or simply benighted, ignorant. These are deficiencies, conditions of some indignity; to point to that indignity—to those deficiencies—is one way of explaining the value of knowledge, of the state of affairs (way of *being*) by which one (so far forth) escapes them. And another way is to point out that it is knowledge, and knowledge alone,[5] that puts us in touch with vast fields of reality, some parts of which we experience but much of which we can know only in true judgments.

Two aspects of Raz's thinking about all this suggest, I think, why the explanation just sketched, though implicit (indeed, explicit, albeit in scattered form) in *NLNR*'s account (pp. 59–79) of knowledge's value, makes no appearance in his essay. (i) His 'value approach to practical reason', unlike mine, predicates value of (in the primary or central instance) *actions*.[6] For him, the 'good- or bad-making properties' that

---

essays) but constitutively, as in the knowledge which *makes possible* such other basic goods as, for example, friendship or excellence in performance.

  [2] See pp. 463, 546–7, and 563–4 in this essay.

  [3] The philosophical concept of self-evidence (that is, of the *per se notum*) is sophisticated, not straight-forwardly self-evident: *NLNR*, 31. Moreover, discerning, among the goods one easily understands, which of them are basic and irreducible and which derivative, which constituent and which complete, is no easy matter: *NLNR*, 81–2, 99. So, *pace* Raz [p. 18], I would not say that 'that these are the basic goods'—i.e. that *this* is the correct list—'is . . . self-evident'.

  [4] Against the relevance of feelings of certitude: *NLNR*, 69.

  [5] True beliefs, falling short of knowledge, put us in touch with those realities, but in a secondary, relatively veiled way—better than nothing.

  [6] That is, activities or omissions. He adds that, of course, 'actions are not the only bearers of value properties. Moreover, often they have value properties in virtue of their relations with something else

'constitute reasons for or against . . . actions' are properties (primarily) of the actions themselves. In my view, however, the value, the intelligible good, the benefit that gives one reason to act, is an aspect of an actual or envisaged purpose. The purpose is a concrete state of affairs[7] attainable by action, and the benefit is that aspect of the state of affairs which contributes to someone's fulfilment, and thus gives action for that purpose some intelligible point not derivative from any other purpose or benefit.[8] To say that action has some intelligible point, some value, is far from saying that it is a *good action*, or even a *valuable* one (in the ordinary sense of these phrases). Action is the carrying out of choice, and one's choices confront a vast array of possible purposes and benefits participating (in perhaps widely differing degrees) in many different basic goods, each realizable more or less fulfillingly (by one's own action) in many, many different persons. Action is good and valuable when, going well beyond the minimum of having intelligible point (benefit), it pursues a purpose not merely intelligible but also responsive to one's opportunities and responsibilities of actualizing a reasonably full measure[9] of fulfilling benefits.

So (ii) knowledge is more and less valuable depending on its subject matter, but Raz dismisses this truth on two grounds, each inadequate.[10] 'Knowledge does not admit of degrees' [p. 21], perhaps, but the objects of knowledge differ greatly in their interest and importance.[11] *Felix qui potuit rerum cognoscere causas*[12]—the emphasis falls on the last word, and to know what *explains* the nature, life cycle, mortality and reproduction of cats is knowledge more worthwhile seeking and attaining than knowledge of a randomly specified fact such as how many were alive in 720 A.D.—though even that fact could be worth knowing, not randomly but rather as (say) confirmation or

---

which has such properties: they may be constituent elements of more complex phenomena that are good . . . or . . . may facilitate the production of some other goods . . . (etc.)' [p. 14].

[7] *Pace* Gardner at p. 151 n. 2.

[8] See *CEJF* I.14, 212–3; 1987f (Grisez, Boyle, Finnis, 'Practical Principles, Moral Truth and Ultimate Ends'), 102–5. Someone might object that this view of Raz's is Aristotle's: 'making [*poiêsis*] has an end other than itself, action [*praxis*] cannot; for good action is itself its end': *Nic. Eth.* VI.5: 1140b6. But this must be taken with qualifications; as the preceding sentence of Aristotle's says: 'practical reasonableness [*phronêsis*] is a true and reasoned state of capacity to act with regard to the things that are good or bad for man [*peri ta anthrôpô agatha*]' (1140b4–5), and the next-following sentence says that Pericles and other people of practical reasonableness see and do 'what is good for themselves and what is good for men in general' (1140b9–10); practical reasonableness (wisdom) is 'a reasoned and true state of capacity to act with regard to human goods [*peri ta anthrôpina agatha*]' (1140b20). So the true sense of the claim about action being its own end is to be found by reflecting that (a) one of the human goods is practical reasonableness itself, which concerns (and should be in charge of) all of one's action; (b) one's choices (and thus the actions that carry them out) *last* in one's will (character) even after they have been carried out (see *CEJF* I.15, sec. II, 239–40; *CEJF* II.8, 137–8; *Aquinas*, 23, nn. 9–10, and 42, n. 68); (c) Aristotle is here concerned with fully reasonable action, not with what makes action intelligible as a choice, a question that can be answered, not by pointing only to the action's intelligibility within, or as, some technique of bringing about some state of affairs, but instead by pointing to some way in which it contributes to the fulfilment of the acting person and/or of one or more other persons.

[9] On this measure, see Boyle, pp. 66–9; Grisez, pp. 444–7; and section 4 (response to Boyle).

[10] Raz, p. 21 n. 14. I respond to that footnote's two arguments in the present paragraph, and add: Granted that any proposition entails or contributes to the entailment of an indefinite number of propositions, still knowledge of explanatory propositions (causal laws and the like) yields *knowledge* of the entailments in a way that knowledge of some bare random fact does not.

[11] See n. 20 in this essay. *Re* degrees of knowledge: consider the value of true *beliefs* in doing science.

[12] Happy are those who have succeeded in finding the *explanations* of things: Virgil, *Georgics* 490.

disconfirmation of some biological or climatological hypothesis of wide explanatory power, or of some historical investigation into effects of early Islamic conquests in Europe and Mesopotamia. And facts and explanations about subjects inherently more important than cats, such as human persons and their communities, are—speaking generally—more important to know. That it matters how important the subject matter of one's knowledge is does not entail that this is not knowledge sought for its own sake, intrinsically valuable just as knowledge. Such knowledge is in many if not all cases one's only available and satisfactory access to this aspect of reality—the past; or to the persons or activities of other spiritual beings like oneself; or to God, the explanation of all that has been, is, or will be.

On the way to his question about knowledge, Raz makes some other critical observations about my accounts of basic goods. I agree with him that it would be a mistake to think that harmony 'explains what is the good of' the basic goods of friendship, practical reasonableness and religion, and even more mistaken to think of it as the one basic value.[13] If harmony earns a mention in relation to some of the items in a list of basic human goods, it does so 'only in the context of something else' [p. 16]: of the relations, for example, between persons, or between the parts of one's psychological make-up.

In reflecting on first practical principles and basic goods, we are seeking neither conceptual (second order) nor metaphysical (first order) truth, but rather truths of the third order (fourth in *NLNR*), truths, that is to say, about what brings order into our choices and actions so that they bear appropriately on human fulfilment.[14] Identifying basic aspects of human fulfilment (basic goods) is only the first stage in identifying what kinds of choice and action bear on human fulfilment *appropriately*, that is, in accordance with the requirements of practical reasonableness. Raz's tendency to run together these two stages of the inquiry by looking immediately for good *actions* shows itself, I think, in remarks of his such as that harmony is not intrinsically good since it need not make music good (it may make it boring); and that 'some friendships and some religions or aesthetic experiences are without merit at all' [p. 16]. The goodness (benefit) of the basic goods is that of giving intelligible point to choice of conduct, not yet the goodness (moral) of an option *reasonably* chosen in preference to alternative options, and of fulfilment in attainable and due measure. Musically appropriate harmony uses discord and its resolution (even if sometimes only at a meta-level) to avoid the boring. But compared with cacophony even boring harmony has some point. So too, in their own ways, do friendships and religions and forms of art even when they are of such a kind, or are pursued in such circumstances, that they ought in reason to be rejected or immediately abandoned because of the harm their pursuit does to human

---

[13] Sensing such a possible misunderstanding, I remark in *CEJF* I.Introduction, 9 that 'essay 14's summary list [of practical reason's first principles], structured around the concept of harmony, is a somewhat over-synthesised construct'.

[14] On the four kinds of order and *scientia*, see *NLNR*, 136–8, 457; *Aquinas*, 20–3; and *CEJF* I.14, 217–20; *CEJF* II.2, 36–8, 66–7. The clarification of the kinds is metaphysical, but denies the 'either conceptual or metaphysical' reduction. On (and against the philosophical weight of) 'conceptual analysis', see *CEJF* IV.6, 11, 35, 41, 85–7, 151, 168, 260–1, 279, 290n, 384; *NLNR*, 278–9, 426, 434n; in this essay, pp. 541–4.

fulfilment in these kinds of ways or circumstances, or because of their injustice or violation of other norms of reasonableness.

NLNR's pages investigating the substantive relationship of friendship say little or nothing about the harmony between friends and much about the mutuality of the friends' valuing of and active interest in each other's well-being, their motivation to cooperation in pursuit of other goods, their appreciation and enjoyment of each other's company, and so forth. The explanation is filled out with occasional reminders of the negativity of friendlessness. And the harms and moral evil that friendship can occasion and facilitate, by act and omission, when pursued in disregard of reason's requirements, are not to be overlooked or downplayed. *Mutatis mutandis*, the same can I think be said of the pages in *Aquinas* investigating practical reasonableness. There is indeed much more to friendship, practical reasonableness, and religion than harmony as it might be understood prior to an understanding of friendship, practical reasonableness, and religion. (And harmony has only a minor role in an account of the good of marriage, and even less, if any, in setting out or explaining the good of life and the good of knowledge.)

But the appropriate filling out of the accounts of these basic goods is not a matter of saying which friendships are good friendships, which religions are good religions, and so on. It is a matter of bringing out (explaining) what is good about friendship, religion, or practical reasonableness. The explanation will be circular, as Raz rightly envisages. The task, moreover, is not too demanding, once one sets aside the demand—at this stage inappropriate—for a specification of which kinds of friendship, etc., are good, that is, reasonable, meritorious, etc. For these are goods whose intelligibility is at the foundation of all the practical reasoning (wicked or virtuous) of everyone capable of deliberating and choosing.

Similarly, to say that human life is a value is not to say that 'there is always a *pro tanto* reason to bring another life into being', nor that 'there is always a *pro tanto* reason to prolong the life of any human being' [n. 10]. Rather, it is to notice that one's life is one's human existence, and that to lose it is to lose a real, intrinsic good: not only all the radical capacity to participate in *human* awareness, feelings, imagination, and so forth, but also one's very reality as a human being.[15] I say a little more about this, in response to Roger Crisp's reflections.[16] For the present, suffice it to note that, in the alternatives Raz offers us, the words 'always', 'bring into being' and 'prolong' all work to render unattractive these alternatives to the 'mere precondition' hypothesis that he argued for in the work he cites [p. 17 n. 10]; the words have this effect by suggesting, once again, that talking about basic goods has a bearing on the goodness of actions more immediate than I think its bearing rationally is. Human life is always to be respected, but the sheer unreasonableness, on countless occasions, of seeking to bring into being a new person (I mean of generating a new human being) is not adequately captured by the qualifier '*pro tanto*'. And 'prolong', too, has connotations of possible excess, relevant when considering the reasonableness or otherwise of action chosen to

---

[15] See *CEJF* III.14, 219–22; *NLNR*, 195.   [16] See p. 466 of this essay.

sustain life in circumstances of triage, or where the means of doing so are burdensome, or intrude upon the process clinically recognized as dying.

2.

Roger Crisp's concluding thought, that philosophy is likely to bring us closer to the truth about well-being (fulfilment) and about its practical implications, is in an important sense undeniable. But there is one respect in which it is deniable. For: each of us pursuing philosophical inquiry and reflection does so within a culture, and some philosophical cultures make getting to truth about such matters more difficult than it need or should be.

Consider the most influential of Oxford philosophers, John Locke, and his sway, for centuries, over those who philosophized on human good and its implications for action. John Austin taught England's first jurisprudence students, nearly 150 years on, that Locke was 'the incomparable man who emancipated human reason from the yoke of mystery and jargon'. As evidence, Austin quoted an extended passage from Locke's *Essay Concerning Human Understanding*, a passage 'which evinces that matchless power of precise and just thinking, with that religious regard for general utility and truth...'[and so forth]. The decisive paragraph is the following answer to the question how we 'know whether [our] actions are morally good or bad':

> Good or evil is nothing but pleasure or pain, or that which occasions or procures pleasure or pain to us. *Moral good or evil*, then, is only the conformity or disagreement of our voluntary actions to some law, whereby good or evil is drawn on us by the will and power of the law-maker: which good or evil, pleasure or pain, attending our observance or breach of the law, by the decree of the law-maker, is [w]hat we call reward or punishment.[17]

This tells us that what makes torture morally bad is not the victims' suffering but the torturer's own pain when, if ever, he is punished by someone who forbad such torture (why?) and had the power to inflict punishment for violation of his decree. The passage, like its extolling by and influence upon Austin (and doubtless Bentham before him), reveals how far mainstream philosophy fell back during the Enlightenment into something like pre-Socratic darkness, making harder, not easier, the approach to truth about human well-being. Kant and Hegel, and their English followers, realized that Locke's hedonist voluntarism could not possibly be the truth about human well-being and responsibility; but their efforts at recovery were crippled by Kant's failure to allow for insight into first practical principles and the basic human goods to which they direct us. In English-speaking legal philosophy, Hart's work is an important, relatively early stage in the laborious recovery from the Benthamite, Austinian (Hobbesian, Lockean) regress and obfuscation.

Another reason to doubt that philosophy *as it is practised* today will facilitate convergence on the truth about human well-being is suggested by Crisp's thought

---

[17] Locke, *Essay Concerning Human Understanding* (1689), Bk. II, cap. xxviii, quoted in Austin, *Lectures on Jurisprudence*, I, 206.

(repeated) that it is 'a tall order' to make plausible the freedom of the will—to 'supply', as he puts it, either some version of compatibilism or some version of libertarianism. Within the conventions and expectations customary in academic philosophy, it seems indeed a tall order. But compatibilism ('soft determinism') is plausibly argued by Anscombe (concluding her inaugural lecture in the chair of Philosophy in Cambridge) to be 'pure nonsense'.[18] And the hard determinist denial of the thesis that there are some free choices is straightforwardly and ineluctably incompatible with responsibility to truth and evidence in the conduct of scientific or philosophical inquiry (or any other form of disciplined thought). That conduct, both within the inner reflections of thinkers, and in their research and their communicating of its results, is a wide domain of choices the freedom of which is evidenced by the normativity of the standards of probity and care (as well as zeal) that bear on them, standards that would be senseless but for the ever-present need to make or execute and reconfirm these choices to be honest and careful in philosophical reflection and discussion. This being so, and the experience of rationally acknowledging these norms and living up to their require-ments in one's research, teaching, and writing being so immanent in that work—not least when the work bears on the truth of determinism—it is, I suggest, a tall order to mount a good case that it is a tall order to make the will's freedom plausible. The usual case gets no closer to engaging with the evidence than a set of reminders about the presumed subjection of everything to physical, chemical, and biological laws. But even when the advances in neuroscience are fully factored in, the supposition that such laws are exceptionlessly universal in scope remains a proposition which—like those laws' presumed applicability without remainder to the manifestly non-material but real and perspicuously human domain(s) of meaning, logical validity, argumentative soundness and error, interpretation, hope, intention, and choice—we are free and rationally entitled to deny.[19] In judging that the appropriate presumption is the reverse of what Crisp thinks it to be, one finds oneself free to return unencumbered to the work of explicating the foundations of value and normativity.

Thematic in Crisp's reflections on these foundations is his questioning how far, and whether, the basic goods have any value to one who is not in a position to enjoy them. In the case of knowledge, I agree that a merely dispositional knowledge that one could never bring to consciousness for contemplation, verification, or falsification, or for any kind of judgment or reflection, is not worth calling the benefit of knowledge.[20] But if

---

[18] Anscombe, *Collected Philosophical Papers*, 172: '...the soft determinist...does think freedom com-patible with physical impossibility...since, being a determinist, he thinks that everything except what actually happened was always impossible...I am at liberty to say that I believe a "can of freedom" which holds in face of physical impossibility is pure nonsense'.

[19] See e.g. *CEJF* II.Introduction, 2–3, 6–8. Those pages should have mentioned the valuable and illuminating work, sophisticated across many fields of science and other disciplines, done by David Hodgson in *The Mind Matters*; see now Hodgson, *Rationality + Consciousness = Free Will*. We were each supervised by Hart during 1962–1965, discussed some of our work together, and were viva'd for our doctorates on the same day. His thesis was published, with some abbreviation, as Hodgson, *Consequences of Utilitarianism*. His works on free will are for anyone not content with the short way I have taken with this question; even without appeal to presumptions, they at least indicate how the 'tall order' can be cut down to size.

[20] I also agree that there is an infinite number of propositions worth not asserting because they deal with matters a knowledge of which is so (relatively) unimportant that it would be a waste of time (see *CEJF* I.4, 86) to get into a position to assert them. And I of course agree that the argument that scepticism about

the deficiency is not so radical, and what is missing is simply the *enjoyment* which perfects the actuation of one's capacity for knowledge (and, *mutatis mutandis*, for health, friendship, excellence, or accomplishment in activity for its own sake, and so forth), I think he is mistaken to conclude that there is no realization of an intrinsic value.

The mistake's source is the same, I think, as a main source of the mistaken thesis[21] that the very life of a permanently unconscious human being is of no value. What in each of these kinds of case impresses us (and so makes plausible the mistaken conclusion) is the *great distance* between the condition (way of being) under consideration—life without consciousness or any savour of knowledge, play, or accomplishment...—and the ways of actualizing the relevant good that are to some extent familiar to us and contribute greatly to its *appeal*—contribute, that is, to the features of its instantiation which arouse our imaginative and emotional interest in purposes and goals instantiating it:

> One may well be overwhelmed by the distance between [the vegetative existence of a person in irreversible coma] and the integral good of a flourishing person. Nobody wants to be in such a condition, and no decent person wants to see anyone else living like that. The good of human life is indeed very inadequately instantiated in such a person's life. Still, the life of a person in irreversible coma remains human life; it is a good, however deprived. True, life of such a deprived and unhealthy kind has little appeal... No human good, considered apart from integral human fulfilment, has the appeal which each of the components of that ideal enjoys when all of them are considered together...[22]

I think the whole section of *NDMR* of which this is a snatch repays a reading.

Instead of further paraphrasing that discussion, I would like to test Crisp's conception of value by taking up what, following James Griffin, he calls 'accomplishment'. He offers this first as a synonym for the value that *NLNR* presented in partial and inadequate fashion as *play*; but in later work I have spoken instead of *excellence-in-performance* for its own sake, whether in work or play.[23] Crisp goes on to broaden and complexify accomplishment, so that it includes practical reasonableness and even, he is tempted to think, religion. But if we resist these extensions, *accomplishment* can do quite well as a term for the distinct basic human good of excellence (for its own sake) in performance. Accomplishment then stands as a fairly clear counter-example to his suggestion that unenjoyed participation in basic human goods is valueless. Enjoyment is, to be sure, an aspect of the reality and goodness of accomplishment. Yet even when one's accomplishment lacks that aspect, and is emotionally dry, subjectively unsatisfying, 'not enjoyable', and 'does not appeal to me now', it can well be understood and

---

knowledge is self-refuting has (without prejudice to its soundness) no purchase on sceptics uninterested in serious rational discussion: see *CEJF* I.4, 83.

[21] See p. 463, n. 16 in this essay.

[22] *NDMR*, 305–6; *CEJF* III.15, 246–7, see also III.14, 219–22 and III.16, 268–9; *CEJF* II.19, 318–20.

[23] *NLNR*, 447–8; *CEJF* I.14, 213, 244n ('skilful performance, in work and play, for its own sake'); *CEJF* II.8, 151; *CEJF* III.5, 88 ('skilful performance...'); *CEJF* IV.17, 361, 369n; *CEJF* V.3, 59 ('skill in work or play'), 156.

intellectually appreciated as good and meaningful as far as it goes, precisely as accomplishment.[24] It is, even then, so far forth fulfilling. We should not be too focused on what is lacking, on the distance—even great distance—between such unappealing accomplishment and the 'real' (full) thing.

Enjoyment—pleasure—is immensely appealing, and pain is immensely repugnant to persons of healthy constitution. Crisp thinks 'it may be an implication of Finnis's view of pleasure as valueless that pain and suffering are also neutral' [p. 35]. But pleasure is not valueless; it is a valuable part of the reality and goodness of each of the basic goods and of full flourishing.[25] And pain is not neutral. So far as it is a means of preservation of life and thus of other basic goods, it is a benefit.[26] But as a vehement proximate cause of the intelligible evil of inner disharmony and loss of integrated psychological functioning and 'personality', it is not merely emotionally repugnant, horrible, but also something which—just in so far as it so operates—we are intelligently and reasonably very interested in avoiding.[27]

Understanding basic goods is a matter of insight into the data of understood possibilities and experienced inclinations[28]; what this insight is and what more is involved are considered at pp. 470–2. Crisp is right to raise [p. 34] Sidgwick's question about the relevance of dissent about self-evident principles of thought such as those that direct us to such goods, and right to take up his inference that we need a theory of error (which will also be an account of how those who fail to share one's reflectively tested judgment affirming the principles are not, in these matters, the epistemic peers of those who do share it). No progress towards such a theory could be made, I think, if we accepted Crisp's thought [p. 30] that 'our beliefs about values are the product of evolution', a thought as obscure and vulnerable as, *mutatis mutandis*, the thought that logic is a product or function of brain states. The remarks about philosophical cultures with which I began these reflections on Crisp's essay go a little way towards a theory of error relevant to this issue of first practical principles. But the most important part of such a theory will consist of dialectical[29] engagement with objections to the principles one has judged true, engagement designed to understand the objections as the indispensable preliminary to refuting them. Refutation's identification of the error or insufficiency or irrelevance of an objection contributes more, and more directly, to the desired theory of error—of error's sources—than any exploration of an error's

---

[24] See *NLNR*, 96–7. See further p. 533, n. 258 in this essay.

[25] *NLNR*, 96–7, 450; at 96 I do not say that '"in the final analysis" pleasure has no value' or is 'valueless', but rather that 'what matters to us, in the final analysis, is knowledge [and the other basic goods there arrayed]', and that if they give pleasure, this is 'one aspect of their reality as human goods, which are *not participated in fully without such experience* of their goodness' (emphasis added).

[26] *NLNR*, 450; *CEJF* IV.17, 362.

[27] *NLNR*, 450.

[28] For some account of this insight into data—for which I would not adopt Crisp's suggestion (too assimilative of understanding to reasoning) that they are 'considerations' that 'determine the intellect'—see *CEJF* I.Introduction, 2; I.2, 45; I.13, 204; also I.1, 31, 33, 39; I.5, 98–9; I.11, 178–9; I.15, 244; and my response to Haldane on pp. 470–2. On how the insights bear on the inclinations, see also nn. 64–6 in this essay.

[29] On dialectic (the Platonic/Aristotelian term) as the (only) way of defending self-evident first principles, see *CEJF* III.5, 89n; the matter is at least mentioned also in *CEJF* I.Introduction, 12; I.2, 45n; I.5, 93–4; *CEJF* II.5, 95; *CEJF* IV.4, 94; IV.11, 273; IV.19, 395; *CEJF* V.9, 145, 150, 161.

possible, more remote propositional grounds, let alone of other, psychological or other natural (cf. 'evolutionary') putative 'causes' of it.

3.

Before reflecting on the role of 'public' philosophizing, **John Haldane** takes us to some truly foundational issues about fact and value. The discussion between us may seem old-fashioned, but I think little or no progress will be made in ethics or political or legal theory, by anyone, without a clarifying attention to these issues.

How can we say anything—anything *true*—about 'norms, values and requirements', beyond describing or endorsing attitudes and commitments? [p. 39]. Would not an objective, true moral proposition (or, indeed, a mistaken one) have to be about some 'existent' moral 'entities: objects, properties or facts'? And are not these too 'exotic and unnatural' to be credible? [p. 41]. Haldane judges this typical contemporary philosophical way of viewing the issue both 'historically atypical' and 'quite unnecessary' [p. 41]. I agree; but showing the needlessness is the harder of the two parts, and his 'traditional' account of the 'metaphysics of animate substance' [p. 43] seems to me to leave the matter unsettled. His account's 'derivation of statements of value from those of fact' [p. 43] goes surprisingly fast; the evaluative terms 'natural *good*', 'benefit', 'abuse', and 'prima facie wrong' [p. 45] emerge abruptly from the account of tendencies, propensities, and inclinations; and even within the biology of subrational animals there loom questions about natural tendencies to aging and death, about the propensities some kinds of being have to perish in or as a result of their reproductive act, and about whether the pertinent 'good' is that of the individual, the species, or the wider ecology in which (in innumerable ways) life for spider is death for fly. But beyond all such questions is the more pressing problem: Can the evaluations (and other normative predicates) derived—let us grant—from true accounts of natural tendencies and inclinations ('immanent teleology') be rightly considered *directive* ('intrinsically prescriptive' [p. 47]), that is, serviceable as evaluative/normative ('first', 'major') premises—principles—for human deliberation towards free choice, that is, for our practical reason(ing)? That they will serve as minor, 'factual', predictive premises in the 'practical syllogism's' movement to its conclusion is indisputable, and not unimportant, but is beside the point when we are asking about practical reason's foundations and starting points either (i) in the way I (and I believe Aquinas) propose[30]—that is, by identifying the substantive *first principles* that give content to the formal first principle 'Good is to be pursued and done . . . ' precisely by directing us to kinds of intrinsic human good—or (ii) in the way recommended by a subsequent tradition[31] and Haldane [p. 43], in which

---

[30] The passage quoted by Haldane [p. 42 at n. 10] from *NLNR*, 33–4 must be taken with the clarifications, disclaimers, and qualifications I heap upon it at *NLNR*, 439. Only taken together with the epistemological principle, which I began to deploy in 1983 (*FoE*, 20–2), does it begin to suffice as an account of the status of first practical principles in relation to 'metaphysical propositions about human nature'.

[31] Haldane rightly uses scare quotes around 'new' and 'traditional' in all his references to schools of natural law theory. The term 'new natural law theory' was forged by an extremely hostile and, I think, uncomprehending critic (Hittinger, *A Critique of the New Natural Law Theory*), and I do not accept it; if one must use a label hereabouts, I would say 'new classical natural law theory', where 'classical' refers to Plato, Aristotle, and Aquinas, whose understanding of the foundations was, I have argued, much

Haldane [p. 43], in which only the first and formal principle is practically or morally prescriptive and the minor premises are propositions ('contingent and known empirically, hence without certainty' [p. 42]) about particular *natural* goods and evils. Why should free human persons treat as foundationally directive for choice the natural goodness, or natural normativity,[32] of the given-in-nature, even in 'human nature'?[33] Why not strike out in new paths, and suppress or transform the immanent teleology, in ways perhaps cautious or perhaps far-reaching?

Questions such as these cannot be pertinently answered, I believe (and am sure Aquinas believed), without referring directly to the intrinsic desirability not only of life and health, but also of knowledge for its own sake, harmony with one's fellow human persons, marital collaboration in procreation and education of new human persons, an appropriate relationship with one's creator, and an integrating of one's inner life and outer action with the requirements of reasonableness.[34] It is this desirability of the kinds of flourishing thus understood and affirmed that is the foundationally *relevant* sort of evaluation, the sort that is inherently directive of a free and rational (intelligent and reasonable) acting person, by being serviceable as a first, major premise in such people's practical reasoning. Such first principles have the type of normativity, the type of *ought* which we need, and which has its developed, more specified form as the fully *moral* ought.[35]

Haldane suggests that the goods and oughts so conceived 'may be too thin or ambiguous' and/or 'too uncertain' to be serviceable as principles for practical, moral reasoning; they need to be filled out and supplemented by resort to an 'anthropology' that is developed somehow prior to practical reasoning and ethics. Neither Aristotle nor Aquinas knows anything about such an anthropology, I believe. You find their anthropology, of a kind sufficiently rich and unambiguous to be serviceable in practical reasoning, in their treatises on ethics, which are treatises unfolding a reflectively general (anticipatory) practical reason. Be that as it may, their 'objects-acts-powers-

---

misrepresented in subsequent scholastic and neo-scholastic theorizing (with occasional exceptions): see e.g. *NLNR*, 45–7. Haldane's essay quite reasonably prescinds from this historical issue.

[32] 'It's spring, so the roses should be budding': *CEJF* I.Introduction, 3.

[33] See 1982a (Finnis and Grisez, 'The Basic Principles of Natural Law: A Reply to Ralph McInerny'), 23:

> One of the principles of *practical* thinking is that knowledge is a good to be pursued; this principle entails that knowledge ought to be pursued. But in the *practical* principle that knowledge is a good to be pursued, 'good' is understood *practically* in the light of the first *practical* principle: Good is to be done and pursued. If 'Knowledge is a good for man' were understood theoretically, simply as a truth of metaphysical anthropology, then it would have no more normative implication than 'Knowledge is good for angels' has practical implication for us.

Again, at 24:

> ... if McInerny wishes to justify a conclusion such as
>
> > Joe ought to go on a diet
>
> he had better not be content with premises such as 'Joe weighs two hundred and fifty pounds' and 'It is not healthy to be overweight.' One must assume a more basic practical premise
>
> > Health is a good to be pursued and protected
>
> which itself is a specification of the very first principle of practical reason.

Nothing in that critique is affected by reading 'healthy' in McInerny's 'evaluative' and *supposedly* prescriptive premise as 'in good psychosomatic human condition'.

[34] See *ST* I–II q. 94 aa. 2 & 3; *Aquinas*, 79–94.   [35] See text and n. 67 in this essay.

essence' principle[36] is rightly taken seriously *on its own merits* by Haldane. Now this is a principle about epistemological order and dependence, *not* in any sense of 'epistemo-logical' bearing on the merely 'evidential' [p. 45], still less the 'contingent' [p. 44] or how 'we choose to arrange our discoveries' [p. 44]. No, it is rather, if you will, *conceptual;*[37] better put, it is concerned with the intrinsic order of *truth-finding*: to know the truth about human nature, one must first know the truth about the forms of human flourishing as that truth is known in reasoning that is practical because inquiring about what is to be done;[38] for only in such inquiring can one come to know the truth[39] about what is both desirable—an intelligibly desirable *object* for one to *act* for—and within one's capacities. My thesis that the first principles of practical reason are understood as identifying (and directing towards) the intelligibly good objects of choices and efforts (and thus of actions, actuations of capacities, and fulfillment of our nature) is a thesis not merely (as Haldane accepts) 'compatible with' [p. 46] or 'consistent with' [p. 47] the epistemological principle; it is a thesis rigorously required by that principle, in that principle's application to a nature such as ours.[40]

But it is certainly reasonable to ask, as Haldane does, how rich and adequate (as opposed to thin and formal) our insights into the first practical principles actually are. Those insights of course deepen or open out into the specifically moral, that is, into conceptions of virtue—so that ideas such as fairness and justice deepen our under-standing of the good of friendship or harmony between persons. Only a saint can really adequately understand human nature (and not all do); the 'metaphysics of animate

---

[36] Haldane [p. 46] rightly summarizes it in this order or sequence, and rightly introduces it [p. 43] as a principle about the 'identification' and 'specification' [p. 43], later the 'real definition' [p. 46], of acts (by their objects), powers (by their actuations), and substances or natures (by their powers). But he does not seem to me to enquire about the significance of this epistemological order for his theory (an evident contradiction of the principle) that a knowledge of human nature is the proper source of our knowledge of the objects of human action.

[37] One could call it metaphysical, provided one does not reduce that to the ontology of beings that are what they are independently of our considerations. It is impossible to sort these issues out without taking into account the theses put on the table by Aquinas in his prologue to the *Ethics*, about the foundational distinction between the natural, logical, moral and technical orders and the corresponding four kinds of science (and epistemology): see n. 14 in this essay.

[38] See *CEJF* I.Introduction, 5–6; I.1, 26–7; I.11, 179; I.13, 204; *Aquinas*, 29–34, 90–4, 102. *CEJF* I.10, 169n, cites some other close students of Aquinas who have independently reached the same conclusions, and to these one can add Martin Rhonheimer; see e.g. Rhonheimer, *Natural Law and Practical Reason*, especially 51, 56. (On knowledge as more than true belief, see p. 460 above.)

[39] Having set up [pp. 40–1] the question of the truth of practical, e.g. moral judgments, and dismissed the 'exotic objects' kind of 'realism', Haldane seems not to return to the question of what account we should give of truth of the kind in question. I have ventured to do so, e.g. in *CEJF* I.Introduction, 8:

> Practical truth is truth. Like non-practical truth it is found by critical attention to all relevant data and questions, coherence with all other truths, and correspondence, not to reality in the same sense as non-practical truth's correspondence (since practical principles and the propositions derived from them concern what is not yet real but might be made real by the actions they direct), but rather correspondence to fulfilment. That is, practical principles have their truth by anticipating—being in an anticipatory correspondence to—the fulfilment whose realization is possible through actions in accordance with them.

See also *Aquinas*, 99–101; also (1987f), 115–20.

[40] That is, the nature of a being existing in all four kinds of order (n. 37), not only the 'order of nature' but also the orders of logic, morality, and arts/techniques: see *CEJF* II.2, sections I and IX.

substances' has to tag along in the wake of some such advanced and practical under-standing, gleaning what it can. But to me it has seemed that the deepening and enriching of our initial understanding and of our verbal summaries ('life and health', 'knowledge', 'marriage', etc.)—the initial part of what Haldane [p. 47] calls 'concept formation'—can and should develop, and can do so independently (to some extent) of specifically moral concerns. I explored this route a bit in the essay from which he has quoted an earlier passage.[41] This sort of exploration is evidently a part of what Aurel Kolnai seems to have had in mind, as the second of the passages Haldane has quoted from him indicates[42]; for the 'feelings' he mentions have nothing to do with experi-ences of or affections toward one's *nature*, and everything to do with the *objects* of one's interest, choice, and action, with the 'matters' about which one should be urgently concerned, and so forth [p. 49].[43]

Thus the synthesis that Haldane rightly desires—between practical knowledge, ontological knowledge, and a 'personalistic phenomenology of value' involving the affective [p. 37; see also p. 54]—is, I am confident, available. Practical knowledge of objects (goods, the desirable, aspects of flourishing) both partly presupposes and partly enhances (greatly) our knowledge of the way things—not least we ourselves[44]—are,

---

[41] *CEJF* I.1, 32–40, especially 39 and 40 (Haldane at n. 11 quotes from 30):

When [the...] practical insight [that knowledge is good and pursuit-worthy] is followed through by chosen commitments to study, reflection, investigation, and so forth, one's original understandings both of knowledge's possibility and of its worth are greatly deepened and enhanced.

I think this mutual reinforcement of theoretical and practical insight is pervasive. So one's originally childish insight into the practical truth that those opportunities are opportunities for me and anyone like me, or into the opportunity of being a friend by valuing and willing the good of another or others for their own sake, is reinforced by knowledge of the capacity of myself and others to make the efforts, commitments, self-disposing devotion to others, and so forth, or to come up with the twisty rationalizations and evasions of betrayal, and so forth. On all this deepened knowledge of possibility there supervenes the enhanced practical understanding of the worth of the person for whom or by whom such acts of will and communication are possible...

So I take the poem [Shakespeare's *Phoenix and Turtle*] to be saying...(iii) that to observe by example the possibility of such devoted, constant, 'true' responsiveness enables one to deepen and reinforce one's understanding of the goods of knowledge, friendship, and practical reason-ableness and thus also one's understanding of the good/value of the persons whose whole lives instantiate and exemplify those goods so awesomely...

See also at *CEJF* I.5, 100.
[42] But Kolnai's position in the third quotation [p. 50], that 'the functioning of nature must be "good" for it is only in that frame of reference, against that background, that we come to contrast good and bad at all' is, I think, simply mistaken, or employs 'good' in a sense quite different from its sense in 'Good is to be done and pursued...'
[43] Similarly in relation to Haldane's analogy with 'a work of art or a performance' [p. 48]. The questions he identifies as pertinent are all focused on the object (the that-toward-which intention and attention is directed)—'What does this mean? What is going on here? What am I trying to say? How does this appear? What does it evoke?...' This is not an anthropological consideration (taxonomy) of '*ways in which* things appear to consciousness' (which would be legitimate but irrelevant) but of 'things [to be made] (as they appear to consciousness)', seeking to (for example) 'see things in a new light' [p. 48] or take someone 'through a series of scenarios real or imagined'. To refer in this context to 'aspects of human nature' is beside the point.
[44] See e.g. *CEJF* III.Introduction, 4–9; Patrick Lee's essay (Essay 15), especially its section II, and my response to it (section 15 at p. 527 in this essay).

independently of our practical reason and freedom; and it partly presupposes[45] and partly enhances (greatly) our affective inclinations. But it is this practical understanding, when sound and correct in its judgments about human goods, that alone explains—provides the *ratio* of, identifies and specifies—the prescriptiveness of whatever we can judge (unaided by revelation) about our opportunities and capacities, about the 'perfection of our nature', and about the 'destination' [p. 47] (flourishing, not the natural as such) we travellers are seeking. Still, this is never a matter of 'aprioristic' understanding or interpretation [p. 47]; and *per se nota* or 'understood in virtue of their very content' should be taken as asserting only non-dependence upon other *propositions*, not independence from the desirability of the states of affairs—states of flesh-and-blood human beings—to the basic kinds of which these first practical principles direct us as to-be-brought-about by chosen actions. The understanding articulated in such principles is no more limited to the initial, preliminary, thin, or formal than any other kind of understanding that supervenes on complex and cumulating data, and emerges and is pursued and assessed in a matrix of other information and of inquiring, attentive, intelligent, reflective, and responsive self-direction.

Like Haldane, I think all these positions argued for in his essay and this response are matters of public reason, and that such arguments do not cease to be matters of public reason if they proceed to specific theses about fundamental political questions and/or about kinds of action that should be excluded from our political communities—even if those theses depart from the consensus of ideas held by those who are considered reasonable by Rawls and by people who accept his idea of public reason. Rawls's idea is indeed irredeemably and fatally equivocal in its criterion ('what all reasonable people could reasonably be expected to endorse'—is 'expected' here normative or predictive?), and unreasonable in seeking to exclude true and warranted judgments on foundational or important matters or issues for authoritative decision.[46] My objection to it is not, however, that 'it licenses anyone who thinks their belief is true to expect that under idealized conditions of inquiry others will share that belief' [p. 54]. Indeed, I hold that under ideal conditions of inquiry (including competence, evidence, attentiveness, etc.) everyone would share my beliefs; and I think it a sign of confusion if someone thinks a belief true without holding that under ideal conditions of inquiry everyone would share it.[47] Thus reasons, in the central sense of that term, seem to me inherently public.[48] But in the non-ideal conditions of inquiry in which we will actually continue to live and communicate with each other, the fact that a moral proposition (or a 'claim of revelation') is 'deeply contested and viewed as beyond rational argument' is no proof, nor even much of an argument, that it is not true and securely believable—though of course in countless cases the contestation and the claims about the proposition's inaccessibility to rational argument are sound, and a sign that it is neither securely believable nor true.

---

[45] See pp. 532–3, n. 258 in this essay (response to Fisher).

[46] See *CEJF* I.16, 259–61; *CEJF* V.2, 52.

[47] On this mark (not criterion) of truth, see *FoE*, 63–6; also *CEJF* I.2, 42; I.5, 93, n. 10; I.16, 260, n. 22; *CEJF* III.1, 46; *CEJF* V.2, 52. If '... is probably true' then 'probably ... everyone would ...', etc.

[48] On public reason(s), see e.g. *Aquinas*, 11ls–12, 255, 257, 320–21n; *CEJF* I.Introduction, 13; I.2, 58; I.16, 259–66; *CEJF* V.Introduction, 4; V.2, 44–5, 47, 52–3; V.4, 84, 86, 102; V.5, 106-7; V.6, 115-6; V.8, 137-8.

4.

The path from first practical principles (and their normativity or directiveness) to specifically moral principles (and their moral normativity and directiveness) is explored in **Joseph Boyle**'s study of the relations between three complementary ways in which Grisez, he, and I have articulated it: one's choices and other forms of willing are to be (i) in line with practical reason's integral directiveness,[49] (ii) in accord with unfettered reason,[50] and (iii) consistent with a will toward integral human fulfilment.[51] He argues that the simplest and most fundamental of these ideas is the first, which 'underlies' the third—the ideal of integral human fulfilment—but has an 'essential expansion' in the second (unfettered reason), without which it would not make clear 'which intermediate moral principles and specific moral norms follow from the most basic moral considerations' [p. 69].[52]

Predicating integral directiveness of practical *reasons* (the propositional content of understanding and reasoning about human goods), rather than of practical reason (the capacity and its activation in such thinking), lets its foundational character emerge the more clearly. That is how I usually articulate it, as for instance in the Introduction to *Reason in Action*:

> [1]...a strictly philosophical moral philosophy (ethics) needs and has a unifying 'last end'. [2] This turns out to be, not an endstate whether in this world or the next, but an ideal of practical reason—integral human fulfilment, not as goal of any plan or project, but as an ideal against which options can be measured as open to such fulfilment or not open to it, and thus as fully reasonable (morally sound) or more or less unreasonable (immoral). [3] For this ideal is the conceptual counterpart or resultant of the idea that the directiveness of each and all of the first practical principles must not be deflected or cut down by sub-rational motivations. [4] That their integral directiveness involves prioritizing and specializations of many kinds is evident, but the true measure of such prioritization is not emotional even when, as in the application of the Golden Rule (fairness), the application of a rational standard for prioritizing legitimizes resort to emotionally shaped preferences (and de-legitimizes an inhuman Kantian or Stoic exaltation of rationality or moral law above spontaneous love and affection). [5] Integral human fulfilment is the fulfilment of all human persons and their communities, precisely *because each of the first practical principles picks out and directs one towards a basic human good which is as good in the lives of others as in one's own.*

---

[49] In *CEJF* I, see Introduction, 12; I.1, 31–2 (referring to the 'integral intelligibility' of the basic goods); I.2, 55; I.11, 180; I.12, 197; I.15, 244, 249.

[50] In *CEJF* I, see Introduction, 12; I.5, 101; I.11, 180; I.13, 210; I.14, 215, 218, 220; I.15, 244, 249, 252, 254.

[51] In *CEJF* I, see I.7, 129n; and Introduction, 13; I.1, 32; I.2, 59; I.5, 101; I.9, 149; I.10, 165, 167, 171–2; I.13, 210; I.14, 220; I.15, 243–5, 251–2, 254. A short synthesis: 'Integral human fulfilment, then, is the ideal of practical intelligence and reasonableness working unfettered by feelings which would deflect it from its full directiveness...[etc.]': *Moral Absolutes* (1991c), 46.

[52] Two reservations: I am reluctant to follow Boyle [p. 57] in conceiving integral human fulfilment as 'the ideal *outcome that would come to be and unfold as the result* of the whole set of possible good choices by everybody' (emphasis added). And I do not think that choosing in line with or on the basis of practical reason's integral directiveness depends upon reflection on options being carried out 'as fully and thoroughly as possible' [p. 62, where Boyle may, however, intend to state only a sufficient, not a necessary condition].

[6] Essay 10's intimations of this ideal of practical reason [are] intimations tailored to showing how far Aquinas employs it as the working integrator of his philosophical ethics . . . [53]

The fifth of these sentences indicates *why* integral human fulfilment is the ideal towards which the first practical principles, taken integrally (all together), direct us. The sense in which reason's integral directiveness underlies the ideal of integral human fulfilment becomes significantly more perspicuous, I believe, when we speak rather of the integral directiveness of practical *reasons*, that is, of the first practical principles. Each of these directs us to a basic element of human flourishing, and understanding their integral directiveness, taken together and fully grasped, includes deploying a metaphysical principle (essential to the metaphysics of morals) implicit in the inference to integral human fulfilment: the *set* implicitly or inchoately referred to in the insight that such-and-such (say, knowledge) is an intrinsic good 'for *me and others* like me' is the set properly denoted as *all human beings* in any way capable of being in any way affected by my choices, that is, all present and future beings who are human in nature.

Boyle's reflections conclude by pointing to the significance of something not mentioned in the paragraph just quoted: the basic human good of practical reasonableness, involving (in his words) the organizing of our very selves by the harmonizing of our feelings and choices under the stable and satisfying direction of reason [p. 72]. I had spoken of this good a few pages earlier in the Introduction to *Reason in Action*, immediately after referring to the metaphysical clarification of the logical structure of each of the first principles:

[1] This universality of the practical principles, and of their normativity for each of us, both reinforces the normativity of the good of friendship, and is capable of qualifying and limiting that normativity.

[2] Here practical reasonableness comes into view as a further basic intelligible good to which a distinct first practical principle directs us. [3] For it is obvious, or soon obvious, that one might respond to one or other or all of these basic human goods and practical first principles unreasonably. [4] The limitations and vulnerabilities of one's life and capacities not only occasion in us an understanding of a further basic good—human life (one's very existence) and health—but also demand that one adjudicate between the normative claims of each and all of the first practical principles in their bearing on the ways one's own choices and actions might affect the future existence and flourishing of oneself and others. [5] That such an adjudication be reasonable is obviously good not only as a means to realizing any of the other intrinsic goods but also in itself. [6] This architectonic good—of pursuing the other goods in one's own and others' lives *well*, fully reasonably, without deflection or distortion by sub-rational motivations—is the matrix of all normativity that is not merely practical but specifically *moral* (ethical). [7] The principle that adequately articulates its content and directiveness is not successfully identified in . . . *Natural Law and Natural Rights*, but can be found in *Fundamentals of Ethics* and . . . [*CEJF* I.14 and 15] . . . [54]

---

[53] *CEJF* I.Introduction, 12–13 (emphasis added).
[54] *CEJF* I.Introduction, 4.

The work most cited in Boyle's essay is 1987f, in which he and I collaborated with Grisez; it is an article that repays re-reading on all the matters in issue in *Reason in Action*. In line with Grisez's preferred way of unfolding practical reason(s), the article speaks of the basic good of harmony between judgment, choice, and performance, rather than of the basic good of practical reasonableness, and says nothing direct about its architectonic character.[55] Again in line with his thinking, the article articulates as 'modes of responsibility' the principles which mediate between the first practical principles and morality's substantive principles and norms.[56] These modes of responsibility, as Grisez's important later work on them makes ever clearer,[57] are to be conceived as reasonable (and reasonableness-shaping) responses to the threat posed by emotions to the rule of reason in our willing, the threat (mentioned in sentence [6] above) that reason will be fettered and its integral directiveness deflected or distorted in its deliverances. In my free-standing work,[58] I have continued to prefer to focus directly on the content of the intermediate principles, as principles of practical reasonableness and as inherently intelligible (especially when the impossibility of consequentialist/utilitarian ideas becomes apparent) both in themselves, and even more as elements of practical reason's integral directiveness and thus as requirements of openness to integral human fulfilment.[59]

5.

Jeremy Waldron's wide-ranging discussion of natural law is implicitly concerned with what I have just called the 'intermediate principles' that, as specifications of the master moral principle of openness to integral human fulfilment, mediate between the *incipiently* moral first principles of practical reason and the *specifically* moral (and fully specified/specific) principles and norms of the natural moral law. But he argues that 'like all law', natural law is and must be 'separable from ethics and morality'.[60] Even

---

[55] See 1987f ('Practical Principles, Moral Truth, and Ultimate Ends'), 137; at 139–40 we say that we have previously referred to *harmony between judgment and choice* as *practical reasonableness*, and that the latter phrase takes the relevant basic good in the sense that it has when taken morally (i.e. considered by unfettered reason and in the light of integral human fulfilment). The article is correct in its premise here: that each basic human good can be understood immorally or amorally, as well as morally. But I think that even the term 'practical reasonableness' can be taken in an immoral or amoral sense, and so is available to name a basic human good, corresponding to the *bonum rationis* that Aquinas identified as the subject of a first practical principle (and thus, implicitly, as a basic human good), in *ST* I–II q. 94 a. 3c, and deployed far more extensively than I had realized until about the time I came to write *Aquinas*: see *Aquinas*, 83–5, 98–9, 106–8, 119, 140, 168, 225n, 308.

[56] 1987f, 127: 'we began [in earlier writings] with an account of the principles of practical knowledge corresponding to the basic goods and moved directly to moral principles such as those requirements of practical reasonableness which demand fairness, forbid revenge, exclude doing evil to achieve good, and so forth. These intermediate moral principles are the modes of responsibility.'

[57] See Grisez, *Difficult Moral Questions*, Appendix 1. On emotions, see p. 533, n. 258 in this essay.

[58] But also in *NDMR*, Ch. X.4–5.

[59] These are matters probed again by Grisez in Essay 27, and touched on in my response to that (pp. 580–1).

[60] [p. 75]; at [p. 73] he speaks of 'natural *law* as opposed to ... natural morality, natural ethics ...', and at [74] of natural law as 'something distinct from natural morality or natural ethics'. On the distinction he draws between morality and ethics, a distinction which, like Habermas, Dworkin (in *Justice for Hedgehogs*), and many others, Waldron draws by reference to an attempted contrast between 'personal virtue' and 'other-regarding actions' [p. 82], suffice it to say that I think the classic tradition from Plato through

when he discusses Kant, he does not allude to the *moral law*, which Kant found 'within' himself, as wonderful as the heavens above him. The term 'moral law' is found only a couple of times in Aquinas, and again in Suarez, but certainly the concept which Aquinas articulates with the terms 'natural law', 'precepts of the natural law', and 'moral precepts of the Law' simply is the concept of 'moral law'. So it is not surprising that Waldron's argument eventually carries him to a less 'provocative' [p. 74] position, that 'perhaps objective morality is the more inclusive category and natural law is a subset of it, distinguished by the *features of forcefulness*' that he had considered as the first two of the four features by which natural law, in his sense of the term, is distinguished from morality.

The first of these two 'features of forcefulness' is deontic character. But I think this does not even begin to distinguish natural law from morality. As I say about the intermediate principles in Chapter V of *NLNR* (immediately before trying to identify them):

> ...the *requirements* to which we now turn express the 'natural law method' of working out the (*moral*) 'natural *law*' from the first (pre-moral) 'principles of natural law'. Using only the modern terminology (itself of uncertain import) of 'morality', we can say that the following sections of this chapter concern the sorts of reasons why (and thus the ways in which) there are things that morally *ought* (not) to be done.[61]

The words I have italicized have meanings and connotations that are as deontic as could be wished. And the severity of this obligation, in relation to at least some kinds of act, is made evident in Chapter VIII.7's discussion (referring back to Chapter V.7) of the *absolute* human rights which correspond to *exceptionless* duties,[62] duties excluding certain types of choice and action *whatever the consequences*.[63]

In the course of his discussion of deontic character and normativity, Waldron contrasts those, such as Locke, who 'identify natural law with reason' with those who 'like Aquinas, associate it [natural law] with inclinations, without insisting as strictly as

---

Aquinas and far beyond rightly rejected it. Aristotle makes the point sufficiently by treating the personal virtue of justice, a virtue entirely concerned with other-regarding action, in the middle of his *Ethics*. Against Habermas on this: *CEJF* I.2, 48. (This is not to say that the virtue of justice is just like the other virtues: see e.g. *S.T.* II-II q. 57 a. 1; *Aquinas*, 137–8; *CEJF* IV.7, 178n.) Pace Waldron [p. 82, n. 40], I doubt that Aquinas's *ad bonum commune naturae* in *S.T.* I–II q. 94 a. 3 ad 1 means 'other-regarding'; the *corpus* of the reply makes no reference to self-regarding v. other-regarding, and strongly tells (like the rest of his account of ethics/morality) against the *practical* relevance of this justice-defining distinction save for purposes of defining the coercive jurisdiction of state government and law (as to which, see *Aquinas*, 222–8, 232–3, 241–2).

   [61] *NLNR*, 103. A similarly programmatic statement is at the end of Ch. V.7 on p. 124: '...as the term "natural law" is used in this book... *everything* required by virtue of *any* of the requirements discussed in this essay is required by natural law. In this use of the term, if *anything* can be said to be required by or contrary to natural law, then *everything* that is morally (i.e. reasonably) required to be done is required (either mediately or immediately: cf. X.7) by natural law, and everything that is reasonably (i.e. morally) required not to be done is contrary to natural law.'

   [62] Of course, I took for granted that these duties are moral, and it did not cross my mind that human rights could be conceived—as some today conceive of them—as merely positive, or as restricted to cases where states are *recognized* as having the authority to intervene. I emphasized (at 225) that such human rights, in their absoluteness, are *not* clearly recognized 'by all or even most people—on the contrary'.

   [63] *NLNR*, 126, 224. On such duties see Finnis, *Moral Absolutes* (1991c); *CEJF* I.5, 101–2; *CEJF* I.12.

Locke does, for example, that all human inclinations must be scrutinized and rationalized by reason before they can safely be regarded as natural law' [p. 78; also p. 84]. He
adds immediately: 'in the case of inclinations, there *is* likely to be a discontinuity
between our apprehension of what we are inclined to do and our apprehension of why
we are inclined to do it'. But this indicates why Aquinas did not make, and could not
possibly have made, inclinations substitute for, or be the subject of or in any way
referred to in, the *first principles of practical reason* (which for him are the first
principles of natural law, and so, by entailment, of morality). A question is not practical
at all if it asks *what we are* [or one is] *inclined to do*, nor if it asks *why we are* [or one is]
inclined to do it, but only if it asks what we have *reason(s)* to do, that is, what it *would be
good* to do, and so, what *is to be* done (in the normative/gerundive, not the predictive/
indicative, sense of 'is to be').[64] Aquinas's account is at least[65] as strict as Locke's in
subjecting inclinations to the rule of reason[66]; the source of normativity for him is the
intelligibility of the goods to which we have *good* inclinations; and the epistemological
primacy, in practical thinking, of reason(s) over nature is affirmed by him with
unambiguous clarity in the passage quoted and commented upon, as of decisive
importance, in *NLNR* at 35–6.[67]

What then of Waldron's second ground for distinguishing natural law from morality? It is that law is enforceable—its norms are appropriately upheld with force
(coercion). Here I think Locke leads[68] Waldron astray:

> In the absence of institutions, Locke maintains that natural law is enforceable by any
> individual. Enforcement is partly a matter of a right to resist and seek reparations for
> violations that concern oneself, but it also includes a more general right to punish
> wrongdoers on account of the danger they pose to all mankind. [p. 79]

But the position massively dominant in the natural law tradition (and Grotius, after an
early deviation, concurred with it) is that—leaving aside all intra-familial issues—there

---

[64] So the International Theological Commission's *In Search of a Universal Ethic: A New Look at the
Natural Law* (2009), sections 2.3–2.4, heads in the wrong direction by making inclinations the guide to the
content of natural law's (or practical reason's) first or first moral principles.

[65] Waldron finds puzzling 'Finnis's... dismissal of the work of John Locke as a "crude attack" on natural
law'. But *NLNR* at 425 is no dismissal of Locke's work; it is a statement that his work *includes* a crude attack
on what I call 'the tradition' 'carried forward from Plato by Aristotle and Aquinas' but subsequently so
enfeebled by misunderstandings that its would-be followers responded inadequately to Hobbes, Locke and
Hume. I had particularly in mind the passage I have quoted in section 2 (464 at n. 17), from Locke's *Essay
Concerning Human Understanding*, a passage indicating that Locke had no *reflective*, philosophically appro-
priated grasp whatever of first principles (of practical reason) in the light of which inclinations might be
tested.

[66] See *S.T.* I–II q. 94 a. 2c and my exegesis and commentary in *Aquinas*, 79–84 and 92–4; also 72–8.

[67] The key sentence in that quotation from *S.T* I–II q. 71 a. 2c is: 'The good of the human being is being in
accord with reason, and human evil is being outside the order of reasonableness... So human virtue... is in
accordance with human nature *just in so* far as [*tantum... inquantum*] it is in accordance with reason...' See
likewise q. 94 a. 3 ad 2: 'all acts of wrongdoing, insofar as [*inquantum*] they are unreasonable, are also [*etiam*]
contrary to nature...'

[68] Actually twice, since he also adopts Locke's thought that 'matters of religious belief are inherently
unenforceable in this sense, because there is nothing that force or sanctions can secure in the way of the
requisite sincere belief'. Thomas Pink's essay [pp. 439–41] argues persuasively (like Kant: see *CEJF* III.2, 68)
that this empirical claim is at best very weak, or more likely simply mistaken. Whether such force or
sanctions *should* be deployed *to* secure such belief is another matter: see pp. 568–72 in this essay.

is no just punishment (in the focal sense of 'punish') of wrongdoers in a state of nature, if such a state of affairs is defined as including no authority.[69] So we should set aside punishment as here a red herring: to punish justly is to claim and exercise responsibility, and thus authority, to *restore* the order of justice in a community. Setting aside any such authority does not, however, leave the norms of the natural moral law unenforceable. Their enforceability includes a right—even in such a 'state of nature'[70]—to resist and seek reparations for attacks not only on oneself but on anyone to whom one has any relevant moral responsibility, including even strangers; and beyond that, it includes the right to intervene to *protect* justice by preventing attacks and other wrongful acts or omissions wherever they can be found and dealt with reasonably, having regard to one's other responsibilities and the rights of other persons and communities (not including the rights forfeited by the wrongdoers, actual or would-be, by reason of their wrongs).[71]

Still, even in this wider sense, is not enforcement appropriate only in relation to violations of justice? Yes, if the coercion envisaged is imposed on adults by state government or law. But the enforceability of the norms of natural law includes their relevance as grounds for parental discipline of children, which appropriately extends far into the domain of self-regarding virtues. And in any case, we are entitled to ask whether Waldron's criteria are indeed necessary conditions for calling natural law *law*. *NLNR* concludes its section on the definition of law by remarking:

> 'Natural law'—the set of practical principles in ordering human life and human community—is only analogically law, in relation to my present focal use of the term: that is why the term has been avoided in this chapter on law, save in relation to past thinkers who used the term. These past thinkers, however, could, without loss of meaning, have spoken instead of 'natural right', 'intrinsic morality', 'natural reason, or right reason, in action', etc. But no synonyms are available for 'law' in our focal sense.[72]

The sense of 'law' focal *in that chapter* includes enforceability by lawful coercive sanctions.[73] But I see no reason to make 'enforcement/enforceable'—at least in any focal sense of those terms—a condition for using the term 'natural law' in the way the tradition since Plato uses it, as synonymous with 'moral law' or 'the precepts of ethics'. Even setting aside the tradition's eschatology (Platonic or Christian), there is good sense in saying both that all morally wrongful acts are contrary to natural law[74] and that such vice is its own punishment. Is not the objectivity and communicability of

---

[69] This tradition creates a notable *aporia* for the mainstream tradition of natural-law thinking about the justification of war: see *CEJF* III.13, 190–4 (1996b, section III), pages which also bring out some of the various different senses of 'in order to punish...'

[70] This is not to concede (or even grant) Waldron's thesis that 'the point of thinking about natural law is to contemplate the absence of such institutions [as courts and police forces]' [p. 79]. It is merely to say that the natural moral law is applicable to *all* human situations in which choice and action are or would be possible.

[71] A brief discussion: *CEJF* III.8, 131 (2003a, section II) and III.13, 187–95 (1996b, sections II–III).

[72] *NLNR*, 280.

[73] *NLNR*, 276.

[74] *ST* I–II q. 94 a. 3 ad 2.

moral principles and norms, taken with their inherent deontic normativity for every-one in the human community, enough to entitle them to the term 'law'?

Waldron's real theme is the *ius gentium*, that set of principles which can be conceived as applicable *de iure* (as true requirements of practical reasonableness) and *de facto* (as accepted in a consensus of overlapping convictions) in and among all peoples, and peculiarly relevant as a *ius inter gentes* (an international law) just in so far as it is only *inter gentes* that we regularly find anything like the philosopher's (and Waldron's) state of nature. So it is perhaps worth noticing *NLNR*'s discussion of the *ius gentium*. This takes the form of a list of 13 'General Principles of Law'[75] which, I argued, are principles not only for courts but also for legislators, and are:

> ...so closely related to the first principles [of practical reason] in combination with the basic methodological requirements of practical reasoning that they should be regarded as derivable *by reasoning* from natural law and thus, in a sense, a part of the natural law. At the same time, they are essentially principles for systems of positive law, and are in fact to be found in virtually all such systems. Hence they are the (or part of the) *jus gentium* in the sense explained (not without obscurity) by Aquinas...part of the natural law by their mode of derivation (by deduction, not *determinatio*), and at the same time of human positive law by their mode of promulgation.[76]

Waldron's discussion of 'ancillary principles' touches on items (ii), (iii), (xii) and (xiii) in my list. Of course, such a mere listing as I made is pitifully slight by comparison with works such as those of Gentili or Grotius or countless others. And Waldron is right that *NLNR* does not set out a system or inventory of principles and norms of natural law, either in his sense of the term or mine. Still, I would not concede that the book contains no more than the 'one or two' deontic requirements and prohibitions that he thinks I 'can eke out' from Chapter V. I have already alluded to the norms against killing, torture, deception, frame-ups, and sterilization articulated in the book's discussion of absolute rights; to these, the justifications of property rights in the context of justice, and of promissory, contractual, and delictual compensatory obliga-tions both there and in the context of obligation as such, add a good many norms, some made explicit but most left implicit; treason and perjury find their place in the discussion of commutative justice; and principles for resolving bankruptcy get a discussion. But where I have tried to justify specific principles and norms, and do the casuistry involved in specifying them precisely, it has almost all been outside *NLNR*, which I thought had enough on its plate.

---

[75] *NLNR*, 288; the list was drawn (296) from a treatise on public international law. For the list and a short commentary, see also 2012b ('What is Philosophy of Law?') at n.1.

[76] *NLNR*, 296. On the intermediate principles or *ius gentium*, see also *CEJF* IV.7, 180, 184n; cf. *CEJF* III.13, 194, 200 on the later Scholastic usage in which *ius gentium* is more a matter of positive law than of natural law. On *ius gentium* in a secondary sense—quasi-universal positive law detached from or contrary to authentic natural law/right, as in slavery, or the outlawing of even non-harmful corporal punishment—see *CEJF* III.12, 179.

II. Intentions in Action

6.

My gratitude for Elizabeth Anscombe's work goes well beyond what I tried to convey in the review essay **Luke Gormally** cites at the beginning of his valuable defence of her position on cases in which (she argued) 'doing this *just is* intentionally[77] killing'. My debts and appreciation appear again, and extensively, in the Introduction to *Intention and Identity*.[78] So he will not be surprised that I resist his theses that my action theory (a) is unfaithful to her *Intention* by relying on an assumption (about 'conceivability') alien to her thought and (b) neglects '*Intention*'s requirement for control of the truthfulness of an agent's act description' [p. 94]. The assumption which he thinks I rely upon is quite as alien to my thought as to hers; and (like her[79]) I think neither action theory nor ethical analysis include any '*requirement* for control' of an acting person's truthfulness: only biographers (including autobiographers), historians, or other spectators, including courts, have any reason to be concerned with truthfulness in agents' descriptions of their acts.

Gormally's essay does us all the service of publishing Anscombe's undated note on certainty and immediacy and their relevance to 'whether doing this is *eo ipso* [by that very fact] doing that' [p. 96]. Unlike *Intention*, the note is suffused with ethical concerns: with what 'gives moral significance' to 'the distinctions employed', with 'the question of your accusability', with what 'absolutely may not' be done or attempted; and with what conduct is or is not 'a great injustice'. While I do not think, and have never thought, that in such ethically suffused analyses Anscombe 'abandoned the standpoint of the acting person' and 'replaced it with the observational standpoint' that looks to 'observable efficient causal behaviour', I do think that they fail as accounts of the acting person's intention (precise choice of action).[80] That failure, and (as I think) the failure of Gormally's critiques of what I have said about craniotomy, stuttering, castration of bulls, and separation of conjoined twins, can most economically be indicated by considering yet again the passage from *Intention* quoted, with my commentary, by Gormally [pp. 97–8].

It is a passage that signals its own importance as a paradigmatic (albeit rigorous) application of the *criteria* of intention. Its context is as the second of two scenarios; in the first, X moves his arm to pump poisoned water to replenish a house's water supply to poison the inhabitants; in the second, Y moves his arm to pump (poisoned) water to replenish the water supply to earn his usual pay as a pumper, and knowing but caring nothing that the water he needs, as usual, to deliver happens on this occasion to be *poisoned* water. About this second scenario, *Intention* said:

---

[77] Note: Anscombe was—I do not complain of this—indifferent to what *CEJF* II, 184 calls 'a nuance of our language ... "unintentionally" connotes accident or mistake or lack of foresight ... [with the result that there can be] a killing which is both intentional and not intentional, for "intentional(ly) is equivocal between "intended" and "not unintentionally"'. In Anscombe's usage in *Intention*, 'intentional act' always means an act done with the intent(ion) [specified by the textual context].

[78] *CEJF* II.Introduction, 3–10; also *CEJF* IV.Introduction, 4.

[79] See text at p. 484, nn. 89–90 in this essay.

[80] About Anscombe's discussion of the potholer, and Gormally's discussion of it, I think *CEJF* II.10, 189–93 (1991b, section II) suffices.

In that case, although he knows concerning an intentional act of his—for it, namely replenishing the house water-supply, is intentional by our criteria—that it is *also* an act of replenishing the house water-supply with *poisoned* water, it would be incorrect, by our criteria, to say that his act of replenishing the house supply with poisoned water was intentional. And I do not doubt the correctness of the conclusion; it seems to shew that our criteria are rather good.[81]

They are. And they show that it is incorrect to hold that craniotomy performed in order to relieve the obstetrical blockage which will imminently kill (both) the mother (and her child) always involves an intent to kill (to shorten the life) or even to harm (impair the functioning and capacities of) the child. In the order of[82] actions, causality, and events *in genere naturae* [considered as natural kinds], this crushing and emptying (and even removing) the child's skull 'just is', '*eo ipso*' harming and killing the child. But this crushing, etc. is neither of those things in the order of intentions or, in Anscombe's idiom, of intentional acts or, in Aquinas's idiom, of acts *in genere moris* [considered as moral kinds] (i.e. as specified—accurately identified—for purposes of applying ethical predicates).[83] For so too, no more and no less, B's pumping of poisoned water into the house 'just was', 'also', '*eo ipso*', poisoning the water supply, yet equally (as Anscombe in *Intention* holds) it simply *was not* the intentional or *in genere moris* act of poisoning the water supply.

Indeed, Gormally's thesis—'it would be part of the practical knowledge [such] a surgeon had of his intentions *that he aimed to kill the child*' [p. 100]—is, I suggest, a *reductio ad absurdum*, or at any rate is straightforwardly incorrect by the criteria which Anscombe judged 'rather good'. Gormally's analysis obliterates the essential act-analytical and humanly real distinction between scenario Y and scenario X. Equally, it obliterates the distinction between therapeutic craniotomy and partial-birth abortion,[84] between jumping from the top of the World Trade Center on '9/11' to escape the oily fireball and jumping to commit suicide, between shooting down a passenger plane to save a skyscraper full of people and shooting it down to kill the passengers, between 'transfixing with an arrow' a drugged or mentally defective child who is killing people with a machine gun and transfixing him in order to kill (or to maim him for more effective street beggary); between giving a life-shortening dose of analgesics as the only dose that will suppress a terminally ill patient's pain and giving the same dose to shorten her life and 'unblock' her bed; and many other like distinctions.

---

[81] Anscombe, *Intention*, 42 (para. 25). Nothing turns on the phrase 'seems to', which is simply the idiom of modesty and subtracts nothing from the basic affirmation that it is *correct* to conclude that his intentions did *not* include delivering *poisoned* water.

[82] That is: considered as a matter of…

[83] See also p. 500 in this essay. Throughout the discussion of pumper Y, do not forget that in most versions of his scenario, he will be morally and should be legally culpable for *murder* (despite his lack of intent to kill): see p. 488, n. 98 in this essay.

[84] In saying this, we should not forget that moral assessment looks not only to what is done *qua* carrying out of intentions (of means and ends) but also to the justice or injustice, virtue or vice, involved in accepting the side-effects of doing so. No one is suggesting that the bare fact that Y did not intend to deliver *poisoned* water is *sufficient* to establish that his conduct was morally acceptable (rather than a very serious homicide that might be called murder). But the fact that the surgeon's therapeutic craniotomy involves no intent to kill or harm, together with the fact that without it both mother and child will soon die, may well be sufficient. These are issues of moral theory, not act analysis. (See also pp. 487–8 in this essay.)

Anscombe's *Intention*'s criteria of intention, and of correct descriptions of an act(ion) *qua* execution of intentions,[85] refute the equations insisted upon in her later, ethically oriented writings, published and unpublished, and in Gormally's essay. That transfixing a man certainly damages him does not entail that trying to transfix him is trying to damage him; performing a therapeutic craniotomy by crushing and removing the child's skull is neither trying to kill the child nor 'constitutive of' (as opposed to having as 'a known concomitant result') killing the child. Pumping water one knows to be poisoned is both 'a contingently inseparable part of' and indeed 'constitutive of' pumping poisoned water and poisoning the water supply; but *Intention* shows that and why and when behaving in this way is not the carrying out of an intention to pump poisoned water and/or to poison the water supply. Gormally notes Matthew O'Brien's attempt to assimilate Anscombe's analysis of scenario Y to scenario Z (in which the pumper's usual job description includes ensuring that water he pumps is drinkable); but he rightly rejects it, observing parenthetically that Anscombe does *not* adopt the inference on which O'Brien founds his scenario. The essay thus leaves *Intention*'s account of scenario Y (and indeed my commentary, as quoted at pp. 97–8) intact.

Just as Y would reject the question 'Why are you (trying to) supply(ing) *poisoned* water?', the therapeutic craniotomist would reject the question 'Why are you (trying to) kill(ing) the baby?', the bull-breeder in our special scenario (castrating solely to fatten) would reject the question 'Why are you trying to sterilize the bull?', the stuttering witness would reject the question 'What are you stuttering for?', and the surgeon trying to separate the conjoined twins would reject the question 'Why are you trying to mutilate the weaker one?' The fundamental arguments of *Intention*, applied rigorously, centre on the A-B-C-D pattern helpfully recalled in Gormally's essay [p. 99] in recounting scenario X. Little or nothing in Gormally's replacements for my treatment of all these scenarios seems to me to adhere to that pattern and that strategy of argument.

As for his criticism of my accounts of that set of scenarios, it all comes down to the thought that they '[assume] that one's actual choice of means can be defined in terms of what is *conceivably possible*' [p. 95], that my 'conception of what makes a means attractive to choice ... is conceived ... in terms of what "one wants and needs", where these can be formulated in terms of what one could confine oneself to doing in some conceivable world' [p. 101], that is, 'in terms of merely conceivable possibilities' [pp. 103, 104], under 'the description of what *ideally* one "needs and wants"' [p. 101]. As Gormally rightly remarks [p. 95], this is an assumption which finds no support in Anscombe's *Intention*. Equally, it contradicts all my own attempts to articulate the correct strategy for understanding and analysing action, and describing it in a form fit for ethical predicates (that is, for assessing choices and actions morally, by comparison of the act, so described, with some true moral standard).

For: all those attempts of mine emphasize that what counts in such analyses and descriptions is the actual practical reasoning of the acting person about what he actually needs and wants in order to accomplish his actual purposes.[86] Ideal or merely

---

[85] See *Intention*, 86–8 (section 48).

[86] Thus *CEJF* II.13, 268: 'We [the authors] have no interest whatever in conducting an act analysis in terms of "conceptual necessity" or "conceptual relations". We spoke of the "conceptual" only in relation to

conceivably possible eventualities are thus completely beside the point. My summary of the act-analysis in *Intention* was also a summary of the action theory I have deployed since the early 1980s:

> The book [*Intention*] ascribes a descriptive and explanatory priority to the description(s) which behaviour has in the practical reasoning (the deliberations) by which the acting person shaped up the proposal he or she adopted by choosing to behave (act or forbear) in this way. This shaping of description(s) in practical reasoning and deliberation is not a matter of finding a description under which the behaviour one is determined to carry out will be acceptable to oneself or others. Rather, it is settled by what one considers a necessary or helpful means to achieving an objective (usually a nested set of objectives) that one considers desirable, in view of the factual context as one understands its bearing on both one's end(s) and the means that one judges serviceable for achieving such end(s).[87]

There is no room in such practical reasoning and deliberation for the merely ideal or merely conceivable.[88] Gormally points to nothing that could warrant his attribution of the 'assumption', save the passage quoted at his n. 12 in which Boyle, Grisez, and I say that 'there could be a form of craniotomy in which, though the usual outcome is the death of the baby, the surgeon nevertheless hopes that cutting and squeezing the skull without emptying its contents will not result in the baby's death'. But this statement was responding to a subordinate argument (the fifth of seven) against craniotomy: that 'this kind of behaviour *never* is done to help the baby'. Our reflection about a possible form of craniotomy was not deployed or hinted at in our replies to the four arguments offered to show that craniotomy is intentional killing. We were merely observing that there could be a procedure in which skull-crushing and decapitation was just the last resort after other procedures, carried out with some hope of success, for non-lethally reducing the skull size to set free the baby, proved unsuccessful. The last-resort procedure would be identical to the normal case, both in its fully foreseen lethality and, *pace* Gormally, in its lack of any intent or 'aim' to kill. This conjunction of

---

Flannery and only because he is interested in conceptual or "logical" necessity. Our understanding of intention and action is entirely in terms of the why and how questions that the acting person addressed in the deliberations that ended in choice and action.' The basic position is summarized at 257: 'A true and morally objective description of such acts is the description they have, prospectively (as acts still to be done), in the proposals the acting person shapes in deliberation and adopts by choice(s). What an act objectively is, and can be known objectively to be, is not affected by what the acting person or others may say about it, or by what others may reasonably (though mistakenly) infer it to be. Nor is the reality of what an acting person is doing described adequately or objectively by describing it only in terms of the purposes that motivated it, omitting what the acting person chose to do as means of pursuing those purposes.' And at 240: 'Foreseen effects of what one does are intended only if they actually are among one's reasons for acting. If they are not, they are part of neither the proposal one adopts in choosing nor the purpose(s) for the sake of which one chooses: they are part of neither the means nor the end(s).'

[87] *CEJF* II.3, 76; likewise at Introduction, 13; II.10, 189, 194; II.13, 255, 260: I.14, 274. The passage at 76 ends: 'In summarizing her book's main thesis in this way, I use terminology (for example, "proposal", "adopt") which is not altogether hers. But her favourable albeit informal and oral response to an exposition and analysis of intention which I gave in her presence in 1980 [now *CEJF* II.9 (1991a)] served, in my mind, to confirm my opinion that her main thesis was, or was in line with, what I have just set out.'

[88] Indeed, there simply could not be a 'proposal...phrased in terms of what is merely conceivably possible' [Gormally, p. 104].

possibilities (spectrum or graded sequence of procedures) we said is a 'sign' that 'the fact that the craniotomy normally results in the baby's death'—with (as we took for granted and could have added) certainty and immediacy—'does not suffice to settle what is or is not the object', that is, the precise and morally decisive intention, of the act. For as the surgeon moved along this possible spectrum of procedures, he would be choosing each step not for its lethality or harmfulness but for its efficacy in reducing the size of the baby, just as *Intention*'s Y chooses to pump water (*known by him* to be poisoned water) not for its character as poisoned or not poisoned but for its replenishing of the cistern with water, and is rightly counted in that book as neither intending to pump poisoned water nor intentionally doing so.[89] A few pages later we took care to say that *such a counterfactual 'sign' is 'no criterion at all' for judging what is and is not intended*.[90] It is at most a device for encouraging attention to the *actual* train of practical reasoning and choice by which the acting person, here the surgeon, comes to shape and adopt the proposal of which his action is the execution.[91] By prompting one to focus on such actual trains of reasoning (and to focus now unconcerned with conceptual possibilities), temporary attention to possible cases helps one break free from the grip of sheer external facts about certainty and immediacy of effects, focussing on which in isolation from actual practical reasoning generates such a *reductio* as Gormally's claim that the surgeon in any craniotomy simply must be aiming to kill.

I agree with Anscombe that there can be checks on the truthfulness of the descriptions that acting persons offer of their intentions and actions, and that such checks operate by bringing to light an actual train of reasoning inconsistent with some feature of such an avowal. But as she stresses, such checks run out, and there are intentions which are real and specific though quite uncheckable. This allows room for deception, including self-deception in relation to what one *did*, in the (even quite proximate) past. But–

> ...the truth about what is intended and being done is available, primarily if not exclusively, to the acting person *in* that acting—*in* that deliberating, choosing, and carrying out the choice—which constitutes the reality to which all accounts of intention and action must conform if they are to be true.

> Each clear-headed and honest person knows what he or she is truly or objectively doing. Such persons know what end(s) they have in view, and what means they have reason, in view of such ends, to choose, and are actually choosing in preference to alternatives.[92]

---

[89] Once again: 'If the answer to the question "Why did you replenish the house supply with poisoned water?" is "To polish them off", or any answer within the range, like "I just thought I would", then by my criterion the action under that description is characterized as intentional; otherwise not.' *Intention*, 43 (section 25).

[90] *CEJF* II.13, 262.

[91] See *Intention*, 86–8 (section 48); Aquinas, *ST* I–II q. 20 a. 1 ad 1: 'actus exterior est obiectum voluntatis *inquantum proponitur voluntati a ratione* [the external action, in so far as it is proposed to one's will by one's reason, is one's will's *object*]'.

[92] *CEJF* II.13, 259; see the whole of each of these paragraphs; also at 255: 'What counts for moral analysis is not what may or may not be included in various descriptions that might be given by observers, or even by acting persons reflecting on what they have done, but what is or is not included within a proposal developed in deliberation for possible adoption by choice. Only the truthful articulation of that proposal can be a description that specifies an act for the purposes of moral analysis.'

Similarly, Anscombe in *Intention* denied that there must be checks on truthfulness, and denied that checks on truthfulness control what (kinds of) intention there is in any given case or type of case.[93] To insist that there must be controlling checks on truthfulness, such that they would lend support to the necessities asserted in Gormally's essay and Anscombe's ethical writings, *would* be to abandon the standpoint of the deliberating and acting person which it was Anscombe's remarkable achievement to have shown is (so to put it) the criterion for the criteria of true action descriptions.

Anscombe, so far as I know, never explained the discrepancy between *Intention* and her ethical writings, including the note now published in Gormally's essay. The nearest the essay gets to tackling the relationship between them is the brief statement that the ethical writings (helpfully exemplified by the quotation at p. 100, n. 24 from her 1982 paper) 'echo what she has to say in *Intention* about the description of means in the light of circumstances as answering the question "How?" about the achievement of one's end. [fn.: *Op. cit.* §26].' But the 'circumstances' discussed in section 26 of *Intention* are the reasons for action (intentions, A-B-C-D series of 'Why?' questions and answers . . .) that make it the case that X's 'moving his arm up and down with his fingers round the pump handle *is*, in these circumstances, operating the pump . . . replenishing the house water-supply . . . poisoning the household'.[94] This discussion of circumstances and means explains how in section 27 she could say that Y's moving his arm up and down with his fingers round the pump handle and replenishing the house water supply with (knowingly) the very same poisoned water is *not* poisoning the household (except as a side effect of his chosen act). So section 26 of *Intention* is precisely *not* echoed, but rather disregarded, in the 1982 article and other ethically oriented writings. The puzzle about the relation between[95] the two sets of work thus remains.

---

[93] After showing that Y need not be intending to pump *poisoned* water, and as postulated does not have that intention even though he knows the water he is pumping is poisoned, *Intention* says:

> . . . there can be a certain amount of control of the truthfulness of the answer . . .
>
> Up to a point, then, there is a check on his truthfulness in the account we are thinking he would perhaps give; but still, there is an area in which there is none . . . (43, section 25)
>
> . . . we can find cases where only the man himself can say whether he had a certain intention or not . . . (44, section 25)
>
> . . . given that it [the spontaneous thought 'I'm only doing my usual job'] survives all the [external tests for truthfulness], it comes under the same last determination: '*In the end* only you can know whether that is your intention or not'; that means only: there comes a point where a man can say 'This is my intention', and no one else can contribute anything to settle the matter. (47–8, section 27)

As Anscombe rightly says, a man 'cannot [truthfully] profess not to have had the intention of doing the thing that was a means to an end of his' (44, section 25). But the paragraph of which that is the final sentence shows that what is a means is here established by the man's reasons for action (e.g. the precise nature of Y's or Z's job commission/contract), considered with subtlety and precision, and has nothing to do with immediacy or certainty of effects.

[94] Anscombe, *Intention*, 46 (section 26).

[95] And to some extent also within the ethical set: e.g. 'if you attack a lot of military targets . . . as carefully as you can, you will be *certain to kill* a number of innocent people; but that is not murder': 'Mr Truman's Degree' (1957), in Anscombe, *Collected Philosophical Papers*, vol. 3, 66 (emphasis added).

7.

Anthony Kenny's renewed reflections on intention begin with the common sense of ordinary language: 'we are only said to intend B by doing A if we do A *in order* to bring about B'. But, by the end, he is saying that the surgeons intended to kill the weaker conjoined twin, and is making the line between what is intended and what is not follow the line between the '(foreseen to be) certain but for a miracle' and the '(foreseen to be) virtually certain'. What pushes him to this commingling of intention with foresight, and of practical reasoning with (knowledge of) sheer cause-and-effect sequences?

He points out, as if it were an objection to my focus on the acting person's practical reasoning, that 'practical reasoning does not operate in isolation from the causal order'. Indeed it does not; as he observes, one's choosing to do A in order to bring about B depends on one's belief that doing so will have that effect. But the deliberation (practical reasoning) that shapes one's intentions looks to effects that yield the benefit one seeks, that is, looks to means that advance, secure or realize one's end(s); all other effects are side effects (as Kenny's own initial examples show: one does not drink alcohol in order to get the inevitable hangover, nor, we can add, walk to cause one's shoe soles to wear). More boldly, he says:

> It is wrong to attribute to a human agent a privileged first-person authority in the description of the action of his that is up for moral evaluation. In fact others may know better than I do what I am up to. [p. 115]

How so? Well, he points out, we can see through X's claim that he is doing A for the sake of bringing about B but not C, if X stops doing A when it ceases to bring about C (while continuing to produce B). Quite so; we realize that this is strong evidence that X was trying all along to get C, strong evidence, that is, about X's practical reasoning all along. Our focus remains steadily on that reasoning, and on causal chains *as they figure in that reasoning* (as we infer it to have been).

But what about my statement that targeters 'merely deceive themselves' if they tell themselves that all they intend to destroy is the military base they select for their aimpoint in a *city chosen for destruction* to shock their enemy into surrender? Kenny says:

> This consideration shows that what people tell themselves is not decisive about what their intention genuinely is. But the sharp distinction that Finnis elsewhere makes between the perspective of the active agent and the cause-effect sequence does not seem to leave room for people to be wrong about their own intentions in this manner. [p. 115]

On the contrary, it is precisely that distinction that makes possible the self-deception. In describing their intentions *for purposes of satisfying conscience* (self-justification), the targeters describe to themselves the cause-effect sequences involved in aiming the bomb onto the targeted military base, and say to themselves that the destruction of the city and its inhabitants is a side effect—which is what it is, *relative to this cause-effect sequence*: those effects are all *outside* the targeted base and will be destroyed *after* it! But this is self-deception, because their reason for targeting something in or near the city was to destroy *the city* and very many of its inhabitants in a shocking, awesome way; *that* destruction was their purpose, their means to ending the war, and was certainly intended, not a side effect in the sense of that term relevant to the accurate act-description needed as the subject matter for moral evaluation.

Kenny's own shift from end-means reasoning (the basis of his sensible 'failure test') to observation of causal sequences and degrees of certainty is made with Lord Bridge's infamous example of the fleeing man who gets on the first plane he sees, discovering as he does so that it is bound for Manchester (and who according to the Law Lord therefore boarded it *with intent to go to* Manchester). Kenny reasons [p. 112] that Lord Bridge was in error because there is no certainty the plane will head for Manchester; many factors short of a miracle could reroute it. To me, such reasoning seems irrelevant:

> The destination does not enter at all into [the fleeing man's] practical reasoning save under the description 'not London airport'; the complete list of his [relevant] intentions is: to elude pursuit, to take a plane, to get away from London Airport, to go into hiding in whatever turns out to be the plane's destination city.[96]

This is a perhaps more realistic example of unconcern with an aspect of the foreseen outcome (here, with the precise destination), the unconcern that Anscombe's *Intention*'s scenario Y was designed to capture (see pp. 480–2 of this essay). Such an aspect of the outcome, however certain, is outside the acting person's intention.

The same is true of the vile surgeon in each of Kenny's two scenarios, who removes the heart of a living person for science or donation. We do not need to add to the unlikelihood of the scenarios by having the surgeon say 'because he would have been perfectly happy if his victim had continued to live without a heart' [p. 115]. In the real world such surgeons would intend death, as part of their plan to avoid investigation and punishment for their atrocious assault. But taking the scenario at face value, we should not tamper with the reality of intention by retreating from the correct account of it with which Kenny began. As I said in my own discussion of such a scenario, the immorality of the conduct consists in something apart from intent precisely to kill:

> Indeed it would [clearly be murder]. But not because D intends to kill P. As Anscombe has elsewhere remarked, such killings may be more callous and heinous than some that are intentional. The surgeon intends to and does deal with the body, that is, the very person of the patient, as his own to dispose of. Though his choice is not, precisely, to kill or even, perhaps, to impair the functioning of the patient/victim—that is, though death and impairment of functioning are side effects—the surgeon's choice *is* precisely to deal with the bodily substance and reality of the other human person as if that person were a mere subhuman object. The moral wrong, on a precise analysis of the surgeon's intent, is a form of *knowingly death-dealing enslavement*; one who inflicts death, even as a side effect, in order to effect such an instrumentalization of another has, in the fullest sense, 'no excuse' for thus knowingly causing death.[97]

So it is morally and legally murder but, the passage concludes, 'we should not ... distort our understanding of intention so as to bring this within the category of murder

---

[96] *CEJF* II.14, 274n (2010a).
[97] *CEJF* II.10, 194. See p. 481, n. 84 in this essay and, on the immorality of the cargo bomber's act, see *CEJF* II.13, 256.

supposed, too casually, to be limited to *intent* to kill (or seriously harm)'; instead we should adjust the definition of murder.[98]

Kenny's other argument is that applying the means-ends account of intention as strictly as I do entails, or 'is uncomfortably reminiscent of', the sort of 'direction of intention' which Pascal, and Anscombe, famously denounced. They were right to do so. But as Anscombe shows in *Intention*, such an interior performance of redescribing one's intentions so as to satisfy conscience or potential critics 'is itself a new action, like clicking out the rhythm of God Save the King on the pump'.[99] My account gives no warrant for that, or any such 'performance in the imagination', in Kenny's happy phrase. Still, Kenny finds a sentence which in isolation could, I suppose, be read as winking at it: '[what is intended] is settled by one's practical reasoning as an agent, by the intelligible benefit one seeks and the means one chooses *under the description which promises to yield that benefit*'.[100] 'But surely', he objects, 'focussing on the description that promises to yield the benefit—rather than the other descriptions indicating the impermissibility of the means—is precisely what constitutes "direction of intention"'. Indeed it is, but my phrase 'description which promises to yield' was (not too happily) elliptical for 'description which indicates how the means is both intended and likely to yield...'; it had nothing to do with focussing on one description rather than another (while holding steady the means selected). As I said on the following page:

> ...the 'doctrine' of double effect [more precisely: about how intended effects differ from side effects] is not about choosing descriptions, let alone just one description. It holds rather that what is *being done* is not settled simply by looking at behaviour, to see what movements are being made, with what awareness and what results. Rather, that is settled by what one chose, under the description which made it attractive to choice (*not: the description which makes it acceptable to onlookers, or to 'conscience'*).[101]

And I usually make a similar caveat when speaking of act descriptions, to exclude any savour of direction of intention.[102] Much in *Nuclear Deterrence, Morality and Realism*

---

[98] Kenny's proposed amendment to the legal definition of murder ('doing an act that causes death with the intent either to kill or to create a serious risk of death') may be compared with mine: killing with intent to kill (or to do grievous bodily harm), or doing without lawful justification or excuse an act which one knows will kill: *CEJF* II.10, 193. (Lord Goff's proposal to extend the *mens rea* of murder to include 'wicked recklessness' is comparable in its motivation and effect: Goff, 'The Mental Element in the Crime of Murder'.) Kenny's definition, on an untampered-with definition of intent, would not catch the heart-removing surgeons he fancifully postulates (but would cover real-world villains who need their victims 'out of the way' and cremated to avoid awkward inquiries). Since Kenny does not mention it, I add that my discussion of the cargo bomber included the statement that he, like the postulated heart surgeon(s), is guilty of murder: *CEJF* II.10, 185. And so is pumper Y in *Intention*'s scenarios (see p. 481, nn. 83–4 in this essay).

[99] Anscombe, *Intention*, 47 (section 27).

[100] *CEJF* II.10, 190 (emphasis added).   [101] *CEJF* II.10, 191 (emphasis added).

[102] See *CEJF* II.Introduction, 13 ('...the idea of choosing and acting "under a description" which is not a mere rationalization but a genuine step in one's deliberation about means suitable for one's purposes...'); *CEJF* II.2, 76 (2009a):

> This shaping of description(s) in practical reasoning and deliberation is not a matter of finding a description under which the behaviour one is determined to carry out will be acceptable to oneself or others. Rather, it is settled by what one considers a necessary or helpful means to achieving an objective...that one considers desirable, in view of the factual context as one understands its bearing on both one's end(s) and the means one judges serviceable for achieving such end(s).

Likewise at 76–7; *CEJF* II.9, 165 (1995a, section II); *CEJF* II.13, 255 (2001a, section III) (quoted at p. 484, n. 92 in this essay).

was a relentless critique of strategies of redescription or rationalization by 'focusing' or 'direction' of intention.

A final point. Much in Kenny's discussion (like, it must be admitted, much in *Intention*) is framed (unhappily, as I think) in terms of what someone might *say*...[103] But in reality:

> The morally significant acts a person does are, objectively, what that person chooses to do for the reasons he or she has for making those choices.... What an act objectively is, and can be known objectively to be, is not affected by what the acting person or others may say about it, or by what others may reasonably (though mistakenly) infer it to be.[104]

Consequently, issues such as whether the acting person does or does not have 'indefeasible authority in describing his own intentions', or whether it does or does not 'lie in his mouth to say that he did not intend' [p. 115], or what a person 'can claim not to intend' [p. 114] are, I think, misframed issues—red herrings.

8.

Kevin Flannery SJ and I are at one about Aquinas's grasp of the realities of action and intention: so profound and, by and large, exact that anyone's understanding of those realities can, even today, gain much from engaging with what he wrote about them. Flannery thinks I have misunderstood those writings (as well as the relevant realities), and he could well be right about that. But is he? I will suggest not.

All the five misunderstandings of Aquinas listed in Flannery's conclusion [p. 131] concern—some directly, some implicitly—the relation between the proposal(s) one shapes in deliberation and the object(s) of the act(s) in which one carries out the proposal one has adopted (by choice if, as is usual, one finds two or more mutually incompatible proposals/options attractive and feasible). The most important of the five are the fourth and fifth.

To see why Flannery thinks I have misunderstood Aquinas in the *fourth* and *fifth* ways listed, consider what he thinks I mean by 'proposal':

> (A1) 'the term "proposal" is ... primarily to be associated with the will rather than the intellect' [p. 120]; (A2) to say that 'a good is proposed *to* the will' goes against Finnis's thesis [p. 130];

---

[103] *CEJF* II.13, 251, put into the craniotomy surgeon's mouth the words which have aroused the critical attention of Gormally and Kenny alike, but did so only because we had postulated (at 250) an objection framed in terms of what the surgeon could and could not say. And we ascribed to the surgeon the words we did, in reply to the objection, only on the hypothesis with which the offending sentence begins:

> Still, a surgeon who performed a craniotomy and could soundly analyse the action, resisting the undue influence of physical and causal factors that would dominate the perception of observers, could rightly say 'No way do I intend to kill the baby' and 'It is no part of my purpose to kill the baby'.

We prefaced this with the remark that the surgeon would 'not be likely to say' such things, given that 'craniotomy immediately causes the destruction of the baby with impressive physical directness'. But if the question arose, he could justly say them, and more accurately, as I have been arguing [e.g. p. 481], than Luke Gormally's saying [p. 100] that he must have been aiming to kill the baby.

[104] *CEJF* II.13, 260 (2001a, section IV).

(B1) 'whereas Aquinas...understands the object as something presented to the intellect...as a...desirable thing, Finnis understands it as a *proposal*: as something coming from the agent' [p. 128]; (B2) 'the object that specifies the moral act *is* the proposal adopted by choice' [p. 121, emphasis added]; (B3) 'Finnis does understand the object of the external act...to be a proposal...' [p. 130];

(C) 'a proposal is an activity of choosing among options that are attractive' [p. 123].

Flannery thinks there are other (erroneous or non-Thomist) features of my concept of a proposal, but these can be considered when we look at the first and second/third of my five supposed misinterpretations.

We can quickly dismiss (C): it is incompatible not only with (A1–2) and (B1–3) but also with everything I have ever said about proposal(s). Proposals are shaped in deliberation *for* adoption *by* choosing[105]; in every choice, at least one proposal is not chosen, so it is simply inconceivable that a proposal could be an activity of choosing. I can take the opportunity to note that, for me, 'proposal' and 'option' are synonymous, in all the contexts relevant to this discussion.[106]

What then about the two versions of (A)? (A1) articulates Flannery's interpretation of my work most clearly, and explains (A2). Unfortunately, (A1) reverses everything I think about proposals. They are, each and every one, what intellect offers to will for adoption by the will.[107] They belong securely on the left, *Reason*, side of the table (schema) that on the next page I transcribe from my book *Aquinas* and offer again for readers' reflection, as a notable improvement on the neo-scholastic table (schema) which I criticized in essays 9 and 12 of *Intention and Identity* and which can be contemplated now on p. 121 of Flannery's essay. The table on p. 491 is exactly as on p. 71 of my book, save that I have inserted the bracketed word 'proposal' at the point where I might have used it instead of, or as substantially synonymous with, 'option'; for in expounding the table on p. 64, I had introduced the term 'proposal' thus:

> *Intentio* and *electio* are analytically distinguishable elements in one's response to the benefits, as one understands them, of the proposal [i] one adopts.
>
> [i *'Proposals' for adoption by choice*...This conception of the **intelligible content of options** is used a great deal by Aquinas, albeit usually in verb form. Thus: 'intelligence moves will in the way an end is said to move (motivate), i.e. in as much as one's intelligence first conceives the intelligible benefit of some purpose {praeconcipit rationem finis} and *proposes* it to one's will': Ver. q. 22 a. 12c; also I-II q. 10 a. 2c; q.

---

[105] Or, though (in respect of external acts) quite rarely, by simple assent of the will (*consensus*): see pp. 494–5 in this essay.

[106] Thus *CEJF* II.Introduction, 3: 'proposal (a kind of synonym for an option)'; *CEJF* II.Introduction, 11:

> The analysis of deliberations towards free choices, when it is fully attentive, draws attention to the strategic role of the proposal, the option which, when competing with alternative proposals (options), must be chosen or rejected, preferred or not preferred, if anything is to be settled and done.

Likewise *CEJF* II.8, 143, 149; II.13, 236; *Aquinas*, 62, 66. Of course, in ordinary usage there can be nuances of difference: 'his options' can refer to possible actions in a situation in which the relevant person has not yet formed any proposals; and someone might say that where only one proposal has any attraction, 'there is no *option*' (but Flannery and I discuss this as a case of 'only one option').

[107] See *CEJF* II.2, 68; II.3, 76; II.8, 142, 143 n. 14; II.9, 155, 163 n. 38; 168 n. 49, 170; II.10, 176, 178, 181, 191 n. 37; II.11, 213; etc.

13 a. 1c; a. 5 ad 1 ['intellectus proponit voluntati suum objectum']; a. 6 ad 3; q. 19, a. 1c; q. 20 a. 1 ad 1.][108]

Reason	Will
one's understanding and reasoning ... *(RATIO)*	one's responsiveness to reasons ... *(VOLUNTAS)*
understanding basic ends/goods *(intellectus finium)*[109]	basic openness to these *(voluntas simplex)*[110]
envisaging a possible purpose for action *(apprehensio finis)*[111]	interest in pursuing that purpose; in some cases, provisional resolution to act if deliberation finds acceptable means *(intentio)*[112]
deliberation (when needed)[113] about means: devising of possible options [proposals] as increasingly specified conceptions of eligible purposes *(consilium)*[114]	assent to increasingly specified conceptions of eligible purposes as interesting and acceptable, an assent which becomes increasingly specific, until it is an
judgments that options A, B ... are each practicable/suitable for me/us here and now *(sententiae, iudicia)*[115]	assent to options A, B ... as each sufficiently interesting to be live options for me/us now *(consensus)*[116]
judgment of preference made in choosing ('This is the thing for me/us to do') *(iudicium electionis)*[117]	formation of definitive intention and adoption of one proposal by choice *(electio)*[118]
self-direction by using the chosen proposal as a 'rule of action' and directive to act *(imperium)*[119]	exertion of one's capacities in carrying out choice *(usus)*[120]
knowledge of action's success in achieving its end *(cognitio finis in actu)*[121]	taking satisfaction in action's achieving its end *(fruitio)*[122]

[108] *Aquinas*, 64, with endnote i from 96 (bold added).

[109] *Ver.* q. 5 a. 1c; see also *ST* I–II q. 94 a. 2; II–II q. 47 a. 6c; *An.* I.8 n. 13 [119].

[110] *ST* I–II q. 12 a. 1 ad 4; q. 15 a. 3c; and see q. 10 a. 1c.   [111] I–II q. 6 a. 2 c; q. 15 a. 3 c.

[112] I–II q. 12, especially a. 1 ad 4 & a. 4c & ad 2 & ad 3; and see q. 8 a. 3.

[113] Sometimes judgment about means needs no prior deliberation: I–II q. 14 a. 4 ad 1.

[114] I–II q. 14.   [115] I–II q. 13 a. 1 ad 2; a. 3c; q. 14 a. 1 ad 2; a. 4 ad 1.   [116] I–II q. 15.

[117] See endnote j. [j. '*Iudicium electionis*' ... The term is found only in early works (see II *Sent.* d. 24 q. 1 a. 3 ad 5; q. 2 a. 3 ad 4; *Ver.* q. 16 a. 1 ad 15; q. 17 a. 1 ad 4 & ad 17). But the idea—that choice includes, so to speak, a judgment in it—is present in the discussions of *electio* in Aquinas's last writings: see *ScG* II c. 48 n. 6 [1246]; *ST* I–II q. 13 a.1 c: 'the act in which one's will tends [definitively] to something proposed to it as good, being an act directed to an end by one's reason, is materially an act of will, though formally an act of reason'. Bourke 1960, 183, is far astray in thinking that the content of the 'judgment of choice' is 'I *will* act' (Bourke's emphasis); like all practical thought, its content is directive, not predictive.]

[118] I–II q. 13.

[119] I–II q. 17; IV *Sent.* d. 15 q. 4 a. 1 sol. 1 ad 3; *Quodl.* IX q. 5 a. 2c. Often also called reason's directive (*praeceptum*) about acting: II–II q. 153 a. 5c.

[120] I–II q. 16.   [121] See I–II q. 11 a. 1 ad 2; a. 4c.   [122] I–II q. 11.

Everything I have written about proposals is inspired by the second and third of those citations: in *ST* q. 13 a. 5 ad 1, Aquinas says 'one's intelligence proposes to one's will its [the will's] object',[123] and in a. 1c he speaks of choice as 'the act by which one's will intends something which is proposed [to will] as being good—good because directed by one's reason to an end',[124] that is, an end presupposed in one's deliberation as desirable, that is, as a benefit. (In short: the proposal articulates one's notion that the envisaged means are good precisely as serving to achieve some purpose/goal/endstate one takes to be beneficial/desirable/worthwhile.)

So it would be absurd to hold that the proposal is primarily a matter of will rather than intelligence. And to say that a good is proposed to the will is not against my thesis; it *is* my thesis.

(B1) involves the same confusion as (A1) and (A2) but introduces a new mistake, repeated in (B2) and (B3). When one chooses, one chooses between incompatible proposals. Each proposal picks out one or more—usually more than one—object(s): to move the handle, to pump the water, to replenish the house cistern, to serve the inhabitants (alternatively: to poison them), to earn one's salary, and so forth. In the theological and now doctrinal theses that have recently installed the term 'object' in the heart of our civilization, 'object' denotes the more 'proximate' (say, pumping water), rather than the more 'remote' (say: earning pay or a reward), in this sequence of means to ends.[125] As the deliberating and acting person envisages matters, the *good* of pumping is that it will replenish the cistern, and the good of doing that is that it will serve (alternative scenario: poison) the inhabitants, and the good of that may be envisaged as (spitefully or vengefully) a good for its own sake, or as a means to a salary (or, alternative scenario, to a medal, or to winning the war ...); and so on. Obviously, the object in every case is a possible *state of affairs* considered as *being brought about by action* choosable *for the sake of the benefit* (whether merely as means or also as end) *thereby attainable.*[126] Equally obviously, the proposal is an *idea of* such states of affairs as *eligible*, that is, *as to be pursued and brought about*; it is a plan framed in terms suitable for acceptance or rejection—for being chosen, or being rejected in favour of an

---

[123] 'Nam *intellectus proponit voluntati suum obiectum,* et ipsa voluntas causat exteriorem actionem.'

[124] 'Sic igitur *ille actus quo voluntas tendit in aliquid quod proponitur ut bonum ex eo quod per rationem est ordinatum ad finem* materialiter quidem est voluntatis, formaliter autem rationis.'

[125] See the definition of 'object' in the encyclical *Veritatis Splendor* (1993) section 78, quoted in *CEJF* II.13, 247:

> By the object of a given moral act, then, one cannot mean a process or an event of the merely physical order, to be assessed on the basis of its ability to bring about a given state of affairs in the outside world. Rather, that object is the proximate end of a deliberate decision which determines the act of willing on the part of the acting person.

On 'object' in the context of what I call proposals, i.e. in the context of deliberation and action, see Pilsner, *The Specification of Human Actions in St Thomas Aquinas,* 70–140, 217–46; Belmans, *Le sens objectif de l'agir humain,* 36–108, 116, 163–247. As an example of complete failure to attend to an action's *object,* which alone (rather than the behaviour described from some other viewpoint) is decisive for the understanding and application of exceptionless moral norms, see the objection raised against the moral norm about contraception in Dummett, *The Nature and Future of Philosophy,* 50–2.

[126] Although Aquinas occasionally speaks as if the object in an act of theft is the thing stolen, his real position is that the object of that act is the (non-consensual) *acquiring of* the thing. Unhappily, later scholastics seeking to disambiguate his position often (notably John of St. Thomas, the Salmaticenses, and Billuart) jumped precisely the wrong way, declaring that the object is the thing stolen.

alternative one prefers (chooses). At the moment of choice, one has two or more proposals, each proposing, picking out, one or more objects as suitable for choice; but as yet one has no object (save to get into a position to choose); and even after one has chosen one of these (sets of objects) in preference to the other(s)—by adopting one of those proposals—the state(s) of affairs which it is now one's object(ive) to bring about remain(s) to be brought about. In short: It is inconceivable that the proposal *is* the object, and equally inconceivable that the object *is* the proposal. In any of its three versions, (B) is not my position, nor anyone else's so far as I am aware.

Of course, one and the same answer can be given ('replenishing the house water supply') to the question 'What's the state of affairs you're bringing about?' and the question 'What's your idea in moving that handle?' That does not make a state of affairs into an idea! But, quite generally, when speaking of ideas, concepts, plans, proposals, etc., we can focus either on the thinking/thought or on its content or on *what that content* is a thought *of* (the object).[127] And when concerned with the thinking (doubtless along with its content), as a fact about the thinker, we can focus more, or less, on the object. So when I was speaking about the significance of choice for the character of the chooser, I said:

> All free choices go to constitute and determine, creatively, the self, the character, the personality, of the one who chooses and carries them out. And in that sense the self is the primary, certainly the nearest, 'object of the action'. Nevertheless, this intransitive effect and significance of choice is normally accomplished without the self, or self-determination, being the *object* of choice, whether 'object' in the sense of the proposal which, in choosing, one does adopt, or 'object' in the sense of one's reason for adopting that proposal...[128]

By '"object" in the sense of the proposal' I meant, as the context quoted makes evident, the object *qua* envisaged-as-choiceworthy in the proposal.

So, to complete the discussion of (B1): the contrast Flannery sees between my work and that of Aquinas, for whom 'the object [is] something presented to the intellect...as a desirable thing', is non-existent. We are, all three, discussing the domain of deliberation and rationally motivated action. Here, the object is a desirable state of affairs not yet existent but capable of being achieved through action. So the 'presenting to intellect' cannot conceivably be other than the intellect *understanding* (a) that some state of affairs is both possible and desirable in itself and (b) that some other state(s) of affairs capable of being achieved by action would bring about the first-mentioned state of affairs. *This* is the 'devising and putting to oneself' of a proposal; like (in this respect)

---

[127] Hence the harmless elision in n. 14 to *CEJF* II.8, 143: 'that which has been proposed—a proposal'. Flannery, pp. 128–9 at nn. 45–6, objects to this, but apparently on the basis of his mistaken idea that proposals are products of the acting person's *will*, a notion that he reads into my phrase (at 142) 'devised and put to oneself'—omitting to notice that even in that sentence as it stands, the devising is a matter of intelligence discerning the merits of the ends and means that hang together to constitute 'a plan or proposal which one has devised and put to oneself in one's practical reasoning and deliberation on the merits of alternative options'; likewise, II.13, 236, and citations in n. 107 of this essay. Geometers devise proofs, climbers routes.

[128] *CEJF* II.8, 138–9 (1987b, section III). Similarly at 149 ('the acting subject retains the character specified, in part, by that object of his choice, that proposal he once freely adopted'). For many other passages relevant to this, see *CEJF* I.15, 239–40.

the devising of a mathematical or logical proof, or a move in chess, it is a matter of discerning intelligible relationships. In the domain of human action as distinct from logic, technique and natural sciences, the relationships discerned are partly evaluative—considerations indicating that such-and-such a state of affairs would be fulfilling—and partly are causal considerations indicating that that fulfilling state of affairs could be achieved thus-and-thus. The entire content of a proposal is provided by one's intellect discerning and making judgments about such (as yet non-existent) objects, each desirable as a *finis* (end) or as an *id quod ad finem est* (means) or, more usually, as both. Aquinas has no other theory of the formation of options for choice than this. Though his accounts of deliberation and action preferred verbs rather than abstract verb-derived nouns like 'option' and 'proposal' (but *obiectum* is just such a verbal noun), Aquinas's meaning and mine are, I believe, identical—and demonstrably so—on all the matters in contention in Flannery's essay.

Now, thirdly, for the *first* of the five 'misinterpretations' collected at the end of Flannery's essay. It concerns *consensus*, the 'act' of will listed as step 6 in the 12-step neo-scholastic schema and as steps 6 and 8 in my more realistic and more Thomist 14-step table. *Consensus*, assent to a proposal, appears twice in my table because deliberation is typically a *process* in which *alternative* options/proposals are developed by intelligence in *more and more specific* form, a process in which will participates as a secondary partner, responding to these developing thoughts about practical possibilities with assent or disapproval. Flannery says my 'position [is] that in human action there *must* always be plural options that are attractive, suitable and practically interesting' [p. 123, his emphasis], whereas in reality, and Aquinas, there are cases 'in which [*consensus*] consists of the favourable assessment of a single option' [p. 131].

But my position is quite different, and is the same as Aquinas's. One of the passages where I *deny* that in rationally guided human action there must always be plural options (and thus the need to choose) is quoted by Flannery, but he writes off these passages as 'verbal inconsistency'. Inconsistent with what?[129] For me the case of plural options is 'the standard case'[130] or 'typical'[131] or 'paradigm'[132] 'common case',[133] contrasted thus with the non-standard or uncommon:

> the case where only one possible course of action is attractive is perhaps rather rare, except insofar as prior choices have effectively and closely shaped one's commitments and dispositions.[134]

---

[129] The only basis I can imagine for Flannery's notion that I think there must always be plural options, and that *consensus* always involves [he says 'presents'] more than one option [p. 122], is a glissade from (P1) 'Any deliberation which ends in *choice* must have yielded . . . (at least) *two* judgments' each affirming the choiceworthiness of an option (incompatible with the other option(s)) to (P2) any rational human action involves choice between at least two options each judged choiceworthy and assented to by *consensus*. I affirm (P1) but have more than once denied (P2), and have never affirmed it (though the schema I present in substitution for the neo-scholastic one outlines the *standard* case, which had disappeared from view in the neo-scholastic diagram, and in general discussion of human action I often speak, for simplicity, only about the standard/common case in which there are two or more options each judged and assented/consented to as acceptable).

[130] *CEJF* II.9, 156.   [131] *CEJF* II.9, 158.   [132] *CEJF* II.12, 226, n. 24.
[133] *CEJF* II.12, 232.   [134] *CEJF* II.9, 156, n. 13.

In the sentence before that remark, I quote Aquinas's consideration of the case where only one possible course of action is attractive:

> If only one [proposed course of action] is found acceptable, *consensus* and choice are not distinct in reality, though they are distinct in concept since here one can say that there is consenting, in that the proposed course of action is [found] acceptable, or that there is choosing, in that this course of action is being preferred to those found unacceptable.[135]

So far am I from holding that there *must* be choice, and that *consensus* could never suffice to settle what one is to do, that I say[136]:

> If one were in a situation where one proposal offered all the benefits of alternative proposals, and some more benefit, then (as Aquinas observes)[137] one would not need to choose; the alternatives would drop out of consideration, leaving one proposal as (in a modern jargon) 'dominant', and one would simply assent to this proposal and start acting on it. Choice (*electio*) as distinct from assent (*consensus*) is a matter of preferring *one* amongst alternative proposals *both* or *all* of which win one's assent as promising benefit and so remain interesting.[138]

And I treat the formation of a procedural intention—an intention to deliberate about means—as perhaps standardly by way of '*consensus* without need for choice'.[139]

So the 'first misinterpretation' is not mine. But before we leave it, what about the neo-scholastic table or schema? Flannery says my 'central criticism of this schema is that it was used by certain neo-scholastics to eliminate true choice' [p. 121]. No, that would have been a quite extravagant claim, and I recorded that the sounder neo-scholastic exponents of 'the schema or diagram' (or table) *often*, 'if elsewhere', attend to 'the fact that, by definition, choice is *between* eligible options...mutually (here and now) exclusive practical alternatives (proposals for action)'.[140] My complaint, here, was

---

[135] *CEJF* II.12, 232, n. 38, translating the Latin (also quoted here and, in part, at II.9, 156, n. 13, which cross-refers to II.12, 232, n. 38) of *ST* I–II q. 15 a. 3 ad 3. Flannery says [p. 124] that I misinterpret this passage by holding that 'even consent to one option involves a choice between attractive options'. On the contrary, n. 38 on 232 is there precisely to make the point that, unlike the 'common case' where '*consensus* is distinct *re* [in reality] as well as *ratione* [conceptually] from *electio*' and *consensus* thus in this common kind of case does not settle what is to be done [text to n. 38], the less common case is one where *consensus* and choice are not distinct in reality, and it is *consensus* that performs the vital function normally played by choice. So I have agreed all along with Flannery's point that in the 'one option' case, 'that which is here called both *consensus* and *electio* is essentially *consensus*...' [p. 123]. *ST* I–II q. 15 a. 3 ad 3 is not 'a problem for [Finnis]' [p. 124]; indeed, like the rest of q. 15 a. 3, it is one of the foundations of my positions so far as they appeal to Aquinas as well as to reality.

[136] *Aquinas*, 66. The next two footnotes are nn. 24 and 25 on that page. On the termination of technical practical reasoning in adoption of a proposal without choice, see also *CEJF* I.15 ('Commensuration and Public Reason'), 243. On 'dominant' options, see also *CEJF* IV.17, 359 (1990d, section II): 'Virtually the only realistic context in which an option can rationally be regarded as dominant is within the context of... "technical" reasoning and action, for example, competitive games.'

[137] I–II q. 15 a. 3 ad 3 (where Aquinas also observes that one's assent to this uniquely attractive proposal could still be called 'choice', inasmuch as this proposal would still, in a sense, be being 'preferred' to the unattractive alternative).

[138] *Electio* in the strict sense (unlike *consensus*) always involves a preferring: II *Sent.* d. 7 q. 1 a. 1 ad 1; d. 24 q. 1 a. 2c ('to choose is to prefer one thing to another {alterum alteri praeoptare}'); I–II q. 12 a. 3c {praeeligit}; q. 13 a. 4 ad 3 {praeeligi}; q. 15 a. 3 ad 3 {praefertur, praeeligitur, praeaccipimus}.

[139] *CEJF* II.9, 157.　　[140] *CEJF* II.9, 155.

that *their schema or table hides* the process whereby, in the most common case, more than one proposal emerges as choiceworthy and acceptable. The feature that I said defied Aquinas's account is something different: that their table (like Flannery's) places *consensus* before a *sententia* or judgment about means, whereas Aquinas 'always and unambiguously locates [*consensus*] after a *sententia* or judgment about means'.[141] About this (my main criticism), Flannery is, so far as I can see, silent.[142] The underlying point of the criticism is that the neo-scholastics were not sufficiently serious and careful about understanding just how human actions are, not slabs of causal behaviour preceded or accompanied by thoughts and urges, but *precisely* the *carrying out of a proposal* shaped in thought and judgment and adopted by a response (that response being, in the standard case, *choice*, motivated by interest in the goods held out, prospectively, in the proposal adopted).

Which brings us to the remaining two 'misinterpretations', listed as *second* and *third*. They are interconnected and, as will not be surprising, are connected with Flannery's misapprehension of what I say about proposals. In some remarks of mine about means, he sees an 'exclusion of technical means from the realm of human action', an exclusion 'closely connected with Finnis's concept of a proposal'. And the sinister meaning he finds in that exclusion is that it 'would allow [Finnis] to exclude from the same realm the procedure that kills the baby whose skull is crushed in the effort to save the life of the mother' in craniotomy [p. 120]. Now such an exclusion would indeed be a stunning misinterpretation of Aquinas's thesis in *ST* I-II q. 13 a. 4 that 'choice is always of human acts'. But Flannery does not and could not cite, from my actual discussions of craniotomy, anything suggesting that I exclude from that action any part whatsoever of the surgeon's chosen performance of manipulating his fingers and his instruments to crush and empty and perhaps remove the baby's skull in order to release it from the birth canal and thus relieve the mother's body of the stresses threatening to kill both her and the baby. One's proposal includes, explicitly or implicitly, *everything* one needs to do (and to try to accomplish) to achieve what one is proposing to achieve.

---

[141] *CEJF* II.9, 154, citing and quoting *ST* I-II q. 15 a. 3c (for more citations see p. 491, n. 115, in my table). At II.12, 232, in the section devoted to *consensus*, I restate this central criticism of the neo-scholastic schema, which 'confused matters pretty thoroughly' because in it '*consensus* precedes ... reason's judgment that such-and-such an option (specific means) is available and suitable for some end in which one is interested'.

[142] But he obscures matters, I think, by adopting John Damascene's locution in preference to Aquinas's, by saying [p. 123 at n. 18] that *consensus* is 'a *sententia* regarding what is set before a person by judgment'. Not only does the last-mentioned pre-*consensus* judgment simply fail to appear in the neo-scholastic schema/table which he himself gives [p. 121], but using *sententia* as a synonym for *consensus* elides the vocabulary of reason and will in a non-Thomistic way.

Flannery asks for evidence that Thomas Gilby (for example) maintains that 'when an action arrives at the stage of *electio*, matters have already been decided' [p. 122]. The page cited by Flannery [n. 16] will do:

> 5. *Deliberation.* The mind investigates the situation ... 6. *Consent.* ... act of approving and promoting the process of finding a way to the desired end ... 7. *Decision.* The practical judgment which selects which course is to be taken, the preference ... verdict, *sententia* ... In moral matters, this judgment is the act of conscience ... 8. *Choice.* After coming to a decision, a further effort of will is required to keep up the momentum of the act.

That is *all* thoroughly misleading, untrue to Aquinas and common sense, and confused; the last sentence is also, in relation to this prominent modern neo-scholastic, the evidence for which Flannery asked.

To see how the just-mentioned '*second* misinterpretation' of Aquinas was arrived at, consider—finally—the misinterpretation listed *third*. This concerns the distinction I draw, following Aquinas, between the third and the fourth of the 'four kinds of order and *scientia*': (3) the realm of voluntary action (*praxis, actio*) which is morally significant and the subject of the moral, economic, and political sciences compendiously called *philosophia moralis*, as distinct from (4) the realm of the practical arts (*technê, ars, factio*), the technologies or techniques which, by bringing order into matter of any kind external to our thinking and willing, yield 'things constituted by human reason'. Flannery thinks that the irreducibility I see in the four orders' distinctness from each other is incompatible with remarks made by Aquinas within a few lines of setting out the distinctions. Suffice it here to say that the remarks quoted by Flannery cannot, I believe, be made to assert or entail any such incompatibility.[143]

We have to get beyond words here. For instance: both the third and the fourth orders are called (by Aquinas) 'practical', matters of 'practical reason', of practical philosophy, of *scientia operativa*, and so forth.[144] And beyond this is the point that is, I think, overlooked in Flannery's reading of my occasional distinction[145] between human actions as morally significant and, on the other hand, 'technical means' *as such*. Those last two words matter, because *every* human *use* of technical means (techniques, procedures, technologies, instruments, etc.) is a morally significant action. The technique or procedure is devised to achieve a specific, definite, limited kind of effect in the world, and can be set out in manuals from which it can be learned. But choosing (deciding) to put the technique into practice, even by way of rehearsal, is itself—as such—not a matter of technique, but rather a choice to act in the open horizon of 'human life as a whole', to devote part of one's one life to doing this. All the intentions and intended performances involved in making (and indeed in carrying out) that choice, all the way down to each intended movement of tongue or hand, are matters of human action.

The remarks of mine which aroused Flannery's suspicion that I have sought to insulate technical means from moral scrutiny were a pedagogical sally: students tend to take the word 'means' as denoting instruments, implements, and suchlike; and Aquinas himself warns (in q. 13 a. 4 ad 1) that, if we are concerned with human action of the kind (and in the sense) relevant to moral evaluation and our fulfilment or perdition, this is a misunderstanding: it is the *use* of instruments, etc., that matters. Similarly,

---

[143] Aquinas's statement, summarizing in headline form the topic of *NE* 1.1:1094a 1–18, is itself made under the heading of *moralis philosophia* and in any case does not imply that human acts *stricto sensu* (i.e. in the third order) are the sole topic of *NE* 1.1:1094a 1–18, in which Aristotle also mentions (fourth-order) crafts (*ars*) and speculative teaching (*doctrina*) (which latter Aquinas says pertains to speculative, non-practical intellect, which in turn would presumably be a matter of the first and second orders).

[144] See *Aquinas*, 23, n. 10: '... and *In Pol.* I.2.12 [53]: "*actio* and *factio* are different in kind (*specie*); for *factio* is the sort of doing (*operatio*) which makes something in matter which is external [to the mind and will] ...; *action*, on the other hand, is the sort of doing which remains [lasts] in the doer (*permanens in operante*) and bearing on the doer's very life". As a matter of word usage, the term *factio* can extend to include *actio* of the last-mentioned kind (*ST* II-II q. 134 a. 2c) just as "art" can be either distinguished from or treated as including *moralis philosophia* and practical reasonableness (*prudentia*).' This, I suggest, dissolves the exegetical points [pp. 126–7] summarized in Flannery's 'third misinterpretation'.

[145] See *CEJF* II.9, 171; II.10, 179; II.13, 264.

I added, with procedures and techniques *as such*, meaning: as pertaining to the domain of technique not the domain of action.[146] To apply my thought to Flannery's concern: the surgeon might use the very same procedures and techniques when performing an emergency craniotomy on a living child as on a dead child, or when doing a partial-birth abortion; but the three actions are very different—the first two share essentially the same intention but have very different morally relevant side effects, while the third has an essentially different intention: to kill the baby. Even if I were mistaken about the intentions in an emergency craniotomy, it would not be because I have excluded or insulated any part of the surgeon's intentional performance from scrutiny as being 'technical means' rather than 'action'. To repeat: every using of technical means is an action, all the way down.

9.

Cristóbal Orrego's searching exploration of questions about the description and evaluation of actions, and of kinds of action, invites us (1) to reflect on the distinction I have drawn several times in the preceding sections, between the description or analysis of actions and the evaluation of the actions thus understood. His essay also invites us (2) to accept, rely upon and develop a thesis of Aquinas about which I have written scarcely anything.[147]

(1) With the broad thrust of Orrego's main argument, and with most of his theses, I am in general agreement. Particular actions can be understood and described, for many purposes quite adequately, without evaluating them as morally good or bad, virtuous or vicious, just or unjust, right or wrong. But a general theory of action, of the kind that issues in stable, grounded classifications of action, cannot be developed independently of conceptions of human good (and ill), and of what is reasonable and unreasonable in human choosing and acting (including omitting). The theoretical situation is strongly analogous to that set out in Chapter I of *NLNR* and Chapter II of *Aquinas*. That is, there is a 'mutual though not quite symmetrical interdependence between the project of describing . . . and the project of evaluating human options with a view, at least remotely, to acting reasonably and well'; 'the descriptions are not deduced from the evaluations, but without the evaluations one cannot determine what descriptions are really illuminating and significant'.[148] And evaluation cannot reasonably stop short of the strenuously moral assessment that proceeds best, I believe, according to the criteria of reasonableness recalled, in outline, in section 4 (in discourse

---

[146] This indeed is not very perspicuously expressed by my explanation in *CEJF* II.9, 159: '(that is, just insofar as they could in principle be replicated by machines and other devices)'. Clearer is *Aquinas*, 64, n. 18:

> 'means' (*id ad quod finem est*) . . . here refers, not to instruments (*organa*) nor even to techniques *precisely as fourth-order realities*, but to some action of the chooser, an action chosen for the sake of its benefit(s). 'Choice is always of human acts': I–II q. 13 a. 4c. (Emphasis added.)

See also *CEJF* I.11 ('Prudence about Ends' (1997), 181, n. 20).

[147] Orrego (p. 144, n. 71 quotes the one passage that bears (rather indirectly and inadequately) on it: see n. 156 in this essay.

[148] *NLNR*, 19, quoted and elaborated in *Aquinas*, 51 with 47–51; see also *NLNR*, 17.

with Boyle). To say all this is to assent to Aristotle's thesis that in a philosophy of human affairs (notably, political theory, or ethics), matters *are* as they are understood to be by the person of practical reasonableness, that is, of virtue (moral soundness)— the morally good person.[149]

(2) Orrego's essay presents this theoretical situation with rather less emphasis, it seems to me, on the mutual interdependence of description and evaluation in the classification of actions. He, like Joseph Pilsner, understands Aquinas to be holding the thesis that 'the primary', 'the essential', 'the basic', and 'most generic' classification or specification of kinds of human act is as (morally) good or bad or indifferent; all other specifications (morally relevant classifications) of acts are subdivisions of these supreme genera: good (kinds of) acts, bad (kinds of) acts, and kinds of acts that, as kinds (i.e. in the abstract), are neither good nor bad.

I very much doubt that Aquinas held the strong thesis thus stated. Certainly he held that the classification of human acts as good and bad (and indifferent) is a classification of intrinsic kinds, and that (against the view of great contemporaries such as Albert and Bonaventure, and others) this classification stated something essential and 'constitutive'[150] about such acts, not merely 'accidental' still less extrinsic. Morally bad acts are against the moral law because they are morally bad 'in themselves', and by virtue of their kind (*ex genere*), not merely because they are morally prohibited (or: contrary to some true moral standard).[151] Their deficiency goes to their essence because (as I would put the gist of his thesis) every morally significant action is chosen as being intelligent, a good thing to do, and somehow reasonable. Thus the critique of the morally bad choice will proceed by showing that, more adequately understood, the act chosen is not *adequately* intelligent, is defective in, and actually opposed to, human good(s), so much so that it is *un*reasonable. The criteria for assessing moral goodness and badness are, in a sense, the very criteria that constituted the act as an object of choice, and are simply (so to speak) extended in their intelligibility—or, in the terminology recalled in section 4, are the very principles that even the morally bad chooser employs—first (and as such not yet moral) principles of practical reason—but understood and applied *integrally* (and now fully and properly morally). But to say so much is not yet to say that this sort of classification is 'the primary', 'the essential', and 'the basic'.[152] The definite article in these phrases entails a unilaterality that jars with the two-way (inter)dependence of description and evaluation, in which neither is simply and exclusively primary or basic.

Aquinas's argument for the 'essential' character of moral evaluation of kinds of act, like Orrego's own account of the matter, indicates that such evaluation is consequent

---

[149] See *Aquinas*, 48–9; *NLNR*, 37, n. 37.
[150] *Sent.* II d. 27 q. 1 a. 2 ad 2.   [151] See *De Malo* q. 2 a. 4c.
[152] None of the 13 passages cited by Pilsner, *The Specification of Human Actions in St Thomas Aquinas*, 61, n. 27, to show that for Aquinas 'good and evil are the essential differences of human action' and 'the primary essential division of human actions', warrants the definite article that Pilsner thus twice deploys. I would say, instead, 'an essential . . .' and 'a primary essential . . .' (in a sense of 'primary' to be nuanced so as not to be exclusive of other primary distinctions that are important in their own right and also contribute to the good/evil distinction among human actions).

on a *prior*—and in that sense more primary, more basic—identification of the kind(s) of act to be specifically evaluated. As Aquinas says in the texts cited by Orrego, 'good and evil in human acts is assessed according as *the act* is [or is not] in line with reason...'[153]; 'the human acts we call moral have their species [as good or bad] from their object *as related to* the *principium* of human acts, which is reason'.[154] These and all such statements about kinds of acts take for granted that the kind has been at least provisionally specified (identified precisely as a distinct act-type or, in Orrego's phrase, 'act description') prior to being 'related to', and assessed for its concordance with, some criterion or principle of reason (and natural law). All but three or four pages of Joseph Pilsner's book-length study of Aquinas's account of specification of actions concern this prior process of identifying kinds of acts by their object (close-in end(s)), their characteristic further objective(s) (end(s)), and in some cases their (other) characterizing circumstances. Specification of actions for purposes of, and preliminary to, moral evaluation is a task of practical reason and philosophy; it proceeds by attending to real differences such as those between causing, foreseeing, and intending, and between an action's objects and its effects. In these respects it differs significantly from—and contributes significantly to—the *further* kind of 'specification' involved in (and issuing in) evaluation itself, practical reason's and philosophy's task of measuring whether an action, or type of action, already specified by its object, further purposes and circumstances, is morally acceptable (good) or unacceptable (bad) by reason's criteria.[155] To call this *further* task, too, one of specification is neither wrong nor confused. But it is 'a source of confusion'.[156]

Nor does the 'specifying' of kinds of act as each 'in its kind' good or bad or neither (i. e. indifferent, neutral)—call this 'good/bad specifying'—do the work that Orrego hopes for when he speaks of explaining how (or showing that) just or chaste acts are

---

[153] *De Malo* q. 2 a. 4c: bonum et malum in actibus humanis consideratur *secundum quod actus concordet rationi* informatae lege divina vel naturaliter vel per doctrinam...

[154] *ST* I-II q. 18 a. 8c: actus humanus quod dicitur moralis habet speciem ab obiecto *relato ad* principium actuum humanorum, quod est ratio.

[155] Hence my argument for the moral significance of the pre-moral difference between intending and knowingly causing: *CEJF* II.10, 194–5; *CEJF* II.11, 213–14; pp. 564–5 in this essay.

[156] *CEJF* II.9, 164, n. 43:

> ...we should not fail to note that Thomas is willing to identify or specify acts by reference to morally relevant circumstances which are *praeter intentionem* [outside the acting person's intention] *and thus in a sense is willing to treat good and bad, and right and wrong, virtue and vice, as if they were somehow categories **specifying** acts within the moral order* (see e.g. *ST* I-II q. 18 aa. [5] and 10), and that this is a source of confusion (italics added).

The passage to which that footnote was cued said:

> The distinction between behaviour *in genere naturae* and acts *in genere moris* is readily misunderstood; people treat it as conveying simply that behaviour understood *in genere naturae* is assessed by comparison with moral norms and consequently judged and described *in genere moris*, that is, with the peculiarly moral predicates such as 'just', 'unjust', 'virtuous', 'vicious', and so forth.

The footnote was misjudged in so far as it implied that Aquinas was only 'in a sense willing' to treat good and bad as specifying categories, and that he did so only indirectly and by way of treating some kinds of circumstances (e.g. fornication *with a married person*, or stealing *from a sacred place*) as changing the specification of actions. Orrego's essay rightly stresses that good/bad specifying was something Aquinas treated as important in its own right. The risk remains of understanding 'specify' equivocally, and of crude misunderstandings (such as the one pointed to in the just-quoted passage, and the rest of *CEJF* II.9).

good, and unjust and unchaste acts bad. For (i) the goodness of act-types that are each 'good of its kind' is only provisionally good; in Aquinas's stock example: restitution of what you have borrowed is a good kind of act, but when the lender is dangerously insane or criminal, restitution of borrowed weaponry or of other means of doing harm may well be morally bad. And (ii) the meta-category 'morally neutral [indifferent] of its kind' has the striking feature that it has both many instances and none! For: many kinds of act, such as walking to the bus stop or pumping water, are neither morally good nor morally bad as such, *yet*—as Aquinas forcefully insists[157]—*no particular human act* (my walking or pumping, on this occasion for this reason or in neglect of that responsibility, etc.) *is morally neutral.* (iii) There is a further asymmetry: any act that is 'good in its kind' may in particular circumstances of motivation, side effects, prior responsibilities, etc., be morally bad, but there are kinds of act, 'bad of their kind', which can never, whatever the circumstances, be morally good to choose or do. Only in relation to this last category does 'good/bad specifying' operate as primary or basic in significance for deliberation and choice. And the notable feature of this category of kinds of acts, exceptionlessly or 'absolutely' unreasonable and wrong and always to be excluded from one's deliberations, is that they are (or at least include) kinds which—as Orrego does not for a moment dispute—can be fully specified (identified) without any evaluative term: choosing to try to kill a non-threatening human person, choosing to seek non-marital sexual satisfaction, and so forth.

In saying that, I am using 'evaluative' in a much narrower and more standard sense than in Orrego's surprising sub-thesis [p. 144] that 'just or unjust and chaste or lustful' are '*non-evaluative* characterizations of human acts'.[158] I think this sub-thesis forgets that, in deliberations and reflections of the kind I believe both of us are engaged in or discussing, predicates such as (un)just and (un)chaste cannot reasonably be applied without the very assessment by reason that Aquinas says is necessary and sufficient to predicate the terms '[morally] good' or '[morally] bad'—an assessment deploying the criteria involved in reason's integral directiveness (*prudentia*) towards integral human fulfilment (*beatitudo*). 'Just', 'chaste', and so forth are paradigmatically *evaluative* predicates, and indeed, in their domain, exhaust evaluation. (That is not to say that nothing further can be said to show the full evil significance of the morally evil, or the

---

[157] *ST* I–II q. 18 a. 9; *Aquinas*, 193, n. 31.

[158] This is articulated in connection with his suggestion that I '[do] not see the connection between non-evaluative descriptions of human acts in their most specific kinds, such as murder or fornication, and the similarly non-evaluative characterizations of human acts in their more generic kinds, such as just and unjust . . .' And the suggestion is made as an *inference* from my remark (*Aquinas*, 87) that the *Summa Theologiae*'s exposition of morality in terms not of goods or types of acts, or of practical reason's norms, but of virtues, though understandable, 'can obscure morality's foundations'. I think Orrego over-interprets this, for it does not at all deny the rational connection (indeed an essential one) between predicating virtue(s) and making right judgments about goods, types of act, and reason's norms. See *CEJF* I.9 (1987a), 150: the 'intrinsic merit' (which I do not question) of Aquinas's decision to focus on human acts and virtues—

> had a regrettable side effect. The rational propositional principles which constitute the *regula vel mensura rationis*, or *medium rationis* [the rule or measure of reason, or mean of reason], which distinguishes virtue from vice never became the central focus of Aquinas's attention. Later theologians and moral philosophers, until almost today, have not repaired the omission; many have seemed not to notice it . . .

full attractiveness to reason of the morally reasonable, just, and chaste.) I think Orrego, in line here with Anscombe it seems, has over-generalized from the rather special case I referred to at the end of the preceding paragraph—of those negative exceptionless norms which pick out, and exclude from further deliberation, certain kinds of acts that are non-evaluatively specifiable even when their moral significance as always wrong flows back into terms commonly used to refer to them ('murder', 'fornication', 'lying', and so forth).

Similarly, I do not think that Aquinas 'tries to prove ... that human virtue is good' or that he thinks 'he has to prove rationally that virtues in general are good' [p. 146]. What Aquinas is doing in the passages cited here by Orrego is not, in my view, any such attempted proving. Rather it is a clarifying of the meaning of 'virtue', 'virtuous'. These are passages to which the often very questionably applied category, 'conceptual clarification', does, I think, properly apply: to speak of virtue is to speak of *good* dispositions,[159] 'good uses of free will',[160] 'good' because appropriate to the agent's nature,[161] particularly in so far as the human agent is rational.[162] That being reasonable makes demands and distinctions of the kind we call moral is not essentially a matter of conceptual clarification, but of understanding how human goods—not, in the first instance, moral goods—can be promoted, respected or disrespected, and damaged, and how one's willing engages with these goods (by way of objects, intentions, side effects, and other circumstances).

III. Justice, Rights, and Wrongdoing

10.

John Gardner's illuminating commentaries on my account of justice are almost silent about two interlinked decisions that shaped that account and differentiate it from his. (1) One was the decision to—

> use the concept of justice with all the breadth that that concept has had in academic discussion since Aristotle first treated it as an academic concept. That is to say, I set aside all the special and limiting shades of meaning that the word 'justice' may have acquired in common parlance ...[163]

This decision was aimed at distinguishing my way of thinking about justice from, notably, Hart's as manifested by his statement, right at the beginning of *The Concept of Law*'s treatment of justice, that—

> Very little reflection on some common types of judgment is enough to show [the] special character of justice. A man guilty of gross cruelty to his child would often be judged to have done something morally wrong ... But it would be strange to criticize his conduct as *unjust*.[164]

---

[159] *ST* I–II q. 54 a. 3c & ad 1; q. 55 a. 4c & ad 2.   [160] I–II q. 55 a. 1 ad 2.
[161] I–II q. 54 a. 3c.   [162] I–II q. 55 a. 2 ad 3; a. 3 ad 3; a. 4 ad 2 & ad 4; q. 19 aa. 3 & 4; q. 94 a. 3.
[163] *NLNR*, 161; also 163: 'I am seeking to *give* the concept of justice ... sufficient breadth for it be worthy of its classical and popular prominence in [the] analysis [of practical reasonableness]' (emphasis added).
[164] Hart, *The Concept of Law*, 157–8 [153].

This sort of reliance on what I called 'common parlance' is what my method set aside from the outset, in favour of an 'academic', that is, initially stipulative way of proceeding. And (2) the two key elements of my stipulative conception of justice, set out in the next paragraphs (the second and third) of *NLNR*'s chapter on justice, were that—

> Justice concerns not every reasonable relationship or dealing *between one person and another*, but only those relations and dealings which are necessary or appropriate for the avoiding of a *wrong*.[165]

So, to summarize the effects of these stipulations, I observed that 'in my theory parents can treat their child with straightforward injustice...regardless of whether or not others are being so treated' by these parents or by anyone else.[166]

Hart's procedure, thus set aside, was the same, so far as I can see, as the procedure expressed in Gardner's repeated phrase, 'to my ear(s)' [p. 155, n. 21, pp. 159, 163]. To his ear, it is strange or warped or misleading to say that torturing people, or ripping them off (scamming or defrauding them), is doing them an injustice, unless the suggestion is that they were wrongly picked out for this treatment, or subjected to it in some other *allocatively* inappropriate respect. In making this point, Gardner of course takes for granted that these are wrongful ways of treating other persons. For me, that wrongfulness, being *to others*, makes such conduct a 'straightforward' injustice; the will to exclude torture and scamming from one's deliberations is a paradigm of the kind of non-distributive justice that in *NLNR* I called commutative.

This definitional divergence, just as it stands, puts a wide gap between our positions. For Gardner [p. 164], 'The just person has no particular eye for wrongdoing. That is not her distinctive department of practical life.'[167] For me, the just person's whole concern is to avoid wrongdoing (*ad alteram*, to [some] other [person]). *That* is justice's distinctive department of practical life. Some wrongdoing of that sort is wrong allocatively, but some—a lot—is not.

Yet this conflict, being between a stipulative definition and a definition intended to be more or less lexicographically ('ear') guided, is merely expositional. It leaves the issues about what is right and wrong in one's attitudes to others essentially untouched. As a strategy for expounding those issues, I continue to prefer the one I articulated in *NLNR*, though I think it is better (as I argued in *Aquinas*) to radicalize it—make it even more general—by setting aside the categories 'distributive' and 'commutative', and looking instead to see what makes various types of *ad alteram* conduct wrongful: sometimes it will be the unfairness of misallocating shares in some 'pool of benefits or burdens'; sometimes it will be unfairness in bargaining or exchange, or in recompensing, or in allowing wrongdoers to flourish at the expense of those they have wronged; sometimes it will be the intended harmfulness (to another or others), just

---

[165] *NLNR*, 162, emphasis added. The third key element or 'necessary and sufficient' condition for the application of the term was/is equality (162–3), understood in a highly analogical way that makes it more explanatory of the (necessity of avoiding) *wrongdoing to another* than a separate condition to be satisfied.

[166] *NLNR*, 163–4.

[167] And its 'want of justice' does not establish—except in special cases such as judicial decision—that a choice/action is unreasonable: [p. 54 after n. 19].

as such, of one's conduct; and sometimes there will be some other source of wrongfulness.[168]

One reason why I prefer my way of ordering or expounding the problems of justice is that it preserves the tradition initiated by Plato, of treating justice as one of four *cardinal* (that is, pivotal) virtues. Of the four, only this one is as such concerned with other persons. Like Gardner and Aristotle, Aquinas can distinguish between justice and, say, *misericordia, liberalitas et aliae huiusmodi virtutes* (what Gardner lists [p. 159] identically as mercy and generosity and—more specific than Aquinas's 'other virtues of this kind'—being 'loyal, honest, humane, diligent, considerate, and so forth'). But Aquinas defends grouping all these under the academic category 'justice':

> since justice is a *cardinal* virtue, certain other virtues, such as mercy, generosity and other like virtues, are linked to it *secundarie*...

and what he means by *secundarie* appears from the example he gives:

> generosity in doing good to others is, by a kind of tracing back to source, attributed to justice as to a principal [primary or source] virtue.[169]

To my 'academic' way of thinking, humaneness, generosity, mercy, and so forth pertain to justice precisely to the extent that they help preserve one from injustice, that is,[170] from wronging another person.

Gardner's procedure of going 'by ear' confronts, or in a sense creates, quite a few problems. A first fruit of his method is his remark that it is 'quite alien' to 'Aristotle's account of justice in the narrow sense' that justice and injustices can only be done to others, and his rejection of my statement that 'doing oneself an injustice' is a kind of metaphorical extension of justice-talk. But this leaves Gardner to confront the arguments that Aristotle brings *against* talking of doing injustice to oneself: good people who assign themselves a share smaller than they are entitled to neither do themselves nor suffer injustice (as distinct from loss).[171] And if it is as clear as Gardner thinks that one can do oneself injustice, how can it be as clear as he thinks [p. 159] that 'one has no

---

[168] As this sentence (which abbreviates a longer list in *Aquinas*, 188) implies, I do not regard 'justice and fairness as essentially equivalent' [Gardner p. 155, n. 21], since fairness belongs more with the allocative department of issues of justice. Torture (properly understood) is always unjust (and therefore to be absolutely excluded), though not always unfair. See p. 506, the final paragraph of this section.

[169] *ST* II-II q. 58 a. 11 ad 1:...liberaliter benefacere...per quandam reductionem, attribuitur iustitiae sicut principali virtuti.

[170] *CEJF* III.4 ('Distributive Justice and the Bottom Line'), 76–7:

> whatever the merits of the issue between the classics and the moderns, you will not begin to understand the classical conceptions of justice unless you accept that, on those conceptions, it is nonsense to speak of an unjust but justified action. That is why one of the most popular classical definitions of justice was 'the constant and perpetual willingness to give/render to each and every person his due/his right(s)/what he is owed/what is his [*jus suum* or simply *suum*]'—the phrase 'constant and perpetual' meaning unconditional: *not* subject to further calculations of utility or other assessments of the 'justified and the unjustified'. What is due to somebody correlates with what ought not to be done, or omitted to be done, to or for him, as judged when *all* the relevant considerations are in. Classical justice is on the bottom line, as American bureaucrats would say.

[171] *NE* V.12: 1136b17–24 and a15–b14 (cf. the unconvincing arguments at V.15: 1138a4, a14–28 and 1138b5–13).

rights against oneself'? If we are going by ear, must we say that one has no right to a fair share of the cake one is distributing?

I am happy to concede that various of my writings too quickly assimilate what is due to X with X's right, a way of speaking that mislocates who it is that has the right that X, if an offender, be punished.[172] I see no reason, however, to concede 'a wedge between justice and duties'. Gardner's explorations of 'deserts' and 'deserves' serve to suggest one reason for my reluctance to use this opaque term: there can be occasions when there is no duty to impose on X the punishment he deserves, since imposing it would unfairly risk harm to others; or the common good could be shifted to a higher synthesis by a healing exercise of mercy (see p. 521 of this essay).[173] As he says, 'that [certain] things are deserved is just one reason among others for giving them'; but, as I stipulated and am maintaining, justice concerns what should be chosen and done (or abstained from) all things considered, and is therefore always tightly connected with duty and *breach* of duty. Correspondingly, when I speak of giving people their due, I refer (unlike Gardner [p. 158]) to what someone has a duty to give them. I think his willingness to cut between due and duty as he does is another problem—that of needless or distracting complexity—created by his method. And the method then carries him on to compounded terminological complexities by persuading him that duty too (like 'due'!) is not a bottom-line predicate: 'duties do not automatically defeat non-duties'. An orderly reflective ('academic') treatment of the truly complex issues of the moral life calls, I believe, for a vocabulary in which some terms are reserved for the all-things-considered, bottom-line judgments. 'Right' and 'wrong', 'duty', and 'unjust' are, I think, all helpfully so reserved, even if common idiom deploys them in varying fashion.

These reflections on Gardner's essay are in line with my complaints[174] about the idiom that courts and draftsmen deploy when they speak of justified or justifiable *violations of right*. I quite understand those locutions, and do not regard them as self-contradictory or even erroneous. But I do say they introduce a needless source of confusion, cross-purposes, and the risk of biasing the courts' assessment of the issues at stake.

---

[172] Similarly, my summary of the issues of justice, in *Aquinas*, 188:

> When will everyone, some people, or someone, be entitled to some action or forbearance of mine, or to some thing which I should provide, respect, or restore?

may be less satisfactory than the simple comprehensiveness of *NLNR*, 162: '[What] relations and dealings are necessary or appropriate for the avoiding of a wrong [to another][?]'

[173] *Pace* Gardner [p. 158], I do not think a just person is concerned 'with the gullible electorate getting the government they deserve'; for the common good may be gravely impaired by such a government, and a just person's ultimate concern is always for the common good (understood as including people's rights and just liabilities).

[174] See e.g. *CEJF* III.1, 40:

> This uncraftsmanlike language of 'interference' with exercises of the right carries an inappropriate implication: that when I am arrested in my cellar for making drugs, bombs, or freeze-proofed wines down there, the unwelcome irruption is not merely into my privacy but also into my exercise of my right. Would it not be more accurate to say that in such use of my cellar, I take myself outside the true ambit of my right? The limitations indicated by the Convention's references to public health, prevention of crime, and so on, are limitations which specify the limits of my right; they are in fact a part—or at least a compendious reference to an intrinsic part—of the right's own definition.

And see the endnote to that passage, at 45.

Another example of the problems generated by trying to systematize from common idiom: Gardner holds that 'each of us has a right not to be tortured' [p. 160], but that torturing is not, as such, an act of injustice [pp. 159–60] and 'talk of rights is implicitly contrastive—it indicates that a duty is owed to one person or group rather than another' [p. 160]. Would it not be better to say that each of us has a right never to be tortured, that torturing is therefore always an injustice, and that there are duties which are owed to everyone, not merely to one person or group rather than another, and even though nothing is up for allocation?[175] Again, does not the concept of allocation, which Gardner's method has led him to make decisive for justice, seem elusive even within the confines of his essay? 'There is a question of justice...only when something is up for allocation' [p. 161], he says, and 'allocative questions arise *only in connection with some legal and more broadly institutional rights*' [p. 164, emphasis added]. But his generous words about my work in the final section of his essay include praise for 'explaining, *without condoning*, the late 20th-century tendency to think of justice as a topic for political and legal philosophers rather than for other moral philosophers' [p. 166, emphasis added].

11.

Matthew Kramer's reflections on retribution offer to adopt my account of it, but on a carefully restricted basis. They (1) abstain from arguing that an account of retribution could be correct as an 'overarching justification of punishment', or that his preference for my account over its principal rival is justified; they (2) minimize (with the most benign of intentions) the place of freedom in my account; and they (3) hold that the account could work as a justification only in 'a liberal-democratic regime'. Since I have elsewhere conspicuously neglected the austerity of (1), I need here say something only about the other two restrictions.

Having sweepingly attacked George Sher's 'suggestion that the unjust gain accruing to every criminal resides in the inordinate freedom which he arrogates to himself through his law-breaking conduct' [p. 168], a suggestion that he thinks 'we should reject altogether', Kramer notes my 'intermittent' and 'occasional lapses' into talk of 'some extra share of freedom supposedly accruing to a criminal' and constituting 'the gain...intrinsic to every offence and...properly counteracted through punishment'. But he benignly discounts it. Instead he says approvingly that I 'usually make clear that it is a criminal's self-indulgence...that constitutes' that gain. Indeed, 'self-indulgence' is the term he headlines to articulate that to which retribution is the fitting response. It is not a term I use in these contexts: to me it suggests, above all, a weak-willed indulgence of desire or inertia. Since the essence of criminal wrongdoing is, in my account, precisely the gaining of an excess of freedom, the nearest I get to speaking of 'self'

---

[175] Gardner thinks [p. 161] that his propositions, just recalled, are 'all...consistent with' my view (*NLNR*, 163) that, as just people, 'we may be interested in...comparing adults' rations with what...is *fitting* for them to have if they are to remain alive and well, regardless of questions of supply and shares'. But *that* kind of concern is what I called commutative justice, of which I went on to say (*NLNR*, 179) that it concerns 'the whole field in which, *problems of allocation of the common stock and the like apart*, the problem is to determine what dealings are proper between persons...'

and 'indulgence' in the same breath is my reference to indulging self-preference—a rather different matter:

> the restoration of a fair distribution of advantages and disadvantages as between citizens is *an aim* of punishment. Of course, the crime and the harm it causes can never be *undone*. But that fair distribution (or balance or order) whose disruption is entailed by the now past crime can be subsumed under a new order by an adjustment of the criminal's position relative to his fellows—an adjustment in the precisely relevant respect, i.e. by deprivations in respect of his *wrongfully (but necessarily profitably) indulged disposition towards self-preference*—so that, taking a period of time rather than one or another moment in the life of a society, a long-term order of fairness is maintained (by renovation). Naturally, it would be better if the order of fairness were never disrupted; but often it is, and at the end of a period one should be able to look back over the *whole* period and say that, because of the adjustments that were made in response to criminal disruption of that order, no one has (overall and taking the period as a whole) been disadvantaged unfairly by attempting to live in strict accordance with that basic order of fairness.[176]

I have quoted all this because Kramer's criticisms of Sher, and of everyone else's talk of freedom in this context,[177] seem to me to overlook what it is that Sher and others, and certainly my own writings, have been referring to—and not by intermittent lapses of language—as the offender's wrongful gaining of freedom. The freedom wrongfully gained is the freedom that *was exercised in* the forbidden act. It is not, as Kramer strangely postulates first, a freedom from the normative demands of the law—a permission. Rather it is the freedom of choice exercised as a *violation* of the law. And that freedom is not in the least an attempt to acquire some new ability (moral, legal, or physical) or 'unpreventedness' [p. 170].

It seems to me that the cause of Kramer's critical attention to such fanciful notions, and neglect of the obvious sense of all this talk of freedom, is that he neglects what the passage just quoted recalls: the temporal framework of retribution. (It is a framework reflected or implicit in his own use of tenses when he refers to, e.g., 'the unjust gain that has accrued to any wrongdoer simply by dint of his having acted athwart the terms of a morally worthy criminal-law mandate' [p. 168].) Retribution has nothing to do with gaining anything new in the way of a future freedom or a future ability. It is not like what biologists, chemists, or physicists would count as gain, but is like what bookkeepers or accountants would. (And not just accountants, but all who are conscious of what they themselves owe to the gifts or services or fidelity of others.[178]) *Before* the offence

---

[176] *CEJF* III.11 ('The Restoration of Retribution'), 164 (emphasis added).

[177] Inconsistently, I think, Kramer quotes with evident approval [p. 182] the passage in *NLNR*, 263 which explains how 'punishment rectifies the disturbed pattern of advantages and disadvantages throughout a community', as Kramer agrees it does; but the quoted explanation is precisely that it rectifies that disturbed pattern 'by depriving the convicted criminals *of their freedom of choice*, proportionately to the degree to which they had exercised their freedom, their personality, in the unlawful act'.

[178] 'Earnings', and '*quantum meruit*', and 'debts of gratitude' are among the many terms, less opaque than 'desert', that assume the need to consider human affairs diachronically, so that present obligations and liabilities are truly (even when defeasibly) entailed by past acts and facts normatively picked out as supplying relevant premises for such propositional consequences. Such diachronic consideration holds

there was, by hypothesis, a fair balance of advantages among a society's members, including the advantage of doing what one wants when one wants. Then, *in* the offending, the offender exercises a freedom others (the law-abiding) deny themselves: the freedom of acting in violation of the law. Thus, *after* that time, the offender stands in the relevant, notional 'books of account' as someone who is 'in profit'—a profit (by hypothesis) unjustly acquired, an 'ill-gotten gain' (nothing, as Kramer rightly notes, to do with loot or psychological satisfactions). And the culpable offender remains in illicit profit unless and until deprived of precisely that sort of gain—excess of freedom of action, the freedom exercised in the self-preference of *doing* what one wants though the law forbids it—by punitive restriction of freedom of action by fine, imprisonment, or some other deprivation of freedom or imposition on the offender's will.[179] Thus a fair equality is preserved, in the relevant respect, over the span of time extending from immediately before the offence to immediately after the imposition of punishment. I doubt that, without this conception of illicitly gainable and licitly annullable freedom, Kramer is in a position to make thoroughly intelligible his thesis—in itself correct— that punishment rectifies the injury done to a community by a criminal's 'pursuing his criminal purposes' [p. 181] in the commission of an offence, a rectification 'by impos-ing on the wrongdoer a disadvantage ... that counterbalances the valuable advantage'— what, precisely?—'which he has [thereby] gained' [p. 181].

I turn to the second remaining restriction (itself double-barrelled) proposed by Kramer when he writes:

> the saliently egalitarian tenor of desert-focused retributivism confines its justificatory reach to liberal-democratic societies. Only in such a society is the ideal of human equality realized sufficiently to render germane the proposition that punitive measures serve to effectuate that very ideal[180] ... [Moreover], a necessary condition for the

---

the whole sequence in view, and the consequences ('Cambridge changes') do not run in only one direction. As Sher (1987) says at 187, in the course of an interesting discussion of how the past matters:

> By [rewarding the deserving and punishing the guilty] we change unrewarded past efforts and acts of virtue into rewarded ones and unpunished crimes into punished ones.

And by performance we change unfulfilled into fulfilled promises, and so forth.

[179] In my lectures on Jurisprudence in Oxford in 2001 and 2004, for example, I summarized the matter thus:

> *Aquinas* 213–4; *NLNR* 261–4, 291: The essence of punishments is that they subject offenders to something *contrary to their wills* – something *contra voluntatem*. This, not pain, is of the essence. Why? Because the essence of offences is that in their wrongful acts offenders 'yielded to their will more than they ought', 'followed their own will excessively', 'ascribed too much to their own preferences'—the measure of excess being the relevant law or moral norm for preserving and promoting the common good. Hence the proposition foundational for e.g. Aquinas' entire account of punishment: the order of just equality in relation to the offender is restored— offenders are brought back into that equality—precisely by the 'subtraction' effected in a corresponding, proportionate suppression *of the will which took for itself too much* (too much freedom or autonomy, we may say). In this way punishment 'sets in order' the guilt whose essence was wrongful willing; and this (re)ordering {ordinativa} point of punishment can either be accounted remedial {medicinalis}, or contrasted with the remedial (deterrent, reformative) (emphasis in original).

For the remainder of this part of the handout, on mercy, see p. 521 at n. 216 in this essay.

[180] A footnote at this point refers readers to 'a suggestion along these lines' at *NLNR* 263, n. 1. But that says no more than that *some* ('*relevant*') kinds of inequality prior to the offence negate the offender's retributive liability to punishment.

satisfactoriness of desert-focussed retributivism as an account of the worthy ends of punishment is that it be conjoined with a liberal-democratic theory of criminalization. [p. 183]

But the retributive aim and justification of punishment, based though it is on the need to restore a disturbed equality among the members of (paradigmatically) a political community, is not confined to political communities that are fair in their distribution of wealth, or liberal or democratic in their constitutional order.

Take wealth first. There are societies in which a small class of very rich people lord it over an unfairly deprived mass. *Qua* unfairly rich individuals, none of the members of the elite have a justified claim that fair equality be restored after it has been disturbed by crime. But *qua* responsible for the governance, for common good, of the political community, the police and judges and jailers, like the legislators whose laws authorize their activities by defining crimes and lawful penalties, have the justified authority retributively to restore equality not only between victims of crimes and the criminals, by enforcing compensation of the former by the latter, but also between the latter and the law-abiding, by depriving offenders of their ill-gotten gains. For although the unjust poverty (or other forms of deprivation) of offenders may excuse and even justify the commission of certain legal offences (such as stealing food to avert starvation), there remain countless offences that are not thus excusable or justifiable. Indeed, most of the offences of poor people who offend are against other poor and vulnerable people, and many of the latter are law-abiding in the relevant sense, that is, willing to abide by laws, even laws inconveniently athwart their desires, provided they are laws compliance with which is compatible with the very necessities of life. Whether or not these law-abiding poor are *entitled* (as Kramer doubts) to have the law punitively upheld, it is *per se* right and just that it be so upheld—and if none but morally tainted rich people can be found to uphold it, no matter: they do not (rightly) uphold it in their own name, or for their own sake, but for the common good of the community for whose common good they are responsible, a common good which has as one of its key elements the maintenance of equality between the law-abiding and the lawless.

Nor did punishment become retributively justifiable only with the advent of the liberal-democratic state in 1928, or 1832, or 1689 or whatever other date or period Kramer may nominate. His position seems to me a *reductio ad absurdum* of the practice, so widespread in legal and philosophy (not to mention theology) in the last and present generation, of treating 'liberal' as a framework term equivalent to 'just' and, by implication here made explicit by Kramer, 'illiberal' or 'non-liberal' (or 'undemocratic') as equivalent to 'illegitimate'. The writings in which I have criticized that practice, especially for its imprecision[181] and its tolerance of superficiality,[182] fail to bring out sufficiently its unsoundness. Notwithstanding the real merits[183] of the complex of political and legal institutions and norms usually referred to today as liberal-democracy, that complex should be judged—though the judgment is difficult and uncertain in many details—to depend, for its existence and its merits, on the

---

[181] *CEJF* III.Introduction, 10; III.5, 94; *CEJF* V.5, 104.
[182] *CEJF* IV.11 ('Hart as a Political Philosopher'), 277–9, and *CEJF* IV.14, 321.
[183] See p. 515 at n. 200 and section 24 (on Ekins) at pp. 560–3.

obtaining (satisfying) of a number of necessary conditions concerning the willingness of various components of the relevant population to consider themselves members of the people of one political community, and to trust other components sufficiently to accept their members as rulers, participate honestly in elections as voters or scrutineers, accept political defeat and adverse criticism, make and adhere to good faith compromises and constituent arrangements, carry out and/or submit to impartial adjudication, pay their taxes, and so forth. Such conditions cannot be conjured up at will; nor is their non-obtaining always (though it often is) a matter of culpability; nor does the culpability or inculpability affect the often obstinate fact of such non-obtaining. A serious question confronts us. Have not the governing elements of many societies that have congratulated themselves on their liberal-democratic order been accepting and instigating norms, policies, tolerances, and intolerances, that are perceptibly and even rapidly undermining those conditions? If so, may not liberal democracy, before very long, become a thing substantially of the past?[184] (Verbally, no doubt, its passing away would be denied, much as the anti-democratic character of many regimes has been contradicted by their self-description as 'People's Democracies' and the like.) Then it will be important that the *criminal law* of such post-liberal, post-democratic political communities need not be entirely or even largely illegitimate, and that the retributive punishing of most kinds of offence could be legitimate, even when carried out by agents of a regime that ought, if the preconditions be in place, to be overthrown in order to be replaced by a more just constitutional order.

The last two paragraphs, though falling short of a complete argument (even when their themes are further explored and developed in the next two sections), may perhaps suffice to put in question Kramer's contention that the equality to be upheld by criminal law and restored by retributive punishment is co-extensive with the forms of equality valued by liberal-democratic polities as such.

12.

Leslie Green is right to interrogate my talk of the 'instrumental' character of the political community's (state's) common good, and of state government and law. Since I have not hitherto sorted out and repaired the defects of my discussion of these matters in *NLNR* and *Aquinas*, and in the 1996 essay that Green considers, I will now try to do so, in outline, with supplementations in my remarks in section 13 (on Tollefsen).

In *NLNR* the idea of common good, including but in no way restricted to the common good of the state, was set forth unsatisfactorily, as I explain in the Postscript:

> The discussion of the common good is too resolute in giving primacy to the [definition given] in the second paragraph on p. 155. This conception—in terms of a set of conditions for the attainment of individual or common objectives—makes the common good (at least seem) *instrumental*. It omits the intrinsic desirability of a

---

[184] Haldane expresses a similar doubt [Essay 3, p. 54] without straying, as I have, into identifying grounds for it. More elaborately: *CEJF* II.6, 113–18; more stringently, *CEJF* IV.11, 274–80; and p. 517, n. 202 in this essay.

communal flourishing which consists not merely in the individual flourishing of each member of the community (family, club, association, team, state ...), but also in the reality that this flourishing was and is assisted by, and in good measure consists in, mutual assistance through all the forms of friendship (though not all the instances of friendship between each person and each other person). There is, in short, the common good that consists in the all-inclusive and intrinsically desirable flourishing of that community (and those communities) as such.[185]

The Postscript comment runs on as follows, shifting attention to the distinct question of the character of *state* community and state governance, in one key aspect (not the one most discussed by Green):

> This is brought out in *Aquinas* at p. 235, together with this rider: it does not follow, and Aquinas himself does not think it follows, that there is or should be someone— even government and law as a whole—responsible for coercively bringing this about, or that the coercive jurisdiction of the state's government and law is defined by this all-inclusive common good. Indeed, that jurisdiction is to be defined rather by the *public good* which, as Aquinas says, is limited to interpersonal relations and external acts which impact directly or indirectly on others.

This aspect of the moral-political limits on government was not discussed in *NLNR* itself, which neither affirmed nor denied the paternalism that, as I showed in *Aquinas*, was rejected by Aquinas and was rebutted in my own writings after 1998. It concerns the issue debated by Mill in *On Liberty* and, much less adequately,[186] by Hart and Devlin. The related but distinct issue taken up in section IV of Green's essay ('Civil Society and the State') can be compressed into the 'instrumentality principle', the essay's name for a proposition (here italicized in sentence [4]) in the following passage from my 'Limited Government' (1996):

> [1] ... the political community—properly understood as one of the forms of collaboration needed for the sake of the goods identified in the first principles of natural law—

---

[185] *NLNR*, 459.

[186] See *CEJF* IV.11 ('Hart as a Political Philosopher'), 267–74: a principal conclusion of this discussion is that Hart's acceptance of Devlin's framing of the issues led him to ignore completely (a) the civil-law tradition of permitting only the enforcement of *public* morality, and (b) the corresponding Thomist, very distinct variant of the Platonic-Aristotelian theory of state concern for the moral character of adult citizens. The superiority of Mill to both Hart and Devlin consists mainly in his attention to historical preconditions. Green [p. 200] quotes his remarks about 'the ancient commonwealths' as if Mill simply 'laid a charge against Greco-Roman political morality', but does not complete the sentence, which goes on to offer a conditional defence of that conception of politics:

> a mode of thinking which may have been admissible in small republics surrounded by powerful enemies, in constant peril of being subverted by foreign attack or internal commotion, and to which even a short interval of relaxed energy and self-command might so easily be fatal, that they could not afford to wait for the salutary permanent effects of freedom.

The only thing wrong with this is the complacency about progress—'salutary permanent effects...': *CEJF* I.18 ('Freedom of Speech'), 308–9; and n. 276 in this essay.

(A further superiority of Mill's discussion is that, alongside discussion of *legal* repression, it includes some consideration, admittedly much less ample, of repression by extra-legal social pressures, which have today become a principal mode of suppressing discussion of issues important—some vitally—to the future of the societies involved: ours. See also *CEJF* I.18 ('Freedom of Speech'), 298.)

is a community co-operating in the service of a common good which is instrumental, not itself basic. [2] True, it is a good which is 'great and godlike'[187] in its ambitious range: 'to secure the whole ensemble of material and other conditions, including forms of collaboration, that tend to favour, facilitate, and foster the realization by each individual [in that community] of his or her personal development'[188] (which will in each case include, constitutively, the flourishing of the family, friendship, and other communities to which that person belongs). [3] True too, its proper range includes the regulation of friendships, marriage, families, and religious associations, as well as all the many organizations and associations which, like the state itself, have only an instrumental (e.g., an economic) common good. [4] But such *regulation of these associations should never (in the case of the associations with a non-instrumental common good) or only exceptionally (in the case of instrumental associations) be intended to take over the formation, direction, or management of these personal initiatives and interpersonal associations.* [5] Rather, its purpose must be to carry out a function which the Jesuit social theorists of the early twentieth century taught us to call subsidiarity (i.e., helping, from the Latin *subsidium*, help): the function of assisting individuals and groups to co-ordinate their activities for the objectives and commitments they have chosen, and to do so in ways consistent with the other aspects of the common good of the political community, uniquely complex and far-reaching in its rationale and peculiarly demanding in its requirements of co-operation.[189]

I have quoted the whole passage, including sentence [3], to indicate that at least some of Green's grounds for rejecting the instrumentality principle seem beside the point. As a limit on government and law, the principle is compatible with extensive regulation, say of marriage—not only with regulating, by direction of state officials or law, what Green calls [p. 198] the social institution of marriage, but even with so regulating some elements of (potential harmful deviations from) the 'common good of marital life' of particular married couples. But it is not compatible with establishing that common good of marital life for any particular couple, or with doing anything else which, like that, would be going beyond regulating to what the principle forbids: trying to 'take over the formation, direction, or management of these personal initiatives and interpersonal associations'. (And see p. 515 at n. 197 in this essay.)

The communities called in the quoted passage 'non-instrumental' are friendships, marriages, and religious communities (self-)understood as instantiating communion of believers with the divine; paradigmatically the Church. Universities, though organized to pursue the intrinsic good of knowledge, are not instances of this type, since their relationship to that good is itself instrumental: the good is one that can in principle be pursued in a solitary way. As for the political community's common good, the 1996 essay called it 'instrumental' because it does not as such instantiate any of the basic human goods (listed on that essay's previous page). In *Aquinas*, however, this way of conceiving the political common good was to be set aside (albeit partially and incompletely) in a much more elaborate analysis of the state and its common good. A main

---

[187] *NE* 1.1: 1094b9.   [188] *NLNR*, 147…
[189] *CEJF* III.5, 89–90 (two footnotes omitted and one abbreviated).

result of that later analysis was stated in *Aquinas* at p. 235 (cited in the *NLNR* Postscript passage above), concluding:

> Thus there is an important sense in which the common good of the political community is all-inclusive, nothing short of the *beatitudo* [all-round flourishing] of its members and the fulfilment of their families. This all-inclusive common good of the state includes the all-round virtue of every member of the state.

At this point, on the same page, the analysis changed direction, to take in a nuanced version of the 'instrumentality principle'. From the just-mentioned all-inclusiveness of the state's common good 'it simply does not follow that law-makers and other participants in state government are responsible for directing and commanding all the choices that need to made if this all-inclusive good is to be attained.' The argument runs on for a page and more, and ends with—

> ... Although rulers are in many respects in charge of their subjects, their direct concern as rulers is only, as we have seen, the promotion of *public good*.
>
> Public good is a part or aspect of the all-inclusive common good. It is the part which provides an indispensable context and support for those parts or aspects of the common good which are private (especially individual and familial good). It thus supplements, subserves, and supervises those private aspects, but without superseding them, and without taking overall charge of, or responsibility for them ... [190]

The summing-up repeats the division of senses of 'common good of the political community':

> In sum: The common good attainable in political community is thus a complex good attainable only if the state's rulers, its families, and its individual citizens all perform their proper, specialised and stratified roles and responsibilities. This common good, which is in a sense *the* common good of the political community, is *unlimited* (the common good of the whole of human life). But there is also a common good which is 'political' in the more specific sense that it is (i) the good of using government and law to assist individuals and families do well what they should be doing, together with (ii) the good(s) which sound action by and on behalf of the political community can add to the good attainable by individuals and families as such (including the good of repelling and overcoming harms and deficiencies which individuals and families and other 'private' groupings could not adequately deal with). This, and only this, specifically political common good is what the state's rulers are responsible for securing and, by legislation and lawful governmental actions (judicial and administrative), should

---

[190] The next paragraph at *Aquinas*, 237 runs, in part:

> Still, the justice and peace which rulers must maintain *are* for the sake of individual and familial well-being and cannot be identified and pursued without a sound conception of individual and domestic responsibilities ... Because the *prudentia* of political rulers must comprehend, though without replacing, the *prudentia* of individuals and families, it is the most complete ... The immediate and direct measure of individual and parental responsibility is not the directives of political authority, but remains the practical reasonableness of individuals and of heads of households.

require their subjects to respect and support. This specifically political common good is *limited* and in a sense *instrumental*. It is what Aquinas, as we have seen, calls public good.[191]

Even though 'instrumental' was qualified by 'in a sense', and was here applied only to the state's '*specifically political* common good', and not to its all-inclusive common good, I have reservations about the term.

For one thing, the proposition that the specifically political common good is instrumental is qualified by a not merely occasional exception, set out in the next few pages of *Aquinas*. Even though property, produce and exchange, and the laws that establish and protect them are, like defence forces, instrumental goods, the restoration of justice, by 'private law' compensation and restitution and by 'public law' retribution, seems to be *an aspect of* the basic human good of *societas* or *philia*.[192] So at least one element of the specifically political common good—that is, of the 'public good' that marks out the domain of the coercive jurisdiction of state government and law—is no mere means, but an intrinsically valuable object for the relevant state action.

And in any case, 'instrumental' does not well fit a form of human cooperative associating—political governance—which cannot be done well, or even adequately, without both a measure of pervasive political friendship and a correct and widely held conception of, and willing favour for, the *all-inclusive common good* of the political community (including those aspects of the all-inclusive common good that fall outside the coercive jurisdiction of state government and law because not elements of the public, specifically political good).

Moreover, the term 'instrumental' was used (in the very essay on which Green focuses) to indicate what is wrong with Augustine's account of marriage as instrumental to procreation.[193] And 'instrument' is used in the tradition to pick out the status or role of animals and slaves.

For all these reasons, the term 'subsidiary'—understood rather as it is in the ('upstream' [cf. pp. 188–9, 195 n. 22]) principle of justice called 'the principle of subsidiarity'[194]—might, I now think, have been better than the term 'instrumental' in the contexts relevant to Green's essay.[195] Or perhaps 'supplementary' would do.[196]

Which is not to say that I doubt the principle Green has named my 'instrumentality principle'. As I have already hinted, I think it is a sound principle (and not merely a strategically absolutized [p. 193] legal precept like 'Congress shall make no law prohibiting the free exercise of religion'). But it is not well rendered as a principle that, as he puts it, 'will certainly ban interference with what we might call the internal aspects of an associational group (its membership criteria, its authority over its

---

[191] *Aquinas*, 235–7, footnotes omitted. This is the substance of Ch. VII.5, headed 'Specifically Distinct Responsibilities for Common Good'. The role of the term 'public good' (*bonum publicum*) in Aquinas's writings had been detailed at 222–8, 230–2.

[192] *Aquinas*, 245, 247.

[193] *CEJF* III.5, 100–1.

[194] See *NLNR*, 146, 159, 169, 188, 194, 197, 233, 292.

[195] I return to the question debated in this paragraph in section 13 (Tollefsen) of this essay.

[196] *Aquinas*, 245–52 (headings).

members)' or that 'directs the state to allow these organisations to do their own thing' [p. 194]. Just as, for example, the privileges of the English Parliament exclude any management, direction, control, or takeover of either House by the courts or the executive, yet do not entail that the criminal law and its officers have no jurisdiction over acts and events within Parliament, so state government and law have some proper regulatory role in relation to even the internal affairs of families and religious associations. The limit excludes any aim to take over their formation, direction,[197] or management. 'Take over', like 'dignity' and 'equal protection', is vague, but like them, is not without content,[198] especially when embedded in a course of argument that shows the worth of individual self-direction and marital equality in freedom, goods clearly basic and at least as important in living a human life as political community properly is.

A word, finally, about two important themes framing Green's contribution: tradition and fallibility. Green presents liberalism as a matter of tradition [pp. 187, 188]. He does not challenge my view that 'liberal' and its cognates are unsuited (largely by reason of their radical ambiguity in historical and current usage) for use as framework terms in moral, political, or legal theory.[199] Nor does he challenge or note my view that, as a matter of historical reportage, the very loose cluster of traditions self-described as liberal can reasonably be regarded as a subset (or cluster of subsets) within the wider tradition of political theory initiated by Plato; and that within that wider tradition certain theories such as Aquinas's (or indeed Kant's)—theories not self-described as liberal—can reasonably be described as liberal,[200] even though their general features are closer to Plato's and Aristotle's theories than many characteristic modern liberal theories are. It is characteristic of a tradition that its members refer with respect, and a certain (even if defeasible) reverence, to founders and exemplars of the tradition, whose theses they treat as presumptively sound even when they reject their arguments and some at least of the theses. That is how Green speaks of Mill and Locke, without affirming any of their arguments or precise positions, and indeed seemingly dissociating himself [pp. 191–2] from a main tenet of *On Liberty* where—at least in the sense it had in that tract—it collides with one of Devlin's counter-examples.

The closest Green gets to affirming one of Mill's own positions is where he adduces Mill's support for the thought that:

> we have reason to believe that in certain areas governments are especially likely to fall into error ... [E]specially in matters of belief, sex, and friendship, there are chasms of incomprehension that make it difficult to know *what it is like* to be in another person's position, and thus difficult to have any accurate appreciation for the effects that one's proposed policy may have on him. [p. 202]

---

[197] Green [p. 196] uses 'direction' to mean what I meant by 'regulation'; by 'direct(ion)' I meant the sort of things that the board of directors of a corporation does—the sort of things that someone who has *taken over* an enterprise as sole owner of it does in managing it.

[198] Grisez, at the relevant point in his very similar account of political community and authority, says 'political society is only one community among others and should be limited so that it will not displace or absorb the others': Grisez, *Living a Christian Life*, 847–8 (11.B.2(b)).

[199] *CEJF* III.5, 94; *CEJF* V.5, 104.

[200] See *CEJF* IV.5, 135; IV.11, 270; IV.15, 334 (with 328). The first-mentioned two note the bifurcation of Aquinas from Plato and Aristotle in this domain.

The proposition that Green recalls at this point, described by Mill as 'the strongest of all' his arguments about liberty of 'purely personal conduct', is left baldly unargued by Mill himself, is bafflingly weak, and seems little strengthened by Green's argument, just quoted. For, *pace* Green, is it not in fact easy enough for mature people to have gained—by experience, report (biography and history and poetry), testimony, and critically tested imagination—an accurate comprehension and appreciation of *what it is like* to hold a belief, experience sexual desires and acts, and acquire, be, and lose friends? And all persons in private or public positions of responsibility for children act, and have to act, on the basis that they have sufficient comprehension of these issues to gauge 'the effects that one's proposed policy may have' on children at an age when those effects are likely to be particularly marked (for good or ill)—to gauge the effects sufficiently, that is, to judge appropriately about what forms of life to hold out to the children for whom they are responsible, and what policies and lifestyles to protect them from. Policies of teaching, say, that 'values' are a matter for individual choice measured only by authenticity, and/or that recreational use of addictive drugs is a lifestyle choice, and/or that sex ('gender') is a matter of self-chosen identities along a spectrum, that femininity and manliness, including the maternal and the paternal, are 'sexist' categories, and that marital sex has no priority of value let alone exclusive worth, are all policies that are at least as substantive, as value-laden and (if believed) as profoundly life-changing *and constraining* as their antitheses. There is no reason to believe (and Green seems not to suggest) that such policies are an 'error-reducing mechanism', or that one can produce such a mechanism by according them some sort of priority because supposedly more value-free and less error-prone.

What, then, would work to reduce error? Green denies [p. 201]—for me, unpersuasively—that he is commending 'a proceduralist response' to either the problem of evaluative disagreement or, by implication, to the deeper, epistemologically intrinsic problem he sums up as 'fallibility'. That deeper problem is indeed real and important. The 'right of free speech' is, as he says, an important and proper response to it. Indeed, it is a response increasingly imperiled and neglected, precisely in and by the attitudes of many powerful people who understand themselves to be liberal egalitarians. It is worth adding that the freedom of speech which is responsive to the problem of fallibility does not properly include exposure of the whole population, or even the whole adult population, to pornography,[201] salacious advertising, and the filmed or cartooned glorification of cultural nihilism by cynically inhuman violence. And such exposure cannot rightly be defended on 'free speech' grounds against the objections to it that can be made on the substantive grounds of its eminently probable harmful effects,[202] effects

---

[201] I doubt that, in the vast mass of writings which since 1965 have offered to reveal 'what it is like' to desire or engage in (say) sexual practices, there is anything that provides a sufficient basis for thinking unwise the previous policies that (i) prohibited or severely limited the circulation of such writings as made these disclosures, and (ii) more relevantly here, prohibited public arrangements for or other promotion of such practices.

[202] Devlin unwisely conducted his famous polemic as an argument about the enforcement not of morals, but of strongly held moral opinions whether false or true: see *CEJF* III.1, 27. The resulting thesis that, as Green not unfairly puts it, 'sexual *non-conformity* will cause social disintegration' is, as Green says [p. 192], 'comically weak' (and see *CEJF* IV.11, 270 especially n. 2). Had Devlin's thesis been, instead, that sexual *immorality* will cause social disintegration or collapse, it is likely—presuming that he had broadly sound

not least when indirect, like the effects on all those harmed in their relationships with persons directly harmed (corrupted) by it.

Fallibility is a reason to favour a dividing, separating, and specializing of powers, a constant discourse and part-professionalization of deliberation, and an elimination of factors promoting immoderate deference (Yes-men). But fallibility—the possibility of error—is not, generically, a reason for cutting back the criminal code, or the strength of the armed forces and their munitions, or the scope of taxation, though there may be many good grounds for pruning *this* criminal code, or *these* forces or taxes, on their (lack of) merits. Nor is fallibility sufficient ground for cutting back on the judicious enforcement of *public* morality, or on other appropriate state-sponsored means of transmitting and defending it. The bad consequences (to the common good, and to assignable individuals) of a decay of public morality are often so grave and irreversible, in vanilla-plain human harms, losses, and vulnerabilities, that to base on the fact of moral fallibility alone a presumption against enforcement of public morality would be just as unreasonable as adopting a presumption-based unwillingness to withdraw one's support for enforcement of some accepted, supposedly moral norm of conduct once one has responsibly judged that that norm was and is morally erroneous.

Green's proposed error-minimizing mechanisms are very much more modest and reasonable than Rawls's programme of 'public reason' and 'political' liberalism.[203] But beyond a certain point, proceduralist responses to the problem of fallibility are fundamentally inadequate. What matters here is not so much the possibility of error as the fact—or absence—of error. Moral truth, as best one can judge it (and taken along with truths, however unwelcome to pious ears, about typical differences in aptitudes and vulnerabilities, and other realities predictably affecting the outcomes of different lifestyles, permissions, and policies), is the only reasonable *foundational and generic* criterion for anyone to deploy in deliberating about whether to (vote to) enforce or otherwise support those aspects of the common good that are conventionally pointed to by the term 'public morality'.[204] Indeed, moral truth is surely the criterion being applied—or more likely misapplied—in the plausibly imagined responses of Green's supposed audience ('you') to the imagined rise of a Natural Law Party [p. 200]. And it is a criterion being applied (even if incorrectly) in the 'liberal-egalitarian' repression of speech and freedom of association that has recently been set in motion by law and

judgments about that (a presumption not defeated by his public support for decriminalization of private adult consensual sodomy)—that he would/will have the last laugh. Already he could be wryly noting the ever growing and ever more manifest probability that the sophisticated, negligent peoples who have adopted beliefs about sex and friendship which the main tradition articulated by Plato, Aristotle, and Aquinas judges immoral will during the coming century be substantially replaced, or at least be socially, culturally, and politically dominated, by people whose immoralities take a partly different form and include (i) an indifference to the main values and principles both of the tradition and its politically liberal subset and of those sophisticated, negligent peoples, and (ii) a strong tendency towards tyranny and lethal sectarian instability. See *CEJF* III.20, 324, 328; *CEJF* V.23, 362–4.

[203] See *CEJF* I.15 and 16 and Introduction, 13; *CEJF* V.2 and 5.

[204] The tolerance- and privacy-favouring, partly prudential considerations set out by Devlin towards the end of his 1958 Maccabean Lecture (Devlin, *The Enforcement of Morals*, 1–25, at 15–21) are appropriate; they do not, however, rest on the fallibility argument (which applies, nonetheless, to qualify if not subvert his general, truth-marginalizing thesis that passionately held moral *beliefs* are to be enforced for their fervour not their truth).

social pressure, in many contexts, against holders of the moral judgments prevalent for a couple of millennia until the late 1990s. Green's proceduralist policies, like the genial course of his dialectic, could helpfully be deployed as an antipyretic against the enthusiastic, even feverish, certainty that those millennial judgments[205] were and are (xeno-, Islamo-, homo-, trans-...) 'phobic' violations of 'identity' rights and egalitarian 'diversity' values—rights and values that those who promote them conceive of as, or as if, a newly discovered true and objective morality. But the main objection to be made to such certainties, rights, and values—to such new-minted conceptions of 'public morality'—is that taken in undiscriminating forms, as they largely are by these enthusiasts, they are mistaken and illusory, as well as harmful.

13.

To **Christopher Tollefsen**'s clarifying account of issues overlapping widely with those just discussed, I have little to add but a caveat about the term 'the state', a further brief note on the term 'instrumental', and some reflections on the real bases for concluding that the coercive jurisdiction of state government and law is limited to public good and external acts affecting others.

In *Aquinas*, I consistently used the term 'state' ('a state', 'the state', 'states') to refer to the entire political community that takes the form of a state amongst the other states (nowadays in an international order of states); and as the modern equivalent of Aristotle's *polis* and Aquinas's *civitas*. Tollefsen [pp. 208, 206] calls this 'political society' or 'a society', and Mill in the passage quoted by Tollefsen calls it 'a civilized community'. Tollefsen then reserves the term 'state' for what I consistently called 'the state's government and law', or 'the state's structure of governing offices and particular rulers and office-holders'. Tollefsen's usage corresponds to that of many others, including Jacques Maritain, on whose usage I commented in stipulating my own.[206] As I there said, each usage is rooted in common speech, but their difference needs to be noted, even if one accepts a strong version of the thesis of representation (*of* the state in my sense *by* the organs and acts of the state in Tollefsen's) that Voegelin explored early on in *The New Science of Politics*.

So when Tollefsen says that the state has an (only) 'instrumental character', he is referring, so far as I can see, to the instrumental character of state governance, whereas I predicated an instrumental character of 'the *specifically political* common good',[207] that is, of 'the common good that specifies the jurisdiction of state government and law'[208]— of what Tollefsen neatly (but in his use of the term 'state', not mine) calls 'that aspect of the more general common good of a society over which the state has authority'.[209] Again,

---

[205] Substantially quite correct: see *CEJF* III essays 20, 21 and 22; *CEJF* IV.5, section xix; *CEJF* V.23, 350–2.

[206] See *Aquinas*, 220, n. 4.

[207] *Aquinas*, 239.

[208] *Aquinas*, 252; also 245: 'the common good which is inter-defined with the responsibilities of state government and law seems indeed to be an instrumental good or set of goods, albeit of pre-eminent complexity, scope, and dignity among instruments'.

[209] Tollefsen [p. 206]; the context suggests that here 'a society' means 'a political society' (in my usage, a state).

I think the difference turns out to be only terminological. For the 'ends to which the state is instrumental' [p. 214], and which he lists at [p. 208] and more summarily at [p. 214], turn out to be wholly or largely ends that are not themselves basic, ultimate, or intrinsic: coordination amongst groups, defence against outsiders and criminals, punishment, and care for those who need and lack the care of other persons. Such 'purposes for which individuals, and the groups they constitute, are not self-sufficient' [p. 214] look 'instrumental' rather than 'intrinsic'. But they do hang together as the 'shared point', a multifaceted good, a common good, of a community, the political community or political society.

Recall here the form of the argument outlined by Tollefsen: political community, like its organs, the state, is *needed as a means* to the performing of functions that individuals, families, religious communities, and other civil associations cannot perform adequately, and that need to be performed adequately. In *Aquinas*, I propose that it is especially the need for impartial and irreparably coercive adjudication that makes state governance ineluctably necessary for the well-being of individuals, families, and other civil associations. As the provider of such coercive adjudication, the state's government, governing by law and in accordance generally with the Rule of Law, can also rightly regulate conduct in many ways needed for the common good of the individuals and groups who are subject to its jurisdiction. But 'subject to its jurisdiction' in turn needs unpacking.

What makes a rule of our law a rule *of our law* is always this: that some past act of constitution-making, enactment, and/or adjudication is treated by us *now* as sufficient reason for accepting that that action laid down or confirmed a rule, and that the rule it laid down or confirmed *then* settled, *and now settles* for us, how (in some main and often decisive aspects) we are going to act now in ways that strongly affect the future well-being of one, some, or all of us. This reference to—or connectedness to—the past doubles up, too. For many of those positive-law rules of ours are treated by us as the decisive reason for us to treat *past* agreements, settlements, and other more or less private or non-official arrangements as *now* legally effective and decisive for the *future* well-being of some, perhaps very many persons among us. The dispositions and willingness referred to by these phrases 'treated by us' and 'for us to treat' are the factual, 'ontological' basis or substance of our law.[210] Without such a basis, in present or prospective fact, the reasons for treating a rule of our law as sufficient reason for action cease to be sufficient. And throughout these references, the 'us' and 'our' refer not to families or ethnic or religious groups or associations, nor to networks of more or less piratical kinds, but to the political community that treats some defined and extensive territory as ours, and as defining the primary and essential jurisdiction of our law. What and which political community? Our country and our fellow countrymen.

Thus, from another angle, we come across the issue, touched on in section 11 (on Kramer), of preconditions for a well-functioning legal system. Willingness to share and act upon a shared conception of the identity and value (despite blemishes) of one's political community may be strongly pre-political, when the political community's boundaries coincide substantially with a cultural, linguistic, perhaps also religious

---

[210] See p. 556 at n. 324 in this essay.

unity, a nation—the sense of which may sometimes exist by reason, rather, of some historical or present shared judgment about the need for mutual defence against some dire enemy. Or such willingness may start as merely the acknowledgement of a shared need for more or less instrumental cooperation, and then develop into a widespread political friendship, so that the state's constitution and governance operate as a cause of a patriotism that is not only or ultimately 'constitutional' but amounts to a shared sense and acceptance of a legitimate community that is political but could outlast the extinguishing of its organs of governance (say, by absorption into an empire) and later still could function as a cause (efficient and final) of political self-determination, a constituent moment, and of a newly independent legal system and one-to-one state governance.[211] The possible directions of causality hereabouts are suggested by Heraclitus's saying: 'The people [*demos*] [of the *polis*] must/should/ought to/need to fight for [its] law as for [its] walls.'[212]

The value of Grisez's work in this area is the clarity with which he articulates the position that the state's government and law, even assuming them to be just and to be greatly facilitated in their tasks by a judicious patriotism of rulers and ruled, are neither the exclusive appropriate object of patriotism, nor the exclusively or all-inclusively appropriate means to the well-being of one's *patria*, one's country and one's fellow countrymen. Thus they can be in the service of a common good which is instrumental even though (a) the coordinated pursuing of it instantiates the basic and intrinsic good of friendship, and (b) the community whose instrumental common good is what government and law serve will often correspond closely to the *patria* or country whose common good is an intrinsically desirable object for the service of everyone whose *patria*, country, and people it is.[213] What I tried to add, in *Aquinas*, was a *reason* for treating the specifically political common good as instrumental even in the face of plausible claims that state government and law could with real efficacy use directly or indirectly coercive measures to promote the all-round good of the relevant community and its members, by directly paternalistic precepts backed up with coercive penalties for non-compliance. The reason was not any of those advanced by Aquinas himself, nor any of Mill's, or Kant's, all of which seem inadequate. Instead, the reason was that 'can' does not entail 'should' or even 'may (is entitled or permitted to)', and that the onus is on those who claim that state government and law are entitled to compel private virtue for its own sake to show why they are.[214]

14.

We are fortunate that **Jacqueline and John Tasioulas** found the sketchiness of my writings on mercy occasion for their illuminating discussion of the relations between law, justice, and mercy, and for their searching, sombre, but surely very playable reading of *Measure for Measure (MfM)*.

---

[211] See further p. 560 in this essay.   [212] Fragment B 44.
[213] See Grisez, *Living a Christian Life*, 837–8, 840, 842–4, 846–51 (11.A.1, 3, 6; B.2); for reservations about the term 'instrumental' see p. 514 in this essay.
[214] *Aquinas*, 242–52.

Their essay recalls and deploys the main elements of Aquinas's reflections on mercy as an emotion (compassion) and as a virtue.[215] It seems to me that his discussion, like theirs, leaves room for us to wonder, and worry, just how it is that mercy is coherent with justice, especially if we are acknowledging the real truth of retributive justice, as well as the real vulnerabilities of potential future victims of leniently treated malefactors. The response to those concerns that I offered in my Oxford lectures on Jurisprudence in 2001 and 2004 is a definition of mercy as:

> a remedy looking to a higher synthesis than restoration of equality [retribution], and seeking to heal a society's disorder by attracting persons to a more constructive pursuit of goods in a fuller friendship.[216]

This summarizes, sketchily, the pages in Germain Grisez's *Living a Christian Life* in which, with the aid both of Aquinas and of John Paul II (who devoted an encyclical to mercy, a document on which Grisez gave classes over many years), Grisez tackled head on, and in detail, the question 'How are justice and mercy related in practice?'[217] A theological version of the idea indicated by 'higher synthesis'—indeed, by the whole of my definition—is articulated in a sub-heading in Grisez's discussion: 'Mercy is the justice of Jesus' kingdom'. And such a slogan is not far, I think, from the sense of *MfM*, as Shakespeare offered it for the royal court's pleasure at Christmastide 1604, and as the courtly audience will surely have taken it.

The play is like other Shakespeare middle-period plays[218] which give the coherent pleasure of a comedy[219] only on the postulate that conversion is possible and is

---

[215] There is little to add: *Aquinas*, 75, n. 57 recalls Aquinas's thesis that (a) it is part of the perfection of the morally good that the acting person be moved to good not only by will but also by sentient desire (*appetitu sensitivo*), but (b) 'it is more praiseworthy to do a charitable (loving) act as a result of rational judgment than from the emotion of mercy/compassion alone (*ex sola passione misericordiae*)': *ST* I–II q. 24 a. 3 ad 1. *Aquinas*, 310, n. 72 restates his thesis that divine mercy, overcoming the deficiencies in creatures [e.g. their non-existence prior to creation], is more fundamental than, and is the very root of, the divine justice by which creatures have what they need to fulfil their natures (*ST* I q. 21 a. 4c; for mercy is a rationally ordered willingness to give to others what they *lack*: *ST* II–II q. 30 a. 6c and ad 1).

[216] Part of this definition was proposed in 1993d, text at n. 63, with a citation to Grisez, *Living a Christian Life*, 644–6.

[217] Grisez, *Living a Christian Life*, 360–71 (6.F); also Grisez, *Christian Moral Principles*, 644–6 (26.H); John Paul II, *Dives in Misericordia* (1980).

[218] Notably *As You Like It* (1600) and *All's Well that Ends Well* (*c*.1604, more likely than recent suggestions of *c*.1607). On the place of conversion in each of them, see *CEJF* II.2, 48, 52–3, 62–4, to which I would add this. In the novella by Thomas Lodge that is closely followed, by and large, in *As You Like It*, the eldest brother's change of heart comes from reflection while imprisoned by the envious usurper: 'brothers that are sonnes of one father, should live in friendship without jarre' and by mistreating his youngest brother he has, he realizes, 'sought to pervert Nature by unkindnesse'. This lonely meditation issues in resolve to be penitent and do some penance, so as to pacify the youngest brother's wrath. When the youngest rescues the eldest from the lion, he discovers the eldest *already* '*reformed*': *Rosalynde* (1590), in Bullough, *Narrative and Dramatic Sources of Shakespeare*, II, 198, 218. In Shakespeare's play, however, it is the rescue itself that, by its example of self-sacrificial mercy, works in Oliver what is not merely a change of heart but a real conversion, like a miracle in its rapidity and completeness: 'my conversion/So sweetly tastes, being the thing I am': 4, iii, 135–6.

[219] That it is from the outset a comedy is well argued in Gless, *Measure for Measure, the Law, and the Convent*, Ch. 1 ('The Problem of Kind'); the book gives a reading of the play *broadly* similar to mine, though on the basis only of distinctly Protestant understandings of the issues and entire unawareness of the possible relevance of Albert and Isabella. It also gives a good sense of the main and radically discordant currents of interpretation that make this a 'problem play' even if, in the end, we judge that it is not a problem play in the

redemptive—remedial—not, or not merely, in the Lutheran sense that a veil is drawn over sins but in the Catholic sense defined by the Council of Trent in 1547 and echoed in the words of Isabella quoted in the Tasioulas essay:

> Why, all the souls that were, were forfeit once,
> And He that might the vantage best have took
> Found out the remedy. How would you be
> If He which is the top of judgement should
> But judge you as you are? O, think on that,
> And mercy then will breathe within your lips,
> *Like man new made.* (II, ii, 74–8)[220]

The direct subject of the renovation (or rather, re-creation) envisaged by Isabella is the (proposed) giver of mercy (Angelo), but only as himself the object already (she reminds him) of remedial divine mercy—so that his new-found mercifulness would be a first, moral effect, so to speak, of that mercy shown to him (and all of us). Isabella's appeal to Angelo here is modelled on the gospel passage behind the play's title, the Sermon on the Mount. The Sermon is sketching the justice of the Kingdom, in which sin and division are healed by mercy:

> Be ye therefore merciful, as your father also is merciful . . . forgive, and ye shall be forgiven. Give, and it shall be given unto you: a good *measure*, pressed downe, shaken together and running over shall men give into your bosom: for with what *measure* ye mete [measure out], with the same [measure] shall men mete [measure out] to you again. (Luke 6: 36–8, *Geneva Bible* 1557)[221]

That a higher synthesis can be accomplished by mercy and forgiveness is something enacted in Shakespeare's comedies and late 'romances', and is made possible, according to the tradition re-articulated at Trent, by conversion, the inward 'making holy and *making new*' whereby one from unjust '*is made*' just, and from enemy [of God] '*is made*' friend.[222] In a conversion not simply moral (as needed for these Shakespeare

---

sense restated by the Tasioulas essay: 'an unsuccessful attempt at overlaying the logic of comedy on an essentially tragic theme'. I regret that 2011a appeared too late to be discussed in their essay.

[220] Citations are to the Arden Shakespeare edition of *MfM* (1965). As to this passage, I agree with Parker, *The Slave of Life*, 113 (and 233) that it articulates Shakespeare's 'solution' to the problems of justice and mercy in this play, and to the end of his last play.

[221] The Rheims (Catholic) version of 1582 ends 'For with the same measure that you do mete, it shall be measured to you again.'

[222] Council of Trent, 6th session, Decree on Justification (January 1547), cap. 7:

The nature and causes of the sinner's justification
. . . justification itself . . . is not only the remission of sins but the sanctification and *making new* {*renovatio*} of the interior man . . . whereby from unjust one becomes just, and from enemy a friend . . .

The causes of this justification are these . . . The final cause [purpose] is the glory of God and of Christ, and life everlasting. The efficient cause is *the merciful God* {*misericors Deus*} . . . The meritorious cause is . . . Jesus Christ . . . by his most holy suffering on . . . the cross . . . Finally, the single formal [essential] cause is 'the justice of God, not that by which he himself is just, but that by which he *makes* us just' [Augustine, *De Trinitate* 14.12.15], namely the justice which we have as a gift from him and by which we are spiritually *made new*. Thus, not only are we considered just, but we are truly called just and *we are* just, each receiving in oneself one's own justice

comedies) but fully religious (as these comedies also hint), the efficient cause of this 'being new made within'—'making new the inner man'—is (the Council had said) God precisely as merciful {*misericors Deus*}, and the 'formal', that is, most essential cause is the justice of God, not in the sense of God's being just but in the sense of his 'making us just' so that we are 'made new {*renovamur*} ... according to the measure {*secundum mensuram*} that the Holy Spirit wills to each respectively [1 Cor 12: 11] and according to each one's particular disposition and co-operation.'

Understood, and played, as achieving comedic resolution,[223] the plot of *MfM* requires that Angelo be reformed—that his heart indeed, as he says without hope or desire of advantage, be penitent (which includes remorse); and that he will be able to live up to the Duke's dispositive injunctions, 'Look that you love your wife: her worth, worth yours' and 'Joy to you, Mariana; love her, Angelo'. The comedy also requires that even Lucio—charming, brilliant, witty, acerbic, yes, but also selfish and a wanton calumniator—will *not*, in his compulsory and punitive marriage to the wench/punk whom he had begot with child and abandoned, be rendered, as he *claims* he fears, merely a cuckold. In setting aside comedy to the extent it does, the Tasioulas essay makes light of Angelo's penitence and takes an indulgent view of Lucio's unmotivated character assassinations of responsible persons.[224] And it takes a gloomy view of Barnardine, once a murderer, yes, but one who for nine years has passed up opportunities to escape and lived harmlessly for little more than drink: hardly likely to be a menace on the streets of Vienna/Brussels/London even if the friar's advices about the hope of 'better times to come' in 'a better place'(cf. 4, ii, 140–4, 206–7; 5, i, 478–83) fail to yield a conversion—and why should they fail to, given the sheer spirit shown by Barnadine in his hilarious refusal to come forth to be executed?

I doubt above all that we should take the essay's downbeat view of the Duke. In allegory, as M.D.H. Parker argued, he is Christian Providence itself (albeit very humanly refracted).[225] Non-allegorically, on the other hand, he could scarcely fail to have been seen by the 1604 courtly audience, as—also—an allusive Albert, the Duke of Austria (born in New Vienna) who at the Pope's behest[226] laid down the ecclesiastical robes he had worn as a (lay) cardinal and archbishop-elect, and left the governance of

---

according to the measure which 'the Holy Spirit apportions to each individually as he wills' (1 Cor. 12:11) and according to one's own disposition and cooperation.

Gless, *Measure for Measure, the Law, and the Convent*, 109–110, accepts the centrality, in the play, of the plea that ends 'Like man new made', but does so without élan and of course attributing the theology to Paul (say, Ephesians 4:24; Colossians 3:10–13) rather than Trent (which emphasized the making new rather than the Lutheranly construable 'putting on' of newness).

[223] Bennett, *'Measure for Measure' as Royal Entertainment*, showed, I think, how the play is a true and brilliant *comedy*, plotted and crafted with supreme skill and control, probably written for presentation at the court at Christmastide 1604. Had she been aware of the (many) powerful allusions to the Archdukes (as Albert and Isabella were universally known) she could not have been as anxious as her book is about the allusions to King James being too strong and direct to be easily acceptable.

[224] Such as the Duke (e.g. 3, ii, 120–36; 5, i, 253–5) and the Duke's *alter ego* (5, i, 130–3, 137–9, 151; 261–3; 302; 331–7) and Friar Peter (5, i, 337–9). On the vulnerability of princes to the effects of such defamation, see the Duke's expostulations at 3, ii, 179–82; 4, i, 60–4; 5, i, 521). See also Stevenson, 'The Role of James I in Shakespeare's *Measure for Measure*', 197–8.

[225] Parker, *The Slave of Life*, 118.

[226] Cf. *MfM* 3, ii, 213.

Belgium in the hands of his cousin[227] for 11 months while he went to marry Isabella, Duchess of Austria, from early girlhood an informal (later a formal) votaress of the Order of St. Clare. As joint rulers of Belgium, Albert and Isabella together had since 1599 been running a remarkably holy and monastic court while very publicly resolved upon trying to beget together an heir and so secure their adopted nation's independence. Certain members, at least, of the English court audience had no need to assume flawlessness of Albert, or of the play's Duke (never named on stage), for them to find themselves entering agreeably into the play's fancy of a new order of governance and society, a new synthesis higher and more godlike than that emergent from their own new monarch's bookish religio-moralism and complicitous tolerance of an English court 'new made' (for many of its members) as grossly drunken and licentious.[228] With sure nerve, Shakespeare has his Hapsburg Duke, garbed as a Catholic ecclesiastic, stand alone before the Scots King of England and declaim in antique, hieratic rhythm an ideology of governance strongly reminiscent of Albert and Isabella's *Pietas Austriaca*[229]:

[227] Cardinal Andrew of Austria. The Duke four times calls his deputy Angelo 'cousin'—a term which, by itself, could be ambiguous between genealogy and friendship, but takes on a strong suggestiveness in light of all the other allusions to the persons and situation of Albert and Isabella. While deputed by the Emperor to govern Cologne in 1582, Andrew (though an ordained priest and bishop publicly committed to the chastity of celibacy) fathered two illegitimate children by Elisa Ferreri. In the 15 months between his handing back the rulership of Belgium to Albert and his death in Rome in 1600 he manifested the great piety and humility that was publicly acknowledged by the Pope and is recorded on his tomb. During his tenure as deputy for the Archduke (September 1598 to August 1599), Andrew more than once sent emissaries to London and Elizabeth's court to negotiate for peace with England: see (2002d) at 62. Of course, Shakespeare took his story of the hypocritical deputy in large part from the Italian Cinthio's *Hecatommithi*; but see also n. 229 on a tantalizing real-life parallel.

[228] See Harrison, *A Jacobean Diary*, 33–4, for an instance very early in the reign.

[229] See van Wyhe, 'Court and Convent', 414, 425–9 and *passim* on Albert and Isabella's distinctive cultivation of the *Pietas Austriaca* (Habsburg piety), in which the Habsburg ideal of a Holy Court (*aula sacra*) was given the specific twist that their court imaged a monastery, demanded chastity of both men and women, but encouraged marriage and provided endowments to those of its ladies in waiting who married. Sexual liaisons with Isabella's ladies were stringently forbidden (and the ladies were inducted into the Isabella's service with ceremonies designed to recall a convent such as the Poor (Discalced) Clare convent that had been central to Isabella's upbringing in Madrid as eldest daughter of the King of Spain). When a maid, some time between 1599 and 1612 (quite possibly in or before 1604) was made pregnant, the offending courtier was required by Albert to marry her with a view to immediate execution (beheading) after the marriage and its consummation—and only the strenuous intercession of the Spanish ambassador and Papal nuncio saved the young courtier. See Brennan, *The Travel Diary (1611–1612) of an English Catholic Sir Charles Somerset*, 292–3. (The courtly English visitor Sir Charles Somerset—brother of the man whose mid-1600 court wedding celebration occasioned, I believe, *As You Like It*—says in his diary (288) that Isabella's ladies 'are kept up as if they were in a Nunnerie' and (287) that the archiducal palace 'is none of the fairest, but the order of it, and the government of it both of the Archduke and his servants quarters, and also of the Infanta [Isabella] and her ladies in her quarter, both for virtue and piety is such that it may be the pattern for many other princes to take example by it'. In the early 1600s, Albert and Isabella walked (as 'cold gradation' at *MfM* 4, iii, 99 may allusively recall) every Saturday the league from the gates of Brussels to a sacred fountain near Laeken, to pray there for their fertility, since unless they bore a successor, Belgium would revert to Spain, a national destiny they honestly, and with an acquired Belgian patriotism, strove to avoid.)

  The envoys of Albert and Isabella were resident in London during the year running up to the peace treaty England signed with them (and Spain) at Somerset House in July 1604; so the ways of the Archdukes would be well known by report in London courtly circles when the play was first staged.

  The playwright maintains judicious deniability, not to mention a surer way to the King's heart, by including in the Duke's speech more than one echo of James's own moral writings: Stevenson, 'The Role of James I in Shakespeare's *Measure for Measure*', 197–9.

> He who the sword of heaven will bear
> Must be *as holy as severe*:
> Pattern in himself to know,
> Grace to stand, and virtue, go:
> More nor less to others paying
> Than by self-offenses weighing.
> (3, ii, 254–60, emphasis added here as elsewhere)

That is to say: what is needed for attaining the right measure(s) is holiness, grace to stand firm and constant in temptation and adversity, and virtue to go forward in life and outwards from oneself, in line with the Duke's original counsel to Angelo: 'if our virtues/Did not go forth of us, 'twere all alike/As if we had them not' (1, i, 34–5). More potent in our image of the Duke than any 'self-referential attitude' or 'arrogating of all acts of mercy to himself' is, I suggest, the brilliance of his resourceful, adaptive mastering of evil as it unpredictably unfolds, and his managing-directing of a five act comedy of his own devising, as the fifth act of our play.[230] His comedy makes sense—as our play makes comedic sense—only if it was devised as above all an awesomely rigorous test and proof of, *pace* Tasioulas, Isabella's mercy, and thus as a final act in the Duke's original, part hidden, part intimated plan to test 'our seemers'.[231]

Isabella's plea for Angelo ends with some incoherence or irrelevance, but it is real enough. In the play's staging of a new order, one which the Duke's science, art, and practice of 'government' (1, i, 3) (including self-government) brings out of the lethal disorder of criminality and legal pseudo-justice, good but not flawless people like Isabella[232] and

---

[230] Bennett, *'Measure for Measure' as Royal Entertainment*, Ch. 5, shows that Act 5, entirely stage-managed (as *MfM*'s audience is enjoyably aware) by the Duke (see 4, v, 1–9 and 4, vi, 3–8), itself consists of five 'Acts'.

[231] Parker, *The Slave of Life*, 121 reasonably sees Isabella's kneeling to plead for Angelo—she who never knelt to Angelo—as the choice, the option for mercy, the passing of the test, to which 'the whole play tends', and with it the Duke's 'goading' (Tasioulas) of Isabella, his 'final twist of the knife' (Parker). On the Duke's plan of testing puritanical attitudes ('Precisian' being then a pejorative synonym for Puritan) for their underlying humanity or lack of it, see *MfM* 1, iii, 48 to the end:

> More reasons for this action
> At our more leisure shall I render you;
> Only this one: Lord Angelo is precise;
> Stands at a guard with Envy; scarce confesses
> That his blood flows, or that his appetite
> Is more to bread than stone. Hence shall we see
> If power change purpose, what our seemers be.

If any of this is right, 'serious considerations of justice and mercy' are for the Duke, not unwanted intrusions on 'the theatrics of his final scene', [p. 234], but rather the very point of those theatrics. For my exegesis and interpretation of his 'The very mercy of the law cries out' speech (as broad comedy, indeed farce), see 2011a, 100–1.

[232] Her harshness in denunciation at 3, i, 135–49, observed by the Duke, was unmeasured in a puritanical way. But though a strict moral analysis cannot fully follow the Duke (3, ii, 270–5; 4, i, 71–5) (and Isabella: 5, i, 448–52), or Helena (and Mariana and the Widow) in *All's Well* (or Leah and her father in *Genesis* 29: 21–4, and Leah's son Judah's widowed daughter-in-law Thamar in *Genesis* 38: 14–26), in justifying the bed-trick (see my discussion in *CEJF* II.2, 58, including n. 54), the fault on the side of those who arrange it seems slight enough when, as in these plays, the man is already and independently resolved on fornication (if not rape) and the deception's well-judged purpose is to convert him—as a consequence of, though not alas in, the sex act—*from* that vicious disposition *to* the marital commitment and fidelity to marriage enacted in the woman's own participatory sex act. So we need not see in Isabella anything so flawed as 'a narcissistic concern with her own chastity rather than with the morality of the situation' [p. 231].

perhaps even the Duke himself have been *made better*—why doubt it?—by, or at least in, being humbled. Much in the play's structure and language invites its audience to sense this as on one level a kind of pageant of the redemption available—as Christmas testifies—by divine initiative and human cooperation—a pageant, that is, of the justice of the eternal kingdom which begins in this world, a higher synthesis made possible by the *healing and converting effects* of mercy and forgiveness, that is, of a kind of eschatological equity. (Equity in particular is the non-standard—exceptional—but apt way of pursuing the law's objective and intention: *common good* in some specifiable respect.) In this world, of course, as responsible persons in the play have stated and repeated,[233] the choice to have mercy on others and forgive them, without a grounded expectation of moral conversion, may well be mere foolish injustice.

15.

The theses **Patrick Lee** argues for in his essay are fundamental and important, and in the culture of our time stand increasingly in need of defence, a defence increasingly likely to go unexamined or ill-understood. The more willing one becomes to attribute rights to subrational animals (say, great apes, or dolphins), the less grasp one can have (if any) of the *equal* entitlement of human beings, *as* rational animals, to basic rights. *Equality* of basic *human* rights entails predicating a radical discontinuity between all human beings and all other animals—the former all having the nature of animals with a radical (basic)[234] capacity for understanding not only desirable options but also the responsibility they have to reflect on those options' alternative merits and choose freely among them; and the latter having a nature that, like even great apes and dolphins, shows no sign of having (even radically) *that* capacity. Most valuable in this essay are Lee's passages of argumentation showing, in quite different contexts, the need to be willing to affirm such discontinuities.

A first instance is his showing, against Singer, that counting dispositional but non-occurrent desires makes no sense unless one is willing to count also the basic/radical capacity for such desires [p. 240]. For it is a capacity of this kind that is more and more actuated and determined as one moves towards (or away from) having the disposition to desire, through stages of *not quite having*, to (or from) actually having that disposition, and then through the stages of not quite having to (or from) actually having occurrent desires, and so forth. The point is not a *sorites* one, but rather a disclosing of what makes it possible to count having a disposition as significant for attributing (better: acknowledging, recognizing) rights or status as a bearer of rights. A second, different kind of instance is the radical discontinuity between, on the one hand, the accumulation of countless small changes that contribute to and accompany the coming together of spermatozoon and oocyte and, on the other hand, the coming into being of the new organism that sets off on a course of life and development fundamentally

---

[233] For example, Escalus, 2, i, 279–82: '[Severity] is but needful. Mercy is not itself, that oft looks so;/ Pardon is still [= always] the nurse of second woe.' Likewise, Angelo, 2, ii, 101–5.

[234] Lee uses 'basic capacity' throughout and, when explicating my use of 'radical capacity', he (rightly) takes for granted (I think) that they are synonymous.

different from the life and course of development of the inherently short-lived cells whose penetration by the one and transforming absorption by the other made that new thing possible and immediately actual [p. 247].

Our confidence that fidelity to truth calls for recognizing the radical discontinuities involved in such predicates as 'is a new substance' or indeed 'is an individual [animal; person]' is a confidence given warrant by the transparency that one's own existence (with its awareness, its concerns, its reflections, and its choices to act) has for oneself.[235] Lee's essay, in its central section and central contribution [pp. 241–3], deploys reflections on this transparent, experiential, non-inferential yet fully secure knowledge, to draw out and put in view the content and implications it has in our understanding of first principles of practical reason, principles that pick out ways in which one's being is not simply a fact but also a locus of opportunities (and vulnerabilities) that *matter*.[236] 'The point', in Lee's words, 'is to uncover the extension of the first practical principles themselves—to make explicit what is known when one apprehends that life, know-ledge, etc., are goods worthy of pursuit for myself and others like me. Implicit in the first principles of practical reason is the truth that what is to be pursued, promoted, protected, is the well-being of *rational* beings' who are, indeed, rational *substantial* beings [p. 242]. This, I would say, is an uncovering not only of the extension of the first practical principles but also of their intension, their meaning (content and normativity) in relation to each of the beings whose flourishing they direct us towards.[237]

That is why, as Lee's title has it, natural law theory has a position on what the subjects of rights *are* (beings of a rational nature), and more fundamentally on how and why it is that there are rights and right bearers at all. For such a theory is not just about goods or values and the directiveness or normativity of propositions picking out those goods as pursuitworthy. It moves back and forth along the sequence traced by the epistemological axiom (that our nature is understood by understanding the objects of the acts which we have the capacity to do and the capacity freely to choose)[238]—'back and forth' because always open to deploying one's understanding of objects to enhance one's understanding of nature(s), and to deploying understanding of nature(s) to enhance understanding of possibilities and thus of objects intelligently judged desir-able. The most far-reaching and fundamental of the kinds of radical discontinuity relevant to human existence and equality is the discontinuity *in kind* between matter and spirit (rational soul), a discontinuity or disparity entirely though mysteriously compatible with the unity of matter and spirit in the human animal, a unity so thoroughgoing that Aquinas will explain the human rational soul as the *act* and *form* of the body. Lee's essay leaves these terms and categories in the sober implicitness of the

---

[235] See *NLNR*, 40: 'There is much to be said for the view that the order of dependence was precisely the opposite—that the teleological conception of nature was made plausible, indeed conceivable, by analogy with the introspectively luminous, self-evident structure of human well-being, practical reasoning, and human purposive action: read Aristotle, *Physics* II.8: 199a9–19.'

[236] This mattering is the objective counterpart of the sense of pre-moral responsibility that Lee [pp. 241–2] and Boyle [p. 58] call to our attention.

[237] See *CEJF* III.Introduction, 5.

[238] See section 3 (response to Haldane) at pp. 469–70.

term 'rational nature', rather as he here leaves the basic good of marriage in the sober inexplicitness of 'other actualizations of our basic potentialities' [p. 241]. One understands the good of marriage not, in the first instance, as an actualization of potentiality but rather as the carrying out of a free choice of commitment to carry out, across a lifetime, a cooperation in activities engaging every level of one's natural reality including the highest levels, at which aspirations to meaning,[239] understanding of responsibilities, and care for what matters define what one is doing. Reflection on such a kind of activity (practice, institution), if informed by practical reason's understanding of its worth, provides one good way among others of coming to terms, philosophically, with 'rational nature'. The essay outlines a firm grounding[240] for that, set out as the authentic and much needed public discourse and reason(ing) it is.

16.

Gerard V. Bradley gives us a really new and penetrating framework for understanding the doctrinal condition of our law[241] about the human and constitutional rights of the unborn. Just how new may be sensed by asking oneself why the preceding sentence did not conclude with the words 'our law about abortion'. Even that most stringent of the early critics of *Roe v. Wade*, Robert F. Byrn, the New York law professor who earlier had personally initiated litigation to defend the unborn,[242] and had sat on the New York Governor's commission of inquiry on abortion law, wrote that 'abortion statutes are the proper vehicle for protecting unborn children'.[243] My only criticism of Bradley's essay is that, as I shall suggest later, it may not quite sufficiently take into account how thoroughly that restriction of doctrinal perspective shapes the course of the *Roe v. Wade* opinion. Be that as it may, the essay reveals the extent and drastic doctrinal consequences of the restriction itself.

The laws of now 38 US states explicitly recognize the crime of fetal homicide, at least 24 of these encompassing some wrongful causing of death at any time after conception.[244] In their present forms these laws all postdate *Roe v. Wade* and, in many cases, represent a deliberate pushback against the thinking behind that remarkable assault on laws and principles in place in every state in the union. But law of comparable purpose and import existed in many jurisdictions long before 1973—in England from at latest 1929, when the Infant Life (Preservation) Act by its first section created the felony of causing (by wilful act done with intent to destroy its life) the death of a child, capable of being born alive,[245] before it has an existence independent of its mother. Bradley's essay

---

[239] On the purpose(s) of such commitment, see p. 543 at n. 297 in this essay.

[240] See further Lee and George, *Body-Self Dualism in Contemporary Ethics and Politics*.

[241] 'Our law' in a wide sense: the travails of US constitutional doctrine in this area are very substantially replicated in the doctrine of European and, say, Canadian human rights law, however unclear the identity may seem at first glance.

[242] See Byrn, 'The Supreme Court on Abortion', 840–2; on the bad, Kelsenian legal philosophy engaged to defeat Byrn's action, see *CEJF* II.1, 27.

[243] Byrn, 'The Supreme Court on Abortion', 856.   [244] *CEJF* I.16, 257n.

[245] This surely meant (as is made plain by a reference to '24 weeks' in the equivalent statutory provision in force in New York in 1967: see Byrn, 'The Supreme Court on Abortion', n. 298) an unborn child who has reached the stage of viability: see Keown, *The Law and Ethics of Medicine*, 181–92.

describes some of the recent applications of fetal homicide law, which bring forcibly to our notice the plausibility of the convicted offenders' unavailing pleas that they are being flagrantly denied the equal protection of the law (as a rule and doctrine, call it Equal Protection). The laws under which they have been convicted punish them for ending somebody's life, with *mens rea* of a kind standard in felony law, and without justification or excuse of a kind standard in homicide law (notably as self-defence or defence of another).[246] Whether or not those laws name the offence (as many do) 'homicide' or (as many do) something else such as 'child destruction', and whether or not they define the unborn-child victim as 'a person', matters little or not at all. These offenders are being convicted and punished for conduct substantially identical to the kind of conduct by mothers and their agents that *Roe v. Wade* and its successors declare incapable of being made a crime. Of course, in some cases the mother and her agents would be entitled, under standard laws against homicide (or child destruction), to be acquitted, their conduct being justified as self-defence[247]; and doubtless very few of those charged now with fetal homicide or child destruction could in practice (given the circumstances of their lethal conduct) avail themselves of such a defence. But the plea of denial of Equal Protection has its bite because the mother and her agents, unlike offenders of the kind highlighted in Bradley's essay, can never now be put in a position where she or they might need to raise such defences, in relation to conduct the same as (if not even more purposefully lethal than) these offenders'.

The essay's discussion of *Roe v. Wade* is expository, drawing out the three Propositions that give rise to these apparent denials of Equal Protection. Proposition One (the unborn are not Fourteenth Amendment 'persons') undergirds the nullification of every state law criminalizing abortion by or at the behest of a woman who deems it to be for her welfare.[248] Proposition Two (the courts are incompetent to determine when human life begins) and Proposition Three (legislatures may determine when persons begin) together undergird the legislation under which the fetal homicide or child destruction laws have been enacted and indeed extended and strengthened, in their application to everyone save the mother and her agents. That the proviso in the last six words involves a denial of Equal Protection was manifestly not contemplated by the court in *Roe v. Wade* or by its early critics, or even, I think, by Bradley in his own 1993 critique of *Roe v. Wade*,[249] a critique incidental to his devastation of Ronald Dworkin's account and defence of the case.

---

[246] Byrn, 'The Supreme Court on Abortion', 853–4, thinks not of self-defence (or defence of another) but only of 'necessity'; Bradley, '*Life's Dominion*: A Review Essay', 345–6, rightly brings into consideration both justification ('justifiable self-defense') and excuse.

[247] Bradley says [p. 256] that the justification defence of self-defence in a trial for homicide extends to cases where the defendant feared (or, perhaps, reasonably feared) that the deceased 'was going to kill, or cause serious bodily harm'. That seems right, though the equivalent defence in child-destruction statutes (such as the 1929 Act in England) is commonly limited to threats to *life*. If, as Bradley says [p. 249, n. 2], the Court in n. 54 of *Roe v. Wade* was stating or implying that the defence of self-defence in general homicide law extends only to defence of *life*, and not to defence (of self or other) against imminent grave bodily harm or imminent rape, that suggests to me (and not only me) that footnote 54 was intended not as an expression of genuine 'worries' but as a debating point, an ironical if not cynical lampooning of Texas's position (and law).

[248] See n. 254 in this essay.

[249] Bradley, '*Life's Dominion*: A Review Essay', 333–59; on pp. 345–6 he canvasses the question whether, in a legal regime that recognized the right of the unborn to Equal Protection (and/or to Due Process), it

All three Propositions are indefensible, though the third has a defensible sense. If told that their proposed Fourteenth Amendment would have the constitutional effect of protecting not only former slaves and their descendants but also unborn children, there is scant reason to think the requisite majorities for ratification would have fallen away.[250] And on any less originalist but still defensible criterion of constitutional interpretation and development, 'any person' in the Constitution should have been taken to include the unborn child, for the purposes of the limited but important protections relevant to, and reasonable in light of, its (his or her) condition, on a footing of equality, and no more than equality, of right to life with its mother.[251] *A fortiori*, by criteria of interpretation sufficiently accommodating to make possible the attribution of constitutional rights such as those announced in *Griswold v. Connecticut*, *Eisenstadt v. Baird*,[252] and *Lawrence v. Texas*, not to mention *Roe v. Wade* itself and many other developments of constitutional doctrine more secure and reasonable than those. The legitimate interpretative development in relation to 'person' should have occurred as soon as the issue was squarely raised. Logically speaking, it is squarely raised by enactments which break free from categories such as 'inducing a miscarriage', and attend instead to 'destruction of the life of the unborn child'. But noticing the logic is another matter.[253]

---

would be compatible with Equal Protection to make the abortionist team criminally liable *but not the mother* requesting the abortion.

[250] Bradley, '*Life's Dominion*: A Review Essay', 344. To the evidence his present essay assembles about opinion in 1866–8, and the different, convergent evidence in Byrn, 'The Supreme Court on Abortion', 835–8, I would add, for example, the statement of the Supreme Court of Iowa in the year of ratification of the Fourteenth Amendment:

> The common law is distinguished, and is to be commended, for its all-embracing and salutary solicitude for the sacredness of human life and the personal safety of every human being. This protecting, paternal care, enveloping every individual like the air he breathes, not only extends to persons actually born, but, for some purposes, to infants *in ventre sa mere* 1 Black. Com. 129.
> The right to life and to personal safety is not only sacred in the estimation of the common law, but it is inalienable. It is no defense to the defendant that the abortion was procured with the consent of the deceased.
> The common law stands as a general guardian holding its aegis to protect the life of all. Any theory which robs the law of this salutary power is not likely to meet with favor.

State v. Moore 25 Iowa 128 at 135–6 (1868); see Byrn, 'The Supreme Court on Abortion', 839.

[251] On the fragility of the reasons adduced in *Roe v. Wade* for denying the constitutional status of 'person' to the unborn, see *CEJF* I.16, 268–9, 275–6n; *CEJF* II.1, 27–8. On fairness between mother and unborn child, see *CEJF* III.19, 307–11.

[252] On the illegitimacy of the interpretative neutrality between good and evil in *Griswold* and *Eisenstadt*, see *CEJF* V.3, 70–1.

[253] I for one never got it into focus. In 1993b I began my survey of 'the legal status of the unborn baby' thus:

> The unborn baby (conceptus, zygote, embryo and foetus) has a fairly well-protected status in English law, except as against his or her mother and her medical advisers or agents or, if conceived outside the womb, against the technicians who have come into possession of the set of gametes from which he or she was conceived. Let me consider first, then, the status of the unborn child as against strangers—meaning always, by 'stranger', someone who is not the mother or her medical advisers or agents or technicians of the sort just mentioned.
> It has never been murder for a stranger to kill an unborn child within the womb intentionally. Nor has it ever been manslaughter for a stranger to cause the death of the unborn child within the womb by some act of gross negligence or some unlawful and dangerous act. Such acts, if intended to kill the unborn child or prevent its live birth, have always been in English law a

As for Propositions Two and Three, they knock each other out, leaving the true position: courts and legislatures alike have the responsibility to judge correctly who are entitled as of right to their protection in relation to their most basic interests. On such a matter, they are not entitled to be agnostic, and not entitled to err. Precisely what forms such protection should in justice take is a matter on which there is properly a margin of appreciation—room for a variety of constitutional, legislative, and common-law positions. Even when strongly urged to do so, no court has shown any inclination to challenge or question the correctness of the judgments implicitly and often explicitly made—about the entitlement of the unborn to protection—by the very many legislatures that have enacted fetal homicide and analogous criminal-law protections for the unborn. Indeed, once the issue is got free from the narrow perspective of concern with 'abortion', 'inducing miscarriage', and the like—of things that happen (or are done) to the mother—the judgment called for by the truth of the matter is obvious enough. But the court in *Roe v. Wade* was not challenged or invited to move beyond that narrow perspective.[254] This neither justifies nor excuses the pervasive juridical ineptness of its judgment—to say nothing of injustice. (Still less does it excuse the open wickedness of *Casey*'s rationale—brought out by Bradley [p. 267]—that the powerful have made their dispositions on the assumption that the powerless will be made not to count, an assumption which the Court said must not be disturbed.) But the hitherto undisturbed narrowness of perspective does go some way to explaining how it is that the resultant juridical dilemma, a dilemma undeniably inherent in *Roe v. Wade*, comes (courtesy of Bradley's essay) as news to many of us, certainly me.

serious offence (called by the leading 17th and 18th century legal writers a 'great misprision', though not a felony), and since 1803 such acts—intended to destroy the life of the unborn child—have been the statutory offence which we commonly call abortion (see below).

The basis is there, but the article never gets closer than half-way:

The unborn are human beings with the rights of persons from conception, above all the fundamental right to life, on a basis of equality. That truth has been more and more clearly articulated and defended by the Church, in the face of ideologies, practices and opinions. A consistent defence of these rights can now no longer admit any difference of principle between abortion and other forms of homicide. Full and equal protection of the state's *laws against homicide should be accepted as extending to the unborn. There should be no special law prohibiting abortion.*

The article includes a response to difficulties commonly raised by people of good will against treating the unborn as persons.

[254] Can it be right to say that 'Proposition One had no point or significance in *Roe* save to block the bringing of abortion under the ordinary laws about killing' or that it 'has no meaning apart from the proposition that the decision to kill the unborn was exempted from the operation of the criminal law's homicide proscriptions, including its provisions about justified use of deadly force'? [p. 252]. No one asked the court to consider or reflect on the operation of the ordinary laws about killing, on the criminal law's homicide proscriptions, or even on the laws creating offences of child destruction (laws in which the position of the mother was not in focus). I know of no reason to suppose that the majority Justices, or most of them, gave those laws (actual or possible) any thought. Proposition One was conceived, I am confident, as a proposition about blocking the application to women and their (medical-professional) agents of any laws against abortion or induced miscarriage. The essay's main arguments remain intact.

On the spell of the term 'abortion', confining thought to woman's pregnancy, consider the effort to make infanticide palatable by styling it 'post-birth abortion': see 2013b ('Capacity, Harm and Experience in the Life of Persons as Equals').

17.

Anthony Fisher OP's disappointment with 20th-century bioethics [p. 269] is amply justified. Indeed, it is felt even more keenly by those who began their philosophical reflections on ethics in the decade and a half after the Second World War. In those days, revulsion at the abuses which the Nazis perpetrated—in some fields developing them in seamless continuity with advanced medico-ethical thinking of the 1920s— seemed capable of reversing the slide, accelerating from the late nineteenth century, into medico- and bio-ethical laissez-faire or (its predictable counterpart) totalitarian appropriation of utilitarian rationalizations. Oaths and declarations were drafted to affirm, for example, that—

> I.5...Concern for the interests of the subject of biomedical research must always prevail over the interests of science and society.

> III.4 In research on man, the interest of science and society should never take precedence over considerations related to the well-being of the subject.[255]

By the turn of the millennium, the World Medical Association had replaced those clauses with—

> 21. Medical research involving human subjects may only be conducted if the import- ance of the objective outweighs the inherent risks and burdens to the research subjects.[256]

As we know, such 'weighing' of incommensurables to pronounce such means 'justified by the end' ('the importance of the objective') cannot fail to be the re-description of something else. This something else might be the application of some conventional standard(s) or criteria of fairness, or it might be directly linked to some emotional motivation, such as group or individual self-preference, a motivation which often enough operates by harnessing reason to rationalize the originating passions behind the relevant preference or policy or conventional standard—those mentioned by the essay as embodiments of 'arbitrary preferences' amongst persons or goods [p. 279]. Bioethics committees have as one of their unadvertised functions the raising of such rationalizations to new levels of sophistication and efficacy.

The essay wonders whether we exponents of the 'new natural law theory' (sad name!) do not share 'a certain suspicion of emotions and passions' in our writings [p. 277].[257] What suspicion we have is not a mite more than reason requires. No theory holds more firmly than ours that emotion is a necessary accompaniment of

---

[255] World Medical Association, *Declaration of Helsinki*; *CEJF* II.17, 296. The Declaration, drafted in 1964, achieved this form in 1975.

[256] *WMA Declaration of Helsinki* revd through October 2008, <http://www.wma.net/en/30publications/ 10policies/b3/index.html> (accessed 27 November 2012).

[257] The other suspicion attributed to us is of state involvement in healthcare; but this is a matter on which I was unaware of any common thought or attitude (or for that matter any diversity) among us, beyond standard general teaching on subsidiarity. Grisez, 'Health Care Technology and Justice' (2010) commends massive state involvement, on a sophisticated basis outlined in that essay, and Boyle's comment ('An Appreciative Response') at 256–7 does not demur. (On 'new natural law theory': p. 468, n. 31.)

rational action,[258] and when guided 'constitutionally'[259] by reasons affords an invaluable support for upright deliberation and choices in face of difficulties and temptations to defect to the lazy, the popular, the selfish, or other non-virtuous alternatives. But almost every form of human deviation from the virtuous is caused, and every form is accompanied and reinforced, by emotion. So, even without appeal to the revealed truths about original sin, philosophy must hold emotion in suspicion—as well as, when contemplating the virtuous or saintly, holding it in unfeigned honour.[260] In today's bioethics, *compassion* is the standard overt guise under which, or 'reason' for the sake of which, philosophers and 'ethicians' set aside—and consciences are obscured from seeing or hearing—the principles and virtues unfolded, expounded, and defended in Bishop Fisher's essay.[261]

18.

John Keown has assembled a comprehensive memorandum on writings and other interventions of mine in and around medical law.[262] After the leisurely weeks of simply academic research into schemes of abortion law,[263] in 1967–69, almost everything in the list was a work of urgent circumstance, done as the extended retreat from basically sound to basically unsound standards, criteria, rules, and practices gathered pace. Keown's first book[264] shows, in abortion law and medical attitudes in England over many centuries, how the long tides of history flow first one way and then turn and reverse with the momentum of a partly unthinking conformism of sentiment. In 1982, while his book was in its gestation, he and I worked together in preparation for one of the television debates noted in his essay's last footnote; it was shown on 2 January 1983, and concerned IVF, then in the infancy of its first triumphs. For our pains, the learned reviewer for the *New Scientist*, a week later, called my case as 'as odious as it was bizarre', mere 'obfuscation masquerading as clarity'. So Keown had no illusions about the nature of the public discourse in which, for 25 years, he has been advancing

---

[258] See 1987f (Grisez, Boyle and Finnis, 'Practical Principles, Moral Truths, and Ultimate Ends'), 99–100, 104–5, 121–2; <http://www.twotlj.org/ppmtue.pdf>. Summarily: *CEJF* I.Introduction, 14–15:

> Just as it is virtually impossible for even the most sophisticated mathematicians to think mathematically without some support from images (diagrams and the like) which they know perfectly well are partly false to mathematical reality, so it is impossible for bodily beings such as us to act without some support from our emotions and therefore from our imagination and memory.

See the whole paragraph; and p. 472 at n. 45 in this essay (response to Haldane).

[259] *Aquinas*, 72–8.

[260] Theology, too: in the encyclical *Caritas in Veritate* (2009), Benedict XVI (whose evocation of emotion in his address on his installation as pope brought the Romantic tradition of his native country into St. Peter's Square) wasted no time in getting to his proposition that love in truth is threatened, in a culture without truth, with 'falling prey to emotions' and subjection to 'the constraints of emotionalism': section 3; see also section 76.

[261] On compassion as ethical solvent, see Grisez, 'Death in Theological Reflection', 158–9, with cross-references to Pellegrino and others.

[262] I could add only some notes on developments in English case law for the shortlived *Bioethics Reporter* edited by James Childress in 1983–1985; whether more (or fewer) than half a dozen persons ever read them will doubtless never be known.

[263] Yielding 1970c (i) and (ii).

[264] Keown, *Abortion, Doctors and the Law*.

comparably odious masquerades—or rather, as I would say, clarifying contributions to honest and civil debate and discourse.[265]

As Keown's latest book makes clear, the founding fathers (or 'grandfather' and 'father') of English medical law, Glanville Williams and Ian Kennedy, have done the damage they have by abandoning *intention* for *causation* of outcomes, in elementary consequentialist fashion.[266] In the case especially of Kennedy, as Keown patiently shows, a body of work which began by affirming the significance and reality of intention developed gradually but inexorably into promotion of active euthanasia, because its author, like his predecessor, lacked a grip on the difference between what is intended and what is caused as a side effect. Neither he nor Williams could give an accurate statement—not even for the purpose of critique—of what they each called 'the principle of double effect'. Nor, more importantly, could they accurately state, even to criticize, the principle (called by Keown the inviolability of life) that killing, by action or omission, with intent to terminate or shorten life is to be excluded from social life.[267]

---

[265] Several of Keown's and my subsequent, separate writings in this and related fields have been in pursuit—almost always trailing too late, I fear—of scholarly deceptions (possibly, self-deceptions of astonishing extent and depth). On the infamous 'Historians' Brief', see his 'Back to the Future of Abortion Law: *Roe*'s Rejection of America's History and Legal Traditions' [2006], in Keown, *The Law and Ethics of Medicine*, 109; and my 1994d ('"Shameless Acts" in Colorado: Abuse of Scholarship in Constitutional Cases'). On analogous fabrications of history in the interests of Progress, see *CEJF* III.20, 323 n. 18; III.22, 359–80 and citations in nn. 91, 109; *CEJF* V.10, 173–4.

[266] Keown, *The Law and Ethics of Medicine*, Chs 2 and 3.

[267] In testimony to the Select Committee of the House of Lords on the Assisted Dying for the Terminally Ill Bill [Joffe Bill] in January 2005, I said:

> At present, there is a clear principle: never intend to kill the patient; never try to help patients to intentionally kill themselves. That is the law, it is the long-established common morality, it is the ethic of the health care profession and it is Article 2 of the European Convention on Human Rights, and so forth. There is a 'bright' line, and though like other laws and principles it is not invariably respected it is not in the least artificial or brittle; it rests on a rational principle that a person's life is the very reality of the person, and whatever your feelings of compassion you cannot intentionally try precisely to eliminate the person's reality and existence without disrespect to the person and their basic equality of worth with others. I think that that principle underlying the clear line is sound and right, though I am not here primarily to ask you to agree with it. Rather I am here to compare the present situation with the situation once any form of euthanasia or legalised assistance in suicide is admitted.
>
> In the new situation, any attempt to draw the line is necessarily artificial. The principles on which any attempted line would be based undermine each other and subvert the attempt to hold a line. If autonomy is the principal or main concern, why is the lawful killing restricted to terminal illness and unbearable suffering? If suffering is the principle or concern, why is the lawful killing restricted to terminal illness? Why must the suffering be unbearable if there is real and persistent discomfort? If suffering is unbearable, why should one have to wait for 14 days? If suffering and terminal prognosis are the concern, why is relief restricted to those who are capable of asking for it?
>
> Each of those questions is not simply a reason for doubting the rationality of any proposed line alternative to the present principled lines; each of the questions is also a reason why there will be much more abuse and secrecy and underground killing than at present, because each of those questions can and will be asked by any doctor faced with a patient demanding euthanasia or assistance in suicide or with a patient not demanding it but suffering or confronting an early death. Patient autonomy pushes the doctor to accede to requests that do not meet the legal criteria of terminality or suffering. Suffering, or terminality, and medical responsibility each push the doctor to set aside the requirement of voluntariness. All this will cause externally reinforced and profound changes in medical and professional ethics, so that intentional death-dealing becomes a clinical option and, of course, also a hospital management option and a nursing home option.

HL Paper 86 II Q. 1973. See Keown, *The Law and Ethics of Medicine*, 238–69.

IV. Philosophy of Law

19.

N. E. Simmonds here explores the relations between practices (individual and social, linguistic[268] and non-linguistic) and the ideas (individual and shared) that, as embodied in them, make them *practices* rather than mere behaviour—especially the ideas of value that settle the intended point(s) (purposes) of those practices. He also expresses, more than once, a doubt about the need for and sense of a general theoretical *description* of law. About both these issues, I have only supplementary observations to make.

On the role of practice, they can begin by adding a few words to his critique of Scott Shapiro's *Legality*. As Simmonds reports, the book moves mysteriously from the fact that elites depict their legal demands 'as activity that is supposed to solve moral problems' to the theoretical position that 'law has a moral aim'—'has' it in the sense that 'even in a legal system staffed by officials who merely pretend to pursue noble aims . . . it would nonetheless be true that the aim of legal activity in that system is moral in nature . . .' To illuminate this dark statement, Shapiro completes it with an analogy: 'much as the aim of assertion is to convey true information even though the asserter is lying'. What is it that makes the aim of assertion the conveying of true information even when the lying asserter aims to convey information he believes (usually correctly) to be false? Simmonds answers: in asserting, one subjects oneself to a special range of normative requirements (inapplicable to non-assertive utterances such as storytelling or poetry recitation). Yes, but how do these normative requirements (even assuming that they make it the case that the asserter *ought to* convey true information) make it the case that the *aim* of asserting *is* truth-conveying (even when the asserter's aim is to convey falsehood)? How does one get this *Is* from that *Ought*?

Taking my cue from Simmonds's general position, I would argue that it is true that 'the aim of assertion is to convey truth' because in the linguistic social practice of assertion—the practice which, by establishing[269] a semantic *type*, makes it possible to intend to assert, in the expectation that one will be understood as asserting—the precise point of a stating or uttering of that type is to indicate that one is intending to convey information one believes to be true. The practice exists, as a relatively precise type or form of practice, *in order to* make the conveying of true information (and of beliefs about the truth of information) possible, expeditious, and reliably intelligible. Liars can

---

[268] Simmonds's invocation of 'the tradition of political thought that stems most evidently from Aristotle directs its gaze outwards, towards established habits of conduct and ways of life'. True, and Aristotle chose to make prominent in his treatise on *Ethics* (his prolegomenon to *political* theory) numerous appeals to 'what everyone would say . . .' On this, see *FoE*, 17–19.

(Note that in the paragraph on p. 17 introducing this section of *FoE*, I say 'The "function" argument is not the deep structure of Aristotle's ethical method; it is an erratic boulder'. But there '"function" argument' should read '"unique function" argument', as it does read on p. 16, summarizing the argument made on p. 15 and recalled on p. 122.)

[269] I do not hold that there were no assertions prior to the establishing of the social practice. Thought heads towards assertion and denials, under the auspices of the self-evident first principle of reason (non-contradiction). And thought can precede language, creating as need be an initially private language: *Aquinas*, 196 (where I speak for myself).

exploit the practice precisely because that is its aim, that is, the shared aim with which people generally engage and participate in it (as speakers and audience); liars can state propositions they believe to be false with the intent and confident expectation that their statements will be taken to be true. Lying assertions are non-central instances of assertions because they abuse, exploit, and indeed oppose the point of the practice in its central form. And this centrality is established not merely or primarily, in my view,[270] by its being statistically typical, but above all because the practice responds to a *need* (for expeditious, reliably intelligible communication of intent to convey a proposition believed to be true).

The preceding paragraph sketches a plain, unmysterious sense in which 'assertion has a truth-conveying aim even when someone is lying' is true. In the practice as available alike to truthful (even if mistaken) speakers and to liars, the aim of that mode of utterance is to convey truth (and genuine belief), though the liar's use (abuse) of the practice has a precisely contrary aim (but is reliant on the practice and its central-case aim). And establishing all this establishes, in turn, why there is a normative requirement of the kind mentioned by Simmonds—a requirement not to abuse the practice. And all this is a plain example of the relation between practices, ideas, and values—between needs, awareness of needs, and more or less effective responses to needs.[271]

What is first in intention is last in execution.[272] So the preceding paragraph ended by putting the need or value first, the awareness and idea second, and the responsive practice last. But of course, once established, practices can be transmitted and adopted without awareness of the need. The idea 'behind' and 'within' the practice may not be adverted to by many or all who use the established practice, except reflectively and occasionally. Two-year olds who learn a practice of swapping playground 'cars' from time to time, and of exclaiming as they do so 'We're sharing', doubtless have not very much idea of what sharing is, or how 'sharing' is used, or of the benefits of the practice of sharing whether then and there or in life at large. But I think Oakeshott is not precise in saying [p. 317] that 'moral ideals are . . . the products of human behaviour, of human practical activity'; behaviour cannot be significant for establishing a practice (such that 'reflective thought' can 'subsequently' find in it a moral ideal) unless it already expresses an intelligent response to need, to intelligible benefit understood as somehow available through action.

---

[270] Simmonds says:

> . . . Shapiro is not simply saying that law *generally* serves moral aims, although it can also be employed to serve wicked aims. If he was to make such a point . . . it would strongly suggest a reliance upon Finnis's notion of 'focal meaning' [p. 322].

Hardly. In my usage *focal meanings* refer and correspond to *central cases* or *central instances*, and centrality of this kind is not a matter of statistical typicality (of what obtains 'generally'), but of considerations such as need, point, purpose, value . . .

(Incidentally, Simmonds at [p. 324] has me speaking of ' "focal instances" ', but neither that expression nor 'focal cases' is ever used in *NLNR* or *CEJF*, where 'focal' is always on the side of language and 'central' always on the side of what language refers to; the point is rather trivial, but the practice, in itself merely stipulative, keeps matters slightly clearer.)

[271] Without setting out to do so, the foregoing paragraph shows the sense in the neo-scholastic distinction (sometimes employed quite questionably) between *finis operis* ('the end/objective of the work') and *finis operantis* ('the end/objective of the person doing it').

[272] *ST* I-II q. 1 a. 1 ad 1; q. 18 a. 7 ad 2; etc.

On the need for and sense of a general descriptive theory of law, I share Simmonds's doubt. Chapter I of *NLNR* assumes throughout that general theory with purely descriptive purpose is possible (and argues that its controlling selection of concepts will nonetheless need to have an ineluctably evaluative element). The rest of the book, as I indicate near the end of Chapter I and stress in the Postscript,[273] is *not* an exercise in descriptive theory, but is evaluative and justificatory in purpose as well as method and content (though like all practical reasoning, its conclusions depend on purely descriptive/predictive premises as well as evaluative premises). But the book does not seek to deflect anyone from a general theory of law purely descriptive in *purpose*. It is only in recent years that I have suggested that the purposes of descriptive theory can and should all be pursued, not outside and parallel with critically evaluative-justificatory theory, but instead as an element within the latter.[274] Behind this shift in my assumptions and position lies a doubt about whether a general sociology such as Weber envisaged and masterfully attempted can ever be properly detached from (the study of) history, which is too open-ended towards the future of human free choices (and their side effects as well as their intentions) to allow a truly general 'social science' modelled, even with all Weberian nuance, on the manifestly successful natural sciences.[275] Still, practical reasonings, and therefore normative ethics, political theory, and legal theory, require extensive empirical information, selected and processed so as to be of service in deliberating about what to do, as an individual, a family, an economy, political community and legal system, an international order and economy, and humankind, all moving into a future which may be substantially just and peaceful, or only patchily so, or may be one calamity after another until the end.[276]

A word, finally, about doing legal theory in the highly convergent ways practised by Simmonds and myself. It prominently deploys distinctions between 'core' (Simmonds) or 'central' (Finnis) cases, on the one hand, and non-core or non-central cases,[277] and instead of banishing the latter ranges of instance to some other discipline studies them for the light they shed on the good reasons people have had (and have and will have) for moving away from them towards the core or central kind of social institution(s) and practice(s) of law. One such more or less borderline kind of phenomenon is the cynical tyranny that can be erected in a community that has an established practice of thinking in terms of law, legal rules, legal requirements, legal rights, etc. Simmonds's essay holds that—

A regime that imposed coercive demands and punished people without any pretence to be enforcing their duties, or protecting their rights, would not be a legal order. [p. 317]

---

[273] *NLNR*, 18, 434.

[274] E.g. *CEJF* IV.1; and 2012b ('What is the Philosophy of Law?').

[275] See the scattered remarks about 'typologies of social forms' in *CEJF* IV.13 ('Critical Legal Studies'), 302, n. 13, 313; IV.9 ('Weber, Objectivity, and Legal-Rational Authority'), 217.

[276] Hence the importance to political theory of the untenability of Mill's optimism about the stable obtaining of the preconditions for political and social 'liberty': see p. 511, n. 186 in this essay.

[277] Shapiro's criticism, *Legality*, 390–2, depends on attributing to me a notion I do not use—that central cases are 'ideal'—and an interpretation of that notion that is Platonic (or, rather, Platonising) rather than, as mine is, Aristotelian.

This thesis seems very similar to Raz's thesis that law must, as a matter of conceptual necessity, claim to be morally obligatory. Against Raz's thesis, I have made the objection[278] which I would now make to Simmonds's. It seems entirely possible for a regime to proclaim:

> Our law, which satisfies all the (say) Hartian criteria (primary rules restricting violence, theft and fraud, secondary rules of recognition, change and adjudication, etc.), imposes legal duties and confers legal rights that have nothing to do with moral rights. Our law imposes legal obligations that are not moral obligations, and has nothing to do with justice in the moral sense etc. but is instead a structure of ordered power designed to pursue our sectional purposes. We as regime will mercilessly enforce this law.

I see no compelling reason why this 'would not be a legal order' (still less why it is conceptually impossible). It is simply very deviant, since being for common good, including justice and human rights, is central to law—is at the core of law as an idea. The deviation is possible because, once legal thought has become conscious of its own source-based character, and equipped with (and dependent on) legal rules about what counts as such a source, one can distinguish sharply between legal right(s) and moral right(s), and so forth.[279] In central-case legal systems, of course, all these distinctions and technical devices[280] remain in the service of moral rights and purposes—not least, of doing *justice* according to law—and it is both an aspiration and an assumption that legal and moral obligations should not and properly do not diverge except in marginal and 'extraordinary' cases. So: wicked and exploitative regimes will no doubt *tend* to find it more convenient and effective to pretend that their law serves common good, justice, and moral rights (as Simmonds postulates).[281] But that is only one kind of deviant case; the other, more shameless, less duplicitous kind (as I have postulated it) remains possible.

20.

Timothy Endicott gives us an account of how to think of central cases that, taken in its completeness, adds much illumination to my own fragmentary accounts.

Along the way, he draws attention to law's 'evaluative complexity'. This is not so much the multiplicity of purposes concurrently served (despite their tension with one another) by good legal systems, statutes, and decisions[282]—though certainly Endicott in no way denies that multiplicity. He has in mind, rather, the admixture of ill with good in law. Rightly, he will not allow us to palm off the bad as merely deviation from the good: often enough, evil takes a distinct form by its *opposition* to good. So, even

---

[278] *CEJF* IV.Introduction, 8, n. 18.

[279] See further p. 539 and p. 554 at n. 318 in this essay.

[280] See further section 23 (Köpcke Tinturé). On law as a fourth-order, technical kind of object (properly in the service of third-order, moral purposes), see *CEJF* I.14 ('Legal Reasoning as Practical Reason'), 219–20; *CEJF* IV.5, 111, 148–9, 155; IV.6, 166, 169–72; IV.14, 326.

[281] And as I do in *NLNR*, 274.

[282] See pp. 545 and 550–1 in this essay.

though evil as such is merely the privation or absence of good and reality, we can and should have a stable account of characteristic vices, in their central and secondary cases, and of *mala in se*, in theirs.[283] And we should have an account of vicious kinds of regime, which as forms of governance, of the overcoming of anarchy and starvation, are deviant but as contemners of *common* good and of the justice that is a key element in the common good are more than deviant—are enemies 'of reasonable governance': 'specifically bad' [p. 332]. '[O]pposition to goods plays a focal and pre-eminent role in the explanation of vicious practices' [pp. 333–4].

So the ironies of legal rule that he points to—ironies because it is a reasonable project for common good that is inflicting these ills [p. 335]—are partly of the form of opportunities and facilities afforded by law (and its procedures) for malicious evasions of justice, prevarication, culpable irresolution, and so forth. But partly these ironies—in one respect more ironically—are intrinsic, '*bound* to be incurred if the system attains the goods that characterize the central case' [p. 338]. These are instances of the, so to speak, inbuilt bad side effects of choices between the goods in two (or more) good options between which (because of the exigencies of the world's materiality and finitude) one has to choose, where the choosing entails the loss—being deprived—of the goods that would have been afforded by the options not chosen (and where not choosing might well entail the forgoing of all the goods promised in all the options). Utilitarians, without falling into the fantasy of an infinity of good, dreamed nonetheless of a model of choice in which the option to be chosen would have *all the value* [pleasure, utility] of options to be rejected *and some more value* [pleasure, utility]. But that is not our world. And there are cases of inbuilt bad side effects that are more piquant, if not more ironical: the pursuit of a good feature such as clarity through explicitness (as in tax statutes) may result in deficiency in the very same property as diminishing marginal value in clarity eventually becomes negative (as explicitness results in complexity that defeats human comprehension and frustrates the need for practical guidance).[284]

The 'irony of law' is not an instance of the central case of irony : deliberate ascription of good qualities with intent to convey the opposite, like Mark Antony's 'All honorable men'.[285] As a matter of intent, law makes sense only as something intended to be for common good; all legal interpretation takes this as axiomatic, too obvious to need articulating. To say this is not for a moment to pretend that all law-making actually has that intent, and that no law-making has the opposite intent. It is merely to say that such instances are not merely to be classified as the deviations they are, but also to be resisted as evils opposed to one of the necessary conditions to having law worthy of the recognition (practical and theoretical) it necessarily seeks. To be sure, 'it is for the

---

[283] Why evil, though dependent on good for its reality and efficacy, is not to be understood as merely a deviation from good, is tersely illustrated by Aquinas by analogy with water's obliterating effect on fire: *De Malo* q. 2 a. 4 ad 8; see also *ST* I–II q. 18 a. 1. See also *NLNR*, 430.

[284] Fuller, *The Morality of Law*, 45, gives a slightly different example: 'making laws readily understandable to the citizen carried a hidden cost in that it rendered their application by the courts more capricious and less predictable' because it abandoned the articulation of 'those elements in a legal system that shape its rules into a coherent whole and render them capable of consistent application...' See also Endicott, *Vagueness in Law*, 188–90.

[285] *Julius Caesar*, 3.ii, 84.

common good that acts of making and applying law should be effective whether they promote the common good or not' [p. 339].[286] But culpable opposition by such powerful people to the common good robs their product of its title to compliance and efficacy even when, as is sometimes the case, the needs of the common good and fairness to the vulnerable provide other sufficient ('collateral') reasons to do what the law requires.[287]

21.

Timothy Macklem rightly asks [p. 353] just how one is able to identify the central purpose, or point, of a practice which people put to different purposes, or of practices whose point is wholly or partly bad [p. 356]. He rightly holds [p. 356] that purposes cannot be shielded from evaluative contention. And he remarks [p. 348] that one can find at least something 'helpful and true' in what I have to say on issues surrounding these questions. But there we part company, since the views he sets out to exemplify this agreeable finding are not mine. I have never thought that either our encounters with the world, or the concepts with which we conduct or reflect on these, are 'undertaken with some species of evaluation in mind'; nor that we are interested in the world 'always and only with what *ought to be* in mind'; nor that in some sense 'all values are facts, and all facts are evaluatively inspired'; nor that 'when we come across an unfamiliar object we seek to grasp ... what the object might be good for' or good as, or in terms of its value [p. 349]; nor that 'comprehension is always ... comprehension of the possibility of value or disvalue' [p. 350]; nor that 'there is no essential divide between description and evaluation, no fundamental separation between law and morals'; nor that description is to be identified with 'evaluative purpose' [p. 351].

Macklem has overlooked my fundamental view that 'there can be non-evaluative, neutral, value-free descriptions' of countless facts or realities, including 'of evaluations, i.e. of the value judgments that particular people or peoples make'.[288] I think there is thoroughly contemplative inquiry and understanding which has no purpose of evaluating the object inquired into and judged about (though there is no escape from 'evaluating' one's hypotheses and arguments for their soundness, validity, etc.). The argument of *NLNR*'s first chapter, about the need for evaluation in the development of a satisfactory descriptive *general theory of human affairs*, is rigorously confined to *general theory*, as distinct from biography, history of particular events, and of constitutions and laws, and so forth, and does not trade on any claims about description or evaluation at large. I happily regard those two activities as essentially distinct.

The entertaining metaphor in the title of Macklem's essay alludes to his view that descriptions of objects (say, handsaws) and practices (say, law) hold steady (as 'placeholders') while the values or point(s) with which these objects or practices are 'infused'

---

[286] This is an aspect of, or gains much of its force from, the patriotism (or, at least, political friendship) that is analogous to the central-case 'warts and all' friendship of Endicott's last paragraph. See also *CEJF* I.1 ('Practical Reason's Foundations'), 40. (I take Simmonds's reference to civility, in this context, at p. 320, to be alluding to the same concept, more coolly articulated.)

[287] *NLNR*, 361, 476.

[288] *NLNR*, 426; see also *CEJF* IV.5, 107; IV.10 ('On Hart's Ways'), 232–5.

(by those who use or engage in them) are 'promiscuous', 'multiple, fluid, transitory, and open-ended' [p. 348]. 'The underlying point of descriptions is to identify an object or practice without thereby identifying it with any value in particular'; descriptions are to be evaluatively permissive [p. 357]. By contrast, he holds, 'unity, relative stability, and closure are central to the concept of point as Finnis deploys it' [p. 348]. So 'Finnis would...take the purpose of a handsaw to be that of cutting wood' [p. 358]. But in truth I am as willing as Macklem is to regard the purpose, or central-case purpose, of handsaws in carpentry as serving to cut wood, or other substances needing cutting, while their purpose or central-case purpose in music-making is to serve as a kind of instrument[289]—just as 44-gallon drums had one purpose in the oil industry, another in old-fashioned park maintenance (as rubbish bins), and another in West Indian steel bands.[290] Nor is there any need, in a plain description of some people's practices, to identify central cases, other than in some easygoing statistical sense, or as one way of reporting what those people regard as more and less important. In such description, the account of purposes should be as promiscuous—open to variety—as people's purposes actually are. And when we move to the level of theory, and need central-case method to sort out and establish a conceptual structure for our account, we should be conscious that—

> The idea of central cases and focal meanings is itself an analogical idea. That is, we should expect the application and even the meaning of 'central case' and 'focal meaning' to shift as we move [from one theoretical context to another] ...[291]

As Macklem reports, 'In analytic philosophy, the conventional approach has been to be as minimal *as possible* about the elements of description so as to be as catholic [promiscuous] as possible about the potential for value and disvalue of engagement in the social practice as so described' [p. 357]. I have emphasized the words 'as possible' because the weakness of 'the conventional approach' is that it lacks a coherent account of possibility/impossibility, and thus instantiates the conceptual dogmatism[292] from which it is a primary aim of the central-case method in analytic philosophy—as practised in the tradition which my work deploys—to free us all up. An instance of such weakness, it seems to me, is to be found in Macklem's pervasive and confident, but undefended, detaching of 'practice' from 'purpose(s)', 'point', and 'value'. He works hard to establish, as least stipulatively, some sort of difference between each of these three terms, but 'practice' floats free from them all, and his essay seems to do nothing to

---

[289] But notice that some instances of the *central case* of saws in carpentry are not instances at all of the handsaws as employed in music. For a backsaw (e.g. a tenon saw) is stiffened with a back that prevents the flexibility without which a saw can scarcely make music because it cannot change pitch. Moreover, the angled sharpness of a saw's teeth is something very central to carpentry, but irrelevant to music-making. An account of saws that failed to make clear the element of the adventitious in the adaptation of (some) saws to music-making would be defective. To ask whether it would also be conceptually defective is to fall into the mythical dimension of 'conceptual analysis'.

[290] On the serviceability of a hammer as the backbone of a garden gnome: *CEJF* IV.1, 42.

[291] *NLNR*, 430.

[292] *NLNR*, 273: 'As we have to stress again and again in an age of conceptual dogmatism, concepts of law and society are legitimately many, and their employment is subordinated to matters of principle rooted in the basic principles and requirements of practical reasonableness (which themselves generate many concepts and can be expressed in many reasonable forms).' Also 265, 277–8, 472. In this essay, p. 462, n. 14.

suggest how we might make sense of a practice, let alone distinguish one type of practice from another, without reference to purpose, point and/or value. Of course, one might simply report differences between one event and another to which someone somewhere has applied the word 'practice' (or some more or less similar term in some other language). One will soon get one's 'vast rubbish heap of miscellaneous facts described in a multitude of incommensurable terminologies',[293] but that is not theory or analytic philosophy. To be sure, making sense of actions, including practices, by reference to their intentions, purposes, and point—that is, by reference to the value the acting persons thought their action/practice would achieve—does not solve the problem of establishing the differences and similarities between one kind of action/practice and another, or what is 'possible' or 'impossible' in descriptions (concepts) of them. But it does bring the descriptive material, *including* descriptions of those 'subjective' values and purposes, into a position where reflection can establish contours and differences by criteria worthy of being called theoretical, or 'conceptual' in a sense which transcends local history and lexicography.[294]

Or consider the matter to which Macklem keeps coming back: marriage. He displays the descriptive openness or promiscuity he favours, by reminding us of 'the ongoing development and extension of the possible purposes of marriage' to include, 'today', arranged ('less than fully voluntary') marriages, same-sex marriages, and ('polygamy aside') marriages accepting of adultery. But this openness is less than complete or even bracing. As Europe (to go no further) 'develops and extends' its population, indeed its citizenry, we will find its social practices and doubtless its law developing and extending to include polygamy more straightforwardly than it is already recognized in British social welfare law or official practice; and will (indeed, do) find marriages 'arranged' in ways that amount to the frankly coercive; and Shia marriages that cover what today, in our undeveloped way, we would call prostitution;[295] and marriage law that frankly rejects the Christian concept of equality between husband and wife and permits divorce at the will of the one but not the other; and polyamory which radicalizes polygamy by making it, too, symmetrical. Macklem says [p. 352] that 'were concepts actually tied to particular purposes (or points) in the way that Finnis contends... [m]arriage between members of the same sex would be logically impossible...' But to say this is to forget the entire nature and purpose of central-case analysis, which is to

---

[293] *NLNR*, 17; see also 4:

> The subject-matter of the theorist's description does not come neatly demarcated from other features of social life and practice. Moreover, this social life and practice bears labels in many languages. The languages can be learned by speakers of other languages, but the principles on which labels are adopted and applied—i.e. the practical concerns and the self-interpretations of the people whose conduct and dispositions go to make up the theorist's subjectmatter—are not uniform. Can the theorist do more, then, than list these varying conceptions and practices and their corresponding labels? Even a list requires some principle of selection of items for inclusion in the list. And jurisprudence, like other social sciences, aspires to be more than a conjunction of lexicography with local history, or even than a juxtaposition of all lexicographies conjoined with all local histories.

[294] See *CEJF* IV.1, 32, 34–5.

[295] On the 'fixed-term/temporary/pleasure marriages' apparently authorized by the Koran 4: 24, see *A Shi'ite Encyclopedia*, Ch. 6a: <http://www.al-islam.org/encyclopedia/chapter6a>.

shift discussion away from sterile or prematurely dogmatic inquiry or assertion about what is 'logically' ('conceptually') possible, or statistically predominant, or historically original, towards discussion of what is fully or less than fully reasonable, and—where it is central cases of human practices (as distinct from artefacts and techniques) that are in issue—this amounts to discussion of what is morally sound as opposed to unsound.

Macklem rightly says [p. 353] that there might be competing *reasonable* conceptions of the point and central case of a practice. But the issue is not about which conception is *most* reasonable, but whether some conceptions and practices, however widespread, are unreasonable. In relation to morally significant choice and action, unreasonableness entails immorality, and immorality entails (in reason) exclusion of the relevant option(s) from deliberation. However widely approved, immoral options cannot be *central* instances of the central cases of practices as understood and described in a sound and critical descriptive theory of human affairs (and see p. 539).

Macklem assures us that the purposes of same-sex sex couplings self- or socially-interpreted as marital are 'reasonable' and 'every bit as at home in the practice' of marriage as the marital purposes of husbands and wives. Less ecumenical is his statement that 'husbands and wives today are bound to respect the other (valuable) purposes for which that practice may also be engaged in now . . .'—other, that is to say, than the purpose of 'uniting heterosexual couples for life' [p. 352]. But husbands and wives are not *bound to respect* those who enter on marriage with a purpose of 'swinging' or open (consensually adulterous) union, or with a purpose of divorcing if ever they find a more attractive and agreeable mate, or of excluding children altogether. Such purposes are not 'as at home in the practice' as the purposes of exclusive fidelity and openness to procreation. As for the purpose of enabling same-sex couples to imitate marriage (with or without the law's denominating their coupling lawful and valid marriage), it is reasonably regarded as including, or encouraging, an immoral (unjust) purpose of generating children necessarily intended to be deprived of their father or their mother (if not of both), since every child engendered 'by' such a union *must* be the child of someone not party to the union. And even when children are no part of the purpose of the 'marriage', the approval by anyone of such a coupling is immoral for the same sort of reason as it is immoral to approve of even consensual adultery, or pre-marital sex.[296] For such approval, being a kind (however qualified) of conditional willingness to engage in non-marital sex acts, corrupts the intentionality of marital sex acts—which are unquestionably central to the practice of marriage—by cutting off the non-illusory self-understanding of chaste spouses that in engaging in intercourse with each other they are experiencing, actualizing, and expressing *their marriage* in both its procreative and its friendship dimensions. And it was only the conjunction of procreation with friendship that made sense of the *practice* of 'uniting heterosexual couples *for life*' in a commitment to sexual exclusivity. A practice that made good sense only on the assumption that its nature and purpose, as a practice,[297] involved procreation was, indeed, open to couples who made that commitment knowing that their union could

---

[296] I have argued this in many places; very briefly at *CEJF* IV.11, 273; briefly in IV.5, 135–8; *CEJF* III.20, 322–3; *CEJF* V.23, 351; at some length in *CEJF* III.22, 373–80.
[297] On this kind of purpose-of-a-practice, see also pp. 535–6 in this essay.

not, whatever they willed or did, result in procreation, but willing to do together *all and only* what other married couples rightly do. So naturally sterile marriages between spouses capable of marital sex acts could be (non-central) instances of the central case of marriage, a central case set which includes all, and only, morally sound (just and chaste) kinds of marriage, and excludes the rest—not from 'the concept of marriage' but from the concept of marriage that deserves legal recognition as just, chaste, and essential to the well-being of political communities.

The point of making philosophical judgments about central and non-central cases in the domain of human affairs, whether the judgments be for purposes of descriptive social theory or for ethics or evaluatively critical or justificatory political or legal theory and practice, is to bring to the surface and make transparent the judgments about human value and morality that control the selection and deployment of concepts and terms for these purposes—instead of hiding those judgments in the murkiness or untheoretical superficiality of 'conceptual' analysis. In that domain, central cases include a reference to purposes, point, and value, but also and just as essentially (*pace* Macklem [p. 356]) to kinds of behaviour and relationships, kinds of *means*. For example, only four or five lines of the 15-line sentence in which *NLNR* offers a definition of law—of the focal meaning of 'law' and central case of law—concern purpose, point and/or value, as distinct from the means that in the conditions of human existence are needed to realize that complex purpose, point, and good.[298]

Macklem's embrace of easy virtue pays insufficient regard, it seems to me, to the problem of evil. May not 'developments' of what he too easily takes to be a single practice be (as I have heavily hinted) rather like, say, the 'development' of constitutional governance in Germany between 1931 and 1936? May not engaging in theatre 'just to discover what theatre might be capable of' [p. 353] bring you to, say, the Roman amphitheatre or the snuff movie? The reforms of family law in the 1960s and 1970s, approved (and more) by energetic but superficial scholars (and ratifying many people's short-term, self-interested desires), hollowed out and watered down marriage; the modern Western institution became a plainly non-central case, ready for subjection—by equally superficial 'human rights' scholars and judicial law-makers—to more extreme degradations such as synchronic as well as diachronic polygamy, open assimilation to sheer concubinage, and state-sponsored same-sex marriage; all with the predictable result (not, of course, without other contributing causes, nor unaccompanied by further harmful impact along the way) that the political communities concerned are on track to incurring a not unprecedented fate: an accelerating diminution in the populations who adopted these ideas, and their colonization and replacement by peoples of (to say no more) alien culture, conceptions of the human, and principles of governance.[299]

The problem of evil is presented on p. 348 as a difficulty for any central-case method such as mine (a method which, overlooking my definition of law, Macklem mistakenly supposes can comprehend only one point per practice); for, he asks, may

---

[298] *NLNR*, 276–7. On ends and means in that definition (and a part-quotation of it), see p. 551 at n. 310 in this essay.
[299] *CEJF* IV.11 (2009), 274–9; and see p. 563 in this essay.

not the point of a practice be wholly or partly bad, and might not law be 'on the whole more of a bad thing than a good thing'? There is, hereabouts, a fair question to be asked, but any reasonable answer to it is going to include this. It is precisely the threat of evil—of the bad consequences of inaction or misdirected action—that makes the point of the central cases of practices and institutions such as law, property, and marriage a complex, non-single point, embracing the complexities of, say, the rule of law, the distinction between private and public domains, a conception of common good as including rights and side-constraints, and so forth. The laboriousness of a book such as *NLNR* results in some measure from its attempt at constant, open engagement with the problem of justifying action by reference to the threat of evil and misdirection.

Again, to criticize the ideas, mistakenly ascribed to me, that 'there is no essential divide between description and evaluation' and 'no fundamental separation between law and morals', Macklem presses once more his celebration of easy virtue:

> ...the objects and practices that description captures are typically susceptible to the ongoing direction of imagination and will, be it human or otherwise, a direction that makes them the bearers of different values and disvalues in different hands and at different times (and also susceptible to misdirection)... [pp. 350–1]

But this is the issue set out in the first two pages of *NLNR*, the issue to which Chapter I and then, with different intent, Chapters III–XII are a response. Yet I do not see in the rest of Macklem's essay much allowance for the problem of misdirection. And may we not see an implicit—and mistaken—response to the problem in his later explicit contrast [p. 356] between, on the one hand, 'imagination and will' and, on the other hand, a 'reason' reduced to 'the governing role... in supervising, however imperfectly, the exercise of those capacities'?[300] For unless will is a response to reasons, and reasons are not merely the slave of passions, but provide more direction (and therefore more supervisory content) than Kantian non-contradiction, appeals to imagination and will as grounds for embracing the 'colonizing' of 'practices' by new 'points' (straddling 'purposes' and 'values') should be resisted like the allures of the Reeperbahn. Macklem's essay does not distance itself from neo-Humean ideas of reason as supervising only means (for their efficiency). This, like his final paragraph's words about 'instantiations' practised 'for good and for ill', leaves us uncertain how a legal theory he could commend would deal with certain instantiations and fruits of 'imagination and will' which a theory of law should be able to judge injustices and corruptions of legal order. Nor should such a judgment earn the rebuke that its author 'believes that practices are inherently constituted by morally valid norms', a belief as absurd as judging 'practices not so constituted deviant by definition' [p. 360].

The philosophical method I defend encourages undertaking a scrutiny to assess how far law (as against anarchy and tyranny, or indeed domination by a saintly hero) is admixed with evil. Indeed, it demands that such a scrutiny be made; *NLNR*'s chapter on unjust laws is quite open-ended. Law is no doubt susceptible to the evils of adopting

---

[300] Taken alone, this phrase of course suggests reason's proper role as constitutional ruler (*Aquinas*, 72–8) over passion and imagination, with reasonable will as reason's activation in choice, effort, and *praxis*. The essay's stress on imagination and will, etc., unsettle that benign interpretation.

poor means and neglecting bad side effects of its own institutions. Can it further be said that law, as I present its central case in *NLNR*, is inadequately open to 'imagination and will', and itself puts too much store by 'unity, relative stability, and closure' [cf. p. 348]? I willingly concede that *NLNR* reads more like, say, Adenauer with his stolid Constitution of 1950 than like, say, Foucault with his theoretical, political, and personal openness, imaginative and wilful, and so attractive to huge crowds of students, as long as he lived.[301]

A word, finally, about circularity. In footnote 2 of his essay, and again, at important junctures, notably on pp. 354 and 357, Macklem suggests that central-case method, appealing to practical reasonableness, entails question-begging (vicious circularity: assuming one's conclusion). Not so. It is not question-begging for logicians to take as their framework concept and criterion of acceptability the idea of a valid argument; nor is it question-begging or viciously circular for them to begin filling out the concept of validity with various axioms (which are not conclusions of any argument), before reaching certain theorems about validity in particular types of argumentative context, theorems which unlike the framework concept and the axioms can be taken to be the conclusions of arguments (proofs). Similarly, in the project of understanding practices, institutions, and other social facts sustained by thought, deliberation, choice, and action, there is nothing question-begging in taking as one's framework concept— whether for descriptive-explanatory general 'sociological' theory or for moral-political-legal theory—the idea of the practically reasonable; nor in beginning to fill out that idea with axioms such as that rational action is always guided by a conception of value or point or intelligent purpose, and that some such conceptions are intelligent, others not so much; nor in identifying starting points (premises) for practical reasoning, and later for adequacy in practical reasoning (ultimately morality), premises that are self-evident, not the conclusions of any reasoning but defensible by dialectical reasoning[302] against objections; nor in proceeding to argue from such principles in combination with regularities of cause and effect to conclusions about the need for and reasonableness of coordinative practices such as law made for common good (relative to which laws made only apparently or partially for common good are non-central cases).

For a problematically circular argument, one may look to Macklem's thought [p. 359] that descriptions of articles or social practices, as 'typically couched', 'are threatened by

---

[301] But see *NLNR*, 220, on imagining future states of society with attention to the quality of human interactions and the need for individual initiative, in a context of 'a wide freedom of cultural and political debate'; also the brief discussion in 'A Grand Tour of Legal Theory' of 'the twin roles of reasonableness *and rationally underdetermined choice* in the positing and maintaining of even a thoroughly decent legal system': *CEJF* IV.5, 118; and *CEJF* IV.10 ('On Hart's Ways'), 255:

> descriptive social theory will be unable to get beyond an endless video of local histories—or a merely statistical ordering of them—unless it makes the judgments about reasonableness that are fundamental to practical social theory. (Hart's theory makes and relies on some.) And practical, morally oriented social theory will be a half-blind guide unless it profits from the practical insights, and the transmissible experience of inner and outer causes and effects, that are made available by history and social theory, perhaps distilled and by imagination and intelligence enhanced in great works of literary art.

[302] See p. 467, n. 29 in this essay.

failures of value only as and when those failures are either comprehensive or critical in character', and that—

> Failures of value are critical in character in all those settings in which achievement of some value in particular through the article or practice is a condition precedent of recognizing the article or practice as falling under the description in question.

More important than this dubious circularity is what Macklem concludes from it [p. 359]: 'failures of value and of definition…cannot be mapped onto one another' but have only a contingent connection—

> *so that* it would be a mistake to suggest either that an unjust law is never a law or that an unjust law never fails to be a law by reason of its injustice, as much of a mistake, and for connected reasons, as it would be to suggest that there is a central case of law and that it is to be looked for in the purpose for which law is most reasonable engaged in. (emphasis added)

But the proposition that unjust laws are not *simpliciter* laws is a thesis, not in a descriptive theory of law such as *NLNR* Chapter I discusses, but in a moral-political-legal theory of law such as is developed in *NLNR* Chapters III–XII, to which the way descriptions of utensils are 'typically couched' is of scant relevance. And, again, the central case of law, whether in descriptive social theory or in the moral-political-legal theory of laws as types of reason, will not be articulated in terms exclusively of law's purpose (or point or value).[303] So there is plenty of material in the central case to motivate retaining the name in the non-central, more or less vicious or primitive cases where the complex defining point, purpose, and value (function) of law is defied or neglected by law-makers or law-appliers.[304]

22.

Julie Dickson's four questions about, or senses of, explanatory priority are interesting. And this interest is indeed enhanced, as she holds, by law's dual character as 'both a social and a normative phenomenon'—or, as I have sometimes said, its 'double life' as both facts and reasons.[305] This dualism or duality is actually a bit more stark, I think, than would appear from her initial account of it. For the 'two main points' she adduces [p. 362] to indicate law's 'social fact' character or properties (its 'social facticity' [p. 365]) seem to me not so much facts about the presence of the law in anyone's environment as, rather, expressions of a doctrine (a reason for predicating) which holds (as lawyers, officials, 'good citizens', and moralists more or less systematically do) that past acts and facts ('social[-fact] sources') have the significance of settling certain present questions

---

[303] See further the discussion at p. 552, point (3), in this essay.

[304] *NLNR*, 11: 'one's descriptive explanation of the central cases should be as conceptually rich and complex as is required to answer all appropriate questions about those central cases. And then one's account of the other instances can trace the network of similarities and differences, the analogies and disanalogies, for example, of *form*, function, *or content*, between them and the central cases' (emphasis added).

[305] Hence *CEJF* IV.10 ('On Hart's Ways: Law as Reason and as Fact'). See also, on 'the double life of the law', *CEJF* IV.Introduction, 1–6, *CEJF* IV.5, 101–2, 107, and *CEJF* IV.20, 397, 402 (and 399–403).

about what to do, by picking out certain standards for answering those questions as valid standards whose propositional content should (legally should) be regarded as supplying the (legally) normative premises for the (legally) right answer. 'Positivist' legal theory is much less securely on the 'fact' side of law's duality than it tends to suppose—as 'legal realists' have not been slow to point out. Attention to law and legal system strictly as social fact would report present conduct of courts and officials, and in so far as it looked at such persons' actual dispositions it would include not only their willingness to look to social-fact sources but also their disposition to decide cases on their view of the merits of the parties, or their own prospects for promotion, demotion, or worse.

Be that as it may, Dickson's enquiry into my answers to the four questions about what has explanatory priority in legal theory focuses on the essay in which I offered to show that considering law as a distinctive kind of *reason* is sufficiently illuminating to yield also a sufficient understanding of it as a distinctive kind of social fact. Her focus is justified; I put that essay first (renamed 'Decribing Law Normatively') in the volume *Philosophy of Law*. But it will be helpful to recall that the first proposition in it which she selects for scrutiny [p. 371] is itself the conclusion of an argument. The proposition is:

> The primary reality of the law is rather in its claim, as itself a moral requirement,[306] on my deliberating about what to decide . . . to choose and do . . . This mode of *our positive law's* existence—as a morally legitimate and compelling, albeit conditionally and only defeasibly compelling, *claim on my action when I am thinking about what to do* as a plain citizen (child or adult), a judge, a police officer, a tax inspector, and executor, and so forth—is the primary reality of *law*. It is primary because the rational force of this claim is fully intelligible even before one knows much about the content of the law and certainly before one has been taught anything about law in general or 'the concept of law'.
>
> That rational force, like all rational force, is at bottom the attractiveness of truth. Because I judge it to be true that, say, the victim's bodily and emotional well-being is as much an instantiation of intelligible human good as the well-being of the bully . . . [307]

The sentence goes on for another 11 lines. No need to follow its course. I have extended the quotation to indicate the argumentation, which had begun some pages earlier with a 'primal scene', an act of bullying in the primary school playground, with an actual or hoped-for conclusion that order is restored by the intervention of a teacher to insist upon rules against bullying, rules of rectification, and so forth—school rules merging perhaps into the law's own standards and demands. If there is going to be law anywhere, with the characteristics that Hart picked out as the central case and that Fuller and Raz elaborated and refined under the name of the Rule of Law, it is not going to spring from the mind of the bully, or of Dickson's London rioters in their rioting, but from the minds and actions of the intervening school authorities in parallel with other, higher, wider, and more potent but logically similar structures of (persons in)

---

[306] On this all too compressed statement about law's claim, see p. 554, n. 317 in this essay.
[307] *CEJF* IV.1, 29 (emphases in original).

authority, and from the desire of law-abiding children and adults for such interventions in what otherwise threatens to be the anarchy of my imagined playground or Dickson's actual London riot districts in 2011. So I am not much moved by her reminders of the very different attitudes to the law displayed by those rioters; my own account, by including the bully in the primal scene, had laid the basis for including the actions and attitudes of Dickson's malefactors.

Now I do not think we need or should leave the rioters with only one side of their attitudes on display. We can be confident that as the owners of property, or of entitlements to social welfare payments and to a fair trial and to scrupulously lawful treatment at the hands of the police,[308] these same rioters have a keen sense of the injustice of unlawful conduct so far as it violates those legal entitlements of theirs. But their allegiance to law is not a central case; it is too infected, I take it, with inconsistency (no need, here, to ask whether also with hypocrisy). And if some small part of the rioting (not the looting and burning) was a protest against actual official misconduct, we have here, again, a *pro tanto* non-central case of legal system.

Nor, most fundamentally, could it be reasonable not give priority to the concerns, beliefs, and dispositions of the sort of people whose choices make the law come into being in a central-case form, and maintain it as such, against the opposition or at best indifference of rioters, other criminals, and opportunists of every social class. Giving that explanatory priority to (people with) those law-shaping and law-supportive concerns, beliefs, and dispositions does not in the least eliminate from the theory's account the law-threatening or law-indifferent concerns, beliefs, and dispositions of persons who are perhaps even a majority.

The other passage of mine on which Dickson has founded her root-and-branch rejection of my methodological stance is note 9 in 'Describing Law Normatively':

> ... Raz asked why law should be thought to be like argument, medicine, or contracts, rather than like novels or paintings or people, that are still novels or paintings or people, even if they are bad. The answer is that, *like argument, medicines, and contracts, law has a focused and normative point to which everything else about it is properly to be regarded as subordinate.* Novels and paintings, on the other hand, can have incompatible points, e.g. to entertain or arouse (like kitsch or porn) or to tell a truth with artistry. People exist in the natural order as living substances even if they are not functioning adequately or at all in the orders of logic and thought, deliberation, and/or exercises of skill.

I have italicized the statement to which Dickson objects. The paragraph to which the footnote was appended gives essential context:

> ... some elements of what has been posited in our community in response to our shared moral need are, in my judgment or yours, so unreasonable that the

---

[308] Indeed, the very first comment quoted in the report cited by Dickson in n. 48, by a 17-year-old Muslim rioter, includes the statement: '*They're supposed to be law enforcement.* I hate the police. *I don't hate the policing system,* I hate the police on the street.' So even this rioter uses the law as a kind of moral standard (perhaps not of a central-case kind, because perhaps dominated by concern with 'perceived' consistency/hypocrisy) by which to criticize the police.

presumptive moral claim on us of these elements is, in my judgment or yours, defeated in whole or part. Posited... rules of the latter kind are analogous to contracts which have been made in full compliance with every formality and other procedural condition specified by the law of contract but are void for illegality. Or, to take two perhaps closer analogies, they are like medicines which prove futile or lethal and are thus not medicinal at all, or like arguments the formal elegance of which only masks their invalidity: no argument. Unjust laws are not laws, though they may still count in reasonable conscientious deliberations, and certainly warrant attention and description. So, too, invalid arguments may win a place both in manuals of rhetoric as the art of persuasion, and in guides to fallacies for young logicians, quack and lethal medicines are sold as medicines and listed in histories of medicine and on warning notices, and contracts void for illegality earn a place both in books on the law of contract and, more interestingly, in books on restitution where their apparent validity, or their widespread acceptance as valid, may affect the success or quantum of a restitutionary claim. It should go without saying that some people are persuaded by fallacies, that parties may for years consider themselves legally bound by a contract in fact void for illegality, and that the police and the hangman may act against me in accordance with unjust laws. The excitement and hostility aroused by the old saying that unjust laws are not laws is quite needless.

So my decision to depart here from my otherwise virtually invariable practice, and say, without verbal qualification, '... is not law', was a matter not of stridency but of argument. The argument from analogy shows plainly, in each case, that the verbally unqualified formula is compatible with all manner of unexpressed but contextually implied qualifications. Arguments that truly are no argument are nonetheless (and *truly*, albeit from another perspective) arguments in many different respects (they perhaps persuade countless dupes, and win elections and convictions and acquittals). And so forth.

Now we can return to the footnote. Its talk of law having 'a focused and normative point' could easily be misunderstood. Law's point is complex, a manifold of points (ends). And because it is articulately reflexive, its characteristic means become for it also ends and part of the 'common good' that includes all its ends. As I said in 'Law as Coordination' (1989):

> The point of law is not merely to ensure the survival of government or the future conformity of the potentially recalcitrant [or, I might have added, the prosperity and defence and demographic sustainability and sound education of the community]. Part of the law's point is to maintain real (not merely apparent) fairness between the members of a community; and this aspect of law's point is unaffected by the detection or covertness of breaches of law. The institution of law gains much of its value, as a contribution to the common good, precisely from the fact that the obligations it imposes hold good even when breach seems likely to be undetectable.[309]

---

[309] *CEJF* IV.3, 72.

But a less constrained view of what I mean by 'the point of law' can be had by looking at a fragment of the 15-line definition of law in *NLNR*, where aspects of law's point appear, compressed perhaps, in the phrases here emphasized:

> ... directed to *reasonably resolving any of the community's co-ordination problems ... for the common good* of that community, according to a manner and form itself *adapted to that common good by features of specificity, minimization of arbitrariness, and maintenance of a quality of reciprocity between the subjects of the law both among themselves and in their relations with the lawful authorities.*[310]

To grasp the complexity of law's ends, consider the drafting of a statute for authorizing the expropriation of certain property for the purposes of a national transport system. The *ends* that a lawyerlike draftsman will bear in mind throughout include not only the construction of a transport system and the minimization of costs to the Treasury but also that the compensation payable should by due process of law yet without undue delay reach all and only persons entitled to it by virtue of their property rights or their investments or long enjoyment, and that alternative schemes and routes should receive public scrutiny and debate in the interests not only of a good transport system but also of local democracy and autonomy and of due process of law, including respect for *audi alteram partem*. Not *one* end, purpose, value, or point, but many, with their appropriate technical and other means, which interact with each other and with the various ends in various ways, all needing lawyerlike scrutiny and judgment.

So, to the four questions:

(1) Does it matter where you start? No. You can start with the social facts about what is called law, and ask why these facts hang together in the way they are taken to, and then whether the human purposes and benefits adduced in the most satisfactory explanation for that factual clustering suggest more satisfactory clusterings, achieving those purposes and benefits *and* some further purposes or benefits. (Think of the way Hart traces the improvement of sets of social rules by the introduction of secondary rules for the remedial purposes he specifies, rules and purposes that in turn are open to the further improvements traced in the Fuller/Raz specification of the elements of the Rule of law; and so forth.) Or you can start as I do in *NLNR*, or, differently, in the 'Describing Law Normatively' essay, go directly to the needs to which law is the generically most satisfactory kind of response, and trace out that complex of ends and means. In no case is the explanation to be dominated by 'the first thing that strikes us about law'—as if there were just *one* such 'first thing'!

(2) Are some of law's defining properties explained by others? Yes. Means, *qua* means, are always explained by their ends. Law is all made—posited, even those parts of it that are made by adopting moral principles whose truth and applicability is not made but discerned. Every such human making is purposeful. So law is a complex of means to a complex of ends, as the definition partly quoted above makes plain, though in

---

[310] *NLNR*, 276–7.

the most compressed fashion.[311] Law 'functions well as the resolver of coordination problems' only when it does so in a way that is not only efficient but also—even at some expense in such efficiency!—fair, respectful of acquired rights, and in line with the desiderata of the Rule of Law.

(3) Is law's point or value also more important than law's other properties in settling what counts as law? No. What is distinctive about law as a means of author-itatively resolving coordination problems is that the means are deployed to settle *what counts as* an admissible and authoritative solution. And law's means involve the techni-que of making and enforcing—but in the normal last resort enforcing *judicially*—brightline rules, conceptions of validity and invalidity, and other devices for linking the present settlement (and thus the future outcome) to past determinations even though a clean-slate solution today would yield a different and more efficient solution. To the extent that a social system departs from these technical means, it departs from the Rule of Law and abandons or at least neglects the procedural *ends* that call for that ideal of governance. So law's ends treat means as decisively important in settling *the* law, and that is distinctive of *law* as a kind of social entity.[312] I think Green[313] is broadly right about this.

(4) What makes law what it is? Social facts. (They are its 'material' and 'efficient' causes.) Unless there is factual acceptance of actual acts of legislation and adjudication, law cannot possibly achieve its normative point or create legal or moral obligations. What makes social facts so utterly central to law? Human needs, vulnerabilities, scarcities, and ways of flourishing or losing out. One of the most important of our needs is for justice in human responses to these problems. So justice is a necessary condition for law's counting as an adequate response to them. Efficacy (social facticity) is another necessary condition. In vain does one assign priority to one of these two necessary conditions. I have never claimed that the 'properties [constituting law's efficacy or social facticity] are of significantly less importance to law's nature than its normative point or value' [p. 377].[314] Footnote 9, in saying that 'like argument, medicines, and contracts, law has a focused and normative point to which everything

---

[311] I think Dickson's account of Dworkin may need amendment in saying [pp. 367, 374] that, for him, all legal propositions flow from law's point (the justification of state collective force). This overlooks, I think, the part that is played in his account by *fit with the materials* given by the community's political-legal history (social-fact sources). True, fit is required by justification, but the happenstance of the community's history *changes* what would otherwise have been the outcome of the other elements in the justification (background rights, and so forth). Even though each element in that happenstance was itself purposive (not happenstance), the conjunction of such results of purposes, votes, accidents of litigation, and legislative process, etc., is not settled by, and not fully consistent with, what would *otherwise* be the best account of the law's justifying point.

[312] See further *CEJF* IV.2, 63–4; *CEJF* IV.3, 71–2; and the entire Introduction to that volume, especially 5.

[313] Quoted at [p. 368].

[314] Recall here the starkness with which *NLNR* makes authority (of which law will be accounted one modality) depend upon the fact of likely present and future compliance:

> Authority (and thus the responsibility of governing) in a community is to be exercised by those who can in fact effectively settle co-ordination problems for that community. This principle is not the last word on the requirements of practical reasonableness in locating authority; but it is the first and most fundamental.

NLNR, 246.

else about it is properly to be regarded as subordinate', says no more, and no less, than the answers just given to questions (2) and (3). Bad arguments, quack medicines, and unjust laws weigh heavily indeed on their victims and on human history; their self-presentation as arguments, medicines, and laws is a principal cause of their deceptiveness and destructiveness. That does not make them arguments, medicines, or laws in the eyes of anyone who, in seeking to bring reason into human activity (including thinking) to the extent that we should, deploys those concepts as developed and refined for collaborative use to articulate rather precise requirements and aspirations of reasonableness.

23.

After three sections in which she gives a most helpful guide to *NLNR*'s forbidding chapter on obligation, and to a main feature of the whole book's modus operandi, **Maris Köpcke Tinturé** raises a plausible objection to one of the perhaps surprising theses implicit in that book, and explicit in more recent work of mine: the thesis that, very strictly speaking, the law does not claim to be morally obligatory. Her sense is that 'we cannot render the law morally intelligible unless we understand it to claim (contextually and implicitly) vis-à-vis the convict that he failed to do what he had a moral obligation to do *in the particular circumstances*...' [p. 395]. The law's moral claim, therefore, is in her view, a claim to be 'non-defeasibly morally binding, binding *semper et ad semper*' across the whole range of conduct to which it has extended its precise specifications (*determinationes*) [p. 394]. Against my thesis that, besides moral normativity, there is legal normativity which is 'so far forth not moral' and 'occupies the same space in practical reasoning as morality', she objects [p. 393]:

> ...what else, other than a *moral* syllogism, could be 'offer[ed]' (*NLNR* 317) to the 'good citizen' for adoption as 'his own' (*NLNR* 341)?

The issue raised in this objection is a narrow one (and not the worse for that). For *NLNR* holds that—

> ...the law creates a...frame of reference [that] gives, at least to those directly responsible for superintending the common good, a right to demand compliance, not merely as something morally obligatory in the broad, moralists' sense, but as something morally owed 'to the community'. The law provides the citizen, like the judge, with strongly exclusionary moral reasons for acting or abstaining from actions. (319)

So the issue concerns the difference between (1) the law's 'creating a frame of reference' and (2) its 'claiming...' And again, the 2008 lectures she cites [p. 379] asserted that—

> Law contextually and implicitly claims both that its rules etc. are reasonable, and that the legally required course of action ought to *prevail in deliberation*, as against reasonable (and of course unreasonable) alternatives...[315]

---

[315] My lecture handout went on:

Does law claim to be morally obligatory? Raz: Yes... Finnis: Strictly speaking, No. Though it (morally) ought to be such that it is morally obligatory, morally justified, and morally justifying (e.g. of judicial action), its *claim* is only that it is *legally* legitimate, authoritative, and binding/obligatory. Like morality, it claims to be decisive in the deliberation, choices, and actions of its subjects. But it does not *purport* to be (or *not to be*) morally obligatory. The meaning of *obligation, obligatory* etc. in law is not precisely the same as the meaning of *obligation*, obligatory, etc. in moral reasoning and judgments.[316]

So the issue concerns the difference between (A) being reasonable in its imposition of legal obligations and (B) thereby imposing moral obligations.

In both these respects, then—(1) v. (2) and (A) v. (B)—the issue is very narrow. And it is also narrower than Köpcke Tinturé suggests when she says that 'Finnis reasons [that] the law cannot intelligibly be said to make a moral claim'. For I think the law 'can intelligibly be said' to make such a claim,[317] but that it need not do so[318] and in fact, and in a sound legal-philosophical view, does not.

Why am I willing to say that the law claims to be reasonable, when I am not willing to say that it also *claims to be* morally obligatory? After all, the law may well be less than fully reasonable, or even be unreasonable. My answer: to speak of 'the law' is to speak of a legal system, not merely of an isolated 'rule' or edict; and to speak of legal system is to deploy, implicitly, criteria of validity and interpretation which strongly affect the judgment of the law's subjects about what conduct the law (say, in a single rule or order) claims of them, as legally obligatory for them; and to do all this is necessarily to conceive of the law as reasonable—controlled by reasons—at least to the extent that it is responsive to such criteria of coherence and validity. So it is right to hold that the law cannot but claim, albeit only implicitly and contextually, to be reasonable.

But to hold that the law claims to be morally obligatory *non-defeasibly* (in parallel with its claim to be *legally* non-defeasibly obligatory) would be to hold that the law—

Why contextually? The basic context is that law is a relationship between persons in the present, a relationship shaped by the systematic willingness of these present persons to treat themselves as in a relationship to persons (not excluding themselves) in the past of their community, and to make this backward reference to originating sources in the interests of future persons of these same community.

[316] The passage ran on:

Legal obligation is, legally speaking [= 'in contemplation of law': *NLNR*, 317], *invariant* in its legal force: 'There are, legally speaking, no degrees of legal obligation, just as there are no degrees of legal validity' (*NLNR* 309). 'This invariability in the formal force of every legal obligation has as its methodological counterpart the legal postulate...that there are no overlapping and conflicting legal duties...' (*NLNR* 311; see also 317). So there is 'legally obligatory' in the legal sense and 'legally obligatory' in the moral sense (*NLNR* 314–320), and the premise that we need to be law-abiding is treated in legal thought as a sheer 'postulate, isolated in legal thought from the general flow of practical reasoning' about the common good (*NLNR* 316–7).

I think Köpcke Tinturé is right to suggest that 'invariant' here means conclusive, non-defeasible.

[317] Hence the passage quoted on p. 548 in this essay, in which I say 'The primary reality of the law is rather in its claim, as itself a moral requirement, on my deliberating about what to decide... to choose and do...' The syntax of 'its claim, as itself a moral requirement' is (not accidentally) ambivalent, falling short of 'its claim to create a moral requirement', but seeming to suggest something more than 'its claim to create a legal requirement (which we should presume to be a moral requirement)'.

[318] See p. 538 at n. 279 in this essay.

even in the central case of law—embodies a moral error, and asserts (albeit implicitly) a moral falsehood. For, in my view (well set out by Köpcke Tinturé [pp. 391–2]), the moral obligation created and imposed by the law is defeasible, and defeasible not only by injustice in its making or content but also by competing moral responsibilities of particular subjects on particular occasions, responsibilities sufficiently serious to prevail over the 'strongly exclusionary moral reasons' created by the law (*NLNR*, 319, quoted earlier in this section). I do not see that Köpcke Tinturé replies to this difficulty—that her view entails that moral falsehood is built into the morally most satisfactory form of political organization.

How then do I reply to her objection that no content has been attributed to 'legally obligatory' to occupy that 'space in deliberation' in which good citizens decide (judge) what they should treat as decisive for their choice of conduct? Well, the law implicitly deploys and holds out the schema of practical reasoning reported in her section I (her intrepid explorer's report: p. 382), but with step *A* so isolated[319] from 'the flow of general ("extra-legal") [straightforward] practical reasoning'[320] that it makes no reference to 'the common good' but just to an unspecified need for all the law's subjects to be law-abiding. That need in turn can be explicated—reintegrated into a flow of general practical reasoning—by good citizens in terms of the common good, by 'good citizens' (uncritical servants of the regime) in terms of the sustaining of the regime, by careerists in the law in terms of what must be done or omitted to promote their own advancement towards wealth or office, and by disaffected or criminally opportunistic citizens in terms of what they themselves need in order to get by without undesired consequences (punishment and the like). In all these specimens of practical reasoning, the law slots into the relevant schema and thereby intelligibly 'holds out its principles and rules as a (non-optional) standard for comparing options and ranking them as obligatory, permissible, or impermissible ... and so forth'. That is 'the place it claims in our deliberations'.[321] What *NLNR* XI.4 predicates of these non-optional standards is that

---

[319] The grounds for this isolation (which is in no way abrogated when the law's model schema of practical reasoning is integrated or slotted into some general flow of practical reasoning, but only when the question arises of 'equitably' interpreting or reforming a particular rule or principle) are well set out in section III of her essay. To the citations given at and in n. 25 of the essay I would add (what ought to have been recalled in *NLNR*, 473) *CEJF* IV.2 (1989b), 64:

> The quality of a legal system that makes it authoritative is its general salience. By holding itself out as a public and privileged identification of a solution for the case of every coordination problem, and by offering grounds for acknowledging that privileged status, the law achieves the salience it seeks in particular coordination problems. The grounds for acknowledging that privileged status are several. The law, if accorded that status, offers the prospect of combining speed with clarity in generating practical solutions to constantly emerging and changing coordination problems, and in suggesting devices by which such solutions can be generated. Its institutions for devising and maintaining solutions secure fairness by the stability, the practicability, and the generality or non-discriminatory character of the solutions, and by the imposition of those solutions on free-riders and other deviants by processes which minimize arbitrariness and self-interested or partisan deviance in the very processes themselves. In short, it is the values of the Rule of Law that give the legal system its distinctive entitlement to be treated as the source of authoritative solutions.

[320] This is the phrase that the Postscript to *NLNR*, at 473, substitutes for 'the unrestricted flow of practical reasoning'.

[321] *CEJF* I.15 ('Commensuration and Public Reason'), 233.

they are 'legally obligatory in the legal sense', a sense in which their obligatoriness is (deemed) invariant, conclusive, non-defeasible, peremptory—as distinct from 'legally obligatory in the moral sense', a sense in which their obligatoriness is presumptive, defeasible, and so forth. And 'morally decent law-makers and law-appliers (who instantiate the central case of law-making and -applying) will try to ensure that the law they make or apply is fit to impose moral obligations that could only be overridden by moral responsibilities applicable in particular kinds of circumstance not provided for by law...'[322] But whatever the practical reasoning into which it slots, the law's schema for practically understanding the legal obligations that the law claims to articulate and impose is one and the same—practical but not *in itself, as such*, moral, though (in the central case): always *apt* for a moral reading by the morally concerned subject, yet far from empty of guidance, as non-optional, for those uninterested in moral concerns.

24.

Exploring my thinking about constitutions, **Richard Ekins** probes a wide range of issues, at a depth which stirs up thought about fundamentals. The issue throughout the following reflections arising from his essay is how the *Ought* of a certain important kind of principle can reasonably, and without fallacy or evasion of responsibility to reason, be judged to be modified by the *Is* of states of affairs (facts) resulting from human choices made, or dispositions formed, otherwise than in accordance with that principle. Can we avoid the sheer opacity about and indeed indifference to this issue that are to be found in Kelsen and Hart[323] as much as in an overtly decisionist Schmitt?

What is it for a people, its members and its rulers and judges, to recognize a constitution as a foundation for and articulation of their willingness to conduct their life together over time as a legally ordered political community? The question can be approached directly, or it can emerge as an outcome of inquiring into a legal system considered as a set of rules, norms, or principles treated as valid or operative not simply at some moment but across a period of time. The period may include events widely and reasonably treated as law-making or law-terminating otherwise than by virtue of rules authorizing them or validating such an effect: *coups d'état* and revolutions. But it will surely also include events purporting to be, and generally accepted as, *authorized* acts of law-making: constitutional devolution or succession. In either kind of case, legal thinking, whether formal or informal, involves the 'general principle of continuity' recalled and quoted by Ekins [p. 397]. As he remarks, it exists as 'a disposition of the political community' [p. 397], a state of willingness to take past acts as settling the present, and in my reflections in section 13 (Tollefsen), I have called this the onto-logical foundation of the law[324]: so far as it is a sheer fact about shared states of mind, it

---

[322] *CEJF* IV.Introduction, 6, n. 13. Of course, in legal systems rendered non-central by their rulers' deviations from or negligence about the common good's requirements—deviations parallel to those of the 'good citizens', careerists, and opportunistic and criminal *subjects* just mentioned in the text of the present paragraph—there may well be no intent to 'offer a moral syllogism' to anyone.

[323] *CEJF* IV.21, 417.

[324] See p. 519, n. 210 in this essay.

is the law's material cause; so far as those states of mind have a particular intellectual content picking out such-and-such a set of propositions of law, it is the law's formal cause.

When he reminds us that 'the continuity and identity of a legal system is a function of the continuity and identity of the society in whose ordered existence in time the legal system participates',[325] Ekins is referring to this ontological, 'factual' existence and character of the principle (as a disposition, a state of affairs). But he adds that the disposition 'follows from the reasonableness of ordering public life in this way', and I agree—provided that 'follows from' is taken as a psychological generalization rather than a logical implication. Principles of the kind that his essay highlights function both as factual (psychological) causes (*principia*, sources) *of* actions, including law's practices and institutions, and as rational justifications *for* judgments (conclusions) in legal, political, and moral reasoning. In their latter sense and significance, principles face critical scrutiny for their justice and contribution to common good. Perhaps Ekins says 'follows from' to signal the difference between such truly general principles (without which 'legal system' would lose much of its sense and legal ordering most of its point) and, on the other hand, principles important in the constitution and political life of one or many political communities but lacking a rational claim to universality.

As an example of the latter, non-universal principles, consider the three articulated in my critique of the Lords' *Belmarsh* decision: (1) citizens can never be excluded from the realm; (2) aliens can be excluded because states need not accept from aliens the risks they must accept from citizens; (3) subject to (2) and employment conditions imposed on entry, 'aliens within the realm have rights and obligations equal to citizens'.[326] Principle (1) did not crystallize until the mid to late 19th century; statutes ordering banishment or transportation of Jesuits, whether British nationals or foreign, were enacted as late as 1829 and not repealed until 1926. Principle (3), on the other hand, is of considerable antiquity in the common law of England. The emergence of (1) in tandem with (3) yields (2), not as a demand of logic but as a reasonable response to the circumstances of an international order of states occupying the whole globe; international agreements that (4) statelessness is to be minimized are a parallel, complementary response. All four principles taken together amount to a humane and highly suitable way of giving effect to a recognition of the fundamental equality of all human persons. But there have been other ways of giving reasonable effect to that truth about equality.

So those are constitutional principles that depend for part of their normative force on their adoption—that is, on a *fact*: widely shared willingness to appeal to and live by these rather than alternatives. Much more radically dependent on such facts—

---

[325] [p. 397], quoting *CEJF* IV.21, 428. Here 'a function of' is used in the quasi-mathematical sense deployed in Ekins's paraphrase: 'the continuity of the law turns on the continuity of the political community...' [p. 398]. But in saying (*CEJF* IV.21, 425) that the general principle of continuity presupposes, expresses, and realizes the mostly general and basic 'function of the law', my essay on revolutions and continuity of law used 'function' in the non-mathematical sense of role and point (purposive function). Ekins reasonably takes this as too obvious to comment on, but there is no harm in my mentioning it here.

[326] For these propositions and those that follow, see *CEJF* III.9 ('Nationality, Alienage and Constitutional Principle'), 133–40.

paradigmatically, on a willingness that prolongs what Ekins calls 'past commitments of the political community' [p. 411]—are the defining principles of each political community's constitution: the standards that pick out (a) which legislature(s), courts, and officials have final[327] authority over some particular person (say, me) and accordingly—since that question deserves a principled answer—(b) the range of persons and places to which that authority, sovereign within its jurisdiction, extends.[328] Ekins states that 'Equivocation about the location of law-making authority is reckless'. The statement may need some qualification. Are there not some circumstances, which may even obtain for long periods, when the common good is better served by tolerating some such equivocation (when pressing for a resolution might stymie agreement necessary for resolution of other matters presently more urgently important for the common good), where, and only where, it can reasonably be assumed that the ambiguity will probably not be successfully exploited by some imprudent or ill-disposed segment of the community? The Statute of Westminster 1931 left a number of matters about the location of law-making authority in and in relation to Australia shrouded in wordy obscurity,[329] and to this day it remains far from obvious just when Australia became an independent political community, though it cannot, on even the most pedantic of legalistic views, be later than the date (3 March 1986) when the Australia Acts[330] came into force.

The general principle of continuity can sometimes resolve uncertainty about some constitutional principle(s) or rule(s) more particular than itself. Consider the principle that the Westminster Parliament can repeal any of its own statutes so far as they relate and extend to territories subject to its legislative authority. Ekins deploys this to answer a hypothetical question he raises about the effect of a repeal of the European Communities Act 1972 on the law-making competence of EU organs in relation to the United Kingdom. In doing so, he assumes that at all times the validity of those organs' acts within the UK has depended on the *ambulatory* force and effect of the 1972 Act, not simply on the criteria of validity in force under EU law considered independently of that Act's continuing validity from day to day.[331] This assumption he links, in turn,

---

[327] For practical purposes, this is the coercive authority to seize my goods or person and dispose of them against my will. The negligence with which theorists of 'globalization' or 'legal pluralism' speak of our being subject to many legal orders—speaking in purportedly descriptive mode but with evident complacency, as if this were obviously something desirable—overlooks the strong desirability of minimizing the number of persons who have this final, centrally legal authority over others, and of fully specifying their identity and modus operandi, and clear limits to their respective jurisdictions.

[328] Constitutional principles central to a Westminster-type constitution, such as that taxes and other charges on the subject must be authorized by *specific* parliamentary enactment, are of real practical importance; my written advice applying that principle underlay the decision to bring the challenge to sewerage charges levied, under plausible but (in light of the principle) insufficiently specific statutory authority, on owners of unsewered properties: *Daymond v. South West Water Authority* [1976] AC 609.

[329] See Twomey, *The Australia Acts 1986*, Ch. 2.

[330] Australia Act 1986 (UK) and the identical Australia Act 1986 (Commonwealth [of Australia]); they were each enacted because of uncertainties—for widely different reasons—about the validity within Australia of either, despite the unanimity of all the political actors in both countries and all States of Australia that the legal changes thus effected were desirable. The 1986 Acts eliminated most of the equivocal 1931 Act.

[331] When he says that those EU criteria have not since 1972 been 'in force in the UK', I take it that that phrase includes *sub silentio* 'otherwise than by virtue of s. 2 of the 1972 Act'. That they have since 1972 been in force in the UK of themselves (and not by virtue of the 1972 Act's continuing validity) was argued by Eleanor Sharpston QC in *Thoburn v. Sunderland City Council* [2003] QB 151.

with the 'point that the UK continues to conceive of itself as a distinct political community, apart from the EU'. I do not dispute the point (and as a citizen hope that this long remains the fact, and 'ever' more obviously so). But Ekins's seeming appeal to this fact can helpfully be reinforced by direct appeal to the principle of continuity. For there have been jurists who, ignoring that principle, or giving it no weight even as a presumption, have said that the House of Lords in *Factortame (No. 2)* carried out a stealth '*revolution*' by changing (or treating as changed) the constitutional principle of parliamentary sovereignty, and indeed the legal concept of UK sovereignty, by treating the law-making authority of Parliament as now simply subject to counter-vailing principles and rules of EU law.[332] Such a view, if not a mere expression of favour for submersion of the UK in a European United State, manifests an unwillingness to think juridically about basic constitutional laws—a premature 'legal realism' which bows to (alleged) 'facts' to impose legal obligations without reason. There can indeed be revolutions which so change the facts about a community's order that responsible juridical thinking will regard the principle of legal continuity as modified, in its application to the new condition of the country's affairs, by the needs of the common good including acquired rights and a stable Rule of Law: modified just as much as is strictly necessary for those purposes, and no more. But an important element in juridical thinking is accurate reading of the judicial decisions to which appeal is made; and in fact no trace of a revolution—of an intent to change the law, or proclaim it changed—can properly be found in *Factortame (No. 2)*.[333]

The first proposition in my last Oxford undergraduate lectures on 'Fundamentals of the Constitution' (2001) was that 'the constitution of the United Kingdom is a matter of common law, as modified from time to time by Act of Parliament'. Was that too unilateral a statement? I would certainly not affirm it if 'is a matter of common law' were to be understood as acknowledging an authority of judges, as supposed *makers* of the common law, to change the constitution by deciding that a rule of the common law constitution needs changing in light of what they judge necessary or desirable, whether for the protection of human rights or democracy or of other concerns or interests they hold sufficiently important. My explanation of 'common law' included the propositions that its determination and statement in the rulings and reasoning of the superior courts in each case '*seeks to identify* the unenacted principles, institutions, and rules *which have already been identified* by the superior courts of record, and modifies them so far as is appropriate to make a them a coherent set *consistent with any Parliamentary enactments that have modified them* or authorised their modification by ministers of the Crown or (occasionally) others'. And it concluded: 'Each of the three great

---

[332] Thus Wade, 'Sovereignty—Revolution or Evolution?', 573. The true position is well stated by Trevor Hartley in a memorandum of evidence to the European Scrutiny Committee of the House of Commons ('The European Union and British Sovereignty') dated November 2010, touching what is now s. 18 of the European Union Act 2011: <http://www.publications.parliament.uk/pa/cm201011/cmselect/cmeuleg/633ii/633we04.htm>. Similar: Adam Tomkins's memorandum at . . ./633we02.htm.

[333] [1990] UKHL 7, [1991] 1 AC 603. I argued this point in Oxford examiners' reports in 1997 and 1998, and the lectures in 2001, giving various textual and contextual considerations overlapping with but going beyond the correct disposal of the matter by Laws LJ in 2002 in *Thoburn* at 185–6 [61].

documents of the constitution is framed in terms of rights and liberties *already old*: Magna Carta (1215), the Petition of Right (1627), the Bill of Rights (1689).'[334]

So the thought that the constitution is a matter of common law need not be an expression of the constitutional 'common law radicalism' denounced by Adam Tomkins and, without that label, by Jeffrey Goldsworthy and by Ekins in his forthright and sound critique of Lord Steyn's pronouncement that 'the supremacy of Parliament is still the general principle of our constitution. The judges created this principle.'[335] The principle, to be sure, is acknowledged by the judges, and could not have become law without that acknowledgement. But it has both its origins and its present operation as a constitutional principle by virtue of the dispositions also of many politically relevant persons and groups besides the courts. I would not adopt Goldsworthy's formulation of the point, when he says: 'the true foundation of the doctrine of parliamentary sovereignty is general consensus among senior officials of all branches of government, supported by public opinion and based on commitments to principles of political morality such as democracy'.[336] Rather, we should go beyond that consensus to its propositional content, where we find the grounds of its normativity; for the consensus is a shared willingness to assent to a normative proposition: that our realm and its people, as a historic and continuing community, should (as it can) defend and promote the rights and well-being of its members by common acknowledgement of the fundamental principles and rules (not least parliamentary supremacy) by which it has lived since the time—now very many centuries ago—when it first began to understand itself as this realm and people and to govern itself accordingly.

In the early-middle maturity of this historical process we find the three books on the governance of England by Sir John Fortescue, eight times a member of Parliament, a former Chief Justice of the King's Bench, and councillor to both Henry VI and (after pardon) Edward IV. All three of these 15th-century books will be taken up into the judicial recognition of parliamentary supremacy and the separation of powers in the *Case of Proclamations* (1611). All three place themselves under the aegis of Aquinas's doctrine of political as opposed to regal governance, the essence of 'political' governance being that the people rule themselves, since their laws do not emanate from the will of the monarch alone, but are made 'with the assent of the whole realm' (as represented in parliament), so that 'political law restrains the power of the king'.[337] If we were, like Fortescue, to adopt the categories of that grand philosophical theorist

---

[334] The clarification was defective in not bringing to light the extent to which Parliamentary enactments, and other non-judicial pronouncements and acts, have been *sources* as well as modifiers of the judicially recognized law of the constitution. My lectures' first proposition also neglected '*convention*(al) principles'.

[335] *Jackson v. A-G* [2005] UKHL 56, [2006] 1 AC 262 at 302 [102]; Ekins, 'Acts of Parliament and the Parliament Acts', 103. Cf. also Wade, 'Sovereignty—Revolution or Evolution?', 574: 'It [the rule about the overriding effect of Acts of Parliament] is a rule of unique character, since only the judges can change it.'

[336] 'Submissions [to the European Scrutiny Committee] on Proposed EU Bill' (November 2010), paragraph 6: <http://www.publications.parliament.uk/pa/cm201011/cmselect/cmeuleg/633ii/633we12.htm>.

[337] Fortescue, *De Laudibus Legum Angliae*, Chs 19 and 9 (Lockwood, *Sir John Fortescue: On the Laws and Governance of England*, 28–9, 17–18). The CUP editor says, Lockwood (1997) xxxviii–xxxix:

> In conclusion, therefore, Fortescue's political thought represents to a large extent the 'Englishing' of Thomist theory . . . King and people are bound together by the *vinculum iuris* [bond of law] and together they deliberate and determine the means to their single destination [the *bonum commune* of the *res publica* and realm itself].

of our civilization we would locate the supreme law-making power (the 'sovereignty' of a later jargon) in 'the whole people (*tota multitudo*)' that is 'a free people (*libera multitudo*) which can make law for itself'.[338] And we would not say that it is common law that confers this status on the people, or on the categories of public person that come to 'represent [bear the *persona* of]'[339] the people for the purposes of making, maintaining, and declaring the law. What the common law does is articulate and supervise the application of a constitutive self-understanding going well beyond, and preceding, the self-understanding and pronouncements of judges,[340] and contributing in due measure to the constancy and coherence of the normative orientation—to the common good of justice and peace for our polity and people—that is decisive for that self-understanding's, that self-*determination's*, relevance to the law and the constitution.

In personal friendship, the universalities of the intelligible basic human goods are given a particularity of concern, affection, and even of commitment, a particularity which adds to those universalities a rational ground for the prioritizing necessitated by our finitude—a ground constituted by the factual happenstance of contiguities of birth, sustenance, upbringing, familiarity, shared interests and memories and information and pride and shame, along with mutual trust as well as appropriate (experience-based) distrust: a set of facts that make reasonable the expectation that common good (in the first place, ours!) can be served by collaboration with *this* person for purposes *we* share. In marriage, this 'taking up of reasons out of the fungibility of goods affirmable by reason'[341] has the rational form of a most thoroughgoing commitment. In political community, formed up around the need for irreparable measures to preserve and enforce justice, the obligations of citizenship or rulership are not quite as pointedly unconditional, but have a *sui generis* solemnity and reach. Only when this is acknowledged (however inarticulately) does it become possible to have constituent practices

---

The *De Laudibus* [*In Praise of the Laws of England*] was published with an English translation in 1567, 1573, 1599, and 1616 (to mention only the Bodleian copies), and later in many other editions.

[338] *ST* I–II q. 90 a. 3c with q. 97 a. 3 ad 3; *Aquinas*, 264; Fortescue, *De Laudibus*, c.13 (Lockwood, *Sir John Fortescue: On the Laws and Governance of England*, 20–2): the people 'wills to erect itself into a kingdom [realm]', this realm 'issues from the people', and the king [ruler], at least in a 'political' realm, 'has power to this end [scil. for the protection of the law, the subjects, and their bodies and goods] issuing from the people'.

[339] *ST* I–II q. 90 a. 3c; q. 97 a. 3 ad 3.

[340] To say this is not, I think, to subtract from the conclusion I reached about the role of judges in post-coup situations (see 1969a, 77):

> In revolutionary situations such as those in Pakistan (1958), Uganda (1966) and Rhodesia . . . the judges have a legal authority to determine controversies (and the principles for determining future controversies) precisely because, being previously lawfully appointed and accepted as the judges in their community, nothing has happened which need be regarded as divesting them of their authority. At these critical times they sit lawfully, but not 'under' any constitution (where by 'constitution' is meant the constitution in the positivist sense, i.e., something that can be promulgated or annulled *uno ictu*, as distinct from that lasting order of society which makes it intelligible and reasonable, *inter alia*, to regard certain men as judges without needing to know under which 'constitution' they sit). [n. Cf. Hegel: 'The existence of the people and a constituent Assembly already presupposes a constitution, an organic constitution, an ordered popular life' . . .]

See likewise *NLNR*, 275–6.

[341] *CEJF* I.1, 40.

and constitutive or determinative 'moments' or 'events', and possible for the normative significance[342] of those to subsist, through adherence to the principle of continuity, in the form of a constitutional order and legal system.

The injustice, unconcealed furor, and consequent wickedness and horrors of the *Gleichschaltung* ('bringing into line', a euphemism) instigated by the National Socialist regime, and ideologized by its prime scholarly juristic theorist Carl Schmitt, as a forcible means to the *Gleichartigkeit* or *Artgleichheit* of national homogeneity as ground for the unrestricted domination of the people by the Executive,[343] have understandably[344] deterred or dampened inquiry and reflection about the preconditions[345] for the emergence and sustainability of the shared understandings and trust that make possible and stable the widely shared disposition[346] whose articulable content is a constitution. But that justified caution is no sufficient justification for carelessness about those preconditions. The 'constitutional patriotism' that some recent, mostly German theorists (not least in reaction to the Nazi exploitation and deformation of patriotism) have proposed as a reputable replacement for patriotism, should rather be regarded as one element in the central case(s) of reasonable and affective patriotism, itself a necessary condition for constitutional government and political liberty. That is to say, a reasonable patriotism includes an understanding that a broadly worthy constitution, in its place in the sequence of constitutional forms of *our* constitution, is one of the fine things—our patrimony and social capital—to which it is good to be attached, in large measure because one is *grateful* that these things were *made to be*, and are *there for us all* in our infancy, maturity and, we hope, in any later dependency.

---

[342] For the ultimate normative basis of this in the possibility the fact affords for cooperation highly promotive of human common good (and avoidance of evils), see *NLNR*, 249–52.

[343] Faye, *Heidegger*, 153, quotes a writing of Schmitt in May 1933:

> German law and the German state no longer [*scil.* since March] rest on the empty and formal 'equality of all before the law' or the deceptive phrase 'equality of all that has a human face', but on the real homogeneity and substantial nature of the entire German people, unified in itself and homogeneous. *Gleichartigkeit* [homogeneity of type/race] is something more, and something more profound than *Gleichschaltung*, which is but a means and an instrument for *Gleichartigkeit*... The decisions concerning magistrates, doctors and lawyers purify public life from non-Aryan elements foreign to the race.

And see the whole of Ch. 6. Also, briefly, Jones, *The Nazi Conception of Law*, 5–6.

[344] But, I believe, needlessly and even damagingly. Excessive recoil of this kind took some time to become prevalent: in September 1957, for example, the Australian Catholic Bishops all spoke with undisguised appreciation of national homogeneity (as something to be valued and retained, not, of course, to be imposed), and of the need for 'cultural pluralism' to give way, after a generation or so, to 'complete cultural integration'. Though perhaps speaking more or less *ultra vires*, as Catholic bishops fairly often do, their grasp of the problem of conditions for common and public good was firmer than many of their successors', who seem relatively inattentive to what John Paul II in 2005 called a tenet of Catholic social doctrine: that 'the family and the nation are both natural societies' which cannot in human history be replaced by anything else; he went on to suggest that the proper remedy for 'unhealthy nationalism' includes essentially a reasonable patriotism: see *CEJF* II.7, 123.

[345] On these see *CEJF* II.6 ('Law, Universality, and Social Identity'), 107–8, 114–18; *CEJF* II.7 ('Cosmopolis, Nation States, and Families'), 123, 125–6.

[346] 1968b, 59:

> What the events of the period under review [in India] do seem to suggest...is a breakdown in the *homonoia* or *concordia* or spirit of harmonious give-and-take and constitutional like-mindedness which the classical theorists of western political institutions insisted upon as the *sine qua non* of constitutional government and order.

And, thankfully, our constitution (like its more or less proximate descendants in other countries) *is* a fine thing precisely because it has been built up to incorporate the goods of discourse and reason, being (in Aquinas's turn of phrase) 'well mixed', dividing sovereign responsibility and consequent authority between legislative, executive, and judicial, prudently trusting the bearers of these responsibilities with a measure of control over each other which can work for the common weal as long as constitutional wariness coexists with an underlying mutuality of trust that all concerned have the same particular commonwealth in mind.[347] All this remains true even if, as now, the popular suffrage is manifestly resulting (in the most banal of predictable ways) in the evasion of long-term problems, and the incurring (via unnecessary but popular expenditures) of vast public debts that are liable in time to result in many serious difficulties threatening even the maintenance of the constitution, and to put pressure on the old and the ill to kill themselves (or acquiesce in their own killing), even before future generations find themselves burdened with unpayable obligations. And it remains true even if, as now, *the people* is represented to itself in the forms of anti-patriotic cultural relativism, racialist self-abasement,[348] legalized will to kill the unborn, contempt for the goods and disciplines of marriage, and in endlessly diverting entertainments occluding much-needed attention to public perils, and suffocating the aspirations—to learning, wisdom and self-government—that characterized the Christian people who 150 years ago won for themselves that popular franchise which, in principle, completed the joining up of our kind of constitution with its Thomistic *Idealtyp*.

25.

From **Neil Gorsuch**'s opening selection of benevolent recollections and travellers' tales there emerges the question how it could be pertinent to recall the definition of a circle for the instruction of a student who has called an argument circular. The essay holds back from framing this—it is for litigants not judges to frame interrogatories—but I will volunteer an anticipatory answer. Some arguments are viciously circular, but some arguments are circular without vice. Without even covertly helping themselves to the desired conclusion by employing it as a premise, they circle from 'point to point' around a set of considerations each of which casts some light upon the others and upon their joint significance. Consider, say, proofs of guilt; or, as I doubtless had in mind[349] when saying what the tale recounts, the elements of an explanatory definition such as of 'circle' by reference to 'centre', 'radius', and 'circumference', where each element in the

---

[347] This division and mixing of responsibilities and authorities is very fittingly extended to the division of sovereign authority found in federations such as Australia's, provided (as close experience of the governmental workings of that federation for over a decade impressed upon me) that the preconditions of underlying trust, shared understanding of history, and fellow-feeling are satisfied (to a degree that there is no recipe or formula for determining).

[348] On willingness to assent (not always tacitly) to a reverse colonization by peoples of profoundly alien culture, etc., see *CEJF* I.19, 323–4; *CEJF* II.6, 117–21; II.7, 125–6; *CEJF* III.20, 328; *CEJF* V.1, 41; and p. 544 in this essay.

[349] From the discussion of this in Lonergan, *Insight: A Study of Human Understanding*, sections 2.6–8; I will have said, I think, '…a locus of points…' On some of what I took and declined to take from Lonergan's work, see *CEJF* Index s.v. Lonergan.

definition must be grasped by insight without deduction, in order to grasp the whole. 'Some wide circles have explanatory power' is how Raz's essay puts it.[350]

The body of the Gorsuch essay recalls some high points in the law's use of intention as a basis for liability, concluding that this use 'is not always and wholly beside the point' and 'can, at least sometimes, be both analytically and normatively justified'. If someone asks, 'Well, *when?*', I would venture to say: (1) When someone *intends* to do harm, whether as an end or as a means, the law can be presumed to treat any resultant damage, so intended, as 'ground for liability' (in the usual lawyers' sense of 'ground', namely, sufficient unless defeated by some specific head of defence). But (2) when someone causes harm *without* intending it either as end or as means, the absence of intent to harm will *often* be irrelevant—no defence; and (3) not rarely, when the 'subjective' foresight or 'objective' foreseeability[351] of the harm is sufficiently plain, the law will mark our sense of the culpability of causing harm in such circumstances by treating the causing of harm as intended. Position (3) involves a fiction and is I believe, unnecessary and regrettable. Gorsuch remarks without evident enthusiasm [p. 415] that such 'deeming' is entrenched in the law of tort, perhaps for good reason 'given that in tort only money, not individual liberty, is at stake'. The problem is that the main peddlers of this fiction, professors of tort law, get an early, straight shot at imbuing young law students with a kind of negligence about the realities of intention.[352]

For intention, under any of its many names and pronominals, is a reality, and one that matters greatly in a person's or society's self-awareness, and in shaping a person's or society's stance in the world. Tort law is rightly unimpressed, in many contexts and heads of liability, by the *absence of* (real) intent, and rightly willing to impose liability, far-reachingly, for negligence. But even tort law should not be indifferent to the moral purpose and purport of those important parts of our law, and of our general stance towards each other, that are concerned to exclude *intent to harm* from social interaction and life. Gorsuch's essay speaks to this with firmness and energy.[353]

The underlying point is that—put at it its briefest—what is intended so figures in the acting person's proposal that it is *adopted*—chosen and *made his or her own*, as end

---

[350] See [p. 18], and in this essay pp. 460, 463, 546–7.

[351] Restatement (Second) of Torts section 8A requires actual belief that the consequences are substantially certain to result, and the modern law has been increasingly hostile to extending the fiction so as to deem that consequences foreseeable but not foreseen to be certain are therefore intended.

[352] The problem is not, of course, confined to tort law and doctrine. At least outside the US (as to which Gorsuch's nn. 4 and 47 speak), criminal law and doctrine have, in relation to accomplices, remained enmeshed in what amounts to a kind of 'felony-murder' liability long abolished in relation to principals; for those who go on a joint criminal venture knowing that one of the venturers may use a lethal weapon are liable for murder, without any further *mens rea* on their part (i.e. without any intent to kill or wound), if eventual use of the weapon causes death with intent *on the part of the user* to kill or seriously injure. See e.g. *Rahman (Islamur)* [2008] UKHL 45, [2009] 1 A.C. 129 at 160 [51] (Lord Brown):

> There are many more murderers under our law than there are people who have killed intentionally. The actus reus of murder is, of course, the killing of the victim; the mens rea (established in *R v Cunningham* [1982] AC 566) is the intention either to kill the victim or at least to cause him some really serious bodily injury—grievous bodily harm as it used to be called, gbh for short. As this appeal illustrates, moreover, there is a further group of murderers too, those who did not intend even gbh but who foresaw that others might kill and yet nonetheless participated in the venture.

[353] See especially his text at pp. 419–22.

and/or means—in the adopting of the proposal, whereas the side effects, however foreseeable and foreseen and perhaps very 'directly' caused, are not adopted, but only accepted or permitted. So, for example, in relation to assisting suicide, the persons 'swept into the dragnet' [p. 422] of a soundly articulated law, will be those who choose to supply the means of (self-)killing. To take (briefly) a relatively difficult example: It is one thing to (1) abstain from treating, out of respect for the autonomy of the person who cannot be treated without autonomous consent; it is quite another thing, as a human reality, to (2) supply lethal dosages or other means out of respect for the suicidal person's autonomy. For (2), unlike (1), entails treating that person's *death* as a (conditional) means, that is, as part of one's purpose (on the ground that, if the suicidal person chooses to go through with it, that is what he 'autonomously' intends/purposes). In (2), the assisting person makes the success of the plan (the bringing about of death) part of his intention, *adopting* it (subject only to a condition whose eventual fulfilment or non-fulfilment is not up to him). To adopt the bringing about of death into one's character as individual or society is to cross a real line[354] into another form of personal and social life, a form of life that Gorsuch's *The Future of Assisted Suicide and Euthanasia* does much to bring into view and make understandable, and (as he foresees and accepts) nothing to make tempting.

V. Philosophy, Religion, and Public Reasons

These two essays include extended, fully public reflections on the content of a religious faith that holds itself out as reasonable, accessible to all reasonable people with the opportunity and capacity to give it a fair hearing, and yet as informed not only by 'natural reason' using the sources and methods of natural science or philosophy, but also by 'public revelation'—communications of the intentions of a transcendent Creator, by means of historical teachings and actions of a small number of people at particular times and places in the past. Faith in this revelation (its occurrence and its communicable propositional content) involves more than assent to its propositional content; it includes a personal commitment both to its author and to orienting one's life according to the way it holds out both as invitation and requirement. But insofar as it is, in a central respect, assent to propositions, it properly includes assent to the propositions (held by the Catholic Church) that none of those propositions contradicts anything to which natural reason (including every science) requires one to assent, and that respect for historical evidence provides much reasonable support for believing, rather than rejecting or doubting, the testimony in reliance on which one assents to those propositions of the faith that are not accessible to the sources and methods of the sciences. In these very substantial respects, then, to hold *this* faith is to believe it a part of public reason, to expect participants in public reason to subject any and every part of its content and its evidences to rational scrutiny, and to entertain a rational hope that a good many will come to share the judgment that everyone should (and under *ideal* epistemic conditions would)[355] assent to it.

---

[354] And see p. 534, n. 267 in this essay.   [355] See p. 472 at n. 47 in this essay.

26.

What is the historic and present content of Catholic teaching about the right to religious liberty, that is, to immunity from coercion 'in religious matters'? **Thomas Pink** gives us a complex, muscular synopsis of the work with which he has recently given new impetus and inflection to that scholarly *quaestio*. The key to the matter turns out to be what is meant by 'coercion' and 'coercive penalties' within the Church and indeed within the state—what the intentionality of and in these social actions is. And that is not the only respect in which there is much of wide interest, going beyond history and Catholic faith, in the five of his theses I would like to address:

A. The religious-liberty right, as affirmed by the Second Vatican Council's declaration *Dignitatis Humanae* [DH], is based on one's metaphysical freedom, that is, one's power of control over one's belief and action. [p. 438: likewise pp. 428, 437, 439]

B. Despite appearances (including *Thesis A*), *DH* bases its declaration on the division of jurisdiction between state government and law, on the one hand, and ecclesiastical (or more generally, religious) authority and law, on the other [pp. 437, 438]: *DH*'s teaching 'involves a model of religious liberty that is jurisdiction-centred rather than purely person-centred' [p. 438] and 'in no way impugns religious coercion as such' [p. 437].

C. The religious repression in 'Catholic states' in former centuries resulted from an ecclesiastical *policy*—now shelved indefinitely—of requiring or licensing baptized Catholics in positions of authority as state governors or law-makers to lend the assistance of state coercion to the Church's exercise of *its own coercive jurisdiction* over heretics and apostates ('all along the real coercive authority in religion was the Church, not the state' [p. 441]).

D. *DH*, while implicitly but plainly ratifying and reinforcing the abandonment of that policy of the Church (regarding 'state coercion under her authority' and 'on her behalf' [p. 437]) by the preceding six or seven popes, carefully left intact the legitimate authority and liberty-right of the Church to make such requests of or impose such requirements on Catholic political leaders, notwithstanding everyone's metaphysical freedom and the state's own lack of *inherent* authority in such matters.

E. For it is an irreversible teaching of the Catholic faith (against Erasmus) that the Church has 'divinely given authority to coerce belief' [p. 441], that is, jurisdiction to coerce and 'pressure' [p. 427] any of the baptized to adhere to the Catholic faith, even those who never adopted it by a mature, personal act of commitment.

The evidence Pink points to in support of *Thesis E*, evidence which received scant if any attention in the Council's public deliberations, and little scholarly attention since, puts all five theses on the table, and shakes up the discussion of religious freedom in a salutary way, even if we conclude that the theses themselves cannot stand.

As to *Thesis A*: It is important not to rest content with the thought that the natural right affirmed by *DH* is 'based on metaphysical freedom'. To be sure, the right is so based in the weak[356] sense that such freedom is amongst its necessary conditions. But normative truths such as duties and correlative rights need premises at least one of which refers to a *good* that *needs* to be promoted, respected, or protected by some sort of action or abstention (no *Ought* from a bare *Is*). Accordingly we find in *DH*'s third sentence: 'the liberty thus demanded pertains above all to those [goods] that are goods of the human spirit (*animi humani bona*), primarily indeed those [goods] that relate to the free exercise of religion in society'. The *DH* drafting committee's report to the Council in November 1964 states that in truth six kinds of freedom (*libertas*) are in play, the sixth being the 'religious liberty-right' itself and the other five being collectively its basis (*fundamentum*).[357] Setting aside, for a moment, the fourth and fifth as pertaining to divine revelation not natural reason, we are left with (i) 'physical' (the fact of *liberum arbitrium*, free will or freedom of choice, which Pink equally reasonably calls 'metaphysical'), (ii) 'psychological', and (iii) 'moral'. Here 'psychological' was used to denote that human *responsibility* which marks us out—as agents answerable for our actions—from other creatures. And 'moral' liberty was said by the committee to be what one needs, by way of immunity from coercive interference, if one is to fulfil one's moral responsibilities (in particular in relation to God) as one judges them to be. The committee's explanation only dimly succeeds in pointing to the relevant *goods*. But taking it with the text as developed through four successive drafts in 1964–65, each more clearly articulating the human good (and need and duty) of being authentically interested in truth (especially about matters of ultimate significance) even when one happens to reach untrue judgments, we can see what the Council was pointing to. It can be summarized with emphasis either on the psychological conditions for seeking truth[358] or on the psychological conditions for entering into an appropriate relationship with the God

---

[356] But of course significant; Pink rightly reminds us [p. 438] that Catholic grounds for affirming the right to religious liberty are 'distinctive' in a culture where very many of those who affirm it deny (in the last analysis, absurdly: see p. 465 in this essay) the ontological reality of free choice.

[357] Hellín, *Declaratio de Libertate Religiosa*, 582–3 (= *Acta Vat. II* IV/1, 183–5): libertas religiosa... fundamentum habet in omnibus aliis libertatibus atque ab ipsis exigitur...

[358] *CEJF* V.2, 49:

> so important is it for each human being to seek, find, and live according to the truth about God and man—religious truth—that coercion, since it prevents, distorts, or tends to render inauthentic that search for religious truth, is wrongful. The wrong done is a wronging of the person whose search for truth, had there been no coercive pressure to conform, might have been authentic and centred on truth (about the most important things) at least as an aspiration, ideal, or goal. So that person (and thus any person) has the right (claim-right) correlative to the government's duty not to commit that wrong.

See also *CEJF* V.4, 94:

> *Dignitatis Humanae*... mak[es] primary one's serious duty to pursue the truth about ultimates and to shape one's life in line with what one judges one has discovered about them, a duty which is only fulfilled if it is pursued with an authenticity which coercion and 'psychological pressure' prejudice, corrupt, and tend to nullify.

Likewise at *CEJF* V.1, 39.

whose existence, nature, and purposes become, to some extent, discernible by way of such search.[359]

In either form, this argumentation is now confronted by the considerations attractively assembled in Pink's Suarezian thesis that coercion can actually aid authentic belief.[360] This is the theory—at once about causality and purpose ('function')—that Pink has primarily in mind when from time to time he refers summarily to 'pressuring belief', as a *project* not unreasonable in kind [pp. 427–8, 430, 439–40]:

> canonical punishments for heresy and the like threatened by the counter-reformation Church, or by the modern Church, are similar *in intended function* to those threatened by today's liberal state: to communicate testimony or witness to the truth given by representatives of the coercing authority... and *by impelling attention to the message and its grounds, to pressure those subject to the authority into believing it.* [p. 440, my emphases]

Such a project, precisely one of inflicting punishment in order to bring about Christian belief (albeit via 'impelled' attention to evidence), was always vigorously rejected by Aquinas. There is no reason to think that he accepted the idea of *compelling the beliefs* of heretics or lapsed Catholics any more than the idea, which he unambiguously rejected, of compelling Jews, Mahometans, or pagans into belief in the Catholic faith. 'Belief is a matter of will [or: is voluntary]'; to an objector who cites this Augustinian maxim as grounds for leaving heretics uncoerced, Aquinas gives a reply that takes the maxim and its soundness for granted: 'the Church does not proceed against heretics with a view to using force to lead them to belief, but instead to prevent them corrupting others, and so as not to leave so great a wrong unpunished'.[361]

---

[359] *Aquinas*, 293:

> The requirement that faith be voluntary and free from coercive pressures... is an implication of the basic good of religion as a personal search for, appropriation of, and adherence in practice to the truth about God as one can grasp it.

But it should be said more plainly that faith goes beyond its necessary and core assent to propositions for their truth and includes also, and also centrally, commitment to the God who is the object (and guarantor) of those propositions, and the commitment, as fundamental option, to live accordingly, both in prayer and in the other elements of one's daily life. See *CEJF* II.2, 52; *CEJF* V.10, 171; V.17, 229; Grisez, *Living a Christian Life*, Ch 1.

[360] Pink puts it thus [pp. 440–1]:

> ... dislike of the threatened penalties is supposed to work by engaging the attention of those threatened, and motivating and directing them seriously to consider a case that is being argued, on the basis of reasoning or credible testimony, and which they had wilfully and culpably been ignoring. In relation to belief the function of coercion is not to replace argument and evidence, but to reinforce them... And certainly in so far as the truth does then actually 'impose itself' on one's belief, one will indeed come to believe the truth just because it is the truth...

[361] *Sent.* IV d. 13 q. 2 a. 3 ad 5. My discussion of Aquinas in this paragraph follows the course of *Aquinas*, 292–3; Pink has criticized that in a longer version of his essay, but I think it accurate and sound. I went a shade too far, however, when I said that Aquinas can be found 'saying' that heretics can rightly be 'compelled... (back) to faith'; the most that is entailed by the structure and language of *ST* II-II q. 10 a. 8 is that 'in *some* sense of "compelled to faith", heretics can rightly be...'; but even that is something Aquinas does not *state*, and such qualms are significant: see p. 569 and p. 575 at n. 391 in this essay.

In Aquinas's more famous, later discussion, in the *Summa Theologiae*, all the weight falls on that last idea: heretics have broken their promise, and like other promise-breakers are punishable by reason of that fault. This last argument is unsound in its reliance on a promise not all heretics had ever actually made,[362] but again there is no trace of a *punitive purpose of inducing belief.* And in a recently discovered sermon probably from the same late period of his life,[363] Aquinas considers how the Gospel parable-saying 'compel them to come in' (Luke 14: 23) applies to heretics; having remarked that one sort of 'compulsion' is the evidence of miracles, he turns to the (or a) literal meaning of 'compel'. He puts the point made by the heretics themselves: 'no-one is to be compelled by punishment to come to faith'. *'Quite so!'* says Aquinas,[364] accepting once again the person-centred application of this premise to persons inside as well as outside the Church. But, he adds, the suffering (*vexatio*) of punishment, like the *vexatio* of floods or other such scourges and miseries, may well have the effect of inducing understanding of the message of the faith.[365] So, once again, we find no acceptance—indeed, a rather forceful rejection—of any *proposal to induce* faith or a return to faith by penalties or coercion, but rather attention to a potential welcome side effect of penalties imposed for other purposes (in the sermon, unstated).

So Suarez, and Pink's rendering of Church teaching, would take what in Augustine probably and Aquinas certainly is treated as, fundamentally,[366] a legitimately welcomed side effect, and propose it instead as a legitimating purpose. And that line of thought seems to me fundamentally incompatible with the central reasoning of *Dignitatis Humanae*, reasoning that does indeed (contrary to *Thesis B*) 'impugn religious coercion as such'.

DH's reasoning (like, no doubt, Aquinas's) goes beyond arguments from unaided natural reason to arguments from revelation. So the drafting committee's type (iv) liberty, 'evangelical [Gospel] freedom', concerns the Christian revelation that our natural human freedom as persons has by divine grace been raised to the (offered and enabled) freedom of sons and daughters in the divine household, a freedom to be lived principally, therefore, as a matter of love. The underlying thought is perhaps even

---

[362] *Aquinas*, 292; *CEJF* V.6, 117.

[363] 1267–71 (discovery announced in 1943): Bataillon, 'Une sermon de s. Thomas d'Aquin sur la parabole du festin', 451–2; Bataillon, 'Le sermon inédit de Saint Thomas *Homo Quidam Fecit Cenam Magnam*', 354; the sermon can be read in the latter, or more conveniently (though without editorial apparatus) at <http://www.corpusthomisticum.org/hhf.html>. Note: a sounder exegesis of Luke 14: 23 can find in the parable nothing about heretics or even about membership of the Church or the divine kingdom: Lagrange, *Evangile selon Luc*, 405–7.

[364] *Certe immo.*

[365] '*Homo quidam fecit cenam magnam*', section 3. The quotation from Isaiah 28: 19, 'vexatio dabit intellectum auditui'—the suffering will give understanding of what is heard [lend understanding to the hearing of it] (Douay: 'vexation alone shall make you understand what you hear'; Knox: 'the very alarm of it will make you understand the revelation at last')—is important, since it is used by Suarez arguing from the punishment of heretics to the compelling of unbelievers. *Vexatio* refers to the undergoing of suffering, deprivation, or fear, etc. (in Isaiah, brought on by 'an overflowing scourge', a 'flood of ruin') and (*pace* Pink's translation of Suarez, *De Fide* d. 20 s. 3 n.17 in the longer version of his essay) should not, I believe, be here translated 'pressure' as a transitive verb which, in relation to human agency, implies intention to impose suffering as the *means* designed to change or induce understanding. Suarez may have seen nothing wrong in such intent, but there is sufficient reason to conclude that Aquinas did not share that complacency, at least in relation to faith.

[366] See pp. 570–1 at n. 371, and p. 576, in this essay.

clearer now, some decades later, in the way brought out in the present pope's remarks about Islam in his address at Regensburg: using force or the threat of force precisely with a purpose of persuasion to faith should be deeply repugnant because it misrepresents the nature of the transcendent creator and of the divine kingdom to which we are invited. My development of these thoughts in 2006 (indeed, by chance, in the week of that address)[367] did not attend to the contention that it can be permissible and appropriate, at least for the Church in relation to its own members, to use coercion precisely with a view to inducing not dull, hypocritical, or irresponsible conformity but belief grounded in evidence, evidence that would be ignored by some people unless they were subjected to coercion or the non-bluffing threat of it. Against that contention, now squarely raised by Pink, I would say three things.

First: it is one thing to compel people (say, convicts, or military draftees) to attend sermons and lectures and other ways[368] of setting out the tenets of and evidences for a religion; it is quite another thing to require (or to 'pressure' by threat of penalising) them, at the end, to *profess or hold* those tenets, or any of them. The Suarezian discussion, so far as I can see, ignores that difference, burying it within the single, equivocal phrase 'compelling belief'—a phrase in the last analysis offensive to pious ears, for the reasons summarized in the preceding paragraph. Whatever could *legitimately* be achieved by requiring profession of faith can be achieved by requiring attendance at lectures and so forth; the rest would be illegitimate humiliation, scandalously encouraged lying and hypocrisy, and so forth.

Second: although the Church, as a 'complete community' *analogous* to the political community,[369] undoubtedly has authority to impose penalties on its members, it would be an abuse of that authority, and a violation of a person's rights, to impose or increase a penalty precisely to induce attention to evidence of the truth of the Church's claims.[370] Punishment can have the beneficial side effect of reforming the offender—where 'reforming' is more properly short for encouraging attention to realities, natural consequences, evidence, and so forth, attention that may yield a change of mind and heart. And modalities of punishment can—and where possible *should*—be adapted, *without increase in the penalty*, to eliciting such effects appropriately (in which case they remain in one respect side effects—not 'the purpose'—and in another respect intended).[371] But the justifying purpose of punishment, distinguishing it from means

---

[367] *CEJF* V.4, 90–5; the relevant part of the Regensburg address is quoted at 91.

[368] During 'basic training' in the Australian Army in 1959, I was pressured (not precisely, if memory serves, compelled) to attend one or two films attractively displaying the 'argument from design' for the existence of a transcendent Creator. The Army's pressure and my resentment of it (absent when coercion or pressure related to *military* matters) only exacerbated my resistance to and repudiation of an argument I now think essentially sound. I do not think the attention-blocking reaction to pressure arose primarily from the thought that the Army was acting outside its jurisdiction.

[369] See Journet, *The Church of the Word Incarnate*, 180, 194. I would say that the core of the *perfecta communitas* analogy is that this is a community which needs (for its Gospel purposes) to be able to act as a community in ways that, whether legislative, executive, or judicial, commit (to some extent) the whole community both internally and in its dealings with other complete communities, such as states.

[370] Suarez himself makes this point with some force in *De Fide* d. 18 s. 3 nn. 8, 9 & 11. And in his treatment of punishment of heretics in d. 20 s. 3 nn. 8–9, where he again quotes Isaiah 28: 19, he makes it clear that the rightness (as he sees it) of the *coactio* (which looks to a future good result, return to faith) depends on the retributive, etc., justice of (and *prior* liability to) the punishment (*punitio*).

intended).[371] But the justifying purpose of punishment, distinguishing it from means taken simply to deprive an offender of the opportunity or means of doing further harm, can only be to restore the order of justice disturbed by culpable offence. Deterrence and reform, in the absence of that retributive purpose (the purpose called in current canon law 'expiatory'[372]) and going beyond straightforward stopping of harm, are contrary to human dignity and rights.[373]

And third: the Church's penal sanctions on its members are coercive only in a relatively weak, extended sense. As the drafting committee said, in rejecting a proposal to include in *DH* 14 some words affirming the Church's responsibility to 'impose its teachings and disciplines on those *freely subject* to it', authoritatively and with sanctions, as 'coercion' [*coactio*] fully compatible with genuine liberty[374]: 'Church action of the kind described is not to be called "coercion" [*non est vocanda coactio*]'.[375] The remark—like the committee's remark (in relation to a proposed amendment of *DH* 10) that 'ecclesiastical punishments … are exercises of the coercive power of the Church … but are not coercive [*non sunt coactio*]'[376]—is scarcely advice for the reform of ecclesiastical law or its terminology, which then as now refers freely to its sanctions as coercive [*coactio, coercere*, etc.]. These were remarks intended to recall to the Council's mind the fundamental significance of what the rejected DH 14 proposal itself had recalled with the word 'freely'. The Church is a voluntary association.[377] The

---

[371] There is a good discussion to essentially this effect in the standard pre-conciliar treatise, Ottaviani, *Institutiones Iuris Publici Ecclesiastici* I, 343–51 (sections 171–4), in the chapter on the Church's coercive authority (*de potestate Ecclesiae coactiva*).

[372] On 'expiatory', see Ottaviani, *Institutiones Iuris Publici Ecclesiastici* I, 343 (section 171). The anti-Erasmian canon discussed by Pink and below is treated at 341 (section 170).

[373] So the commentary on current canon law cited by Pink summarizes its treatment of 'the Church's coercive power' by saying that it—

> must be understood as a *potestas propria* of external forum, with the purpose of safeguarding, or restoring, if applicable, social juridical order, as a necessary assumption for the ecclesial common good in which it is possible for a person to realize himself as a person and as a Christian.

Marzoa *et al.*, *Exegetical Commentary on the Code of Canon Law*, IV.1, 225 (ad can. 1311).

[374] The proposed insertion would have ended by appealing to the example of Christ, 'who again and again harshly condemned, precisely for their unbelief, those who should have acknowledged the truth: "who does not believe will be condemned" (Mark 16:16)'. The drafting committee do not comment on this argument, but rebuff the proposal by saying that *DH* is not about the Church's responsibilities but its rights, and does not concern 'the question of liberty within the Church itself'.

[375] Hellín, *Declaratio de Libertate Religiosa*, 175; *Acta* IV/6, 770.

[376] Hellín, *Declaratio de Libertate Religiosa*, 131; *Acta* IV/6, 761; the previous sentence of the same response of the drafting committee says that the coercion (*coactio*) dealt with in Part I of *DH* is 'intrinsically unjust' (*de se iniusta*). So the committee were treating '*coactio*' as synonymous with '*coercitio*', the word used in the text of *DH* throughout.

[377] Marzoa *et al.*, *Exegetical Commentary on the Code of Canon Law*, IV.1, 200:

> Canonical penal law … is operative where, as the [drafting] Commission [for the Code of 1983] lucidly explained, a member of the Christian faithful wants to participate in the goods that the Church offers with a view to salvation … The law of the Church does not obligate, nor does penal law compel, entering the Church, nor even *remaining* in the Church. What it does obligate (and *ius coactivum* has its field here) is a certain behavior *to the degree to which the adherent wishes* (this wish as such is not a subject of canon law) to be so considered, and as such to enjoy the status of a member. Where then is the opposition between 'the freedom of the act of faith' and penal law? There can be no opposition where there is no meeting. The act of faith and [Catholic] penal law cannot meet, because [Catholic] penal law *presupposes* and finds its point of departure in the very free act of faith or adhesion to the Church.

(Emphasis in original)

penalties for heresy and apostasy, as for the other offences known to canon law, are just what you would expect: deprivation of the benefits of membership (excommunication, deprivation of ecclesiastical office, and the like). They are justifiable not as intended to pressure to faith but as intended to protect the household and vindicate its due order.[378]

Matters have not always, alas, been so clear. We can see things beginning to go wrong when we look at the early 7th-century ruling of the assembly of bishops at Toledo, cited (for its first part) by *DH* and (for its second part) by Pink. Its first part states, in six different, equally forceful ways, that non-believers (Jews) are not to be converted by force or impulsion, or unwillingly, but only by persuasion. Its second part addresses the fact that some people have recently (in fact, less than 20 years earlier) been converted *ad Christianitatem* by *coactio*[379] 'in the time of' (a delicate way of saying, by the order of) Sisebut the Visigothic king of northern Spain—a flagrant royal violation of the principle of freedom in faith, just stated. Yet the bishops then rule that these people should be compelled (*cogantur*)—by Church or State is left unspecified, as is the envisaged mode of compulsion—to hold to the faith to which they had committed themselves and in whose sacraments they had participated; the reason given is that otherwise God would be blasphemed and that same faith (and commitment) would be treated as worthless and contemptible.[380] The intentionality and meaning of such 'compelling to keep the faith', left unclear at Toledo, will later be disputed, as they are, implicitly, by Aquinas as against Suarez.

Charles Cardinal Journet, friend of Pope Paul VI and closest modern theological student of these matters, said (by implication) in one of the Council's plenary sessions on *DH* that the '*christianitas*' we see referred to in such documents as Toledo's was a *temporal*[381] *and political* order (in which the Church played a part the precise lineaments of which I will not attempt to define).[382] That order was created in large measure by the initiative of over-enthusiastic secular rulers such as this King Sisebut, but was in important ways endorsed and enthusiastically supported by the Church's own

---

[378] Pius XII said to the ecclesiastical judges in 1946:

> a member of the Church may not without fault deny or repudiate the Catholic truth he has once known and accepted. And when the Church, having certain proof of the fact of heresy or apostasy, punishes the guilty party by excluding him from communion with the faithful, she remains strictly within the field of her competence, and acts, so to speak, as guardian of her household rights [*suo diritto domesticó*].

Acta Apostolicae Sedis 38 (1946) 395. The previous page is cited in *DH* 10, no doubt for the passage, a couple of sentences earlier (*quoted* in the *drafts* of *DH*: Hellín, *Declaratio de Libertate Religiosa*, 131, n. 15; 209, n. 9), where it is made explicit that the principle of willing adhesion that excludes coercion to faith applies equally to persons entering *or returning* to the faith.

[379] This *vis vel necessitas* is not identified, but is said to have been essentially the threat of whipping.

[380] Friedberg, *Corpus Iuris Canonici*, I, 161–2 (Decret. I d. 45 c.5, abrogated formally in 1917).

[381] On this key word, see *CEJF* V.4, 92–5.

[382] *Acta* IV/1 at 425 (21 September 1965). In his great treatise of 1941 (Journet, *The Church of the Word Incarnate*, 214–62), Journet calls this 'consecrational Christendom' (*la chrétienté sacrale*) as distinct from the 'secular Christendom' (*la chrétienté profane*) that is the temporal order of Church and State that Christians should hope for in the modern world. In either sense, 'Christendom/*chrétienté*' is to be distinguished from Christianity or Catholicism (*le christianisme*), the (community of) faith itself, in which the distinction between sacred (spiritual, ecclesiastical, Church) and secular (temporal, political, civil, state) is fundamental and permanent.

authorities. We can see some of its lineaments firmly outlined in the preamble to the English statute *De Haeretico Comburendo* of 1401, introducing into English law truly coercive penalties for heresy and apostasy.[383] Parliament makes clear that it is acting to assist 'the Church of England' because the [Oxford-based] heretics now troubling the Church by their anti-Catholic teaching and preaching 'may excite and stir [people] to sedition and insurrection, and make great strife and division among the people' and subvert the Church which has brought great honour and other benefits to the realm for centuries; and since the Church's own penalties ('censures') for this are ignored, evaded and derided by the heretics, it is right for the sake of the 'honour and prosperity' of the realm to accede to the request of the Church's authorities for state assistance, which will be given in the form of public burning of those whom the Church has found guilty of persistence in heresy[384]—all this with a view to extirpating the heresy from the realm, a realm conceived implicitly as a (part of) *christianitas*, Christendom.

The rationale for this political construction, Christendom, whether at large (facing an Islam aggressive from many directions) or in particular realms such as the England of King John or King Henry IV (or King Sisebut's Hispania), was not fundamentally different from that envisaged by Mill, without disapproval, for Greek city states, in the passage I have quoted[385] in my response to Leslie Green: the belief that the political community could not survive its external enemies or internal subverters without the unanimity on fundamentals that was available by shared (e.g. national) adherence to a single faith, a faith which, moreover, treated everyone, king, noble, or peasant, as fundamentally equal in a life lived meaningfully, charitably, and hopefully towards eternity. Though acting in (in a broad sense) the interests of the Church and at the request of its authorities, the rulers of the state conceived their extremely coercive repression of heresy and apostasy as the exercising of an inherently secular state jurisdiction—to repress disturbers of the political community's politically needed and honourable unifying ideology (*christianitas*)—rather than as the exercising of the Church's coercive jurisdiction by an agency conveniently free from the limitations of the Church's capacities and character.[386] So I very much doubt *Thesis C*.

Experience, accumulating over many centuries,[387] showed that that degree of ideological unity is too rarely if ever so necessary that it should take priority over the real

---

[383] 2 Hen IV c. 15; 2 *Statutes of the Realm*, 127–8.

[384] The last burning pursuant to a writ of the form instituted by *De Haeretico Comburendo* was of two Arian Englishmen in March 1612 by order of King James and the very learned, anti-Catholic Archbishop of Canterbury, George Abbot, a Balliol man who had been Master of University College Oxford for 13 years (1597–1610) and whose portrait may be seen to advantage in Univ's Hall.

[385] See p. 511, n. 186.

[386] The distinction, though real and important, is a fine one, and Journet (*Church of the Word Incarnate*, 275; also 262) is doubtless right that in looking at the historical records of the vast episode of (consecrational) Christendom one will often be legitimately uncertain whether those involved in a particular event, practice, or institution held the view just articulated above, or a view (later favoured by Suarez (*De Fide* d. 23 s.1 n.2) and many another theologian) in which the state's government and law chose, or should have chosen to act, fundamentally as well as superficially, as agents of the Church's mission, authority, and jurisdiction. Journet's own conclusion (252–4, at 254) was that 'by reason of the spiritual values invested in the temporal common good in a consecrational regime, it was this temporal common good itself which the Church required to be defended, by temporal means used in accordance with their own laws'.

[387] The second of *DH*'s two parts begins with the proposition (*DH* 9) that the requirements of human dignity have become more fully apparent to human reason 'through the experience of centuries'.

human and religious goods which are opposed by encumbering and distracting a person's approach to the great religious questions with the looming prospect of undergoing pain and loss to be imposed by human will if one fails to give those questions answers with the content demanded by those administering this threat. Amongst the goods proximately imperilled by coercion of religion is a living sense that religious truth, and the religious community organized around it, is in some important ways higher and of higher significance—that is, rationally has a more directive, because all-embracing, status in deliberation—than the requirements of one's political community.

Is the Church prevented by its own irreversible doctrinal commitments from holding now that state government and law cannot rightly be invited or permitted to threaten or apply coercion *with the purpose* (object) of advancing or protecting the interests of the true faith and church or the objective spiritual good of the unfaithful person in question, as distinct from the purpose of protecting public order (i.e. the rights of others, public peace, or public morality)?[388] Not, it seems to me, by Trent's anti-Erasmian canon, as *Thesis E* would have it. For that canon does not even teach (let alone irreformably)[389] that *the Church* has jurisdiction to apply coercion with a purpose of pressuring its members to faith or back to faith. Erasmus had expressed the view that if children at the age of puberty—in the context of a quasi-monastic process and ceremony of recommitment proposed *by* Erasmus[390]—declined to ratify the faith undertaken for them by godparents at their infant baptism, they should not be 'compelled by' any 'penalty' 'other than deprivation of the sacraments' (and should not be 'excluded from worship or sermons'); theologians in the 1520s and 1530s and the Council fathers and their theologians in 1547 thought the whole proposal both belittled infant baptism and would, if instituted, needlessly invite defections by adolescents. The Council condemned anyone who holds the whole Erasmian proposal (as deliberately reworded in ways one of which I shall discuss in a moment); Pink quotes the text of the canon (no. 14 in the decree on baptism) at [p. 428]. Leaving aside mere logic chopping about the single negation of a pair of propositions, it is fair to say that the condemnation, so far as concerns the present discussion, commits the Church to no more than the following:

> There is at least one baptismal promise bearing on Christian life, the keeping of which might be required of at least some adolescents (of those who decline to commit to keeping it) by threatening them with, and if need imposing, some punishment (besides deprivation of the sacraments) for not keeping it.

---

[388] For better or worse, I do not see that *DH* condemns as *intrinsece malum* (exceptionlessly wrong by reason of its object) the precise rationale of *De Haeretico Comburendo* as I have reconstructed and articulated it above; see the references to public order in section 7 of *DH*, and *CEJF* V.4, 94–5.

[389] The modern theological historian of the Council reminds us that 'the canons, with their appended anathemas, are not to be regarded, without more ado, as so many definitions *de fide*...': Jedin, *A History of the Council of Trent* I (1961), 381. But I do not rely on this important nuance at all in what follows.

[390] I am not insinuating any criticism of Erasmus, whose way of advancing (*Collected Works* vol. 45, 20, 21–2; *Opera Omnia* VII **3 (1522)) and subsequently defending (*Opera Omnia* IX 459 (1526), 562–3 (1532)) his two-part suggestion, decades before its condemnation, seems to me admirable, and ecclesial.

Canon 14 in its final form had carefully removed from Erasmus's wording everything that made the issue explicitly one of *faith*, of subscribing or not subscribing to the articles of faith, and of *compelling to faith* by penalties.[391] The decree articulates the issue instead as one of reaffirming baptismal 'promises' and of (un)willingness, and 'being compelled', to *live a 'Christian life'*. Now canon 7 in the same decree had said that baptism creates an obligation (called a debt) not only 'to faith alone' but also 'to observance of the whole law of Christ' (the greater part of which is the natural moral law explicit or implicit in the moral precepts of the Ten Commandments). And although candidates for baptism in the Church's main rites, personally or (if infants) by their godparents/sponsors, made a profession of faith, they also made what have long been popularly known as the baptismal vows (or promises)[392]—to renounce Satan, his empty promises and all his pomps (attractions)—promises, that is, to live a Christian life.[393] Punishing children for misdeeds against justice, charity, chastity, self-respect, etc., is a far cry from compelling, or pressuring, to faith.

Moreover, a reading of the Council proceedings strongly suggests that the distinction I have just outlined was fully intended. Nearly a third of the more than two dozen theologians who addressed the fathers on the baptism canons (in their early-draft form) expressed no view on the Erasmian proposition. For a week, those who did speak to it seem to have focussed on the implications of Erasmus's proposed ceremony of rededication (so to call it) for the Church's established teaching on baptism. But then, on 25 January 1547, a Spanish theologian reminded the fathers of Toledo's decree 'that Jews may be compelled to hold onto the [Christian] faith they have once received'.[394] And the synthesized report of the theologians, delivered on 29 January, focussed its entire (brief) commentary about the Erasmian proposition on the analogy between the Toledo decree about compelling the retention of faith once accepted and the non-release of an adolescent (or anyone else) who 'has once accepted the faith'.[395] But on 19 February something remarkable happened. The General of the Augustinian order, Jerome Seripando, fearless, indefatigable, and eloquent theological heavyweight

---

[391] Cf. Erasmus, *Opera Omnia* VII at **3v; IX at 459, 562: 'omnia tentanda sunt ne quis [instructus in ... communibus *fides articuli*] resiliat a prima *fide*. Quod si non potest obtineri, fortassis expediet illum *non cogi*...'; Erasmus's main Parisian opponent, Nicolas Beda, accused him of wanting to leave the adolescents free not to profess 'the Christian religion' (562). Erasmus's replies shift the debate somewhat towards the issue of 'leaving free' the moral conduct of the (imaginary) youths in question: secular law could deal with their thefts, blasphemies, rioting, etc. (563).

[392] 'Baptismal promises' was and is not, it seems, a technical theological term, and Trent uses the Latin word for 'promises' that Erasmus happened to use. Seripando's tract of Jan./Feb. 1547 (see n. 396), right after discussing the Erasmian article, lists a number of *vota* (vows, undertakings) made in baptism, besides the obligation of holding the faith: 'bene vivendi secundum commune modum, furtum non facere, etc.' [living rightly by generally accepted standards, abstaining from theft, etc.]: *Conc. Trid.* XII, 757 ll. 4–7.

[393] Castellani, *Liber Sacerdotalis ad consuetudinem sanctae Romanae Ecclesiae aliarumque ecclesiarum*, 18r; Trent's phrase *ad Christianam vitam* doubtless was used because this *Liber Sacerdotalis*, approved by the Pope in 1520, exhorts priests conducting baptisms to instruct candidates (or in infancy their godparents/sponsors) 'in faith and morals and the Christian life': 14r. At the beginning of the baptismal ceremony, after the candidate or sponsor has asked for the faith that offers eternal life, the priest is to say that eternal life is loving God with all one's mind and heart, etc., as the first and greatest commandment, and, as the second, loving one's neighbour as oneself, etc.: 15v.

[394] *Conc. Trid.* V 855 line 20: '[haereticus] cap. *De Iudaeis* dist. 45: quod Iudaei cogantur fidem acceptam retinere'.

[395] *Conc. Trid.* V 864 lines 444–5.

amongst the prelates (voting members) of the Council, spoke to the Erasmian proposition:

> In this article, assuming it were to be condemned on account of the censure of it by the Parisian theologians [in 1527], we should attend to the actual words of Erasmus, who did not say that they [the recalcitrant adolescents] should go free but that they should not be compelled by any punishment other than excommunication, until they revert. 'For if you compel by whatever other punishment, he will not on that account be a good Christian; if you burn him, he will not be saved; if you tolerate and teach him, perhaps he will revert, enlightened by God. You may say: Give an example to others. What example? If not that they are to be Christians by force and fear.'[396]

The Erasmian rhetoric—an appeal to a deep current in Christian self-understanding— must have had its impact. Nominally only one of four theologians appointed then to prepare the final draft of the canons on baptism, Seripando had the pen and on 21 February[397] settled them in the form presented to the prelates on 27 February and adopted by the Council on 3 March. All reference to faith was stripped out; the after- echo of Toledo was retained in the reference to 'compelling'. A Spanish maximalist could take it as reaffirming 'compulsion to keeping the faith', but the commitment of the Church's teaching authority, controlled by the logic of negation well understood by all the theologians concerned, was to nothing that contradicted the Erasmian revulsion against *that* form, that purpose, of compulsion.

So I see no reason to accept *Thesis E*.

As to *Theses B* and *D*: Pink is surely right to say that *DH*'s declared purpose of saying nothing about freedom and authority within the Church leaves it logically possible that the Church retains a jurisdiction, over its members, to 'coerce to faith'. But has it ever definitively claimed a jurisdiction properly so described? And is he right to contrast the 'jurisdiction-centred' and 'person-centred' 'models of religious liberty' in the way he

---

[396] *Conc. Trid.* V 965 lines 10–16:

> In hoc articulo, si damnandus esset, propter censuram Parisiensem consideranda sunt Erasmi verba, qui non dicit, esse dimittendos, sed non cogendos alia poena quam excommunicationis, donec resipiscant. *Si enim compellas quacumque alia poena, non propterea Christianus bonus erit; si comburas, non salvabitur; si toleres et doceas, forte illuminatus a Deo resipiscet. Dices: Do exemplum aliis. Quod exemplum? Nisi ut Christiani sint per vim et metum.*

(Italics in *Conc. Trid.* V denote quotation by the speaker/author.) I do not find the quoted passage in the several places in Erasmus that I have seen mentioned as the places where he articulates and defends the proposition. The last two, most cutting, sentences, beginning 'You may say . . .' were not in the written tractate that Seripando prepared and put about in the Council sometime between 31 January and 8 February—*after* the Spanish theological intervention of 25 January and the theological synthesis of 29 January: *Conc. Trid.* XII 756 lines 42–7; Gutiérrez, 'Hieronymi Seripandi "Diarium de Vita Sua" (1513–1562)', 68 n. 401; Jedin, *Papal Legate at the Council of Trent: Cardinal Seripando*, 398.

[397] Gutiérrez, 'Hieronymi Seripandi "Diarium de Vita Sua" (1513–1562)', 68, n. 401; *Conc. Trid.* I 616 l. 36 and n. 396. On Seripando's admiration of Augustinian and Erasmian thought, see Marranzini, 'Girolamo Seripando dopo Hubert Jedin', 360; on his profound humanistic formation, see Jedin, *Papal Legate at the Council of Trent: Cardinal Seripando*, 24–70; on his intense interest in human freedom in our personal spiritual relationship to God, and especially to Christ, a relationship essentially of call and response, see Jedin, *Papal Legate at the Council of Trent: Cardinal Seripando*, 84–6, 326–38; Marranzini, *Dibattito Lutero Seripando su 'Giustizia e Libertà' del Cristiano*, 168–72. On his resort to strong coercive power over recalcitrant ill-living members of his monastic order in the 1540s, see Marranzini, *Dibattito Lutero Seripando su 'Giustizia e Libertà' del Cristiano*, 221–2.

does, and to use this contrast to suggest that it is theologically open to the Church to change its present 'policy' and authorize states to impose in its behalf (and on its members) penalties intended to coerce them back to faith (whether directly or by Suarezian attention-stimulating means)?

Start with the question whether it is really the case that 'the historical Catholic view is jurisdiction-centred'. I see no sign of that in Aquinas's treatment of these matters, though the relevance of jurisdiction is not of course denied. St. Thomas's ground for asserting, prominently, that unbelievers 'cannot rightly *in any way* be coerced into faith'[398] is, as we have seen, the (too tersely expressed) person-centred ground unpacked and amply deployed in each of *DH*'s two Parts. What *DH* does is generalize this argument, this jurisdiction-indifferent or jurisdiction-transcending argument. The same good of dignity, responsibility, and authenticity in inquiries and commitments about religious matters, the good that unconditionally excludes trying to coerce someone into faith, equally excludes trying to coerce someone *back to faith*. And can it make a difference whether the attempt is by the Church (or another religious body), or by state government or law in the interests of the state or in the interests of the Church (or, at the Church's nod, in the interests of the person in question)? The specified conclusions which *DH* draws from the premise it articulates reach only as far as the state (and its government and law) and other social bodies, but the premise reaches Church and state alike, jointly or severally. So I would set aside *Theses B* and *D*.

The Church's responses to a Catholic's heresy or apostasy, though described in its own law as coercive 'penalties' on ('*coactio*' of) an 'offender'—since after all they follow adjudged facts, are applied perhaps 'against this person's will', and involve deliberately depriving that person of some good—nonetheless do not have the precise object or further intent of coercing that person back to faith, and could not have that object or intent consistently with the premise of principle taught in *DH*. Rather, they are responses necessary or appropriate to mark the incompatibility of externally manifested[399] unbelief with membership of the Church, and to protect the ecclesial community against the effects of that incompatibility. In an important sense—the sense relevant to the issues dealt with in *DH* and Pink's essay, and articulated twice to the members of the Council by its drafting committee[400]—such action is not coercion. That is to say: if properly undertaken by the Church's authorities, it is neither intended to be, nor justifiable as, coercive of belief.

27.

Though **Germain Grisez**'s far-reaching account of origins and ends moves from reasons to reasons, one might overlook its own origin as response after response to *questions*—from questions to questions. Knowledge, explanatory knowledge for its

---

[398] *ST* I–II q. 10 a. 8c.

[399] It is a canon-law requirement of liability for these offences (can. 1364.1) that they be certainly manifested by external conduct: can. 1330.

[400] See p. 571 at nn. 375, 376 in this essay. This section 26 benefitted from the critical acumen of Sherif Girgis.

own sake, is the good which beckoned as the rationale for the whole inquiry whose results Grisez summarizes, and which beckons even if the inquiry results in a certain displacement of contemplative knowledge from too exclusive and unilaterally dominant a place in the account of human destiny.

Nothing should deflect the reader from following straight through the commanding and illuminating sweep of Grisez's account, from beginning to end. In this essay, he has focused the account on the *moral ought*, and the sense that it gains as one locates it in wider, more adequate accounts of reality as including the origin of the moral ought, like everything else, in the practical understanding and choice of the Creator, and its end-state in the everlasting community of divine and other persons that was revealed by Jesus of Nazareth. I add only some side notes.

(1)

The essay's formulation of the first principle of morality gains its simplicity, compared with our earlier formulations, by taking it to be simply a response to the problems created for reason by feelings. The earlier formulations, revisited in Boyle's essay (and my comments on that), are responsive to those problems but also to the problems created for reason by reason's own very first practical principles, picking out and directing us towards the basic human goods. These are the problems entailed by the multiplicity of basic goods, and by the multiplicity of lives in which they could be actualized and protected by one's choices. The old formulations remain sound, and I would say primary, because they articulate reason's synoptic response to the latter, more intrinsic set of problems. The relationship between the formulations is, I believe, somewhat as set out in the passage from *Reason in Action* quoted on pp. 43–4 of this essay. To that I would add two things. (i) In *Aquinas* I show how the principle of *love of neighbor as oneself* is taken by Aquinas as directing us towards the widest, ultimately all-embracing community of human persons:

> Here then is a first, architectonic, and master principle of morality..., a principle conceived by Aquinas—or at least ready to be interpreted by his careful reader—as the import, the specifically moral significance, of the first practical principles when taken together, integrally.[401]

---

[401] *Aquinas*, 128. The passage continues with thoughts relevant to the course of Grisez's essay:

> Aquinas will, of course, be the first to raise some further questions. The answers to these questions are to enhance both the content and the normativity of even this master principle of morality by reference to an even more ultimate principle, directing us towards some even better good, for the sake of which all human persons—self and communities of neighbours—should be loved. But these questions arise in relation to every other fundamental element in our knowledge, and we can leave them for later reflection [in Ch. X.4]. Provided those further questions and their answer are not suppressed, Aquinas is content to say that moral principles and norms—and the moral ought—are *all* implicit in or referable to this one principle.

In Ch. X.4 that 'even more ultimate principle' is articulated, after the proofs of the existence (and something about the nature) of God, thus:

> ...the master moral principle or first precept of the natural *moral* law...can now be more adequately stated: one should love one's neighbour as oneself *by reason of* the divine goodness as it is participated, reflected, and imaged in that neighbour as in every human being...

So one of Grisez's first names for the general moral principles that specify (begin to make specific the implications of) the master moral principle was, as he records in footnote 7 to his essay, 'guidelines for love'. When reason, guided not only by the first practical principles but now by the master moral principle and such immediate specifications of it as the Golden Rule, reflects on why these are indeed the foundations and proper developments of the moral ought, it will be looking not only to 'parts of oneself' that might otherwise be neglected or ill-treated but also to the equivalent aspects of the make-up of others[402]—without overlooking that 'neighbour *as oneself*' itself directs us to the rational grounds for duly prioritizing oneself and one's own (family, friends, associates, neighborhood, country, etc.).

(ii) If one employs Grisez's 'simpler' version of morality's master principle, one must take 'feelings' as tantamount here to 'inclinations'. For reason's adjudication among the competing directions given by different first principles, and among the different persons to whose good those first principles direct us, must avoid being deflected or corrupted by spiritual inclinations such as pride (as distinct from 'pride of life') and the associated kind of envy (of others for their excellence or success, that it is theirs not mine)—inclinations to displace the reasonable order of priorities amongst self and others *simply* because it does not assign unilateral priority to oneself.[403]

(2)

The essay condenses its account of questing (questioning) reason's discovery of the transcendent creator and creative will, and of the bearing of that will on the directiveness of practical reason and moral principle, by saying—

> When we understand that directiveness as guidance provided by our Creator, our sense of its dependability deepens, and with that the normative force of the moral *ought* which it generates increases, and general moral obligation emerges. [p. 499]

That thought, as developed in the rest of the passage, *Aquinas*, 314, is about the understanding of these matters that is available to natural reason and the 'natural religion' that reason unaided by divine revelation makes possible for us. For the understanding of the yet richer conception—made available by divine revelation completed in Jesus—of completed integral human fulfillment, see briefly *Aquinas*, 327–34.

[402] That will be said at least implicitly later in the essay ([p. 450, in the sentence defining the single ultimate end of all morally good acts; and in the essay's last sentence]). It may well be that the essay at this earlier point is implying, without saying, that unreasonable neglect or ill-treatment of others neglects or ill-treats that part of oneself that I call (the good of) practical reasonableness (Aquinas's *bonum rationis*). As to Aquinas, incidentally, (i) I see no ineluctable inconsistency between what he says in *ST* I–II q. 89 a. 6c & ad 3 about a child's first acts of responsibility (on which see *Aquinas*, 41, n. 68) and what is said in Vatican II, *Lumen Gentium*, 16, about the salvation of those who have no 'express acknowledgment' of God; (ii) I am inclined to understand most if not all of what Aquinas says about each person's having one last end at a time as statements about what rational consistency requires of one (even when one is operating with one or more mistaken premise), just as I am disinclined—again, as a matter of correct interpretation—to take literally what he (frequently) affirms (and not infrequently seems to deny) about 'everyone' understanding without mistake the principles of practical reason: see *Aquinas*, 100, endnote u. (And see n. 407 in this essay.)

[403] See *ST* I q. 63 a. 2, on how a purely spiritual being, without passions/feelings, can make wrong choices.

Grisez goes on to explain how practical principles become understood as principles provided by the Creator, and as bases for cooperation with the Creator, so that non-compliance with them is now non-cooperation and indeed disobedience:

> Therefore, whenever one is aware of a moral *ought*, one is aware not only of practical reason's moral demand but of moral obligation, of being bound to obey the Creator. [p. 499]

In both these passages, I take 'moral obligation' as being given a stipulative sense, as a sort of technical term to mark the gain in context, significance, intelligibility, and consequently in force. One can appropriate the term like this without taking the view that 'moral obligation' is a term rationally unavailable to—or empty in the mouths of—persons who fail to understand moral principles and oughts as having the dependability and force of guidance from the Creator. Anscombe did hold some such view; it was put too broadly, so as to include even the moral 'ought', and was widely misunderstood, but even when accurately interpreted, and narrowed to 'obligation', seems mistaken.[404]

(3)

'Integral *communal* fulfilment', which the essay introduces as it nears the end of its second section and moves towards its discussion of the Kingdom revealed to be that fulfilment's embodiment (so to speak), is here defined [n. 20] as 'the realization of the Creator's purpose in creating, friendship with him, and the happiness of increasing well-being and flourishing in themselves and other created persons'. This is a concept intended to include the whole content of the 'integral *human* fulfilment' about which we have so often written. And it is a concept that was always implicit in 'integral human fulfilment', since one of the basic human goods is religion, understood as a harmony (or, in a sense, community) of purpose (and interaction) between human persons and the divine. In so far as 'fulfilment' in 'integral communal fulfilment' refers to the willing, formation, and consummation of community between human and divine persons, the phrase says what it should. In so far as it *seems*, by virtue of our syntax, to refer to a willed and effected fulfilment of the divine person(s) as it refers to the willed and effected fulfilment of the human persons in that community, it can grate against our apprehension of the transcendence, otherness, and inherent perfection of God (already pointed to in the essay's initial discussion of *what* the Creator must be, and always given unsurpassed emphasis in Grisez's philosophical writings on God). Aquinas can, with due precautions,[405] predicate *beatitudo* of God, because that word is relatively free of the connotations that 'fulfilment' has of a moving from incomplete to complete. As I say, the definition of the phrase 'integral communal fulfilment' preserves the necessary distinction between the divine and human participants in the community referred to, a distinction also underlined when the essay speaks of a duality of *shaloms*: those who die in Christ 'will share fully in the *shalom* of God while also sharing fully in the human *shalom* of the definitive kingdom' [p. 454]. But the phrase itself rather

---

[404] *CEJF* II.3, 74–5; *NLNR*, 297, 343.   [405] *Summa contra Gentiles* I c. 100 n. 2.

eludes or elides these distinctions; 'integral human fulfilment', though it too can be, and has not rarely been, misunderstood, may prove more serviceable a term.

(4)

Imagination has some of the rigidity of syntax. It balks as much at 'time's beginning' as at 'time without beginning', at 'space without limits' as at 'the limits of space', at 'there are free choices' and at 'there are no free choices', and much else related to the intersection of the material and the spiritual, intersections as humdrum and mysterious as the meaningfulness of a word uttered in a sentence heard or read, and understood. Reason must pick its way cautiously, endangered by excess of denial as of assertion. And when it comes to determining precisely what was and was not asserted by Jesus of Nazareth and those who received and handed on what his words and conduct taught, one must take into account everything stated, especially everything apparently asserted, in all the books which they and their close successors judged authentic witnesses to revelation: the biblical canon. This necessity holds especially when one is assessing all that was said, and is said to have happened, that bears directly on aspects of those special intersections of eternal and temporal, transcendent and this-worldly, that mark out what we call revelation, and its communications about a world beyond this one, and beyond the life and lives that we see (or know to be) passing and ending. Taken in relative isolation, or pressed too unilaterally, without the control both of the whole canon and of the reflection and judgments of the community whose canon of scripture it is, many terms and statements push imagination even to the point of recalcitrance.

So the passage from Vatican II's *Gaudium et Spes* quoted and discussed in Grisez's essay [p. 455], as also in essays of mine, is prefaced by: 'We do not know the time for the consummation of the earth and of humanity, *nor do we know how all things will be transformed.*' The Church has long strongly discouraged all projects of investigating the scriptures to learn more about the date or antecedents of the end-time, and similarly these short sections (38–9) in *Gaudium et Spes* express the level of generality at which the Church has long encouraged the faithful to remain in their meditations on, and imagining of, the objective counterpart to reason's ideal, 'integral human fulfilment'.

What matters, it seems to me, are propositions at a level of generality that, without oppressing or seducing imagination,[406] convey the truths asserted in revelation (all its elements taken into consideration), truths about the lastingness of unrepented choices into an existence beyond death, an existence involving eventually the whole person (rather than only of some spiritual remnant) in society with other human persons fulfilled in human goods and now seeing the divine person(s)—that incomparable glory—somehow as we are seen[407]: all this in a manner compatible with a justice that

---

[406] For example: among the many statements made about the completed City is—

> ...the glory of God is its light, and its lamp is the Lamb. By its light shall the nations walk; and the kings of the earth shall bring their glory into it,...they shall bring into it the glory and the honour of the nations. [*Revelation* 21: 23–4, 26]

But is this conveying something about the proper order of this world (and thus about political thought), or only about the next?

[407] For understanding Aquinas (cf. n. 402 in this essay), it is significant that—

takes due account of everyone and everything in human history.[408] For ours is a history the eventually evident pattern and significance of which could only emerge in (and surely as an important element in) that eventual sharing in the Creative understanding—somehow 'seeing' as we have all along been 'seen' (by an understanding, a *knowing*, that has not been all-absorbingly contemplative).

Bibliography

Acta Synodalia Sacrosancti Concilii Oecumenici Vaticani II (Rome: Vatican Polyglot Press) vol. IV/1 (1976), vol. IV/6 (1978).

Anscombe, G.E.M. ([1957] 1985), *Intention* (Oxford: Blackwell).

Anscombe, G.E.M. (1981), *The Collected Philosophical Papers of G.E.M. Anscombe*; vol. 2, *Metaphysics and the Philosophy of Mind*; vol. 3, *Ethics, Religion and Politics* (Oxford: Blackwell; Minneapolis: University of Minnesota Press).

Austin, John (1869), *Lectures on Jurisprudence or the Philosophy of Positive Law*, 3rd ed., ed. Robert Campbell (London: John Murray).

Bataillon, Louis-Jacques (1974), 'Une sermon de s. Thomas d'Aquin sur la parabole du festin', *Revue des Sciences Philosophiques et Théologiques* 58: 451–6.

Bataillon, Louis-Jacques (1983), 'Le sermon inédit de Saint Thomas *Homo Quidam Fecit Cenam Magnam*: introduction et édition', *Revue des Sciences Philosophiques et Théologiques* 67: 353–69.

Belmans, Theo (1980), *Le sens objectif de l'agir humain* (Rome: Libreria Editrice Vaticana).

Benedict XVI (2009), Encyclical Letter *Caritas in Veritate* dated 29 June 2009, <http://www.vatican.va/holy_father/benedict_xvi/encyclicals/documents/hf_ben-xvi_enc_20090629_caritas-in-veritate_en.html>.

Bennett, Josephine W. (1966), *'Measure for Measure' as Royal Entertainment* (New York: Columbia University Press).

Boyle, Joseph M. (2010), 'An Appreciative Response' in Christopher Tollefsen, *Bioethics with Liberty and Justice: Themes in the Work of Joseph M. Boyle* (London; New York: Springer), 242–58.

Bradley, Gerard V. (1993), '*Life's Dominion*: A Review Essay', *Notre Dame Law Rev.* 69: 329–91.

Brennan, Michael G. (ed.) (1993), *The Travel Diary (1611–1612) of an English Catholic Sir Charles Somerset* (Leeds: Leeds Philosophical & Literary Society).

Bullough, Geoffrey (1958), *Narrative and Dramatic Sources of Shakespeare* vol. II (London: Routledge & Kegan Paul).

Byrn, Robert M. (1973), 'The Supreme Court on Abortion: An American Tragedy', *Fordham Law Rev.* 41: 807–62.

Castellani, Albertus (1523), *Liber Sacerdotalis ad consuetudinem sanctae Romanae Ecclesiae aliarumque ecclesiarum* (Venice).

[though he] never softens his thesis that it 'consists in' the intellectual vision of God, the narrow philosophical argument which advances that claim (a claim often stated also, in so many words, in his theological work) broadens out, in its theological (i.e. revelation-based) counterpart, to affirm a yet more complete fulfilment. The definitive expressing of God's goodness in heavenly human happiness—blessedness {beatitudo}—will include also the participation, body and soul, of many human persons [IV *Sent.* d. 49 q. 2 a. 3; *ST* I-II q. 3 a. 3 ad 3, q. 4 aa. 5, 6 & 8] in an order (peace) such that 'that *beatitudo* consists in two things {in duobus consistit}: seeing God and love of neighbour.' [*In Matt.* 5 ad v. 8]

Aquinas, 327; see also 329–31, 333–4, 318–9. Must not the 'two things' be of unimaginably disparate significance?

[408] On this question of ultimate justice (and peace—of how 'all manner of things shall be well'), perhaps most vital of all questions for its impact on evangelization, see Grisez, *Christian Moral Principles*, 446–51 (18.G-I)(on perdition) and writings now awaiting publication.

Concilium Tridentinum Diariorum, Actorum, Epistularum, Tractatuum, ed. Societas Goerresiana, vol. V, ed. S. Ehses (Freiburg im Breisgau: Herder, 1911); vol. XII ed. V. Schweitzer (Freiburg im Breisgau: Herder, [1930] 1966).

Devlin, Patrick (1968), *The Enforcement of Morals* (Oxford: OUP).

Dummett, Michael (2010), *The Nature and Future of Philosophy* (New York: Columbia University Press).

Dworkin, Ronald (2011), *Justice for Hedgehogs* (Cambridge, MA and London: Harvard University Press)

Ekins, Richard (2007), 'Acts of Parliament and the Parliament Acts', *Law Quarterly Review* 123: 91–115.

Endicott, Timothy A.O. (2000), *Vagueness in Law* (Oxford: OUP).

Erasmus, Desiderius (1706), *Desiderii Erasmi Opera Omnia* (Leiden: Petrus Vander).

Erasmus, Desiderius (1974), *Collected Works of Erasmus*, vol. 45, *Paraphrase on Matthew* (Toronto: University of Toronto Press).

Faye, Emmanuel (2009), *Heidegger: the Introduction of Nazism into Philosophy in Light of the Unpublished Seminars of 1933–35* (New Haven, CT: Yale University Press).

Friedberg, Emil (1922), *Corpus Iuris Canonici* (Leipzig: Tauschnitz).

Fuller, Lon L. (1969), *The Morality of Law*, rev. ed. (New Haven, CT; London: Yale University Press).

Gless, Darryl J. (1979), Measure for Measure, *the Law, and the Convent* (Princeton, NJ: Princeton University Press).

Goff, Robert (Lord Goff of Chieveley) (1988), 'The Mental Element in the Crime of Murder', *Law Quarterly Review* 104: 30.

Gorsuch, Neil (2009), *The Future of Assisted Suicide and Euthanasia* (Princeton, NJ: Princeton University Press).

Grisez, Germain (1983), *The Way of the Lord Jesus* vol. 1, *Christian Moral Principles* (Chicago, IL: Franciscan Herald Press; now St Paul's: Alba House), <http://www.twotlj.org/G-1-V-1.html>.

Grisez, Germain (1993), *The Way of the Lord Jesus* vol. 2, *Living a Christian Life* (Quincy: Franciscan Press; now St Paul's: Alba House), <http://www.twotlj.org/G-2-V-2.html>.

Grisez, Germain (1997), *The Way of the Lord Jesus* vol. 3, *Difficult Moral Questions* (Quincy: Franciscan Press; now St Paul's: Alba House), <http://www.twotlj.org/G-3-V-3.html>.

Grisez, Germain (2000), 'Death in Theological Reflection', in *The Dignity of the Dying Person*, Proceedings of the Fifth Assembly of the Pontifical Academy for Life, ed. Juan de Dios Vial Correa and Elio Sgreccia (Vatican City: Libreria Editrice Vaticana, 2000), 142–71; reprinted in *Linacre Quarterly*, 69:1 (February 2002): 1–32; also at <http://twotlj.org/death.html>.

Grisez, Germain (2010), 'Health Care Technology and Justice' in Christopher Tollefsen, *Bioethics with Liberty and Justice: Themes in the Work of Joseph M. Boyle* (London and New York: Springer), 221–39.

Gutiérrez, Davide (1963), 'Hieronymi Seripandi "Diarium de Vita Sua" (1513–1562)', *Analecta Augustiniana* 26: 5–193.

Harrison, George B. (1941), *A Jacobean Diary* (London: Routledge).

Hart, H.L.A. ([1961] 2012), *The Concept of Law*, 3rd ed. Leslie Green (Oxford: OUP).

Hellín, Francisco Gil (2008), *Concilii Vaticani II Synopsis in Ordinem Redigens Schemata cum Relationibus necnon Patrum Orationes atque Animadversiones: Declaratio de Libertate Religiosa Dignitatis Humanae* (Rome: EDUSC).

Hittinger, Russell (1987), *A Critique of the New Natural Law Theory* (Notre Dame, IN: University of Notre Dame Press).

Hodgson, David (1967), *Consequences of Utilitarianism: A Study in Normative Ethics and Legal Theory* (Oxford: OUP).

Hodgson, David (1991), *The Mind Matters: Consciousness and Choice in a Quantum World* (Oxford: OUP).

Hodgson, David (2012), *Rationality + Consciousness = Free Will* (New York: OUP).

International Theological Commission, *In Search of a Universal Ethic: A New Look at the Natural Law* (2009), <http://www.vatican.va/roman_curia/congregations/cfaith/cti_documents/rc_con_cfaith_doc_20090520_legge-naturale_en.html>.

Jedin, Hubert (1947), *Papal Legate at the Council of Trent: Cardinal Seripando*, trans. F.C. Eckhoff (St. Louis and London: Herder).

Jedin, Hubert (1961), *A History of the Council of Trent*, trans. Ernest Graf (London: Nelson).

John Paul II (1980), Encyclical Letter *Dives in Misericordia* dated 30 November 1980, <http://www.vatican.va/holy_father/john_paul_ii/encyclicals/documents/hf_jp-ii_enc_30111980_dives-in-misericordia_en.html>.

Jones, J. Walter (1939), *The Nazi Conception of Law* (Oxford: OUP).

Journet, Charles (1955), *The Church of the Word Incarnate: An Essay in Speculative Theology*, trans. A.H.C. Downes (London; New York: Sheed & Ward).

Keown, John (1988), *Abortion, Doctors and the Law: Some Aspects of the Legal Regulation of Abortion in England From 1803 to 1982* (Cambridge: CUP).

Keown, John (2012), *The Law and Ethics of Medicine: Essays on the Inviolability of Human Life* (Oxford: OUP).

Lagrange, M.-J., OP (1921), *Evangile selon Luc* (Paris: Gabalda).

Lee, Patrick and George, Robert P. (2007), *Body-Self Dualism in Contemporary Ethics and Politics* (New York: CUP).

Lockwood, Shelley (1997), *Sir John Fortescue: On the Laws and Governance of England*, ed. Shelley Lockwood (Cambridge: CUP).

Lonergan, Bernard J.F. (1957), *Insight: A Study of Human Understanding* (London: Longmans, Green; New York: Philosophical Society).

Marranzini, Alfredo (1981), *Dibattito Lutero Seripando su 'Giustizia e Libertà' del Cristiano* (Brescia: Morcelliana).

Marranzini, Alfredo (1997), 'Girolamo Seripando dopo Hubert Jedin' in Giuseppe Alberigo and Iginio Rogger, *Il Concilio di Trento nella Prospettiva del Terzo Millennio* (Brescia: Morcelliana).

Marzoa, Ángel, Jorge Miras and Rafael Rodríguez-Ocaña (2004), *Exegetical Commentary on the Code of Canon Law* (Montreal: Wilson & Lafleur; Chicago, IL: Midwest Theological Forum).

Ottaviani, Alfredo (1936), *Institutiones Iuris Publici Ecclesiastici*, 2nd ed. (Vatican: Vatican Polyglot Press).

Parker, M.D.H. (1955), *The Slave of Life* (London: Chatto & Windus).

Pilsner, Joseph (2006), *The Specification of Human Actions in St Thomas Aquinas* (Oxford: OUP).

Rhonheimer, Martin (2000), *Natural Law and Practical Reason: A Thomistic View of Moral Autonomy*, trans. Gerald Malsbary (New York: Fordham University Press).

Shapiro, Scott J. (2010), *Legality* (Cambridge, MA: Harvard University Press).

Sher, George (1987), *Desert* (Princeton, NJ: Princeton University Press).

Stevenson, David L. (1959), 'The Role of James I in Shakespeare's *Measure for Measure*', ELH: *English Literary History* 26: 188–208.

Tollefsen, Christopher (2010), *Bioethics with Liberty and Justice: Themes in the Work of Joseph M. Boyle* (London and New York: Springer).

Twomey, Anne (2010), *The Australia Acts 1986: Australia's Statutes of Independence* (Leichhardt, NSW: Federation Press).

van Wyhe, Cordula (2004), 'Court and Convent: The Infanta Isabella and Her Franciscan Confessor Andrés de Soto', *The Sixteenth Century Journal* 35: 411–45.

Voegelin, Eric (1952), *The New Science of Politics* (Chicago & London: University of Chicago Press).

Wade, H.W.R. (1996), 'Sovereignty—Revolution or Evolution?', *Law Quarterly Rev.* 111: 568–75.

World Medical Organization (1996), 'Declaration of Helsinki (1964)' [as revised in 1975 and 1983], *British Medical Journal* 313 (1997): 1448–9.

Bibliography of the Published Works of John Finnis

1962a 'Developments in Judicial Jurisprudence', *Adelaide L Rev* 1 (1962) 317–37.

b 'The Immorality of the Deterrent', *Adelaide Univ Mag* 1962, 47–61.

1963 'Doves and Serpents', *The Old Palace* 38 (1963) 438–41.

1967a I.17 'Reason and Passion: The Constitutional Dialectic of Free Speech and Obscenity', 116 *University of Pennsylvania L Rev* 116 (1967) 222–43.

b IV.8 'Blackstone's Theoretical Intentions', *Natural L Forum* 12 (1967) 63–83.

c 'Punishment and Pedagogy', *The Oxford Review* 5 (1967) 83–93.

d 'Review of Zelman Cowen, *Sir John Latham and Other Papers*', LQR 83 (1967) 289–90.

1968a III.10 'Old and New in Hart's Philosophy of Punishment', *The Oxford Review* 8 (1968) 73–80.

b 'Constitutional Law', *Annual Survey of Commonwealth Law 1967* (London: Butterworth, 1968), 20–33, 71–98.

c 'Separation of Powers in the Australian Constitution', *Adelaide L Rev* 3 (1968) 159–77.

d Review of Neville March Hunnings, *Film Censors and the Law*, LQR84 (1968) 430–2.

e 'Natural Law in *Humanae vitae*', LQR 84 (1968) 467–71.

f 'Review of H. Phillip Levy, *The Press Council*', LQR 84 (1968) 582.

g 'Law, Morality, and Mind Control', *Zenith* (Oxford: University Museum) 6: 7–8.

1969a 'Constitutional Law', *Annual Survey of Commonwealth Law 1968* (London: Butterworth, 1969), 2–15, 32–49, 53–75, 98–114.

b 'Review of Herbert L. Packer, *The Limits of the Criminal Sanction*', *Oxford Magazine* 1 (1969) 10–11.

1970a I.6 'Reason, Authority and Friendship in Law and Morals', in R. S. Khanbai, B. Y. Pineau, and R. A. Katz (eds), *Jowett Papers 1968–1969* (Oxford: Blackwell, 1970), 101–23.

b 'Natural Law and Unnatural Acts', *Heythrop J* 11 (1970) 365–87.

c (i) 'Abortion and Legal Rationality', *Adelaide L Rev* 3 (1970) 431–67.
   (ii) 'Three Schemes of Regulation', in Noonan (ed.), *The Morality of Abortion: Legal and Historical Perspectives* (Cambridge, Mass.: Harvard University Press, 1970).

d 'Constitutional Law', *Annual Survey of Commonwealth Law 1969* (London: Butterworth, 1970), 2–4, 27–34, 37–50, 65–81.

1971a IV.21 'Revolutions and Continuity of Law', in A.W.B. Simpson (ed.), *Oxford Essays in Jurisprudence: Second Series* (Oxford: OUP, 1971), 44–76.

b 'The Abortion Act: What Has Changed?', *Criminal L Rev* (1971) 3–12.

c 'Constitutional Law', *Annual Survey of Commonwealth Law 1970* (London: Butterworth, 1971), 2–4, 17–31, 33–42, 51–60.

1972a III.11 'The Restoration of Retribution', *Analysis* 32 (1972) 131–5.

b IV.18 'Some Professorial Fallacies about Rights', *Adelaide L Rev* 4 (1972) 377–88.

c 'The Value of the Human Person', *Twentieth Century* [Australia] 27 (1972) 126–37.

d 'Bentham et le droit naturel classique', *Archives de Philosophie du Droit* 17 (1972) 423–7.

e 'Constitutional Law', *Annual Survey of Commonwealth Law 1971* (London: Butterworth, 1972), 2–5, 11–25, 28–41.

f 'Meaning and Ambiguity in Punishment (and Penology)', *Osgoode Hall L.J.* 10 (1972) 264–8.

1973a III.3 'Review of John Rawls, *A Theory of Justice* (1972)', *Oxford Magazine* 90 no. 1 (new series) (26 January 1973).

b III.18 'The Rights and Wrongs of Abortion A Reply to Judith Jarvis Thomson', *Philosophy & Public Affairs* 2 (1973) 117–45.

c 'Constitutional Law', *Annual Survey of Commonwealth Law 1972* (London: Butterworth, 1973), 2–8, 23–56, 62–6.

1974a   'Constitutional Law', *Annual Survey of Commonwealth Law 1973* (London: Butterworth, 1974), 1–66.

   b   'Commonwealth and Dependencies' in *Halsbury's Laws of England*, vol. 6 (4th edn, London: Butterworth, 1974), 315–601.

1975   'Constitutional Law', *Annual Survey of Commonwealth Law 1974* (London: Butterworth, 1975), 1–61.

1976a   'Constitutional Law', *Annual Survey of Commonwealth Law 1975* (London: Butterworth, 1976), 1–56.

   b   Chapters 18–21 (with Germain Grisez), in *The Teaching of Christ*, (eds R. Lawler, D. W. Wuerl, and T. C. Lawler) (Huntingdon IN: OSV, 1976), 275–354.

1977a   I.3 'Scepticism, Self-refutation and the Good of Truth', in P.M. Hacker and J. Raz (eds), *Law, Morality and Society: Essays in Honour of H.L.A. Hart* (Oxford: OUP, 1977), 247–67.

   b   'Some Formal Remarks about "Custom"', in International Law Association, Report of the First Meeting [April 1977] on the Theory and Methodology of International Law (1977), 14–21.

1978a   'Catholic Social Teaching: Populorum Progressio and After', Church Alert (SODEPAX Newsletter) 19 (1978) 2–9; also in James V. Schall (ed.), *Liberation Theology in Latin America* (San Francisco: Ignatius Press, 1982).

   b   'Conscience, Infallibility and Contraception', *The Month* 239 (1978) 410–17.

   c   'Abortion Legal Aspects of', in Warren T. Reich (ed.), *Encyclopedia of Bioethics* (New York: Free Press, 1978), 26–32.

1979   V.18 'Catholic Faith and the World Order Reflections on E.R. Norman', *Clergy Rev* 64 (1979) 309–18.

1980a   *Natural Law and Natural Rights* (Oxford: OUP, 1980).

        Legge Naturali e Diritti Naturali (trans. F. Viola) (Milan: Giappichelli, 1996).

        Ley Natural y Derechos Naturales (trans. C. Orrego) (Buenos Aires: Abeledo-Perrot, 2000).

        Prawo naturalne i uprawnienia naturalne (trans. Karolina Lossman) Klasycy Filozofii Prawa (Warsaw: Dom Wydawniczy ABC, 2001).

        自然法与自然权利 ([Mandarin] trans. Jiaojiao Dong, Yi Yang, Xiaohui Liang) (Beijing: 2004).

        Lei Natural e Direitos Naturais (trans. Leila Mendes) (Sao Leopoldo, Brazil: Editora Unisinos, 2007).

   b   'Reflections on an Essay in Christian Ethics: Part I: Authority in Morals', *Clergy Rev* 65 (1980) 51–7: 'Part II: Morals and Method', 87–93.

   c   'The Natural Law, Objective Morality, and Vatican II', in William E. May (ed.), *Principles of Catholic Moral Life* (Chicago: Franciscan Herald Press), 113–49.

1981a   [*British North America Acts: The Role of Parliament*: Report from the Foreign Affairs Committee, House of Commons Paper 1980–81 HC 42 (21 January 1981) (87 pp)].

   b   'Observations de M J.M. Finnis' [on Georges Kalinowski's review of *Natural Law and Natural Rights*], *Archives de Philosophie du Droit* 26 (1981) 425–7.

   c   [Foreign Affairs Committee, *Supplementary Report on the British North America Acts: The Role of Parliament*, House of Commons Paper 1980–81 HC 295 (15 April 1981) (23 pp)].

   d   [Foreign Affairs Committee, *Third Report on the British North America Acts: The Role of Parliament*, House of Commons Paper 1981–82 HC 128 (22 December 1981) (17 pp)].

   e   'Natural Law and the "Is"–"Ought" Question: An Invitation to Professor Veatch', *Cath Lawyer* 26 (1981) 266–77.

1982a   (with Germain Grisez) 'The Basic Principles of Natural Law: A Reply to Ralph McInerny', *American J Juris* 26 (1982) 21–31.

   b   'Review of Anthony Battaglia, *Towards a Reformulation of Natural Law*', *Scotlish J Theol* 35 (1982) 555–6.

1983a   'The Responsibilities of the United Kingdom Parliament and Government under the Australian Constitution', *Adelaide L Rev* 9 (1983) 91–107.

     b   *Fundamentals of Ethics* (Oxford: OUP; Washington, DC: Georgetown University Press, 1983).

     c   'Power to Enforce Treaties in Australia—The High Court goes Centralist?', *Oxford J Legal St* 3 (1983) 126–30.

     d   'The Fundamental Themes of *Laborem Exercens*', in Paul L. Williams (ed.), *Catholic Social Thought and the Social Teaching of John Paul* II (Scranton: Northeast Books, 1983), 19–31.

     e   ['In Vitro Fertilisation: Morality and Public Policy', Evidence submitted by the Catholic Bishops' Joint Committee on Bio-ethical Issues to the [Warnock] Committee of Inquiry into Human Fertilisation and Embryology, May 1983, 5–18].

1984a   I.10 (i) 'Practical Reasoning, Human Goods and the End of Man', *Proc AmCath Phil Ass* 58 (1984) 23–36; also in (ii) *New Blackfriars* 66 (1985) 438–51.

     b   IV.2 'The Authority of Law in the Predicament of Contemporary Social Theory', *J Law, Ethics & Pub Policy* 1 (1984) 115–37.

     c   ['Response to the Warnock Report', submission to Secretary of State for Social Services by the Catholic Bishops' Joint Bioethics Committee on Bio-ethical Issues, December 1984, 3–17].

     d   'IVF and the Catholic Tradition', *The Month* 246 (1984) 55–8.

     e   'Reforming the Expanded External Affairs Power', in Report of the External Affairs Subcommittee to the Standing Committee of the Australian Constitutional Convention (September 1984), 43–51.

1985a   III.1 'A Bill of Rights for Britain? The Moral of Contemporary Jurisprudence' (Maccabaean Lecture in Jurisprudence), *Proc BritAcad* 71 (1985) 303–31.

     b   IV.9 'On "Positivism" and "Legal-Rational Authority"', *Oxford J Leg St* 3 (1985) 74–90.

     c   IV.13 'On "The Critical Legal Studies Movement"', *American J Juris* 30 (1985) 21–42; also in J. Bell and J. Eekelaar (eds), *Oxford Essays in Jurisprudence: Third Series* (Oxford: OUP, 1987), 145–65.

     d   'Morality and the Ministry of Defence' (review), *The Tablet*, 3 August 1985, 804–5.

     e   'Personal Integrity, Sexual Morality and Responsible Parenthood', *Anthropos* [now *Anthropotes*] 1985/1, 43–55.

1986a   'The "Natural Law Tradition"', *J Legal Ed* 36 (1986) 492–5.

     b   'The Laws of God, the Laws of Man and Reverence for Human Life', in R. Hittinger (ed.), *Linking the Human Life Issues* (Chicago, IL: Regnery Books, 1986), 59–98.

1987a   I.9 'Natural Inclinations and Natural Rights: Deriving "Ought" from "Is" according to Aquinas', in L. Elders and K. Hedwig (eds), *Lex et Libertas: Freedom and Law According to St Thomas Aquinas* (Studi Tomistici 30, Libreria Editrice Vaticana, 1987), 43–55.

     b   II.8 'The Act of the Person' *Persona Veritá e Morale*, atti del Congresso Internazionale di Teologia Morale, Rome 1986 (Rome Cittá Nuova Editrice, Rome, 1987), 159–75.

     c   III.2 'Legal Enforcement of Duties to Oneself Kant v. Neo-Kantians', *Columbia L Rev* 87 (1987) 433–56.

     d   IV.4 'On Positivism and the Foundations of Legal Authority: Comment', in Ruth Gavison (ed.), *Issues in Legal Philosophy: the Influence of H.L.A. Hart* (Oxford: OUP, 1987), 62–75.

     e   IV.12 'On Reason and Authority in Law's Empire', *Law and Philosophy* 6 (1987) 357–80.

     f   Germain Grisez, Joseph Boyle, and John Finnis, 'Practical Principles, Moral Truth, and Ultimate Ends', *American J Juris* 32 (1987), 99–151. (Also, with original table of contents restored, in 1991d *Natural Law*, vol. 1 (ed. Finnis).)

     g   *Nuclear Deterrence, Morality and Realism* (with Joseph Boyle and Germain Grisez) (Oxford: OUP, 1987).

h   'Answers [to Questions about Nuclear and Non-nuclear Defence Options]', in Oliver Ramsbottom (ed.), *Choices: Nuclear and Non-Nuclear Defence Options* (London: Brasseys' Defence Publishers, 1987), 219–34.

i   'The Claim of Absolutes', *The Tablet* 241 (1987) 364–6.

j   ['On Human Infertility Services and Embryo Research', response by the Catholic Bishops' Joint Committee on Bioethical Issues to the Department of Health and Social Security, June 1987, 3–12].

1988a   **V.21** 'The Consistent Ethic A Philosophical Critique', in Thomas G. Fuechtmann (ed.), *Consistent Ethic of Life* (Kansas City: Sheed & Ward, 1988), 140–81.

b   **V.20** 'Nuclear Deterrence, Christian Conscience, and the End of Christendom', *New Oxford Rev* [Berkeley, CA] July–August 1988, .6–16

c   'Goods are Meant for Everyone: Reflection on Encyclical *Sollicitudo Rei Socialis*', *L'Osservatore Romano*, weekly edn, 21 March 1988, 21.

d   '"Faith and Morals" A Note', *The Month* 21/2 (1988) 563–7.

e   Germain Grisez, Joseph Boyle, John Finnis, and William E. May, '"Every Marital Act Ought to be Open to New Life" Toward a Clearer Understanding', *The Thomist* 52 (1988) 365–426, also in Grisez, Boyle, Finnis, and May, *The Teaching of Humanae Vitae: A Defense* (San Francisco: Ignatius Press, 1988); Italian trans. in *Anthropotes* 1988/1, 73–122.

f   'Absolute Moral Norms: Their Ground, Force and Permanence', *Anthropotes* 1988/2, 287–303.

1989a   **II.5** 'Persons and their Associations', *Proc Aristotelian Soc*, Supp. Vol. 63 (1989) 267–74.

b   **IV.3** 'Law as Coordination', *Ratio Iuris* 2 (1989) 97–104.

c   **V.11** 'On Creation and Ethics', *Anthropotes* 1989/2, 197–206.

d   'La morale chrétienne et la guerre entretien avec John Finnis', *Catholica* 13 (1989) 15–23.

e   'Russell Hittinger's Straw Man', *Fellowship of Catholic Scholars Newsletter* 12/2 (1989), 6–8 (corrigenda in following issue).

f   'Nuclear Deterrence and Christian Vocation', *New Blackfriars* 70 (1989) 380–7.

1990a   **I.12** 'Aristotle, Aquinas, and Moral Absolutes', *Catholica: International Quarterly Selection* 12 (1990) 7–15; Spanish trans. by Carlos I. Massini-Correas in Persona y Derecho 28 (1993), and in A.G. Marques and J. Garcia-Huidobro (eds), *Razon y Praxis* (Valparaiso: Edeval, 1994) 319–36.

b   **IV.16** 'Allocating Risks and Suffering Some Hidden Traps', *Cleveland State L Rev* 38 (1990) 193–207.

c   'Natural Law and Legal Reasoning', *Cleveland State L Rev* 38 (1990) 1–13.

d   **IV.17** 'Concluding Reflections', *Cleveland State L Rev* 38 (1990) 231–50.

e   **V.16** 'Conscience in the Letter to the Duke of Norfolk', in Ian Ker and Alan G. Hill (eds), *Newman after a Hundred Years* (Oxford: OUP, 1990), 401–18.

f   Joseph Boyle, Germain Grisez, and John Finnis, 'Incoherence and Consequentialism (or Proportionalism)—A Rejoinder' *American Cath Phil Q* 64 (1990) 271–7.

g   'The Natural Moral Law and Faith', in Russell E. Smith (ed.), *The Twenty-Fifth Anniversary of Vatican II: A Look Back and a Look Ahead* (Braintree, MA: Pope John Center, 1990) 223–38; discussion (with Alasdair MacIntyre) 250–62.

1991a   **II.9** 'Object and Intention in Moral Judgments according to St Thomas Aquinas', *The Thomist* 55 (1991) 1–27; rev. version in J. Follon and J. McEvoy (eds), *Finalité et Intentionnalité: Doctrine Thomiste et Perspectives Modernes*, Bibliothèque Philosophique de Louvain No. 35 (Paris: J. Vrin, 1992), 127–48; shortened and revised version in 'Autour de la question de la fin et des moyens', *Catholica* 21 (1990) 53–61; 'Object and Intention in Moral Judgments According to St Thomas Aquinas', *Catholica: International Quarterly Selection*, Spring 1991, 3–8.

b   **II.10** 'Intention and Side-effects', in R.G. Frey and Christopher W. Morris (eds), *Liability and Responsibility: Essays in Law and Morals* (Cambridge: CUP, 1991), 32–64.

c   *Moral Absolutes: Tradition, Revision and Truth* (Washington, DC: Catholic University of America Press, 1991).
Absolutos Morales: Tradición, Revisión y Verdad (trans. Juan José García Norro) (Barcelona: Ediciones Internacionales Universitarias, EUNSA SA, 1992).
Gli assoluti morali: Tradizione, revisione & verità (trans. Andrea Maria Maccarini) (Milan: Edizioni Ares, 1993).

d   'Introduction', in John Finnis (ed.), *Natural Law*, vol. I (International Library of Essays in Law and Legal Theory, Schools 1.1) (Dartmouth: New York University Press, 1991), xi–xxiii.

e   'Introduction', in John Finnis (ed.), *Natural Law*, vol. II (International Library of Essays in Law and Legal Theory, Schools 1.2) (Dartmouth Aldershot, Sydney, 1991) xi–xvi.

f   'A propos de la "valeur intrinsèque de la vie humaine"', *Catholica* 28 (1991) 15–21.

g   'Commonwealth and Dependencies', in *Halsbury's Laws of England*, vol. 6 re-issue (4th edn, London: Butterworth, 1991), 345–559.

1992a   I.14 'Natural Law and Legal Reasoning', in Robert P. George (ed.), *Natural Law Theory: Contemporary Essays* (Oxford: OUP, 1992), 134–57.

b   III.7 'Commentary on Dummett and Weithman', in Brian Barry and Robert E. Goodin, *Free Movement: Ethical Issues in the Transnational Migration of People and of Money* (University Park, PA: U. Penn. P., 1992), 203–10.

c   III.15 'Economics, Justice and the Value of Life: Concluding Remarks', in Luke Gormally (ed.), *Economics and the Dependent Elderly: Autonomy, Justice and Quality of Care* (Cambridge: CUP, 1992), 189–98; Section II of this appears in translation in 'A propos de la "valeur intrinsèque de la vie humaine"', *Catholica* 28 (1991) 15–21.

d   V.9 *'Historical Consciousness' and Theological Foundations*, Etienne Gilson Lecture No. 15, Pontifical Institute of Mediaeval Studies, Toronto (1992).

e   V.17 'On the Grace of Humility: A New Theological Reflection', *The Allen Review* 7 (1992) 4–7.

1993a   II.16/III.19 'Abortion and Health Care Ethics', in Raanan Gillon (ed.), *Principles of Health Care Ethics* (Chichester: John Wiley, 1993), 547–57.

b   'The Legal Status of the Unborn Baby', *Catholic Medical Quarterly* 43 (1993) 5–11.

c   II.19 *'Bland* Crossing the Rubicon?', *LQR* 109 (1993) 329–37.

d   'Theology and the Four Principles: A Roman Catholic View I' (with Anthony Fisher OP), in Raanon Gillon (ed.), *Principles of Health Care Ethics* (Chichester: John Wiley, 1993), 31–44.

e   'The "Value of Human Life" and "The Right to Death": Some Reflections on *Cruzan* and Ronald Dworkin', *Southern Illinois University L J* 17: 559–71.

1994a   II.12 'On Conditional Intentions and Preparatory Intentions', in Luke Gormally (ed.), *Moral Truth and Moral Tradition: Essays in Honour of Peter Geach and Elizabeth Anscombe* (Dublin: Four Courts Press, 1994), 163–76.

b   'Law, Morality, and "Sexual Orientation"', *Notre Dame L Rev* 69 (1994) 1049–76; also, with additions, *Notre Dame J Law, Ethics & Public Policy* 9 (1995) 11–39.

c   'Liberalism and Natural Law Theory', *Mercer L Rev* 45 (1994) 687–704.

d   '"Shameless Acts" in Colorado Abuse of Scholarship in Constitutional Cases', *Academic Questions* 7/4 (1994) 10–41.

e   Germain Grisez and John Finnis, 'Negative Moral Precepts Protect the Dignity of the Human Person', *L'Osservatore Romano*, English edn, 23 February 1994.

f   'Beyond the Encyclical', *The Tablet*, 8 January 1994, reprinted in John Wilkins (ed.), *Understanding* Veritatis Splendor (London SPCK, 1994) 69–76.

g   Germain Grisez, John Finnis, and William E. May, 'Indissolubility, Divorce and Holy Communion', *New Blackfriars* 75 (June 1994) 321–30; also trans. as 'Lettre ouverte … au sujet de l'admission à la communion eucharistique des divorcés "remariés"', *Catholica* 44 (1994) 59–70.

h   '"Living Will" Legislation', in Luke Gormally (ed.), *Euthanasia, Clinical Practice and the Law* (London: Linacre Centre, 1994), 167–76.

i   'Unjust Laws in a Democratic Society: Some Philosophical and Theological Reflections', in Joseph Joblin and Réal Tremblay (eds), *I cattolici e la società pluralista: il caso delle leggi imperfette: atti del I Colloquio sui cattolici nella società pluralista: Roma, 9–12 Novembre 1994* (Bologna: ESP, 1994), 99–114.

1995a   **II.11** 'Intention in Tort Law', in David Owen (ed.), *Philosophical Foundations of Tort Law* (Oxford: OUP, 1995), 229–48.

b   **III.14** 'A Philosophical Case against Euthanasia', 'The Fragile Case for Euthanasia: A Reply to John Harris', and 'Misunderstanding the Case against Euthanasia: Response to Harris's First Reply', in John Keown (ed.), *Euthanasia: Ethical, Legal and Clinical Perspectives* (Cambridge: CUP, 1995), 23–35, 46–55, 62–71.

c   'History of Philosophy of Law' (465–8), 'Problems in the Philosophy of Law' (468–72), 'Austin' (67), 'Defeasible' (181), 'Dworkin' (209–10), 'Grotius' (328), 'Hart' (334), 'Legal Positivism' (476–7), 'Legal Realism' (477), 'Natural Law' (606–7), 'Natural Rights' (607), in Ted Honderich (ed.), *Oxford Companion to Philosophy* (Oxford: OUP, 1995).

1996a   **III.5** 'Is Natural Law Theory Compatible with Limited Government?', in Robert P. George (ed.), *Natural Law, Liberalism, and Morality* (Oxford: OUP, 1996), 1–26.

b   **III.13** 'The Ethics of War and Peace in the Catholic Natural Law Tradition', in Terry Nardin (ed.), *The Ethics of War and Peace* (Princeton, NJ: Princeton University Press, 1996), 15–39.

c   **IV.7** 'The Truth in Legal Positivism', in Robert P. George (ed.), *The Autonomy of Law: Essays on Legal Positivism* (Oxford: OUP, 1996), 195–214.

d   'Unjust Laws in a Democratic Society: Some Philosophical and Theological Reflections', *Notre Dame L Rev* 71 (1996) 595–604 (a revised version of 1994i).

e   'Loi naturelle', in Monique Canto-Sperber (ed.), *Dictionnaire de Philosophie Morale* (Paris: Presses Universitaires de France, 1996), 862–8.

1997a   'Natural Law—Positive Law', in A. Lopez Trujillo, I. Herranz, and E. Sgreccia (eds), *'Evangelium Vitae' and Law* (Rome: Libreria Editrice Vaticana 1997), 199–209.

b   **I.15** 'Commensuration and Public Reason', in Ruth Chang (ed.), *Incommensurability, Comparability and Practical Reasoning* (Cambridge, Mass.: Harvard University Press, 1997), 215–33, 285–9.

c   **III.21** 'Law, Morality and "Sexual Orientation"', in John Corvino (ed.), *Same Sex: Debating the Ethics, Science, and Culture of Homosexuality* (Lanham, MD: Rowman & Littlefield, 1997), 31–43.

d   **III.22** 'The Good of Marriage and the Morality of Sexual Relations: Some Philosophical and Historical Observations', *Am J Juris* 42 (1997) 97–134.

1998a   **I.16** 'Public Reason, Abortion and Cloning', *Valparaiso Univ LR* 32 (1998) 361–82.

b   **III.16** 'Euthanasia, Morality and Law', *Loyola of Los Angeles L Rev* 31 (1998) 1123–45.

c   **V.3** 'On the Practical Meaning of Secularism', *Notre Dame L Rev* 73 (1998) 491–515.

d   *Aquinas: Moral, Political, and Legal Theory* (Oxford: OUP, 1998).

e   'Public Good: The Specifically Political Common Good in Aquinas', in Robert P. George (ed.), *Natural Law and Moral Inquiry* (Washington, DC: Georgetown University Press 1998), 174–209.

f   'Natural Law', in Edward Craig (ed.), *Encyclopaedia of Philosophy* vol. 6 (London: Routledge, 1998), 685–90.

1999a   **I.2** 'Natural Law and the Ethics of Discourse', *American J Juris* 43 (1999) 53–73; also in 'Natural Law and the Ethics of Discourse', *Ratio Juris* 12 (1999) 354–73.

b   **III.12** 'Retribution Punishment's Formative Aim', *American J Juris* 44 (1999) 91–103
c **IV.20** 'The Fairy Tale's Moral', *LQR* 115 (1999) 170–5.

d   **V.6** 'The Catholic Church and Public Policy Debates in Western Liberal Societies: The Basis and Limits of Intellectual Engagement', in Luke Gormally (ed.), *Issues for a Catholic Bioethic* (London: Linacre Centre, 1999), 261–73.

e   'What is the Common Good, and Why does it Concern the Client's Lawyer?', *South Texas L Rev* 40 (1999) 41–53.

2000a   II.1 'The Priority of Persons', in Jeremy Horder (ed.), *Oxford Essays in Jurisprudence, Fourth Series* (Oxford: OUP, 2000), 1–15.

b   II.17 'Some Fundamental Evils of Generating Human Embryos by Cloning', in Cosimo Marco Mazzoni (ed.), *Etica della Ricerca Biologica* (Florence: Leo S. Olschki Editore 2000), 115–23; also in C.M. Mazzoni (ed.), *Ethics and Law in Biological Research* (Boston: Kluwer, 2002), 99–106.

c   'Abortion, Natural Law and Public Reason', in Robert P. George and Christopher Wolfe (eds), *Natural Law and Public Reason* (Washington, DC: Georgetown University Press, 2000), 71–105.

d   'On the Incoherence of Legal Positivism', *Notre Dame L Rev* 75 (2000) 1597–611.

e   'God the Father', in Peter Newby (ed.), *Occasional Papers from the Millennium Conferences at the Oxford University Catholic Chaplaincy* No. 1 (Oxford, 2000), 24–6.

2001a   II.13 '"Direct" and "Indirect": A Reply to Critics of Our Action Theory' (with Germain Grisez and Joseph Boyle), *The Thomist* 65 (2001) 1–44.

b   III.6 'Virtue and the Constitution of the United States', *Fordham L Rev* 69 (2001) 1595–602.

c   'Reason, Faith and Homosexual Acts', *Catholic Social Science Review* 6 (2001) 61–9.

2002a   IV.5 'Natural Law The Classical Tradition', in Jules Coleman and Scott Shapiro (eds), *The Oxford Handbook of Jurisprudence and Philosophy of Law* (Oxford: OUP, 2002), 1–60.

b   V.22 'Secularism, the Root of the Culture of Death', in Luke Gormally (ed.), *Culture of Life—Culture of Death* (London: Linacre Centre, 2002).

c   'Aquinas on *jus* and Hart on Rights: A Response', *Rev of Politics* 64 (2002) 407–10.

d   Patrick H. Martin and John Finnis, 'The Identity of "Anthony Rivers"', *Recusant History* 26 (2002) 39–74.

e   Patrick H. Martin and John Finnis, 'Tyrwhitt of Kettleby, Part I Goddard Tyrwhitt, Martyr, 1580', *Recusant History* 26 (2002) 301–13.

2003a   III.8 'Natural Law & the Re-making of Boundaries', in Allen Buchanan and Margaret Moore (eds), *States, Nations, and Boundaries: The Ethics of Making Boundaries* (Cambridge: CUP, 2003), 171–8.

b   IV.1 'Law and What I Truly Should Decide', *American J Juris* 48 (2003) 107–30.

c   V.10 'Saint Thomas More and the Crisis in Faith and Morals', *The Priest* 7/1 (2003) 10–15, 29–30.

d   'Secularism, Morality and Politics', *L'Osservatore Romano*, English edn, 29 January 2003, 9.

e   'Shakespeare's Intercession for *Love's Martyr*' (with Patrick Martin), *Times Literary Supplement*, no. 5220, 18 April 2003, 12–14.

f   '"An Intrinsically Disordered Attraction"', in John F. Harvey and Gerard V. Bradley (eds), *Same-Sex Attraction: A Parents' Guide* (South Bend, IN: St Augustine's Press, 2003), 89–99.

g   'Nature and Natural Law in Contemporary Philosophical and Theological Debates: Some Observations', in Juan Correa and Elio Sgreccia (eds), *The Nature & Dignity of the Human Person as the Foundation of the Right to Life: The Challenges of Contemporary Culture* (Rome: Libreria Editrice Vaticana, 2003), 81–109.

h   Patrick H. Martin and John Finnis, 'Tyrwhitt of Kettleby, Part II: Robert Tyrwhitt, a Main Benefactor of John Gerard SJ, 1599–1605', *Recusant History* 27 (2003) 556–69.

i   Patrick H. Martin and John Finnis, 'Thomas Thorpe, 'W.S', and the Catholic Intelligencers', *Elizabethan Literary Renaissance* (2003) 1–43.

j   Patrick H. Martin and John Finnis, '*Caesar*, Succession, and the Chastisement of Rulers', *Notre Dame L Rev* 78 (2003) 1045–74.

k   'Commonwealth and Dependencies', in *Halsbury's Laws of England*, vol. 6 re-issue (4th edn, London: Butterworth, 2004), 409–518.

l   [Abortion for Cleft Palate: The Human Fertilisation and Embryology Act 1990] *Sunday Telegraph*, 7 December 2003.

m   'An Oxford Play Festival in 1582' (with Patrick Martin), *Notes & Queries* 50 (2003) 391–4.

2004a   **II.18** 'Per un'etica dell'eguaglianza nel diritto alla vita: Un commento a Peter Singer', in Rosangela Barcaro and Paolo Becchi (eds), *Questioni Mortali: L'Attuale Dibattito sulla Morte Cerebrale e il Problema dei Trapianti* (Naples: Edizioni Scientifiche Italiane, 2004), 127–39.

b   **IV.22** 'Helping Enact Unjust Laws without Complicity in Injustice', *American J Juris* 49 (2004) 11–42.

2005a   **I.1** 'Foundations of Practical Reason Revisited', *American J Juris* 50 (2005) 109–32.

b   **I.4** 'Self-referential (or Performative) Inconsistency: Its Significance for Truth', *Proceedings of the Catholic Philosophical Association* 78 (2005) 13–21.

c   **II.2** ' "The Thing I Am" Personal Identity in Aquinas and Shakespeare', *Social Philosophy & Policy* 22 (2005) 250–82; also in Ellen Frankel Paul, Fred D. Miller, and Jeffrey Paul (eds), *Personal Identity* (Cambridge: CUP, 2005), 250–82.

d   **IV.6** 'Philosophy of Law' (Chinese trans.), in Ouyang Kang (ed.), *The Map of Contemporary British and American Philosophy* (Beijing: Dangdai Yingmei Zhexue Ditu, 2005), 388–413.

e   'On "Public Reason"', in *O Racji Pulicznej* (Warsaw: Ius et Lex, 2005), 7–30 (Polish trans.), 33–56 (English original); <http://ssrn.com/abstract=955815>.

f   'Restricting Legalised Abortion is not Intrinsically Unjust', in Helen Watt (ed.), *Cooperation, Complicity & Conscience* (London: Linacre Centre, 2005), 209–45.

g   'A Vote Decisive for … a More Restrictive Law', in Helen Watt (ed.), *Cooperation, Complicity & Conscience* (London: Linacre Centre, 2005), 269–95.

h   'Aquinas' Moral, Political and Legal Philosophy', *Stanford Encyclopedia of Philosophy* (2005); <http://plato.stanford.edu/entries/aquinas-moral-political/>.

i   Patrick H. Martin and John Finnis, 'Benedicam Dominum: Ben Jonson's Strange 1605 Inscription', *Times Literary Supplement*, 4 November 2005, 12–13.

j   Patrick H. Martin and John Finnis, 'The Secret Sharers: "Anthony Rivers" and the Appellant Controversy, 1601–2', *Huntingdon Library Q* 69/2 (2006) 195–238.

2006a   **V.4** 'Religion and State Some Main Issues and Sources', *American J Juris* 51 (2006) 107–30; <http://ssrn.com/abstract=943420>.

b   'Observations for the Austral Conference to Mark the 25th Anniversary of *Natural Law and Natural Rights*', *Cuadernos de Extensión Jurídica* (Universidad de los Andes) no. 13 (2006), 27–30.

2007a   **III.9** 'Nationality, Alienage and Constitutional Principle', *LQR* 123 (2007) 417–45; <http://ssrn.com/abstract=1101495>.

b   **IV.10** 'On Hart's Ways: Law as Reason and as Fact', *American J Juris* 52 (2007) 25–53; also in Matthew Kramer and Claire Grant (eds), *The Legacy of H.L.A. Hart: Legal, Political & Moral Philosophy* (Oxford: OUP, 2009), 1–27.

c   'Natural Law Theories of Law', *Stanford Encyclopedia of Philosophy* (2007); <http:// plato. stanford.edu/entries/natural-law-theories/>.

2008a   **I.5, II.7, V.8** 'Reason, Revelation, Universality and Particularity in Ethics', *American Journal of Jurisprudence* 53 (2008) 23–48.

b   **II.6** 'Universality, Personal and Social Identity, and Law', address, Congresso Sul-Americano de Filosofia do Direito, Porto Alegre, Brazil, 4 October 2007; Oxford Legal Studies Research Paper 5/2008; <http://ssrn.com/abstract=1094277>.

c   **III.20** 'Marriage: A Basic and Exigent Good', *The Monist* 91 (2008) 396–414.

d   [**V.13**] 'Grounds of Law & Legal Theory: A Response', *Legal Theory* 13 (2008) 315–44.

e   'Common Law Constraints: Whose Common Good Counts?', Oxford Legal Studies Research Paper 10/2008; <http://ssrn.com/abstract_id=1100628>.

f   *Humanae Vitae: A New Translation with Notes* (London: Catholic Truth Society, 2008).

2009a   **II.3** 'Anscombe's Essays', *National Catholic Bioethics* Q 9/1 (2009) 199–207.

     b   **IV.11** 'H.L.A. Hart A Twentieth Century Oxford Political Philosopher', *American J Juris* 54 (2009) 161–85.

     c   **V.1** 'Does Free Exercise of Religion Deserve Constitutional Mention?', *American J Juris* 54 (2009) 41–66.

     d   **V.2** 'Telling the Truth about God and Man in a Pluralist Society: Economy or Explication?', in Christopher Wolfe (ed.), *The Naked Public Square Revisited: Religion & Politics in the Twenty-First Century* (Wilmington, DE: ISI Books, 2009), 111–25, 204–9.

     e   'Endorsing Discrimination between Faiths: A Case of Extreme Speech?', in Ivan Hare and James Weinstein (eds), *Extreme Speech and Democracy* (Oxford: OUP, 2009), 430–41.

     f   'Discrimination between Religions: Some Thoughts on Reading Greenawalt's *Religion and the Constitution*', *Constitutional Commentary* 25 (2009) 265–71.

     g   'Commonwealth', in *Halsbury's Laws of England*, vol. 13 (5th edn, 2009), 471–589.

     h   'Why Religious Liberty is a Special, Important and Limited Right', Notre Dame Legal Studies Paper 09-11; <http://ssrn.com/abstract=1392278>.

     i   'The Lords' Eerie Swansong A Note on *R (Purdy) v Director of Public Prosecutions*, Oxford Legal Studies Research Paper 31/2009; <http://ssrn.com/abstract=1477281>.

     j   'The Mental Capacity Act 2005 Some Ethical and Legal Issues', in Helen Watt (ed.), *Incapacity & Care: Controversies in Healthcare and Research* (London: Linacre Centre, 2009), 95–105.

     k   'Debate over the Interpretation of *Dignitas personae*'s Teaching on Embryo Adoption', *National Catholic Bioethics* Q 9 475–8.

2010a   **II.14** 'Directly Discriminatory Decisions: a Missed Opportunity' *LQR* 126 (2010) 491–6.

     b   Law as Idea, Ideal and Duty: A Comment on Simmonds, *Law as a Moral Idea*', *Jurisprudence* 1 (2010) 247–53.

     c   'Invoking the Principle of Legality against the Rule of Law' *New Zealand Law Review* [2010] 601–16; also in Richard Ekins (ed.), *Modern Challenges to the Rule of Law* (Wellington: Lexis Nexis, 2010), 129–42.

     d   'The Other F-word' *The Public Discourse*, 20 October 2010 (address at Princeton University, October 2011) <http://www.thepublicdiscourse.com/2010/10/1849/>.

2011a   'Exceptionalism and Exceptionless Moral Norms in *Measure for Measure' Journal of Law, Philosophy and Culture* 5 (2010 [2011]) 103–10.

     b   'Equality and Differences', *American J Juris* 56 (2011) 17–44.

     c   *Reason in Action: Collected Essays of John Finnis* volume I (Oxford: OUP, 2011), 1–15.

     d   *Intention and Identity: Collected Essays of John Finnis* volume II (Oxford: OUP, 2011), 1–15.

     e   *Human Rights and Common Good: Collected Essays of John Finnis* volume III (Oxford: OUP, 2011), 1–16.

     f   *Philosophy of Law: Collected Essays of John Finnis* volume IV (Oxford: OUP, 2011), 1–19.

     g   *Religion and Public Reasons: Collected Essays of John Finnis* volume V (Oxford: OUP, 2011) 1–14.

     h   Abstracts of Introductions and all 106 essays for *Oxford Scholarship Online* edition of *Collected Essays of John Finnis*.

     i   Foreword to Anthony Fisher OP, *Catholic Bioethics for a New Millennium* (Cambridge: CUP, 2011), viii–x.

     j   Preface to *Fundamentos de Ética*, trans. Arthur M. Ferreira Neto, Coleção Teoria e Filosofia do Direito (Rio de Janeiro: Elseveira Editora, 2012), vii–xi.

     k   'Reason Will Get us Out of this Bunker': commentary on the Pope's address to the Bundestag, *Il Sussidiario*.net, 27 September.

2012a   'Natural Law Theory: Its Past and Its Present' in
       (i) Andrei Marmor (ed.), *The Routledge Companion to Philosophy of Law* (London: Routledge, 2012), 16–30;

      (ii) *Amer. J. Juris.* 57 (2012) 81–101.

b   'What is Philosophy of Law?' *Rivista di Filosofia de Diritto* 1 (2012) 67–78; *Amer. J. Juris*
       59 (2014).

c   'Social Virtues and the Common Good', in the *Truth about God, and Its Relevance for a*
       Good Life in Society: Proceedings of the XI Plenary Session of the Pontifical Academy of
       St Thomas Aquinas, 17–19 June 2011 (Vatican City, 2012) 96–106.

d   'Coexisting Normative Orders? Yes, But No', *Amer. J. Juris.* 57 (2012) 111–17.

e   'Equality and Differences', the H.L.A Hart Memorial Lecture 2011, Oxford Legal Studies
       Research Paper 72/2012; <http://ssrn.com/abstract=2180410>.

f   'Response [to Seven Papers]', *Villanova Law Rev.* 57 (2012) 925–55.

Table of Contents of the Collected Essays of John Finnis

VOLUME V RELIGION & PUBLIC REASONS

Index

Introductory Note

References such as '178–9' indicate (not necessarily continuous) discussion of a topic across a range of pages. Because the entire work is about 'reason', 'morality', and 'law', the use of these terms (and certain others which occur constantly throughout the book) as an entry point has been minimized. Information will be found under the corresponding detailed topics.

Lightning Source UK Ltd.
Milton Keynes UK
UKOW06f0126190115

244699UK00004B/8/P

9 780198 738107